PEOPLES AND CULTURES
OF NATIVE SOUTH AMERICA

The Natural History Press, publisher for The American Museum of Natural History, is a division of Doubleday & Company, Inc. The Natural History Press publishes books and periodicals in all branches of the life and earth sciences, including anthropology and astronomy. The Natural History Press has its editorial offices at Doubleday & Company, Inc., 277 Park Avenue, New York, New York 10017, and its business offices at 501 Franklin Avenue, Garden City, New York 11530.

Daniel R. Gross was born in New York and raised in Atlanta. After receiving his B.A. in philosophy at the University of Chicago, he moved to New York where he took a Ph.D. in anthropology at Columbia University in 1970. Since 1965 he has spent nearly three years in Brazil doing ethnographic research. Much of his work concerned traditional society and religion in the arid Northeast, where he worked among peasants. He has also published papers on socioeconomic change from an ecological point of view, dealing with the introduction of sisal agriculture to an area formerly dominated by subsistence farming. More recently he conducted preliminary field work among the Western Gaviões (Timbira), an Indian group living in Pará State in north Brazil. He is married and lives in New York, where he is Assistant Professor of Anthropology at Hunter College of the City University of New York.

APPROXIMATE LOCATIONS OF SOME GROUPS MENTIONED
IN THIS BOOK ON A MAP OF MODERN SOUTH AMERICA

1 Guajiro	14 Tenetehara	26 Tapirapé
2 Chibcha	15 Eastern Timbira	27 Shavante
3 Otavalo	(Canella)	28 Karajá
4 Tukano	16 Tupinambá	29 Terena
5 Cubeo	17 Sherente	30 Caduveo
6 Yanomamö	18 Inca	31 Guayaki
7 Warao	19 Sharanahua	32 Abipon
8 Carib	20 Aymará	33 Araucanian
9 Jívaro	21 Sirionó	34 Tehuelche
10 Amahuaca	22 Nambikwara	35 Alacaluf
11 Mundurucú	23 Bororo	36 Ona
12 Apinayé	24 Mehinacu	37 Yahgan
13 Marajó Island	25 Kuikuru	

PEOPLES AND CULTURES

OF NATIVE

SOUTH AMERICA

AN ANTHROPOLOGICAL READER

EDITED WITH INTRODUCTIONS BY
DANIEL R. GROSS

PUBLISHED FOR
THE AMERICAN MUSEUM OF NATURAL HISTORY
DOUBLEDAY / THE NATURAL HISTORY PRESS
1973 GARDEN CITY, NEW YORK

ISBN: 0-385-05725-3 Trade
ISBN: 0-385-05728-8 Paper
Library of Congress Catalog Card Number 77–171295

Contents

Acknowledgments

No book is complete without giving recognition to those who helped it come about. In addition to the contributors to this volume, I should like to thank the following people for their assistance: Iria Barricklo, Kate Brown, Loretta Caruso, Marguerite Fabio, Elizabeth Knappman, Leslie Kotarsky, Edward Lanning, Sally McLendon, Karen Rauhauser, Christopher J. Tavener, Terence Turner and Andrew P. Vayda. Silêde Gross, my wife, more than anyone helped me to bring this book to completion.

Brooklyn
New York
July, 1972

PART I: PREHISTORY

Introduction to Late Pleistocene Environments and Early Man in South America

To understand how cultures have adapted to different areas of the world it is necessary to know something about the environments of those areas. The student studying a particular people should always begin by examining the main features of the natural environment in which they live. In South America this is easily accomplished by consulting any of a number of geographical works such as Preston James (1959). But an understanding of how the earliest migrants to South America lived requires us to know about environments that no longer exist.

Fortunately a number of scholars in different disciplines are attempting to reconstruct the environments that existed in South America at the end of the Pleistocene, the dawn of human habitation. A recent attempt by James J. Hester is reprinted here. On the same topic, anyone concerned with the reconstruction of prehistoric life in South America should consult *Early Man in the New World* by Kenneth Macgowan and Joseph A. Hester, Jr. (1962).

Hester had most of his training at U.C.L.A. where he earned his Ph.D. degree in anthropology in 1954. He has since taught at a number of institutions in California including Occidental and Stanford. He is presently teaching at San Jose State College.

1. LATE PLEISTOCENE ENVIRONMENTS AND EARLY MAN IN SOUTH AMERICA *

JAMES J. HESTER

Any consideration of the early human population of South America must take into account the unique geography of that continent. The geography of South America is quite different from that of North America. This difference conditions our thinking with respect to the entire subject of early human migrations in the New World as the specific geographic features served as corridors or barriers to migration and influenced the climate. Therefore, our initial inquiries into South American geography will be structured in terms of this contrast.

The major portion of the South American land mass is located near the equator, between 10° north latitude and 30° south latitude. This is in contrast to North America where the largest land mass is located between 30° and 70° north latitude. The approximate median latitude for South America is 10° south latitude whereas that for North America is 50° north latitude, 40° closer to the pole.

A second physiographic feature of South America is the nearly continuous range of mountains extending from Colombia to Tierra del Fuego. This mountain chain influences the vegetal communities so that they trend in a North-South direction with their altitudinal limits being high near the equator and steadily lowering toward the more southerly latitudes. These vegetal zones as they occur today were mapped by Anderson et al. (1958, p. 21). This north-south orientation of vegetal zones is not duplicated in North America with the exception of the Sierra Nevada and Rocky Mountains.

Reprinted by permission of the author and publisher from *The American Naturalist* Vol. 100 (1966), No. 914, pp. 377–88.

* Presented at a symposium, "Reconstructions of Past Biological Environments, Part I," sponsored by the American Society of Naturalists, and held in Berkeley, California, December 27, 1965, as part of the A.A.A.S. meetings.

In areas removed from these mountain ranges, the North American vegetal communities are much more influenced by latitude.

South American climate is also conditioned by the fact that the southern hemisphere contains much more water than land. The greater absorption of heat in summer and its radiation in winter by a water body, as contrasted with a land mass, results in an oceanic climate characterized by cooler summers and warmer winters. The net result of this factor is that by latitude South America has a smaller range of temperature extremes than does North America.

Another major feature of the geography concerns the relative importance of the exposure of portions of the continental shelf during glacial periods. The most striking aspect of this exposure was the width of the Argentine shelf, which during periods of maximum low sea level nearly doubled the South American land mass south of 40° south latitude.

The major result of the combination of these geographic factors was the limiting of continental glaciation, a factor in strong contrast to the Pleistocene record for North America (Donn, Farrand, and Ewing, 1962). However, before we examine the data concerning the past climate of South America in detail, we shall consider more fully the factors already mentioned.

SIGNIFICANCE OF THE ANDEAN RANGE

The majority of all land not in the Andean Chain lies below 500 meters in elevation. Due to the equatorial position of most of this land, it is assumed that even during the glacial maximum much of the area of Venezuela, Brazil, and the Guianas, would not have been particularly favorable for human occupation. On the other hand, early human migrants entering South America by way of the Andes easily could have followed the same environmental zone for several thousand miles. These early migrants practiced a big game hunting economy with the animals hunted being adapted to specific vegetal zones. Their hunters would have exploited these game herds wherever they were found and thus would have followed these zones to the southern end of the continent. On the other hand, a movement of only 100 miles or so to the east or west would have forced the hunters to enter quite different environmental zones and to change their economy.

THE OCEANIC CLIMATE

Temperature gradients have been computed for a land mass corresponding to that of North America (105° east longitude, through central Asia), for a land mass similar to South America (130° east longitude), and for the Southern Hemisphere Ocean (Van Loon, 1966, Fig. 9). These gradients demonstrate that South America today possesses a continental climate only as far south as 30° south latitude at which point it rapidly changes to a more moderate oceanic climate (Fig. 1). This shift actually results in

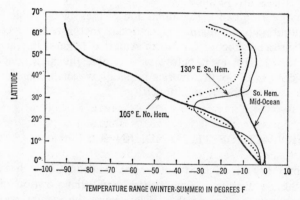

TEMPERATURE RANGE (WINTER-SUMMER) IN DEGREES F

FIG. 1. Comparison of modern temperature gradients for a land mass corresponding to that of North America (105° east longitude), for a land mass corresponding to that of South America (130° east longitude), and for the Southern Hemisphere Ocean (after Van Loon, 1966, Fig. 9). Dotted line shows a hypothetical temperature gradient for South America ca. 20,000 years ago during the glacial maximum.

reversal of the normal temperature gradient with temperatures less variable between 40° and 60° south latitude than they are at 30°. One result of this factor would appear to be that the more southerly latitudes in South America had a warmer climate through time than the same latitudes in North America. A second result is that the reverse temperature gradient contributes to the southerly extension of vegetal zones, normally (on larger land masses) present closer to the equator.

THE CONTINENTAL SHELF

Soundings of the sea floor taken recently off the coast of Argentina indicate the presence of a series of former beaches at various depths. The depths of these beaches below modern sea level and their age as determined by radiocarbon analysis of shells from cores taken from these beaches (Fray and Ewing, 1963) are as follows:

Depth of beach below sea level	Radiocarbon age in years before present
More than 80 fathoms	35,000
80 fathoms	18,700
30 to 40 fathoms	15,000
65 fathoms	11,000

Continuous soundings by the Lamont Observatory vessel "Vema" indicate that the Falkland Islands are connected to the continental shelf at a depth of 80 fathoms below modern sea level (Grinnell, unpublished). With the drop in sea level recorded between 35,000 and 18,700 years ago, a land bridge would have connected the Falkland Islands to the mainland. This land bridge could have made possible the occupation of the Falkland Islands by prehistoric man during this interval. An additional feature resulting from the presence of the exposed continental shelf would be its effect as a land mass on the climate. The continental shelf at its maximum exposure doubled the land mass south of 40° south latitude. The presence of a greater land mass should have contributed to an increasing continentality of the climate, i.e., colder winters and warmer summers than at present. The effect of this feature on the temperature gradient ca. 20,000 years ago at the height of the late Wisconsin glacial maximum has been illustrated in a hypothetical curve in Fig. 1. This graph is only plotted to show the inferred direction of change of the temperature gradient. No statement of the amount of this change is implied.

Raised beaches reported along Beagle channel and other parts of Tierra del Fuego are now believed to be of tectonic origin rather than indicative of former high stands of sea level. Unfortunately, these beaches are not yet dated by radiocarbon (Urien, 1965). The fact that some have associated artifacts suggests they may be more recent than the submerged beaches reported by Fray and Ewing.

PALEO CLIMATE

Data concerning the past climate of South America are not available from many areas. However, excellent studies of fossil pollen and other climatic data are known from the Savanna de Bogata, Ecuador (Van der Hammen and Gonzalez, 1960), and from southern Chile and Tierra del Fuego (Heusser, 1965; Aüer, 1956, 1958, 1959). Additional limited pollen studies include researches in British Guiana (Van der Hammen, 1965), the Orinoco Delta (Muller, 1959), and the Argentine Shelf (Groot, 1964). The most outstanding feature of these studies (even though they are few in number and represent only a small fraction of the continent) is that they suggest climatic shifts in South America were synchronous with some of those known from the late Wisconsin of North America (Flint, 1963; Hafsten, 1961). Graphs of fluctuations in South American pollen species are presented by Aüer (1958) and Van der Hammen and Gonzalez (1960). Climatic inferences by Heusser (1965) based on similar pollen data are summarized below:

Zone 1	16,000–12,000 B.P.	cool and wet
Zone 2	12,000–11,000	drier and warmer
Zone 3	11,000–10,000	cooler and wetter
Zone 4	10,000–8,500	cool but warmer later becoming wetter
Zone 5	8,500–6,500	warmer and drier
Zone 6	6,500–4,500	cooler and wetter
Zone 7	4,500–2,500	cool but warmer, not as wet
Zone 8	2,500–present	wetter, cooler in recent centuries

Corroborative data concerning past climatic fluctuations are provided by fossils present in deep sea cores collected throughout the southern ocean. Species of radiolaria found in these cores may be divided into types typical of a cold water environment and types preferring a warm water environment. Graphs of fluctuations in the distribution of these species through time (Hays, 1965, Figs. 33, 34, 35) may be correlated with graphs obtained from land based pollen studies. In addition, plots of the quantity of calcium carbonate in these deep sea cores record nearly identical fluctuations to those plotted from warm water radiolaria (Hays, 1965, Fig. 28). Additional substantiation of these climatic fluctuations are provided by the diatoms (Donahue, 1965, p. 103) and ice rafted detritus (Conolly and Ewing, 1965) from deep sea cores in the same area.

Perhaps of most importance to this study is the fact that a poleward migration of species of warm water radiolaria, radiocarbon dated at 6,000 and 6,700 years ago, suggests a two degree southward shift at that time of the Antarctic Convergence (the line where waters circulating around the south pole meet the subtropical currents). This fact may be inferred from the modern southern limit of these radiolaria species which is almost identical to the latitudinal position of the Antarctic Convergence. This southern displacement of the convergence would have resulted in a warmer climate in the Antarctic Islands 6,000 to 8,000 years ago than today, as the antarctic storm tracks are closely correlated with the position of the convergence (Van Loon, 1966, Fig. 8). From a climatic standpoint, the Antarctic Islands may have been habitable at that time. However, occupation of these islands would have required the use of boats, a cultural trait not yet demonstrated by the archaeological record.

A final climatic feature is the record of Pleistocene glaciation. Most of the available information is summarized by Patterson (in preparation) as follows: "In the northwestern part of South America—the area which now comprises the countries of Venezuela, Colombia, Ecuador and northern Peru—there were numerous cirque and small piedmont glaciers in regions with elevations greater than 3,300–3,800 meters above sea level; these glaciers were isolated from one another by vast areas at slightly lower elevations. The glaciers coalesced in the high mountain ranges of central

Peru, so that there was a large continuous glacier varying in elevation from 3,500 to 4,000 meters above sea level which extended
from Cajabamba (8° S. lat.) to the Cordillera de Huanzo (15°
S. lat.). Less extensive piedmont glaciers occurred in the mountain
ranges forming the Cordillera Oriental from north of Cuzco to
the eastern shores of Lake Titicaca. The high plateau of Bolivia,
northern Chile, and northwestern Argentina was largely unglaci-
ated, except for isolated peaks and small mountain ranges with
elevations greater than 4,600–5,200 meters above sea level. Glaciation reappeared in the mountains along the border between Chile
and Argentina; the ice coalesced about 30° S. lat. at elevations
of 3,100–3,500 meters above sea level and extended southward
along the Andes to Tierra del Fuego. . . ." According to Van
der Hammen and Gonzalez (1960) and Aüer (1958, Appendix
I), the vertical displacement of the snow line and vegetal zones
during the glacial maximum was 1,200 to 1,300 meters. Utilizing
these data I have attempted to plot the limits of the Wisconsin
maximum glaciation for South America. In addition, although relatively little data are available, I have also attempted to plot the
vegetation zones for the same time period, ca. 20,000 years ago
(Fig. 2). Sources consulted include Van der Hammen and Gonzalez (1960) for Ecuador, Van der Hammen (1965) and Muller
(1959) for the Guianas, and Aüer (1958) and Heusser (1965)
for Tierra del Fuego. The plotting of these zones also takes into
account the high quantity of Ephedra pollen in sediments from
the Argentine Basin (Groot et al., 1965), a factor which is interpreted as indicating a rainshadow desert in northwest Argentina.
Using as a primary determinant the 1,200 to 1,300 meter lowering
of the modern limits of each vegetal zone, I have constructed a
hypothetical map (Fig. 2) which gives us one parameter as a basis
for understanding of the prehistoric habitation of South America.
The rationale for the construction of this map is a simple logical
construct, i.e., the map is based on a 1,200 to 1,300 meter lowering
of the modern vegetal zones. The major determinant of specific
zones is thus elevation, a factor which led to the plotting of co-
niferous and deciduous forests on the Guiana and Brazilian highlands. Underlying this mapping is the assumption that these latter
zones have been pinched off the tops of these highlands by post-
glacial warming.

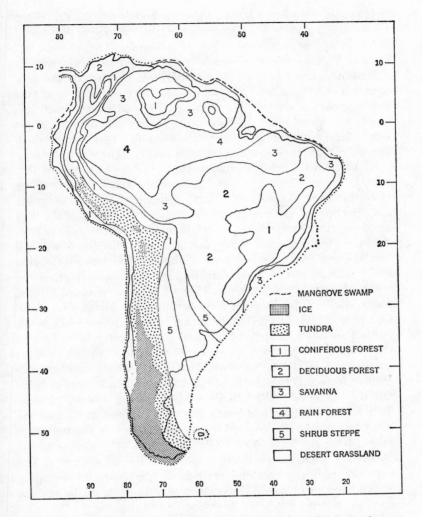

FIG. 2. Hypothetical map illustrating glaciation and vegetal zones in South America ca. 20,000 years ago. The outline of the modern continent is shown as a heavy black line. The dotted line is the shoreline during the glacial maximum.

It should be pointed out that this methodology is based on the results of the glacial age climatic change, the lowering of the vegetal zones being the combined effect of changes in temperature and rainfall. This method thus stands in contrast to that employed by Patterson wherein he seeks to explain these changes by the construction of a theoretical climatic model. The model proposed here is geographic in nature. The plotting of vegetal zones, based primarily on elevation, is a method which ignores differential changes due to local variations in temperature and rainfall (details of which are only available for a few specific areas). Therefore, there is no doubt that the resultant map is inaccurate, or to put it another way, is more accurate in some areas than others. However, my intent has been to construct a map which would serve to delineate the direction of environmental change, a map which could then be of use in understanding prehistoric man's population of the continent. In this respect it is of interest to note that the downward displacement of the vegetal zones along the Andean range during the Wisconsin glacial maximum did not appreciably increase the width of these zones north of 30° south latitude. It is only in the region south of this line that these vegetal zones increase in width. One result of this fact is that the region between 30° and 50° south latitude featured the largest areas of tundra and cold steppe on the continent. Therefore, this area would have been favorable to the hunting of the faunas typical of these zones. Another geographic feature is that much of the area available to human habitation south of 30° south latitude was the exposed continental shelf. This region was level and sandy (Grinnell, unpublished), and the coast line may have featured numerous lagoons of the type now known from the Texas Coast (Emery, 1965). The climate of the continental shelf was probably very dry, as the area is today. The exposure of the continental shelf along the coast of Argentina would have also affected the position and direction of the oceanic currents, a subject beyond the scope of this paper.

Another feature of this ancient landscape was the presence of numerous lake basins. These lake basins have been noted along the entire Andean chain from Venezuela to Chile and are especially frequent on the Bolivian Plateau (Royo y Gomez, 1956; Sievers, 1914). Another important area of lakes not mentioned heretofore (to my knowledge) is Tierra del Fuego. A number of the valleys in Tierra del Fuego now flooded by the sea, such as the Strait of Magellan, would have been altered into lake basins which collected rainfall runoff with the lowering of sea level during glacial periods. An area featuring such lakes, especially if they overflowed flushing out the residual salts, might have been a suitable environment for early man and his prey animals.

EARLY HUMAN HABITATION

The archaeology of the early sites in South America is poorly known. The reason for this is that scientists have only recently begun to classify the data through systematic typological and chronological studies. At this writing, although more than 50 sites are considered to belong to early cultures, only a half dozen have been dated by radiocarbon analysis. Initial attempts to group these early sites into a continent-wide chronology are those of Lanning and Hammel (1961), and Lanning (1965). In these chronologies, the earliest level, the "Andean Biface Horizon," is dated by radiocarbon at approximately 10,000 to 11,000 years ago. Another chronology has been proposed by Krieger (1964) in which he groups sites into three stages based on typological considerations. His stages are: "Preprojectile Point" (which might more appropriately have been termed non-projectile), "Paleo Indian," and "Proto Archaic." A serious discrepancy exists between these chronologies, as the earliest levels in the chronologies proposed by Lanning and Hammel are assigned by Krieger to his latest period, the "Proto Archaic." At this time it seems futile to attempt to bring order into this situation through comparative typological studies. What is needed is a large-scale program of dating of these assemblages by radiocarbon. It is only after the application of such an independent method of analysis that we will be able to determine whether or not those assemblages without projectile points should be assigned to the earliest time horizon. Another independent examination consists of comparing the geographical and elevational position of each of these sites with our evidence for the position of late Pleistocene climatic zones and ice sheets (Fig. 3). It is obvious from this comparison that many of these sites are located in positions which could not have been occupied until after the

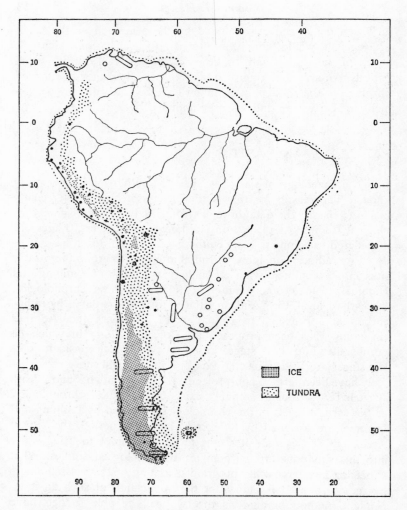

FIG. 3. Map illustrating correlation between early human sites in South America and Pleistocene glaciation. Dots—"Early Lithic" sites according to Lanning and Hammel (1961, Fig. 1); circles and ovals —"Preprojectile Point" sites listed by Krieger (1964); dots within circles—sites listed by Lanning and Hammel as "Early Lithic" and Krieger as "Preprojectile Point." Note number of sites in areas covered with ice or tundra vegetation during the glacial maximum.

withdrawal of the ice 11,000 years ago. The only other possible explanation would be that these sites were occupied during an interglacial period and would thus be greater than 25,000 years of age. So far not one radiocarbon date supports such a viewpoint.

Although most of this evidence suggests that early man probably occupied South America during the post-glacial period, the "Preprojectile Point" sites in Argentina (Fig. 3) remain as possible evidences of glacial age man in South America. These sites are undated, they are in an area that was not glaciated, and they possess artifact types which could be very ancient.

It is also of interest to note that the occupation of Fell's and Palli Aike Caves (Bird, 1938) occurred almost immediately after Tierra del Fuego was deglaciated, suggesting that early man was moving in direct response to glacial advances and retreats. Prehistoric migrations within South America during the late Pleistocene appear to have been little hampered by glaciation, with the exception of direct east-west movement across the Andes. In fact, the local topography and climatic zones favored north to south population movement (on both sides of the Andes) as soon as the continent was first occupied, a feature recognized by Sauer (1944, Map 2) and Lothrop (1961). Such north-south migrations would have involved little change in environment as contrasted with east-west movements. There is little evidence today to alter Sauer's map of the migration routes used by the earliest inhabitants of South America. However, a specific understanding of this occupation and its chronology is dependent upon more precise identification of the area occupied by each of the Late Pleistocene ice lobes and the radiocarbon dating of the occupation sites.

SUMMARY

The early human occupation of South America was favored by an unusual set of geological and climatic factors which channeled population movements in a north to south direction. Because of the exposure of the continental shelf and the ameliorating effect of the oceanic climate, the area between 30° and 50° south latitude may have featured favorable environmental zones for human habitation. Therefore, it is no accident that the earliest dated cultures are known from the southern end of the continent. This factor is a logical result of the climatic and geographic factors influencing human migrations in South America, influences which may have resulted in this north to south migration requiring only a brief span of time. The exact chronology of this migration is inadequately known. However, comparison of the geographical location of the early sites with the presumed location of the late Pleistocene ice masses suggests that a majority of these sites are of post-glacial age. The presence of any sites of glacial age is yet to be demonstrated.

Introduction to Archaism and Revival on the South Coast of Peru

One of the problems confronting archeologists is the proper dating of cultural material obtained in field research. There are many methods in use including so-called "absolute" techniques like radiocarbon and dendrochronology, and "relative" techniques like stratigraphy and seriation. But even when such material is precisely located in time, further problems in interpretation may remain. One of these is the possibility that certain items, e.g. ceramic pieces, may be stylistic anachronisms. In other words their manufacture may be of one period, yet their style imitative of some earlier period. To give a contemporary example, how might an archeologist of the future interpret the long skirts, epaulettes, and wide-lapelled suits which are enjoying a revival in the clothing fashions of today? Would he conclude that his site had been disturbed? Or that the people who used these items were dressing in their grandparents' clothing? Or could he conclude, as Menzel has here, that such items are in fact archaisms and as such are significant in understanding the lives of those who made use of them?

Anthropological archeologists are no longer content to excavate and classify the "treasures" of dead civilizations. More than ever archeology belongs to the discipline of anthropology because its practitioners like Menzel are concerned to use archeological data to reconstruct the behavior patterns of extinct peoples (cf. Deetz 1967). Readers who would like to pursue the subject of Peruvian archaeology should consult Rowe and Menzel (1967), Lanning (1967), Bennett and Bird (1964) and Mason (1968).

Prehistory

Dorothy Menzel has a great deal of experience in Andean archeology. She holds a Ph.D. degree from the University of California at Berkeley and presently holds posts at the Lowie Museum of Anthropology and the Institute of Andean Studies.

2. ARCHAISM AND REVIVAL ON THE SOUTH COAST OF PERU

DOROTHY MENZEL

Recent studies of late prehistoric pottery styles of the South Coast of Peru have brought to our attention some examples of cultural archaism, phenomena which are of considerable theoretical interest to archaeologists and students of culture change. Archaism is defined as the deliberate attempt by a later people to imitate or revive features of culture of an earlier period. Such attempts may differ widely in motivation and in their general effect on the respective cultural features in question. Present studies have revealed at least two examples of archaism which show marked differences in kind.

Art historians have noted the existence of archaistic and revivalistic movements in so many instances in the Old World that one gets the impression that the phenomenon is not an unusual one. Some of the best-known examples are those of Neo-Babylonian Mesopotamia and Saite Egypt in the sixth century B.C., a period in which art styles and religious ideas of some 2000 to 1300 years earlier were revived. Another well-known example is that of the Hellenistic period in the Mediterranean, in the first century B.C., during which there was an archaistic taste among art collectors leading to the imitation of sixth and fifth century Greek art. During the Ming dynasty in China in the fifteenth century A.D., after a period of Mongol rule, there was an attempt at revivals of bronze art of the Chou and T'ang dynasties, respectively 2000 and 800 years earlier. However, such archaistic revivals are not necessarily confined to art styles, or to only one aspect of culture. The Renaissance in Europe was in part an archaistic movement on an immense scale, affecting first art and literature, then philosophy and science, and finally even political theory. Although these phenomena are

Reprinted by permission of the author and editor from *Men and Cultures*, edited by Anthony F. C. Wallace, pp. 595–600. Philadelphia: University of Pennsylvania Press, 1960.

known and have to be studied mainly from archaeological material, archaeologists have paid little attention except as they furnish one more dating problem. It is time that we started looking at them as problems in culture history as well.

One of the places in the New World where examples of archaism are most striking is prehistoric Peru. As early as 1925, A. L. Kroeber recognized the fact that the Late Chimu style of the North Coast of Peru revived many features of the earlier Moche style, after a period during which foreign influences had virtually wiped out the local tradition. In the recent studies of South Coast pottery styles of the later periods, it has been possible to study several examples of archaism in very close detail.

One type of archaism present in the late styles of the Ica valley is a form of antiquarianism involving the collection and imitation of antiques. It had a particular vogue during the period of the Inca occupation in the late fifteenth and early sixteenth centuries, but the phenomenon is known from much earlier times on the South Coast as well. The earliest evidence of a taste for the antique has been reported by Lawrence E. Dawson for the later phases of the Nazca styles of about the eighth or ninth centuries A.D. Some 400 years later, antique specimens appear in burials of the Chulpaca style of the Late Intermediate period. Two burials with pottery of this style in the Museum of Anthropology at Berkeley contained also one Nazca vessel each. The Nazca specimens are definitely ancient pieces and not later imitations, and the Nazca style had no traceable influence on the styles of the Late Intermediate period. It is interesting that no attention is paid to the Nazca style in the archaizing activities of later periods. The taste of later collectors seems to have run exclusively to Epigonal and Chulpaca art which developed from a tradition foreign to the South Coast.

The Inca-period vogue of antiquarianism which revives post-Tiahuanacoid styles first appears at a time just preceding the Inca conquest of the area. A grave-lot of this period (Late Soniche) included one jar, in the Epigonal style of about 300–400 years earlier, which is so authentic that it is presumably another reused ancient specimen. Subsequently, during the Inca occupation, collectors' items and later imitations of Epigonal and Chulpaca pottery represent six percent of the pottery found in burials of that time. While one or two vessels may be reused ancient specimens, the majority of the specimens are copies of ancient prototypes with varying degrees of faithfulness. In most cases elements in shape features and design techniques betray the later origin of the vessels. With the end of Inca administrative control in the sixteenth century came an abrupt change in the local style, and the antiquarianism of the Inca period largely seems to have gone out of fashion.

The antiquarianism just described has in common with the examples from the Old World cited earlier that it revives stylistic elements of much earlier times not in the memory of those living. An interest in the antique is traditional in this area. It probably had its origin in the occasional accidental discoveries by the later inhabitants of earlier specimens, perhaps uncovered through the disturbance of earlier burials by natural or human agencies. Such discoveries must have been made at all times, but the antiques clearly proved of greater attraction in some periods than in others. Imitations, in particular, seem to be confined to certain periods. An important distinction of this type of antiquarianism in the Ica valley is that it does not affect the contemporaneous style as a whole but is restricted to isolated specimens.

A second type of archaism occurs in Late Ica pottery in the early Colonial period which differs from the earlier antiquarianism just described in that it revives on a large scale features of one particular style of the recent past. There is very clear evidence that this early Colonial archaism is a nativistic revival, the result of a reaction at Ica against the Inca occupation which preceded it. To date virtually the only nativistic revivals which have come to the attention of anthropologists have been described by ethnologists, such as the Ghost Dance of the American Indians or the Cargo cults of the South Pacific. It is a valuable addition to our knowledge to be able to document such a movement from archaeological evidence as well.

The early Colonial or Tajaraca B pottery of the Ica valley represents a wholesale reversion to the local style which immediately preceded the relatively brief Inca occupation period. Its main distinguishing feature is the fact that no vessel found is free from its stylistic effects, in contrast to the archaism described earlier. This revival coincides with an almost complete loss of features of Inca origin; both such features and local stylistic features which are closely associated with the Inca occupation are pointedly ignored. The emphasis which dominates the revival is the reversion to the Soniche style, the last fully standardized style which preceded the Inca occupation. However, although a few vessels come very close to being perfect replicas of their Soniche prototypes, such close replicas are extremely rare, and the majority of vessels have some characteristic which betrays their later origin. This is due to the fact that changes in the local style independent of Inca influence, which had taken place during the period of Inca occupation and for a brief interval preceding it, persisted, though in somewhat altered form. Traces of such changes are found in combination with classic Soniche features as well as with additional innovations in patterning and design. The result is a distinctive new ware characterized by a number of stylistic anachronisms.

Many of the revivals of classic Soniche features are amazingly faithful. Such accuracy undoubtedly was possible because of the shortness of the intervening period. The Inca occupation lasted about sixty years. There must have been enough older people living at the time of the Spanish conquest who remembered the art of their youth or had close contact with those who did, so that there was direct continuity of artistic experience to supplement the heirloom specimens available as models.

Information on the historical background of the revival, based primarily on archaeological evidence, contributes a good deal to our understanding of the circumstances which led up to this early Colonial reaction at Ica. In the first place, on the basis of studies of pottery styles from a number of South Coast valleys, we can make some inferences about the status of the Ica valley among its neighbors in the period preceding the Inca conquest. Ica clearly had a position of prestige as regards artistry in pottery making. This prestige manifests itself in the amount and kind of stylistic influence which Ica pottery had on that of neighboring valleys. Such influence is discernible to the north at least as far as Chincha, and to the south in the Nazca drainage, at Acari and at Chala, over an area of about 500 square kilometers. The evidence also indicates that the artistic prestige of Ica originates with the Chulpaca style, some 200–300 years before the Inca conquest, and is found with increasing strength through successive Ica style phases up to and including the Inca period. Not only do elements of the Ica styles strongly influence the styles of adjacent valleys, but, in addition, trade pieces or local imitations of Ica ware are found in conspicuous percentages side by side with vessels of the local styles. In contrast, no comparable influences from neighboring valleys are found at Ica, where stylistic change is based predominantly on local development unaffected by outside influences. This is particularly true of the Soniche style which served as the basis for the Colonial revival. Compared with the earlier styles, the Soniche style reaches a high point in homogeneity and standardization, and foreign influence is virtually nonexistent.

Unfortunately, the studies to date are based almost entirely on pottery, and consequently it is not known whether Ica prestige extended also to other forms of artistic expression. However, it is known from historical sources that in terms of political and military power and size of population Ica was not important in the area in which it exerted artistic influence. Early chroniclers agree that in these respects the Chincha and Cañete valleys were more important at the time of the Inca conquest and up until the advent of the Spaniards. Ica prestige, then, was based on artistic achievement rather than political power, and pottery was either the main, or at least an important, expression of that achievement.

The history of succeeding political events, starting with the Inca conquest, is another important aspect of the antecedents which led up to the Ica revival. Inca conquest techniques are known from historical sources and have been described by Rowe (1946) in the Handbook of South American Indians. The Inca pursued a policy of enlightened self-interest designed to establish complete political control of a large and well-functioning empire. Their policies were ruthless, uncompromising and sweeping in their aim to establish such control, but they also brought efficient administration and material well-being to the provinces as an important means to this end. A conspicuous aspect of the conquest program was the manipulation of cultural symbols standing for the national self-consciousness of conquered peoples. The Inca attempted to divert these symbols from representing exclusive pride in local tradition to representing pride in membership in the Inca empire. Historic sources give us only sporadic glimpses of the effect of this manipulation on the affected peoples. These sources do show that the policy affected many aspects of culture, including dress, architecture, religion and local leadership, but the information is rather general and selected; it is here that the archaeological data provide important additional information on how the program was carried out. In the first place, pottery studies demonstrate that on the South Coast, at least, this Inca policy was extended with particular emphasis to pottery art as an important symbol of local distinctions. In all the valleys for which studies have been made, the Inca conquest brought fundamental and arbitrary changes to local pottery styles. At Ica, in particular, new categories of pottery vessels became important symbols of new social distinctions and prestige associated with the Inca. The new wares have very little in common with the local tradition and are primarily composed of arbitrary combinations of Inca elements and local innovations. These new types clearly originate at Ica but have a wide distribution, specifically in the former sphere of Ica prestige on the South Coast, and sporadically as far away as the highlands. No comparable prestige ware emanates from the other South Coast valleys, and it is evident that the local prestige pattern continued under the Inca domination, though it was divorced from its former associations. Pottery of the local Ica tradition continued side by side with the new wares, but the evidence is that it was relegated to a position of inferiority in relation to the latter and to Inca pottery. Thus, the sum of historical and archaeological evidence shows that the Inca conquest interfered in a number of ways with local pride and independence, although it did not bring economic or general physical hardship to Ica.

The advent of the Spaniards to Peru in 1532 brought with it the destruction of the Inca administrative system as a functioning unit and the dissolution of local controls. Subsequent civil wars and chaotic conditions prevented effective administrative control by the Spaniards until 1570, when the Spanish administration began to enforce residence by Indians in certain designated towns under the so-called "reduction" policy. Thus, during a period of about forty years, there was a relaxation of controls over dominated peoples, and it was during this period that the Ica revival took place.

The above historical and stylistic observations readily reveal the nature of the Ica pottery revival. It was unquestionably a reaction to the Inca occupation, based on frustration rather than extreme hardship. The primary point of sensitivity at Ica involved local pride in prestige based on pottery artistry of some two to three hundred years' standing. Ica prestige did not diminish in this respect under the Inca, but it became second to foreign prestige wares, such as Inca and North Coast pottery, and a symbol of Inca domination. It is thus not the loss of prestige but rather the alteration of its symbolic associations and status which caused the reaction at Ica. It is no accident that the nativistic reaction manifested itself so emphatically in pottery, since pottery was a major symbol of local pride and independence in pre-Inca times.

It is of considerable interest that no comparable revival occurred in the neighboring South Coast valleys in the instances in which the pottery could be studied in detail. Early Colonial ware at Chincha, Acari and Chala continued without noticeable changes from that of the Inca period. Archaeological evidence shows that pre-Incaic pottery in those valleys had a secondary prestige position in relation to Ica and so would not have been suitable symbols of local pride. This does not preclude the possibility that nativism could have manifested itself in some other form in those valleys. Surface collections in the Pisco and Nazca regions to the immediate north and south of Ica turned up one revivalistic pottery vessel from each valley. The characteristics of these specimens are such that they indicate Ica influence rather than an independent local revival. Their presence in those valleys seems to be the result of a continuation of the historic prestige pattern in the area. It is quite possible that, had South Coast cultures not been destroyed by Spanish domination, Ica influence might have continued to grow in the old pattern and eventually again might have influenced pottery development in the neighboring valleys.

As may be seen, the above examples of stylistic revival, as studied from archaeological data, are capable of revealing a good deal of significant information about the culture history of the area. Aside from pointing to their historical significance, we can also emphasize the special difficulties they create for archaeological interpretation. They produce a situation where degree of similarity cannot be used as a basis on which to infer nearness of time, a type of inference commonly made by all archaeologists and which usually works reasonably well. In such cases only careful data on associations in the ground and on stylistic antecedents make a reasonable chronological arrangement possible.

Introduction to The Agricultural Basis of the Sub-Andean Chiefdoms of Colombia

With the exception of the Chibcha (Kroeber 1944), the sub-Andean chiefdoms of Colombia are poorly known in the ethnographic literature. This is because they rapidly became extinct after contact with Europeans; indeed, they were already under pressure from the highly developed Andean peoples from the south. Furthermore, it would appear that the chiefdom level of social organization is an extremely unstable one, for all over the Americas, the peoples at this evolutionary level succumbed rapidly to foreign intervention. There even is evidence (see Meggers and Evans in Chapter 4 of this volume) that such a society collapsed on its own on Marajó Island. In the southeastern United States, the Caribbean area, and the northern Andes, such peoples flourished, but today they are known only from the accounts of early travelers and archeological remains (e.g. Swanton 1911; Rouse 1962).

These chiefdoms, however, are extremely important since they provide a link between the uncomplicated polities of lowland South America and the high civilizations of Mexico and Peru. Chiefdoms are characterized by large settlements bound together into confederations under hierarchically arranged rulers; social strata including priests, warriors or nobles, commoners, and slaves; and a redistributive economy with surpluses of land, labor or agricultural goods managed by the elites. The more we learn about such peoples, the better we can understand the evolution of social stratification and the state in South America and elsewhere (cf. Fried 1967; Carneiro 1970b).

One of the most interesting problems which these societies present is that of explaining the ecological basis of their differentiation from less highly organized lowland types. The transition from unstratified, tribal societies to chiefdoms apparently took place in the absence of any significant technological innovations. In this selection, Gerardo Reichel-Dolmatoff has gathered together and analyzed the sparse sources available on the chiefdoms that existed in Colombia.

Gerardo Reichel-Dolmatoff, born in 1912, is research professor at the Instituto Colombiano de Antropología in Bogotá and served as Chairman of the Department of Anthropology, Universidad de los Andes, from 1963 to 1969. He has worked in Colombia for over thirty years, carrying out archeological and ethnological field research. His publications include *Los Kogi* (1951), *The People of Aritama* (1961), *Colombia: Ancient Peoples and Places* (1965), and *Amazonian Cosmos* (1971).

3. THE AGRICULTURAL BASIS OF THE SUB-ANDEAN CHIEFDOMS OF COLOMBIA

GERARDO REICHEL-DOLMATOFF

The particular nature and scope of agriculture as it was practiced by the Sub-Andean natives of Colombia, must be viewed and evaluated as a phenomenon which is intimately related to the unique geographical and cultural position this country occupies in tropical America. Two seashores, three great mountain chains, large rivers and alluvial plains, innumerable intermontane valleys, and a general situation between the Equator and the Caribbean Sea, form an environment of extremely complex geographical and meteorological features. Temperature, prevailing air currents, precipitation, and soil characteristics vary with latitude, elevation, and slope-exposure. While north of Latitude 8° N the yearly cycle is marked by a distinct dry season of some four months and a rainy season of corresponding duration, south of Latitude 8° N there are two shorter dry seasons alternating with two wet periods of equal duration. On the other hand, Colombia is and has always been the gateway to South America, located on one of the major crossroads of cultural exchange. Diffusion and stimuli reached Colombia from north and south and spread—at different rates and at different times —from there to other regions, leading to a wide variety of local cultural developments.

Within this mosaic of micro-environments, ecological niches, and local cultures, the so-called Sub-Andean chiefdoms form an intelligible type of socio-cultural systems characterized by a recurrent configuration of certain traits. The Colombian chiefdoms (and here I shall include the Muisca and the Tairona) were small, class-

Reprinted by permission of the author and the Fundación La Salle de Ciencias Naturales, Caracas, from *Antropológica*, Supplement No. 2. *The Evolution of Horticultural Systems in Native South America*, edited by Johannes Wilbert, Caracas, 1961, pp. 83–89. The appendices and references to this article have been omitted.

structured village federations, politically organized under territorial chiefs. The precise character of this chieftainship varied from group to group, and while some were hardly more than village headmen, others were warchiefs or became eventually the leaders of small incipient states. But all had in common the concept of the respected or feared authoritarian leader who had to be obeyed. Religious life centered around the priest-temple-idol cult. Subsistence, in the widest sense, was based upon agriculture and trade. Warfare was highly developed and included such elements as cannibalism, head trophies, and the taking of captives either as sacrificial victims or as slave laborers.

The organization of these local chiefdoms was oriented not only toward the maintenance of a stable food supply but toward the acquisition of a surplus which would support the existing social differentiation, political power, specialization, and the carrying on of warfare and trade. The relative amount, nature and use of this surplus depended on many local factors, but all Sub-Andean peoples did show this more or less marked capacity to develop the natural resources of their respective territories far beyond mere biophysical needs and beyond what these groups considered to be their cultural subsistence level. In many cases the surplus consisted of privately owned stores of maize and in some chiefdoms there were communal stores of food in case of war, or special fields to be planted by the community and the harvest of which was used to support the warring members of the group. Large stores of cotton cloth, salt, dried fish, and other industrial products were used for trading or were acquired for personal prestige reasons.

Native techniques and tools of agriculture were limited to brand-tillage, the digging-stick, and the stone-ax. However, specific land use and permanency of settlements and fields depended in a large measure on the recognized regenerative capacity of the local soils and, with it, on rainfall and temperature distribution, slope-exposure, population density, and crop variety. In the rich alluvial soils of the intermontane basins where convectional rains are frequent, or on the temperate western slopes which receive abundant and evenly distributed orographic rainfall, this brand-tillage did not have the character of rapidly shifting slash-and-burn cultivation, but permitted the maintenance of large permanent fields which produced high yields for long periods. But even in the less favorable areas brand-tillage apparently did not lead to rapid soil depletion but proved to be a highly efficient agricultural system. Not only were there ample forest reserves but in many valleys the particular soil and rainfall conditions permitted intensive cultivation of plots over long time-spans. From several descriptions it is evident that new fields were not necessarily cleared in virgin forest or secondary growth in fallows, but that also grassy slopes and plains were profitably used for agriculture. The Anserma Indians, e.g., simply beat down the grass with sticks, burned it and grew on such fields up to two yearly harvests of maize with an average yield of 1:100. The fact that villages were moved occasionally was certainly not always due to local soil depletion but may have been caused by many other factors.

The use of fertilizers seems to have been unknown and no data are available as to systematic crop rotation, but it seems that mixed cropping was the rule and that maize was usually planted together with beans and squash. In many regions where seasonal differences of temperature and rainfall were slight, crops were staggered and the fields were perennially productive. About a dozen local groups practiced small-scale irrigation and terracing, and fruit trees were often irrigated but, with the possible exception of the Tairona, these engineering works could be handled by small and loosely organized groups and were not an important factor in concentrating population nor in fomenting political cohesion or control. The geographical distribution of irrigation and terracing does not show any significant clusters nor does it show a marked culture-physiography accord. The Tairona Indians practiced terracing and irrigation on steep wet mountain slopes *and* on the arid foothills. The Guane Indians irrigated their fields lying in the high semi-arid Andean valleys, and several of the Cauca tribes constructed large irrigation ditches on the floodplains. In the Northern Lowlands the fertile soil deposited by the yearly inundations of the large rivers was made ample use of for short-term cropping but drainage ditches seem to have been unknown.

Notwithstanding this relatively low technological level of agricultural practice—as far as tools are concerned—the total inventory of crops was of considerable variety. In practically all regions maize was the most important food plant. Next in importance followed the root crops such as sweet manioc, racacha, sweet-potato, and yam. The highland dwellers grew at least two local types of potato and, besides, quinoa, ulluco, oca, topinambur, and cubios, a tuberous nasturtium. Other root crops were achira, yautia, and groundnuts; kidney and lima beans were widely cultivated. A large number of more or less cultivated fruits included avocado pears, papaya, guava, custard apple, pineapple, soursop and others. The peach palm provided an important and very common source of food, and squashes, pepino, tomato, caimito, hogplums, and peppers were widely used. The greatest number of species was grown on the fertile temperate slopes of the Cordilleras.

It is important to point out here that the Colombian Sub-Andean tribes, even those which inhabited the tropical lowlands, *did not* cultivate bitter manioc but used only the non-poisonous varieties. From these, however, no storable cakes or flour were prepared but the tubers were consumed as soon as they were harvested. This then shows an essential difference from the cassava and farinha economy of the Amazon forest where there existed techniques for storing this food and where important surpluses could be accumulated in this form.

Although the list of food plants known to the Sub-Andean groups is impressive, it is clear that crop diversity is not equivalent to food abundance. Although Colombia occupies a most important place in the field of plant domestication and diversification of native domesticates, it is doubtful whether crop productivity—under the agricultural and social system outlined above—was ever sufficient to support a dense population for long time periods. There seems to be but little time-depth to the archaeological sites which may be correlated with these slope and valley agriculturalists and we must consider then some of the probable causes of this discontinuity of occupancy.

Chronic inter-tribal warfare was a characteristic feature of Sub-Andean culture. Although in most cases it seems to have been closely related both to religion, by providing sacrificial victims, and to social stratification, by putting a premium on bravery and thus defining rank and status, the ultimate motives of these persistent wars and raids must be sought in economic causes. As a matter of fact, closer analysis reveals that warfare was most violent between groups which occupied territories that differed markedly in agricultural productivity. Telling examples are the wars between the highland Muisca and the slope-dwelling Panche; the Pijao raids into the Cauca Valley, and the violent wars fought just at the edge of the fertile rainbelt which extends in a west-easterly direction across the Central Cordillera, at about Latitude 5° N. In all these cases the main aggressors were inhabitants of regions with a relatively low precipitation and one single yearly harvest of maize, while the invaded territories were of higher rainfall, extremely fertile soils, and two or even three yearly harvests. In many cases it would seem that the 80-inch isohyet was practically a military frontier.

But warfare, if successful, was profitable not only with regard to the fertile lands conquered or looted; it also provided slave laborers who were made to work in the fields or as domestic servants. On the other hand, the drinking bouts which preceded or followed the organization of a war party were important occasions to affirm social cohesion and personal rank, and the possibility of or need for alliances with neighbors offered to local chiefs the opportunity to expand their influence and power. Additional factors which contributed to this pattern of warfare were many. On the one hand, population pressure in narrow fertile valleys seems eventually to have reached limits where expansion by organized force became the solution. On the other hand, the necessarily migratory nature of shifting cultivation practiced by neighboring Tropical Forest groups, marauding parties of which penetrated into the Sub-Andean chiefdoms, frequently led to border conflicts and occasionally to wars of extermination. Also the general migratory movements of the many different groups which followed the rivers or coasts or crossed the Cordilleras either in search of new land or retreating under the pressure of foreign intruders, were a danger to any permanently settled community which did not or could not defend its territory. Defensive action and acquisitive aggressive intrusion thus led to a type of warfare which contributed to the characteristic pattern of territorially restricted political cohesion and to a frequent shifting and relocation of habitat and political power.

But quite apart from these considerations, it is also evident that warfare—in combination with human sacrifices, wide-spread cannibalism, and institutionalized infanticide—was also a mechanism to control population increase. Besides, quite often, cannibalistic practices may have been simply the result of a deficient food situation. In many Sub-Andean chiefdoms cannibalism was simply part of the food quest and reached proportions where the consumption of human flesh became a standard food habit.

Wherever warfare was absent or less developed, as among the Tairona, the Sinú, the Malibú, or in the Muisca heart-land, not only the settlement pattern varied but there was also a definite trend toward large ceremonial centers and a theocratic system of government. It is possible that here we observe already a later phase of developments where the particular combination of physical environment, technological knowledge, and political leadership had made possible the consolidation of once scattered groups into small incipient states. It seems, however, that after this initial step had been taken, the principal controls went into the hands of a group of priests while the functions of military and political chiefs were rather restricted.

Another factor, next to warfare, which appears to be significantly related to agricultural developments is trade. Most Sub-Andean Indians were great traders and it seems that in many cases wealth—and with it social rank and political control—was based not so much on surplus food production, stability of food supply, or war honors, than on successful trade of such industrial products as gold, cotton cloth, and salt. Among those lacking these industries trading may have been an incentive to local agricultural production, but among the producers of these goods—notably the Muisca, Tairona, and some of the principal Cauca tribes—it might have been at times an inhibiting factor as trading for food would have been preferred to producing it locally.

There are then several aspects which set Sub-Andean agriculture apart from that of its closer or more distant Tropical Forest neighbors. In the first place, the extraordinary geographical and biotic diversity of the Sub-Andean territories offered a total ecological advantage with its great variety of habitat niches which made possible the cultivation of a wide range of food plants. Most natural factors concerned with agriculture were more propitious: soils, temperature, rainfall distribution, moisture, drainage. In the second place, incipient water control and a conscious choice of profitable land led to greater productivity per total area. To these advantages was joined the political hability of taking possession of fertile crop lands, especially in those regions where maize yielded abundantly. It should be kept in mind here that the Sub-Andean peoples were essentially seed farmers. Although the highly caloric products of vegetative planting were of no small importance in their diet, their staple crop was maize.

The real intensification of agriculture stemmed from the fact that the Sub-Andean peoples had learned to recognize the inherent advantages of certain regions such as western slopes with abundant, evenly distributed rainfall, where temperature and soil conditions induced the rapid growth of high yielding plants and permitted a wide variety of crops. Tropical Forest agriculture in Colombia, on the other hand, was limited mainly to lowland regions where precipitation is often irregular, disastrous flooding is frequent, and altitudinal variation is lacking. Their agriculture, then, included fewer crops, small yields and, above all, it lacked the capacity to produce the storable surplus provided by maize farming on fertile slopes.

Nevertheless, the specific nature or relative efficiency of Sub-Andean agricultural practices was not wholly conditioned by a given environmental potential, as far as differential suitability of the physical factors is concerned, but there were also cultural factors at play which influenced choice and emphasis. There are instances where irrigation was practiced in regions of fairly high rainfall, and others where preference was given to root crops although the country was well suited for maize farming. The Muisca, at the cost of chronic warfare, preferred the variety of temperate crops to a more intensified irrigation agriculture of their own highland complex of food plants. The Tairona, under the pressure of population increase, did not try to expand by conquest but resorted to the intensive exploitation of a narrowly limited territory through complex irrigation and terracing systems. It is evident that similar environments or opportunities did not evoke the same cultural responses, for the Sub-Andean peoples' adaptation to and use of the physical environment varied greatly.

Archaeological evidence obtained so far seems to suggest that the beginnings and the eventual growth of the Sub-Andean culture pattern were closely related to the cultivation of a developed form of maize. Although a primitive type of maize may have spread into Colombia already much earlier and might have coincided with incipient plant domestication on the mountain slopes of the interior, the Preformative and Formative stages seem to have been largely limited to a littoral, riparian, and lagoonal environment. The domestication of certain root crops which thrive in regions of low or irregular precipitation led probably to the sporadic settling of interfluvial regions, but definite independence from a riverine environment was made possible only through maize farming. Now, maize cultivation, if it is to be profitable, requires a great deal of water and sunshine, but productivity depends not so much on the quantity of precipitation and insolation as on their seasonal distribution. To a certain degree, the specific requirements of this crop which in itself is, of course, a cultural product, led the way to those regions where productivity was high because of a particularly favorable combination of physiographic and meteorological factors. At the same time, this environment included a wide range of other highly productive food plants. It was maize cultivation which brought about the expansion of population over the flanks of the mountain systems, a region which, until then, could have been hardly more than a hunting territory or the occasional habitat of small-scale migratory farmers of the Tropical-Forest level.

This movement into the rugged, mountainous interior had far-reaching consequences. The general orientation toward agriculture led to a type of warfare which necessarily was only of a local nature because the social units carrying on war were themselves based on a technology-ecology which was also local. This reinforced the regional character of small chiefdoms whose political power was under constant threat. The spread into the mountains was also followed by decentralization, cultural isolation, and regionalism in, what I have termed, the Colombian micro-environments. Although through the centuries there certainly was a notable cultural advance as shown by crop diversity, social and religious complexity, and major achievements in metallurgy and ceramics, the eventual population pressure did not lead to a more intensified agricultural system nor to an integration of wider political controls, as in the Andean Cultures, but rather led to migrations and small local but highly destructive wars. The great territorial extension of the Chibcha peoples was a passive spread, not a military conquest, and possibilities for wider political expansion and cultural development were limited by the provincialism of circumscribed economic adaptation.

Most notably, there was also a partial return to the riverine environment, a step which definitely limited further agricultural developments. Those who did not choose to compete in the struggle for the fertile slopes settled in areas which were marginal to the core-land of intensive maize farming. Although some of them created relatively complex local cultures, the discontinuity of such factors as occupancy, population density, favorable environment, and cultural impulse, inhibited further advance.

Introduction to An Interpretation of the Cultures of Marajó Island

The authors of this article were among the first archeologists to conduct modern research in the tropical forest regions of South America. The highlands and drylands of South America have been subjects of archeological investigation for decades, but it was only in the fifties that prejudice and pessimism regarding tropical forest archeology began to be overcome. For their research Meggers and Evans chose a fascinating problem, not only for its exotic aspects but also for its relevance to South American prehistory and to cultural theory. The area investigated is the vast island called Marajó, located at the mouth of the Amazon River. On this island in pre-Columbian times, there flourished briefly a society dubbed Marajoara which manufactured pottery far superior to the ware produced by any other nearby people. It also left behind large burial mounds, a type of monument virtually unknown in Amazonia. What was the origin of this people? Were they intruders from a distant land, or was their elaborate cultural pattern native to Marajó? Aside from the intrinsic interest of solving such a puzzle, the answers to such questions are relevant to the broader problems of tracing the migration of peoples and the diffusion of cultural elements in aboriginal South America.

In the following article Meggers and Evans conclude that Marajoara culture was intrusive, and this led them, along with further research, to a series of hypotheses regarding the peopling of the Amazon basin (Evans 1965, Evans and Meggers 1968, Meggers and Evans 1957, 1961). That the issue is still debated is evident from Lathrap's article in Chapter 6 of this volume.

The explanation of the downfall of the Marajoara society that Meggers and Evans offered has generated even more interest and debate. From this research Meggers went on to write her famous article "Environmental Limitations on the Development of Culture" (1954) in which she argued that agricultural productivity imposes an upper limit on cultural evolution in a given area. In regard to Amazonia, she pointed out that the tropical rain forest with its weak soils did not permit large, permanent settlements (generally agreed to be a prerequisite of cultural development), because the only viable form of agriculture is the extensive, slash-and-burn type. Robert Carneiro addresses himself to this problem in Chapter 7 of this volume. The issue is relevant to other problems as well, for example, in the explanation of the classic Maya collapse (Meggers 1954, 1957a; William Coe 1957; Dumond 1961; Willey and Shimkin 1971). Meggers has expanded and updated her theoretical arguments in an article (1957b) and in a recent book (1971).

Betty Meggers and Clifford Evans are members of the Department of Anthropology, Smithsonian Institution, Washington, D.C. In addition to their work on Marajó, they have carried out excavations in Ecuador, Venezuela and Guyana.

4. AN INTERPRETATION OF THE CULTURES OF MARAJÓ ISLAND

BETTY J. MEGGERS AND CLIFFORD EVANS

Since the middle of the 19th century, when they were first seen by travelers and natural scientists, the ceramics of the mounds of Marajó have been acclaimed as an advanced and versatile expression of artistic and technical skill. In recent years other Amazonian ceramic styles have been discovered and their relative crudity has served to accentuate the superiority of Marajoara pottery. This superiority led to speculations about its origin, many based on unscientific considerations. In 1949, Willey reviewed the archeological evidence then available from the Amazonian lowlands and postulated that Marajó was a center from which influences moved north, west, and south to affect the ceramics of distant areas.

The impossibility of evaluating conflicting interpretations in the absence of more exact chronological and distributional information led us to undertake fieldwork at the mouth of the Amazon in 1948–49. Survey and stratigraphic excavations at sites on the north coast and in the center of Marajó revealed the presence of four other cultural phases and permitted establishment of a relative chronology within each phase. For environmental reasons, knowledge of these cultures is limited to what can be deduced from the pottery. The climate prevents survival of perishable objects and stone of the kind suitable for tools does not occur locally. What we know of living Amazonian tribes indicates that weapons and tools were made from wood, bone, and cane. Except for a few pottery ear plugs and beads, we find no ornaments, and we deduce that these were also made from feathers, seeds, and other perishable materials. The discovery of an occasional sherd rounded into a disk and perforated through the center leads us to postulate the

This paper is a revised version of "Uma interpretação das culturas da Ilha de Marajó," Instituto de Antropologia e Etnologia do Pará, Publ. 7, Belém, 1954.

existence of textiles, although no nets or fabrics remain. A non-pottery-making people living in a humid climate like the Amazon basin leaves no clues for the reconstruction of its history; a pottery-making people leaves a record in broken pottery that an archeologist can decipher and from which he can reconstruct many aspects of their culture. The following pages will show how this can be done.

The earliest of the Marajó ceramic styles, the Ananatuba Phase, has been found at a number of sites on the northern and eastern parts of the island. The refuse deposits are thicker and the sherds more concentrated than in any of the other phases except the Marajoara Phase, indicating that villages were moved less frequently than in later times. The pottery is hard and smooth, with a cream to tan surface. Only two percent is decorated with well executed incised designs.

The seemingly peaceful and undisturbed life of the Ananatuba Phase population ended with its conquest and assimilation by a group with a different ceramic complex. In this Mangueiras Phase, the great majority of the sherds are once again from undecorated small bowls and jars, probably cooking vessels. The common form of ornamentation was brushing and scraping of the exterior surface with a stick or bunch of twigs producing parallel and criss-cross scratches. The Mangueiras potters apparently admired the Ananatuba Phase incised designs, however, since they began to copy them [cf. Menzel in Chapter 2 of this volume—Ed.].

A third group, the Formiga Phase, appears in the same general area after the decline of the Ananatuba Phase but contemporary with the latter part of the Mangueiras Phase. Compared to the preceding two, its occupation of Marajó appears to have been brief. It also differed in settlement pattern, sites occurring in the savanna rather than in the forest. The pottery is poorly made and has a reddish to grayish hue. Decorated sherds, comprising four percent of the total, are not characterized by any well defined style.

When Europeans first visited the mouth of the Amazon, they found the islands of Mexiana, Caviana, and Marajó occupied by a tribe they called the Aruã. At one time it was believed that these were the Indians who built the mounds, but archeological research has revealed small glass beads from European trade associated with a type of pottery that is much simpler than that from the mounds and different from that of any of the other phases just described. The frequency of decoration is the lowest of all in the Aruã Phase (less than one percent) and consists predominantly of a row of rings impressed with the end of a hollow piece of cane around the neck or shoulder of burial jars. Like the Marajoara Phase people, the Aruã practiced secondary burial in large urns, but these were grouped on the surface of the ground rather than interred in mounds. Villages are smaller and less permanent than in any of the other phases and are located along tidal streams in the forest near the coast.

Of these four phases, three are earlier and one (the Aruã) is later than the Marajoara Phase. Except in the Formiga Phase, sites are located on natural elevations not conspicuously higher than the surrounding land, but which always remain above flood level during the rainy season. The villages were typically on small streams in patches of forest. Sites average 50–75 meters in diameter, with deposits of pottery refuse varying in thickness from 5 centimeters (in the Aruã Phase) to about a meter. The sherds are evenly distributed and mixed with a relatively small amount of dirt. This is the situation that one would expect to encounter in a present-day village anywhere among the more sedentary tribes of Amazonia. The pottery, simple and utilitarian in construction and form, is not standardized in shape or size. Neither is it skillfully decorated. These features are evidence that it was made by each woman for her own use rather than by specialists whose production supplied the whole village. The small area and shallow depth of refuse deposits indicate that villages were small and occupied for only a short time. Like surviving Tropical Forest Indians, these prehistoric tribes of Marajó moved from place to place as their fields were exhausted or the hunting grew poor. Except for the Aruã, we have no evidence of their burial pattern. Apparently there was no well developed belief in an after-life, urn burial was not practiced, and the bodies were disposed of in ways that leave no record for the archeologist.

This way of life contrasts sharply with that of the Marajoara Phase. The Marajoara sites, concentrated in the savanna on the eastern half of the island with Lago Ararí as a center, are prominent features in the otherwise flat landscape. These mounds were built with soil gathered basketful by basketful and emptied on the site.

By analogy with living tribes in other regions, we know that this kind of construction requires a social organization that can plan and carry out long-range programs, a society divided into ruling and ruled segments, and occupational division of labor. While some people built the mounds for use as dwelling sites or cemeteries, others worked in the gardens or went hunting or fishing to supply them with food.

This division of labor is evident also in ceramics. Marajoara pottery, both in form and decoration, shows itself to be the product of a special group of artisans. The uniformity of shape and size in the utilitarian vessels, the decoration of two or more jars in almost identical elaborate patterns and colors, the skillful execution of complex excised designs, the use of one or two slips on the same vessel, and other complicated decorative techniques are all indications that pottery making was a specialized craft. In addition to vessels, one finds figurines, pipes, stools, pot rests, spindle whorls, and tangas (pubic coverings) of pottery, as well as anthropomorphic and zoomorphic adornos.

The mounds were constructed for two purposes: as habitation sites and as cemeteries. In the village mounds, pottery is relatively sparse and nearly always undecorated. The large amount of dirt mixed with the sherds and the fire-reddened layers one above the other, which mark successive floor levels, indicate that the Marajoara Phase people did not use a house elevated on piles. Instead, they built directly on the ground, using the surface as the house floor, which they covered from time to time with clean dirt. Since such a floor would become damp in the rainy season if placed on the natural ground surface, the motive for construction of the habitation mounds appears to have been the need of a dry house site.

Cemetery mounds are in general larger than those built for habitation. The existence of an elaborate ritual centering on death and the belief in an after-life are evident from the large jars manufactured for burial, and from the small bowls, probably once containing food offerings, the tangas, and animal bones found inside the burial jars. A distinction in social status is implied in the contrast between this kind of burial and other skeletal remains that were interred directly in the earth with no protecting jar and no offerings except an occasional tanga.

This is Marajoara culture in its earliest form on Marajó. It appears fully developed, with a suddenness that makes it certain that it represents an intrusion. Its history on Marajó is one of steady decline. The pottery becomes less expertly made, the burial urns become smaller and less elaborately decorated, cremation takes the place of secondary burial, and tangas and other ritual objects cease to be made. These are small changes, but they are hints of decreasing population size, of waning governmental strength, and of increasing emphasis on individual self-sufficiency rather than division of labor. In other words, the Marajoara Phase, which entered the island as a higher developed culture, regressed or declined slowly to the level of simple, undifferentiated society characteristic of the earlier and later occupants of Marajó.

It is of interest to examine the reason for this decline. Anthropological and archeological research has shown that cultures advance as the productivity of human labor increases. In a culture where subsistence depends on hunting, fishing, and gathering of wild plants, life is a constant food quest. All the able-bodied members of a family must devote most of their time to subsistence activity. There is no specialization of occupation except by sex and little political organization or social distinction. The semi-nomadic life that reliance on game and wild plants requires makes anything but the most temporary kind of shelter useless. It also discourages the development or elaboration of material goods, because only a bare minimum can be transported by a people frequently on the move. Remains of tribes in this stage have not been found archeologically in Amazonia as yet.

The discovery of agriculture transformed this way of life. By domesticating plants and making them work for him, man was able to increase the fruits of his labor immensely. With a reliable source of food for daily needs and a surplus for feasts or to store against the possibility of future want, there was no longer any need for everyone to devote all his time to food getting. Some of it could be spent on making life more convenient and comfortable. Permanent dwellings and larger population concentrations were possible. This produced changes in social organization, with the development of social stratification and the beginnings of division of labor by occupation. Women no longer had to spend their days in search of wild roots and fruits, and could devote the time left over from household duties to the perfection of their skill in weaving, pottery making, and basketry. Ritual was elaborated and directed toward placating the spirits of the forces of nature that could assure the success of the harvest. Slash-and-burn agriculture makes possible the beginnings of all these things. In dryer areas, like Peru and Mexico, where agriculture could be intensified, the cultures continued to develop and differentiate. In these areas, tribes grew into confederacies and empires, with rigid social classes, great bodies of governmental and religious officials, as well as craftsmen and specialists of all types, none of whom contributed to subsistence activities. A necessary adjunct of this division of labor was elaboration of mechanisms for distribution. The spirits of nature evolved into powerful gods; great temples were erected, and sacrifices were made.

In the tropical forests, this elaboration was prevented by factors inherent in the environment. The poor soil will permit the use of a field for only a few years. Then it must be allowed to revert to forest to recover its fertility, and new land must be cleared. As that near the villages ceases to be productive, the fields move farther away until it finally becomes necessary to relocate the village to keep it within practical distance of the gardens. The yield per unit of land is not sufficient to support a large number of people and villages must consequently remain relatively small. This in turn keeps the division of labor and the development of social stratification at a minimum.

The more advanced culture of the Marajoara Phase was out of adjustment with the resources of the tropical forest environment. The social organization was dependent on occupational division of labor, which required a few to produce food for the whole community. Arriving on Marajó with an already highly developed social organization, the population was able to maintain this level long enough to build the large mounds and to inhabit them for an unknown length of time. Subsistence activities, however, required more time and labor than they had in the previous home of the group and this brought a concomitant reduction in the labor available for other pursuits. The sequence was the opposite of the one just described: the division of labor decreased, the villages grew smaller, and with fewer people, less specialization, and weaker political control the culture inevitably declined in complexity. The mounds in the headwaters of the Rio Anajás, which were excavated during the 1948–49 season, probably were not occupied during the last stages of the Marajoara Phase. Although the pottery is inferior in the upper levels to what it was in the lower and earlier ones, it is still superior to that of any of the other phases. What finally became of the Marajoara people may be discovered through more archeological work. They may have died out or moved away from Marajó, or they may have been conquered and absorbed by the Aruã, who moved onto the island from Mexiana, Caviana, and the Territory of Amapá.

This cultural-ecological theory has two parts. It asserts that 1) a society with advanced social stratification and occupational division of labor cannot evolve in a tropical forest environment where agriculture is by slash-and-burn, and that 2) should such a culture penetrate into the tropical lowlands, it will not be able to develop further or even to maintain the level it has already achieved, but will decline until it reaches the simplicity characteristic of existing tropical forest tribes. There is no archeological evidence that the elaborate Marajoara Phase culture evolved from the preceding Mangueiras and Formiga Phases on Marajó Island. Instead, the evidence indicates that it arrived at the peak of its development and slowly but steadily declined.

If the theory is correct, the origin of Marajoara culture should not be sought within the limits of the lowland tropical forest. The presence of several unusual techniques of pottery decoration (such as excision, incisions made with a double-pointed tool, double slipping, and red or white retouch of incisions), as well as ceramic artifacts such as stools, tangas, spoons, spindle whorls, and figurines, should make it a simple matter to identify its place of origin. Analysis of the distribution of these and other Marajoara Phase traits shows the majority to occur in northwestern South America, especially in highland Colombia. This suggests that the Marajoara Phase evolved somewhere within this area. In addition to possessing the requisite cultural elements, this part of South America also has an environment suitable for a high level of cultural development. Although the indigenous cultures did not attain the climax achieved in Peru, they advanced much farther than those of the tropical forest.

For reasons yet to be discovered, the ancestors of the Marajoara

Phase were forced to abandon their homeland. They moved into the lowlands in search of a new location, finding the land unsuitable or the occupants unfriendly until they arrived at the mouth of the Amazon. On Marajó Island, they probably met with little or no resistance from the small and loosely organized Mangueiras and Formiga Phase peoples, whom they may have absorbed. The fact that they chose to settle on the open savanna rather than in the forest may be indicative of the nature of their previous environment. This pattern of settlement also placed villages within easy communication of one another and reserved the forested portions for slash-and-burn agriculture and for hunting.

This brief interpretation of the archeology of Marajó Island summarizes some of the principal results of the 1948–49 fieldwork. It has shown that not one but five distinct cultures occupied the island and that none of them originated there. All were simple cultures, comparable to those of surviving Amazonian tribes, except the Marajoara Phase, which possessed a more highly developed social and religious system as well as more elaborate pottery. By showing that the island of Marajó was not a center from which influences emanated to distant parts of Amazonia, but was instead the recipient of successive immigrants from different sources, our research has answered one question only to raise several more. In view of the vast expanse of the archeologically unknown portions of South America, it is certain to be a long time before a reliable reconstruction of aboriginal cultural development in the lowlands will be achieved.

POSTSCRIPT (1972)

Since publication of the foregoing article in 1954, additional fieldwork has been conducted on Marajó by Hilbert and Simões. Charcoal samples obtained by Simões (1969) show that the Ananatuba Phase was in existence by 980 B.C. and the Marajoara Phase by A.D. 500. Archeological complexes sharing many of the Marajoara Phase techniques of ceramic decoration have been described from the middle Amazon by Hilbert (1968), from the Rio Napo in eastern Ecuador by Evans and Meggers (1968), and from the Ucayali in eastern Peru by Lathrap (1970). None of these complexes contains the full range of diagnostic Marajoara traits, however, and existing carbon-14 dates indicate them to be several centuries more recent. The existence of a high proportion of the significant features in highland Colombia at a sufficiently early time to be ancestral to the Marajoara Phase, as well as ecological considerations, makes this a promising source area, but no complex yet described incorporates all of the relevant traits. In short, subsequent archeological work has not produced evidence to refute or to validate the interpretations proposed two decades ago. The place of origin, impetus for emigration, route of movement, and duration of migration of the bearers of Marajoara culture remain to be ascertained. We hope that the coming two decades will bring increased understanding of this intriguing and important prehistoric event.

Introduction to Urban Settlements in Ancient Peru

Emphasizing the rise of urbanization in Mesopotamia may distract us from the fact that parallel developments took place in the New World. In South America there is only one area where an extensive network of cities grew up: Peru. Yet in spite of the colossal size of some of these settlements, they have been neglected in the literature of prehistory and evolution in the Americas.

"Urban Settlements in Ancient Peru" helps to fill this gap. Readers interested in further information on urbanization in the New World should look at the Mayan and the Mexican material (Sanders and Price 1968, Adams 1966, Coe 1966, Palerm 1955, Blanton 1972). Material is accumulating at a rapid rate and soon new understanding will be achieved regarding the development and nature of urbanism throughout the New World.

John H. Rowe is one of the most important figures in South American archeology and ethnology. His contributions to the study of the Andean area are numerous and indispensable. Rowe holds the Ph.D. degree from Harvard University as well as doctorates from Cuzco and Brown universities. He is Professor of Anthropology at the University of California at Berkeley.

5. URBAN SETTLEMENTS IN ANCIENT PERU

JOHN H. ROWE

There were urban settlements in ancient Peru which were comparable in size and cultural importance with the great cities of antiquity in the Old World. Large urban settlements were built in Peru much earlier than is generally recognized; one preceramic site of this character is known from the central coast. The story of the urban pattern in Peru in later times is not one of simple expansion through the growth of existing settlements and the establishment of new ones, however. Many sites of large urban centers were occupied for relatively short periods and then abandoned. Whole districts with a flourishing urban tradition lost it and shifted to other patterns of settlement. The most striking example of the loss of an urban tradition is found in the southern sierra, where there was a general abandonment of urban settlements toward the end of the Middle Horizon which invites comparison with the abandonment of Roman cities in the Dark Ages. At the time of the Spanish conquest the only parts of Peru where there were large urban settlements were the central sierra and the north coast.

The evidence relating to the rise and fall of urban settlements in Peru is still scattered and fragmentary, and any interpretation of it is bound to be tentative. A review of the subject may, however, serve to clarify the problems involved and suggest fruitful lines of research for the future.

Two introductory digressions are necessary before we can discuss the evidence from specific sites. We need an explanation of the system of dating to be followed and a discussion of what we mean by an urban settlement.

In this review dates will be given in terms of the system of pe-

Reprinted by permission from *Ñawpa Pacha*, Vol. 1 (1963), pp. 1–27. Institute of Andean Studies, Berkeley, California.

riods of relative time which I have used in earlier publications.[1] The periods are defined with reference to a master sequence, the sequence of changes in the pottery style of the valley of Ica. There are seven periods in all in this system, covering the span of time from the introduction of pottery at Ica to the abandonment of the traditional cemeteries a little over a generation after the Spanish conquest. The periods are named Initial Period, Early Horizon, Early Intermediate Period, Middle Horizon, Late Intermediate Period, Late Horizon, and Colonial Period.

The Early Horizon begins with the beginning of Chavin influence in Ica pottery and ends when slip painting replaces resin painting in this valley as a method of executing polychrome designs on pottery. The Early Horizon can be subdivided into ten smaller time units (epochs) on the basis of a recent analysis of the Ocucaje pottery style.[2] The Early Intermediate Period, which follows the Early Horizon, is characterized by the presence of Nasca style pottery in Ica and can be divided into eight epochs on the basis of L. E. Dawson's studies of Nasca pottery. The next period, the Middle Horizon, begins with Phase 9 of the Nasca style, which, elsewhere on the coast, is associated with strong influences from the Ayacucho area in the sierra. It lasts until the beginning of the Chulpaca style at Ica and can be divided into four epochs. The Late Intermediate Period lasts from the beginning of the Chulpaca style at Ica to the beginning of the Tacaraca A style, an event which apparently coincides rather closely with the conquest of Ica by the Incas in about 1476. The Late Horizon is the period of Inca domination at Ica and of the Tacaraca A phase of the local pottery tradition. It ends with the beginning of the Tacaraca B style, close to the time of the Spanish conquest of Ica, an event which took place in 1534.[3]

Archaeological units from other parts of Peru are dated to one or another of these periods or their subdivisions on the basis of evidence that the units in question are contemporary with a particular unit of pottery style at Ica. Direct evidence for dating of this kind is available in those periods labelled "horizons," because in these periods there was an expansion of trade; certain highly distinctive pottery styles were distributed over large areas, and imported vessels in these styles are found associated with ones in the local traditions. In the Early Horizon the Chavin and Paracas styles were widely distributed in this way, while in the Middle Horizon a spread of the Pacheco-Conchopata style is followed by an even wider distribution of the style of Huari. One phase of the Cajamarca pottery tradition had a wide distribution at the same time that the Huari style did. In the Late Horizon Inca style vessels from Cuzco were widely traded and imitated, and a number of other styles had a more restricted spread.

In the periods which lack the "horizon" label trade was much more restricted, and arguments for contemporaneity are generally indirect, except when closely neighboring valleys are involved. As more local sequences become known, however, there is no reason why detailed cross-dating on a valley to valley basis cannot be achieved.

The Colonial Period and the Late Horizon can be dated by historical records and reliable traditions. Our only source of dates in years for earlier sections of the Peruvian chronology is the method of radiocarbon dating. Relatively few radiocarbon determinations are available for ancient Peru, and not all the determinations which have been announced are on reliably associated samples and consistent with one another. The most consistent determinations available in June, 1962, suggest the following approximate dates for the beginning of the periods named:

1400 B.C.—Initial Period
600 to 700 B.C.—Early Horizon
100 to 150 A.D.—Early Intermediate Period
800 A.D.—Middle Horizon
1100 A.D.—Late Intermediate Period

The determinations used for these estimates are based on the Libby half-life value of 5568 years for radiocarbon.

The assignment of cultural units to periods in this study is based on archaeological evidence independent of radiocarbon dates, except in a few cases which will be discussed individually.

This study is concerned with urban settlements in ancient Peru. For the purposes of the present argument, an urban settlement is an area of human habitation in which many dwellings are grouped closely together. The dwellings must be close enough together to leave insufficient space between them for subsistence farming, although space for gardens may be present. In the case of a site where the foundations of the dwellings have not been excavated, an extensive area of thick and continuous habitation refuse provides a basis for supposing that the settlement was an urban one.

The intent of this definition is to exclude clusters of dwellings so small that they could be interpreted as belonging to the members of a single extended family. Twenty dwellings is perhaps the minimum number which would provide this exclusion.

It will be convenient in our discussion to distinguish four kinds of urban settlements, according to whether or not they include residents who are engaged full time in occupations other than hunting, fishing, farming and herding, and whether or not there is a separate rural population in the area. I am proposing to use the word "pueblo" to designate an urban settlement in which all the residents are engaged in hunting, fishing, farming or herding at least part of the time, and "city" to designate one which includes residents engaged in other activities (manufacturing, trade, services, administration, defense, etc.). If the urban settlements have around them a scattered rural population, I propose to call them "synchoritic," a term coined from the Greek word *chorites,* countryman. If all the people engaged in rural occupations reside in the urban settlement itself, so that the countryside has virtually no permanent residents between the settlements, I propose to call the settlements "achoritic." The four kinds of urban settlements, then, are the synchoritic pueblo, the achoritic pueblo, the synchoritic city and the achoritic city.[4]

People who live in an urban settlement but are engaged in hunting, fishing, farming or herding must travel to work, and they can only work effectively in the immediate neighborhood of the settlement. The productivity of land and water in the accessible area therefore limits the number of people engaged in these rural activities who can live together in a single urban settlement. The maximum figure under favorable conditions in native North America seems to have been about 2,000; at any rate, the largest pueblo-type settlements in the Southwest and on the Northwest Coast apparently did not exceed this figure. There is no reason to think that the limit was higher in ancient Peru.

The population limit just discussed sets a ceiling for the total population of pueblos but not for that of cities, since cities also include residents engaged in occupations which can be carried on within the city itself. We thus have reason to suppose that any urban settlement with a population in excess of 2,000 is or was a city and not a pueblo, even though specific evidence relating to the occupations of the inhabitants is not available. Unexcavated archaeological sites with habitation areas of great extent fall into this category. I propose to refer to urban settlements estimated to have had less than 2,000 inhabitants as "small," and ones estimated to have had more than 2,000 as "large."

The distinction between synchoritic and achoritic urban settlements has a bearing on the problem of the destruction of cities. By definition, some of the residents of a city are not themselves directly engaged in the production of food and raw materials of animal and vegetable origin, and these people must obtain such necessities from the producers. In the case of synchoritic cities, some or all of the producers live outside the city proper. The spatial distinction facilitates the development of a social distinction between urban and rural residents. If the urban residents control the market, as is usually the case, they are in a position to exploit the rural residents in various ways, arousing thereby an understandable resentment and hostility among the latter. Then if the cities are weakened by political and economic instability the countrymen may take a violent revenge, destroying the cities which have become a symbol of oppression. In the case of achoritic cities, resentment between the producers of food and raw materials and the rest of the urban population might also arise and could easily lead to violence. The producers, however, being themselves city dwellers, would be more likely to try to take over the city government than to destroy their own homes and shrines. As a pattern of residence, the pattern of synchoritic cities contains an element of potential instability which is not present in the achoritic city pattern or in any of the other patterns of urban settlement.

This general theory is a development out of Michael Rostovtzeff's more specific argument that the antagonism of the rural population to the cities in the Roman Empire was the major factor in the destruction of Roman cities in the west in the 3rd and 4th centuries A.D.[5] The best documented example is the destruction of Augustodunum (Autun) in 269 by a coalition of local "peasants" and Roman soldiers, the soldiers themselves having been recruited from the rural population.

Any discussion of urban settlements in ancient Peru necessarily involves reference to ceremonial centers as well. Ceremonial centers occur in Peru; they may be combined with urban settlements in various ways or provide a kind of alternative to them. A ceremonial center is a grouping of public buildings housing common facilities, such as shrines, meeting places, markets, and law courts, which is used seasonally or at prescribed intervals by the population of a considerable surrounding area. Between the occasions when a ceremonial center is used it is either closed and empty or houses only a small permanent population of caretaker personnel. The general population which makes use of the center may be entirely dispersed in the surrounding countryside, or it may be clustered in urban centers.

Ceremonial centers may be found even in an area where large cities also occur. In the Andean area today there are a number of rural churches which attract very large numbers of people once a year for a religious festival and fair, and some of these ceremonial center churches are located not far from major cities. Cities do generally provide competing facilities, however.

We can now turn to the archaeological evidence for urban settlements in ancient Peru. The story begins on the Peruvian coast before the first appearance of pottery in this area, but after cotton began to be used as a textile fiber. In the stage bounded by these two events the coast dwellers drew their subsistence primarily from hunting sea mammals, fishing, and gathering shellfish, although some plant cultivation was practiced as well. Many of the known habitation sites are on waterless sections of the coast which were attractive because of the abundance of shore resources. Small urban settlements of the pueblo type are very common, the best known being that at Huaca Prieta in Chicama. At a few of these sites public buildings can be identified. At Rio Seco, for example, there are two mounds about 4 meters high, each consisting of two levels of rooms which had been deliberately filled with stone to provide a raised substructure for an important building.[6] The preceramic population of the coast did not live exclusively in pueblo type settlements, however; there are also many very small habitation sites. At Ancón, where Edward P. Lanning and I have been making a systematic survey, some of the small sites are set back from the shore, probably to take advantage of supplies of *Tillandsia,* an epiphytic plant which was used for fuel in dry areas.

The possibility that there were also preceramic cities is suggested by the size of the Haldas site, situated 329 kilometers north [of Lima] on a dry shore just south of Casma. Lanning tells me that the preceramic occupation refuse at Haldas covers an area about two kilometers by one and averages 50 cm. in thickness. There is also a complex and imposing temple structure at this site, and part of it was built before the introduction of pottery. The University of Tokyo expedition of 1958 secured a sample for radio-carbon dating consisting of cane used to wrap stones laid in the floor of the temple, and this sample (Gak-107, run in 1960) yielded a date of 1631 B.C. ± 130.[7] If the area covered by pre-ceramic refuse at Haldas is continuous and was all occupied at the same time, the population of the site must have been well over 10,000. Further excavation at this site is urgently needed.

The temple at Haldas was enlarged in the Initial Period, but there are only about 300 square meters of Initial Period habitation refuse. The shrinkage of population which this figure suggests may be the result of a shift to the Casma Valley following the introduc-tion of maize cultivation. Maize appears in the refuse at Haldas shortly before pottery.[8] In any case, Haldas appears to have be-come a ceremonial center rather than an urban settlement in the Initial Period.

There were urban settlements elsewhere on the coast in the Ini-tial Period, however. The Hacha site in Acarí is one; it has habita-tion refuse covering an irregular area about 800 by 200 meters along an abandoned channel of the Acarí River. This occupation is dated by two radiocarbon determinations: UCLA-154 (1962), 1297 B.C. ± 80, and UCLA-153 (1962), 997 B.C. ± 90, both run on charcoal samples.[9] At this site there are remains of several structures with walls of packed clay which were probably public buildings; one of the structures is earlier than the 1297 B.C. char-coal sample. Ordinary dwellings were probably constructed of flim-sier materials, as they were in later times. Pottery is common and distinctive. Although the Hacha site is located about 21 kilometers from the sea, marine shellfish are prominent in the refuse. In the refuse associated with the radiocarbon date of 997 B.C. the cultivated plants represented, in approximate order of abundance, are cotton, gourds, lima beans, squash, guava, and peanuts.[10] No trace of maize has been found. Relatively little excavation has been carried out at Hacha, and the data are still insufficient to determine whether it was a pueblo or a city.

In the sierra the site of Qaluyu, located in the northern part of the Titicaca basin near Pucara, probably also qualifies as an urban settlement of the Initial Period. Qaluyu is a stratified site with two distinct phases of occupation. The later one, associated with Pucara style pottery, is Early Horizon in date. The earlier occupation is characterized by a distinctive pottery style called Qaluyu which occurs in a stratigraphically early position at Yana-mancha, near Sicuani, as well as at Qaluyu itself. Although there is no way to relate the Qaluyu style to the Ica Valley sequence directly, its consistently early position in local sequences and the absence of common Early Horizon stylistic features argue for a date in the Initial Period. There are two radiocarbon dates from Qaluyu based on charcoal samples associated with Qaluyu style pottery, namely P-156 (1958), 1005 B.C. ± 120, and P-155 (1958), 565 B.C. ± 114.[11] The two samples were taken from about the same depth in a short test trench and should not be so far apart; they cannot both be accepted in the first sigma. The earlier one fits the archaeological evidence better.

The accumulation of habitation refuse at Qaluyu forms a low mound several acres in extent. A road has been cut through the mound, and the Initial Period occupation is exposed in the road cut. The extent of this exposure suggests that Initial Period refuse underlies virtually the whole mound, but further excavation would be necessary to establish its limits. No buildings have been excavated at this site, and the case for its being an urban settlement of some kind rests on the probable extent of the refuse.

The site of Marcavalle near Cuzco yields pottery in a local version of the Qaluyu style. The refuse covers at least an acre.

For the Early Horizon, many sites have been recorded which qualify as urban settlements, both on the coast and in the sierra. Several are large enough to be considered large cities, the ones now known being located in the Titicaca basin, in the Ica Valley on the south coast of Peru, and in the Mosna Valley in the northern sierra. Let us discuss the large sites first.

At Pucara in the northern part of the Titicaca basin are the ruins of a very large urban settlement with imposing public buildings. Pucara is a "one period" site and the type site for the Pucara pottery style. No earlier pottery has been found there, and there was no later occupation until the Late Intermediate Period. There is no direct evidence by which to relate the Pucara style to the Ica sequence, so radiocarbon dates provide the only basis for correlation. Six radiocarbon determinations have been made on charcoal samples from a refuse deposit at Pucara (P-152, P-153, P-154, P-170, P-172, and P-217).[12] Five of these determinations agree very well and suggest a date in the first century B.C. The sixth, P-154, agrees only if taken in the second sigma. A date in the first century B.C. should fall in the latter part of the Early Horizon, perhaps Early Horizon 8 or 9.

Both public buildings and private houses at Pucara were built of adobe on stone foundations, and the collapse of the adobe superstructures has buried the foundations so that only the largest buildings can be distinguished on the surface without excavation. There were at least three large buildings, probably temples, on a terrace called Qalasaya at the foot of the great Rock of Pucara. The residential area was on the flat plain between this terrace and the river and was apparently very extensive.[13]

The area around Pucara is good farming country where potatoes and quinoa can be grown, and there are catfish in the Pucara River. Good pottery clay is available near the river, and there is a considerable pottery making industry at Pucara today. If ancient Pucara was a city, as its size suggests, its economy probably involved pottery manufacture, trade, and religious activities as well as farming.

The Pucara settlement at Qaluyu, only three or four kilometers away, also covers a substantial area, though a less extensive one than at Pucara itself. As the local farmers have recognized, the mound at Qaluyu is shaped like a catfish, a fact which suggests some deliberate planning. According to Manuel Chávez Ballón, there is another very large Pucara site at Tintiri on the road from Azángaro to Muñani. No one has yet looked for small habitation sites between these urban settlements.

The site of Tiahuanaco, at the southern or Bolivian end of Lake Titicaca, covers an area at least 1½ by 1¼ kilometers. The full area over which sherds occur on the surface has never been mapped, but the reports of visitors indicate that it is immense. The surface remains represent a Middle Horizon occupation, but there is evidence that the site was already important in the Early Horizon. Since this evidence has never been brought together, a review of it is in order.

Bennett apparently dug into an occupation level of Early Horizon date at the bottom of his Pit V, located east of the Acapana, the level in question being his Level 9 (4.00 to 4.60 meters). It was set off from the deposit above by a thin layer of clay. Bennett collected 116 sherds from Level 9, 111 of them being plain ones.[14] The most significant of the decorated sherds was a small one with a stepped design in red and black, the color being outlined by incision. When I examined this sherd in Bennett's collections at the American Museum of Natural History in 1941 I identified it as Pucara Polychrome.[15] The identification was based on the colors, surface finish, and technique of decoration, the design being too simple to be diagnostic. It may be, of course, that the sherd in question belongs to a local style related to Pucara rather than to the Pucara style proper, but, as Bennett noted, it is quite different from later Tiahuanaco pottery.

The evidence of radiocarbon determinations confirms the early date here assigned to Level 9. Alfred Kidder II and William R. Coe dug another pit adjacent to Bennett's Pit V in 1955 to secure samples for radiocarbon dating. Sample P-150 (1958), animal bones from 3.25 to 3.50 meters depth, corresponding to the lower part of Bennett's Level 7, gave a date of 246 A.D. ± 104. Sample P-123 (1958), damp charcoal from 3.50 to 3.75 meters depth, corresponding to Bennett's Level 8, gave a date of 141 A.D. ± 103.[16] In the light of this evidence, a date in the first century B.C. for Level 9 is entirely reasonable.

Some sculpture in the Pucara style has been found at Tiahuanaco also, notably the two kneeling figures in red sandstone which stand at the sides of the door of the Tiahuanaco church. These are ancient statues which were reworked for Christian use early in the 17th century. The reworking did not extend to the backs of the figures, however, and enough is left of the back of the headdress on one of them so that we can recognize it as a work in the Pucara style or in a style closely related to it. The Spanish chronicler Bernabé Cobo gives a circumstantial account of the finding of these statues, and his account suggests that they were dug up near the church, rather than in one of the areas where there were ruins on the surface.[17] Perhaps the reason why more remains in the Pucara style have not been found at Tiahuanaco is that the area of the modern town has not been explored.

In 1858 the Swiss naturalist J. J. von Tschudi purchased a small stone carving in the purest Pucara style at the town of Tiahuanaco.[18] This carving, now in Bern, was in use as a cult object at the time of Tschudi's visit and consequently lacks provenience. It may very well have been dug up at Tiahuanaco also, however.

Since 1957 Carlos Ponce Sanginés and Gregorio Cordero Miranda have been excavating at Tiahuanaco for the Bolivian government, working mainly in and near the Qalasasaya. They have found a new pottery style in their lowest levels which is probably of Early Horizon date also. Ponce assigns the new style to his "Epoca I" and describes it as very distinctive, including painted pieces, plain polished pieces, and modelled ones. The painting is most commonly in red on yellow, with some incised motifs and feline designs drawn in black and white.[19] I propose to call the new style Qalasasaya for convenience of reference. The head of the principal figure on an incised and painted bottle of this style illustrated by Ponce has a number of features which occur in the same combination at Ica, where they are limited to Early Horizon 10.[20] This observation suggests a date immediately following the Pucara occupation. On the other hand, a radiocarbon sample which is supposed to date "Epoca I" materials gives a date of 239 b.c. ± 130 (GaK-52, organic carbon from Qalasasaya Pit E-14, Layer 6).[21] The radiocarbon determination suggests that the Qalasasaya style is earlier than Pucara. More evidence is clearly needed to settle the problem of dating, but the indications are that the Qalasasaya style belongs sometime in the Early Horizon.

So far we have no evidence regarding the extent of the Early Horizon occupation at Tiahuanaco, but if there were urban settlements at the other end of the lake at this time there may very well have been an important one at Tiahuanaco also.

The Ica Valley is one of the larger valleys on the Peruvian coast, but its water supply in ancient times was very limited. The Ica River carried water for three months of the year at most, and in some years it carried no water at all. On the other hand, one good soaking of the land a year was enough to ensure a crop of maize and squash.

In the earlier part of the Early Horizon the population of Ica seems to have been distributed in numerous small settlements along the edges of the valley. Some of them were certainly large enough to qualify as pueblos. In Early Horizon 9 times, however, there was an abrupt concentration of the population in a few very large urban settlements. Two of these settlements have been located, namely Tajahuana, on a dry plateau beside the river, about half way down the valley, and Media Luna in the oasis of Callango, far below. According to L. E. Dawson, who discovered it, Media Luna is an area of continuous, concentrated habitation refuse over a kilometer across, with fifteen small adobe mounds and some remains of adobe walls on the flat. The mounds presumably represent temples or other public buildings. There are no fortifications at this site. The Tajahuana site is only slightly smaller. The whole area is covered with stones representing the foundations of small rectangular houses, and there are a number of mounds about the same size as the ones at Media Luna. Tajahuana is elaborately fortified with multiple walls and a dry moat on the side of easiest access.

Both of the sites described were occupied only during one epoch of the Early Horizon, perhaps for a century or a century and a half, and then never occupied again. They apparently represent achoritic cities, without smaller settlements between them, but we have no evidence of the nature of their economic life. In the next epoch, Early Horizon 10, settlements were substantially smaller but very numerous, suggesting that there had been a redistribution of the population rather than a decline in numbers. Whether pueblos or small cities, the new settlements were synchoritic. The situation suggests that the striking concentration of population in Early Horizon 9 reflects some kind of political planning.[22]

There is no indication that the urban settlements of Early Horizon 9 depended in any way on large scale irrigation works. There was probably never enough water at Callango to irrigate any very large area, while the Tajahuana site is located close to the river bank and adjacent to a marshy area. The sites in the Ica Valley which depend on major irrigation canals all date to Early Intermediate Period 7 or later.

In the northern sierra of Peru we have evidence of urban settlements in the Mosna Valley east of the Cordillera Blanca. The principal site in this valley is Chavin, where there is an impressive temple which is famous for its stone sculpture. Archaeological research has been largely concentrated on the temple. Wendell C. Bennett, who excavated there in 1938, suggested that the temple was a ceremonial center for seasonal use with a very small resident population.[23] However, Marino Gonzales Moreno, the Peruvian government commissioner at the site, who is a native of Chavin as well as a very able archaeologist, showed me evidence that the whole area occupied by the modern town, which is adjacent to the temple on the north, is underlain by Early Horizon refuse and constructions. An area perhaps a kilometer long and half a kilometer wide is involved. There is also a considerable area of habitation refuse on the other side of the river. Chavin thus appears to have been a large city. There are reported to be a number of smaller sites of the same period within a few kilometers of Chavin itself, so it was probably a synchoritic city.

Chavin was certainly a religious center, and it has a favorable location for trade. The Mosna Valley is a natural route of communication between the sierra to the west and the tropical lowlands along the Marañón. Whether the site was also a manufacturing center cannot be determined on the basis of the evidence now available. A city the size of Chavin is likely to have had considerable political power.

Chavin was not a ceremonial center in the settlement pattern sense during the Early Horizon, but it may have become one during the Early Intermediate Period. Most of the habitation area of the city had been abandoned by the end of the Early Horizon, but later structures and refuse around the temple indicate continued use of the ceremonial part of the site.

If Tiahuanaco was already a city in the Early Horizon it may have had a continuous urban life through the Early Intermediate Period. All the other known Early Horizon cities, however, were either entirely deserted or at any rate had ceased to exist as cities before the end of the Early Horizon. The break is particularly remarkable in the northern Titicaca basin, because we have no idea what followed it there. Although a certain amount of exploring has been done, no habitation sites have been found which can be attributed to the Early Intermediate Period; we do not even know what kind of pottery was in use.

Apart from the large city sites we have been discussing, the known Early Horizon habitation sites are mostly small urban settlements, probably of a pueblo character. Some examples are Llawllipata, near Pomacanchi; Chanapata, at Cuzco; Pozuelo, in the Chincha Valley; and the Tank Site at Ancon. There are also, of course, many important sites which I do not have sufficient information about to discuss from the point of view of this survey; Kotosh, La Copa, Pacopampa, and Chongoyape fall into this category.

For the Early Intermediate Period many sites representing large cities are known from southern and central Peru, but none has been reported in the north.

There are large urban sites of the Early Intermediate Period in the south coast valleys of Pisco, Ica, Nasca, and Acarí. The site of Dos Palmas in Pisco comprised an area of habitation nearly half a kilometer long and some 300 meters wide when it was photographed from the air in 1931 by the Shippee-Johnson Expedition. By 1957, when Dwight T. Wallace visited it on the ground, the area had been brought under irrigation and the site largely destroyed. The photograph of 1931 shows the habitation area densely packed with the fieldstone foundations of small rectangular rooms, interrupted by four or five small open plazas. The pottery is in a local style datable to Early Intermediate Period 3.

In Ica there is a great habitation site of Early Intermediate Period 1 and 2 on the slopes of a hill at the edge of the Hacienda Cordero Alto. The population then seems to have shifted to the other side of the valley, where there is an equally large site of Early Intermediate Period 3 to 5 on the slopes of Cerro Soldado. The Cerro Soldado site consists of the fieldstone foundations of small houses scattered over the slopes of a large rocky hill overlooking the Ica River. A shrine can be identified on one of the spurs of the hill. No habitation site attributable to Early Intermediate Period 6 has yet been found in Ica, although burials of this period are known there. In Early Intermediate Period 7 there was a large city on the Pampa de la Tinguiña, a broad alluvial fan subject to occasional flooding. The surviving area of habitation is just under 600 meters across and was probably originally half again as large, the missing sections having been washed out in flash floods. The ruins consist of fieldstone foundations of buildings, a number of small mounds, and at least one plaza. An imposing adobe palace associated with this site was destroyed by the owner of the neighboring hacienda in 1959. Tinguiña is a "one-period" site, abandoned before the end of Early Intermediate Period 7 and never reoccupied.

The story of settlement in the ravine of Nasca has not been traced systematically, and only one large urban site is known there. This site is Cahuachi, which comprises shrines, plazas, cemeteries, and habitation areas extending along the side of the valley for over a kilometer. Strong's excavations there in 1952 indicated an occupation from Early Horizon 10 to Early Intermediate Period 3.[24] It is not easy to determine how much of the area of Cahuachi was used for habitation. The houses were constructed of perishable materials, so that their foundations do not show on the surface, and some of the surface pottery is derived from looted tombs rather than from refuse. Nevertheless, the habitation area was clearly extensive.

The largest urban site in the valley of Acarí is Tambo Viejo, at the south edge of the modern town of Acarí. The Early Intermediate Period habitation area at this site is about a kilometer in length and half a kilometer in width, comprising fieldstone foundations of small rectangular rooms, a number of small mounds, probably representing shrines or public buildings of other kinds, and plazas. The site is surrounded by fortification walls of fieldstone and adobe. The earliest occupation is represented by pottery datable to Early Intermediate Period 2 and representing an old local tradition. The site seems to have been rebuilt and enlarged in Early Intermediate Period 3 and abandoned before the end of this epoch. The Early Intermediate Period 3 occupation is associated with Nasca style pottery and very likely represents an actual Nasca invasion.

Further up the Acarí Valley at Chocavento is another fortified habitation site, closely similar to Tambo Viejo but about half as large. Still further up valley there are two additional sites of the same sort, one at Amato and the other at Huarato. Both are smaller than Chocavento. All of these sites appear to have been built and abandoned in Early Intermediate Period 3. It is not unlikely that all these Acarí sites represent achoritic urban settlements, that is, ones in which the farming population of the valley was concentrated; their size bears some relation to the amount of farm land available nearby. The size of Tambo Viejo indicates that it, at least, was a city. These sites of Early Intermediate Period 3 represent the peak of urbanization in the Acarí Valley. In all subsequent periods the habitation sites in this valley were relatively small.

The fact that Cahuachi in Nasca and the urban settlements in Acarí were deserted at about the same time is suggestive, in view of the evidence that the fortified settlements in Acarí represent an invasion from Nasca. Perhaps Cahuachi conquered a little empire on the coast which was destroyed after a generation or two. The situation could be clarified by further study of habitation sites in the Nasca area.

There are a number of Early Intermediate Period sites in the area around Ayacucho in the sierra which are large enough to qualify as large cities. The extent of these sites must be traced from the distribution of pottery fragments; there are no architectural remains of the Early Intermediate Period visible at the surface. In the immediate environs of Ayacucho there are three large habitation sites of the Early Intermediate Period, Acuchimay, Chakipampa (Tello's "Conchopata"), and Nawimpukyu. All three continued to be occupied into the Middle Horizon, and the last two have remains of Middle Horizon buildings. The great site of Huari, about 25 kilometers north of Ayacucho, also had an extensive Early Intermediate Period occupation as well as the Middle Horizon one for which it is famous. At Churukana, a short distance east of Huari, there is a very large Early Intermediate Period habitation site which is not obscured by any later occupation.

Tiahuanaco either continued to be occupied or was occupied again in the Early Intermediate Period. The Early Intermediate Period pottery style at this site is the Qeya style, the major component of Bennett's "Early Tiahuanaco" category, corresponding to Ponce Sanginés's Epoca III. The name Qeya is derived from the name of the type site, Qeya Qollu Chico on the Island of Titicaca, where it was found isolated in burials excavated by A. F. Bandelier in 1894. Bandelier's collection from this site is at the American Museum of Natural History; it is referred to but not described in his report.[25] The two pits, V and VIII, in which Bennett got "Early Tiahuanaco" refuse are located half a kilometer apart, a fact which suggests the presence of an extensive habitation area. Ponce Sanginés dates the construction of the Qalasasaya to his Epoca III, so the site also had large public buildings in the Early Intermediate Period.

On the central coast the sites of Pachacamac and Cajamarquilla were large urban settlements in the Middle Horizon and the Late Intermediate Period, and at both sites the occupation can be traced back to the Early Intermediate Period. We do not know the area involved or the character of the early occupation, however. The site of Maranga, between Lima and Callao, includes a cluster of great temple mounds which were built during the Early Intermediate Period and abandoned early in the Middle Horizon. No extensive habitation area has been found associated with these mounds, and it is very likely that they constituted a ceremonial center.

There was a moderate sized settlement of urban character at Playa Grande, on the desert coast south of Ancon.[26] The habitation area at this site was about 400 meters across and included at least seven public buildings. There was no water available for irrigation at Playa Grande, and the population must have been engaged in fishing, gathering shellfish, and hunting sea mammals, like the inhabitants of the settlements along the desert coast before the introduction of pottery. I hesitate to argue that the existence of an urban settlement at Playa Grande implies general use of this pattern in the neighboring valleys. Occupational convenience might encourage the formation of urban settlements by fishermen, even though contemporary farmers preferred a different pattern of residence.

Schaedel has argued that urbanization began on the north coast in the Middle Horizon or Late Intermediate Period, and that the earlier pattern in this area was one of ceremonial centers.[27] He reached these conclusions on the basis of a survey of major architectural remains on the north coast carried out between 1948 and 1950. The procedure followed was to locate large ruins on aerial photographs and then to visit the sites on the ground. This procedure provides an excellent basis for studies of monumental architecture, but it yields only part of the information needed for the study of settlement patterns. Many habitation areas on the coast cannot be identified at all on aerial photographs and can be recognized on the ground only by the presence of ancient pottery, bone fragments, and shell. Except in areas where stone was very abundant, ordinary houses on the coast were generally framed with poles and closed with matting or with canes smeared with mud. Such houses leave no remains except a floor and some post holes which, if not covered by a layer of refuse, weather away within a few centuries. Generally the floors are covered with refuse and can be found by excavation. The data for the Early Intermediate Period collected in Schaedel's survey may reflect the pattern of scattered residence and ceremonial centers which he suggests, but they could also result from a pattern of urban residence in flimsy houses which left no remains of the sort he was mapping.

Apart from Schaedel's survey, data on north coast settlements in the Early Intermediate Period are not abundant. The problem is complicated by the fact that, for certain valleys (e.g., Casma and Lambayeque), the pottery of the Early Intermediate Period has not been identified.

The extensive survey of ancient sites carried out in the Virú Valley by J. A. Ford and Gordon R. Willey in 1946 indicated what Willey has called a small or medium sized village pattern for settlements of this valley in the Early Intermediate Period.[28] The Huaca Gallinazo, which is the largest habitation site associated with Gallinazo style pottery, is described as covering an area of 400 by 200 meters.[29] These relatively small settlements may have been associated with ceremonial centers, if that is the function served by the so-called "castillos." The Virú evidence can hardly be said to contradict Schaedel's generalization. On the other hand, it does not support his interpretation very strongly, because Virú, which is not a very large valley, had no major urban settlements even in the Late Intermediate Period when such settlements were fairly common on the north coast.

The fact that later sites on the central coast, such as Pachacamac and Cajamarquilla, were already occupied in the Early Intermediate Period leads us to ask whether the same might not be true of some of the large late urban settlements on the north coast. Heinrich Ubbelohde-Doering did some digging at the great site of Pacatnamú in the Pacasmayo Valley in the hope of finding an early occupation. The earliest pottery he found, however, dates to Middle Horizon 1.[30]

The Middle Horizon was marked by a great expansion of the Huari culture centering in the Ayacucho area, an expansion which probably involved military conquest. Its traces have been found through most of Peru, in the sierra from Sicuani to Cajamarca and on the coast from Ocoña to Chicama. There was a parallel expansion of the Tiahuanaco culture in the basin of Lake Titicaca and in northern Bolivia, reaching the coast in the extreme south of Peru and in northern Chile. These expansion movements are significant for our story, because the Huari culture certainly had a well established tradition of large cities by the beginning of the Middle Horizon, and the Tiahuanaco culture probably did also.

There seems to have been a concentration of population and probably also of power at Huari in the Middle Horizon. The great urban settlements in the environs of Ayacucho were abandoned at the end of Middle Horizon 1, while the major occupation at Huari dates to Middle Horizon 2 and 3. The site of Huari is enormous. According to Bennett, the "major core" of the ruins covers an area at least 1.5 kilometers square. The masonry structures represented by the ruins now visible above ground were probably public buildings; the habitation area around them can only be traced from the distribution of surface sherds.[31]

Tello reports the existence of another large site like Huari at Hatun Wayllay on the Lircay River in Huancavelica.[32] A 16th century writer describes what appears to be another such site at Cabana in the province of Lucanas in the southern part of the modern Department of Ayacucho.[33]

A striking feature of the Huari expansion was the construction of very large building complexes consisting of plazas, corridors and rectangular rooms laid out according to a formal plan. The walls are very high, with few doors and windows, and refuse is virtually absent. These elaborate complexes probably housed government stores rather than people. There is a comparatively small complex of this type at Huari itself, in the Capilla Pata sector. The larger ones are Pikillaqta, at the lower end of the valley of Cuzco, Wiraqocha Pampa, near Huamachuco, and a site on the Pampa de las Llamas in the valley of Casma on the north central coast.[34] The existence of these formal storage complexes provides evidence that the expansion of Huari was not simply a matter of peaceful penetration or raiding. It represents the formation of an imperial state with a well organized administration.

Pikillaqta has an extensive Middle Horizon habitation site associated with it. The habitation site is located on the next hill (Raqch'i), an elevation formed by an old lava flow. Here there are pockets of soil, including some fairly extensive fields, among the outcrops of lava, and Middle Horizon sherds occur on the surface. Presumably the buildings were of adobe.

There are many Middle Horizon habitation sites of various sizes in the area of Huari expansion, usually marked by refuse without standing ruins. Waywaka, near Andahuaylas, is relatively extensive; Yanamancha, near Sicuani, and Zukzu, at Urcos, are small.[35] Evidently, the entire population was not concentrated in large cities.

On the south coast there is a small Middle Horizon 1 habitation site at Pacheco in the ravine of Nasca, associated with a shrine of Ayacucho type. No really large Middle Horizon habitation site has yet been identified on the south coast, although some extensive cemeteries of this period are known, particularly in the Nasca drainage. However, little enough survey work for habitation sites has been undertaken in this area so that it would be dangerous to infer that no large Middle Horizon site exists.

Pachacamac continued to be occupied throughout the Middle Horizon, but the occupation of this period is covered by later construction and could only be traced by excavation. Many Middle Horizon burials have been found at Pachacamac, however, and the pottery in them represents a local variant of the Huari style. This Pachacamac variant is distinctive, and its influence can be traced over most of the central coast and as far south as Ica.[36] Since Pachacamac was a great city in the earlier part of the Late Intermediate Period, it is reasonable to suppose that it was already one in the Middle Horizon when it was such an important center of influence.

The north coast was an area of large cities in the Late Intermediate Period. One of them, at any rate, namely Pacatnamú in the Pacasmayo Valley, can be traced back to the beginning of the Middle Horizon, as we have already noted. If Schaedel is right in claiming that there were no large cities on the north coast before the Middle Horizon, the easiest way to account for the rather abrupt appearance of such cities is to suppose that they represent a pattern of settlement introduced by the already urbanized conquerors from Huari.

Tiahuanaco reached its greatest extent in the Middle Horizon, and most of the famous sculpture from this site is of Middle Horizon date. No other really large Middle Horizon city has been found so far in the area of Tiahuanaco expansion. This fact may be significant, or it may simply reflect inadequate exploration. There has been relatively too much attention paid to carved stones and not enough to house foundations and habitation refuse. For example, when Bennett was excavating the cut stone ruins of a Tiahuanaco temple at Lukurmata he noted the presence of house foundations and habitation refuse but did not trace the area of habitation.[37] Some small Tiahuanaco habitation sites are known; there is one on a hill at Juliaca, for instance.

Both Huari and Tiahuanaco were abandoned toward the end of the Middle Horizon, and there was no sizable later settlement at either site. Furthermore, in a large part of southern Peru and Bolivia the abandonment of cities was general; there were virtually no large cities in this area in the Late Intermediate Period and the Late Horizon. The entire pattern of settlement in large cities was eliminated and not reintroduced until after the Spanish conquest.

The abandonment of the great cities in the south coincides approximately with the decline and eventual elimination of Huari and Tiahuanaco influence in local pottery styles. The Late Intermediate Period was a time of marked local cultural diversity and relative isolation, contrasting in both respects with the Middle Horizon. Some evidence regarding political conditions in the Late Intermediate Period can be derived from Inca traditions, and these traditions describe a situation of extreme political fractionation in the sierra at the time of the beginnings of the Inca dynasty. Evidently, the great imperial states of the Middle Horizon fell at about the time that the cities were abandoned. There thus appears to be a formal parallel in Peru to the situation in western Europe at the time of the abandonment of the Roman cities.

The general absence of large cities in the south in the Late Intermediate Period was noted by the University of Tokyo field party which surveyed the area in 1958. The expedition report, in discussing the site of Churajón in the Arequipa area, says that it is "the only city site of the Urbanist period that has ever been recognized in the southern Andes."[38] The "Urbanist period" of this statement is approximately equivalent to the Late Intermediate Period. There is some question, however, whether Churajón qualifies as a city in terms of the criteria used in this study. The Tokyo party reports two habitation areas at Churajón, one of 2,000 square meters and the other of 5,000 square meters. The 5,000 square meter area, however, includes tombs and agricultural terraces as well as dwellings. The habitation areas described sound like small urban settlements, and probably pueblos rather than cities.

The largest urban settlements in southern Peru datable to the Late Intermediate Period which I have visited are Mallawpampa at Curahuasi, Qaqallinka and Timirán near Arequipa, and Sahuacarí and Otaparo in the Acarí Valley.[39] Probably all of these sites continued to be occupied in the Late Horizon. They cover areas at least 300 meters across and include the remains of fieldstone foundations as well as habitation refuse. These sites need be no more than relatively large pueblos. The sites which Max Uhle visited at the southeast end of Lake Titicaca between Achacache and Huaycho sound similar.[40]

In the area around Cuzco many Late Intermediate Period sites have been identified. Some are very small, representing perhaps no more than half a dozen houses, while others have an area of refuse 200 to 300 meters across and evidently represent pueblos or small cities. Examples of the larger sites are Qencha-qencha in the valley of Cuzco and Kuyu (Pukara Panti-lliklla) near Pisac.

The Ica Valley seems to have had a pattern combining small settlements and imposing ceremonial centers in the Late Intermediate Period. The major ceremonial center was at Old Ica in the Pago de Tacaraca where there is a large cluster of adobe temple mounds but little habitation refuse. Smaller clusters of mounds, probably representing subsidiary centers, occur at Macacona and Chagua (La Venta). The habitation sites of this period are numerous but small in area and scattered all over the valley.

In central Peru there are some Late Intermediate Period cities of large size. I have visited two near Huancayo, Patan-qotu and Qotu-qotu. The University of Tokyo expedition estimated that Patan-qotu extended for two kilometers along the bank of the

Mantaro River, and Qotu-qotu may be nearly as large. The latter site continued to be occupied into the Late Horizon.[41]

Pachacamac on the central coast was a very large city in the early part of the Late Intermediate Period. Indeed, most of the buildings now visible in the central and southern part of the site appear to be Late Intermediate Period constructions. The city declined in size, however, and was at least partly in ruins when the Incas took it. The best evidence for this fact is provided by the excavations which Arturo Jiménez Borja carried out in the central part of the site in 1957–58. Jiménez cleared a small temple of the Late Intermediate Period in this area and found the courtyard filled with over a meter of very dirty Inca refuse. Part of the facing of the south wall of the courtyard had fallen out, perhaps during an earthquake, and the layers of Inca refuse continued into the gap in the face of the wall. There is thus no question that this building was in a ruinous condition when the Incas began to use it as a dump. Miguel Estete, who accompanied the first Spanish exploring party to reach Pachacamac, in 1533, reported that much of the city was in ruins in his time. He says: "It must be something very ancient, because there are many ruined buildings, and the town has been walled, although most of the wall has now fallen in; it has its main gates giving access to the interior and its streets."[42]

Cajamarquilla, in the valley of Lima, was a large city in the Late Intermediate Period, as we have already noted. No one has succeeded in identifying early Spanish references to it, and its ancient name is unknown. No evidence of Inca occupation has been found there. It is thus at least possible that Cajamarquilla was abandoned before the end of the Late Intermediate Period.

The north coast was the most highly urbanized part of Peru in the Late Intermediate Period, with many large cities of imposing size. I have not explored this area myself and have nothing to add to the descriptions of north coast city sites published by Schaedel and Kosok.[43]

For the most part, the patterns of settlement of the Late Intermediate Period carried through into the Late Horizon. Whatever changes occurred were the result of Inca planning, so we need to add some comments on Inca practice.

As we have seen, the Cuzco area, where the Inca state began, had a pattern of small urban settlements and even smaller clusters of houses in the Late Intermediate Period. Cuzco, the Inca capital, was a small urban settlement at the time the Incas began their expansion; Inca traditions were quite explicit on this point. Pachakuti, the first great Inca conqueror, who ruled from about 1438 to about 1471, rebuilt Cuzco to make it a more appropriate capital for the new empire. He planned a core of palaces, temples, and government buildings with a ring of small urban settlements around it. The residential settlements were separated from one another and from the core area by open fields. Since the service personnel in the core area probably grew to number at least 2,000, the core itself was technically a large city by the criteria we are using. However, Pachakuti's intent appears to have been to build a ceremonial center with a cluster of small urban settlements dependent on it.

The administrative centers which the Incas established in the provinces tended to follow the model of Cuzco, except when they were attached to already existing native settlements. The Inca administrative center in Acarí, for example, consisted of government buildings with satellite settlements located some distance away.[44] If there were any Inca settlements which were planned as large cities, they were some of the great regional centers in the north, such as Pumpun, Wanuku (Huánuco Viejo), and Tumipampa.

Where the native population was very scattered, the Incas tried to consolidate it in urban settlements to facilitate government control, but the settlements so formed were not large and had a minimum of public buildings, aside from a shrine or two. The settlements established for the colonization of uninhabited country were likewise small. Machu Picchu, which was the largest of a group of Inca colonies in the rough country between Ollantaytambo and Vilcabamba, contained a total of only about 200 rooms for all purposes.[45] The Incas were not city builders in the sense that their predecessors of the Middle Horizon had been.

Such, then, is the record of urban settlement in ancient Peru as it appears in the present state of archaeological knowledge. There are still great gaps in what we know and extensive areas where no archaeological survey has ever been undertaken, but the present record is sufficient to support a few conclusions and to make it possible to ask some useful new questions.

In the first place, Peru has a long and persistent tradition of urban settlement. From far back in preceramic times the urban pattern is found generally wherever patterns of residence have been investigated. Scattered settlement in family groups is also found, but in combination with urban settlement rather than as an alternative to it. There are a few cases of what appear to be achoritic urban settlements, as in Ica in Early Horizon 9, in the Lake Titicaca basin at the time the Pucara cities were flourishing, and in Acarí in Early Intermediate Period 3. In Ica and Acarí the achoritic pattern is associated with fortification of the settlements and may be a deliberate military measure.

So little excavation has been carried out in Peruvian urban settlements that it is usually not possible to distinguish a small city from a pueblo. We can only be sure we are dealing with cities when we find habitation areas so extensive that they fall into the "large" category.

Large cities are not as generally characteristic of Peruvian settlement patterns as small urban settlements. Some large cities were built at some time or other in most parts of the sierra and the coast, but usually only part of the area was urbanized at any one time. The concentration of population in large cities appears to have been most general during the Middle Horizon.

The earliest large city so far known is preceramic Haldas on the coast, an isolated phenomenon in the present state of knowledge and one which deserves careful investigation.

The basin of Lake Titicaca was the home of a long tradition of large cities. This tradition goes back to the Initial Period (Qaluyu) and was very likely continuous from that time until the end of the Middle Horizon. There may have been a general abandonment of large cities in the northern part of the basin near the end of the Early Horizon, bringing an end to such cities as Qaluyu and Pucara, but it is at least possible that the occupation of Tiahuanaco was not interrupted until the general crisis at the end of the Middle Horizon.

There was a large city at Chavin in the Early Horizon, but it is not yet clear whether it was unique or merely one of many such settlements in the northern sierra at that time. If the latter, it may be possible to find links between the northern tradition and the Lake Titicaca one. Similar difficulties attend the interpretation of the occurrence of cities on the south coast in the Early Horizon.

A large unexplored area separates the south coast from Lake Titicaca. The south coast urban tradition appears to have been continuous until the Middle Horizon, although individual sites were abandoned on many occasions.

The expansion of Huari in the Middle Horizon is the expansion of a culture of cities which had its center in the Ayacucho area. Large cities in this area can be traced back well into the Early Intermediate Period, and designs on pottery indicate contacts with the urbanized south coast in Early Intermediate Period 7 and with Tiahuanaco in Middle Horizon 1. The origins of the urban tradition in the Ayacucho area are still obscure, because there has been so little exploration in the sierra. Large cities may well go back to the Early Horizon here, in which case a link with other Early Horizon occurrences of cities should be sought.

It was probably the influence of the Huari culture which was responsible for the introduction of large cities to the north coast. This area appears to have had only small urban settlements and ceremonial centers in earlier periods. Once it accepted the large city pattern, however, the north coast became highly urbanized and maintained its urban tradition until the time of the Spanish conquest.

The power of Huari and Tiahuanaco collapsed at the end of the Middle Horizon, and their fall was accompanied by a general abandonment of cities in southern Peru. Thereafter, the prevailing pattern of settlement was one of small urban settlements and dispersed dwellings. The fact that the abandonment of cities was general over a large area suggests that there was a reaction against cities as such, and we are reminded of the hostility of the rural population to the cities in the later Roman Empire. Like the Roman cities, the Peruvian ones of the Middle Horizon did have a rural population around them. It is interesting that the reaction took place in the areas where the urban tradition was very old and not on the north coast where large cities were a new phenomenon.

The story of ancient Peruvian cities has some important implications for general theories of the development of cities. In the first place, in Ica, where I have had an opportunity to study the relationship between cities and irrigation, large cities appear first and major irrigation canals were only built later. It would be difficult to argue that there was any relationship between irrigation and the development of cities in this area, unless it was that the growth of cities produced a pressure on the land which was met by irrigation projects on an unprecedented scale.

In the second place, the Peruvian data throw some light on the relationship between cities and ceremonial centers. Except for the late and somewhat peculiar case of Cuzco, there is no example in our Peruvian data of large cities developing out of ceremonial centers. When large cities replaced or were added to ceremonial centers, as occurred on the north coast, the cities represent the intrusion of foreign ideas coming from another area where the urban tradition was much older. The ceremonial center, therefore, is not a necessary stage in the development of the city.

The Peruvian evidence also shows very clearly that the large city is not such an advantageous institution as to spread consistently at the expense of other patterns of residence. We have seen how large cities disappeared over a considerable area in southern Peru at the end of the Middle Horizon and were replaced by a pattern of small urban settlements. At Ica an urban pattern was replaced by a ceremonial center one in the Late Intermediate Period. During this same period Pachacamac was transformed from a large city into a ceremonial center, which is all it was when the first European visitors saw it. Something similar had happened at Haldas in the Initial Period.

The ceremonial center is obviously in some sense an alternative to the city, providing the kinds of public institutions and services which are present in large cities, but without a permanent concentration of population. It would be possible to argue from the Peruvian data that ceremonial centers represent a secondary development out of cities. They clearly do so in some cases, but it would be going too far beyond the evidence to maintain that the prior existence of cities is a necessary condition for the development of ceremonial centers.

POSTSCRIPT   by John H. Rowe   1971

The dates in years given in this article are based on the radiocarbon measurements available in 1962. The measurements reported between 1962 and 1964 suggested earlier dates (see Rowe and Menzel 1967: v–vi and 16–30). Developments in radiocarbon age determination since 1964 will certainly necessitate further revisions of the absolute chronology for the Andean area. However, since the argument of this paper is based as far as possible on *relative* dating (Horizons and periods), it will not be affected significantly by changes in the radiocarbon scale.

The distinctive character of the settlement pattern of Cuzco, referred to in this article, has been further explored in another paper: "What Kind of a Settlement Was Inca Cuzco?" (Rowe 1967:59–76).

NOTES

1. Rowe, 1960a, 1960b, 1962b.
2. Menzel et al., 1964.
3. A summary of the archaeological sequence in the Ica Valley is given in Rowe, 1962a.
4. As the reader will note in the text which follows, this study suffers to some extent from the fact that the categories used in it grew out of my attempts to compare and interpret field data. The field observations were not made with these particular distinctions in mind and often fail to include the most pertinent details. Such deficiencies can be taken care of by further fieldwork, however, and the inductive approach calls for no apology.
5. Rostovtzeff, 1957, vol. 1, pp. 496–501.
6. These mounds are described by Engel, 1958, pp. 89–90. My data, however, were provided by E. P. Lanning, who participated in the excavations at Rio Seco.
7. Kigoshi et al., 1962, p. 91, and information provided by Rosa Fung de Lanning. See Engel, 1958, fig. 4, for an inaccurate plan of the Haldas temple.
8. Information provided by E. P. Lanning.
9. Sample UCLA-154 was collected in 1961 by J. H. Rowe and Dorothy Menzel and consisted of wood charcoal and carbonized seeds associated with a thin layer of ash on a clay floor at the foot of and continuous with the longest section of packed clay wall at the south end of the site. The ash represents the remains of a substantial fire which burned the face of the wall. The construction of the wall should, therefore, be earlier than the date of the sample. Sample UCLA-153 was collected in 1959 by Gary S. Vescelius, Hernan Amat Olazabal, and Dorothy Menzel, all at that time working on the joint archaeological project sponsored by the U.S. Educational Commission in Peru and the University of San Marcos. It consisted of wood charcoal from a layer of undisturbed refuse on the lee side of a sand hill at the north end of the site. Both samples were submitted to the laboratory by J. H. Rowe. Since the site had been dated in the Initial Period on the basis of the archaeo-

logical relationships of its pottery, textiles, and stone work, both dates are acceptable.

10. Preliminary identifications by J. H. Rowe and L. E. Dawson, not checked by experts.
11. Ralph, 1959, p. 57.
12. Ibid.
13. For photographs of the Pucara site see Kidder, 1943, and Rowe, 1958.
14. Bennett, 1934, pp. 378–85 and Table 1.
15. Rowe, 1944, p. 56.
16. Ralph, 1959, p. 55.
17. Cobo, lib. XIII, cap. XIX; 1956, Tomo 92, p. 197.
18. Rowe, 1958, pp. 260–61.
19. Ponce Sanginés, 1961, pp. 33–35.
20. Ibid., 1961, p. 22, top figure; comparison with Ica by Dorothy Menzel.
21. Kigoshi et al., 1962, p. 91.
22. Early Horizon 10 was also a time when the Ica Valley had a relatively unified pottery style. See Menzel et al., 1964.
23. Bennett and Bird, 1964, pp. 98–101.
24. A sample of the pottery from the Cahuachi excavations is illustrated by Strong, 1957, who also provides a plan and aerial photograph of the site. Strong generously permitted L. E. Dawson, Dorothy Menzel, and me to examine his original sherd collections, and the dates here assigned to Strong's materials are based on Dawson and Menzel's observations. I have also visited Cahuachi personally.
25. Bandelier, 1910, pp. 172–73 and plate XXI.
26. Stumer, 1953, pp. 44, 48, and fig. 1; Tabío, 1957, p. 5.
27. Schaedel, 1951a, p. 22; 1951b, pp. 234, 242–43; cf. Willey, 1953, pp. 412–13.
28. Willey, 1951, p. 198.
29. Willey, 1953b, pp. 132–33; Bennett, 1950, pp. 25–29.
30. Ubbelohde-Doering, 1959, pp. 6–26. The excavator's stylistic attributions of the pottery found in burials E-I, M-XI and M-XII are erroneous. These are all Middle Horizon 1 burials, dated by the Moche V style vessels they contained. All dark incised ware is not Chavin; all utilitarian face-neck jars are not Gallinazo, and so forth. The eclecticism reflected by the variety of decorated vessels in these burials is a common characteristic of Middle Horizon 1 burials elsewhere on the coast as well.
31. Bennett, 1953, p. 18 and fig. 2.
32. Tello, 1942, pp. 683, 684.
33. Monzón, 1881, p. 210.
34. McCown, 1945, pp. 267–73, figs. 5 and 13; Rowe, 1956, pp. 142–43; Kubler, 1962, plate 162; Tello, 1956, pp. 49–51 and fig. 2. Pikillaqta is dated by a find of small stone figures in Huari style. Wiraqocha Pampa is dated by its resemblances to Pikillaqta and to the Capilla Pata sector of Huari. The site on the Pampa de las Llamas is the group of rectangular plazas and associated buildings lying northeast of Huaca Mojeque at the foot of Cerro San Francisco. I know it only from Tello's plan and description, which provide very inadequate evidence for dating. My grouping of this site with the sierra ones is no more than a guess based on certain features of its formal plan.
35. Waywaka and Yanamancha are discussed briefly in Rowe, 1956, pp. 143 and 144.

36. Menzel, 1958, pp. 40–41.
37. Bennett, 1936, pp. 491–92 (sections K and L).
38. Ishida and others, 1960, p. 468.
39. Qaqallinka ("Casa Patac") and Timirán ("Dos Cruces") are described briefly in Ishida and others, 1960, pp. 467 and 462. For Sahuacarí and Otaparo, see Menzel, 1959, pp. 130–31.
40. Rowe, 1954, p. 107.
41. Ishida and others, 1960, p. 471.
42. Estete, 1938, p. 87.
43. Schaedel, 1951a, 1951b; Kosok, 1960.
44. Menzel, 1959, p. 130.
45. Plan in Bingham, 1930.

PART II: SUBSISTENCE AND ECOLOGY

Introduction to The "Hunting" Economies of the Tropical Forest Zone of South America: An Attempt at Historical Perspective

Donald Lathrap has devoted a considerable amount of his time and energy to excavating the remains of ancient communities in the tropical areas of South America. In this article, originally delivered at the Symposium on Man the Hunter held in Chicago in 1966, Lathrap explores the notion, supported by other researchers, that the Amazon basin is not to be considered a single ecological zone but that it should be divided into at least two distinct zones: riverine and slightly elevated upland environments. The main contrast between the two is found in differential productivity, both in agriculture and animal biomass.

This distinction has a number of significant implications regarding the ethnology of the Amazon. One is the suggestion that certain societies which concentrate largely on hunting and gathering for subsistence do not represent a prior stage of cultural evolution to the denser agricultural populations, but rather may be devolved from just such societies. This has interesting theoretical implications in that it departs from a unilineal model of evolution which some anthropologists may have adopted. This model also has important implications for the interpretation of particular ethnographic cases (e.g. the Sirionó, Holmberg 1950) and for the reconstruction of migration patterns in the peopling of the Amazon basin (cf. Meggers and Evans 1961, and the introduction to Chapter 7 of this volume). M. K. Martin (1969) makes a similar case using a regional cross-cultural sample.

This article demonstrates how much remains to be learned about the history and evolution of culture in South America. Much of the needed research is documentary in nature; hopefully some of the readers of this volume will equip themselves with the necessary skills in archeology, historical linguistics, ethnohistory, languages and anthropological theory and carry it out. As can be seen from reading this article and those reprinted here by Meggers, Carneiro and Oberg, a lively and healthy debate is still alive regarding many of the issues.

Trained at Berkeley and Harvard, Donald Lathrap has carried out extensive research in eastern Peru. He is the author of several important articles and a recent book *The Upper Amazon* (1970). Dr. Lathrap is Professor of Anthropology at the University of Illinois, Urbana.

6. THE "HUNTING" ECONOMIES OF THE TROPICAL FOREST ZONE OF SOUTH AMERICA: AN ATTEMPT AT HISTORICAL PERSPECTIVE

DONALD LATHRAP

The Amazon Basin contains the largest block of tropical rain forest in the world. The patterns of human utilization of this region and the history of how these patterns evolved through time is of considerable interest as a major chapter in the progressive expansion of human populations, and in the adaptation of such populations to diverse ecological settings.[1]

At the time of the first European contact, the Amazon Basin showed a considerable range of cultural pattern in terms of size and complexity of social units, complexity of material culture, and even in basic patterns of subsistence activity. The flood plain of the main stream of the Amazon and of its major tributaries sustained large, sedentary populations engaged in intensive root-crop farming combined with fishing and the hunting of aquatic mammals and reptiles. The exact size and complexity of sociopolitical units attained by these riverine societies, as of A.D. 1500, continues to be a matter of controversy since all such societies were very early disrupted by the effects of slave raiding, missionization, and diseases introduced by the Europeans. While it is clear that none of these societies rivaled the kind of sociopolitical unit which had been typical of the central Andes for the last 500 to 1,000 years before Columbus, it is equally clear from the various reviews of the early sources (Métraux, 1948a; Nimuendajú, 1952a; Palmatary, 1960, 1965; Rowe, 1952) that such riverine groups were far larger and more complex than the presently surviving remnant groups repre-

Reprinted by permission from the author, editors and publisher from Richard B. Lee and Irven DeVore, editors, *Man the Hunter,* Chapter 3, pp. 23–29 (Chicago: Aldine Publishing Company, 1968); copyright © 1968 by the Wenner-Gren Foundation for Anthropological Research, Inc.

senting tropical forest culture. An even greater discrepancy exists between our knowledge of the contact period riverine societies of the Amazon Basin and the generalized notion of "tropical forest culture" or "tropical forest stage" which has been developed by Meggers and Evans (Meggers, 1954, 1957a, 1957b; Meggers and Evans, 1956).

The demographic and cultural situation in the slightly elevated regions between the major rivers was in sharp contrast to that of the flood plains. The interfluve areas were characterized by scant populations organized into small, widely dispersed and mobile social units. These groups typically showed simple and relatively unproductive agricultural systems and relied heavily on the hunting of terrestrial and arboreal game for their sustenance. Unlike the groups inhabiting the more accessible and economically more valuable flood plains, the simple, dispersed Indian societies of the interfluve have in many instances survived until recently without major modifications in culture (Carneiro, 1964, p. 9).[2]

The presentation of a full, composite ethnographic picture of all such simple non-riverine groups is far beyond the scope of this paper, but certain key points in the above generalizations should be documented. In the area with which I am most familiar, the Peruvian Montaña, groups such as the Cashibo, Amahuaca, Remo, and Mayoruna are completely characteristic. A recent comparison of the agricultural practices of the Isconahua group of Remo, with those of the Shipibo, a riverine Panoan group, has shown the relative inefficiency of the Remo system and suggested that this inefficiency was an adjustment to the poorer agricultural potential of the interfluvial zone, the Remo's accustomed habitat (Momsen, 1964, pp. 76–77). Carneiro's excellent discussion of Amahuaca agriculture indicates equally rudimentary practices. For instance, he says: "At best, the Amahuaca are reluctant weeders" (1964, p. 14). The Shipibo on the other hand appear to be rather systematic and finicky on these matters.

Points which are crucial to the present discussion are the great importance which the hunting of terrestrial and arboreal game had for these interfluvial groups, and the degree to which the dependence on such game affected all other aspects of their culture. Carneiro has repeatedly demonstrated (1960, 1961, 1964) that it is not agricultural potential which directly controls the size and

mobility of tropical forest social groups. In the Amahuaca case
he gives a clear demonstration that the agriculture system, rudimentary as it is, is still capable of producing far more vegetable
foods than the people are able to use (1964, pp. 17–18). It is
the absence of significant aquatic resources (1964, p. 10) leading
to a dependence on terrestrial hunting for the protein necessary
to the diet which largely controls the nature of the social group.
Carneiro is worth quoting at length on this point:

> First of all, it should be kept in mind that the Amahuaca
> are still hunters almost as much as they are gardeners. Con-
> sequently, considerations having to do with the availability
> of game are very important to them. Even though three or
> four families settled in one locale for a year do not hunt out
> the game animals within the usual hunting radius of the set-
> tlement, they nevertheless probably make a noticeable inroad
> in their numbers. By the end of a year it has become
> necessary to walk farther to find game, and this is a decided
> inconvenience. If this inconvenience were counterbalanced
> by an equal or greater inconvenience in building a new settle-
> ment each year, the Amahuaca might not move so frequently.
> But Amahuaca houses can be built in three days and
> Amahuaca families are independent units perfectly free to
> pick up and move when and where they want to. Thus the
> Amahuaca, in deciding to move their settlements, do not
> have to overcome the inertia that would face a society which
> had a large village, substantial houses, and centralized
> political authority. In short, since the resistance to moving is
> small, the forces required to bring it about can likewise be
> small (1964, p. 16).

Holmberg (1950) paints a far bleaker picture of the results of
the necessary dependence on terrestrial hunting by such interfluvial groups. While probably somewhat extreme in terms of the
average situation for such groups throughout the Amazon Basin,
his description of hunger and life among the Sirionó still stands
as the most detailed coverage of the kind of economic patterns
shared by such groups.

A final factor which characterized the primitive groups on the interriverine uplands is that they were typically denied access to the flood plain environment by the warlike activities of the riverine groups. It was the continual threat of slave raiding, head taking, and in some instances cannibalism which held the non-riverine groups in their less favorable environment. Nimuendajú's discussion of the territory of the Tukuna illustrates the point admirably:

> The Tukuna did not then inhabit the banks of the Amazon-Solimões, for fear of the Omágua, who occupied the islands of that river throughout its course in Tukuna territory and even far beyond, while the banks of the Putumayo-Içá were held by Aruak tribes—the Mariaté, Yumána, and Pasé (1952b, p. 8).
> The most feared enemies of the ancient Tukuna—one might say their only enemies—were the Omágua. [The Omágua] attacked by canoe, with great spears. They captured many: some of them were sacrificed to their idols and the rest served as slaves in their husbandary (1952b, p. 65).

Marcoy's general discussion of the attitude of the riverine Shipibo toward the non-riverine Cashibo is equally telling, and his description of the crucifixion of a Cashibo unfortunate enough to fall into Shipibo hands is even more graphic (1873, vol. 2, pp. 162–63).

Concerning the relation between the riverine Arawakan and Tucanoan tribes of southeastern Colombia and the interfluvial Macú, Métraux says:

> The *Arawakan* and *Tucanoan* tribes of the upper Rio Negro, Caiarí-Uaupes, and Tiquié Rivers have since time immemorial waged merciless war against the *Macú,* whom they enslave or reduce to serfdom. Some small groups of *Macú* come to work for the sedentary *Uanana* and *Desana* and, after a few months, disappear again into the bush. The *Tucano* of the Tiquié River subjected a large group of *Macú* to their rule, but on the slightest suspicion of sorcery, they were prompt to attack them and sell their captives to the Whites (1948b, p. 866).

Carneiro also alludes to the constant hostility between the Amahuaca and their riverine neighbors as a factor tending to maintain their small, highly mobile, social units (1964, p. 16).

It is the culturally simple groups of the slightly elevated interfluvial regions of the Amazon Basin who are of possible interest to this symposium. It is clear from the foregoing discussion that they are typically dependent on the hunting of terrestrial and arboreal game for the essential protein complement of their diet, and arguments have been presented suggesting that the hunting practices of such people are a more important factor in conditioning their total way of life than are their relatively rudimentary and inefficient agricultural systems.

There has been a tendency to treat these people as unmodified representatives of a very early and primitive stage of tropical forest culture. Thus in a recent description of the Isconahua group of Remo, we find the authors, Whiton, Greene, and Momsen saying: "Their culture was that of incipient tropical forest slash-and-burn and close to neolithic man" (1964, p. 123). The suggestion has also been made that some, perhaps most, of these peoples represent groups of primitive hunters only slightly modified by trait-unit diffusion from their more advanced agricultural neighbors, and thus show a large degree of cultural continuity from a pre-Neolithic period or stage. Métraux is explicit about such an interpretation (1948b, p. 861), while such a view appears implicit in most of Steward's discussion of the same problem (1948b, pp. 896–99). Some such view would also appear to be implicit in Needham's emphasis on the anomaly of a system of asymmetric prescriptive alliances occurring in a "small-scale, hunting and collecting society" such as the Sirionó (1961, p. 252).

There is reason to question both of these interpretations and to suggest that many, perhaps all, of these simpler and less sedentary groups are the degraded descendants of peoples who at one time maintained an advanced form of tropical forest culture. In the remainder of this paper I hope to develop a simplified model of the historical background of such peoples.

I will assume that man entered South America with an economy oriented toward the hunting of big game, the large grazing animals typical of the grasslands and savannah. If the earliest inhabitants of South America indeed did function as predators on the grazing fauna, it is unlikely that they initially would have extended their range beyond that of the major element of their subsistence.

Such hunting groups appear to have entered South America before 15,000 B.C. (Rouse and Cruxent, 1963a, p. 537) and to have extended their range to the Straits of Magellan by 9000 B.C. (Lanning and Hammel, 1961, p. 147). There is insufficient space to review the distribution of Late Pleistocene and Early Post-Pleistocene sites in South America, but the available evidence is compatible with the hypothesis that the earlier occupations were confined to areas of relatively open vegetation: seasonal grasslands, high grasslands, open thorn forest, etc.

For groups with a technology and social system well adapted to cooperative hunting on the grassland, the tropical forest would not have been an attractive environment for permanent occupation or intensive utilization. The more common forms of game, both animals and birds, had as their typical habitat the upper levels of the forest canopy or were semi-aquatic to aquatic. In terms of mammalian fauna, the floor of the tropical forest away from the rivers supported a poverty of species and a low density of individuals. Gilmore comments on the generally unfavorable nature of the tropical forest as a hunting territory (1950, p. 354), and information on groups such as the Sirionó suggests that even for a people with a technology specifically adapted to the problems of hunting within the tropical forest, the tropical forest is far from prime hunting territory.

One would expect that most of the areas of more open vegetation including the east Brazil highlands, the llanos of Venezuela and Colombia, and parts of the Guiana highlands would have been occupied before groups with a specifically hunting orientation would have attempted a direct penetration of the central block of tropical forest within the Amazon Basin. Indeed, there is no direct archeological evidence that such penetration ever took place. The earliest demonstrable penetration of the tropical forest of the Amazon Basin is oriented to the far richer riverine resources.

The more astute students of tropical forest culture, such as Sauer, Lowie, Steward, and Goldman, have all observed that tropical forest culture is less an adaptation to the forest as such, than to the riverine environment within the tropical forest. Since this point has been consistently ignored by those who tend to see the tropical forest as a uniform environment, it may be well to offer extensive documentation. Sauer's emphasis on the importance of riverine resources suffuses his whole discussion of the origin of the tropical forest pattern of cultivation (1952, pp. 40–49). And Lowie comments:

> At the core of the area the diagnostic features are: the cultivation of tropical root crops, especially bitter manioc; effective river craft; the use of hammocks as beds; and the manufacture of pottery.
>
> The very wide distribution of certain traits in the area is correlated with navigation. Thanks to their mobility, the canoeing tribes were able to maintain themselves in the midst of boatless populations, to travel with ease over periodically inundated tracts, and to diffuse their arts and customs over enormous distances (1948, p. 1).

Steward makes the same points even more strongly:

> The distribution of culture elements and complexes reveals at least one broad pattern. The basic Tropical Forest cultures occur mainly in the areas accessible by water routes, both the coast and the great rivers. . . . The inference is clear that what is thought of as a typical Tropical Forest or selvan culture—a developed agriculture and a technology manifest in twilled and woven baskets, loom weaving, cotton hammocks, ceramics, and other material traits—flowed along the coast and up the main waterways stopping where streams were less navigable . . . (1948b, p. 883).

Goldman's statement of the Cubeos' view of their ecological setting has an almost poetic force:

> The river forms a wider community of related sibs. With some exceptions the sibs have aligned themselves along a river on the basis of degree of closeness and of rank. Sibs

that have segmented from a parental sib ordinarily occupy an adjacent site. The river is the most important territory. It is a highway and a link between related sibs, the source of ancestral power, and the economic zone of the men, fish being the main source of animal protein. Even most land animals are hunted along the river banks.

The orientation of the Cubeo is toward the river and not toward the forest. Whereas the forest is undifferentiated terrain, the rivers are known to every turn and outcrop of rock or other feature. The river is the source of the ancestral powers, of benefits as well as of dangers. The forest is a source mainly of dangers (1963, p. 44).

The advantages of the riverine environment over the slightly elevated interriverine zone include not only the greater availability of animal protein, but also a much higher agricultural potential. Sauer discusses the difference between the two zones in terms of land form (1950, p. 324), while Sternberg stresses the very real difference in agricultural potential of the lands lying within the Amazon Basin:

> Or take the prospect of an unlimited extent of rich crop land. The luxurious forest which mantles most of the region has commonly been interpreted as an unconditional promise of inexhaustible fertility. The very real productivity of bottomlands, periodically flooded and rejuvenated with silt-laden waters, has thus been ascribed to the enormous area corresponding to the generally acid and poor soils of the terras firmas, or uplands (1964, p. 13).

Thus it cannot be too strongly emphasized that the deep alluvial soils within the active flood plains have a far greater agricultural potential than the laterized and heavily eroded soils on the slightly elevated uplands back from the rivers. My Shipibo friends inform me that such deep, alluvial soils in certain parts of the central Ucayali flood plain will support continuous root-crop agriculture for up to fifteen or twenty years.

Sauer has stressed that the tropical forest agricultural pattern is essentially one of carbohydrate production, with the fat and protein requirements of the diet supplied by a technologically sophisticated utilization of the prodigious fish, aquatic mammal, and aquatic reptile resources of the flood plain (1952). Evolved tropical forest culture involves not just developed root-crop agriculture, but a developed set of fishing practices, including fish poisoning and effective water craft. Archeological manifestations suggesting all of these accomplishments appear early along the major rivers within the Amazon Basin.

Along the flood plain of the central Ucayali River in the Montaña of eastern Peru we find remains of such cultures as early as 2000 B.C. (Lathrap, 1958; 1962; 1965a, pp. 797–98; 1965b, p. 12). The elaborate and technologically sophisticated ceramic style designated Early Tutishcainyo cannot be derived from any early central Andean ceramic style. It does, however, show certain basic similarities to the earliest examples of tropical forest culture known from the flood plains of the Lower Orinoco in Venezuela, suggesting that both ceramic styles may have derived from some common source along the intermediate network of rivers (Cruxent and Rouse, 1959; Lathrap, 1963; Rouse and Cruxent, 1963b). The geographical setting in the central Ucayali presents the grossest kinds of obstacles to a meaningful estimate of settlement pattern and density of occupation for the earliest complexes. Given the degree to which jungle litter tends to camouflage all land surfaces, given the fact that the activity of the more numerous colonial ants tends to bury all ancient land surfaces under three to six inches of culturally sterile deposit, and most importantly given the destructive power of the continually meandering river which erases all traces of early settlements not located at the precise edge of the flood plain, the available evidence suggests that Early Tutishcainyo already represents a dense occupation of the suitable ecological niche.

In the course of the long cultural sequence which follows Early Tutishcainyo on the central Ucayali there exists evidence for at least three instances of complete ethnic replacement; two of the intrusive ceramic styles, so strongly suggesting the entrance of new ethnic groups, are clearly derived from the central Amazon. The long archeological sequence on the central Ucayali fully substantiates the picture of cultural development which Steward sketched on the basis of ethnographic distribution alone:

Culturally, the *Chuncho* (the Indians of the Montaña) belong with the Tropical Forest peoples. They appear to represent a series of migratory waves that had spent their force
against the barrier of the Andes, where representatives of
many widely distributed linguistic families . . . subsided into
comparative isolation (1948a, p. 507).

A series of waves of migration, basically in an upstream direction, is also suggested by the distribution of languages in two of
the more fully studied South American linguistic stocks, Macro-
Arawak and Tupí-Guaraní. Noble (1965) has presented a detailed
reconstruction of the proto-language of Macro-Arawak including
estimates of the degree of relationship among the various languages within Macro-Arawak. Rodrigues (1958) has presented a
brief statement as to the classification of the various Tupí-
Guaraní languages. A full treatment of the significance of these
classifications for the understanding of South American culture
history is beyond the scope of this paper, but I am at present engaged in preparing a manuscript which will attempt to evaluate
the distribution of the languages of these two stocks in terms of
past population movements. In attempting to summarize what is
a complex picture, one might say that the more divergent, and
presumably more anciently dispersed branches of Macro-Arawak
tend to be near the headwaters of the major western tributaries of
the Amazon, while the more closely related Maipuran languages
within Arawak tend to dominate the mainstreams of the western
segment of the Amazon, the Rio Negro, and the Orinoco [cf.
Sorensen, p. 316, this volume—Ed.]. Likewise the more divergent
branches of Tupí-Guaraní are ranged near the headwaters of the
various major southern tributaries of the Amazon, while the more
closely related languages within the family dominate the broader
flood plains of the lower reaches of these rivers, much of the main-
stream of the Lower Amazon, the Atlantic coast of Brazil, and
much of the flood plain of the Paraná. The most economical explanation for these observations (especially when they are coupled
with Noble's demonstration of an ultimate relationship between
Proto-Arawak and Proto-Tupí-Guaraní, relating to a period before
the dispersal of these two stocks) would be that the proto-
languages of the two stocks occupied adjacent stretches of the Cen-

tral Amazon between 3000 and 2000 B.C. with Proto-Arawak on the upstream side. From this hearth, colonization spread outward, mainly in an upstream direction, along all available waterways. Certain marked congruences between the distribution of ceramic styles and the distributions of particular linguistic families or subfamilies suggest the possibility of indicating the archeological concomitants of these major migrations demonstrable on linguistic grounds, and I hope fully to explore this possibility in the aforementioned forthcoming paper.[3]

The pattern of outward migration suggested by all of these converging lines of evidence could best be explained by intense and continuing population pressures of the flood plain of the Central Amazon, the most favorable environment for the support of tropical forest culture. Such continuous expansion by groups moving out to colonize further areas of flood plain progressively pushed smaller or militarily weaker groups farther upstream or off the flood plains entirely. In presenting this view I am, of course, in complete accord with Vayda's argument that warfare among tropical forest farmers has profound economic and demographic effects even though it may have a religious or recreational rationale (Vayda, 1961b).

This extreme and continuing competition for territory is understandable, if one realizes the limited amount of flood plain—the only ecological niche really suitable to tropical forest culture—available in the Amazon Basin. Sternberg summarizes the point nicely:

> It has been seen how the uplands are generally poor, and it must be granted that they occupy the major part of the Amazon region, comprising more than a million square miles and leaving only a slight fraction of the area to the fertile *várzeas,* or floodplains. Nevertheless, one is dealing with lands of continental dimensions and this small fraction represents no insignificant area: the *várzeas,* rejuvenated every year by the silt brought down by the river, occupy some twenty-five thousand square miles . . . (1964, p. 324).

Considering that these processes have been continuous from about 2500 B.C. up to the time of the contact, it is clear that a large number of ethnic groups were forced off the flood plains into less favorable environments.

Most of the primitive groups inhabiting the tropical forest uplands away from the major flood plains can be interpreted as the wreckage of evolved agricultural societies forced into an environment unsuitable to the basic economic pattern. Deprived of the riverine resources, such groups had to rely on the hunting of forest game to provide the protein and fat essential to the diet. A more intense orientation to hunting the relatively scarce game available led to more nomadism, a decline in agricultural productivity, and a still greater dependence on wild food.

I am convinced that this picture accounts for all of the simpler groups within the Tupí-Guaraní, Arawak, and Panoan linguistic stocks. As we gain more knowledge the interpretation may be extendable to other groups, whose cultural and linguistic affiliations are less clear such as the Tukuna, Mura, and Macú. The speed with which this kind of cultural devolution can take place is suggested by the relatively minor linguistic differences between the riverine Panoans such as the Shipibo and Conibo and the very "primitive" interfluvial Panoan groups such as the Cashibo and Remo.

While the "hunting" cultures of the tropical forest zone of South America offer highly explicit examples of the cultural and demographic effects of a dependence on hunting in an area where hunting is neither profitable nor easy, they probably instruct us not at all about the nature of pre-Neolithic hunting cultures.

NOTES

1. This paper is a somewhat expanded version of the presentation given at the symposium [on "Man the Hunter"—Ed.]. It has benefited from the symposium discussions, and through advice given by my wife Joan W. Lathrap and Dr. Frederic K. Lehman.

2. In view of the discussion which followed the presentation of this paper, it is perhaps advisable to make explicit that the Gê and Bororo groups of the east Brazil highlands fall outside the territorial and ecological limits set for this paper.

3. Readers familiar with the literature on South American archeology will

know that Meggers and Evans have presented a markedly different model of demography and population movements in the Amazon Basin (1961). Other archeologists who have worked under their close supervision have followed the Meggers-Evans hypotheses rather slavishly (for example, Hilbert 1962a, 1962b). That the Meggers-Evans model is not mentioned in the text of this paper does not indicate that I am ignorant of its existence. Rather I find that all of the data presented by Meggers, Evans, and Hilbert, as opposed to their speculation about the data, can be accommodated quite easily in my own model.

*Introduction to Slash-and-Burn Cultivation Among the Kui-
kuru and Its Implications for Cultural Development in the
Amazon Basin*

Robert Carneiro's article is a response to the ideas of Betty Meggers (1954) regarding limitations imposed by agricultural potential on cultural development. In her article, Meggers used the four-
part typology from the *Handbook of South American Indians*
(Steward [Ed.] 1947: Vol. V, 669 ff.) to show that each cultural
type was limited to areas with different agricultural potential. The
"marginals" such as the Fuegian and Patagonian peoples, for
example, lived in areas where agriculture was impossible with the
available technology. The tropical forest peoples, according to
Meggers, were limited to a tribal level of development (small,
politically unorganized, autonomous villages) because of the poor
soils of the areas they inhabited. In support of her argument,
Meggers described the prehistoric Marajoara society (see Meggers
and Evans in Chapter 4 of this volume), a chiefdom with complex
organization and social elites which migrated down the Amazon
from the Río Napo in Ecuador. This society collapsed, according
to Meggers, because tropical soils could not support the intensive
agriculture on which it depended.

Carneiro does not deny that a minimum level of subsistence
productivity is a prerequisite to cultural development. He attempts
to show, however, that Meggers' estimate of the potential productivity of the South American forest is too conservative. Using a
formula he devised for estimating the carrying capacity of a slash-
and-burn system (see Carneiro 1960), Carneiro calculates that

the Kuikuru of the upper Xingú River could have sustained villages of up to 2,000 without degrading the environment or being forced to move. Thus, Carneiro argues that while a certain level of subsistence productivity is a *necessary* condition of cultural development, it is nonetheless not a *sufficient* condition. According to him, many tropical forest dwellers had the capacity to produce far more food per capita yet they did not take advantage of it (cf. Carneiro 1964). He goes on to suggest that other natural and social factors must be considered in order to account for cultural evolution in South America. Carneiro's contribution to the theory of cultural development has been to emphasize the role played by warfare and conquest. He has recently expanded his "circumscription theory" of the origin of the state (1970b) outlined here utilizing new data and including material of the Yąnomamö (see Chagnon in Chapter 8 of this volume).

Robert L. Carneiro received his doctorate from the University of Michigan and now is Curator of South American Ethnology at The American Museum of Natural History in New York. Other articles on the Kuikuru can be found under his name in the bibliography and in Gertrude Dole's article in this volume. Carneiro has also made substantial contributions to anthropological method and theory in his explorations of scale analysis and the sociology of Herbert Spencer.

7. SLASH-AND-BURN CULTIVATION AMONG THE KUIKURU AND ITS IMPLICATIONS FOR CULTURAL DEVELOPMENT IN THE AMAZON BASIN

ROBERT L. CARNEIRO

I.

The Kuikuru of central Brazil are a more or less typical Tropical Forest society whose mode of subsistence is slash-and-burn agriculture. They occupy a single village near the Kuluene River, a headwater tributary of the Xingú. At the time that field work was carried out among them in 1953–54, the Kuikuru village consisted of 9 large, well-built thatched houses, and had a population of 145. The village is situated in an extensive tract of forest within which the Kuikuru make their garden clearings.

The most important crop plant grown is manioc (*Manihot esculenta*), at least 11 varieties of which are cultivated. All of these varieties are poisonous. In the form of a gruel or as beijú cakes manioc makes up approximately 80 or 85 per cent of the Kuikuru diet. Other cultivated plants, including maize, provide only 5 per cent or less of their food, while fishing accounts for most of the remaining 10 or 15 per cent. Hunting is of almost no importance, providing less than 1 per cent of the food supply.

In clearing a garden plot steel axes, machetes, and brushhooks are now used. Before 1900, however, the Kuikuru felled trees and cleared undergrowth with stone axes and piranha mandibles. The system of swidden cultivation employed by the Kuikuru is very similar to that practiced by primitive cultivators in forested regions generally. Shortly after the end of the rainy season the for-

Reprinted by permission of the author and the Fundación La Salle de Ciencias Naturales, Caracas, from *Antropológica*, Supplement No. 2. *The Evolution of Horticultural Systems in Native South America*, edited by Johannes Wilbert, pp. 47–67. 1961.

est vegetation is cut and left to lie where it falls for several months in order to dry out. Just before the next rainy season it is piled up and burned. Planting begins about the time of the first rains. The ground is not fertilized other than by the wood ashes resulting from burning which are washed into the soil by the rains.

Burning does not completely consume the fallen trees, and charred logs and stumps can be seen throughout the fields. The Kuikuru simply plant where they can between these obstructions. Manioc is always planted from cuttings, which are inserted into low mounds made by hoeing up the loose soil. Between 4 and 10 cuttings are planted in each mound. The mounds are located about 4 or 5 feet apart, and in a manioc plot of average size (around 1½ acres) there are some 1,500 of them.

Gardens are weeded by hand as well as with hoes. In addition to weeding them, it is also necessary to fence them in order to protect them from the ravages of peccaries. As a preventive measure fencing is not entirely successful, since peccaries often manage to get into the plots anyway by rooting their way under the fences. According to the natives' account, the amount of damage that peccaries do to the manioc crop is considerable.[1]

Virtually all horticultural work is done by men, including clearing, burning, planting, weeding, and fencing the plots. Women only dig up the tubers and carry them back to the village.

Manioc tubers develop to a harvestable size in about 5 or 6 months after the cuttings are planted, but the Kuikuru prefer to wait 18 or 20 months before pulling them out of the ground. This is because at this age the tubers are considerably larger and have attained their highest proportion of starch, about 25 per cent (see Barrett 1928:373). A Kuikuru garden produces about 4 or 5 tons of manioc tubers per acre per year. Of this amount only a part—perhaps not much more than half—is actually consumed by the Kuikuru. The rest is lost to peccaries, and to leaf-cutter ants who in their unobtrusive way carry off rather large amounts of manioc flour from the village.[2]

Gardens are replanted progressively, new cuttings being put into the ground where old plants have been removed after harvesting. This method of replanting has the effect of staggering the times at which the tubers from the second planting reach optimal conditions for harvesting. A third crop may be planted in a garden, staggered in the same way as the second, but after three plantings the plot is abandoned and a new one cleared.

In selecting a new garden site a Kuikuru has a rather wide choice. Within the 4-mile radius which the Kuikuru are willing to walk to cultivate a manioc plot there are some 13,500 acres of usable forest. This area of arable land is so large in relation to (1) the amount of land under cultivation at one time (about 95 acres), (2) the rate at which land is abandoned (about 40 acres a year), and (3) the time required for an abandoned plot to become reusable (about 25 years), that the Kuikuru are not faced with the prospect of ever having to move their village because of depletion of the soil (see Carneiro 1960). Indeed, the Kuikuru have lived in the same locale continuously for the past 90 years. It is true that during this period of time they have occupied four different village sites, but these sites have all been located only a few hundred yards from each other, and the reasons for moving from one to another have always been supernatural, never ecological.

The subsistence economy of the Kuikuru is one of abundance and reliability. There is never a shortage of food, let alone any danger of starvation. When planting, the Kuikuru make allowance for the depredations of peccaries and leaf-cutter ants by planting more than they themselves could consume. So great in fact is the reservoir of manioc in a growing field that even a large and unexpected loss of flour may be no more than an inconvenience. Thus on one occasion when a family lost several hundred pounds of manioc flour (a two-months' supply) in a house fire, the woman of the family simply made good her loss by digging up and processing more tubers; she did not attempt to borrow manioc flour from any other family.

The extra manioc planted by the Kuikuru to defray losses incurred to peccaries, ants, house fires, and the like cannot of course be called a surplus even if it is an amount over and above their own consumption. It is, rather, an *obligatory margin*. The Kuikuru however do produce a *seasonal* surplus of manioc, for during the dry season a number of families move to small garden houses near the plots where women convert thousands of tubers into flour which is later stored in the village. This laying up of stores of manioc flour makes it possible for the women to forego the usual routine of going to the fields to dig up roots every 2 or 3 days during the early months of the ensuing rainy season. Instead, they can spend their time gathering piquí fruits, making hammocks, or in some other activity.

There is no doubt at all that the Kuikuru could produce a surplus of food over the full productive cycle. At the present time a man spends only about 3½ hours a day on subsistence—2 hours on horticulture, and 1½ hours on fishing. Of the remaining 10 or 12 waking hours of the day the Kuikuru men spend a great deal of it dancing, wrestling, in some form of informal recreation, and in loafing. A good deal more of this time could easily be devoted to gardening. Even an extra half hour a day spent on agriculture would enable a man to produce a substantial surplus of manioc. However, as conditions stand now there is no reason for the Kuikuru to produce such a surplus, nor is there any indication that they will. The reasons for this failure to produce a surplus of food when, from the standpoint of time and technology it would be perfectly feasible to do so, will be dealt with in a later section of this paper. There we will also consider the implications of this fact for cultural development in general.

II.

The conditions of subsistence which exist among the Kuikuru are, at a number of points, at variance with generally held beliefs about the potentialities and limitations of slash-and-burn agriculture in the Amazon basin. I would like now to examine some of these conventional opinions in light of the evidence provided by the Kuikuru as well as other relevant data from Tropical Forest tribes and elsewhere.

Permanence of Settlement. It is commonly asserted in the literature on swidden agriculture that because shifting cultivators soon exhaust all of the surrounding soil, they find it impossible to maintain their villages in the same location for more than a few years (e.g., Childe 1953:198). We have seen, however, that the Kuikuru have lived virtually on the same spot for 90 years. Furthermore the Waurá, a neighboring society, have likewise maintained their village in the same locale for many decades (Lima

1950:5). A similar degree of village permanence is reported to exist among the tribes of the Rio Uaupés in northwestern Brazil (Brüzzi, 1962).

We see therefore that the mere fact of practicing shifting cultivation does not necessarily prevent a society from maintaining an essentially sedentary community. If it is true that many Tropical Forest Indians do move their villages at rather frequent intervals, as is indeed reported, then this fact calls for a more refined explanation. To show what form such an explanation would take let us examine the pattern of settlement and movement that prevails among a number of tribes of the Peruvian Montaña.

Except for tribes living along the lower Ucayali, the villages of most Montaña Indian groups are small, with an average population of perhaps 30 persons or even less. Yet despite their small size, these communities are reported to move frequently, the cause usually being given as "soil exhaustion." This fact appears to present something of a paradox. How could villages of such small size exhaust the surrounding forest soil so rapidly when the Kuikuru, five times their size, do not? The explanation suggested below is inferential, but it is the only one which seems to me to resolve the dilemma.

Villages in the Montaña are not only small with regard to number of inhabitants, they also consist of very few houses which are of modest size and of exceedingly simple construction. These houses usually have a rectangular framework of 6 upright posts, a thatched gable roof, and no walls. They are quickly and easily built, which means that they can be just as quickly and easily *rebuilt*. Thus it is probably easier, after a site has been occupied for a few years, to relocate a village at a spot right next to un-cleared forest than it would be to walk perhaps even half a mile from the old village to cultivate new garden plots. The successive clearing, planting and abandoning of adjacent areas of forest is therefore a factor in bringing about periodic village relocation, but to say without further qualification that soil exhaustion caused the village to be moved would obviously be a misleading oversimplification.

We can elaborate and generalize this explanation so that it will apply to all shifting cultivators living in areas where, for all practical purposes, the forest is unlimited. In deciding whether or not to move their village, swidden agriculturalists must weigh two inconveniences against each other. One is the inconvenience of walking an increasingly longer distance to cultivate a plot. The other is the inconvenience of rebuilding the village in a different location. If walking the requisite distance to the nearest available garden sites is less bother than moving the village, then the village will remain in the same location. However, if moving the village is less of an inconvenience than walking the additional distance to the fields, then the village will be moved. In a region like the Montaña, where communities are small and dwellings are simple, relocating the village will presumably appear to be the lesser inconvenience before it becomes necessary to walk even a moderate distance to clear a garden. On the other hand, in an area like the Upper Xingú, where communities are larger, and where houses are of good size and carefully built, it is less trouble to walk 3 or 4 miles to the garden plots than it is to rebuild the village closer to them.

The conclusion to which we are led is that village relocation in the Tropical Forest cannot so facilely be attributed to soil exhaustion as it has been the custom to do. Depletion of the soil in the immediate vicinity of a village merely creates conditions under which moving the village becomes, not an ecological necessity, but simply the more convenient of two courses of action.[3]

The preceding argument has considered only some of the factors involved in determining whether or not a village site is to be moved. Other important ones exist. For example in areas where warfare is prevalent the desire for security from attack may lead to successive relocations of the village having nothing to do with the agricultural cycle.[4] Among tribes for whom hunting still constitutes an important part of subsistence, the depletion of game animals in the vicinity of the village may dictate moving long before other conditions would warrant it.

Thus a variety of factors capable of affecting settlement patterns must be known in some detail before we can be sure of why a particular society has moved its village. Lacking this information we are not justified in assuming that the village must have been moved because of soil exhaustion.

Settlement Size. Villages in the Tropical Forest are typically rather small in size. According to the map in the *Handbook of*

South American Indians showing community size for aboriginal
South America (Steward 1949:676), the median village size for
societies in the Amazon basin seems to fall into the class interval
50–150. The reason most commonly advanced to explain why communities in this region should be so small is that slash-and-burn
cultivation does not permit large concentrations of population to
occur (see, for example, Meggers 1954:807). Meggers has gone
so far as to propose the figure of 1,000 as the upper limit for
settlement size in the Tropical Forest.

It is not easy to find population figures for Indian villages in
Amazonia under aboriginal or near-aboriginal conditions. I have,
however, come across at least one instance of a native community
in Amazonia exceeding 1,000 in population. This was an Apinayé
village on the Tocantins River which in 1824 had 1,400 inhabitants
(Nimuendajú 1939:12). There is no reason to suppose that this
village was unique in exceeding the figure of 1,000. Elsewhere
(Carneiro 1960) I have calculated that under the prevailing system of shifting cultivation, the present-day habitat of the Kuikuru
could have supported, on a completely sedentary basis, a village
of about 2,000 persons.

It is very unlikely that even a few centuries ago, when the Upper
Xingú basin was at its maximum density of population, it supported
communities even approaching the figure of 2,000. If Meggers is
too conservative in setting 1,000 as the upper limit of settlement
size in Amazonia, she is nevertheless correct in stressing the fact
that the vast majority of Indian villages in the Tropical Forest
had considerably fewer than 1,000 inhabitants. Certain limiting
factors did indeed operate to keep community size in the Amazon
basin well below 1,000, but slash-and-burn agriculture was by no
means the only, or even necessarily the principal one. I would
like to argue that a factor of greater importance has been the ease
and frequency of village fissioning for reasons not related to subsistence. The Kuikuru themselves, for example, came into existence
as a separate village as the result of such a split some 90 years
ago. Other instances of village fission are on record (e.g., Crocker
1958).

The facility with which this phenomenon occurs suggests that
villages may seldom get a chance to increase in population to the
point at which they begin to press hard on the carrying capacity

of the land. The centrifugal forces that cause villages to break apart seem to reach a critical point well before this happens. What the forces are that lead to village fission falls outside the present discussion. Suffice it to say that many things may give rise to factional disputes within a society, and that the larger the community the more frequent these disputes are likely to be.[5] By the time a village in the Tropical Forest attains a population of 500 or 600 the stresses and strains within it are probably such that an open schism, leading to the hiving off of a dissident faction, may easily occur.[6] If internal political controls were strong, a large community might succeed in remaining intact despite factionalism. But chieftainship was notoriously weak among most Amazonian villages, so that the political mechanisms for holding a growing community together in the face of increasingly strong divisive forces were all but lacking.[7]

Of perhaps equal importance with weak chieftainship as a factor encouraging fission is the fact that no great ecological deterrents exist to discourage a faction from splitting off from a parent community. Land suitable as a habitat for a dissident group is easily to be found. Thus the combination of weak integrative forces and absence of external deterrents keeps at a fairly low level the threshold of internal dissension that need be reached before a split is precipitated.

Food Productivity. It is sometimes affirmed that the reason why the horticultural Indians of Amazonia did not attain a higher level of culture was the low productivity of their mode of subsistence. For example, in attempting to account for the decline of Marajoara culture Clifford Evans writes that "the tropical forest environment . . . does not permit the intensive agricultural production resulting in high yield per man-hour of output that is essential for the continuing support of an advanced level of cultural development" (1955:90).

The belief that slash-and-burn cultivation with manioc as its principal crop is not especially productive is, however, quite erroneous. As a matter of fact it can be shown that Tropical Forest horticulture, as represented by the Kuikuru, is considerably more productive than horticulture as practiced by the Inca. This is true whether we compare the food productivity of the two societies in terms of food yield per acre, or food yield per man-hour of labor.

The manioc tubers grown by the Kuikuru produce something over 4,000,000 calories per acre per year. After we subtract from this figure the caloric value of the manioc wasted and that lost to peccaries and ants, we find that the Kuikuru obtain for their own consumption well over 2,000,000 calories per acre per year.

Figures for food productivity in Peru during Inca times are not readily available, but on the basis of estimates of present-day maize production under conditions similar to those of aboriginal times, it appears that an Inca *chacra* (garden) in the highlands yielded at most 25 bushels of maize per acre per year. On the coast, where irrigation and a warmer climate permitted the harvesting of two corn crops a year, the production of maize would have been no more than 50 bushels per acre per year. Translated into calories, the 50-bushel yield is equivalent to about 700,000 calories, or about a third of that of Kuikuru manioc plots.[8]

Let us now compare food production per unit of human labor. We have seen that the Kuikuru gardener spends an average of about 2 hours a day on manioc cultivation. His Inca counterpart, to judge from descriptions of horticultural practices in ancient Peru (Rowe 1946:210) and from observations of similar practices in modern times (Mishkin 1946:415), must have spent considerably more time on agricultural labor.

The reason for these surprising differences in productivity is not far to seek. Manioc is such a high-yielding crop plant that even when indifferently cultivated it yields far more digestible matter than maize or any other grain crop grown under the most intensive cultivation. If conditions of cultivation are held constant, it will also out-yield any other root crop, although not by as wide a margin.

In view of the foregoing evidence it would appear that whatever the factors that enabled the Central Andes to outstrip the Tropical Forest in cultural development (and we shall examine these later), greater food production per unit of land or per unit of labor was not one of them.

The Possibility of Food Surpluses. Another widely-held belief about slash-and-burn agriculture is that it cannot produce a food surplus. Since everyone seems to agree that without the possibility of such a surplus a society cannot develop the craft specialists, centralized political controls, elaborate religious complexes, social classes, and other characteristics of advanced culture, whether this allegation is true or false is a crucial point. Therefore if it can be demonstrated that Amazonian cultures could not, through the limitations of their mode of subsistence, produce a surplus of food, their failure to evolve beyond the Tropical Forest level would be accounted for.

It is true that over the yearly cycle of production Amazonian cultivators almost never actually produce more food than they need for themselves and their families. Nevertheless, taken by itself this piece of evidence is inconclusive. It is of critical importance that we distinguish between the existence of the *technological feasibility* of surplus food production and the *actualization* of such a surplus. It seems to me that what was said above about Kuikuru horticulture clearly indicates that manioc cultivators in the Amazon basin are technically capable of producing food well in excess of what they need for their own consumption. We noted that the Kuikuru do produce a seasonal surplus of manioc, and suggested that with only a very moderate increase in the time and effort devoted to farming they could produce a surplus over the entire year.[9]

Documented cases of true surplus production of manioc by Tropical Forest tribes are on record. For example, during the 1850's the Mundurucú of the Rio Tapajós produced a yearly surplus of between 180,000 and 300,000 pounds of manioc flour which they sold to White traders from the town of Santarem (Bates 1864:273).[10]

The implications of this evidence are clear: production of a true food surplus is not a matter of agricultural technology alone. The presence of certain additional factors—economic incentives or political compulsion—appears to be required before a people's economic system can be made to generate the food surplus which is an inherent potential of almost every agricultural society. Tropical Forest cultivators certainly possessed the technical capability to produce a yearly surplus of food. But with very few exceptions they lacked both the economic and political stimulus necessary to achieve them.

Alleged Absence of Leisure Time. The availability of leisure time is generally held to be a prerequisite for the development of advanced cultures. Leisure is another kind of surplus. It is a surplus of time over and above that required to carry out necessary activities, especially those connected with subsistence. The assumption is sometimes made that since the village tribes of the Amazon basin never attained an advanced level of culture, they must *ipso facto* have lacked leisure time. Once again the facts show otherwise.

We have seen that the Kuikuru, who in this respect are probably not far above average among Tropical Forest tribes, have considerable amounts of leisure time. Thus insofar as a high level of culture depends upon the availability of abundant leisure, one might have expected it to be attained by the Kuikuru. But despite the leisure time available to them the Kuikuru are like the great majority of other Amazonian tribes in showing no tendency to develop features of a higher level of culture. We are forced to conclude, therefore, that the mere presence of leisure time is not enough. It must be organized and directed by certain kinds of special mechanisms before it can be made to yield significant social consequences (cf. White 1959:292–93). If this view is correct, then it is the absence of the conditions which give rise to such mechanisms, rather than a lack of leisure time, that has kept the Kuikuru and other tribes of the Tropical Forest from achieving more complex forms of society.

Poverty of the Soil and the Abandonment of Plots. Virtually all slash-and-burn horticulturalists in the Amazon basin, as indeed in most other parts of the world, abandon their garden plots after only 2 or 3 years of cultivation. Most writers, in trying to account for this fact, attribute the early abandonment of fields to the exhaustion of soil fertility. Is this explanation really true? This is an issue of sufficient importance to deserve being considered in some detail here.

It is known that the soils underlying tropical rain forests are poorer in mineral content than the soils of drier and more temperate regions. In addition to having a lower initial fertility, garden plots carved out of tropical rain forest suffer more than those in temperate areas from the leaching of minerals by rainfall and from biochemical decomposition of humus. But even taking all of these facts into account is it actually the case that after only two or three years of cultivation a swidden is so depleted of plant nutrients that it is no longer suitable for planting? The experimental evidence bearing on this problem that I have been able to examine makes such a conclusion appear to be highly questionable. Since this evidence has appeared in sources generally unfamiliar to anthropologists it seems worthwhile to cite some of it here.

Carefully controlled and long-term experiments on the duration of soil fertility under conditions resembling those encountered in slash-and-burn cultivation have been carried out in Rothamsted, England, and at the Missouri Agricultural Experiment Station in the United States. These experiments have shown that even after three decades of continuous cropping, with no fertilizer whatever being added to the soil, fields in temperate areas are able to produce about 70 per cent of the crop yield they produced during the first three years of cultivation (Lawes and Gilbert 1895:168; Miller and Hudelson 1921:32). It does not seem likely that the rate of soil depletion is enough greater in a tropical rain forest environment to force abandoning a field after only 2 or 3 years, when in a temperate rainy climate an unfertilized field can be cultivated at a 70 per cent level of productivity for 30 years. But however suggestive this evidence, it is still based on work undertaken in temperate areas. Now let us review some of the evidence stemming from agronomic research carried out in the tropics.

For more than a decade experiments designed to determine the degree of soil depletion taking place under native agricultural techniques were conducted at the agricultural experiment station at Ibadan in Southern Nigeria. Some of the results of this work were summarized by H. Vine, Senior Agricultural Chemist of Nigeria, as follows (1953:65):

> "1. Yields can be maintained at a good level for considerable periods of continuous cultivation on these soils without the use of fertilizers.
> 2. Fertility is lost rather slowly if continuous cultivation is prolonged for more than about 10 years."

Of the three principal plant nutrients, nitrogen, phosphorus, and potash, it is generally believed that nitrogen is the one in most critical supply and the one most easily dissipated in tropical soils. Accordingly, some further observations of Vine's are particularly interesting:

> "The experiment started on land newly cleared from young secondary forest, and the results strongly suggest that the gradual decomposition of constituents of the humus accumulated in such conditions can provide a nearly adequate supply of nitrate for 10 years or more in these soils" (1953:66).

When the time and resources needed to cultivate an experimental plot over a number of years and to make periodic analyses of the soil are not available, significant information on soil fertility may still be obtained by sampling the soil of contiguous tracts which are at different stages of the cycle of swidden cultivation. Such a study was carried out in Fiji by Cassidy and Pahalad (1953). The investigators selected three sites in the wet southeastern part of the island of Viti Levu where the rainfall is 120 inches a year. At each site there were, adjacent to one another, (1) areas of virgin forest (or at any rate of forest that had been growing undisturbed for at least 30 years), (2) areas currently under slash-and-burn agriculture which were being cultivated without the addition of fertilizers, and (3) fallow areas which had been abandoned earlier after a regime of swidden cultivation and which were reverting back to forest.

Soil samples were taken from various layers of the soil profile from each of the three phases of cultivation in each of the three sites. Analyses were made of the soil to determine the total amount of nitrogen, and the amount of available phosphate and potash. The most significant of Cassidy's and Pahalad's results (1953:83) are given in Table I.

Cassidy and Pahalad comment on these results as follows: "A statistical examination of the data in Table II [Table I here] shows that the apparent difference in nutrients after cultivation could have been due to chance except in the case of available potash. Here the cultivated plots were significantly higher than both virgin and reverted plots, and it must be concluded that cultivation had brought about a definite release of potash to the soil" (1953:84).

TABLE I.

CONDENSED RESULTS OF SOIL ANALYSES OF THREE SITES ON VITI LEVU, FIJI, INVOLVED IN A CYCLE OF SHIFTING CULTIVATION.

	Depth of Layer	Phase of Cycle	Total Nitrogen	Available Phosphate (p.p.m.)	Available Potash (m.e./100 g.)
Site A	(0-12")	Virgin (30– yrs.)	.221[11]	14[11]	0.27[11]
(Ovea)	(0-12")	Cultivated (4 yrs.)	.193	15	0.55
	(0- 9")	Reverted (8 yrs.)	.135	15	0.35
Site B	(0- 6")	Virgin (50– yrs.)	.338	28	0.29
(Navuniasi)	(0- 6")	Cultivated (5 yrs.)	.404	22	1.12
	(0- 6")	Reverted (25 yrs.)	.290	20	0.25
Site C	(0- 7")	Virgin (30 yrs.)	.388	7.4	0.50
(Qeledamu)	(0- 8")	Cultivated (10 yrs.)	.244	10.2	0.54
	(0- 4")	Reverted (8 yrs.)	.303	17.4	0.65

These findings are very striking, particularly in view of the fact that the three cultivated plots had been under continuous cultivation for 4, 5, and 10 years respectively, significantly longer than the 2 or 3 years of successive planting characteristic of the average plot under slash-and-burn cultivation.

For a number of years the Carnegie Corporation of Washington maintained an experimental milpa in Yucatan which was cultivated following the same slash-and-burn techniques employed by the Maya Indians of the surrounding region. Every year an analysis was made of the soil in order to determine the amount of loss of mineral nutrients it had sustained. The results of this experiment are described by Morley as follows:

"After the harvest, each successive year, specimens of soil have been taken from this cornfield; and, over a period of ten years, the annual analyses of these specimens have shown no appreciable decrease in the amount of necessary nitrogenous salts, nor a sufficient amount of deterioration in the chemical composition of the soil to account for the diminishing yearly yield" (1947:148).

Morley suggests that the decrease in crop yields observed in the experimental milpa resulted from the increased competition offered the maize plants by weeds and grass. Indeed, there is reason to believe that the invasion of weeds and grass may be the principal reason why shifting cultivators in general abandon their garden plots not long after they begin to till them. At first the crop plants in a garden cleared in the middle of a forest face little competition from other plants, but by the end of three years of cultivation enough seeds of herbaceous plants have been blown in to bring about very heavy competition from weeds and grass. This competition, in which weeds and grass have a distinct advantage, leads to a considerable decline in the yield of the crop plants.

Moreover, to attempt to cope effectively with this invasion by thorough weeding is extremely tedious, and the older the plot, the more difficult it becomes. Thus the amount of time required to weed an old plot may be fully twice as much as that required to weed a new one (Conklin 1957:104). In fact, it often takes more time to *weed* an old garden than to *clear* a new one (Morley 1947:147). In view of these facts it seems quite apparent why shifting cultivators generally should prefer to abandon a 2- or 3-year-old plot and clear another one elsewhere. It would be foolish to do anything else as long as enough wooded land was available.

Thus we see that the abandonment of a plot after a brief period of cultivation can best be understood, not as a necessary consequence of rapid soil depletion in the tropics, but rather as the most economical way of carrying on subsistence farming under the prevailing conditions of technology and environment.

Supposed Lack of Evolutionary Possibilities. A number of writers have maintained that slash-and-burn agriculture, however primitive, is nevertheless the most advanced system of cultivation that can develop in a tropical rain forest environment. Consequently, it is argued, a high level of culture cannot be attained in areas like the Amazon basin. Betty Meggers, one of the most unequivocal advocates of this point of view, has expressed this opinion in the following terms: ". . . the environmental potential of the tropical forest is sufficient to allow the evolution of culture to proceed only to the level represented by the Tropical Forest culture pattern; further indigenous evolution is impossible" (1954:809).

Considerable evidence exists however that while most societies living in regions of tropical rain forest are relatively simple slash-and-burn cultivators, some of them are considerably more advanced. There are a number of instances of complex cultures, a few of them deserving to be called civilizations, which developed and flourished in a tropical rain forest environment. The lowland Maya are probably the best known example,[12] but one can also cite the Anuradhapura culture of Ceylon, the early states of the Malabar coast of India, the Mon Khmer civilization of Cambodia, various states of Java and Sumatra, and the Polynesian cultures of Tahiti and Hawaii.

Of course most of these higher cultures subsisted not by simple swidden agriculture but by more intensive and permanent forms of cultivation. But these more highly evolved farming techniques had undoubtedly been preceded by simpler ones. The fact is, therefore, that swidden agriculture is not a *cul de sac*. Under certain conditions, which it is possible to specify, the agricultural systems of societies inhabiting the rainy tropics do evolve from simple shifting cultivation to more settled and specialized forms of agriculture.

The Evolution of Slash-and-Burn Cultivation as Exemplified in Melanesia. The development of slash-and-burn into something more advanced has received very little attention from anthropologists, probably because its very occurrence lay virtually unrecognized. Recently however a study has appeared, written by the agronomist Jacques Barrau, in which the evolutionary steps undergone by shifting cultivation in various parts of Melanesia have been set forth in a very clear and illuminating manner (Barrau 1958). In this study, which was based on a survey of 17 native groups extending from one end of Melanesia to the other, Barrau convincingly argues that the horticultural systems of many of these tribes represent different stages of a general evolutionary process that has occurred to varying degrees all over Melanesia. Out of a very rudimentary form of slash-and-burn cultivation, which at one time probably covered all of Melanesia, there have developed more intensive, sophisticated, and productive agricultural systems.

In New Caledonia and in certain areas of New Guinea slash-and-burn agriculture in its typical form can no longer be said to exist. Instead it has been superseded by a kind of fallow field system in which plots are cultivated for 2 or 3 years successively, fallowed for 3 to 5 years, and then recultivated. Only after several of these cycles have been completed is the plot taken out of production for an extended time. During the period of fallow tall grass covers the plots, but the time that elapses between abandonment and re-cultivation is too short for woody vegetation to reestablish itself. Ordinarily, dense grassland turf such as this is avoided by primitive cultivators because it is extremely hard to work. But in New Caledonia it is turned over with long digging sticks by several men working together. The clods of turf pried loose by this technique are broken up with clubs.[13]

To cope with problems of excessive ground water some advanced Melanesian cultivators construct drainage ditches. Others build terraces to combat seasonal droughts. In order to maintain the fertility of the soil at a high level, especially when the land is to be kept under cultivation for a considerable proportion of the time, several Melanesian groups use compost obtained from rotting organic matter, and also employ a rotation of crops. A few societies in New Guinea plant their crops on mounds made more fertile by topsoil piled onto them from surrounding ditches.

Intense, semi-permanent systems of cultivation have been developed in Melanesia as a result, apparently, of increases in population. Some parts of Melanesia have attained surprisingly great concentrations of population. In the Baliem valley of central Dutch New Guinea, for example, the total native population is estimated at 60,000, with a density of more than 100 persons per square mile (Brass 1941:557). One section of the Wahgi valley in Northeast New Guinea has a population density of at least 450 persons per square mile (Brown and Brookfield 1959:25). It is in areas such as these that the most advanced systems of cultivation also occur.

Shifting cultivation in its typical extensive form can be practiced only so long as sizable reserves of forest are available from which new plots can be cleared as old ones are abandoned. However in any region of shifting cultivation where the population increases at a significant rate, a reduction in the available forest reserves necessarily occurs. Ultimately, with continued increase in population, the forest disappears, either virtually or completely. When this happens, no choice is left to the horticulturalists but to till the only form of land available to them, namely, grassland. No longer can fallowed land be allowed to revert to secondary forest as was the custom before. Now necessity dictates that it be cleared and planted after a very few years under grass. Unquestionably, cultivating the grasslands is more tedious and time-consuming than cultivating the forest. But it is not as impossible as primitive swidden farmers, blessed with ample forest reserves, are inclined to believe. It can be done and done successfully, even with no better tools than the digging stick or the hoe.

Expansion of the Theory. The two principal propositions that emerge from the foregoing discussion seem to me to be the following: (1) Soils developed under tropical rain forest can support systems of cultivation more advanced than slash-and-burn, and (2) these more advanced systems arise in response to the increasing pressure of human numbers on the land. These two conclusions suggest a general theory of cultural development which encompasses other spheres of culture in addition to subsistence. I would like now to present the theory in brief form and then apply it to aboriginal South America in an attempt to account for the major features of cultural evolution in that continent.

Our exposition of the theory may begin, or rather, resume, at the point where population pressure has led to an intensification of agriculture. This result has occurred not only in parts of Melanesia, but in a number of other regions of the world as well. But not in all. Those regions where a notable intensification of agriculture followed an increase of population are distinguished by an important characteristic: *They are regions where the area of cultivable land was distinctly circumscribed.* Areas of distinctly circumscribed arable land are, typically, narrow valleys, sharply confined and delimited by mountains or deserts. It is in such areas that most of the early advances in agriculture, and in other aspects of culture, took place.

It is a curious and significant fact that these advances were not made in areas of broad and uninterrupted expanses of arable land, regardless of their degree of fertility. The forested plain of northern Europe, the Russian steppes, the Eastern woodlands and the Prairies of the United States, today the most important areas of cultivation in the world, initially lagged far behind the narrow river valleys and littorals in their agricultural, and therefore cultural, development. The reason for this relative backwardness becomes evident in the light of our theory: With extensive and unbroken agricultural land at hand, population increase was followed by the dispersion of peoples. With serious pressure on the carrying capacity of the land thus avoided, the ecological impetus required to turn extensive into intensive cultivation would have been absent.

The same squeeze in available arable land that led to the development of more intensive farming in certain areas of the world, gave rise to another important cultural phenomenon as well: competition between one tribe and another over land. In areas like the Amazon basin, where cultivable land is abundant and population relatively sparse, competition over land is not well marked. But in areas of the world that begin to experience a shortage of agricultural resources, desire for land emerges as a predominant cause of war. In parts of the Wahgi valley of New Guinea, for example, where land resources are severely limited and population has largely filled up what land there is, warfare over land is beginning to assume important proportions (Brown and Brookfield 1959:41–42).

Warfare, it should be noted, has entirely different consequences in an area of restricted arable land and dense population than it does where land resources are extensive and population is sparse. A village or tribe consistently a loser in war can, in an area of extensive land and moderate population, move somewhere else where, safe from attack, it can continue to subsist about as well as before. However, in a circumscribed, densely settled area a defeated group could not make a strategic withdrawal. There would be no place for it to go; all of the arable land would be occupied. Instead, it would have to remain where it was and suffer the consequences. And the consequences of defeat under these conditions would generally be, first, the payment of tribute, and, at a later stage, outright incorporation into the territory of the victor. Under the necessity of having to pay tribute in kind, the vanquished group would have to work their lands even more intensively than before. While food production had not as a rule previously exceeded domestic consumption, a clear surplus would now have to be wrought from the soil in order to meet the demands of the dominant group.

The ever-increasing need for more arable land would continue to act as a stimulus to war; and warfare, through the process of conquest and amalgamation, would lead to an increase in the size of political units. At the same time it would also give rise to confederacies and alliances, as each tribe or chiefdom sought to strengthen its military position. The culmination of this process locally would be the political unification of an entire valley under the banner of its strongest chiefdom. The ultimate military and political result of the process over part or all of a continental area would be the formation of a large conquest state encompassing and controlling many valleys.

As a society continued to expand through successful competition against its neighbors, corresponding and related changes would take place in its internal structure. Brave warriors and skilled military leaders would rise in status, wealth, and power, and would form the nucleus of a noble class. The military organization that had brought success in warfare would become elaborated and part of it would be redirected to the effective control and utilization of the peoples it had subjugated. War prisoners, at first merely slaughtered or sacrificed, would later come to be exploited economically as slaves. They would be put to work for the benefit of the emerging state, perhaps side by side with "citizens" conscripted by means of the corvée. A large part of this forced or drafted labor would be directed toward meeting the increasing agricultural needs of a rapidly expanding society: the drainage of swamps, the building of terraces, the cutting of irrigation canals, and the like. The incorporation of slaves into the conquering state would complete the stratification of society into four major classes: chiefs (or kings), nobles, commoners, and slaves.

Craft production would be immensely stimulated, not only by the demands made on subject peoples for tribute and taxation, but also by the rise of a class of craft specialists. These artisans would come largely from landless segments of the population throughout the state, and they would gravitate toward the centers of political and religious activity. Their technical achievements in ceramics, weaving, metallurgy, architecture, and the like would enrich the culture of the state and enhance its prestige. The magnificence of the social and religious superstructure thus erected would obscure the origin of the state. It would be difficult to infer from the later history of the state that a shortage of land among simple farming peoples and the ensuing competition between them had given the original impetus to its formation.

Implications for South America. Finally, let us apply the theory just elaborated to the continent of South America in order to see if we can make its ethnographic features and culture history more intelligible. We may begin by looking at the horticultural tribes of the Amazon basin. From the earliest days of cultivation in this region, perhaps 2,000 years ago, the technique employed must have been that of slash-and-burn. Since the introduction of shifting cultivation into the Amazon basin, this region has undoubtedly experienced a steady increase in population. However, this increase had been of sufficiently short duration and had taken place within such a vast area, that at the time of earliest white contact it had not resulted in any very dense concentrations of population. If a tendency to overcrowding developed here and there from time to time, it evidently led to the moving away of the "surplus" population, thus relieving the pressure. Indeed, this mechanism has been suggested as the principal means by which Tropical Forest peoples and cultures spread throughout the Amazon valley. With population able to disperse in this manner, no ecological pressure developed which might have led to the intensification of cultivation. With little or no shortage of forest soil, competition over land did not assume significant proportions. Warfare occurred, but its principal causes appear to have been something other than the need for more land. And a village or tribe that met defeat in warfare could easily move to a safer locale which at the same time was suitable for cultivation, thus avoiding subjugation and amalgamation. We see therefore that none of the forms of social development that, according to our theory, are contingent upon competition over land and subsequent conquest could have been expected to develop in the Amazon basin within the period of time available.

The Circum-Caribbean Area. When we turn the Circum-Caribbean area we find that the differences from Tropical Forest culture to be noted here appear to go hand in hand with ecological differences. Perhaps the most striking feature of the geographical distribution of Circum-Caribbean cultures is that they are found in habitats which, however else they may differ from one another, have one feature in common, namely, they are regions where the areas of cultivable land are *circumscribed*. The mountain valleys of Colombia, the coastal strips of Venezuela, and the islands of the Greater Antilles, all centers of Circum-Caribbean culture, share this characteristic.

Ethnologists who try to account for the higher development of cultures in the Circum-Caribbean area than in the Tropical Forest frequently ascribe this differential to the superior soil of the former area. But many areas that supported a Circum-Caribbean level of culture—Puerto Rico, Hispaniola, and the Venezuelan coast, for example—had essentially the same type of soil as the Amazon basin. We must therefore look for other determinants than soil to explain the observable cultural differences.

Technological factors likewise do not offer a solution to the problem. The digging stick was virtually the sole agricultural implement of both Circum-Caribbean and Tropical Forest peoples. Even such a relatively simple tool as the hoe was absent or virtually so from the entire Circum-Caribbean area, just as it was from the Tropical Forest. It is true that some irrigation and terracing were carried out in the Circum-Caribbean region, but only to a very limited extent. Furthermore, terracing and irrigation are more the product of the organization and direction of labor than they are of mechanical innovation as such.

With soil and technology thus eliminated, we may now consider the explanation proposed earlier: the higher culture level of the Circum-Caribbean area was the result of a series of events which began with competition over land among agricultural societies inhabiting areas of circumscribed arable land. The form of social organization assumed by Circum-Caribbean chiefdoms was an outgrowth and reflection of this competition. The food surpluses known to have been produced by Circum-Caribbean peoples were an actualization of a potentiality present, but never realized, among Tropical Forest cultivators. The process which produced the Circum-Caribbean chiefdoms proceeded at different rates and to different degrees in the various valleys, littorals, and islands of the Circum-Caribbean area. In fact, the cultures encountered here by the Spaniards in the 16th century represented almost every stage and gradation of this process, from just above Tropical Forest to solidly sub-Andean.

The Andean Area. Cultural development in the central Andes was essentially a continuation and elaboration of the evolutionary trends observable in the Circum-Caribbean area. One might say that in the Central Andes these trends merely reached their logical culmination. In matters of subsistence, cultivation in Peru brought agriculture to its highest point of intensification in the entire hemisphere with the establishment of permanent, irrigated, and heavily fertilized fields in the coastal valleys. In the sphere of political organization, the Incas carried the process of conquest and amalgamation to the point of creating a vast empire, in which vanquished tribes and petty states alike were carefully fitted into the administrative structure.

Although the Inca empire went far beyond Circum-Caribbean chiefdoms in almost every phase of culture, it still revealed very clearly the factors which underlay this elaborate development. There is scarcely a better example anywhere in the world of an environment in which cultivable land was restricted in area and circumscribed in boundaries than the already mentioned coastal valleys of Peru. Along the course of the rivers and as far as irrigation canals could extend, these valleys were literally gardens. Beyond, there was nothing but desert. The relevance of this fact for our theory can be seen from the following observation made by Cieza de León (1959:18–19):

". . . although I have described Peru as being three desert and uninhabited mountain ranges, by the grace of God there are valleys and rivers I have mentioned; if it were not for them, it would be impossible for people to live there, which is the reason the natives could be so easily conquered and why they serve without revolting, because if they did so, they would all perish of hunger and cold".

The Inca empire also provides us with a remarkable demonstration of how far culture can advance through the large-scale and efficient organization of labor, without the necessity of a correspondingly extensive development of technology. Donald Collier (1958:282) has pointed this out clearly and succinctly enough to be worth quoting:

"Peruvian technology is notable for its lack of labor saving devices and its failure to exploit sources of power other than human muscle. Instead, production was accomplished by means of the organization of human effort, craft specialization, enormous patience, and an amazing virtuosity in uti-

lizing the simple tools and techniques. During the Expansion-
ist stage a kind of mass production of crafts was achieved
not by means of new tools or techniques but simply by a
reorientation of ends and more intensive organization of production".[14]

Conclusion. A theory of cultural development has been advanced in this paper which explains the broad features of native
culture history in South America more fully and coherently than
any other single theory previously put forward to account for the
same phenomena. The theory would appear to have another scientific advantage in that it shows civilization and the stages of society that led up to it to be, not subtle and unlikely products,
to be accounted for by the invocation of "genius" or chance, by
the vagaries of diffusion or of "historic accidents," but rather,
as strictly determined cultural manifestations, the inevitable outcome, under certain specifiable conditions, of a complex but intelligible process.

NOTES

1. Some writers have the mistaken idea that because of the prussic acid
in bitter manioc, "animals do not eat the . . . roots of this plant" (Gourou
1953:28). Actually, as long as it is growing undisturbed the manioc tuber
does not contain any prussic acid as such, but only a cyanogenetic glucoside
(manihotoxine). It is only after the tubers are pulled out of the ground and
exposed to air that an enzyme in the root begins to act on the cyanogenetic
glucoside in such a way as to liberate the prussic acid (Watt 1908:767).
Thus, since peccaries go after the roots while they are still growing underground, they can eat them with impunity. [Cf. Carl Spath 1971—Ed.]
2. On one occasion, the famous naturalist Henry Walter Bates almost lost
the contents of two bushel baskets of manioc flour to leaf-cutter ants in the
course of a single night (Bates 1864:14–15).
3. In the discussion that followed the oral presentation of this paper it was
objected that this explanation is anthropocentric. If the argument has been
worded anthropocentrically it was done so only to make the explanation
appear more immediate and direct. The explanation offered here could easily
be translated into a purely culturological one, since this is, in fact, what it
actually is. In this instance, as in so many others involving human behavior,
individuals may be regarded as objects on which cultural forces act. The

overt behavior of individuals thus may be conceived of as the *resultant* of a cultural *parallelogram of forces,* in which cultural forces of different magnitudes pull in different directions and produce an effect which is a summation of them all.

4. Warfare may combine with factors related to cultivation to affect the length of time a village can be maintained in the same location. In some parts of Borneo, for example, head hunting raids were once so common that it was not considered safe to make gardens very far from the village. Accordingly, the area deemed safe for cultivation was small, and villages had to be relocated about every twelve years (Chapple and Coon 1942:189).

5. "Other factors being constant, the degree of solidarity [of a society] varies inversely with the size: the larger the group the less the solidarity" (White 1959:103).

6. Such a split seemed to have been in the process of occurring among the Chukahamay (Txukarramãe), a Northern Cayapó group of the middle Xingú, in 1954, according to Orlando and Claudio Villas Boas (personal communication), who on the occasion of establishing the first peaceful white contact with that group, found themselves caught in the middle of an internal dispute which threatened to divide the village into two.

7. Father John M. Cooper is said to have described the power of Tropical Forest chiefs in this way: "One word from the chief and everyone does as he pleases."

8. The difference is less if we compare the productivity of manioc with that of potatoes, which, I am informed by John Murra, were the staple food crop of the highland peasants of Peru in pre-Columbian times. Nevertheless, the comparison still shows Kuikuru horticulture to be more productive, since it is unlikely that the yield of potatoes in the Andean highlands exceeded 80 bushels per acre, equivalent to about 1,500,000 calories.

9. Meggers has argued that even if Tropical Forest cultivators did produce a surplus of manioc, they could not preserve it. Thus, she writes that manioc "cannot be stored in the humid warm climate [of the Amazon basin] without sprouting or rotting" (1957:82–83). While it is true that manioc tubers will begin to rot shortly after exposure to the air (being roots and not stems they will never sprout), it is also true that if manioc is reduced to flour it can be preserved indefinitely in that form, or as beijú cakes baked from it.

10. It may be of interest here to cite an instance of surplus food production from the island of Fiji, where a similar type of cultivation was carried out in a similar environment. During one religious celebration the chiefs of Somosomo, a district of Fiji, made a presentation of 10,000 yams to their gods (Tippett 1958:145). At a military review on another occasion a supply of 40,000 yams and a wall of *yaqona* roots 7 feet high and 35 feet long were brought forth (Tippett 1958:153).

11. Cassidy and Pahalad give the analysis for the 0-6" and 6-12" levels separately, but for greater comparability I have averaged the two here and made the average apply to the 0-12" level as a whole.

12. Meggers (1954:817), in order to defend her theory against a seeming exception, has contended that while Maya civilization may have *maintained* itself in the Petén, it must have *originated* in some area other than the tropical lowlands of Guatemala. But this opinion has been challenged, for example by Coe (1957, especially p. 331).

13. This is precisely the way in which Inca farmers of the Andean high-

lands dealt with the grasslands they cultivated, except that their digging stick, the *taclla,* had a footrest and was thus a somewhat more efficient tool.

14. Cieza de León was very much impressed by the same thing: "There is no disputing the fact that when one sees the fine handicrafts they [the Incas] have produced, it arouses the admiration of all who have knowledge of it. The most amazing thing is how few tools and instruments they have for their work, and how easily they produce things of finest quality . . . They also make statues and other large things, and in many places it is clear that they have carved them with no other tools than stones and their great wit" (1959:175–76).

Introduction to The Culture-Ecology of Shifting (Pioneering) Cultivation Among the Yąnomamö Indians

The Yąnomamö are one of the few unacculturated indigenous groups of large size remaining in South America. Although we do not know their total population there may be as many as ten thousand people living in the dense jungle area of the Orinoco basin in southern Venezuela and north Brazil. Known also as the Shirianá and Waica, this group has recently become more widely known thanks to Napoleon Chagnon and his associates (see James Neel in Chapter 10 of this volume). One of the most valuable aspects of Chagnon's work among the Yąnomamö is his description and analysis of Yąnomamö warfare (Chagnon 1968a; 1968b). Chagnon has observed at close range a warfare pattern undisturbed by contact with national populations and the influx of firearms.

Many of the peoples of lowland South America engaged in chronic and bitter raiding in which lives were lost and captives were taken (cf. Florestan Fernandes 1949a, 1952; R. Murphy 1957; J. Siskind in Chapter 13 of this volume). Similar behavior occurs in Melanesia and elsewhere. The natives give many reasons for these wars or feuds: supernatural influences, vengeance, a desire to capture enemy women, etc. But anthropologists have reduced the warfare patterns to a few basic types in terms of mortality rates, frequency of raids and residential outcomes. Andrew P. Vayda (1961) suggested that some of these patterns may be related to slash-and-burn agriculture practiced in Melanesia and South America, a system which requires a group to have far more

/

land at its disposal than it is actually cultivating at any one time. Vayda suggested that warfare among such peoples as the New Zealand Maoris may have played a functional role in a total adaptive system, providing a mechanism for the periodic redistribution of people over the land. The implications of such a functionalist approach are great: warfare need no longer be viewed as a basic character flaw, or as the result of aggressive emotions and instincts, but rather as part of a total adaptive system consisting of feedback mechanisms which serve to maintain crucial variables within tolerable limits.

Napoleon Chagnon's article presents a negative instance of the process discussed by Vayda. The long-distance moves of Yąnomamö villages are precipitated well before the village has approached the limits of agricultural productivity. Warfare is the primary factor in stimulating these moves but it does not yield the adaptive results in terms of man-land relationships seen by Vayda. Indeed, unlike many other slash-and-burn agriculturalists, the Yąnomamö do not utilize secondary-growth forests but have a limitless amount of virgin forest land in which to cut their plots. Chagnon treats warfare in Yąnomamö society as part of the environment and views many aspects of their lives as an adaptation to it. In this, he agrees with Carneiro (in Chapter 7 of this volume) that it is necessary to consider superorganic as well as natural features of the environment.

Napoleon Chagnon took his bachelor's, master's and doctoral degrees at the University of Michigan and presently teaches at Pennsylvania State University. His research has resulted in a number of publications listed in the bibliography. A forthcoming book (Chagnon, in press) will expand the discussion and data presented here.

8. THE CULTURE-ECOLOGY OF SHIFTING (PIONEERING) CULTIVATION AMONG THE YĄNOMAMÖ INDIANS[1]

NAPOLEON A. CHAGNON

This paper describes the slash-and-burn (swidden) cultivation system of the Yąnomamö Indians, viewing the system from the perspective of settlement pattern.[2] By focusing on settlement pattern it is possible to demonstrate that two distinct ecological determinants are involved in the nature of village movements. In brief, Yąnomamö adaptation is effected to a *physical* and a *social* component of their cultural ecology and their settlement pattern can only be understood by considering the effects of both.[3]

With the techniques, crops, tools and traditions of cultivating the Yąnomamö adapt to the physical aspect of their ecology—to the terrain, forest, soil, rainfall and geography. This adaptation results in one type of settlement pattern that I will call village "micro-movements." The nature of the second adaptation is rather more complex, for it involves the socio-political relationships that independent villages have with each other in a milieu of chronic warfare. For the moment I will just mention that warfare dictates a second type of village movement that will be called "macro-movement."

Before describing their swidden system let me just mention that it differs somewhat from the typical slash-and-burn practices of most tribal peoples. The Yąnomamö practice a variant and somewhat rare form of swidden cultivation known as "pioneering" cultivation. That is, as a producing garden is abandoned, new, virgin jungle is cleared and once-used land is permanently abandoned by the original cultivators.[4] Perhaps the best known pioneering cultivators are the Iban of Sarawak described by Freeman (1955).

Reprinted by permission from the *Proceedings* of the VIIIth International Congress of Anthropological and Ethnological Sciences, September, 1968, Tokyo, Japan. Two original maps containing detailed information on specific settlement movements have been deleted.

Because Yąnomamö cultivation is of the pioneering type, models of shifting cultivation, such as that developed by Conklin (1961), are not easily applied to it. Conklin's minimum definition of shifting cultivation is ". . . any continuing agricultural system in which impermanent clearings are cropped for shorter periods in years than they are fallowed" (ibid, p. 27). By its very nature, pioneering cultivation lacks a fallow period so that some of the systematic entailments found in the more common varieties of shifting cultivation, particularly the "cycle" phenomenon of land reuse, are absent. In addition to lacking the systematic entailments of land reuse, Yąnomamö cultivation also departs appreciably from most types of systematic swidden cultivation because of the pressures of warfare: gardens are often cleared as need dictates, not simply because it is convenient to clear during one season rather than another (*infra*). If, however, a village experiences a relatively long period of peace, then cultivation techniques and scheduling take on the attributes of a "system" and regular clearing-burning-planting cycles result.[5]

THE YĄNOMAMÖ

The Yąnomamö Indians number some 10,000 individuals and are distributed in 125 widely-scattered villages. Although they have occasionally and erroneously been called nomadic hunters and gatherers, they in fact rely very heavily on cultivated foods: in some areas upwards of 80–90% of their caloric intake comes from garden produce.[6] Hunting, fishing, and collecting wild foods, especially seasonally-ripe palm fruits, provides the rest of the fare.

Economic dependency on cultivated foods varies both regionally and annually. For parts of the year, wild palm fruits are heavily exploited, not because gardening is insufficiently productive, but because the Yąnomamö delight in varying their diet. Again, some areas of the tribal distribution are characterized by a much more intensive commitment to cultivation, a factor that will be explained below as a form of adaptation.

The mainstay of the Yąnomamö diet consists of several varieties of plantains and bananas.[7] Perhaps as much as 75% of their food is provided by these crops. Next in importance are several root crops, especially manioc, taro and sweet potatoes, the fruit of a cultivated palm tree and a host of other, much less significant foods such as maize, pineapples, lechosa, gourds, peppers and avocadoes. Gardens are also important to the Yąnomamö economy in that they provide cane for arrow manufacturing, cotton for hammocks and decorative garments, fibrous plants, pigments, hallucinogenic drugs, magical plants used in sorcery and, most important, tobacco. In total, the Yąnomamö probably utilize some 50 species of cultivated plants, and their way of life is highly dependent on their gardening.[8]

The Yąnomamö occupy the low-lying areas of the tropical forest, preferably regions where there are few or no large rivers, since travel is always on foot.[9] Most villages lie between 450' and 700' elevation, but in the Parima mountains, a chain of high hills running north and south through the length of the tribal territory, some villages are found as high as 2,500'. With few exceptions,[10] the entire tribal area is covered with forest. There is a marked dry season from November to April, the peak falling in February. The remainder of the year is characterized by moderate to heavy rainfall, May and June being the wettest months. There is considerable yearly variation in rainfall, some years having particularly abundant rain during even the dry season. However, even in the wettest years the Yąnomamö can effect adequate burning since only smaller tree limbs, brush and leaves are burned. If the timber has been lying on the ground for several months, a few days of sunny weather is sufficient to result in a good burning.

The Yąnomamö prefer to do the heavy work of gardening—cutting the large trees—during the wet season, since it is somewhat cooler at that time. Very little agricultural work is done during the peak of the dry season, largely because intervillage visiting and feasting take place at this time of the year, for as the dry season approaches, swamps and rivers that were impassable during the wet season can be easily crossed and friendly groups can entertain each other.

When a new area is colonized, first considerations are to the defensibility of the area. This refers not only to the particular topographic features of the potential site, but its general location with respect to enemy and allied villages. Enemy villages will rarely be closer than two or three days walking distance[11] from each other. Friendly villages, on the other hand, might be as close as a half-day's walk, but if possible, at least a day's journey is considered a more desirable distance; even friendly groups do not trust each other completely. A migrating group will move in the direction of friendly villages and away from enemies, taking advantage of natural obstacles such as large rivers, swamps and hills to separate themselves from their enemies. Once the general area is selected, the specific garden location is decided by topographic features, drainage, water supply and vegetation type. Thus, political factors dictate the general area of settlement and natural features the particular location.

EXPANSION OF THE YĄNOMAMÖ: MACRO-MOVES

Focusing on the macro-movements of Yąnomamö villages, i.e., those long moves brought about by warfare, we note that there has been a general movement away from the center of the tribal distribution. The map shows the general direction of movements for seven historically-distinct clusters of villages. These clusters are lettered A-G.[12]

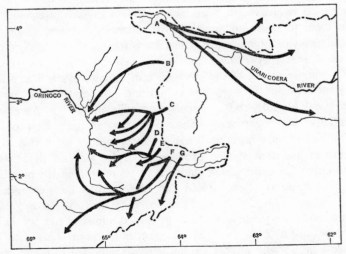

MAP. "Macro-Movements: General Direction," showing the recent expansion of seven clusters of Yąnomamö villages in phylogenetic form.

Closer inspection will reveal that movements at the tribal periphery, village cluster "A" for example, tend to be considerably longer than the moves at the tribal center. Migration is not as much of an option to villages at the center (clusters C, D, E and F) where the frontier area is considerably restricted.[13] That is, villages of the center tend to be surrounded by neighboring groups around whom it is difficult to migrate.[14]

Compared to the periphery,[15] warfare is considerably more intense at the center and an elaborate alliance system has developed that enables the members of independent villages to establish peaceful, but tenuous, social ties whose functions are to reduce the possibility of warfare between the allied groups. These alliances revolve around trading, feasting and exchanging marriageable females (Chagnon, 1968a, 1968b, 1968c; Chagnon and Asch, 1968). Correlated to this—and in large measure the basis for it—are local shortages of resources that appear to be deliberately created. These resources include dogs, bows, arrows, tobacco, cotton, cotton hammocks, drugs, clay pots and other materials that any Yąnomamö group is technically capable of producing. Yet each village has a set of items that it obtains from its allies and another set that it provides in the reciprocal trading. Thus, temporary trading networks emerge that link allied villages to each other and enjoin them to visit and feast. As the alliances dissolve, so do the trading networks; when new friends are found, a new trading network emerges between the partners.

One consequence of the emergence of alliance systems as adaptive mechanisms is a greater commitment to cultivation. Where reciprocal feasting and alliance occur, villages tend to have substantially larger gardens.[16] Thus a village at the center of the tribal distribution must not only produce enough food to feed its members but it must also produce a surplus beyond this that is used either for entertaining guests at feasts or to feed the members of a beleaguered village should they be forced by their enemies to take refuge with that ally. Thus, alliance necessitates a greater commitment to gardening which in turn diminishes the possibility of migrating to a new area when enemies threaten. This is so because a group with a large garden is more reluctant to move, since starting a new garden elsewhere involves extreme difficulty, both in terms of the labor involved[17] and the privations that are endured during the first year or two when the crops ripen in cycles.[18]

A common settlement pattern at the center of the tribal distribution, then, is for a group to take refuge with an ally during periods of particularly intense raiding. When raiding diminishes or ceases, the group moves back to its garden. In many cases, a group will establish a new garden while it lives with its allies, since this makes possible the option of moving to a new area should raiding continue for a protracted period. A group that takes refuge usually must cede women to its protectors, something that most Yąnomamö are reluctant to do. Hence, they attempt to become economically self-sufficient as soon as possible and make every attempt to establish a new garden if the war seems as though it will continue indefinitely.

Figure 1 illustrates the relationship between dependence on cultivated foods, warfare, obligations to allies and macro-movements.

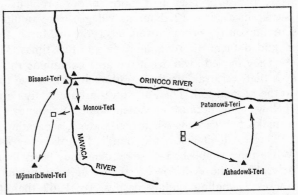

FIG. 1. "Movements of Monou-teri and Patanowä-teri During 1965–66 (Schematic)," illustrating settlement pattern while new gardens are being cleared during periods of intensive raiding.

The members of Patanowä-teri and Monou-teri villages are close relatives (Chagnon, 1968a) and have a common origin. In approximately 1940 they separated from each other (Chagnon, 1966; 1968a; 1968b) and entered into prolonged hostilities that gradually diminished over time. In November of 1964 they renewed their hostilities when a group of Monou-teri men abducted seven Patanowä-teri women at the village of Bisaasi-teri where the latter had been invited to a feast. The abduction led to mutual raiding and killing between the two villages. The Monou-teri immediately made a new garden to their west, being forced to move by the intensity of Patanowä-teri raids. But because the garden was new, the Monou-teri had to rely on their allies, the Mǫmariböwei-teri and Bisaasi-teri, for food during most of the year that the new garden was being established. Thus, they alternatively lived in their own garden during the wet season,[19] moved to their new garden to work at clearing and planting (hauling their food with them from the old garden), thence to the Mǫmariböwei-teri village until their hosts wearied of them when food supplies became critical, then to one or more of the three Bisaasi-teri groups and, finally, back to their own garden. In this fashion they managed to avoid being raided and managed to remain together as a corporate group.[20]

Similarly, the Patanowä-teri were obliged to move because of the warfare pressure. They had more serious problems than the Monou-teri, since some 12 different villages were raiding against them simultaneously. From November 1964 to March 1966 their enemies raided them approximately twenty-five times, killing ten people.[21] They moved away from the area containing the majority of villages that were raiding them, although their move took them closer to the Monou-teri. The Patanowä-teri are a large group (see Table, below) and, because of violent internal disputes[22] they decided to make two gardens when they moved, separating into two distinct villages, albeit just a few hundred yards away from each other. While they established these gardens they lived alternatively with their allies, the Ashidowä-teri, and at their producing garden,[23] thereby avoiding raiding parties. By 1967 their two new gardens were producing but the Patanowä-teri still had their old gardens to rely on, which they maintained whenever they returned to them.[24]

The type of movement shown in Figure 1 and just discussed differs in kind from the type of movement associated with techniques of gardening proper. Figure 2 shows the micro-movements of the village of Bisaasi-teri from about 1960 to 1968, i.e., those movements associated with the techniques of cultivation. The Bisaasi-teri moved to the mouth of the Mavaca River in about 1960 and established two separate gardens and villages. The villages are labeled A and A′ in the diagram, the gardens a1 and a′. The

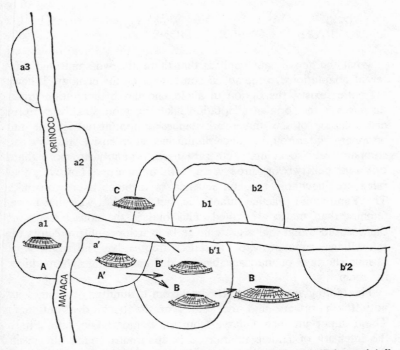

FIG. 2. "Micro-Movements of Bisaasi-teri, 1960–68 (Schematic),"
illustrating the establishment of new gardens as old ones are abandoned.

two groups were, of course, related to each other, but were on
somewhat strained terms.[25] One group, A, was too small to be
viable in a competitive milieu, so it remained close to the parent
village for purposes of defense. When gardens a' and a1 were
abandoned,[26] new ones, b'1, b1 and a2 were made. Village
A' fissioned at this time to produce villages B and B'. When these
gardens became "old women", i.e., barren, gardens a3, b2 and
b'2 were made. Finally, village B' moved across the Orinoco
River in 1966 and established a new garden, c.[27] The important
features in this figure are (1) that *new* land is cleared when gardens are abandoned[28] and (2) the movements associated with
gardening are different from the macro-movements determined by
warfare.

DEMOGRAPHIC CONSIDERATIONS

What the above data imply is that there are two somewhat different adaptations to the *social* component of the ecology. Where a frontier exists, the option to avoid enemies by migrating great distances is the form of adaptation taken by groups at the periphery. Because of the immense distances separating villages at the periphery, intergroup conflict diminishes in intensity. Raiding is, comparatively speaking, quite rare here, probably no more than one raid per two or three years.[29] In both areas, however, the raids are inevitably the consequence of disputes over women.[30] The Yąnomamö practice infanticide, but in such a way that more females than males are killed. This bias is the consequence of their attitudes that males grow up to be warriors and protectors of the village, so males are killed less frequently. The result is a serious shortage of marriageable females and chronic competition for them.

The table gives age and sex data from a number of villages at both the periphery and the center of the tribal distribution.[31] Three important facts emerge from the demographic data. First, the intensity of female infanticide is apparently much higher at the center where greater emphasis on masculinity and warfare exists. For the age category 0–14 years, there is a 21% excess of males at the periphery compared to 57% at the center. The overall shortage of females in the two areas is also revealing: for all age categories combined, there is a 15% excess of males at the periphery compared to 30% at the center. Second, villages at the tribal center are considerably larger than villages at the periphery, averaging 76 as opposed to 53 inhabitants.[32] Third, the range of village size is different in the two areas. At the periphery, villages may be as small as 25 people and rarely exceed 100, whereas villages at the center are never smaller than 40 and may get as large as 250.[33]

I have discussed the relationship between village size and warfare elsewhere (Chagnon, 1966; 1968b). In brief, the tactics of Yąnomamö warfare require the participation of approximately 10 men between the ages of 17 and 40 years. While these men are raiding an enemy village, a few additional men are left with the women and children to defend them. Men who fall between the ages of 17 and 40 years represent approximately ⅓ of the population. Since it takes between 10 and 15 men to successfully conduct warfare, then a village is militarily viable only if it comprises about 40 people. Where military pressure is intense, villages never fall below 40 people, nor do villages of less than about 80–85 people fission to produce new villages.[34] It appears that the reasons for the differences in village size at the periphery and center correspond to differences in the intensity of warfare in the two areas.

There are a number of additional differences between villages at the center and periphery (Chagnon, 1968b). Noteworthy among these is the rather elaborate development of types of fighting (Chagnon, 1967) at the center. These include chest pounding duels, side slapping duels, club fights, spear fights, raiding and treacherous feasts. Some of these types of contests are entirely lacking at the periphery. Of special interest is the fact that these are graded forms of aggression, each a more serious level of fighting than the previous one. And, they appear to be responses to intensive warfare and aggression: some of them might even be considered as alternatives to killing for they permit ritualized and relatively innocuous contests that satisfy grievances without loss of life. Another striking feature of the center is the considerable authority wielded by headmen during times of warfare, which is to say, much of the time. Finally, the attitudes about extra-marital sexual liaisons differ in both areas. At the center, trysts inevitably lead to fighting and often to killing and village fissioning. At the periphery, the affairs are tolerated if not institutionalized.[35] A corollary of this is the surprisingly high incidence of polyandry in some villages at the periphery, all of which may be summarized by concluding that there is a more equitable distribution of the sexual services of women at the periphery and, therefore, a great reduction in one of the major causes of Yąnomamö disputes.

SUMMARY AND CONCLUSION

There are two types of movement characterizing Yąnomamö settlement pattern, each an adaptation to different components of the cultural ecology. One type of movement is a response to the physical demands of gardening while the other is to the nature of the social milieu within which Yąnomamö groups compete as political entities. There is a major difference in the type of adaptation to the social aspect of the ecology when the central Yąnomamö groups are compared to the peripheral groups. Lack of a frontier at the center reduces the possibility of avoiding competitive neighbors by migrating, and villages adapt to this milieu by entering into elaborate alliance patterns with their neighbors. The objective of such alliances is to reduce the possibility of warfare between the principals in the alliance. Where there is a frontier and vast tracts of unoccupied land, competing hostile villages essentially avoid each other by moving great distances.

Three theoretical points are suggested by these data. First, the concept of cultural ecology should be broad enough to embrace inter-group social relationships as a component. A number of students of this problem have persuasively argued this point (Harding, 1960; Sahlins, 1964). Second, more attention should be given to pioneering slash-and-burn systems in view of the fact that they were, no doubt, far more widespread than they are at the ethnographic present. Third, and most intriguing, is the similarity between the effects of territorial circumscription (Carneiro, 1961) and the sociocultural events at the center of the Yąnomamö tribe. One conclusion that can be drawn from the above data is that where warfare is intense and migration out of the area not feasible, there is selection for larger local groups and more elaborate inter-group relations. The key to the developments appears to lie in the absence of an accessible frontier, so that a tribal population need not expand to the limits of its ecological zone before basic social changes are detectable. For all intents and purposes, Yąnomamö villages for which long migrations are not practicable or possible are in fact circumscribed, not by geographical features, but by competing social entities.

It is somewhat ironic, but not unusual, that the forms of Yąnomamö adaptation to this competitive milieu reinforce the competition and intensify the adaptation: the more Yąnomamö villages change, the more they remain the same, for female infanticide not only results in more warriors, it also results in more war. And, the more that alliances and feasting function to relate groups to each other, the less likely this adaptation will permit of migration, for feasting involves a greater commitment to agriculture and, therefore, larger gardens.

TABLE

AGE AND SEX DISTRIBUTION IN YĄNOMAMÖ VILLAGES

A. (Central Villages)

Village		*0 – 14*	*15 – 24*	*25 – 39*	*40 – 50*	*51 –*	*Totals*	
08A,B,C	M	62	25	26	12	4	129	215
Patanowä	F	31	17	23	11	4	86	
08J	M	9	4	5	2	2	22	40
Yeisi	F	6	3	8	1	0	18	
08L	M	17	15	12	6	0	50	89
Yabroba	F	15	10	9	4	1	39	
08N	M	15	3	13	2	1	34	59
Makorima	F	6	5	9	2	3	25	
08S	M	15	5	13	3	3	39	72
Kashorawä	F	13	7	6	6	1	33	
08T	M	10	4	7	6	0	27	45
Yabitawä	F	6	3	8	1	0	18	
03C	M	21	9	5	4	2	41	76
Monou	F	15	7	9	2	2	35	
03A	M	14	6	3	2	4	29	63
Ora	F	11	10	5	3	5	34	
03A′	M	7	7	6	2	3	25	56
Bakadu	F	8	6	9	5	3	31	
03B	M	12	6	6	0	4	28	52
Koro	F	9	8	2	2	3	24	
Möwaraoba	M	21	8	14	5	3	51	73
	F	9	4	9	0	0	22	
Totals	M	203	92	110	44	26	475	840
	F	129	80	97	37	22	365	

AGE AND SEX DISTRIBUTION IN YĄNOMAMÖ VILLAGES (*cont'd*)

B. (Peripheral Villages)

Village		0 – 14	15 – 24	25 – 39	40 – 50	51 –	Totals	
03K	M	37	14	5	5	1	62	
Hakama	F	18	9	7	3	4	41	103
03L	M	6	3	1	1	1	12	
Wutähai	F	6	3	3	1	0	13	25
03M	M	10	6	0	1	0	17	
Shashana	F	4	6	0	3	1	14	31
03N	M	11	2	3	2	0	18	
Fenema	F	6	7	1	1	0	15	33
03Q	M	12	4	4	0	0	20	
Fafanabäk	F	11	2	7	1	2	23	43
03S	M	7	1	5	0	0	13	
Huduwä	F	7	1	2	2	0	12	25
03T	M	10	6	9	3	1	29	
Ora	F	12	3	7	5	2	29	58
03U	M	15	3	6	2	0	26	
Ashikama	F	16	2	8	2	0	29	55
03W	M	15	9	11	6	0	41	
Parimi	F	15	5	14	6	2	42	83
03Y	M	4	2	4	3	0	13	
Amnasbäk	F	5	3	2	0	1	11	24
03X	M	21	14	15	8	6	64	
Borabäk	F	24	7	5	4	4	44	108
03R	M	12	5	4	6	0	27	
Horeba	F	8	8	7	1	0	24	51
Totals	F	132	56	63	30	16	297	
	M	160	69	67	37	9	342	639

NOTES

1. The 19 months' fieldwork on which this paper is based was supported by a USPHS Fellowship F1 MH-25, 052 and attached grant MH 10575-01 BEH R04 and an AEC Area Grant AT(11-1)1552. My participation in the XII ICAES was made possible by a Travel Grant from the National Science Foundation, GS 2130.

2. The concept of "settlement pattern" has been most frequently employed in archaeological analyses. That it is a useful concept for ethnological analyses of contemporary populations has been amply demonstrated by Carneiro (1960; 1961). Other cultural anthropologists, working with archaeologists, have also demonstrated the utility of this concept in establishing cultural types (see Meggers, 1956; cf. also the discussion of this approach in Leeds, 1961). It would appear that any cultural-ecological analysis of human societies would do well to focus on community settlement patterns, since one of the major objectives of such analyses is to isolate the parameters that determine size, composition and spatial location of human populations.

3. Schuster, a German ethnologist who spent some 10 months with the Yąnomamö also recognized multiple causes for Yąnomamö settlement movement (1958). However, he related this to as asserted "nomadism", a sort of "call of the wild" philosophy (". . . traditionell bewahrte Reminiszenzen an die . . . rein wildbeuterische Epoche der Waika [Yąnomamö] . . ." [1958:120]) which he attributed to the Yąnomamö. His work was undertaken in a village that, during his stay, was giving refuge to another village. The pressure on the agricultural systems during this period was considerable, since the refugees lived with their hosts for approximately a year and subsisted largely on the products of their gardens during this time. Consequently both hosts and refugees were obliged to spend considerable periods of time away from the hosts' garden, usually at work in other gardens or visiting other allies, giving their settlement pattern a decidedly "nomadic" flavor. These situations appear occasionally in the history of every Yąnomamö group. For the particulars involved in this (Schuster's) case, see Chagnon, 1966 (Chapter V, discussion of Mahekodo-teri, the village in which Schuster [and Zerries, 1964] did his field work). In defense of Schuster, I should like to point out that he is the first ethnologist to have recognized the importance of intervillage alliances among the Yąnomamö and the extremely complicated basis for them.

4. The Yąnomamö never clear abandoned sites. At present, land is so abundant that all groups, even those at the center of the tribal distribution where population density is at its highest, utilize only virgin jungle. The warfare pattern is such that a group is usually driven out of an area long before it exhausts the cultivable land available.

5. Yąnomamö linguistic categories referring to gardens imply systematic land use but not one that sees once-used land as potentially cultivable. The portion of the garden first established is called the "rectum" (*bei kä bosi*) when productivity begins to fall off. The portion that is added by clearing

140   *Subsistence and Ecology*

adjacent virgin jungle is called the "nose" (*bei kä hushibö*) which also becomes "rectum" as its productivity declines and a new "nose" is added. If a new garden, i.e., one that is not connected physically to the old one, is cleared, the old garden is called "old woman" (*sua pata*) to emphasize its barrenness. Similarly, cultivated peach palm trees are called "old men" (*waro pata*) when they cease to produce.

6. Although early accounts of the Yąnomamö, especially those of Koch-Grünberg (1922, 1923), describe the Yąnomamö as hunting and gathering people, all serious students of their culture have recognized the fact that they are emphatically agricultural (Zerries, 1958, 1964; Becher, 1957, 1960). The reaction of Zerries is very instructive in this regard: "Zu unserer grossen Überrashung müssten wir aber gleich zu Beginn unserer Forschungen feststellen, dass die Waika [Yąnomamö] vor allem von der Kultivierung der Mehlbanane (plátano) in hohem Masse abhängig sind." (1958:177) as is the comment by Schuster that, with respect to Plantains, ". . . von denen sich die Waika [Yąnomamö] heute zu etwa neunzig Prozent ernähren." (1956: 120).

7. In some areas, especially where the Yąnomamö are in contact with the Carib-speaking Makiritare (Dekwana), manioc is at least as prominent as plantains. Plantains, it should be pointed out, are post-Columbian in origin (Reynolds, 1927; Simmonds, 1959), so the Yąnomamö have established their present agricultural biases in less than 400 years. Mythological references (Chagnon, 1968a) suggest that manioc was formerly more significant.

8. See Chagnon, 1968a and 1968b for a more detailed discussion of the social organization of the Yąnomamö and the role of agriculture in their way of life.

9. In most areas the Yąnomamö are aware of crude forms of water craft such as log rafts and bark canoes, the proto-type of the latter being the bark troughs that figure prominently in their feasting. In other areas, the Yąnomamö are completely ignorant of any form of water craft (Seitz, 1967; & personal communication), which I discovered in 1968 much to my consternation (Chagnon, in press).

10. In some areas, especially in the Parima "mountains" that form the border between Brazil and Venezuela north of the Orinoco headwaters, there are small, sporadically distributed savannahs.

11. This refers to walking during the dry season. A day's journey in the dry season may require two or three days of walking in the wet season when trails are inundated and detours over higher ground necessary.

12. This map is largely calculated guesswork, based on distances in sleeps and compass bearings given to me by Yąnomamö informants. Most of the area is not only unexplored, it is also unmapped. See Chagnon, 1966, for more discussion of how village locations are determined for cartographic purposes. That warfare is the cause of the movements, see Chagnon 1966 for a discussion of village movements defined as clusters "D" and "F" on this map. [A more detailed map from the original has been omitted here—Ed.]

13. Two other factors might be relevant in explaining why village movements are much shorter in the area I have called the tribal center. First, the terrain is quite rugged here, low "mountains" being a characteristic feature of the landscape. It might conceivably be true that villages at the center need not migrate great distances in order to avoid their enemies. Secondly, Yąnomamö mythology implies that the center of the tribal distribution is the

homeland of Man (Chagnon, 1968a), and for those groups endorsing this myth, there might be "sentimental" reasons for remaining as close as possible to certain mythologically-prominent mountains. However, the general pattern has been that groups with an unpopulated frontier tend to move long distances.

14. I have no adequate explanation for the reluctance of Yąnomamö groups to migrate past each other, save for their overtly expressed fears that moving into an area where strange Yąnomamö reside is potentially dangerous, largely because they leave behind them villages with which they have maintained alliances in the past. This concern—reluctance to move around other tribal groups—occurs frequently in ethnographic accounts of other tribes.

15. The notion of "periphery" maintained in this paper is difficult to define precisely. There is a difference between the western and eastern periphery of the tribal distribution in that western groups are decidedly more warlike. Most of my comments on "periphery" are based on only two months' personal experience in the easternmost extension of the Yąnomamö distribution and on published works of (and private discussions with) Ernest Migliazza, who spent some five years in this area as a linguist for the Baptist Mid-Missions and the Museu Goeldi of Pará, Belem. I believe that the western periphery is more warlike because of the recency of the Yąnomamö penetration of this area from the center of the tribal distribution (Chagnon, 1966), whereas the eastern area has probably been occupied far longer (Schomburgk, 1841 refers to "Krishana" people here in the early 19th century who appear to be Yąnomamö).

16. This statement is based only on impressions; having visited some 40 gardens in both the central and the peripheral area (and flying over others), I am impressed with their greater size at the center of the distribution.

17. Transporting just the plantain cuttings involves an enormous amount of work, for they weigh upwards of 10–15 pounds apiece. It is for this reason that newly-established gardens occasionally have a preponderance of such crops as maize, since maize seeds are far more readily transported. With respect to plantains, even if smaller cuttings are used, a man can only carry 10 or so for a great distance, and hundreds of plants are needed to establish a garden. Smaller cuttings take longer to mature so the Yąnomamö must choose between a garden with many plants that will mature after a long time or one with few plants that will produce earlier returns, or a garden predominantly of maize.

18. Maize is sometimes used as an "emergency" crop (see footnote 17, above) because it is easily transported and produces a return in a short time.

19. Raids are rare in the wet season since (foot) travel is very difficult.

20. In 1968 the village of Monou-teri no longer existed. Raids from Patanowä-teri were so intense that the population, some 76 people, joined the three Bisaasi-teri groups shown in Figure 1. This fusion could be permanent.

21. Raiding is much less intense at the periphery.

22. There were two killings within the village of Patanowä-teri during this period, both the result of disputes over women. In addition, there were a number of fights that did not result in fatalities.

23. I should add that the Patanowä-teri have lived in this general area for some 45 years (Chagnon, 1966). They have been forced out of it on a num-

ber of occasions, but have managed to return. The name "Patanowä" in fact translates as "highly valued (garden) location."

24. In 1968 they entertained one of their old enemies in a peace-making feast at their *old* garden. Asch and Chagnon, 1968.

25. See Chagnon, 1968a for the sociology of village fissioning.

26. In Figure 2 gardens shown with the same hachure were made at approximately the same time.

27. By this time the total population was large enough to permit village fissioning. A factor that may have promoted this was the addition of a group of Patanowä-teri that fled their village after a serious fight (see footnote 22) and joined the Bisaasi-teri. Also, 76 Monou-teri joined the group in 1967, swelling their numbers even further (see footnote 20).

28. This is because villages never stay in one area long enough to exhaust the virgin jungle available to them, so they never have to use once-cleared land.

29. This estimate is based on missionary accounts and on the genealogies I collected from groups in the area. The latter indicate that death by warfare is appreciably lower, and I presume this is because warfare is likewise less frequent, as claimed by the missionaries.

30. Sorcery occasionally figures in the initial cause of disputes, but fights over women are by far more numerous.

31. The table includes only villages for which my census data are 100% complete for age estimate and sex. I have additional data on many more villages, but these do not include age estimates for 100% of the population. The only thing I can say about the unpublished data is that they confirm the conclusions reached in the discussion of those groups included in the table.

32. The data mentioned in footnote 31, which is complete for population size and sex distribution (but not age estimate), indicate that the average village size at the center is substantially higher than the table implies, 90 people being closer to the true average (Chagnon, in press).

33. In 1968 I contacted a recently-separated group (73 individuals) of Yąnomamö from the village Möwaraoba-teri. The village numbered well over 250 before the split took place, and my informants claimed that they intended to reunite after tempers cooled off. They also claimed that villages to their south, presently uncontacted, were even larger (Chagnon, in press).

34. If one of the groups that results from a fission is less than 40 people, it usually joins a different village. (See footnote 27.)

35. Ernest Migliazza, personal communication. (See footnote 15.)

Introduction to Cultural Influences on Population: A Comparison of Two Tupí Tribes

The Tapirapé and the Tenetehara are probably historically related since the languages they speak are both of the Tupí family. Proceeding on the assumption that these two peoples diverged from a common base, Charles Wagley examines the factors that are responsible for the differences between them. In spite of the linguistic similarity, the differences are considerable. The Tapirapé, who formerly occupied an area west of the Araguaia River in Brazil, have an elaborate system of social organization involving ceremonial subdivisions and complex ritual observances, much like other central Brazilian societies (e.g. the Mundurucu, see Robert Murphy in Chapter 12 of this volume; or the Apinayé, see Roberto Da Matta in Chapter 16 of this volume). The Tenetehara, inhabiting a dense jungle area in northern Maranhão State (hundreds of miles to the east of the Tapirapé), exhibit a simpler, more generalized social structure. Another difference between the two is found in what Wagley refers to as the implicit "population policies" of each group. The Tapirapé had stringent rules limiting family size while the Tenetehara had no such limitations.

The methodology which Wagley employed was to hold constant historical factors (based on the assumption mentioned above), thereby eliminating some of the potential causes of variation. This is the way in which anthropologists seek to attain the same kind of controls which other kinds of scientists achieve in laboratory experiments. Of course, a full-scale test of any hypothesis would necessitate construction of a large sample in which cases which conform to the predicted association have as great a chance of appearing as those which do not. On a basis of his limited test, Wagley eliminated environmental differences as the source of the variation between the two societies, although his contention that the Tenetehara and Tapirapé habitats are comparable has been disputed (Yarnell 1970).

Wagley concludes that the difference in population policy between the two tribes is related to differences in ideology and social structure and not technology and environment. Wagley's conclusion may be surprising in view of his use of a methodology championed by Julian Steward, the pioneer of cultural ecology (1955).

Wagley's discussion is also relevant to an important aspect of evolutionary theory. His suggestion that the Tenetehara survived because their society was more "malleable" anticipated the point elaborated by Elman Service in his article "The Law of Evolutionary Potential" (1960), published several years later. In this article, Service adapts Gauze's ecological principle to anthropology, arguing that more highly adapted (i.e. complex) structures may be less adaptable to sudden and unpredictable changes than those that are less formal.

Charles Wagley is an authority on tropical forest societies of South America, and carried out field work among both the Tenetehara and the Tapirapé (Wagley and Galvão 1948a, 1949). He has also conducted extensive research on non-indigenous communities in Brazil and is known for his classic study *Amazon Town* (1964), a set of essays he edited on race in Brazil (1952) and a general introduction to Brazilian culture (1971). Wagley earned his B.A. and Ph.D. degrees at Columbia University and taught there for nearly thirty years where he was Director of the Institute for Latin American Studies. He is a past president of the American Anthropological Association, and now teaches at the University of Florida.

9. CULTURAL INFLUENCES ON POPULATION: A COMPARISON OF TWO TUPÍ TRIBES

CHARLES WAGLEY

Contact with European civilization has had a varied effect upon the population trends of native societies. Frequently conquest warfare, slavery, bad labor conditions, disruption of aboriginal subsistence methods, and above all foreign disease have brought a rapid population decline which has led in many cases to the total disappearance of aboriginal groups as distinct ethnic units. In other instances, native groups have made an adjustment to the new circumstances. After an initial epoch of sharp decline in population, a few native groups have not only regained their former population level but actually increased in number several times fold. The depopulation of many Melanesian Islands, the decimation of the coastal Tupí speaking peoples of Brazil, and the rapid disintegration of the aboriginal groups of the Antilles are well known examples of sharp population decline following European contact from which the groups never recovered. The multiplication of the Navajo during the last century and the population growth of the Polynesian Island of Tikopia after European contact are examples of recovery and expansion (cf. Firth 1939:39–49).

In many cases, these differences in population trend following European contact may be explained in terms of the nature of contact with Europeans to which the different native groups have been subjected. Epidemics have varied in frequency and in intensity among native groups and the systematic exploitation of native peoples through slavery and other forms of enforced labor has taken heavier toll upon native population in some areas than in others. On the other hand, introduced crops, domesticated animals, new instruments, and new techniques have sometimes raised the

Reprinted by permission of the author and the director of the Museu Paulista from the *Revista do Museu Paulista,* Vol. 5 (1951), pp. 95–104.

aboriginal subsistence level and made possible an expansion of population.

Yet, the causes of such different trends in population among native groups after European contact cannot always be sought in the contact situation alone. The variables which allowed one group to absorb the shock of new disease and other disrupting accompaniments of European contact and to revive, or which led to quasi—or total extinction of a people may also be found in the culture and the society of peoples concerned. Each culture has a population policy, an implicit or explicit set of cultural values relating to population size. The social structure of each society is closely inter-related with a specific population level. A modification of the external environment, such as that brought about by contact with Europeans, generally calls for change both in cultural values as well as in social structure. In addition to environment, technology, and other material factors, cultural values and social structure act also to determine population size and demographic trends in face of modified external circumstances. A rapid decrease in population due to new disease or an increase in population resulting from an increased food supply calls for adjustments in population policy (implicit or explicit) and in social structure. It is the purpose of the present paper to examine the relationship between these social and cultural factors and the population trends following European contact of two Tupí speaking tribes of Brazil.

The two Tupí speaking tribes in question are the Tenetehara of northeastern Brazil and the Tapirapé of central Brazil.[1] After more than 300 years of contact with Luso-Brazilians the Tenetehara in 1945 still numbered some 2000 people—not much less, if at all, than the aboriginal population. On the other hand, by 1947 the Tapirapé with less than forty years of sporadic and peaceful contact with Luso-Brazilians had been reduced to less than one hundred people, the remnant of an aboriginal population which must have numbered more than one thousand. While the Tenetehara still maintained a functioning social system and continued as a distinct ethnic group, Tapirapé society was in 1947 almost totally disorganized and the Tapirapé as a distinct people were clearly on the road to extinction.[2]

A partial answer to this very different reaction to Luso-Brazilian contact may be found in the nature of the acculturation process which each has experienced. Although the first decades of Tenetehara relations with Europeans were marked by slave raids, massacres, and epidemics, the protection of the Jesuits during more than one century (1653–1759) seems to have given the Tenetehara time to make adjustments in their culture and society to changing external circumstances. The missionaries were able to prevent the movement of colonists into Tenetehara territory; and after the expulsion of the Jesuits in 1759, the increased importation of African slaves into Maranhão eased the pressure for Indian slaves. Close relations with the missionaries, and later with the civil authorities and the rural Luso-Brazilian population, presented the Tenetehara with new culture patterns, new attitudes which either replaced aboriginal elements or were incorporated in their culture as alternative patterns. The missionaries urged larger families in order to have numerous innocents to baptize. Warfare was prohibited in the area.[3] The Tenetehara learned that children might be useful in collecting babassu nuts for sale to Luso-Brazilians. Steel instruments and new plants (such as rice, bananas, lemons, etc.) made agriculture more productive. The sale of babassu nuts, copaiba oil, and other forest products brought the Tenetehara imported products. Although Tenetehara culture and society were modified, the aboriginal and the borrowed elements slowly combined to form a new culture and a new social system which at least met the minimum requirements for survival.

The Tapirapé, on the other hand, have had only intermittent contact with Luso-Brazilians. Since about 1911, the Tapirapé have had occasional contact with Luso-Brazilians. A few Tapirapé have visited Luso-Brazilian settlements and missionary stations on the Araguaya River and a few Luso-Brazilians have visited Tapirapé villages. Tapirapé contact with Luso-Brazilians has been limited to relatively short periods and to small groups of people. They have acquired a few axes, hoes, some salt, cloth, beads, and other material objects from their occasional visitors but, on the whole, their culture was little modified by borrowed patterns and elements from Luso-Brazilians. Yet the presence of Luso-Brazilians brought about a crucial modification in their environment. With the arrival of Luso-Brazilians in the area, the Tapirapé were subjected to a series of foreign diseases. If the memory of older

Tapirapé informants may be trusted, foreign disease (common colds, measles, and smallpox) came at first via the neighboring Karajá sometime before their first meeting with Luso-Brazilians. Since about 1911 to 1914, however, foreign disease acquired directly from Luso-Brazilians, has steadily decimated the Tapirapé. Unlike the Tenetehara, before the Tapirapé were presented with a broad segment of Luso-Brazilian culture, which might have provided them with alternative patterns and values with which they might have made adjustments to their new circumstances, they have been practically wiped out.

Still, the difference in population trends after Luso-Brazilian contact of these two tribes cannot be explained entirely in terms of the differences in the contact continuum. The first fifty years of contact between the Tenetehara and Europeans was more violent than anything the Tapirapé have experienced. In the early 17th century organized slave raiding parties penetrated into Tenetehara territory and armed forces such as the one led by Bento Maciel Parente in 1616 made war upon the Tenetehara. Epidemics, which raged in the early 17th century among the Indian populations of northeast Brazil, certainly reached the Tenetehara. From time to time smallpox, measles, and other diseases have taken a heavy toll among these Indians. The impact of the dominant culture upon the Tenetehara was more intense than it has been upon the Tapirapé. In addition to differences in the nature of the contact continuum, factors inherent in the society and the culture of the two tribes were responsible for the reaction of these societies to Luso-Brazilian contact and for the population trends which followed. Since the Tenetehara and the Tapirapé have historically related cultures sharing many patterns and institutions common to most Tupí speaking tribes, a comparison of the two societies and cultures should allow us to determine the variables responsible for their contrasting reactions.

The subsistence methods of the tribes were in aboriginal times basically similar. Both were tropical forest horticulturalists depending upon hunting, fishing, and forest fruits to supplement their diet. For fishing, the Tenetehara had an advantage since their villages were normally situated near rivers and streams while the Tapirapé villages were located inland many kilometers from the river. In hunting, the Tapirapé had the advantage of nearby open plains country where hunting was more productive than in the tropical forest. Neither tribe had a land problem: the nearest village of the Karajá, who were Tapirapé neighbors, was at least two hundred kilometers away and the Timbira neighbors of the Tenetehara were savanna people offering no competition for forest land. Both tribes during aboriginal times had sufficient territory to move their villages every five or six years when suitable garden sites near their villages had been used up by the slash-and-burn system of horticulture. The two tribes inhabited similar physical environments and they had approximately the same technological equipment to cope with it. Their technology and their subsistence methods must have limited the maximum population of any one village and there are indications that approximately two hundred people was the average village size for both groups. On the other hand, a lack of territory evidently did not enforce a limitation on the number of villages for the tribe. Yet while the Tapirapé tell of only five villages in aboriginal times many times that number are reported by early observers for the Tenetehara. Although specific data is not available, it seems that in aboriginal times Tapirapé population was relatively small and stable while the Tenetehara population was at least twice as large and probably expanding.

This difference in population level between the two tribes in aboriginal times was related to the population policies held by the two groups as well as to differences in social structure of the groups concerned. These cultural values relating to population level are explicit in attitudes toward family size and in positive actions to limit families. Among the Tenetehara infanticide is indicated only in the case of the birth of twins since they are believed to be the result of sexual relations between the mother and a dangerous supernatural and in the case of infants with certain supernaturally caused abnormalities. Since there is a low incidence of twins and since in several known cases "abnormal" children have been allowed to live, infanticide has had little or no effect upon Tenetehara population trends. The Tenetehara tell of one or two formulas thought to produce abortion. The long taboos imposed on both parents during the pregnancy of the mother and during the early infancy of the child are a source of irritation and discomfort which would seem to tend to discourage large families. But, in general, there is little planned effort among the Tenetehara to limit family size. Men seem proud of several children; women are eager to bear children and they will leave a husband whom they believe to be sterile.

In contrast, the Tapirapé value small families. They take specific steps to limit their families and have explicit ideas as to maximum family size. Not only do the Tapirapé bury twins at birth as do the Tenetehara (and for similar reasons) but they believe that a woman should not have more than three live children.[4] In addition, the three children of a woman should not be of the same sex. In other words, if a woman has two living daughters and her third child is also a girl, it is usually buried at birth. Similarly, if she has two male children and her third is a male, infanticide is in order. Furthermore, all men who have sexual relations with a woman during her pregnancy are considered fathers to her child. More than two co-fathers leads to complications. All co-fathers are expected to observe taboos on sexual relations and on the eating of certain meats during the pregnancy of the woman and the early infancy of the child. If there are three, four, or more co-fathers one of them is certain to break these taboos thus endangering the health of the infant; consequently the woman is urged to bury the child.[5]

On an overt level, the Tapirapé justify these checks on population by saying, "We do not want thin children" or "They would be hungry". They enlarge upon such statements by adding that it is difficult for a father to supply a large family with meat from hunting. In aboriginal times, manioc was plentiful and no one lacked the tubers with which to manufacture flour but meat was especially scarce during the rainy season when the forest is partially flooded and the paths to the savanna country are impassable. In addition, a complex set of food taboos make the job of supplying meat for a family more difficult. Children before adolescence are allowed to eat only specific meats and women are prohibited others. When a Tapirapé says "I am hungry" he generally means by implication: "hungry for meat". Although empirical data are not available, it is my impression that meat is (and was in the past) just as scarce in Tenetehara villages, and during the rainy season fish are extremely difficult to catch. The Tenetehara, with roughly the same food supply as the Tapirapé, do not feel called upon to impose drastic limitations upon the family size. Population control among the Tapirapé seems not to result from a direct limitation imposed by food supply but from culturally derived values. In other words, although family limitation among the Tapirapé has a basis in subsistence, it does not derive from a minimum starvation situation. Family limitation seems to be related to a desire for a specific food, which the organism needs but which is also selected by Tapirapé culture as particularly desirable.

This population policy of the Tapirapé with its explicit concept of maximum family size and the use of infanticide to limit the number of children must have maintained Tapirapé population in aboriginal times on a stable level. Even then, the balance between a stable and a declining population must have been a delicate one. With an increase in the death-rate from new disease for which they did not have an acquired immunity, this delicate equilibrium was thrown off balance. After Luso-Brazilian contact, the population declined rapidly. Tapirapé concepts of population limitation remained unchanged in face of modified circumstances and families were not large enough to replace the adult population. The less rigid population policy of the Tenetehara was conducive to a large population during aboriginal times and it made the Tenetehara less vulnerable than the Tapirapé to modifications in the external environment. Without doubt numerous Tenetehara died from new diseases, from war, and from slavery after contact with Luso-Brazilians, but their desire for large families must have allowed them to replace their population in at least sufficient numbers to survive until they were able to adjust to the new circumstances.

Secondly, differences in social structure between the two tribes were also important in determining aboriginal population size as well as population trends after Luso-Brazilian contact. An extended family based upon at least temporary matrilocal residence and a widely extended bilateral kin group were basic social groupings of both the Tapirapé and the Tenetehara in aboriginal times. Tenetehara social structure was in fact limited to the extended family and the bilateral kin group. The Tapirapé, on the other hand, also had two other sets of social groups which were lacking in Tenetehara society. First, there were patrilineal ceremonial moieties limited to men. Each moiety was divided into three age-grades—boys, young men or warriors, and older men. Second, both men and women among the Tapirapé belonged to one of eight "Feast Groups" which were non-exogamous. Membership in these "Feast Groups" was patrilineal for men and matrilineal for women, although these rules were often modified by the personal desires of a parent. Both Tapirapé men's moieties and age grades and the "Feast Groups" were basic to all ceremonials and important in economic production and distribution. The masked dances with impersonation of forest spirits performed by the men during the dry season were a function of the men's moieties. The "Feast Groups" met at intervals during the dry seasons at their traditional stations in the central plaza for ceremonial meals. At such times, as Herbert Baldus has shown, these "Feast Groups" functioned as a mechanism for food distribution in a season when more food was available than a family would normally consume. (Baldus 1937:88 ff.) The "Feast Groups" sometimes formed to collect honey and to hunt. The age grades of the men's moieties also frequently acted together economically; they organized work parties for clearing of large garden sites and they went out on large cooperative hunts after herds of wild pigs.

In aboriginal Tapirapé society ceremonial life and many important cooperative subsistence activities were based upon this balanced set of associations. A Tapirapé village in order to assure adequate representation in the various age grades of the men's moieties as well as in the "Feast Groups" by necessity had to consist of about 200 people or more. A small village of fifty to a hundred people, for example, would not have provided sufficient number of males of the proper ages to allow the age graded moieties to carry out their ceremonials nor to organize their cooperative subsistence activities. Tapirapé village organization was therefore not conducive to a process of "splitting off" of groups from one village to form another. The size of Tapirapé villages was limited by their technological equipment within their tropical forest environment yet the social structure made the formation of numerous small villages difficult. In contrast, the less formalized social structure of the Tenetehara allowed for villages of varying size within the limits of their ecological adjustment. Extended family groups easily might break off from a larger village to form a new settlement fully able to carry out the cooperative economic activities and even ceremonials of the society. This process is constantly occurring in contemporary Tenetehara society. When tensions arise between extended families, one group simply splits off from the parent village to join another or to form a separate village without serious effects on the ceremonial or economic system. Tenetehara social structure offered a favorable condition for an expanding population after Luso-Brazilian contact among the Tapirapé seriously affected population.

Tapirapé social structure seems also to have been more vulnerable to disorganization in face of a rapid change in population size. Rapid depopulation after Luso-Brazilian contact among the Tapirapé seriously affected the normal functioning of their highly segmented and balanced social structure. By 1940, the lack of men had thrown the system of reciprocal and competitive activities of the men's age-graded moieties out of balance. There were not enough men of the "older" age-grade of either moiety nor of the young men "warrior" age-grade of one moiety to form functioning units to reciprocate in cooperative garden clearing and to participate in group hunts. Several of the "Feast Groups" had been disbanded for lack of numbers. Ceremonials in 1940 had not been abandoned but they were performed in an attenuated and disheartened manner. There was little motivation to accumulate the meat, the forest fruits, and the garden products which important ceremonials require among the Tapirapé.

Ceremonials and cooperative economic activities in Tenetehara society are organized by extended family and kin groups. Lack of numbers, of course, creates difficulties in carrying out ceremonials and in organizing economic activities but it does not have the effect of disorganizing the society. Cooperation of large extended families in gardening and in collecting babassu nuts and copaiba oil is still the general pattern among the Tenetehara. Tenetehara social structure was maleable to change. Adjustment to new circumstances after Luso-Brazilian contact must have been easier for the Tenetehara than for the Tapirapé.

This brief comparison of the cultural values and of those aspects of social structure of the Tenetehara and of the Tapirapé in terms of their effect upon population size and on population trends after Luso-Brazilian contact suggest several general hypotheses. First, the available information concerning the population size of these two tribes in aboriginal times indicates that the Tenetehara were much more numerous than the Tapirapé. Yet both tribes were tropical forest peoples with roughly similar technological equipment. It seems to the writer that this difference in population size between the two tribes was functionally related to ideological values and to social structure and not to differences in technology and environment. In other words, such differences in population can hardly be interpreted strictly in Malthusian terms. While population potentials are certainly limited by food supply, the level of technology, the application of medical knowledge, and other material factors, social institutions and culturally derived values are influential in determining trends in population size within the limits set by such "natural" factors.

Second, the social structure and the cultural values of any society are functionally related to a given population level. With change in population size, both the cultural values regarding population size and social structure must be adjusted. The Tapirapé concept of family size remained unchanged in face of modified conditions (i.e. higher death-rate caused by foreign disease) with the result that the adult population was no longer replaced by births. A rapidly declining population disrupted Tapirapé socio-ceremonial organization and affected the internal system of production and distribution. The Tenetehara with a more maleable social structure than that of the Tapirapé were able to survive the initial impact of Luso-Brazilian contact until the protection of the Jesuits allowed them to make necessary adjustments to the new circumstances.

Finally, this comparison between the Tapirapé and the Tenetehara calls to mind other primitive societies whose social structure must have been functionally related to population level and to demographic trends in face of European civilization. In Brazil, the Ramkokamekra (Eastern Timbira) with their complex moiety system and the Apinayé with their kiye marriage classes, to mention only two examples, had social systems comparable to that of the Tapirapé. Such social structures depended upon a balanced representation of population in each of the numerous social units. A sudden decline of population might easily throw such highly segmented societies out of balance, so to speak. Without sufficient representation in one or more of these social units reciprocal socio-ceremonial affairs become impossible or may be carried out in a highly attenuated manner. Again, the social structure of the Karajá of the Araguaya River is based essentially upon extended family and kinship ties and lacks the highly segmented social units which cross cut villages and even family groups. Like that of the Tenetehara, Karajá social structure would seem to be less vulnerable to change in population size and more conducive to population growth. In addition to technological equipment and subsistence methods, social structure and cultural values also influence strongly the final adjustment of each society to its environment. Differences in social structure and of value systems between societies must be taken into account in studies of population size and of population trends in any natural area, such as the Tropical forest of South America.

NOTES

1. Basic descriptions of the Tapirapé and the Tenetehara have been published elsewhere: Cf. Wagley and Galvão (1948a, 1948b, and 1949). Baldus (1937, 1944–49, 1948b, 1949b, Ms.). Only directly pertinent descriptive data is presented in this paper.

2. Cf. Wagley (1940) and Baldus (1944–49, Vol. 103; 1948b, 1949b), for discussion of Tapirapé depopulation and disorganization. Baldus (1948b: 137–38), who found the village called Tampiitáua inhabited by 130 individuals in 1935, and only 62 in 1947, mentions that during this lapse of time several inhabitants had emigrated to another Tapirapé village very far from Tampiitáua, but that their number seems to be lower than the number of those who came from there to Tampiitáua. According to information received by this author, the other village is smaller than Tampiitáua, so that in 1947 the whole tribe probably counted less than a hundred members. In the same year, shortly after Baldus' visit, the Tapirapé were attacked by Kayapó Indians and lost several individuals.

3. There are no indications that the Tenetehara shared the warfare-cannibalism complex of the Tupinambá, but the lower reaches of the Mearim-Grajaú-Pindaré River system and the Island of Maranhão at its mouth were inhabited by Tupinambá groups. Métraux (1948c:95). See also Fernandes (1949a).

4. Baldus (1944–49, Vol. 123:55) was told the same regarding the limitation of number of children of the Tapirapé family, but the contrary in relation to twins. According to information given to him by these Indians, the Tapirapé appreciate twins and, therefore, husband and wife eat twin or double bananas, i.e., with two fruits in the same peel.

5. Genealogies indicated that these rules are adhered to almost without

exception. In 1939, during my residence in a Tapirapé village, one woman hesitated in allowing her third male child to be buried. Less than a month after its birth, she appeared one day without the infant and announced that he had died of a cold. Another woman whose child had four fathers allowed the child to live only to have it die of an intestinal disorder. The villagers took a definite "I-told-you-so" attitude.

Introduction to Lessons from a "Primitive" People

Until recently, modern anthropologists have avoided extrapolating from data about contemporary primitive peoples to make statements about prehistoric man. This was a reaction to excesses committed by nineteenth-century evolutionists. But with the development of new techniques of analysis and the passage of time, such extrapolations have once again begun to be made. To cite only one example, hunter-gatherer peoples (those who have neither domesticated plants or animals) have long been thought to live constantly at the brink of disaster since they have no control over the rates of reproduction of the species on which they depend. Before ten thousand years ago, all men were only foragers, thus paleolithic man was thought to have suffered from poor health, poor nutrition, and to have had practically no respite from the constant search for food. Recent studies among the !Kung people of Botswana (R. Lee 1969) among others have shown, however, that even in marginal environments such as the semi-arid Kalahari, small bands of people using a very simple digging-stick-and-bow technology were capable of feeding themselves adequately with an enviable lack of effort. Their nutritional levels and life expectancies as well as hours of work compare quite favorably with many peoples living in societies technologically far more advanced.

Other researchers have utilized data describing free-ranging, terrestrial, non-human primates to reconstruct aspects of prehistoric human behavior (e.g. Sussman 1972). Still others have relied on genetic, nutritional and morphological studies among contemporary peoples for similar purposes (e.g. Stini 1971). Such reconstructions are all incapable of direct confirmation, but many anthropologists are highly optimistic regarding the fruits which such studies can bear.

In the following selection Dr. James V. Neel, the renowned geneticist, draws on recent studies regarding the genetics and behavior of contemporary South American peoples to derive some important lessons for modern man. Some of his conclusions are startling, such as the suggestion that polygyny combined with endogamy in small populations may have played a eugenic function, whether intended or not. His conclusions provide a stimulus for further research before populations like these become extinct.

James V. Neel is Lee R. Dice University Professor of Human Genetics at the University of Michigan Medical School.

10. LESSONS FROM A "PRIMITIVE" PEOPLE

JAMES V. NEEL

The field of population genetics is in a state of exciting intellectual turmoil and flux. The biochemical techniques that are now so freely available have revealed a profusion of previously hidden genetic variability. The way in which this variability arose and is maintained in populations—to what extent by selection, past and present, and to what extent by simple mutation pressure—is currently a topic of intensive discussion and debate, and there is little agreement among investigators as to which are the most promising approaches to the questions.[1] At the same time, it is becoming increasingly clear that the breeding structure of real populations—especially those that approximate the conditions under which man evolved—departs so very far from the structure subsumed by the classical formulations of population genetics that new formulations may be necessary before the significance of this variation can be appraised by mathematical means.

Some 8 years ago, as the new population genetics began to emerge, my co-workers and I began the formulation of a multidisciplinary study of some of the most primitive Indians of South America among whom it is possible to work.[2] Scientists in the program ranged from the cultural anthropologist to the mathematical geneticist. The general thesis behind the program was that, on the assumption that these people represented the best approximation available to the conditions under which human variability arose, a systems type of analysis oriented toward a number of specific questions might provide valuable insights into problems of human evolution and variability. We recognize, of course, that the

Reprinted by permission of the author and publisher from *Science*, Vol. 170 (1970), pp. 815–22. Copyright 1970 by the American Association for the Advancement of Science.

groups under study depart in many ways from the strict hunter-gatherer way of life that obtained during much of human evolution. Unfortunately, the remaining true hunter-gatherers are either all greatly disturbed or are so reduced in numbers and withdrawn to such inaccessible areas that it appears to be impossible to obtain the sample size necessary for tests of hypothesis. We assume that the groups under study are certainly much closer in their breeding structure to hunter-gatherers than to modern man; thus they permit cautious inferences about human breeding structure prior to large-scale and complex agriculture.

I will present here four of our findings to date and will consider briefly some possible implications of these findings for contemporary human affairs. You will appreciate that I am the spokesman for a group of more than a dozen investigators, whose individual contributions are recognized in the appropriate source papers. The article is tendered with no great sense of accomplishment—we the participants in the endeavor realize how far we are from the solid formulations we seek. On the other hand, some of the data are already clearly germane to contemporary human problems. Thus, it will be maintained on the basis of evidence to be presented that, within the context of his culture and resources, primitive man was characterized by a genetic structure incorporating somewhat more wisdom and prudence than our own. How he arrived at this structure—to what extent by conscious thought, to what extent through lack of technology and in unconscious response to instinct and environmental pressures—is outside the purview of this presentation.

The studies to be described have primarily been directed toward three tribes: the Xavante of the Brazilian Mato Grosso, the Makiritare of southern Venezuela, and the Yanomamö of southern Venezuela and northern Brazil. At the time of our studies, these were among the least acculturated tribes of the requisite size (>1000) in South America.[3-8]

The four salient points about the Indian populations that we studied to be emphasized in this presentation are (i) microdifferentiation and the strategy of evolution, (ii) population control and population size, (iii) polygyny and the genetic significance of differential fertility, and (iv) the balance with disease.[9]

MICRODIFFERENTIATION AND THE STRATEGY OF EVOLUTION

The term "tribe" conjures to most an image of a more or less homogeneous population as the biological unit of primitive human organization. We have now typed blood specimens from some 37 Yanomamö, 7 Makiritare, and 3 Xavante villages with respect to 27 different genetic systems for which serum proteins and erythrocytes can be classified. A remarkable degree of intratribal genetic differentiation between Indian villages emerges from these typings.[8, 10] One convenient way to express this differentiation in quantitative terms is to employ the distance function developed by Cavalli-Sforza and Edwards.[11] On the basis of gene frequencies at the Rh, MNSs, Kidd, Duffy, Diego, and haptoglobin loci, the distances between seven of the central Yanomamö villages and the distances between seven Makiritare villages are shown in Tables 1 and 2. The mean distance between the seven Yanomamö villages is 0.330 unit, and between the Makiritare, 0.356 unit. Table 3

TABLE 1.

MATRICES OF GENETIC DISTANCES BETWEEN PAIRED VILLAGES OF THE MAKIRITARE INDIANS (SEVEN VILLAGES, SIX LOCI).[18]

Village	Distance matrices					
	BD	C	E	F	G	HI
A	.362	.558	.353	.345	.268	.336
BD		.250	.221	.432	.314	.296
C			.393	.588	.485	.444
E				.379	.249	.273
F					.394	.383
G						.158

gives the distances between 12 Indian tribes of Central and South America, selected for consideration solely because 200 or more members have been studied for these same characteristics and the tribes were relatively free of non-Indian genes (admixture estimated at less than 5 percent).[12, 13] The mean distance is 0.385

TABLE 2.

MATRICES OF GENETIC DISTANCES BETWEEN PAIRED VILLAGES
OF THE YANOMAMÖ INDIANS (SEVEN VILLAGES, SIX LOCI).[18]

Village	Distance matrices					
	B	C	D	E	H	I
A	.227	.228	.385	.157	.416	.243
B		.367	.506	.144	.537	.360
C			.298	.295	.346	.297
D				.464	.154	.364
E					.486	.296
H						.350

unit. Thus the average distance between Indian villages is 85.7
(Yanomamö) to 92.5 (Makiritare) percent of the distance between tribes. To some extent—an extent whose precise specification
presents some difficult statistical problems—these distances result
from stochastic events such as the founder effect of E. Mayr, sampling error, and genetic drift. But we have also begun to recognize
structured factors in the origin of these differences. One is the
"fission-fusion" pattern of village propagation, in consequence of
which new villages are often formed by cleavages of established
villages along lineal lines (fission), and migrants to established
villages often consist of groups of related individuals (fusion).[14]
A second such factor is a markedly nonisotropic (that is, a nonran-
dom and "unbalanced") pattern of intervillage migration.[8] A third
factor will be discussed below (see "Polygyny and genetic significance of differential fertility").

This situation, of subdivision of a population into genetically
differentiated and competing demes, is one repeatedly visualized
by Wright,[15] beginning in 1931, as being most conducive to rapid
evolution. Competition between these demes can only be termed
intense.[4, 6] On the basis of the genetic distance between these Indian tribes and an estimated arrival of the Indian in Central and
South America some 15,000 years ago,[16] we have with all due
reservations calculated a *maximum* rate of gene substitution in the
American Indian of 130,000 years per gene substitution per
locus.[13] This rate is approximately 100 times greater than an esti-

TABLE 3.

MATRIX OF PAIR-WISE GENETIC DISTANCES FOR 12 SOUTH AMERICAN TRIBES.[18]

Tribe	Cakchiquel	Cayapa	Cuna	Guayami	Jivaro	Pemon	Quechua	Shipibo	Xavante	Yano-mamö	Yupa
Aymara	.260	.301	.355	.485	.370	.381	.288	.393	.374	.514	.450
Cakchiquel		.297	.224	.364	.342	.302	.278	.363	.250	.439	.326
Cayapa			.283	.446	.289	.346	.224	.486	.343	.473	.328
Cuna				.327	.381	.283	.331	.466	.227	.479	.239
Guayami					.444	.469	.398	.645	.410	.437	.433
Jivaro						.402	.270	.521	.375	.536	.433
Pemon							.319	.460	.371	.510	.354
Quechua								.433	.336	.479	.392
Shipibo									.335	.660	.479
Xavante										.549	.249
Yanomamö											.452

mate of *average* rate based on amino acid substitutions in the polypeptides of a wide variety of animal species.[17] For the present, we equate allele substitutions to amino acid substitutions on the assumption that the basic event in both cases is the partial or complete substitution of one codon for another. There is, of course, no logical discrepancy between these estimates, since one of them is a maximum estimate.[18] On the other hand, part of the apparent difference may be valid. Thus, it seems a reasonable postulate that, all over the world in man's tribal days, the single most important step in the formation of a new tribe probably consisted of a village or a collection of related villages breaking away from its tribe and moving off into relative isolation. These villages, perhaps more than the breakaway units of other animal populations, tended to consist of related individuals, thus providing unusual scope in man for what we have termed the "lineal effect" in establishing subpopulations whose gene frequencies are quite different from those of the parent population.[19]

There is a current tendency to regard much of evolution, as measured by gene substitution, as non-Darwinian—that is, not determined by systematic pressures.[17] We have recently argued that no matter whether one assumes a predominantly deterministic or indeterministic stance, the above-mentioned aspect of the social structure of primitive man resulted in genetic experiments of a type conducive to rapid evolution.[18] Conversely, the current expansion and amalgamation of human populations into vast interbreeding complexes must introduce a great deal of inertia into the system.

POPULATION CONTROL AND POPULATION SIZE

The total human population apparently increased very slowly up to 10,000 years ago.[20] If we may extrapolate from our Indian experience, the slowness of this increase was probably not primarily due to high infant and childhood mortality rates from infectious and parasitic diseases (see "The balance with disease"). We find that relatively uncontacted primitive man under conditions of low population density enjoys "intermediate" infant mortality and relatively good health, although not the equal of ours today.[21-23] However, most primitive populations practiced spacing of children. Our data on how this spacing was accomplished are best for the Yanomamö, where intercourse taboos, prolonged lactation, abortion, and infanticide reduce the average *effective* live birth rate to approximately one child every 4 to 5 years during the childbearing period.[24, 25] The infanticide is directed primarily at infants whose older sibling is not thought ready for weaning, which usually occurs at about 3 years of age.[25] Deformed infants and those thought to result from extramarital relationships are also especially liable to infanticide. Female infants are killed more often than male infants, which results in a sex ratio of 128 during the age interval 0 to 14 years.[24] An accurate estimate of the frequency of infanticide still eludes us, but, from the sex-ratio imbalance plus other fragmentary information, we calculate that it involves perhaps 15 to 20 percent of all live births.

There have been numerous attempts to define the development in human evolution that clearly separated man from the prehominids. The phenomena of speech and of toolmaking have had strong proponents, whose advocacy has faltered in the face of growing evidence of the complexity of signaling and the ingenuity in utilizing materials that are manifested by higher primates. Population control may be such a key development. Among 309 skeletons of (adult) fossil man classified as to sex by H. V. Vallois, 172 were thought to be males and 137 were classified as females, which gives a sex ratio of 125.6.[26] These finds were made over a wide area, and they extend in time depth from Pithecanthropus to Mesolithic man. I am aware of the controversy that surrounds the sexing of fossil skeletons, as well as the question of whether both sexes were equally subject to burial. Nevertheless, one interpretation is that preferential female infanticide is an old practice. In contrast to man, it appears that most higher primates must utilize their natural fecundity rather fully to maintain population numbers. I conclude, as has been suggested elsewhere,[25] that perhaps the most significant of the many milestones in the transition from higher primate to man—on a par with speech and toolmaking—occurred when human social organization and parental care permitted the survival of a higher proportion of infants than the culture and economy could absorb in each generation and when population control, including abortion and infanticide, was therefore adopted as the only practical recourse available.

The deliberate killing of a grossly defective child (who cannot hope for a full participation in the society he has just entered) or of the child who follows too soon the birth of an older sibling (and thereby endangers the latter's nutritional status) is morally repugnant to us. I am clearly not obliquely endorsing a return to this or a comparable practice. However, I am suggesting that we see ourselves in proper perspective. The relationship between rapid reproduction and high infant mortality has been apparent for centuries. During this time we have condoned in ourselves a reproductive pattern which (through weanling diarrhea and malnutrition) has contributed, for large numbers of children, to a much more agonizing "natural" demise than that resulting from infanticide. Moreover, this reproductive pattern has condemned many of the surviving children to a marginal diet inconsistent with full physical and mental development.

We obviously cannot countenance infanticide. However, accepting the general harshness of the milieu in which primitive man functioned, I find it increasingly difficult to see in the recent reproductive history of the civilized world a greater respect for the quality of human existence than was manifested by our remote "primitive" ancestors. Firth,[27] in protesting the disturbance in population balance in the Pacific island of Tikopia when Christianity was substituted for ancient mores, expressed it thus:

> It might be thought that the so-called sanctity of human life is not an end in itself, but the means to an end, to the preservation of society. And just as in a civilized community in time of war, civil disturbance or action against crime, life is taken to preserve life, so in Tikopia infants just born might be allowed to have their faces turned down,[28] and to be debarred from the world they have merely glimpsed, in order that the economic equilibrium might be preserved, and the society maintain its balanced existence.

POLYGYNY AND GENETIC SIGNIFICANCE OF DIFFER-
ENTIAL FERTILITY

The three Indian tribes among whom we have worked are polygynous,[4, 5, 21] the reward in these nonmaterial cultures for male
achievement (however judged) and longevity being additional
wives. This pattern is found in many primitive cultures. As brought
out in the preceding section, women seem to be committed to a
pattern of child spacing, which in the Yanomamö results, for
women living to the age of 40 years, in a lower variance in number
of reported live births than in the contemporary United States.[24]
By contrast with our culture, then, the mores of these primitive
societies tend to minimize the variance of number of live births per
female but maximize the variance of number of children per male.

One of our objectives is to understand the genetic consequences
of polygyny. The translation of generalizations such as the above
into the kind of hard data that can be employed in either deterministic formulations or stochastic procedures based on population
simulation designed to explore the genetic consequences of polygyny has proved quite difficult. A single example will suffice. We
have earlier directed attention toward the unusual reproductive performance of certain headmen among the Xavante,[21] and N. A.
Chagnon has similar unpublished data for the Yanomamö. During
the past 2 years, J. MacCluer, in collaboration with Chagnon and
myself, has been trying to develop a computer model that simu-
lates the genetic and demographic structure of the Yanomamö.
The basic input has consisted of Chagnon's detailed demographic
data from four villages. One of the several objectives of this simulation is to derive a better estimate of the amount of inbreeding
than is possible from pedigree information in which the genealogical depth is so shallow, with particular reference to the complications introduced by polygyny. For some time there were great
difficulties in reconciling certain aspects of the inbreeding results
after 150 simulated years with the results of the first 20 simulated
years (during which the real, input population dominated the findings), even though in many other respects—age at marriage, mean
number of children, and distribution of polygyny—there was a good

accord with the facts. During the first 20 simulated years, the members of the (real) population were, on the average, more closely related to each other than those in the simulated population at 150 years, so that, even when the model specified the maximum opportunity for consanguineous marriages consistent with field data, the level of inbreeding declined with time.

The reason finally became clear when the distribution of number of grandchildren per male was considered. Table 4 contrasts the actual distribution in the input data with that predicted by the simulation program after 150 years on the assumption of no correlation in fertility between successive generations. It is clear that the assumption is incorrect. Note the disproportionate number of grandchildren born to some few males, a situation that greatly increases the possibilities for marriages between first cousins or half-first cousins. Added genetic significance is lent to this phenomenon by the fact that the four males whose living grandchildren outnumber those of any male in the computer population represent two father-son combinations. One reason for this "familial" fertility seems to be that, if because of the polygyny of his father a young man possesses many sisters or half-sisters (who can be "traded"), that young man has an advantage in forming alliances and obtaining extra wives; thus, polygyny begets polygyny. The phenomenon does not appear to be primarily genetic. Clearly here is the explanation of why, when MacCluer programmed for the maximum rate of marriage between relatives (but did not incorporate in the model this aspect of fertility), there was an apparent decline in consanguinity as the real world of input was replaced by the simulated world. To be sure, we might have recognized this aspect of polygyny in Indian culture before we programmed the model, but I prefer to view the development as an example of how simulation forces one to look at the real population more carefully. This degree of differential fertility must be another factor in the marked genetic microdifferentiation between villages. Since the number of wives a man obtains and holds also depends on personal attributes, unquestionably determined genetically to some extent, here is an example of an interaction between the genetic system and the social system. Such interactions occur at all cultural levels, but it was unexpected to find this one emerging so strongly in these circumstances.

Table 4. The number of grandchildren (who reach adult life) per male, for all males with at least one grandchild, in the input (real) population and the artificial population after 150 years of simulation. The simulation is based on the assumption of no correlation in fertility between generations.

No. of grandchildren per male	Initial population	Artificial population after 150 years	No. of grandchildren per male	Initial population	Artificial population after 150 years
1	28	17	26		
2	11	9	27		
3	11	10	28	1	
4	7	7	29		
5	10	9	30		1
6	9	6	31		
7	5	9	32		
8	5	5	33		
9	1	5	34		
10	7	5	35		
11	3	5	36		
12	2	3	37		
13		7	38		1
14		5	39		
15	1	2	40		
16	2	3	41	1	
17		3	42	1	
18		1	43		
19	1	1	44		
20	2		45		
21	1	2	46	1	
22	1	2	.	.	.
23		1	.	.	.
24	1	2	.	.	.
25	1		62	1	
			Total	114	121

The *possible* genetic implications of polygyny are clear, but some of the facts necessary to a meaningful treatment are still lacking. Thus, one of our projected future investigations is an attempt to contrast certain mental attributes of polygynous with nonpolygynous males. In many respects, Indian culture is much more egalitarian than our own. The children of a village have the same diet and, by our standards, a remarkably similar environment. There are minimal occupational differences, and we do not find the differentiation into fishing villages, mining villages, or farming communities encountered in many cultures. Even with allowance for the happy accident of a large sibship, the open competition for leadership in an Indian community probably results in leadership being based far less on accidents of birth and far more on innate characteristics than in our culture. Our field impression is that the polygynous Indians, especially the headmen, tend to be more intelligent than the nonpolygynous. They also tend to have more surviving offspring. Polygyny in these tribes thus appears to provide an effective device for certain types of natural selection. Would that we had quantitative results to support that statement!

THE BALANCE WITH DISEASE

Inasmuch as viral, bacterial, and parasitic diseases are commonly regarded as among the important agents of natural selection, a particular effort has been directed toward assaying the health of primitive man and the characteristics of his interaction with these disease agents. We have reported that the Xavante are, in general, in excellent physical condition,[21, 22] and we have similar unpublished data on the Yanomamö and Makiritare. In terms of morbidity, perhaps the most important disease is falciparum malaria, which is probably a post-Columbian introduction.[29] Fortunately for our view of the health of the pre-Columbian American Indian, we can find villages in which malaria does not seem to be a problem. Figure 1 presents our working concept of the Yanomamö life expectancy curve, to be improved as more data become available.[23, 24] Although infant and childhood mortality rates are high by the standards of a civilized country such as present-day Japan, they are low in comparison with India at the turn of the century, especially since there was probably gross underreporting in the data from India. Note the relatively high Yanomamö death rate during the third, fourth, and fifth decades, a substantial fraction of which is due to warfare. One way to view the differences

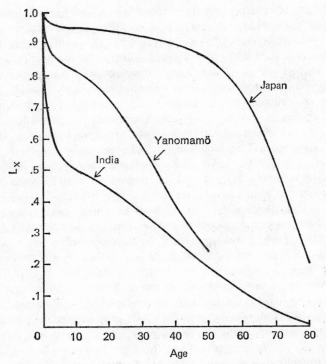

FIG. 1. "Life curves" for three types of populations: a highly urbanized and industrialized country (Japan in 1960); a densely populated, primarily agricultural country (India in 1901); and an unacculturated tribal population (the Yanomamö)[after 23]. Probability of survival is indicated by L_x.

between these three curves is that the advent of civilization dealt a blow to man's health from which he is only now recovering.

Dunn[30] has properly emphasized the degree to which the ecological setting influenced disease patterns in primitive man and the difficulty in reaching generalizations. Even so, certain common denominators may be emerging. For instance, the pattern of acquisition of immunity to endemic diseases in the Indian and possibly other primitives can already be seen to differ in a number of respects from the pattern in most civilized communities.[23] Among the Xavante and Yanomamö, for example, we find gamma globulin levels approximately two times those in civilized areas.[31] Newborn infants presumably possess a high measure of maternal antibody acquired transplacentally. From the first, these infants are in an intimate contact with their environment that would horrify a modern mother—or physician. They nurse at sticky breasts, at which the young mammalian pets of the village have also suckled, and soon are crawling on the feces-contaminated soil and chewing on an unbelievable variety of objects. Our thesis is that the high level of maternally derived antibody, early exposure to pathogens, the prolonged period of lactation, and the generally excellent nutritional status of the child make it possible for him to achieve a *relatively* smooth transition from passive to active immunity to many of the agents of disease to which he is exposed. The situation is well illustrated by the manner in which concomitantly administered gamma globulin reduces the impact of a rubeola vaccination while still permitting the development of effective immunity. To be sure, civilized tropical populations also have relatively high globulin levels,[21] so that there should be high placental transfer of passive immunity; however, because of the higher effective birth rate, the child of the *civilizado* is seldom nursed as long as the Indian child and thus falls prey to weanling diarrhea and malnutrition.

By his vaccination programs, then, modern man is developing a relatively painless immunity to his diseases, similar in some ways to the manner in which the Indian seems to have developed immunity to some of his diseases. A danger for both groups is the sudden appearance of a "new" disease. Burnet[32] has described some of the possible consequences for civilized societies in the appearance in the laboratory of strains of pathogens with new combinations of antigenic and virulence properties, and Lederberg[33] has labeled this threat as one of the hidden dangers in experiments related to biological warfare. At the other extreme, we have recently witnessed at first hand the consequences of a measles epidemic among the Yanomamö, known from antibody studies to be a "virgin-soil" population with respect to this virus.[34] Although the symptomatic response of the Indian to the disease may be somewhat (but not markedly) greater than our own, much of the well-recognized enhanced morbidity and mortality in such epidemics is due to the secondary features of the epidemic—the collapse of village life when almost everyone is highly febrile, when mothers cannot nurse their infants, and when there is no one to provide for the needs of the community. After witnessing this spectacle, I find it unpleasant to contemplate its possible modern counterpart—when, in some densely populated area, a new pathogen, or an old one such as smallpox or malaria, appears and escapes control, and a serious breakdown of local services follows.

This relative balance with his endemic diseases is only one aspect of the generally harmonious relationship with his ecosystem that characterizes primitive man. There is an identification with and respect for the natural world, beautifully described by Radcliffe-Brown,[35] Redfield,[36] and Lévi-Strauss,[37] among others, which we, who have walled it off so successfully while penetrating its secrets, find difficult to understand. In general, the religion of the tribes among whom we have worked is a pantheism in which both the heavens and the immediate environment are peopled by ubiquitous spirits, of human and nonhuman origin, whom it is vitally important to propitiate at every turn. To some extent their apparent respect for their ecosystem probably stems from ignorance and technical incompetence, but, in common with White,[38] I believe that it also reflects the difference between a religion that regards man as a part of a system and one in which he is the divinely appointed master of the system.

A PROGRAM

In a world in which our heads are spinning under the impact of information overload, studies of primitive man provide, above everything else, perspective. Civilized man is a creature who each year is departing farther and farther from the population structure that obtained throughout most of human evolution and that was presumably of some importance to the evolutionary process. At the same time he is not only living far beyond a reasonable energy balance but is despoiling the resources for primary production so as to narrow increasingly the options available to redress the imbalances. The true dimensions of the dilemma that our present course has created are only now emerging.[39] The intellectual arrogance created by our small scientific successes must be replaced by a profound humility based on the new knowledge of how complex is the system of which we are a part. To some of us, this realization carries with it the need for a philosophical readjustment which has the impact of a religious conversion.

We various members of the scientific community are all deeply engaged these days in speculating on the role that we will play in the next major cultural cycle. I find much of relevance to contemporary problems in my field, human genetics, in our studies of primitive man. It is clear that our primary objective—to understand the origin and significance of polymorphic variability—still eludes us. But there are other insights. In the light of our recent experiences among the Indian tribes, I shall now briefly consider some possible emphases in human genetics in the immediate future. In keeping with the new humility incumbent upon us all, it is not surprising that my suggestions are rather conservative; they are designed to preserve what we have rather than to promote unreal hopes of spectacular advances. They constitute in many respects an attempt to recreate, within limits, certain conditions that we have observed. These suggestions do not stem from any romanticism concerning the noble savage: Indian life is harsh and cruel, and it countenances an overt aggressiveness that is unthinkable today. Obviously the world should not return to a state of subdivision into demes of 50 to 200 persons constantly involved in a pattern of shifting loyalties and brutal conflict vis-à-vis neighboring demes. Nor are we likely to return to polygyny, with number of wives in part a function of one's "fierceness"—demonstrated by a series of duels with clubs or stylized bouts of chest poundings. Clearly we do not wish to abandon modern medical care to permit natural selection to have a better opportunity to work. But there are other, less disruptive aspects of primitive society for which there is a modern counterpart. These are enumerated below as a series of principles.

STABILIZATION OF THE GENE POOL

First principle: Stabilize the gene pool numerically. Throughout the world, primitive man seems to have curbed his intrinsic fertility to a greater extent than has the civilized world in recent centuries. Exactly how those curbs were relaxed with the advent of civilization is unclear, but the agricultural revolution undoubtedly played a part. Although it is currently fashionable to indict the great religions, on the basis of the Old Testament injunction to "be fruitful and multiply," their precise role (until recent times) is in my opinion unclear. The remaining pockets of dissent with the principle of population limitation are rapidly disappearing; the next 5 years will convince even the most reluctant. But by what precise formula should population limitation be accomplished? I have previously urged a simple quota system, set at three living children per couple on the thesis that failure to marry, infertility, and voluntary limitation to less than three would result in a realized average of approximately two children who reach the age of reproduction.[40] I now wonder whether failure of contraception will not result in so many well-intentioned persons exceeding their quota that these guidelines are not sufficiently stringent; I would therefore amend the earlier suggestion to include provision for voluntary sterilization after the third child. You will recognize that this proposal implies relative stabilization of the present gene pool, a move that will tend to conserve all our present bewildering diversity but hinder evolution. It makes no value judgments about any specific group. There would be less opportunity for changes in gene frequency than with present patterns of differential fertility.

Such a policy cannot succeed if some religions and governments simply continue their present half-hearted admonitions and leave the rest to science, while other religions and governments actually oppose effective population control. What has been signally lacking thus far is a clear statement at every possible level of responsibility of the implications of continuing the present rate of population increase. Also lacking has been an administrative framework within which all peoples move toward population control simultaneously, thus dispelling deep-rooted fears that some sectors are being subjected to a subtle form of genocide. Bills now pending in the U.S. Congress—S. 2108, S. 2701, S. 3219, S. 3502, H.R. 11550, H.R. 15165—carry the hope that the United States will shortly be facing these questions much more forthrightly than in the past.

PROTECTION OF THE GENE POOL

Second principle: Protect the gene against damage. If, as we have implied, polygyny among the Indian has eugenic overtones, there is no acceptable modern counterpart in view. However, we can at least protect the gene pool from obvious damage. The world of primitive man is remarkably uncontaminated. This fact, plus his lower mean age at reproduction, probably results in lower mutation rates than our own,[41] but we have no direct evidence.

Until recently, the principal concomitant of civilization that appeared capable of damaging the gene pool was an increasing exposure to radiation. Now concern is shifting to the many potentially mutagenic chemicals being introduced into the environment as pesticides, industrial by-products, air contaminants, and so forth. The magnitude of this problem is currently undefined. About 6 percent of all newborn infants have been found to have defects partially or wholly of genetic origin.[42] Let us assume that half of these defects (3 percent) result from recurrent mutation. Doubling the mutation rate would *eventually* double that 3 percent.

For all the work that has been done on the genetic effects of radiation, involving both man and experimental organisms, there still remain large areas of ambiguity, especially as regards the effects of low-level, intermittent, or chronic-type doses, such as characterize most human exposures. The current working estimate of the "doubling dose" of radiation of this type is 100 to 200 roentgens.[42] In general, current man-made human exposures in the United States [probably less than 3 rem to the gonads in 30 years][42] appear to be of the order of perhaps $\frac{1}{30}$ to $\frac{1}{60}$ of the "doubling dose," a price society thus far seems prepared to accept for the benefits of the medical uses of radiation and the development of nuclear sources of energy. It may be that genetically effective exposures to the chemical mutagens are as low or even lower, but we cannot be certain.

The technical advances of the past 20 years now render it possible and feasible to screen a representative 20 proteins in newborn infants for evidence of mutational damage;[43] hence we need no longer rely, as in the studies at Hiroshima and Nagasaki, on the potential genetic effects of the atomic bombs, on such imprecise indicators of genetic damage as congenital malformations, survival rates, and sex ratio. A society that can afford to send man to the moon surely has the resources and the intelligence to monitor itself properly for increased mutation rates. If a significant increase is detected, however, the task of identifying the responsible agent or agents will, because of the many possibilities, be extremely difficult, and that agent, when identified, may be so relevant to the welfare of society that, as with radiation, the goal will be to minimize rather than to eliminate exposures. Despite these difficulties in detection and control, immediate steps to determine the facts are needed.

GENETIC COUNSELING AND PRENATAL DIAGNOSIS

Third principle: Improve the quality of life through parental choice based on genetic counseling and prenatal diagnosis. Both the pressures on the social system and its services and the increasing demands of society on the individual render it imperative that full advantage be taken of all morally acceptable developments that promise to minimize the number of unfortunate individuals incapable of full participation in this complex society. We will not return to infanticide, but there are ethical alternatives. Genetic counseling, which defines the high-risk family, represents one such development. In the past, once the identification had been made, the individuals who wished to limit the entry of defective children into the population had only two alternatives: to practice birth control or to apply for voluntary sterilization. Recently the possibilities inherent in prenatal diagnosis based on fetal cells obtained through amniocentesis during the first trimester of pregnancy have been receiving active attention.[44] Where accurate diagnosis is possible and the presence of a defective fetus is established, the parents can be offered an abortion, usually with reasonable prospects of a normal child in the next pregnancy. Thus far the conditions that can be accurately diagnosed in the very early stages of pregnancy and the numerical impact of these entities are relatively small.

The moral issues that are involved cannot be evaded, and it is better in this time of reappraisal for society to face them forth-rightly. At what point is the artificial termination of a pregnancy no longer ethical, even when the fetus concerned is incapable of marginal participation in society? Just what defects are of such gravity as to justify intervention? To what extent should persuasion be employed in implementing these new possibilities? In my opinion, once the principle of parental choice of a normal child is established, it seems probable that in large measure the parental desire for normal children can be relied on to result in the purely voluntary elimination of affected fetuses.

REALIZING THE GENETIC POTENTIAL OF THE INDIVIDUAL

Fourth principle: Improve the phenotypic expression of the individual genotype. It is a sobering thought that the relatively egalitarian structure of most primitive societies, plus the absence of large individual differences in material wealth, seems to ensure that, within the culturally imposed boundaries, each individual in primitive society leads a life (and enjoys reproductive success) more in accord with his innate capabilities than in our present democracy. In the difficult times ahead, society clearly needs the fullest possible participation of all its members. In the past, a very major effort has gone into the provision of special services for the physically and mentally handicapped. A retreat from such compassion is unthinkable, but it is apparent that a similar effort directed toward realizing the genetic potential of the underprivileged or the gifted would have far more impact on the solution of our problems.

Much of the thrust of the geneticist and those with allied interests has been directed toward the treatment of specific genetic diseases. Obviously these efforts need not only to be continued but to be greatly expanded. And equally obviously, the Indian contributes no insight into a program in this field of endeavor. Others are speaking eloquently to the needs and potentialities of this type of investigation.

But an even greater effort should be directed toward what I have elsewhere termed "culture engineering",[45] which merges at one extreme with the euphenics of Lederberg.[46] There is presumably an environment (or group of environments) in which the still poorly understood potentialities of the human animal find the fullest and most harmonious expression. Although our present environment-culture reduces the impact of a number of previously important causes of mortality and morbidity, it creates a host of other "casualties of our times".[47] The challenge to culture engineering is, of course, greatest in the realm of the mind. It is not enough to think in terms of better schools and more attractive housing; the subtle and lasting influence of prenatal and early postnatal influences is becoming increasingly apparent.[48] Experimental mammalian models are yielding fascinating evidence on the complexity of these interactions.[49] It is doubtful whether our precipitous and helter-skelter attacks on our present world will yield an optimum environment. We cannot escape the consequences of the peculiar position in which we have placed ourselves; we must now cautiously and reverently accept the full responsibility for shaping our own world.

SUMMING UP

The foregoing principles constitute an extremely conservative program in human genetics, which advocates for the present a return to as many of the features of the population structure under which we evolved as is consistent with our present culture. The urgent need to understand the biomedical and social significance of human genetic variability as a basis for an eventual, more definitive program should be clear, and yet we seem to be retreating from support of the necessary research while we are squandering billions in pursuit of dubious military goals.

There has been no mention in this presentation of that brand of genetic engineering concerned with controlled changes in transmissible genetic material. This omission is not due to oversight or limitations of time. My thesis is clearly a plea for a profound respect for ourselves and the system in which we function. It would be inconsistent with that thesis to suggest that, with our present limited knowledge of the human genome, we should in the near future think of intervening to alter it in ways we cannot completely understand. Research along these lines with experimental organisms is inevitable and desirable—but I question the wisdom of attempting, in the foreseeable future, to apply the results of that research to man.

The past decade has witnessed spectacular triumphs in the "inner space" of the cell and the "outer space" of the cosmos. Perhaps this decade will in retrospect be seen as the first of many decades of spectacular advances in our understanding of *"intermediate* space"—the biosphere—the space defined as that narrow life-supporting zone wherein occur the interactions between intact humans and other organisms and their environment which by definition are an ecosystem. As we realize the full complexity of intermediate space, it seems very probable that the scientific challenge to produce new knowledge will be equaled by the challenge of integrating the applications of that new knowledge smoothly into the ecosystem. In the most sophisticated way we can summon, we must return to the awe, and even fear, in which primitive man held the mysterious world about him, and like him we must strive to live in harmony with the only biosphere that we can be certain will be occupied by our descendants.[50]

REFERENCES AND NOTES

1. J. V. Neel and W. J. Schull 1968.
2. The term "primitive" is employed in the usual sense: preliterate; relatively untouched by civilization; with a very simple technology and with subsistence based on hunting, gathering and elementary agricultural practices; and with a social structure in which concepts of kinship play a dominant organizational role.
3. O. Zerries 1964.
4. D. Maybury-Lewis 1967.
5. N. A. Chagnon 1968a.
6. N. A. Chagnon 1968b.
7. T. Asch and N. A. Chagnon 1970.
8. H. Valero 1971.
9. Since this is not a formal review, I shall draw primarily on our own work in discussing our concrete findings. The reader will recognize, however, that there is considerable background literature, although much of it unfortunately lacks the quantitative detail necessary to precise formulations and the construction of population models.

10. J. V. Neel and F. M. Salzano 1967; T. Arends, G. Brewer, N. Chagnon, M. Gallango, H. Gershowitz, M. Layrisse, J. Neel, D. Shreffler, R. Tashian, L. Weitkamp 1967.
11. L. L. Cavalli-Sforza and A. W. F. Edwards 1967.
12. R. H. Post, J. V. Neel, and W. J. Schull 1968.
13. W. Fitch and J. V. Neel 1969.
14. J. V. Neel and F. M. Salzano 1964.
15. S. Wright 1931.
16. J. M. Cruxent 1968.
17. M. Kimura 1968; J. L. King and T. H. Jukes 1969.
18. J. V. Neel and R. H. Ward 1970.
19. J. V. Neel 1967.
20. E. S. Deevey 1960.
21. J. V. Neel, F. M. Salzano, P. C. Junqeira, F. Keiter, D. Maybury-Lewis 1964.
22. E. D. Weinstein, J. V. Neel, F. M. Salzano 1967.
23. J. V. Neel 1971.
24. J. V. Neel and N. A. Chagnon 1968; N. A. Chagnon, unpublished data.
25. J. V. Neel 1969.
26. H. V. Vallois in S. L. Washburn (Ed.) 1961:214.
27. R. Firth 1958:xxvi and 605.
28. A reference to infanticide by suffocation.
29. F. L. Dunn 1965.
30. F. L. Dunn in R. B. Lee and I. DeVore (Eds.) 1968:221.
31. J. V. Neel, W. M. Mikkelsen, D. L. Rucknagel, E. D. Weinstein, R. A. Goyer, S. H. Abadie 1968; T. Arends unpublished data.
32. F. M. Burnet 1966.
33. J. Lederberg 1969.
34. J. V. Neel, W. R. Centerwall, N. A. Chagnon, H. L. Casey 1970.
35. A. R. Radcliffe-Brown 1952:219.
36. R. Redfield 1953.
37. C. Lévi-Strauss 1966.
38. L. White, Jr. 1967.
39. P. R. Ehrlich and J. P. Holdran 1969 and H. R. Hulett 1970.
40. J. V. Neel 1969.
41. J. V. Neel 1969:389–403.
42. United Nations 1962.
43. J. V. Neel and A. D. Bloom 1969.
44. J. Dancis 1968; J. W. Littlefield 1969; H. L. Nadler and A. B. Gerbie 1969; R. B. DeMars, G. Sarto, J. S. Felix, P. Benke 1969.
45. J. V. Neel 1961; also R. Dubos 1969a.
46. Euphenics is defined as the reprogramming of somatic cells and the modification of development. See J. Lederberg 1963.
47. A. B. Ford 1970.
48. Pan American Health Organization 1969; N. S. Scrimshaw and J. E. Gordon 1968.
49. R. Dubos 1969b.
50. This article is adapted from a paper delivered as the Second Annual Lasker Lecture of the Salk Institute for Biological Studies on 21 May, 1970. The investigations described have been supported in large measure by the

U. S. Atomic Energy Commission. Principal colleagues in these studies include Dr. Miguel Layrisse and Tulio Arends of Venezuela, Dr. Francisco Salzano and Manuel Ayres of Brazil and Drs. Napoleon Chagnon, Jean MacCluer, Lowell Weitkamp, Richard Ward, and Walter Fitch of the United States.

PART III: SOCIAL AND POLITICAL ORGANIZATION

Introduction to Types of Social Structure Among the Lowland Tribes of South and Central America

For as long as there have been specialized ethnological studies on South America, there have been attempts to construct classifications of the myriad aboriginal peoples living on that continent. Classifications are useful because they reduce the diverse and numerous sociocultural and linguistic units to a more manageable number of units. Moreover, classifications may serve as adjuncts to a comparative, ethnological enterprise. The criteria used to form a classification will vary, of course, with the theoretical approach taken.

One of the earliest attempts to classify South American Indians appeared in Clark Wissler's book *The American Indian* (1917), in which he describes and classifies all the aboriginal peoples of the New World, and states the known distributions of environmental, genetic, technological, and sociocultural traits. A major concern in Wissler's time was to trace the diffusion of traits in an attempt to reconstruct the history of particular peoples. This "diffusionist" approach held that man is essentially uninventive and that distinctive cultural patterns could be explained in terms of the form and content of the contacts of a particular historical society with other societies. Accordingly, Wissler's classification is known as a culture-area classification. It delimits areas surrounding "culture centers" which are thought to be the foci of radiation (Wissler 1917:257 ff., 370 ff.). Wissler's classifications are based on what is apparently an intuitive grouping, taking "all traits into simultaneous consideration" (1917:218).

Wissler divides South America into the Chibcha, Inca, Guanaco, Amazon, and Antilles areas (1917:245–57). Within each area, he selected a single people or tribe as "most typical." Another culture-area classification was made by David B. Stout in 1938, based again on culture content, but which discriminated nine culture areas. Father John Cooper proposed a simpler scheme in 1942, based largely on environmental factors, but taking into account racial, linguistic and cultural traits. Cooper's aim in discriminating the Marginal, Silval, and Sierral culture areas was to lay a basis for a scheme of migration and diffusion which would explain the distribution of culture traits in South America in historical times. The main center of diffusion in South America, according to Cooper, was the Sierral (Andean) area, which, in turn, was closest to the "avenue of ingress" from Central and North America. Rejecting earlier theories, Cooper suggested that the simpler Silval and Marginal peoples were not degenerated complex societies but represented different levels of cultural development which were correlated with degree of isolation from the main pathways of diffusion. By its simplicity and implicit evolutionist tone, Cooper's areal classification approaches the status of a cultural *typology*.

When Julian Steward became editor of the monumental *Handbook of South American Indians,* he was faced with the immediate problem of how to organize the mountain of ethnographic material which began to pour in during the early 1940s. His initial solution took the form of a culture-area classification (very much like Father Cooper's), grouping societies together on a basis of such diverse aspects as location, social organization, religion, myths, language, ceramic styles, etc. The first four volumes of the *Handbook* reflect this somewhat haphazard scheme. They are titled respectively *The Marginal Tribes* (1944), *The Tropical Forest Tribes* (1945), *The Circum-Caribbean Tribes* (1945), *Andean Civilizations* (1944). But when he came to write an "interpretative summary" of South American cultures for Volume V, Steward (1945:669 ff.) confessed that he had made numerous misclassifications owing to a lack of rigorous criteria. In this essay, Steward modifies his classification, producing a cultural *typology* based not on area or total content, but specifically on sociopolitical and religious patterns. The typology still reflects an interest in culture areas and historical reconstruction, but it represents an important leap forward from the particularist anthropology of Boas and his students to a concern with cultural causality and law. As Steward later wrote:

> If a taxonomic system is to be devised for the purpose of determining cross-cultural parallels and regularities rather than of stressing contrasts and differences, there is needed a concept which may be designated "culture type" (1955:23).

The "culture type" is different from the culture area, primarily in that it is defined in terms of a few selected elements, the culture core, which is, "the constellation of features which are most closely related to subsistence activities and economic arrangements" (1955:37). Steward and Faron (1959) later revised Steward's 1945 typology in the light of new data and further analysis but the main outlines of the typology remained substantially the same.

The next classification to follow Steward's 1945 typology was that of George Peter Murdock (1951), who more or less systematically employed nine criteria to form a classification of twenty-four areas. Murdock made some useful criticisms of Steward's four-part scheme, and his own more complex scheme might be of greater use for the construction of cross-cultural samples (an area in which Murdock has pioneered) to avoid including historically related cases. But this extremely particularistic typology does little to advance the goals of comparison and generalization.

Kalervo Oberg, author of the next selection, has returned to a set of social and ecological criteria to construct a typology of sociopolitical types in lowland South and Central America. Not only does this classification contribute numerous suggestions for research, but it also stands as a genuine cultural typology, untainted by a historical particularist approach. These types therefore facilitate comparisons to societies outside South America.

The reader may want to compare this typology to other recent typologies of South America or Latin America which attempt to deal not only with native populations but with contemporary national populations as well (Wagley and Harris 1955; Eric Wolf 1955; Elman Service 1955). For a discussion of classifications of South American indigenous languages, see Arthur Sorensen's article in Chapter 18 of this volume.

Born in Canada and educated at British Columbia, Pittsburgh and Chicago, Dr. Kalervo Oberg has had a long and illustrious career as an ethnologist and consultant on economic development. He has conducted ethnographic research and acted as a consultant in Surinam, Ecuador, Peru, Africa, New Mexico and Brazil. He is perhaps best known for his monographs on the ethnology of the Terena and Caduveo (1949) and the tribes of the upper Xingú River (1953).

11. TYPES OF SOCIAL STRUCTURE AMONG THE LOWLAND TRIBES OF SOUTH AND CENTRAL AMERICA

KALERVO OBERG

I. THE PROBLEM OF CULTURAL TYPOLOGY

Steward's fourfold classification (Marginal, Tropical Forest, Circum-Caribbean, and Andean civilizations) of the Indian cultures of pre-Columbian America south of Mexico stands as a landmark in the ordering of the vast body of descriptive material brought together in the *Handbook of South American Indians*. It appears to me that in the ordering of this material and in his theoretical and interpretative passages Steward had three major objectives in mind: (1) to classify tribes or other culture-carrying units on the basis of certain typical culture traits; (2) to distinguish broad cultural strata or levels and to indicate the developmental interrelationship of these levels; and (3) to determine, in so far as possible, the concrete historical processes by which these developments have taken place (Steward 1949). With this approach, which is at once taxonomic, developmental, and historical, I am in complete agreement. Steward has gathered the material and has indicated basic approaches, and it remains for others to develop these approaches or to create new ones in order to derive more meaning from the material. In this paper I will attempt not only to describe the major types of social structure under which I believe all sociopolitical units in this area can be listed but will attempt also to account for these types in terms of those cultural elements, environmental factors, and the derivatives which appear to be intimately associated with them. Admittedly this approach is narrow, for large segments of culture content will be omitted.

If one is concerned with the typology of culture, one must of

Reproduced by permission of the author and the American Anthropological Association from *American Anthropologist*, Vol. 57, No. 3 (1955), pp. 472–87.

necessity consider certain functionally interrelated constellations of variable cultural forms, which, in turn, poses the problem of defining the unit to be used for comparison. Is there an isolable, social, culture-carrying unit which in the locus of the cultural process, which accepts the discoveries and inventions of its members, which absorbs or rejects outside culture traits, and which in the process is itself modified? In short, is there not a social organism which exists in an environment, somewhat comparable to a biological organism which is studied and classified by biologists? It is suggested here that, although varying tremendously in size and complexity, social organisms of this kind do exist and that they can be classified in terms of their structures. Once established, these major structural types can be separated into subtypes and the subtypes can be further separated into types based on their cultural content, the latter types depending on the elements which the classifier wishes to select as criteria. Here only the major structural types and some of the associated cultural elements and environmental factors are outlined.

Considering pre-Columbian America south of Mexico, there appear to be sociopolitical units which fall into six major classes of social structure: (1) Homogeneous Tribes, (2) Segmented Tribes, (3) Politically Organized Chiefdoms, (4) Feudal Type States, (5) City States, and (6) Theocratic Empires. These structural types reveal increasing complexity, each successive type on the scale of complexity being distinguished by the structural feature or features which by addition creates greater complexity. It is assumed: (*a*) that the development of more complex structure consists in the reorganization of social relationships on the basis of such constant factors as kinship, age, sex, territory, and status, associated with such prime social functions as economic pursuits, warfare, the settlement of internal disputes, ritual, ceremonial, recreation, and artistic activities; (*b*) that the immediate precondition for the reorganization of social relationships is the increase in population density and the appearance of a food surplus above subsistence needs; (*c*) that population density and the food surplus, in turn, are directly related to the totality of conditioning factors which influence food production. Only the first three structural types will be analyzed here, for they characterize social organization of the lowland tribes of America south of Mexico. Before going on to describe these structural types it seems necessary to discuss their preconditions and the complex conditioning factors which affect them.

II. FOOD PRODUCTION, THE FOOD SURPLUS, POPULATION, AND SOCIAL STRUCTURE

The relationship among food production, population density, the size of population aggregates, and the appearance of a food surplus above subsistence needs is evidently a complex one. Among both food gatherers and food producers improvement in the resource base or an improvement in the methods of exploitation usually means an increase in population density and the appearance of larger bands or villages. This process continues until the population in a given area reaches an optimum size, after which the population either expands territorially or limits its growth. As territorial expansion is not always possible internal checks to population growth must be operative, although perhaps not consciously recognized by the people themselves. There is considerable evidence to indicate that the small Indian tribal groups in central Brazil limit population growth. Illegitimate infants, deformed infants, and often twins are destroyed at birth; and more important is the fact that in many tribes women insist on a long nursing period (about three years) during which if they become pregnant they practice abortion and infanticide.

The fact that these same tribes raid each other for women and children, which seems to contradict a desire to check population growth, relates to different population problems. In small population groups the ratio between males and females born does not always balance, and the capture of women and children is one way of correcting this imbalance; the Terena, for instance, practice infanticide so that a male birth follows a female birth, or vice versa, by this means endeavoring to make the sexes numerically equal. Another factor is the ideal population structure which fits their particular kind of social and economic conditions. Economic processes and defense lay emphasis on the age group between 15 and 40, the younger and the older age groups being considered a burden. A low birth rate associated with the capture of young women and children able to walk and feed themselves appear to correlate with this type of population structure.

The information in the *Handbook* indicates that with the intensification of agriculture there is both an increase in population density and the appearance of a food surplus above subsistence needs. How does this come about? Increased productivity of land can have a number of consequences. If subsistence needs alone provided the incentives, cultivators would utilize smaller plots of land, the population of a given area would increase, and the cultivators would have surplus time to devote to domestic crafts, group rituals, arts, ceremonies, and sports. On the other hand, if cultivators worked full-time on areas as large as they could manage, they would produce a surplus above subsistence needs. But this surplus above subsistence needs would not come about automatically; some incentive or force would be necessary for its production. Craft specialization, occupational groups, and markets would be one condition that could provide this incentive. But if craft or regional specialization had not reached a level to create a market to absorb surplus food supplies, or had done so only to a limited extent, then we would have to look for other social motives and forces capable of bringing into being, concentrating, and utilizing the surplus.

These motive forces and incentives are evidently inherent in any tribal situation. Surplus time, we saw, would lead to a proliferation and elaboration of pre-existing noneconomic activities by group members as a whole. Surplus food supplies, on the other hand, would make possible the appearance of specialized groups to carry on some or all of these activities by the permanent withdrawal of members from agricultural production. Tribal rituals would become the prerogative of special priests, leading eventually to the formation of temples and priesthoods. Marked differences would appear in the nature of warfare, the status of war captives, and intertribal relationships. Instead of incorporating war captives into the tribe as husbands and wives, they could now be used as slaves; weaker tribes could be periodically plundered, or conquered and forced to pay tribute. Warfare, in both its acquisitive and defensive aspects, would tend to become permanent with the appearance of military establishments. But this would mean political organization with corresponding increase in the powers of chiefs, leading ulti-

mately to the appearance of a state organization. These developments in social organization are not directly caused by the capacity
of cultivators to produce increasing surpluses. Surplus producing
capacity is only the precondition. In fact these structural developments must take place to bring the surplus into being.

Major differences in surplus producing capacity are undoubtedly
related to technological developments. Intensive agriculture based
on irrigation is certainly a different technological system from
digging-stick, slash-and-burn agriculture. But the agricultural tool
system does not explain the appearance of a food surplus and of
complex social structures in the Circum-Caribbean lands, for the
hunting tribes practicing supplementary agriculture and the tropical
forest tribes who did not produce a surplus used basically the same
tool—the digging stick—with slash-and-burn as the method of clearing the land. It would thus appear that highly significant increases
in agricultural production can be brought about by factors other
than improvements in agricultural implements. Soil fertility and
its relationship to rainfall is a variable factor of great importance.
According to soil scientists, tropical rain forest soils in general are
low in fertility and quickly depleted by cultivation. Grasslands are
often composed of rich soils but owing to the heavy turf are not
easily accessible to digging-stick methods of agriculture. This is
true today in Brazil in the case of hoe agriculture. Once land goes
into pasture it is removed from cultivation until covered by second
growth which, when again cut down and burned, makes the soil
available to the hoe cultivator. The Circum-Caribbean lands evidently provided variable climate and soil conditions. Our sources
indicate the sporadic use of irrigation and the cultivation of two
crops a year, which would indicate reasonably rich soils.

Even though the list of crops cultivated in this area do not differ
much from those known to the cultivators in the Amazon rain
forest, there is a strong likelihood that there was a more varied
and balanced use of these crops. I have observed that although
the Indians in the Amazon Basin know a wide variety of plants
they tend to confine themselves to a narrow pattern of cultivation,
growing those plants that give the best yields and depending on
the river and forest for many other food products. The fact that
many of the Circum-Caribbean tribes lived away from rivers would
indicate that they had a much more balanced diet provided by

the cultivation of foods such as manioc, maize, potatoes, beans, peanuts, arrowroot, squashes, and a wide variety of fruits. With this more intensive cultivation there is the probability that some selection was practiced, which in time would lead to greater yields per species than was common in the Amazon forests.

Our sources indicate that there was an improvement in the methods of cultivation. Although the digging stick was still the primary tool, and slash-and-burn the prevailing mode of clearing the land, the use of such fertilizers as urine mixed with ashes and the irrigation of cultivated areas indicate a longer period of use of a given parcel of land. With a wider range of food plants used, some rotation no doubt was practiced, land passing from maize to root crops and on to fruit tree cultivation. Abandoned lands would in time be covered by trees and undergrowth and in due course would again be ready for another cycle of cultivation.

The increased possibilities of food production through agriculture would tend to draw productive effort away from fishing, hunting, and wild food gathering. Our sources state that the fields of the Circum-Caribbean tribes increased in size and that fishing and hunting in fact did become of minor importance in the pattern of subsistence activities, in contrast to the tropical forest tribes.

There are indications that some tribal groups in the Circum-Caribbean region domesticated the Muscovy duck and the guinea pig, and bred a vegetable-eating dog for human consumption.

III. SOCIAL STRATIFICATION

Social stratification, as distinct from individual differences in status due to purity of descent and prowess in social activities, appears to be closely associated with the capacity of social units to produce economic surpluses with consequent changes in both internal and external relationships. The Guaicuruan horse-using tribes of the Chaco represent stratification in its simplest form. The introduction of horses, sheep, and cattle into this area created a source of wealth which could be raided through surprise attacks and the driving off of the livestock. The capture of Indian slaves to take care of the livestock and to perform menial tasks for the owners now took on an economic aspect. The economy could now support a class of raiding warriors and the slave class itself. The economic characteristic of this organization was its dependence upon the *surplus producing capacity* of the Spanish settlements and of other Indian tribes which had acquired livestock. The Guaicuruan chiefly class did not concentrate and employ their traditional tribal productive surpluses for social purposes, for the tribe itself was not yet a surplus producing economy. Control by the chiefs over their warrior bands depended upon the individual success of these chiefs in war and on the acquisition of *loot* in which the warriors shared. The chiefs had no judicial control over the tribesmen nor control over their domestic, hunting, and agricultural activities. Although no permanent political structure appeared, a class of wealthy chiefs and a large class of slaves did appear, with the general run of tribesmen forming an intermediate class.

Social stratification on the Northwest Coast of North America was likewise related to the appearance of two kinds of economic processes: a subsistence economy based on fishing and hunting and a potlatch economy based on the surplus producing capacity of the fur trade, the surplus being used for prestige-earning ceremonies which in turn led to the appearance of a wealthy class with high social status. As in the case of the Guaicuru, no political organization appeared, the chiefs remaining ceremonial, economic, or war leaders of kinship groups, their ties to the members of their respective groups being composed of kinship rights and obligations.

This type of social stratification is clearly different from one in which the class position of the chiefs rests on political and economic powers not shared by other members of the tribe. Among the Arawakan Taino the chiefs were territorial chiefs with judicial powers backed by penal sanctions and with rights to requisition surplus wealth for both military and religious purposes. The private wealth of the chiefs was acquired by means of the agricultural labor of female slaves captured in war, while male captives were often reserved for religious sacrifices. Although this type of political structure and the social stratification associated with it was made possible by the surplus producing capacity of the economy, the political bond between tribesmen and chief was one of clientship rather than of kinship or serfdom. The tribesman provided food supplies and his services to the chief's war party as a matter of duty, in return for a share of the loot and for protection against counterraids. The chiefly class due to its greater wealth and to political prerogatives not shared by other tribal members was now able to express this social difference through distinctive social symbols and social behavior.

With the appearance of feudal-type social structure, social stratification takes on a new form. Tribal bonds as cohesive forces are replaced by an estate-like politically organized central nucleus which may well have originally been a conquering tribe to the head of which conquered peoples are linked by serfdom and the payment of tribute. Tribute payment makes possible a greater concentration of wealth for the display-use of the ruler and of the ruling class, the maintenance of a permanent military establishment, and for a priesthood.

Social stratification is in essence a horizontal segmentation of the sociopolitical unit, in contrast to vertical segmentation along kinship lines. Social stratification can appear among both Homogeneous and Segmented Tribes under conditions which make possible the acquisition of an economic surplus from foreign societies. This surplus is in the nature of a windfall and does not alter the basic economy of the tribe itself. If stratification appears among Homogeneous Tribes without a sib structure, it may well bring about an increase in population density through the addition of slaves, but as the tendency of stratification is to create endogamous horizontal groups this would work against the development of sibs and moieties. In other words, a Homogeneous Tribe may pass directly into a class-structured society without passing through a unilinear kinship phase. In a sib-structured tribe social stratification would tend to weaken the social importance of the sib structure.

The argument put forth in this paper is that the increase in the size of population aggregates is sufficient to account for the appearance of sibs and moieties. An alternative development may be the appearance of stratification under the special conditions just described. But a formal political organization and a class structured society can arise only when the economy of the sociopolitical unit itself is able to produce a surplus food supply above subsistence needs.

IV. TYPES OF SOCIAL STRUCTURE

A. HOMOGENEOUS TRIBES

These are small tribal units in which all relationships are in terms of kinship, the tribe being the only corporate named group. Internal structure reveals only evanescent conjugal families and extended families built around unnamed patri- or matrilineages, depending upon the rule of residence. This group operates within a defined territory which it will defend if threatened. In some cases the use of organized force against other groups is of such minor importance that political cohesion does not appear, tribal unity being maintained by periodic joint rituals, intermarriages, visits, exchanges of presents, and a consciousness of common descent. In other words, a homogeneous tribal group is an internally self-perpetuating, corporate, sociopolitical group identified by a name and an origin myth which defines true membership bilaterally through both father and mother back to the mythical ancestors. Most southern hunters and many tribes in the tropical forest and in the Circum-Caribbean area belong to this structural type. Good samples are the Yahgan, the Nambicuara, and the Upper Xingú tribes.

Homogeneous Tribes can be broken down into subtypes on the basis of kinship structure, residence and marriage rules or settlement pattern. If settlement pattern is selected we get: (1) a loosely integrated group made up of dispersed family groups, (2) groups made up of interrelated extended family bands, (3) a large single band, (4) a village tribe, or (5) a multivillage tribe. These differing forms of settlement can, if intensively studied, be accounted for by the differences in the physical environment, the nature of the ecological adjustment, and related subsistence activities.

I differ to some extent with Steward's definition of sociopolitical groupings as his definition pertains to the small tribal units which he calls Marginal. My experience has led me to believe that neither the conjugal family nor the extended family is the effective sociopolitical unit under native conditions. Although it is true that conjugal families and extended families can and do operate permanently as spatially separated economic units, as among the Guató and Mura, or temporarily, as among the Nambicuara and the Upper Xingú Basin tribes, these units are not self-insuring against economic and political risks nor are they self-perpetuating in time. Marginality in the economic sense implies a margin of subsistence with sporadic and uncertain surpluses. Lack of success in hunting and fishing, incapacity due to illness or injury, may drive a conjugal family to the verge of starvation. Economic insurance is secured through dependence upon near relatives. During the eight days the writer spent among one of the Guató groups he observed the presents of food given to an elderly couple who lived some distance from their relatives, and was informed at the same time of the custom among women of looking after each other's children if the mother was not able to do so. An extended family, on the other hand, although economically more secure, is, in a sense, politically marginal. An extended family usually protects its members, property, and sometimes its terrain against encroachments by the other extended families of its own group, but for security against outside attack related extended families band together.

Even more important than economic and political security is the fact that due to the incest bar these units are not self-perpetuating but depend upon one another for their re-creation through intermarriage which in time establishes lines of descent and unnamed lineage groups in accordance with the prevailing kinship system. A conjugal family which is always bilateral cannot come into being without the presence of two independent lineages. This is likewise true of an extended family. A Homogeneous Tribe, therefore, although composed of two or more lineages and their interlinking bilateral conjugal and extended families, contains no named corporate kinship groups, the only corporate kinship group being the tribe itself, the members of which define their totality of relationship in kinship terms.

The Yahgan local group, for instance, represents a very loose form of tribal unit. Although each conjugal family or a group of two or three families made up independent hunting groups, there was, nevertheless, a larger named group.

Each of the five dialectic regions was broken up into local groups, each of which appears to have been composed, mostly at least, of members related by blood or marriage (Koppers, 1926, p. 5). Each such local group had its own territory—that of Ushuaia, for instance, occupied 20 miles (32 km.) of coast line on Beagle Channel—and its own name derived from its locality. Like the dialectic groups, these local groups had no chiefs. The local group's chief function was that of holding the čiéxaus initiation rite. The leader chosen therefor had authority only so long as the rite lasted. As the čiéxaus rite was an educational device contributing greatly to social conformity and solidarity, the local group's political function was chiefly an indirect pedagogical one. Loyalty to fellow members of a local group existed, but was not as strong as that to one's own kinship group [Cooper 1946:94].

Another characteristic of these small homogeneous kinship societies is that they appear to have a minimal structural size below which they cannot fall without breaking down, and a maximum size beyond which they change structurally into something else. I am also inclined to believe that the social norms, that is, the kinship system, marriage and residence rules, and the ways of acquiring a wife, found among simple homogeneous tribes are designed to protect group survival on the minimal level. With numerical increase these norms persist and at some maximum point of expansion form the bases for a restructuring of the group. This process of growth and ultimate structural transformation is due more to the changes in the dimensions of the factors which affect structure than to necessary formal changes in them. Thus, the same technological system can form the basis of a homogeneous tribelet of minimal size, an expanded multilineal homogeneous tribe, or a complex segmented tribe, the basic variables being the carrying capacity of the resource base, the radius of operation from a given center, the man-tool productivity differential, and the consequent numerical increase and concentration of population.

The magnitude of the *minimal* structure among such groups depends upon the demands put upon it as an operational unit, in the first place, by the exigencies of the physical and social (foreign tribes) environment and, in the second place, by the kinship system that integrates it and maintains its continuity in time. The evidence in the *Handbook* and the summary statement by Murdock (1951) show that the predominant type of kinship system among the Marginals (tribes having no sib structure) in the south is Hawaiian and that as one proceeds northward Iroquoian terminology appears. These two types of kinship system which appear to predominate among the bilateral descent groups, which are here termed *Homogeneous Tribes,* give rise to two magnitudes of minimal tribal structure: (1) the two-lineage structure, and (2) the four-lineage structure. A bifurcate-merging system with Iroquoian terminology appears, from available data, to be associated with cross-cousin marriage, which can operate with the presence, originally, of two unrelated lineages that begin and continue exchanging marriageables—young men or women, depending upon the rule of residence. So long as marriageables are available the structure will continue. It can, of course, continue if marriages outside the named tribe can be arranged or if women can be captured from other tribes. These incorporations occur but under native conditions are uncertain. If more than two lineages exist in the tribe (sociopolitical unit) there is naturally no problem. But unless the two lineages which constitute the minimal level can continue exchanging marriageables the structure will break down.

The case of the Iwalapetí in the Upper Xingú Basin shows the breakdown of a tribal unit but also the possibilities for its reformation. The 28 remaining members were reduced to a patrilineage and were forced to marry out. But their children, owing to the cross-cousin marriage rule, can marry and reform the village. Kanato, my Iwalapetí informant, explained that he and his sister could reform a village of two houses if he and his sister both raised sons and daughters. At present he has a daughter and his sister a son. His brother-in-law is a Trumai who has consented to move to the old Iwalapetí village site once their children become of marriageable age. All that will be necessary will be an exchange of daughters between Kanato and his sister's husband. The nucleus of this tribe could be a two-house or two-family system which, with luck, could grow into two extended families and on to several lineage segments forming the basis of a dual division. The 25 Trumai, also, live in a two-house village, each house being occupied by a patrilineage (Oberg 1953).

Hawaiian kinship terminology, on the other hand, presupposes a larger effective social unit on the minimal level than a unit with

Iroquoian terminology associated with cross-cousin marriage. Whereas a cross-cousin marriage system can operate with the minimum of two lineages, a Hawaiian system with a defined second-cousin marriage rule appears to demand a minimum of four lineages, presupposing exchange of marriageables between lineages.

As the Hawaiian system of terminology predominates among the nomadic and seminomadic tribal groups of the southern part of the South American continent there must be something in the hunting-collecting mode of nomadic life which favors the prevention of the effective social unit from falling below a certain minimal size (four lineages or four extended families). This larger group need not be associated with collective activities but may appear due to the economic hazards faced by the conjugal family or extended family. Among hunting groups the burden of the hunt rests upon the adult males. Thus only less than half of the population are the effective food gatherers. Surplus producing capacity is low. Sickness or injury to the adult males spells danger. Dependence upon relatives meets these risks. In contrast, the smaller groups with cross-cousin marriage on the margins of the tropical rain forest are associated with agriculture. Even though men may clear and plant the fields, women take care of the fields and can plant and harvest along with children. The available working force proportionally is larger in these tribes, making it possible for a smaller social unit to survive.

Matrilocal residence among a significant number of Homogeneous Tribes may best be explained by observing the contexts in which it occurs, for what this practice does in a particular context is pretty well the explanation of its existence. Among the Caduveo and Umotina, both tribes being hunters, fishers, and supplementary cultivators, the native belief is that it gives the head of a conjugal family control over a greater number of men for economic purposes. In a society where the most useful producers and protectors are males between the ages of 15 and 40, this desire is understandable. Yet one may well ask what does a father gain by exchanging his sons for sons-in-law? The answer is that he does not really exchange sons for sons-in-law but trades his daughters for the labor power of his sons-in-law. The tie between fathers and sons is strong. The father rears his sons, trains them in economic activities, and assists them in their initiation into the religious life of the tribe.

When the sons leave home they remain sons, the father being able to call on them for assistance whenever necessary. The sons-in-law that live with him are under his control and act toward him as sons. It is true that if daughters went out in marriage the father would have sons-in-law, but his hold over them would not be as strong as over his own sons due to the absence of so deep a personal bond. It would appear that sons make a better second line of defense and security than do sons-in-law.

It follows, however, that sons away from home are helpful only if they are within a reasonable distance. If environmental circumstances favored a dispersal of extended families into widely ranging hunting groups, this advantage would be lost, the male members of the extended family depending upon brother and son relationships within either their own extended family or related male lineages for economic and political security. Although each case should be examined in terms of its special context, evidence points to the fact that the more nomadic Fuegian, Pampean, and Chaco hunting bands with strong lineages as predominant economic groups, practice patrilocal residence. Among the larger, more stable tribes further to the north, matrilocal residence appears to be more common. It goes without saying that control over manpower is just one factor related to the practice of matrilocal residence. Among sedentary groups where property is significant or where women are the prime cultivators the factors favoring matrilocal residence are quite different. The importance of patrilocal and matrilocal residence is that among Homogeneous Tribes it establishes unnamed patri- or matrilineages which appear to be the precursors of patrilineal and matrilineal sibs.

The numerical expansion of these minimal sociopolitical tribelets can lead to (*a*) budding through the permanent spatial separation of lineage segments, or (*b*) larger spatial concentrations which change their inner structure. When the resource base is narrow, that is, restricted to sea and shore line, to plains, or to dense tropical forests, the carrying capacity is limited by the availability of resources exploited by a given technology. As the group increases, the distance to be traveled from a campsite limits the size of the group; a point is reached when some will have to move to more distant areas. In these circumstances a segment of a lineage will separate and establish itself in a new region. But for reasons of economic and political security and marriage it will maintain its connections with the tribal core, periodically meeting with the rest of the tribe for ceremonies or trade. This type of organization prevailed among the southern hunters and is ably described in the *Handbook*. However, completely new sociopolitical units may appear when several lineage segments begin to meet to form an intra-marrying group, due to the increasing distance that separates these lineage segments from their original home center. Specific carrying capacities and travel distances appear to be important factors in determining the size of population units and their interrelationships.

In more favorable environments, which usually means an exploitation at one and the same time of river, swamp, savanna, and gallery forest for agriculture a much wider range of resources becomes available, as is true in eastern Brazil. Agriculture alone is a narrow adaptation and provides a large yield per cultivator only under favorable soil conditions, but when combined with fishing, hunting, and gathering, a heavier concentration of people in one settlement is possible. Here, again, each resource base has to be judged in its own right. Shallow, slightly muddy streams are more favorable for shooting fish with a bow and arrow than deep clear streams. Timbó fishing requires still, shallow pools of warm water for maximum success.

An area which is composed of several kinds of resource bases in close proximity permits a concentration of population. As a consequence the number of conjugal and extended families increases. As individual kinship relationships are determined by lineage ties, the problem of interlineage relationship arises. In a group of 50 to 100 individuals, kinship relationships can be determined on the basis of direct personal knowledge. So-and-so is my brother because he is the son of my father's brother. But in a group of 500 to 1,000 individuals separated into numerous lineage segments, exact relationship requires tracing descent genealogically back to some common ancestor. To overcome this, individuals are categorized on the basis of lineage interrelationships. So-and-so is my brother because he is a Turtle like myself. This same principle of creating named divisions in the original unity of the named sociopolitical unit, after it reaches a certain size, gives rise to named associations for games, rituals, and ceremonials. Individuals know their places, their functions, and obligations to other individuals in tribal life in terms of these new groupings. Individuals who have gone through the puberty rites together or who have similar supernatural experience give recognition to the common bond by thinking of themselves as a group, and express this group identity by a name. The principle underlying this process may well be related to the "span of attention" and "span of control" which are important in the organization of large administrative groups. The capacity of a single individual to know intimately the interrelationships of a number of other individuals is limited by his "span of attention." In a situation where control is necessary this difficulty is overcome by a delegation of authority to a leader of a named section or team. When control is not essential this difficulty is overcome by classing individuals into named groups.

B. Segmented Tribes

These are tribal units which are composed of named unilinear kinship groups, such as sibs and moieties, often with the addition of named associations and age grades. The precondition of increasing size of population aggregates related to an increase in the food supply is sufficient to account for the appearance of segmented tribes. As this type of structure is familiar to all students of social organization no detailed description is necessary. As unilinear kinship structures vary, a number of subtypes can be easily distinguished.

Segmented Tribes appear when it becomes necessary to identify and classify groups rather than individuals. A simple, bilateral system identifies and classifies only living named individuals, but it now becomes essential to identify and classify lineage segments. As a lineage is unilateral, all that appears to be necessary is to identify the relationships of lineage segments through unilateral descent and to give this grouping of lineage segments a name by which it can be identified in time generation after generation. In a Homogeneous Band or Tribelet with a name, an individual is a member of but a single named corporate group. Now, however, he is, in addition, a member of a corporate unilineal kinship group.

A dual division is implicit in a minimal two-lineage or two-extended-family tribelet perpetuated on the basis of cross-cousin marriage. Similarly, sibs are implicit in the segmentation of the two lineages into additional units. The numerically small tribes of the Upper Xingú Basin, who have the cross-cousin marriage rule, have the potentialities of moiety formation. Among the numerically larger Carajá villages with cross-cousin marriage the division into moieties has already taken place. Natural increases or incorporation of outsiders may also give rise to sibs through the same principle of lineage grouping and naming.

It would appear that with an increase in numbers a minimal four-lineage system with Hawaiian kinship terminology could separate into four named marriage classes, as among the Apinayé, or into four exogamous sibs. But it seems that a dual division is also implicit in this system, assuming a defined second-cousin marriage rule and an exchange of marriageables between the lineages. Lineage A would exchange marriageables with lineage B, but as the offspring of these unions would be siblings they would be prohibited from marrying. Lineage A then exchanges with lineage C and similarly lineage B with D, to maintain a balance. In the following generation lineage A can again exchange with lineage B and lineage C with D. With a defined second-cousin marriage rule the four lineages would divide into two halves, consisting of A and D on one side and lineages B and C on the other, the lineages belonging to each side never exchanging with one another.

Although it will be difficult to trace the transformation of a simple four-lineage system into a structure with moieties, sibs, and associations, the writer agrees with Steward that such possibilities are implicit in the simpler structures.

> Such developments cannot be attributed to diffusion from more advanced Tropical Forest neighbors, for they lacked them. The associations must be interpreted as crystallizations of the sex and age cleavages implicit in the Marginal cultures [Steward 1947:94].

To me, numerical increase and concentration appear to be the principal factors affecting this change. If a greater body of information can be gathered to substantiate this thesis, it will help to explain the apparently anomalous fact that tribes with the same type of technology can have social structures which differ as widely in complexity as do Homogeneous and Segmented Tribes.

C. Politically Organized Chiefdoms

Tribal units belonging to this type are multivillage territorial chiefdoms governed by a paramount chief under whose control are districts and villages governed by a hierarchy of subordinate chiefs. The distinguishing feature of this type of political organization is that the chiefs have judicial powers to settle disputes and to punish offenders even by death and, under the leadership of the paramount chief, to requisition men and supplies for war purposes. Unity is achieved by federation, the acceptance of political authority resting on common interests and ultimately on the recognition of common tribal descent. There are no standing armies, permanent administrative bodies, subject tribes, or payments of tribute. Wealth in the form of property and slaves acquired through war, along with war honors, set the chiefs apart as a class with the highest status. The relatives of chiefs and outstanding warriors constitute a class with high rank, often described as a nobility, followed by the great body of common tribesmen. Slaves, as always, constitute the lower class. Chiefs have large numbers of wives, are carried in litters, live in large houses, are addressed by a string of titles, and often speak to the commoners through an intermediary. The Calamari, Quimbaya, Tolú, Cenú, and Mompox of the northern lowlands of Colombia appear to have had this type of social organization, and a good example of this type of structure is provided by the Arawakan Taino of the Antilles as described by Rouse (1948:528–29) in the *Handbook:*

On Hispaniola the Spaniards observed five provinces, or chieftainships, not counting that of *Ciguayo,* which will be discussed below in connection with those people. These provinces are shown on map 10. Magua, in the northeastern part of the island, was the most populous. The wealthiest and most aristocratic was Xaragua to the southwest; it was the model of refinement in customs and manners. As shown on map 10, each province had its own chief, called a "cacique." In addition, there are said to have been some 30 subchiefs in control of local districts within each province and 70 to 80 headmen in charge of the villages of the province.

Each chief, subchief, or village headman seems to have governed the village in which he resided. He organized the daily routine or work, arranging for hunting, fishing, and tilling the soil. He was also responsible for the storage of extra provisions and for their ultimate distribution among the villagers. His was the largest canoe in the village and he probably directed transportation. He acted as host to visitors and conducted relations with other villages, through their chiefs, subchiefs, or headmen. He was the leader at feasts and dances, and, having learned the songs by heart, he also directed the singing. His were the most powerful zemis in the village, and he organized their worship by the villagers. His authority is said to have been despotic; he could order the death of his subjects, and they had to obey his commands to the letter.

The authority of the headman apparently extended no farther than his own village, but the subchief also had a certain control over the other villages in his district, while the chief's authority extended over the entire province. The chiefs and subchiefs exacted no tribute from their subordinate villages, but they had the power to requisition agricultural or military services. This power may have been quite nominal and dependent largely on the personalities of the chiefs and subchiefs for there is some evidence that it shifted considerably from time to time.

The precondition for this type of social structure is the appearance of a food surplus and its association with the new feature of political organization and marked class stratification.

Although not specifically the task of this paper, I would like to add short notes on the remaining three of my six major types of social structure in order to show that the same basic forces were operative in their formation as in the three simpler types.

D. FEUDAL TYPE STATES

When tribal cohesion, as the basis for territorial political organization, is replaced by the institution of serfdom maintained by military power, we may speak of the existence of a Feudal Type

State. This type of organization appears to be associated with the presence of a strong ruler, a hereditary nobility, and a specialized priesthood. To the landscape dotted with villages and homesteads are added two new features, the palace and the temple. These developments are made possible not so much by a greater surplus producing capacity of the cultivators but by a greater concentration of wealth at the disposal of the ruler, nobility, and priesthood through tribute payments and other exactions collected from a large conquered population. A slash-and-burn, digging-stick economy can maintain this type of structure provided that the ruler can control a great number of digging sticks. The Chibcha of Colombia seem definitely to have reached this stage of development. The information concerning the Nicarao of Nicaragua appear to indicate that they too had a Feudal Type social structure.

E. CITY STATES

With the appearance of City States in the coastal valleys of Peru, like Chan Chan for example, there is a radical change in social structure as well as in the underlying economy which supported them. Intensive agriculture based on irrigation made possible large permanently settled population aggregates. The capacity of cultivators to produce a surplus increased to a point where craft industries could develop far enough to lead to the appearance of occupational groups, which, in turn, gave rise to markets in which both domestic and foreign commodities could be exchanged. To the palace and the temple are added the market place and the workshops of the artisans, living quarters of those who serve the rulers, nobles, priests, and the headquarters of specialized officials who constitute a government. Urban society develops an overlay of cultural features not shared by the people of the countryside, who maintain the older folk ways of the village and homestead. Urbanization creates a separation between country life and city life, a division which is considered the basis of civilization.

F. THE THEOCRATIC EMPIRE

By linking the political and tribal units of varying complexity of the highlands and the coastal plain into an empire, the Inca were able to organize the economy of an enormous area. The productivity of irrigation agriculture was sufficient not only to support a dense rural population but to maintain a political and religious superstructure. Land was divided into three parts, the produce of one part going to the upkeep of the state, the produce of another for the maintenance of the religious organization, while the third part sustained the rural workers. Although these parts were not necessarily equal, the system does indicate a surplus producing capacity far superior to any in pre-Columbian America south of Mexico. This surplus was concentrated through the agricultural tax, and was used for the support of the ruler, the upper class, the priesthood, the army, the officials, and the craftsmen. Labor service built and maintained the temples, roads, and other public works. These sociopolitical tendencies were inherent in the antecedent sociopolitical structures and developed due to the availability of a surplus food supply and the consequent possibility to withdraw large segments of the population from agricultural production.

SUMMARY

Progressive increases in food supply are considered the preconditions for the appearance of levels of increasing social complexity. The tendencies toward greater complexity, however, are inherent in the preceding configuration of social relationships. The first step in this process is the segmentation of a homogeneous kinship society into unilateral kinship groups due to the increase in population density. A second level is reached when a surplus above subsistence needs appears, permitting the withdrawal of individuals for the development of nonsubsistence activities. As the surplus increases this process continues, eventually leading to urbanization, pronounced social stratification, and the territorial state.

Although the development of nonsubsistence activities is the force which extracts the surplus from the food producing process, it is not the cause of surplus producing capacity. The capacity to produce is related, on the one hand, to a knowledge of resources and technological devices and methods, and, on the other, to the highly variable conditions of the resource base. It is for this reason that particular subsistence techniques have not been emphasized. The correlation between social structure and such subsistence techniques as food gathering and agriculture is not a close one on the simpler levels of society. It is not the subsistence technique itself but the consequences it has on food supply that counts. Under favorable ecological conditions hunting, fishing, and the collection of wild food plants permits a greater density of population than rudimentary agriculture under unfavorable conditions. Moreover, slash-and-burn, digging-stick agriculture varies so much by specific environments that each situation should be evaluated separately in order to weigh its influence upon social structure. This statement in no way denies the effect of major developments in subsistence practices, like irrigation agriculture, and their correlation with social complexity. In this paper the relationship between social organization and subsistence and other economic activities has not been discussed, for the correlation here is of a different order.

Introduction to Social Structure and Sex Antagonism

In this contribution, Robert F. Murphy argues that while the psychological bases for hostility between the sexes are universal, its expression will depend on the social structure of particular societies. The Mundurucú are particularly interesting in this respect since the two sexes form "true social groups" divided not only in economic function, but also residentially and ritually. Such opposition between the sexes is found in many societies around the world but it is particularly common among the peoples of central Brazil such as the Tapirapé (see Wagley in Chapter 9 of this volume), the Bororo (J. C. Crocker 1969), the Timbira (Nimuendajú 1946) and others, all of whom have exclusive men's cults, men's houses (or sleeping areas) along with uxorilocal postmarital residence patterns. Ritually expressed sex antagonism may thus be regarded as a common trait of much of central Brazil, a parallel which calls for explanation.

The Mundurucú are a particularly interesting tropical forest people from a variety of points of view besides the subject of this paper. They present perhaps the only documented case of a transition from a patrilocal, patrilineal society to uxorical, patrilineal (Murphy 1956, cf. Murdock 1949:216 ff.). *Mundurucú Religion* (Murphy 1958) is one of the few monographs devoted especially to religion and myth in South America and its material has been extensively utilized by C. Lévi-Strauss (1969). Murphy has also subjected Mundurucú warfare practices to a functional analysis, finding that a hostile posture toward outside peoples contributed to the internal social cohesion of the Mundurucú, compensating in part for the disharmony between residence and descent rules (1957; see also Wilson 1958; Vayda 1961b). The transition from tribal life based on horticulture and hunting to a dependent status as gatherers of natural rubber has been described in a classic article called "Tappers and Trappers . . ." (Murphy and Steward 1956) which exemplifies parallel processes of culture change through a comparison to fur trapping among the Northeastern Algonkians of North America. One of the conclusions of the latter article is that, "When the people of an unstratified native society barter wild products found in extensive distribution and obtained through individual effort, the structure of the native culture will be destroyed and the final culmination will be a culture type characterized by individual families having delimited rights to marketable resources and linked to the larger nation through trading centers" (1956:353). This process has numerous parallels in South America, including not only the other groups which turned to rubber gathering but also gatherers of Brazil nuts (cf. Laraia and Da Matta 1967) and riverine fishermen. The principal source on the Mundurucú is Murphy's *Headhunters' Heritage* (1960), which should be consulted by students interested in learning more about this people.

Robert F. Murphy is Professor and former Chairman of the Department of Anthropology at Columbia University in New York. In addition to his work with the Mundurucú, Murphy has carried out research among the Tuareg (or "blue people") of North Africa, and he is very much interested in structural studies and dialectics. He is the leading exponent of Irish social anthropology, and has recently written a book from this point of view (Murphy 1971).

12. SOCIAL STRUCTURE AND SEX ANTAGONISM

ROBERT F. MURPHY[1]

THE PROBLEM

Theories of social and cultural evolution have tended to deal with the quantifiable as units of study. In a quite crude way, anthropologists have spoken of the "cumulative" nature of culture, its tendency to expand in gross inventory of cultural items. Others have dealt on a more sophisticated level with man's growing control over the environment and sources of energy. And still others have oriented their interest toward the social system and an implicitly quantitative gradient of complexity, or structural differentiation. This, I believe, has had great methodological merit, for we have thereby avoided qualitative judgment and the intrusion of wholly subjective criteria of evolutionary level. But in so doing, anthropology has elected to deal with culture only in terms of mass of traits or with problems having a societal rather than symbolic locus. Little attention has been given to the evolution of the cultural symbols themselves, except in terms of methodologically untidy references to the emergence of scientific rationalism, of man's increasing grasp of the reality principle.

It is perhaps extremely doubtful that all or even the greater part of cultural symbolism can be encompassed by a general evolutionary theory, and this is certainly not my intent in this paper. I wish rather to discuss a limited aspect of symbolic behavior and to relate it through functional analysis to social structure, a realm in which evolutionary process is more readily discernible. The particular symbols to be discussed are those that are amenable to analysis in terms of Freudian theory; that is, cultural forms that are clearly projections of unconscious psychological materials and processes.

Reprinted by permission of the author and the editors of the *Southwestern Journal of Anthropology*, Vol. 15, No. 2 (1959), pp. 89–98.

The notion that the psychic ontogeny of the individual recapitulates phylogenetic experience is well known in anthropology, though primarily through its notoriety. The student of the subject receives, however, the disturbing impression that although the theoretical explanation of recapitulation given by psychoanalysts is erroneous, it nonetheless has a strong element of empirical validity. Kroeber (1948:304), for example, in his descriptive generalization upon the face of "progress" says:

> the outstanding physiological events of human life; and the persistent tendency of technology and science to grow accumulatively—these are the way in which progress may legitimately be considered a property or an attribute of culture.

Kroeber attempts no explanation of his second and third criteria of progress, but there is nonetheless a clear implication in his statement that things that are normally repressed in higher civilizations are often institutionalized and formalized in primitive societies. Freud, of course, dealt with the same problem in *Totem and Taboo* and arrived at the conjecture that the early experiences of mankind are perpetuated by the "collective mind," a metapsychological concept analogous to the "racial memory" of Jung. Freud (1952:158) was aware that his hypothesis was untestable and he wrote of the problems involved in this view: "It must be admitted that these are grave difficulties; and any explanation that could avoid presumptions of such a kind would seem to be preferable." It is the purpose of this paper to attempt such an explanation. As such, it is frankly exploratory.

The problem at hand is extremely broad and can, perhaps, be best approached on the level of system discourse. I choose, however, to make my point through analysis of the men's secret society among the Mundurucú Indians of central Brazil. The use of such an example has a certain merit inasmuch as similar organizations and their related symbolic complexes have been studied by psychoanalytically-oriented scholars and also because the widespread distribution of closely analogous phenomena makes comparative study possible. Men's secret societies in such diverse locales as Africa, Melanesia, Australia, and South America exhibit regularities of such a high order that they have long attracted the attention of anthropology. Webster (1908) considered them in terms of his overall scheme for the evolution of associations. Lowie (1947:313), on the other hand, thought the similarities between the cults to be so great that they could only be explained by diffusion. It must be admitted that secret society culture was no doubt frequently communicated from group to group and may even have been brought to the New World by a migrant Paleo-Mongoloid population. But this hardly explains the persistence of the complex or the bases of receptivity in the borrowing groups. And beyond this, secret societies are fundamental to the social structures of many primitive peoples and are not things that are simply copied and borrowed, like a pottery design. In short, some special explanation of a sufficient causal—and functional—kind is necessary to explain their wide distribution in the face of vast geographical discontinuities.

THE MUNDURUCÚ MEN'S CULT

The physical and social separation of the sexes among the Mundurucú is quite complete. The dwelling houses, of which there are usually three to five in each village, are the residences of the females and prepubescent boys. Each houses an extended family, the membership of which is determined by matrilocal residence; it is thus composed of a group of women related in the female line. These units are not, however, matrilineages in the formal sense of the term, and they have no legalistically identifiable corporate character. Formal descent is traced, rather, through the male line, for the Mundurucú have patrilineal clans, phratries, and moieties. The unilineal descent groups lack local nuclei due to the rule of residence, and their membership is scattered throughout the several Mundurucú villages.[2] The corporate character of these unilineal descent groups has, accordingly, become almost obliterated. The relative absence of such corporate units has had an interesting effect. The presence in many matrilocal societies of formally constituted matrilineages within which men exercise decision-making functions militates against the distant removal of a man from his natal household. The absence of such units in Mundurucú is correspondingly accompanied by absence of local endogamy. Villages are by no means exogamous, but most of their adult men come from other communities through marriage.

Those men who leave their native villages for residence in that of their wife are not tightly incorporated into a household unit, for all post-pubescent males reside in the village men's house. There, they sleep, eat, work and relax. Only the passage of time and the arrival of children establishes closer bonds with the household of the wife. For the most part, the life of the male is centered on the men's house, and each sex is a self-consciously solidary unit as opposed to the other, and mutual antagonism is often displayed on ritual, and other, occasions. Opposition between the sexes as groups is, of course, complemented by the residence arrangement; the village males are outsiders and the females are natives; lines of sex antagonism are thus coincident with those between affinals.[3]

The social segregation of the sexes is continued within the division of labor. Men hunt, fish, and clear land for gardens. The women plant, harvest, process manioc flour and all other foods, and tend to the household chores. The only tasks in which men and women work together are the planting of manioc and the collection of fish killed with timbó poison. Communal work is common among the Mundurucú, but it rarely transcends sex lines. The men of a village often hunt as a group, and all the women of the community usually help each other in manioc processing. Thus, the sexes often operate as work groups, but their tasks are well-defined and do not overlap. Beyond the basic sexual division of labor there is little further differentiation of work; the hereditary shamans and chiefs ply their specialties but they otherwise take full part in economic production.

Mundurucú culture is strongly male-oriented. The most highly valued body of traditional activity relates to warfare and hunting, and these pursuits are also the subject of the principal Mundurucú ceremonies. The woman is supposed to be docile and submissive, obedient and faithful to her husband. In actual practice, however, the separation of the sexes and the marginal participation of the men in the extended families of their wives inhibits the direct and personal exercise of authoritarian control of men over women.

There are, however, ritual techniques for the ordering of relations between the sexes that are an integral part of the total men's organization. Attached to each men's house is a small, completely enclosed chamber that houses the village's sacred musical instruments (*karökö*). These consist of a set of three hollow wooden cylinders, into the open ends of which are inserted reeds. When the reed is blown, the cylinder emits a deep vibrant sound. The instruments are completely taboo to the sight of the women, and the doorway to the *karökö* chamber is arranged in the form of a baffle in order to prevent even a casual and inadvertent female glance. The instruments are believed to harbor spirits that protect the villagers from harm and aid in the maintenance and increase of the supply of game animals. In order to secure this benevolence, the supernaturals must be pleased by a daily offering of food and the frequent playing of the instruments. Through their control over the *karökö* the men thus play a vital part in the promotion of animal fertility and social well-being.

That the sacred musical instruments are secret to the women has further significance in the rationalization of sex roles and the validation of the superordinate position of the male. The necessity of secrecy is based upon the belief that the sex controlling the *karökö* thereby achieves dominance. This is seen most clearly in the myth of the discovery of the instruments. According to this tale, three women were walking in the forest when they heard music that seemed to emanate from a lagoon. They investigated but saw nothing except fish swimming in the waters. Each woman caught one of these fish, and it immediately turned into a *karökö,* giving a set of three. The women played these instruments daily until discovered by one of the men, who induced them to bring their find to the village. They did so, but the power contained within the *karökö* enabled them to seize the men's roles and prerogatives. The women occupied the men's house, and the men lived in the dwellings. While the females did little but play the instruments the men had to make manioc flour, fetch water and firewood, and care for the children. Their ignominy was complete when the women visited the dwellings at night to force their attentions upon them ("Just as we do to them today," added one informant). But the women did not hunt and therefore could not make the ceremonial offerings of meat to the *karökö* spirits. The men, as the hunters, threatened to withhold the offerings of game, and thereby incur the displeasure of the spirits, unless the women yielded the instruments. The women were forced to submit and sex roles became as they are today. But the men must still guard the *karökö* from the women if they are to keep their dominance.

I was unable to obtain an actual case in which a woman spied upon the sacred instruments, but the Mundurucú men were firm in their insistence that any such violation would be immediately punished by dragging the offender into the underbrush and submitting her to gang rape by all the village men. Such offenses are no doubt rare, but the same punishment is meted out to women who, in other ways deviate markedly from sex-ascribed roles. These cases of gang rape usually concern women guilty of flagrant and aggressive promiscuity. Lest the impression be given that this is punishment for sin, puritanically defined, it should be made clear that most women indulge in an occasional pre- or extra-marital liaison. These peccadillos are the subject of gossip, but they are strictly private delicts. As such they are the proper concern of the offended husband, who usually attempts, with variable outcome, to beat his wife. On the other hand, when a woman is openly promiscuous and actually takes the initiative in sex relations, she is then manifesting behavior appropriate only to the male and thereby intrudes upon and threatens the masculine role. Her acts are thus a community concern, a public delict, and her punishment becomes the proper duty of all the village men.

Another occasion upon which gang rape is common has a peculiarly modern setting. Missionaries have established a boarding school among the Mundurucú and have gathered there some forty students ranging from about six to sixteen years of age. Parents are induced, usually against their will, to send their children there; the inmates generally make every effort to escape. Now when a boy flees the school, he has universal sympathy, but when an adolescent girl runs away, she is raped by the men of the first village near which she passes. Actually, there is considerable sympathy for her desire to leave the school, but none for the measures she has taken. By running away, she has placed herself beyond masculine protection, and she has also flouted male authority, albeit that of foreign missionaries whose objectives find limited support among the Mundurucú.

Gang rape occurs sporadically in many societies, including our own, but it seems bizarre in an institutionalized form. Actually, the Mundurucú are not at all unique, and we have numerous accounts of it in the ethnographic literature. Mead (1932:91–92), for example, reports gang rape among the Omaha. Although wanton women are stated to be the victims, her evidence suggests that these wantons are aggressive and selective in their love affairs, a clear parallel to the Mundurucú. The same author elsewhere states that the age mates of an Iatmul husband may "rape his recalcitrant wife into submission" at his request (Mead 1949:52). Another example is reported by Wagley, who observed the gang rape of a Tapirapé woman who refused to join the other females in manioc processing.[4] The woman in this case was unmarried and she was turned over to the village men for punishment by her brother. The action of the Tapirapé brother suggests that the deviation of a female constitutes a crisis that requires direct and immediate action regardless of bonds of kinship. The latter become eclipsed and secondary, and the maintenance of sex roles and sex groupings can thus be seen as a primary structural element in the society. This is evident in Mundurucú gang rapes. Not only are the exogamic restrictions connected with moieties and clans disregarded, but in at least one instance a true patrilateral parallel cousin took part in the assault.

INTERPRETATION AND ANALYSIS

The symbolic behavior discussed in this paper, however exotic, is nonetheless quite meaningful. Using a Freudian analysis of symbols, one of the most striking features of the whole complex is the form of the sacred musical instruments themselves.[5] Such objects, usually called flutes or trumpets in the literature, are quite commonly used for roughly the same purposes in men's secret societies in other groups. Functionally, they are equivalent to the more widely distributed bull roarer. Both emit deep, vibrant sounds and are used in some way to control the female portion of the population.[6] The bull roarer has usually been interpreted as a phallic symbol by students of Freudian inclination. I accept this view and would extend it to the more clearly phallic tubular wind instruments. The identification of the latter as a phallus depends upon much more than their external form, persuasive though this may be, for the Mundurucú men consciously believe their power and dominance to rest in their possession of the *karökö*. Moreover, the fertility and well-being aspect of the sacred instruments and their spirits gives the men a role in a normally female realm. It is instructive to compare these phases of the Mundurucú men's cult with that of the Mountain Arapesh:

> Among the Arapesh the *tamberan* is the embodiment, in some noise-making device, of the spirit of the male rituals in which the adult men assert their solidarity, reaffirm their masculinity, and produce growth and welfare for all the people.[7] (Mead 1940:426).

Thus far, I have stated that the secret instruments are phallic in form and, as the repositories of male power, in function. From this viewpoint, the men ritualize their role with the symbolic equivalent of the male organ. That this interpretation is not completely far-fetched can be seen in the ritual of rape, for here the men quite actively and vigorously maintain their position with the real penis, and not a surrogate flute. And as one informant quipped with no little humor, "We tame our women with the banana." Here is the expression in verbiage and social action of phallic sadism and the fantasy of the penis as a weapon and a source of power. It should be noted, lest the impression be given of grim genital retribution, that the Mundurucú men look upon these subjects with some hilarity. Gang rapes are carnival occasions that become the topic of endless anecdotes told in men's houses. And the men also refer to the vagina as "the crocodile's mouth," a marvelous bit of imagery that expresses perfectly the latent antagonism between the sexes, so patently a part of all vagina-dentata motifs. That these subjects are looked upon as humor does not negate their significance; humor, after all, is a fruitful source of otherwise inaccessible data.

The forms of these secret musical instruments, whether flutes or bull roarers, obviously do not frighten or cow the women, phallic though they may be, for the women never look upon them. Rather, they serve as ego-props for the men themselves, and reflect an insecurity, a threat, that is clear in the Mundurucú myth recounted above. This tale is a true social charter inasmuch as it explains and legitimizes sex role differentiation. But in common with the origin myths of men's cults in many other societies, it refers to a period when the women held sway over the men. It is noteworthy that sex role differences are not viewed as being necessarily in the nature of things, given in biology and taken for granted, but depend rather upon a mythological self-assertion by the men. And the boundaries between the sexes must be constantly maintained through ritual and other more directly defensive measures against intrusions upon the male domain. The cultural evidence indicates that not only are the men insecure about their status, but there is fear that the women would attempt to arrogate their prerogatives, if allowed.

The cultural symbolism involved in the Mundurucú men's secret society may be seen as projections of the classic psychological themes of sex antagonism and ambivalent, perhaps incomplete, sex role identification. Sex antagonism is generally attributed in the psychoanalytic literature to the Oedipal situation and ambivalence toward the mother, thence through the mother-image to females, in general. The symbol system manifests another motif of Oedipal origin, that of castration anxiety, or general fear of emasculation. This is most evident in the vagina-dentata theme, but it also underlies the theme that male tenure of masculinity, and its social concomitants, is not absolute. It is at this point that the organ-envy component of sex antagonism becomes significant, for the cultural data imply a recognition by the men that the women desire their power.

Now if these are indeed the sufficient psychological bases of the symbolic accoutrements of the men's cult among the Mundurucú, and in other societies, we are faced with a number of difficult problems. First, the psychological factors outlined above are well-nigh universal in human ontogeny, if not completely so, whatever the culture. Also, is not sex antagonism, latent or manifest, equally a part of all human experience? Is it not ontogenetically functional to successful sex differentiation? Why then if sex differentiation, both social and psychological, is not completely determined by heredity and if females threaten males in most, if not all, societies, are we not all swinging bull roarers or playing sacred flutes? After all, any explanation of the men's cult that pretends to generality must tell us not only why it is present in some societies, but why it is absent in most.

I offer the hypothesis that though the psychological bases for these projective symbols approach universality, their integration into certain cultural systems is a function of social structure. A cursory survey of the ethnographic literature shows the men's cult to occur most commonly in societies that show rough typological congruence to the Mundurucú, and thus supports my previous analysis of the place of the organization in the latter group. This type society is simple and relatively undifferentiated. In such groups, the primary line of sex differentiation is not crisscrossed or blurred by multiple modes of role designation. Moreover, the division of labor is usually minimal—that is, between men and women. But we do not find the men's organization among the structurally most simple people in the world, such as the Polar Eskimo and Shoshone. It tends, rather, to occur in societies having larger local groups and in which economic cooperation is a stable and daily affair. In such a setting, members of each sex are in daily association and engage in common pursuits, frequently in cooperation, to the virtual exclusion of the other sex.[8] In short, the sexes are true social groups, and the locus of social control over the women is vested in the males as a social entity. Sexual solidarity is too strong in systems of this type for role regulation and enforcement to be otherwise. Institutionalized sex antagonism in these societies is thus not just functional to the sex differentiation of the individual, does not just provide a form of abreaction of primary experiences, but it also maintains the internal solidarity because of the fundamental importance of sex-role differentiation to the structure of these societies that we find that other modes of role ascription are suspended on those occasions when social control over women is forcibly exercised.

Related to this opposition between the sexes, there is a tendency also for men's organizations of the type under discussion to be associated with unilocal residence. Unilocality, especially when accompanied by frequent marriage outside the local group, as in Mundurucú, keeps consanguines of one sex together while sending those of the opposite away. Members of the opposite sex thus tend to be outsiders and affines, and the forms of opposition common to the latter relationships complement sex antagonism.

Moreover, in such systems, overt acts of hostility against women who are also close are less likely to occur; the role conflict inherent in our Mundurucú and Tapirapé examples is thus avoidable. Finally, that men's secret societies and their concomitants appear more frequently among patrilocal societies than in matrilocal ones may well derive from the fact that the latter tend toward local endogamy. Coextensive segregation along lines of both kinship and sex is thus inhibited.

CONCLUSION

I have explored in this paper a theoretical framework for the study of the evolution of symbols: a framework that recognizes some empirical validity in the Freudian recapitulation theory but which attempts a rather different explanation. My general thesis is quite simple. It states that the stuff of the unconscious tends to be expressed in cultural symbols where it serves some function in terms of social structure. And insofar as the latter can be studied in evolutionary terms, so also can we see certain projective institutions in an evolutionary perspective.

It will be noted that I have not attempted to relate the symbolism of the Mundurucú, or any other, men's cult to their specific techniques of child-rearing or to their modal personality types. Roheim (1934:165), for example, does this in his attribution of the Australian men's cult to an aggravated Oedipal situation. The sufficient psychological bases of these phenomena are too general in all cultures for such particularistic considerations to be relevant. It is this very similarity of human psychic development that accounts for the close parallels between men's secret societies throughout the world. If we are to seek efficient causes for the institutionalization of this unconscious material, however, we must look to social structure. That we Americans do not have bull roarers and so forth could hardly be due to absence of the Oedipal experience and mutual organ-envy. We have them with a vengeance. The symbolic behavior characteristic of the men's cult is absent because our society is not structured along the simple lines that would make such rites functional. If our primitive contemporaries use techniques that seem to derive from primal experiences, it is because they are grappling with primal problems.

NOTES

1. The author acknowledges with gratitude the support of a Faculty Research Fellowship of the Social Science Research Council during the writing of this paper. The helpful comments and criticisms of L. Bryce Boyer, M.D., are also gratefully noted.

2. See Murphy (1956).

3. This ideal form of opposition represents only a tendency, of course, for marriages between men and women of the same village are frequent. Also, the families of chiefs are patrilocal, and other patrilocal marriages occur sporadically.

4. Charles Wagley, personal communication.

5. I am deducing from Freudian findings here, not trying to prove them. My argument obviously rests in part upon the validity of this psychology, and in part upon its own internal coherence and its success in explaining a body of data.

6. The noise is commonly explained to women and uninitiated males as the voice of spirits; this is not the case among the Mundurucú. Whatever the rationalization of the sound, the acoustical qualities show strong parallels. This may well be purely accidental, but it merits further consideration.

7. See also Bettelheim's (1954) essay on the institutionalization of womb-envy in puberty ceremonies.

8. Lowie (1947:310) recognized the significance of the division of labor in producing what he called "sex moieties," although he did not systematically pursue this lead.

Introduction to Tropical Forest Hunters and the Economy of Sex

Long before the current interest in sexual politics arose, anthropologists were concerned with sex roles in different societies (cf. Margaret Mead 1935, 1949 and Robert Murphy in Chapter 12 of this volume). In the next article Janet Siskind advances a novel hypothesis relating sex roles and sexual behavior to the ecological adjustment of a lowland South American society. This imaginative proposal is particularly interesting in that it attempts to show how features of ideology may contribute to the adaptation of a group to its natural surroundings. It also provides a plausible psychological basis for a very prevalent pattern of male-female relationships in South America and elsewhere. In this case, women are both objects and actors in a system of incentives for behavior —hunting—whose outcome is beneficial to group survival.

Janet Siskind pursued her graduate studies at Columbia University and is presently Assistant Professor of Anthropology at Rutgers, State University of New Jersey, in Newark. This paper was researched and written while Dr. Siskind was Ogden Mills Fellow at The American Museum of Natural History in New York.

13. TROPICAL FOREST HUNTERS AND THE ECONOMY OF SEX

JANET SISKIND

The Sharanahua of the upper Purús River have been pacified for over twenty years, and only older men remember the days of raiding for women. They say those were bad years ("long ago before we were civilized") but their words seem to contrast with their enjoyment of the scenes they enacted, as one man after another picked up the war spears that had been made for me, gestured covetously at an imaginary woman, and demonstrated a thrust through the neck of her imaginary husband.

Frequent fissioning of villages and continuous raiding used to be common in many tropical forest Indian societies. While anthropologists have suggested that these patterns are ecologically adaptive in adjusting population numbers to their available resources (Vayda 1961; Goldman 1963), the data of the field worker show that this objective is rarely a motivating factor. Fission occurs as a result of social tension, and raiding is aimed at stealing women or revenge for previous raids (Carneiro 1970b; Chagnon 1968a; Goldman 1963).

These are not incompatible statements, if we can relate social tension and the motivation for raiding to an ecological cause. Our Indian informants need not be aware of this relationship, but it must be a mechanism that works. That is, the ecological factor must increase social tension and encourage raiding at times and in places where the results are adaptive.

My hypothesis is that an artificially or culturally produced scarcity of women provides a density-dependent mechanism that functions to disperse groups of hunting-and-gathering or hunting-and-agricultural populations in accordance with the availability of game, where game is the limiting factor. This hypothesis applies to hunting populations in which women provide the bulk of the food supply and where it can be established that protein resources are the limiting factor and their procurement the responsibility of men. In applying this hypothesis to South American tropical forest hunters and agriculturalists I will show how this mechanism produces social tensions and provides the motivation for raiding.

It is important to differentiate between "limiting factor" and "scarcity" (or "scarce"). "Limiting factor" is an ecological concept defined in a standard textbook as "the factor that first stops the growth or spread of the organism" (Clark 1954:20). The limiting factor may be salt or water, sweet potatoes or fish. It is whatever factor in the environment of a particular population can be shown by analysis to set the upper limit of density. For human societies the limiting factor or factors may be culturally as well as biologically determined since differing technologies create different environments.

"Scarcity" as used by economists is a relationship between culturally defined desires and culturally available means for their satisfaction such that the means are never sufficient to meet the desires.[1] Scarcity is in the eye of the native, as material desires are those that motivate the informant. Thus, in our own society scarce items include cars, hi-fis, and food, whereas the limiting factors might include oil or copper. In tropical forest hunting societies the anthropologist can attempt to demonstrate that game is the limiting factor, but his informants will tell him in words or in actions that women are the scarce items for which they strive.

Until fairly recently most students of South American tropical forest Indians assumed that for groups who combine slash-and-burn agriculture with hunting or fishing, land would be the determining factor that led to frequent moves of settlements. Carneiro showed in 1960 [see Carneiro in Chapter 7 of this volume–Ed.] that slash-and-burn agriculture is not necessarily incompatible with permanent settlement. In a more recent article, Carneiro contrasts the two major ecological zones of the Amazon basin: "one consisting of areas lying along the major rivers, and the other of areas located away from them" (1970a:245). In the interfluvial habitats of this latter type:

> . . . it is hunting, not fishing, which must be relied on for the bulk of the protein in the diet. This fact is of special significance for settlement pattern, since a heavy reliance on

hunting is incompatible with sedentary village life. Even communities as small as 15, which are characteristic of the Amahuaca, severely deplete the game in their vicinity in a year or two [245].[2]

The Sharanahua, who are culturally and linguistically closely related to the Amahuaca, were also residents of the interfluvial habitat, although in the past twenty years they have moved to the headwaters of a large river, the upper Purús. They used to live in larger settlements than the Amahuaca and used to move their villages every two to five years. Their subsistence is still based on the interfluvial pattern. A rough breakdown of their subsistence activities in 1966 showed that agriculture supplied 60% of the bulk of their diet, hunting 30%, fishing and gathering 5% each.[3]

In 1966 the village at which I worked, Marcos, was a year and a half old and consisted of eighty-nine people. The Sharanahua at Marcos compared their own game resources to those of their kinsmen at Curanja, a village of about one hundred people, ten miles upriver. The men at Curanja left early in the morning to hunt and did not return until late afternoon or early evening. Since at Marcos hunters expect to return by noon or shortly after, this late return is considered a sign that game is poor. The settlement at Curanja had been there for ten years. It was the site of a Dominican mission and, within a year after the mission was closed, the village dispersed. There had been continual references to the poverty of game, but no one ever suggested that it was difficult to find land for their gardens. It would appear that game, not agricultural land, is the limiting factor. I will discuss later why this rational dispersal as game drops off is not adaptive.

It is necessary to differentiate between a limiting resource and other important resources. Among the Sharanahua, sweet manioc is the most commonly eaten food. It is the bread and potatoes of every meal and snack. Bananas, plantains, maize, peanuts, and numerous gathered nuts and wild fruits are important as well. The loss of agricultural products in the diet would be as serious as the loss of animal protein. Yet, given the population size and available land, if one needs more vegetables, one simply works harder and plants more. There is no evidence that labor is a limiting factor here, although it could well be in other locations or with other crops. If, however, more time were spent on hunting, the Sharanahua would rapidly reach a point of diminishing returns, when more effort yields less game until finally this resource is exhausted. This distinction between "limiting" and "important" remains the same when vegetal foods are gathered rather than planted. If at some future time fish or domesticated animals provide a great increase in available protein, settlement size or duration may increase to a point where agricultural land becomes the limiting factor.[4]

With game identified as the probable limiting factor it is possible to apply directly the logic of students of animal ecology to the problem of population dispersion in accordance with the distribution of natural resources. In 1954 David Lack observed that "gregarious species tend to be spaced over the available ground, but unevenly, being nearer to each other where food is more plentiful" (274).

The problem of dispersion arises in part because of the variability of natural resources. If animals were evenly spaced throughout the interfluvial habitats of the Amazon basin, and if each species stayed together, the problem of spacing out hunting populations might be more easily solved. However, naturalists' reports and ethnographers' descriptions indicate that the Amazon basin is inhabited by the same species throughout its expanse. But in some areas game is far more abundant than in others, and there are few natural ecological boundaries that prevent the migration of game from one area to another.

It is, perhaps, for this reason that clear-cut tribal or group territories do not occur among South American hunters, since control of a territory usually would not lead to control of the game within it. In addition, the relatively small size of hunting groups in relationship to their hunting ranges would make active defense of a territory extremely difficult. This is not true of the riverine habitat, where control of the flood-plain and fishing resources in a lake or along a stretch of river was practicable.

The other problem of spacing populations is their tendency to increase. Thus:

If an animal is introduced to a new and favorable area, it at first increases rapidly, but it is soon checked, and thereafter its numbers, like those of other animals, fluctuate between limits that are extremely restricted compared with what is theoretically possible. It follows that natural populations are in some way regulated, and that the controlling factors act more severely when numbers are high than when they are low [Lack 1954:275].

A problem that I am not approaching in this paper is the regulation of population by direct limitation of births or by mechanisms that increase or decrease mortality. James Neel, who has worked for many years with tropical forest populations, points out that "most primitive populations practiced spacing of children" (in Chapter 10 of this volume). A Sharanahua woman practices abortion in order to space children at approximately three-year intervals, and they claim to possess a medicine that prevents conception permanently. Although the two problems of population regulation, dispersion and limitation, intersect, here I am only taking up dispersion.

In recent years many anthropologists and demographers as well as zoologists have been influenced by Wynne-Edwards' book *Animal Dispersion in Relation to Social Behavior* (1962). While some of his ideas are controversial, his outline of the problems that all animal populations confront in relationship to their resources is generally accepted and provides an extremely useful framework for studying hunting cultures. Wynne-Edwards follows Lack in observing that the limiting or dispersion of natural populations does not take place through the exhaustion of resources and subsequent starvation or migration.

He points out that the overexploitation of natural resources "reduces both the yield per unit effort and the total yield; in some circumstances, if sufficiently severe, it can damage the stock beyond recovery and even lead to its extermination" (1962:7). Recent studies of hunting and gathering peoples (Lee and DeVore 1968) support the observation made by Carr-Saunders (1922) that most primitive hunters are healthy and well-fed. Neel finds "that relatively uncontacted primitive man under conditions of low population density enjoys 'intermediate' infant mortality and relatively good health" (Chapter 10 of this volume). The evidence of long-time settlement of the tropical forest without exhausting the game supply as compared to the rapid extinction of game in "civilized" areas indicates a conservation-oriented adaptation of tropical forest cultures.[5]

Wynne-Edwards uses examples of modern fisheries to show that "the size of the optimum catch is not self-evident" (1962:7). That is, for any predator, human or animal, modern or primitive, game may fluctuate within a safe range, but there is a point where continual depredations will push this resource to extinction. The point at which it is noticeable that game is sparse may already be too late. It is for this reason that I suggested that rational dispersion, breaking up a village after game has become sparse, is usually not adaptive.

Since it has been shown that overexploitation usually does *not* occur, "it is impossible to escape the conclusion . . . that *something must, in fact, constantly restrain them, while in the midst of plenty, from over-exploiting their prey*" (1962:7). The restraint cannot be permanently set, for example, at four animals per person per month, since both populations and resources fluctuate over time.

Wynne-Edwards continues: "food is generally the ultimate factor determining population density" (11), but "it cannot be invoked as the proximate agent in chopping the numbers, without disastrous consequences" (13). He argues that a density-dependent mechanism must exist to regulate animal numbers. By density-dependent mechanism he means an indicator that is sensitive to a worsening balance between resources and population size, a homeostatic device that is triggered either by increasing population or decreasing resources and disperses or limits populations until the balance is readjusted.

"Free contest between rivals for any commodity will readily provide such an indicator . . . One of our guiding first principles, however, is that undisguised contest for food inevitably leads in the end to over-exploitation" (14). Within all human hunting societies direct competition over protein is eliminated by sharing meat. The *maloca* or communal house typical of the interfluvial Indians promoted conformity to the cultural rule that meat should be shared.[6]

To follow Wynne-Edwards one step further: "a conventional goal for competition has to be evolved in its stead; and it is precisely in this . . . that social organization and the primitive seeds of all social behavior have their origin" (14). Women are the conventional goal of competition between tropical forest Indian men. They are the incentives for hunting and the goal of raiding.

When I first went to the field I believed, as many anthropologists do, that hunting was an enjoyable occupation in and of itself; that, as Holmberg put it: "such pleasant occupations as hunting . . . and collecting . . . are regarded more as diversions than as work" (1969:101). After slogging through the tropical forest in the rainy season, wading through swamps up to the hips, picking off ticks, and avoiding stinging ants, I would question the idea that hunting is far more joyful than gathering or agriculture. I agree with Holmberg's second thought, when, apparently ignoring what his informants told him, he described at length that the food quest is "always punishing because of the fatigue and pain inevitably associated with hunting, fishing, and collecting food" (249).

If it were possible to measure the relative pleasure of a series of occupations, hunting would probably be no better nor worse than a multitude of others. Both the pleasures and the pains of hunting are related not only to the actual activity but to the implication that a good hunter is a virile man. Thus among the Shavante: "Hunting is the most common expression of virility. Shavante men enjoy it for its own sake and delight in it, if they are good at it, because it enables them to make a public exhibition of their manliness" (Maybury-Lewis 1967:36). Even the Yąnomamö feel obliged to provide meat for their wives and children, although not out of a sense of cherishing: "they genuinely abhor hearing their children cry for meat; this calls into question their abilities as hunters and marksmen, both of which are associated with prestige" (Chagnon 1968a:91).

Virility implies a positive response from women. Further, the culturally structured idea that a successful hunter is a virile man carries a sting: the unsuccessful hunter is by social definition not virile. Shavante women "receive an unsuccessful hunter with a marked coldness, even when there is plenty of other food in the household" (Maybury-Lewis 1967:36). Holmberg described the plight of one Sirionó, Enía, "who was regarded by everyone as a poor hunter . . . he was very unhappy about his lack of hunting ability, for he was being constantly insulted at drinking feasts and was almost daily ridiculed by his wife for returning from the forest empty-handed. Once he had possessed two wives, one of whom he lost" (1969:275). Holmberg taught Enía to use a shotgun, which improved his hunting and his prestige, and helped to gain him a second wife. Perhaps the most succinct expression of the connection between hunting and virility was made by a Sharanahua woman when the men of her household returned from the hunt tired, depressed, and empty-handed. In a voice that carried throughout the house she said, "There is no meat, let's eat penises."

In 1967 I kept a record of the hunting efforts of ten Sharanahua men over a month's time. The Sharanahua have two basic patterns of hunting. In the first, each man decides for himself whether or not to go hunting. He usually hunts alone and brings the game back to his own household. My record showed that older men hunted more often than younger men. Generally men with two wives hunted more often than single men or men with only one wife.

In contrast, during the special hunts—the second pattern—the young men (single or with one wife) always hunted actively. During one special hunt, despite the Sharanahua's fear of the forest at night, three young men stayed out until nine o'clock. They returned carrying two white-lipped peccaries. There are major differences between these two hunting patterns, which explain the sudden enthusiasm of young men in the special hunt. Nowadays, households are separated and no one but the women of the household knows whether or not a man has returned with game. Men face the ridicule of their wives if they return empty-handed, but single men have no one to impress in their own households.

The special hunt is started by the women. Early in the evening, all the young women go from house to house singing to every man. Each woman chooses a man to hunt for her, a man who is not her husband nor of her kin group, though he may be her cross-cousin, her husband's brother, or a stranger. The men leave the following day and are met on their return by a line-up of all the women of the village, painted and beaded and wearing their best dresses. Even the older men will not face this line without game, but, if unsuccessful, they beach their canoes and slink to their households by a back trail. The choice of partners is usually a choice of lovers, and many partnerships are maintained for years. I found it possible to chart the ups and downs of love affairs in the village on the basis of partnerships in the special hunts.[7] Most of the features of the special hunt were part of everyday life thirty years ago, when the Sharanahua lived in *malocas,* and men always had an audience for their hunting efforts.

For the Sharanahua as for other tropical forest Indians the incentive for hunting is to gain access to women, either as wives or as mistresses. One can see variations on a single theme from the crude gift of meat "to seduce a potential wife" among the Sirionó (Holmberg 1969:166); the elaboration of the special hunt among the Sharanahua; to the young Shavante's provisioning his father-in-law with game after the consummation of his marriage. "The partition for the newly-weds is therefore erected as a public statement by the wife's kin that the marriage has been consummated and that the young husband is now contractually bound to them. He is expected to send portions of the game he kills over to their household" (Maybury-Lewis 1967:92). Whether men prove their virility by hunting and thus gain wives or offer meat to seduce a woman, the theme is an exchange of meat for sex.

This theme is not unusual, but it cannot be understood by a direct appeal either to biology or psychology. That is, I know of no real evidence that women are naturally or universally less interested in sex or more interested in meat than are men. On the contrary, in terms of the reality of hunting societies, a more natural exchange would be hunted game for vegetable produce. Perhaps one of the major contributions of the symposium volume *Man the Hunter* (Lee and DeVore 1968) is the presentation of data from several hunting societies that lead to the thought that a more appropriate title for a discussion of this stage in human cultural evolution would be "Woman the Gatherer." Lee and DeVore point out that "Modern hunters . . . depend for most of their subsistence on sources other than meat, mainly vegetable foods, fish and shell fish. Only in the arctic and subarctic areas where vegetable foods are unavailable do we find the text book examples of mammal hunters" (1968:7). Women provide the bulk of the food supply in all other hunting and gathering societies. Although in tropical forest societies men are agriculturalists as well as hunters women are the primary producers of agricultural and gathered crops as measured by hours of subsistence labor. The exchange of meat for sex is an economic system, a system in which men strive to be good hunters in competition with other men in order to gain possession of or access to women.

A law basic to economic theory is that competition occurs only over scarce items. If women are to be the incentive for male hunting efforts, they must be scarce, since competition can occur only over scarce items. The traditional example of air as a free good may soon be lost, but at this date no one yet competes for unpolluted air. Scarce women are the "substitutes for the ultimate goal that should never be disputed in the open—the bread of life itself" (Wynne-Edwards 1962:13).

There are three common cultural means of making women scarce: (1) to limit sexual access by social rules of sexual morality; (2) to practice polygyny; and (3) to alter the sex ratio through selective infanticide or other means. Although it may be difficult to imagine a human society with no rules of sexual morality, that is, where sexual intercourse is left completely to individual choice and preference, a little thought will show that in such a society there would be no competition over sex. The strongest would not monopolize all the women, since he would have no investment in exclusive rights. The most beautiful might win all the men, but so would the rest of the women. Although rules of morality are in some areas applied to men as well as women, the double standard is more common, and there appear to be no cases of men being limited by sexual mores while women are immune. Rules of sexual morality can produce a short supply of sexually receptive women even in a monogamous system, since in hunting societies the necessity for spacing children usually leads to post-partum sex taboos.

Neither polygyny nor female infanticide alone can produce scarcity unless they are combined with rules of sexual morality, but either one will increase it. The choice of cultural means is influenced by factors outside of this discussion. Thus, polygyny seems related to the importance of women's labor; female infanticide may be used as a device for limiting the population by reducing the number of females who will grow up to reproduce.

Various combinations of polygyny and limited sexual access

appear the most common practice for tropical forest hunters. Even where the actual number of polygynous marriages is numerically small, its effect, as Harner (1963:57) has pointed out, is to produce an artificial shortage of women. Among the Sharanahua, though a minority of marriages are polygynous, these reduce the number of marriageable women in the preferred age categories, 16–20, and lead to marriages with child brides. This passes down the shortage of women to a still younger category. For my argument, however, numbers are less important than a belief that one should have more than one wife. This keeps married men in the competition, and women must, therefore, be won.

The scarcity of women is thus a cultural artifact which produces competition between men and provides incentives for hunting. It also provides the incentive for the widespread pattern in the tropical forest of raiding other villages or tribes for women. The practice of raiding itself keeps groups at a distance from one another, thus dispersing hunters, and a perennial motive of acquiring more women is a self-fueling reason to keep raiding.

The problem now is to outline how competition over women may increase as game decreases in relation to population and how this increased competition leads to a dispersion of hunting groups before any tightening of the belt or damage to the game occurs. The model described here is fairly close to the potlatch model of Suttles (1960) and Vayda (1961a), the pig feast model (Vayda, Leeds, and Smith 1961), and Rappaport's (1968) analysis of the ritual of *kaiko*.

Taking two imaginary villages within raiding range, let us assume that game is extremely abundant—monkeys fall out of the trees into the arms of the expectant hunters, tapirs stroll to the streams, herds of peccaries trample their way through the nearby gardens. This is only a slight exaggeration of what Chandless (1866) described on the upper Purús in 1869 when the Indian groups were few and scattered. Every man is a good hunter; only a small amount of time need be expended on the chase; women within the village are content; and young men raid for women back and forth between the *malocas*.

This idyll begins to shatter as game becomes less plentiful. Differences in hunting luck or skill begin to show. The less successful hunters go out more frequently, and their wives are cold and verbally castrating, even though they are receiving meat through the sharing system. Husband's brother is the better hunter, and women are notoriously fickle. If poorer hunters hunt increasingly more often, while better hunters stay in the village with time on their hands and virility in their hearts, the chances as well as the suspicion that they are involved in love affairs increase. As social tension increases a village may fission, and less successful men may leave for a better area while each still has a wife.

Within a *maloca* the poor hunters are less likely to raid for women, since they will stand a good chance of losing them to the better hunters in their own *maloca*. If the entire *maloca* is hunting poorly, the men will not be likely to raid since more women will put even more pressure on all the men to hunt. If the men of one village are continually more successful than another, they will increasingly raid the other, taking women and occasionally killing other hunters until finally the weaker village flees. This outcome to tropical forest patterns of raiding is suggested by Carneiro (1970:735).

Basic to this argument is that differences in hunting skills among men are apparent only when game is not abundant. In hunting societies boys typically begin to handle a bow and arrow from the day they can walk. The only really poor hunter at Marcos, whose efforts invariably met with failure, had spent three to four years of his childhood with a Peruvian trader.[8]

My data show that hunters with less skill or luck even up their odds by hunting more often. In a location that is relatively rich in game such as the area around Marcos, the two most active hunters went out eleven times in one month. They contributed more meat than other men, but their ratios of success to the number of hunting trys were not nearly as high as the ratios of some of the men who hunted less frequently.

Direct testing of this hypothesis is difficult since estimating the point of diminishing returns on hunting presents as many problems to an anthropologist as to an Indian hunter, and a decade would be a sensible time period for testing it. In addition, contact has eliminated raiding throughout most of the tropical forest and has reduced or influenced the fissioning and re-establishment of settlements. It would be somewhat simpler to test a corollary of this hypothesis cross-culturally.

The corollary is that in areas where the balance between game and population density is most delicate, that is where game is more difficult to get and where population density is stabilized at a lower amount of protein per person, the scarcity of women will be more extreme to provide a more refined or more responsive index of competition. Competition will be more intense and village cohesion more fragile. If my hypothesis is correct, all other things being equal, in areas of abundant game in relation to population, sex mores would be more relaxed, and the distribution of women would be relatively equal; in areas of sparser game in relationship to population density, sex mores would tend toward the puritanical, and the distribution of women would be unequal.

Although Chagnon does not present figures on protein intake in his monograph (1968a), the Yąnomamö appear to tend toward the extreme of low protein. "Game animals are not abundant, and an area is rapidly hunted out . . . I have gone on five-day hunting trips with the Yąnomamö in areas that had not been hunted for decades . . . we did not collect even enough meat to feed ourselves" (33). Chagnon estimates that 85% of the food produced by the Yąnomamö is domesticated crops, yet none of these yield an adequate source of protein.

Yąnomamö men severely punish their wives for infidelity (82). Twenty-five per cent of the men in one village had two or more wives (75); one important man "has had five or six wives so far" (14), another man is described as having four wives (94). Since the Yąnomamö also practice female infanticide (74), they are faced with a relatively severe shortage of women. They raid frequently, which, as Chagnon indicates, leads to dispersion: "a Yąnomamö group would remain indefinitely in the area it settled were it not for the threat of raids from warring neighbors" (39).

The Sharanahua tend toward the other end of the scale. Game is relatively abundant. In a typical special hunt, eight men hunting for one day returned with two white-lipped peccaries, one large monkey, and one bird. During these special hunts sexual license is expected, and in everyday life extra- and pre-marital love affairs are common and rarely punished. While 20% of the men have two wives, none has more, and female infanticide is not practiced. The Sharanahua no longer raid, but even in the past they appear to have been moderate in their raiding.

In order for this type of mechanism to work, the participants must be unaware of the artificial nature of the goal for which they are competing. At the point where hunters become aware that "a woman is just a woman" and that the distribution system permits some men to lie in their hammocks while others search for game, the system breaks down. Therefore, it is essential that certain beliefs be shared by all the actors in this scheme. It is necessary to believe that men are hunters, that good hunters get more women, that women are scarce, that scarce (virtuous) women are good, and that non-scarce (loose) women are bad. These are common themes in a wide array of South American myths,[9] and these are part of the consciousness structured by a hunting society.

For the sake of examining my hypothesis I have presented a simplified model of tropical forest culture. Culture is multi-determined and, in order to clarify one strand of determinants, many others must be put aside. As one ecologist warns, "It is not always easy to single out the limiting factor and sometimes two or more factors combine to provide the limiting influence" (Clark 1954:20). The effect of combining agriculture with hunting, village life with roaming game, has certainly influenced marriage and raiding patterns in the tropical forest. Settled hunters have problems that nomads can ignore. Villages can be moved but not far, or else all the crops of the previous planting will be wasted, and new crops take six months to a year and a half to grow. This is probably one of the reasons for dispersion occurring by means of the conventional raiding patterns peculiar to this area.

I suggest that my hypothesis could be applied beyond the region of the South American tropical forest, but that different methods of dispersion should be investigated. For example, today among the Sharanahua and other Indians where raiding is outlawed, men are often forced out of their own villages by the rule of matri-locality as fathers hold onto their scarce daughters. In other regions dispersion may occur through complex systems of marriage in which competition based on the scarcity of women is intensified by the wide extension of incest taboos. The assumption of studies of marriage as a series of exchanges between groups is precisely that women are economic, that is scarce, items. Only a careful analysis of field data can establish what the limiting factor or factors are in any cultural-ecological niche. It will prove productive to examine the relationship between such factors and the culturally defined mode of allocating scarce women.

NOTES

1. Although economists avoid defining a concept as basic to their discipline as scarcity, accepting instead that "a world without scarcity . . . is not our world" (Alchian and Allen, 1965:13), their use of it indicates that it is culturally determined. Thus economists make statements such as: "material wants are for practical purposes, insatiable, or unlimited" yet they add: "this is particularly so in the United States" (McConnell, 1966:24).

2. Lathrap also divides the Amazon basin into these two habitats: "By way of contrast the jungles away from the major rivers have meager game resources. The fishing potential of the smaller tributaries is limited . . . The extreme fragility of the game resources in the jungles away from the rivers was a dominant factor affecting human utilization of these areas" (1970:36).

3. This proportion seems to be changing as the Sharanahua adapt more to the large-river habitat. When I returned to Marcos in 1969, three men had learned to make fish nets, and fishing seems to be gradually becoming more important.

4. This is what Harner suggests occurs with a shift from game to fish as the source of protein (1970:71).

5. The primitive cultures the anthropologist studies tend to be conservative and, therefore, conservation-oriented. There is no implication in the light of culture history that the cultures described here are either typical of human culture or permanently stable. Progress and the destruction of natural resources may be far more typical of human history than the temporary, although for a few thousand years, conservation-based cultures of the South American tropical forest.

6. Although the Sharanahua (Siskind 1968) and the Sirionó (Holmberg 1969) often avoid sharing by eating meat secretly, this simply affirms their own belief that meat should be shared.

7. Similar special hunts are reported for the Cashinahua (Kenneth Kensinger), the Canella (Nimuendajú 1946), and the Krīkati (Dolores Newton personal communication).

8. Enía, the poor hunter described by Holmberg, had a very similar history of being away from native life and the automatic learning of hunting skills during childhood.

9. The two myths that seem particularly related to these themes are those that describe the tapir who seduces women, in which the relationship between meat and sex is graphically illustrated, and both free game and free sex are appropriately eliminated from society. The other set of myths that deal with these cultural principles are those that explain the origin of women, in which it can be seen that women are different from men; that men previously got along without women, i.e. did not need women's labor; and that there are not very many women, i.e. women are scarce.

Introduction to Privacy and Extra-Marital Affairs in a Tropical Forest Community

Using the social structure of a small tropical forest Indian community as his framework, Thomas Gregor focuses on a subtle aspect of social life neglected by structural analyses: privacy and the lack of it. Gregor's approach is influenced by Erving Goffman (1959) and Robert Murphy (see Chapter 12 in this volume and his discussion of image management in "Social Distance and the Veil," 1964). These writers make an analogy between social life and a stage, with the actors upon it realizing social goals through the manipulation of roles. Perhaps the most important aspect of this approach is the way in which information is managed by actors. Each one seeks to limit and otherwise control the kind and amount of information held by the others regarding his motives, goals and activities.

The Mehinacu are, like the Kuikuru, one of several small tribes located in the Upper Xingú Reservation in Brazil. Gregor has described ritual isolation among them in another article (1970) and also discusses privacy in a cross-cultural context (J. R. Roberts and Gregor, 1970). Further information on the sex lives of Xinguano Indians may be found in Carneiro (1958). Further information on the peoples of this region may be found in R. Murphy and B. Quain (1955) and Oberg (1953) as well as the items cited in the introductions to Dole's and Carneiro's articles.

Thomas Gregor holds a Ph.D. degree from Columbia University and is presently Assistant Professor of Anthropology at Cornell University, Ithaca, New York. In addition to his research in Brazil he has conducted field work among the Jicarilla Apache.

14. PRIVACY AND EXTRA-MARITAL AFFAIRS IN A TROPICAL FOREST COMMUNITY[1]

THOMAS GREGOR

I

Sex in nearly all societies is a matter of considerable delicacy, demanding privacy and discretion. Extra-marital sex requires even more careful management, since an affair is a potentially disruptive involvement challenging the stability of vital social relationships. What strategies do lovers employ to conceal secret trysts in a community where everyday conduct is highly visible, and where there are few barriers to the flow of information? In this article we describe the techniques of conducting extra-marital affairs among the Mehinacu Indians of central Brazil, and explore the significance of securing privacy[2] in primitive communities.

The Mehinacu are a one-village tribe of fifty-seven Arawakan-speaking Indians living along the headwaters of the Xingú River. They and their culturally similar though linguistically distinct neighbors[3] subsist primarily on the slash-and-burn horticulture of manioc, and fishing. Kinship among the Mehinacu is reckoned bilaterally, and extends to every member of the tribe, although the precise genealogical connections are often unknown. Residence is ideally matri-patrilocal, but admits of so many exceptions that the actual pattern is best described as *de facto* ambilocal. Marriage is usually village endogamous to a classificatory cross-cousin. Ordinary social relationships are egalitarian in character, so that neither the chief nor the shaman are exempt from the day-to-day tasks of fishing and maintaining a garden.

Like many other tribes in the tropical forest of South America, Mehinacu men and women lead somewhat separate lives. They not only work apart, but conduct separate ceremonies, intertribal sporting events, and trading sessions. This separateness is supported by codes of pollution which hold that contact with the opposite sex can compromise the performance of the sex roles. Men are genuinely concerned about the dangers of female sexuality. Excessive intercourse is said to threaten a man's health and skills by stunting his growth, weakening his strength as a wrestler, and undermining his ability to fish and hunt. Menstrual blood is considered especially dangerous, because it causes sickness and cramps. A house's daily production of processed manioc flour is routinely thrown out if one of the women is found to be menstruating. There are times when even the mere thought of a woman may be foolhardy. A daydream about a wife or a mistress while alone in the forest is said to attract a demon in the guise of a beautiful woman who can carry a young man off to his death. Paralleling these beliefs are a set of restrictions that regulate the women's contact with the men, including rules against certain kinds of sexual behavior, and injunctions against caring too much for a man.

The exclusiveness and separation of the collective activities of men and women are insured by severe punishments. If a woman enters the men's house in the center of the village or looks inside to see the sacred flutes she will be gang-raped by the men of the tribe. Similarly, the Mehinacu believe that if a woman sees a bull-roarer used during certain men's ceremonies her hair will fall out. Corresponding to these sanctions are penalties for men who interfere with women's activities. During one woman's festival any man from another tribe who inadvertently enters the village will be badly beaten by all the women of the tribe. In ancient times, according to Mehinacu legend, the women gang-raped any man who witnessed this festival.

Further reinforcing the separation of the sexes are codes of ritualized and informal sex antagonism. There are ceremonies in which the men intimidate the women with bull-roarers, sing songs designed to sexually shame them, and taunt them with clay phalluses and wax genitalia. The women, for their part, have rituals during which they tease the men with songs, cover them with caldrons of watery garbage, and gouge them with their teeth and nails. This ritualized sex antagonism has a less formal concomitant in gossip and banter, since the men often make deprecatory remarks about the women's genitalia and their behavior during coitus. The women, though somewhat less outspoken, frequently gossip maliciously about the men as a group and as individuals.

Remarkably coexisting with the pattern of separation and antagonism between the sexes is an extraordinary degree of mutual sexual attraction. The Mehinacu attitude toward sex emphasizes its sportiveness and opportunities for mutual enjoyment. The men frequently comment on the excitement of sexual relations, using the terms *weiupei* (voluptuous itching) and *awirintiapai* (succulent, delicious) to describe their sensations. The sexual joking that accompanies everyday male interaction is often of an almost Rabelaisian character,[4] taking immeasurable delight in the description of conquests and seductions. The women are expected to be more demure about sex, but according to our informants nearly all of them have orgasms and enjoy intercourse. Corresponding to the positive attitude toward sex is a high level of sexual activity. Male adolescents say that they have sexual relations every day, and men in their twenties only slightly less often.

Extra-marital liaisons make up a large percentage of Mehinacu sexual activity, as the men report having relations with their mistresses four to five times more often than with their spouses. Coitus with a mistress is said to be considerably more pleasurable than with a wife. Properly, such affairs are limited to women who are not proscribed by the incest taboo or other sexual prohibitions. Only classificatory cross-cousins who are neither the spouses of brothers or brothers-in-law nor certain other affinal relatives are eligible for extra-marital relations. If this system were practiced faithfully, however, many Mehinacu would find themselves in the intolerable situation of having only one, two, or even no women with whom they could legitimately conduct an extra-marital affair. The system of extending kinship is very flexible, however, so that frequently a young man can make a case for insisting that a girl is a cross-cousin rather than some other category of relative. This possibility is especially practicable when both of his parents are Mehinacu, since he may then be able to trace putative genealogical links through either of his parents' lines. One of these alternative methods of working through his relationship to the girls is likely to produce the desired result of placing her in the cross-cousin category.[5] Sexual affairs such as these which are often in marginal violation of the incest taboo only excite passing village interest.

The couple in question seems to experience little anxiety or conflict over their relationship once it is established. Affairs in violation of the respect owed brothers and affinal kin, however, are a somewhat more serious matter, and are not undertaken lightly.

One consequence of the Mehinacu willingness to engage in sexual relationships which are nominally proscribed by the incest taboos is that extra-marital liaisons are numerous. One young man conducts regular affairs with at least ten of the Mehinacu women, which is better than fifty percent of all the adult women in the community. In general, a man participates in extra-marital affairs with most of the women who are more or less of his own generation, and who are not explicitly proscribed by the incest taboo or by the rules of respect owed affinal kin.

In part, it is possible to account for the prevalence of extra-marital relationships among the Mehinacu in terms of their role in maintaining the cohesiveness of the community. On the simplest level, discreetly conducted affairs keep the population of the community together. Lovers and mistresses often become very fond of each other,[6] and regard long absences from the village as a privation they would prefer to avoid. This sentiment is significant, because the solidarity of Mehinacu society is somewhat precariously maintained. The boundaries of the group are not conspicuously structured by exogamy or warfare, and some of the Mehinacu actually leave the tribe for extended trips to other villages or dry season home sites. The persistence of the tribe as a social unit is important in the long run, however, since during times of sickness or crop blights, mutual cooperation can help insure survival. Interest in sexual affairs, then, seems to function as a centripetal force which encourages continued residence in the village, and motivates the traveler to return home.

Sexual affairs are not only a source of stability in village membership, but they are also an important basis of economic distribution within the community. Lovers are expected to provide their mistresses with regular gifts of food,[7] and occasional presents of more substantial items, such as combs, baskets or shell necklaces. Women seem to be under somewhat less obligation to reciprocate, but they often give their paramours a spindle of spun cotton, or even (though very rarely) a hammock. These exchanges are a small but still significant part of the total economy. A house with a num-

ber of sexually active women can count on a modest but regular
supply of fish throughout the year, even during the rainy season
when the total catch begins to decline. A bachelor whose mother
and sister do not provide him with a new hammock or cotton
for his belt and arm bands can often secure these goods from his
mistresses. Even married men can benefit from this system, since
their wives can acquire necessary articles, such as baskets, which
they may lack the skill to make.

Perhaps the most remarkable consequence of extra-marital sexuality among the Mehinacu is its effects on the village kinship
system. The Mehinacu believe that a newborn infant is literally
composed of accumulated ejaculate from repeated instances of sexual intercourse. If a woman does not have sexual relations frequently enough during pregnancy then it is said that her child will
be born too small. On the other hand, if she has sexual relations
too frequently the child may be too large or she may even have
twins. This theory of conception and paternity is logically incorporated in Mehinacu kinship. If a woman has sexual relations during pregnancy with many lovers, they are all considered to have
jointly produced the child together with the mother's husband.
These co-genitors are to a degree recognized as their offspring's
sociological fathers. A child is ideally instructed to refer to his
mother's paramours as *papa* (father, or father's real and classificatory male siblings), and when he is mature he must avoid sexual
contact with these men's daughters since such relations are considered incestuous. In practice this method of extending paternity
is applied flexibly, so that a woman is unlikely to inform her children about the extra-marital affairs she subsequently regretted.
Liaisons in serious violation of the incest taboo, with deviant individuals, or with suspected witches do not seem to become incorporated in the kinship system. Paternity is selectively extended
to men with whom the mother has had enduring and valued relationships. The net effect of this system of extending consanguineal
kinship is to bridge genealogically distant relationships, helping to
insure that no Mehinacu is outside the orbit of kinship.

Even though extra-marital sex among the Mehinacu is a frequent
and socially useful activity,[8] it must be concealed and engaged
in privately. As in our own society sexual intercourse is an intimate
event, and couples are ashamed to be seen. It is also said, however,

to be enjoyable to watch, and a few of the villagers can relate with enthusiasm how they have seen some of their fellow tribesmen copulating. The Mehinacu cannot therefore reliably count on each other's discretion, but must actively attempt to conceal the act of sex.

A second reason for hiding sexual liaisons is more unexpected. Despite their relatively permissive attitudes toward sex and the high frequency of extra-marital affairs, the Mehinacu have a double standard. The men believe it is a good thing for them to have many lovers, but bad for women and especially bad for their wives.[9] A husband may become so jealous about his wife's extra-marital activities that he will publicly beat and denounce her. She, in turn, may violently berate him about his amorous adventures and even swing at him with a fiery brand. Although extreme jealousy of this kind is only typical of the younger couples, even the most mature and liberal spouses have at least the right to expect that their mate's liaisons will be managed discreetly. Sexual jealousies may serve a useful function in that liaisons must be hidden and limited to relatively brief assignations. In this way affairs pose less of a threat to the stability of marriage than if they were not concealed. Nevertheless, jealousy and the interest in voyeurism create difficulties. All overt sexual activity, and especially extra-marital sex, must be carefully hidden. As we shall see, however, managing this kind of activity out of the public eye is extremely difficult in the relatively open setting of the Mehinacu village.

II

Extra-marital affairs are of intense interest to the entire Mehinacu community. Not only are such relationships intrinsically dramatic, but as we have seen they are of great importance in shaping the economic system and network of kinship in which everyone participates. All the villagers are therefore interested in learning about the couples who are conducting extra-marital affairs, the gifts they have exchanged, and their chances of parenthood. This high level of curiosity is difficult to frustrate, since social relationships are rendered highly visible by the physical setting and spatial design of the community.

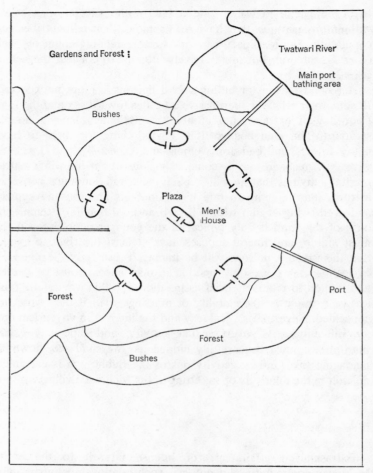

FIG. 1. Map of the Mehinacu village (in 1967). Areas within the center of the village and the main paths are highly visible. The maze of paths around the plaza, represented by the network of thin lines, is hidden from sight by bushes and forest.

Five large communal houses are grouped around an open plaza with a small men's house in the center. Any activities that might take place on the plaza, such as arranging liaisons or going to a rendezvous, would be easily visible to villagers sitting in the men's house and in the doorways around the circumference of the plaza. The main paths around the village are also highly public regions. These trails are nominally owned by the Mehinacu chiefs and maintained by all the men of the village, who take pride in their construction. One trail extends almost a mile and a half into the forest, and in places it is wide enough for two small cars to travel side by side. Part of the motivation for building these roads on such a grand scale is to be able to identify visitors from other tribes long before they arrive in the Mehinacu village. Movements in and out of the community by the Mehinacu themselves, however, are also easily visible. An amorous couple returning from an extramarital liaison would be spotted instantly by one of the villagers.

When social activities are not immediately visible they may often be observed indirectly. Footprints, for example, are almost as well-known as faces, and the barefoot Mehinacu leaves visual records of his whereabouts and activities that his fellows are astonishingly adept at reading. A print of a heel and a buttock, for example, may be enough to establish the identity of a couple that had sexual relations alongside the path. Personal property, such as canoes, arrows, or axes left in public view may also indicate the intentions and whereabouts of the owner.

When conduct is not immediately or indirectly observable it is often audible. The Mehinacu build their homes of thatch, which hardly obscures sound at all. Discussions are easily detectable through the wall of a house, and when listening conditions are good it is even possible to overhear boisterous conversations in a nearby residence. In point of fact, listening conditions are often excellent in the Mehinacu village, for unlike the urban situation to which many of us are accustomed most of what is audible is also socially meaningful. Relevant sounds are never masked by the noise of traffic or machinery. Instead background sounds consist of crying children, the conversations and disputes of spouses, the playing of flutes in the men's house, and the whistling of boys as they go to bathe in the morning, all of which tend to reveal the activities and the location of the villagers. The community is so permeable to sound that the Mehinacu signal to each other with a series of conventionalized falsetto whoops. There are separate calls indicating that food is being brought into the village, that a visitor is approaching, that the men of the tribe have reached agreement over an important issue, and that valuable trade goods have just exchanged hands. So effective are these calls as devices of communication that it is possible for a villager to keep abreast of most of the public social events of the day without ever leaving his hammock. The openness of the community to sound makes it understandably difficult to conduct or directly arrange an extra-marital affair within the confines of the village. The following lines from the ceremonial song of the cricket dramatically illustrate the Mehinacu alertness to the sounds that could expose such a relationship:

> I hear the hammock pole and the cords creaking
> I hear my mother having sexual relations
> Pilaw! Kule! Pilaw, Pilaw, Pilaw!

The last line consists of Mehinacu onomatopoeic words for the sounds of intercourse.

The final source of social information in the community is the gossip network. Small communities have notoriously efficient gossip systems, due in large part to the face-to-face character of social relationships and the relatively few message links required to spread a story to every member of the society. The Mehinacu are not exceptions to this pattern, and rapidly disseminate information about each other's activities and misconduct. The men claim that the women are especially culpable for passing along compromising tales, and certainly they seem somewhat more tolerant of gossip than the men. One of the sanctioned activities of women who are friends, for example, is to tell each other "little lies." On the occasions I was able to trace the movement of an especially choice story through the village the women did in fact appear to be at the core of the process of transmission. In particular, groups of women who work together in the arduous and time-consuming preparation of manioc flour rapidly spread the story to their kinsmen and friends until it was known throughout the village.

Extra-marital affairs are especially vulnerable to exposure through gossip, since information about sexual liaisons inspires enormous interest. Stories of sexual escapades not only name the participants in adulterous relationships, but may even detail their behavior during coitus, describing their sexual performance and the size, odor, and color of their genitalia. These intimate reports spread quickly through the gossip network, to the great embarrassment of the villagers most directly concerned.

By now it must be apparent that in the arena of the Mehinacu community privacy is a scarce commodity. If a villager is to retain control of information concerning his activities he must take advantage of the relatively few back regions his community provides, and carefully manage his conduct to foster the impressions he wishes to convey. As we shall describe below, the techniques of retaining such informational control are especially intricate in the case of extra-marital relationships.

III

Extra-marital affairs are invariably initiated by men, and only after careful forethought. A young man who plans to approach a girl sexually for the first time is highly vulnerable since rejections are often received as personal humiliations. In fact, a scorned suitor can be a dangerous enemy since sickness in women, even the oldest and most dilapidated crones, is often attributed to revengeful sorcery. When the proposed liaison is marginally in violation of the incest taboo (and many affairs are) a rebuff can be especially upsetting. One consequence of these hazards is that a young man directly propositioning a girl for the first time would never do so anywhere within the community where he might be seen or overheard. Instead he waits until she is outside the village on the way to the gardens or the river so that he will be reasonably confident they will be unobserved. He may then seize her by the wrist and propose sexual relations. A very forceful way to proposition a girl, according to one informant, is to ask "Don't you like me?", for after this question it is difficult to turn him down without risking his anger. If he is rejected on the grounds of violating the incest taboo he may respond by pointing out the ways in which their relationship may be considered to belong in the proper kinship category. A final rejection in this situation is a great embarrassment, and the young man will not be likely to misread the nature of their relationship again. An alternative to the direct approach is to arrange a sexual affair with the help of an intermediary. An already established lover or even the girl's brother or cousin will often set up such relationships for his male friends in exchange for a small gift. In this way an attractive girl rapidly accumulates numerous lovers.

Once an extra-marital affair has been established lovers may only have sexual relations when they happen to come upon each other in the gardens or on the paths around the village. If they wish to meet on a more regular basis, however, they must secretly prearrange a time and a place for each liaison. This problem is not easily resolved, since there are few opportunities for lovers to speak to one another privately within the village. Common solutions are to use a child as an intermediary or to set a tentative date after each assignation. The preferred time for an affair is when the lovers' spouses are outside the village. When a man is on a fishing expedition his wife can predict with a fair degree of accuracy when he is likely to return. If a liaison has been prearranged she will wait until she can see her lover leaving the village, thereby signaling that he is ready. A few moments later, perhaps after telling the women of her house that she is going to defecate, she leaves the village on a different path and proceeds to a small cleared area in the woods which they have agreed on in advance. There are many such areas in the forest encircling the village that have been carefully chosen so that they are secluded, invisible from the main paths, and free of biting ants. Each of the Mehinacu men uses several of them distributed around the periphery of the community. The area selected by the lovers for their liaison will be the one closest to the back door of the girl's house, so she will not be forced to cross the central plaza, or make a circuitous route through the forest.

When the couple meet, they may exchange small gifts such as combs or cotton thread, and then have sexual relations with a minimum of conversation or foreplay. According to our informants the most frequent position is both couples sitting on the ground facing each other, with the woman's legs over the man's thighs. An alternate position is for the woman to lie down on a large log or on the ground with the man on top of her. After intercourse the lovers may sit together for a while, assuring one another that they enjoyed the experience, that they care for each other, and that they fear their spouses will discover their relationship. They may also proclaim their faithfulness by saying that they do not have any other lovers, though each may realize that such assurances are not to be taken altogether seriously. They will return to the village as they came, rejoining their families as if nothing had occurred.

A device that is routinely used to mask sexual intrigues is prevarication. Since the open setting of the community makes it virtually impossible for lovers to conceal all their preparations for a tryst, they routinely use mendacity to conceal the intentions that lie behind their conduct. In the late afternoon, when a young man puts on his best shell belt and carefully decorates his hair with red dye, his wife may want to know what he is planning to do. He will routinely explain he is going to the men's house in the center of the village. Since the men often adorn themselves with no intention of engaging in an affair the wife is likely to credit this fabrication, or at least realize that she is not expected to inquire further.[10] If the wife tends to be suspicious about her husband's activities, his efforts to mislead her will grow more elaborate. Quite frequently a husband will tell his wife that he is going fishing or gardening. He will carefully dress up to suit the part, putting on bark ankle wrappings, rubbing his body with oil, and shouldering a gun, canoe paddle, or hoe, whichever prop best suits his story. In reality, of course, he is meeting his mistress, who may be busy deluding her kinsmen into thinking that she is going to bathe, or to harvest manioc in her husband's garden.

Not all intrigues are conducted as discreetly as the one described above. Frequently it is impossible to plan a rendezvous in advance or wait until a woman's husband is a safe distance from the village. Such circumstances call for bolder strategy. One young man waits until his mistress' husband goes to the men's house to wrestle or work on handicrafts. He then slips out the back door of his house and sneaks along the maze of hidden forest paths that surround the village (see Fig. 1) to a hiding place a short distance from the girl's back yard. He does not dare call her or enter the house. Speaking to her publicly would give away his purpose, and entering a neighbor's house simply is not done unless there is a trading session or a ceremony in progress. An hour may go by as the young man waits patiently. At last, the girl steps outside her house to urinate or to throw some household refuse into the bushes. He calls to her by pursing his lips and making a small sound such as one might use to summon a kitten. They go behind a bush to have intercourse as quickly as possible, not having forgotten that the cuckolded husband is only a few yards away. They use a standing position in this situation, the girl raising one knee with her arms about her lover. As soon as they are finished, hardly having spoken a word, the young man races off through the forest to his own house, while the girl goes back to her work as nonchalantly as possible. Her husband may even return to the house at this point, never suspecting that he has been cuckolded in the short time of his absence.

Another kind of liaison requires even greater boldness and daring, as it occurs within the houses at night. For long periods during the height of the rainy season it is often too wet to have sexual relations comfortably out of doors. At such times a man usually waits until he knows that his mistress' husband has left the village on a predawn fishing trip, or on a visit to another tribe. Making certain that his wife is sleeping soundly he quietly slips over to his girl friend's house. Entering, he expertly finds his way in the darkness through the tangle of hammock cords at his chest and the clutter of bowls and benches at his feet, until at last he comes to his mistress in her hammock. Although she may not have been expecting him she is glad he has come, for as the Mehinacu say, a woman likes sex best of all in her hammock at night with her lover. In this situation the couple make as little noise as possible for fear of waking those who are sleeping nearby.

When the girl's husband is present, having sexual relations in her hammock (which is usually suspended just a few feet below her husband's) is considered too risky. As a result, they may have intercourse on the floor of the house, either in the cleared regions facing each door, or even in a narrow vermin-infested area between the thatch walls and the house poles. Either of these alternatives is said to be an indelicate choice, and some informants speak deprecatingly of their comrades who employ them.

The nocturnal adventures of lovers are the most dramatic feature of their relationship, and certainly under the most immediate pressure from the low levels of privacy available in the community. Presents exchanged by lovers, however, must also be concealed from the cuckolded spouses since such gifts are a tangible symbol of their relationship. When a man returns from a successful fishing trip he will almost invariably detach one of his choicest fish, one whose flesh is very oily, and have it delivered to his mistress. He must do this before entering the village, for the moment he is spotted his return will be announced by all the men of the village, who call out "Ki-ki-ki-ki-ki-Kupati!" (Fish!). After the community's attention has been focused on him in this way he has no choice but to go directly to his own house and give his wife the fish for cooking. Publicly delivering the fish to his mistress would not only reveal their relationship, but could suggest they considered each other husband and wife. The paramour can circumvent this difficulty by keeping away from the main paths and central plaza, and delivering the fish to the back door of his mistress' house. If her husband is home, however, it is advisable to send the gift with one of the girl's kinsmen. Children are frequently used for errands of this kind, but it is also possible to recruit an adult, such as the mistress' brother. When he delivers the fish it will seem to the cuckolded husband that the gift has come from his brother-in-law, rather than his wife's lover. Gifts that are neither as disposable nor as casually distributed as food are more difficult to explain. A man may tell his wife that the spool of cotton thread given him by his mistress was actually a present from his sister, a plausible though statistically unlikely explanation. Similarly, a woman with a new basket from her lover will try to lead her husband to believe that it was made by her brother or some other close kinsman.

Gifts and the activities of lovers are not the only evidence of extra-marital affairs. The reader will recall that these relationships have important effects on the Mehinacu system of kinship, since paternity is selectively extended to a child's mother's paramours. Surprisingly enough, even these relationships must be concealed. The sensitivity of these bonds of kinship is partially explained by the fact that the relationship of lovers is often very stable, enduring for most of a lifetime. The use of the kinship term *papa* for the children of such an affair is an offensive reminder to the cuckolded spouses of their mate's past indiscretions and continued infidelity. For this reason a mother instructs her child to call her paramours *papa* only when her husband is out of earshot. Similarly, the paramour will urge the child to use the term *papa* very discreetly, because he is afraid the mother's husband will find out and become angry.

The paternal relationship also affects the conduct of persons other than the paramour and his mistress' children. The Mehinacu chief, for example, is the father of our informant's wife. One of the other villagers, however, is clandestinely her father by virtue of his long-standing affair with the chief's spouse. This father is therefore considered our informant's father-in-law. Neither the paternal nor the affinal relationship is performed or mentioned in the chief's presence, since they are embarrassments he does not wish to confront. Submerging these roles requires care, but is not as difficult as might be expected. The father-child relationship, for example, is understandably poor in content. The only positive behavior associated with it other than the occasional use of the proper kinship terms is a discreetly given present of one fish when the child is able to walk. The kinship term *papa* is even acceptable to the cuckolded chief in this case since he recognizes his wife's paramour as his classificatory brother.

The affinal ties that develop from the extension of paternity to the chief's daughter are also relatively easy to conceal. Among the Mehinacu, father and son-in-law must never use each other's names, and must avoid physical and social contact. The prohibition on naming does not expose our informant's affinal relationship with his wife's mother's paramour, however, since parents-in-law and children-in-law can legitimately refer to each other with kinship terms that are also used for consanguineal kin. The avoidance taboos which our informant and the paramour are obliged to honor are also inconspicuous, since these evasions are dramatically apparent only when father and son-in-law live in the same house. Co-residence of a Mehinacu with his wife's true father and her mother's paramours, however, is unlikely (though possible), given the close relationship of kinsmen within the domestic unit. If the villagers are discreet they can therefore hide many potentially embarrassing consanguineal and affinal relationships from their fellow tribesmen.

IV

We have seen that extra-marital affairs among the Mehinacu can have positive results in terms of the social and economic integration of the village. The jealousy of husbands and wives, however, requires that liaisons be concealed if these benefits are to be realized. Considerable ingenuity is needed to keep extra-marital involvements out of the public eye in the highly exposed setting of the Mehinacu village. Strategies to establish privacy take advantage of the natural and man-made back regions surrounding the village, and the cover that darkness affords within the community. Affairs are invariably arranged and conducted outside the village or within the houses after nightfall. Intermediaries are used to set up rendezvous, convey messages, and deliver presents. Remarkably, there is even an underground kinship system wherein the relationships engendered by extra-marital affairs are performed discreetly so as not to embarrass or anger the cuckolded spouses. Finally, when spouses are indiscreet, or the arrangements and consequences of an affair are impossible to hide, prevarication is the last line of defense, permitting lovers to mask their intentions, even if they cannot conceal their actual conduct.

The significance of this pattern is that the public character of village social life constitutes an important strain on the performance of social relationships, a strain with which the Mehinacu must come to terms. Although I have chosen to make this point by analyzing the management of extra-marital sexuality, privacy and back regions have functions other than concealing misconduct. Areas of low visibility and barriers to the flow of information are required to rehearse ordinary role performances (Goffman 1959:112), to maintain the appearance of meeting the conflicting demands of different members of a role set (Merton 1957:345), and to differentiate social groups (Schwartz 1968, Simmel 1950). The analysis of privacy-setting devices could therefore have been applied to many aspects of everyday Mehinacu conduct, such as the efforts of husbands and wives to smooth over hostility out of the public eye, the techniques of audience segregation employed by men in their somewhat antithetical relationships as kinsmen and comrades, and the sanctions utilized by the sexes to separate group activities and differentiate their roles (Gregor 1969, Roberts and Gregor, 1970).

The wide variety of institutions and conduct which depend on barriers to the flow of information suggests that privacy-setting devices may be of considerable ethnographic and structural significance in the exposed setting of the Mehinacu community. Since social relationships are often highly public in character in other primitive communities, the analysis of devices that restrict the flow of information offers a fresh approach to a broad range of social conduct in small societies. There is ample theoretical justification for this position in the writing of Simmel (1950), Goffman (1959), Murphy (1964), and others, but ethnographic studies very seldom focus directly on the availability of social information within a community. Usually such material must be inferred from a description of etiquette and the settlement pattern. Only when devices that restrict the flow of information have an outlandish or bizarre appearance do they attract the specific attention of anthropologists. Hence there is a considerable literature on affinal taboos and the use of masks in ceremonies as well as systematic analyses of such topics as the use of the veil among the Tuareg (Murphy 1964) and seclusion customs among the Mehinacu (Gregor 1970). We have seen, however, that less dramatic techniques of managing social information have significant structural implications that may be well worth the ethnographer's attention.

NOTES

1. This paper is based on ten months' field work among the Mehinacu Indians during 1967 with the financial support of the Public Health Service and the National Science Foundation, and the sponsorship of the Museu Emilio Goeldi and the Museu Nacional in Brazil. I am grateful to these institutions, and to Roberto Cardoso de Oliveira and Claudio and Orlando Villas Boas for their advice and assistance in the field.

2. The term "privacy" in this paper will be used in the broad sense suggested by Alan Westin (1967:7): "Privacy is the claim of individuals, groups, or institutions to determine . . . when, how, and to what extent information about them is to be communicated to others." When privacy in this sense is minimal, we use the term "exposure."

3. The general culture pattern of the Xingú region is described in Galvão (1953) and Lévi-Strauss (1948a). The most relevant comparative material from this culture area is Robert Carneiro's description of extra-marital sexuality among the Carib-speaking Kuikuru (1958).

4. Ribaldry is apparent in sexual joking among men, in songs that are sung for certain ceremonies, and in myths and stories. The tale that follows is an illustration of the kind of humor that is common among the Mehinacu and, incidentally, reveals some of the latent antagonism that characterizes the relationship of a man and his in-laws:

"A long, long time ago there was a mother-in-law whose husband had died. She had no lovers. Her son-in-law who lived with her had a long rod of beeswax which he used in hafting his arrow points. One day the son-in-law noticed that his wax had a peculiar smell. Later that night, after the fires had almost died out and everyone was sleeping, he saw his mother-in-law get up, take his wax rod, return to her hammock, and push it in and out of her vagina. The next evening he took the wax and rubbed it up and down with hot pepper. He then went through all the houses in the village and dumped out their supply of water. During the night his mother-in-law once again took the wax rod and settled down to use it; but immediately she burned with pain. She raced about the house searching for water, but there was none. She ran to each house in the village, but to no avail. Finally she dashed to the river and squatted down in the water. She stayed there a long time."

5. Manipulating kinship to place women in a category that makes them available for sexual relationships is by no means unique to the Mehinacu. Murphy writes of the Tuareg: ". . . the ethnographer soon discovers that a Tuareg has more cross-cousins, especially female ones, than any other type of kin" (1967:167).

6. The relationship of lovers may endure an entire lifetime. At death, in what may be the only public recognition of their affection the bereaved lover's hair is cut by his mistress' brother, and he places a final gift in her grave to express his mourning.

7. A man supplies his mistress with fish, monkey, and fowl. Fish, however, are taboo to a woman during her menstrual flow. Her chances of obtaining any protein intake at all during menstruation would be poor if she had to rely solely on her husband, since monkeys and birds (the only other animals the Mehinacu eat) are difficult to hunt. Gifts of meat to a mistress at this time may therefore have an important nutritional effect even though the total amount may be small compared to the food distributed by other methods.

8. The structural and economic functions we have attributed to Mehinacu sexual permissiveness do not in and of themselves account for the widespread network of liaisons and affairs. A speculative explanation is that heightened sexual activity is the reciprocal of the codes of separation and exclusion we have documented. Taboos and restrictions permit the sexes to remain aloof, so that they do not have complete mutual knowledge of one another. Areas of ignorance constitute a source of attraction and fascination, of which sexuality is the most obvious expression. Evidence for this hypothesis derives partly from the Mehinacu preference for sexual involvements with mistresses rather than wives. It is as if the too well-known personalities and anatomies of wives held less interest and mystery than those

of their mistresses, who remain more or less unknown quantities. Cross-cultural data provide some additional support for the relationship of high levels of sexual activity with distance-setting devices. Hence, at a level of significance = .0033, societies which residentially segregate adolescents of the opposite sex also are permissive about premarital sexuality (Textor 1967: table 371).

9. To a certain extent this standard is incorporated in the kinship system. It is considered a positive good for a man to have sexual relations with his wife's sisters, but a similar relationship between a woman and her husband's brothers is prohibited.

10. Husband and wife are obliged to cooperate in avoiding the evidence of extra-marital activities. One of the qualities of a good wife is that she does not ask too many questions about her husband's activities and where-abouts. Discretion thereby permits spouses to evade information that might tend to compromise their relationships.

Introduction to Social Structures of Central and Eastern Brazil

In this selection, Lévi-Strauss explores a structuralist mode of interpretation. The structuralist position (Lévi-Strauss 1963, orig. 1945) is analogous to a linguistic approach insofar as it seeks to elucidate the unconscious patterning of cultural behavior. But unlike certain linguistic approaches where elements are analyzed in terms of their meaning (read function) in a given context, the structural approach focuses on the interrelationships between the terms. The structuralist tests models of social structure against information gathered from native informants. These models do not necessarily correspond to the native's own view of how his society is constituted. The analyst's model subsumes both the native's model and the actual functioning of a society, and without it, neither of the latter are intelligible. Moreover, these underlying structures are said to pertain to a collective unconscious of all mankind and are therefore found among a great diversity of societies, often bridging the gap between "primitive" and "civilized" societies.

Here Lévi-Strauss focuses his principal attention on the Sherente of central Brazil, who are one of the Gê groups celebrated for their elaborate social organization (cf. Da Matta in Chapter 16 of this volume). The Sherente claim to have eight patrilineal clans allocated in exogamous moieties in each village. This system would accord (as among the Yąnomamö) with Iroquois kinship nomenclature and bilateral cross-cousin marriage. But the pattern of Sherente kinship terms as reported by Nimuendajú (1942) seems to accord best with a system of matrilateral cross-cousin marriage, while this form of marriage is explicitly prohibited by the Sherente. Furthermore, the pattern of certain ritual exchanges made among the Sherente suggests that there had to be at least three distinct descent groups, or else such paradoxes might have occurred as a man taking his daughter-in-law's side against his own son. Once this complex set of structural contradictions has been laid out, the remaining analytic task is a purely logical one. Interestingly, and in contradistinction to a functionalist approach, Lévi-Strauss's solution is to provide a diachronic model, a speculative account of changes the Sherente must have passed through. No evidence is provided, however, to support the imputed chronological sequence. As usual, Lévi-Strauss leaves us with some fascinating suggestions, namely that, like ourselves, primitive peoples frequently attempt to conceal hierarchical systems with egalitarian-appearing models, and endogamous marriages with models of exogamic structures (cf. Lévi-Strauss 1944).

Maybury-Lewis (1956) has re-examined the specific argument made about the Sherente in the light of his own, more recent field work among them, and has concluded that Lévi-Strauss drew faulty conclusions from faulty data. While not demurring from the structuralist method employed, Maybury-Lewis demonstrated that "the features of aboriginal Sherente social structure are, so far as we know, consistent with a system of patrilineal exogamous moieties . . ." (1956:132).

One of the pioneers of the structuralist approach, Claude Lévi-Strauss's work has had a profound influence not only on anthropology but also on letters, criticism and philosophy. In addition to numerous theoretical works, Lévi-Strauss has published a good deal based on his own ethnographic research among Brazilian Indians. His autobiographical book describing his work in Brazil, *Tristes Tropiques* (1964, translated into English under this title), is indispensable reading for anyone interested in South America or contemplating anthropology as a career. Lévi-Strauss is Professor at the Collège de France.

15. SOCIAL STRUCTURES OF CENTRAL AND EASTERN BRAZIL

CLAUDE LÉVI-STRAUSS

During recent years our attention has been focused on the institutions of certain tribes of central and eastern Brazil which had been classed as very primitive because of their low level of material culture. These tribes are characterized by highly complex social structures which include several systems of criss-crossing moieties, each with specific functions, clans, age grades, recreational or ceremonial associations, and other types of groups. The most striking examples are furnished by the Sherente, who have exogamous patrilineal moieties subdivided into clans; the Canella and the Bororo, with exogamous matrilineal moieties and other types of groups; and finally, the Apinayé, with non-exogamous matrilineal moieties. The most complex types, such as a double system of moieties subdivided into clans, and a triple system of moieties lacking clan subdivisions, are found among the Bororo and the Canella, respectively. (These tribes have been described by Colbacchini, Nimuendajú, and the present author, as well as earlier observers [see bibliography—Ed.]).

The general tendency of observers and theorists has been to interpret these complex structures on the basis of dual organization, which seemed to represent the simplest form.[1] This followed the lead of native informants, who focused their descriptions on the dual forms. I do not differ from my colleagues in this respect. Nevertheless, a long-standing doubt led me to postulate the residual character of dual structures in the area under consideration. As we shall see, this hypothesis later proved inadequate.

Reprinted by permission of the author and publisher. Chapter VII of *Structural Anthropology*, pp. 120–31, by Claude Lévi-Strauss, translated by Brooke Grundfest Schoepf, © 1963 by Basic Books, Inc., Publishers, New York.

We propose to show here that the description of indigenous institutions given by field-workers, ourselves included, undoubtedly coincides with the natives' image of their own society, but that this image amounts to a theory, or rather a transmutation, of reality, itself of an entirely different nature. Two important consequences stem from this observation, which until now had been applied only to the Apinayé: The dual organization of the societies of central and eastern Brazil is not only adventitious, but often illusory; and, above all, we are led to conceive of social structures as entities independent of men's consciousness of them (although they in fact govern men's existence), and thus as different from the image which men form of them as physical reality is different from our sensory perceptions of it and our hypotheses about it.

Our first example will be the Sherente, described by Nimuendajú. This tribe, which belongs to the central Gê linguistic family, is distributed in villages, each composed of two exogamous patrilineal moieties subdivided into four clans. Three of these clans are considered by the natives as the original Sherente clans; the fourth is attributed by legend to a foreign "captured" tribe. The eight clans, four in each moiety, are differentiated by ceremonial functions and privileges; but neither these clans, nor the two athletic teams, nor the four men's clubs and the related women's association, nor the six age grades function in the regulation of marriage, which depends exclusively upon the moiety system. We would expect, then, to find the usual corollaries of dual organization, namely, distinction between parallel-cousins and cross-cousins; merging of patrilateral and matrilateral cross-cousins; and preferential marriage between bilateral cross-cousins. This, however, is only rarely the case.

In another work whose conclusions we shall review briefly,[2] we have distinguished three fundamental types of marriage exchange; these are expressed, respectively, by preferential bilateral cross-cousin marriage, marriage between sister's son and brother's daughter, and marriage between brother's son and sister's daughter. We have called the first type *restricted exchange,* implying the division of the group into two sections, or a multiple of two, while the term *generalized exchange,* which includes the two remaining types, refers to the fact that marriage can take place between an unspecified number of partners. The difference between matrilateral and patrilateral cross-cousin marriage arises from the fact that the former represents the richest and most complete form of marriage exchange, the partners finding themselves oriented once and for all in an open-ended global structure. Patrilateral cross-cousin marriage, on the contrary, is a "borderline" form of reciprocity, links groups *only* in pairs, and implies a total reversal of all the cycles with each succeeding generation. It follows that matrilateral marriage is normally accompanied by a kinship terminology which we have called "consecutive": Since the position of the descent groups in relation to one another is unchanging, their successive members tend to be merged under the same term, and differences of generation are ignored. Patrilateral marriage, on the other hand, is associated with an "alternating" terminology, which expresses the opposition of consecutive generations and the identification of alternating generations. A son marries in the direction opposite from his father—yet in the same direction as his father's sister—and in the same direction as his father's father—yet in the opposite direction from that of his father's father's sister. For daughters, the situation is exactly the reverse. A second result follows. In matrilateral marriage, we find two separate and distinct terms for two types of affinal relatives: "sisters' husbands" and "wives' brothers." In patrilateral marriage, this dichotomy is transposed into the descent group itself, in order to distinguish first-degree collateral relatives according to sex. Brother and sister, who always follow opposite paths in marriage, are distinguished by what F. E. Williams, in Melanesia, described as "sex affiliation"; each receives a fraction of the status of the ascendant whose matrimonial destiny he or she follows or complements, that is, the son receives the status of his mother, and the daughter that of her father—or vice versa according to the situation.

When we apply these definitions to the Sherente, we immediately perceive certain anomalies. Neither the kinship terminology nor the marriage rules coincide with the requirements of a dual system or a system of restricted exchange. Rather, they contradict one another, each pattern being associated with one of the two fundamental types of generalized exchange. Thus the kinship vocabulary offers several examples of consecutive terms, as, for instance:

father's sister's son = sister's son
wife's brother's son = wife's brother
father's sister's husband = sister's husband = daughter's
husband

The two types of cross-cousins are also distinguished. However, marriage (for male Ego) is permitted only with the patrilateral cousin and is prohibited with the matrilateral cousin, which should imply an alternating terminology, and not a consecutive one—as is precisely the case. At the same time, several terminological identifications of individuals belonging to different moieties (mother and mother's sister's daughter; brother, sister, and mother's brother's children; father's sister's children and brother's children; etc.) suggest that this moiety division does not represent the most essential aspect of the social structure. Thus, even a superficial examination of the kinship terminology and marriage rules leads to the following observations: Neither the terminology nor the rules of marriage coincide with an exogamous dual organization. The terminology, on the one hand, and the marriage rules, on the other, belong to two mutually exclusive patterns, both of which are incompatible with dual organization.

On the other hand we find indices of matrilateral marriage which contradict the patrilateral pattern, the only one for which we have evidence. These are: (1) plural union—a form of polygyny usually associated with matrilateral marriage and matrilineal descent, although in this case the descent is actually patrilineal; (2) the presence of two reciprocal terms among affinal kin, *aimapli* and *izakmu,* which leads us to believe that affines maintain a unidimensional relationship with one another, that is, that they are sisters' husbands or wives' brothers, but not both at the same time; (3) finally, and above all, there is the role of the bride's maternal uncle, which is unusual for a moiety system.

Dual organization is characterized by reciprocal services between moieties which are, at the same time, associated and opposed. This reciprocity is expressed in the set of special relationships between a nephew and his maternal uncle, who belong to different moieties regardless of type of descent. But among the Sherente, these relations, restricted in their classic form to the special *narkwa* bond, seem to be transposed to the husband or bridegroom, on the one hand, and to the *bride's* maternal uncle, on the other. Let us examine this point further.

The bride's maternal uncle performs the following functions: He organizes and carries out the abduction of the bridegroom as a preliminary to the marriage; he takes in his niece in the event of a divorce and protects her against her husband; if the niece's husband dies, he forces her brother-in-law to marry her; together with her husband, he avenges his niece if she is raped. In other words, he is his niece's protector with, and if necessary against, her husband. If, however, the moiety system had a truly functional value, the bride's maternal uncle would be a classificatory "father" of the bridegroom, rendering his role as abductor (and as protector of the wife of one of his "sons," thus hostile to the latter) absolutely incomprehensible. There must, therefore, always be at least three distinct descent groups—Ego's group, Ego's wife's group, and the group of Ego's wife's mother—and this is incompatible with a pure moiety system.

On the other hand, members of the same moiety often reciprocate services. At the occasion of female name-giving, ceremonial exchanges take place between the alternate moiety to that of the girls and their maternal uncles who belong to the officiants' moiety. The boys' initiation is performed by their paternal uncles who belong to the same moiety; at the giving of the name *Wakedi* to two boys (a privilege reserved to the women's association), the maternal uncles of the boys accumulate game that is then taken by the women of the opposite moiety, which is therefore the moiety of the uncles as well. In short, everything happens as though there were a dual organization, but in reverse. Or, more accurately, the role of the moieties is lost. Instead of moieties exchanging services, the services are exchanged within the same moiety, *on the occasion* of a special activity held by the other moiety. Three partners, therefore, are always involved instead of two.

Given these conditions, it is significant to discover, at the level of the associations, a formal structure which corresponds exactly to a law of generalized exchange. The four men's societies are organized in a circuit. When a man changes his association he must do it in a prescribed and immutable order. This order is the same as the one governing the transfer of feminine names, which is a privilege of the men's societies. Finally, this order krara→ krieriekmū→ akemhā→ annōrowa→ (krara)

is the same, although inverted, as that of the mythical origin of
the societies and of the transfer, from one society to another, of
the obligation to celebrate the Padi rite.

Another surprise awaits us when we turn to the myth. The myth
actually presents the associations as *age grades,* created in a succession from youngest to oldest. For mask-making, however, the four
associations are grouped in pairs linked by reciprocal services, as
though they formed moieties, and these pairs consist of age grades
which are not consecutive but alternate, as though each moiety
were composed of two marriage classes in a system of generalized
exchange. (See Figure 1.) We find the same order in the rules
of *aikmā*—the commemoration of the deaths of illustrious men.

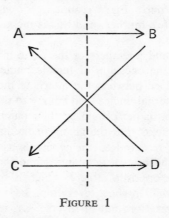

FIGURE 1

The following outline sketches the main features of the preceding discussion:

1. There are no rigid barriers between exogamous moieties, associations, and age grades. The associations function as marriage
classes. They fulfill the requirements of the marriage rules and kinship terminology better than the moieties do. On the level of myth,
the associations appear as age grades, and in ceremonial life they
are grouped within a theoretical moiety system. Only the clans
appear extraneous and seemingly indifferent to this organic whole.
Everything functions as if the moieties, associations, and age grades

were awkward and fragmentary expressions of an underlying reality.

2. The only possible historical evolution that could account for these contradictory characteristics would be:

a. Originally, three patrilineal and patrilocal descent groups with generalized exchange (marriage with mother's brother's daughter);

b. the introduction of matrilineal moieties, leading to

c. the formation of a fourth patrilocal descent group (the fourth clan of each present moiety, or the "captured tribe"; the origin myth of the associations likewise affirms that there were originally three clans);

d. a conflict arising between the rule of descent (matrilineal) and the rule of residence (patrilocal), resulting in

e. the conversion of the moieties to patrilineal descent, with

f. the concomitant loss of the functional role of the descent groups, which are changed into associations through the phenomenon of "masculine resistance" which appeared with the introduction of the original matrilineal moieties.

The Bororo head the list of our other examples, which we shall sketch more briefly. First, we must note the remarkable symmetry between Sherente and Bororo social organization. Both tribes have circular villages divided into exogamous moieties, each with four clans and a central men's house. This parallelism goes even further, despite the opposition of terms that is due to the patrilineal or matrilineal character of the two societies. Thus the Bororo men's house is open to married men and that of the Sherente is reserved for bachelors; it is the scene of sexual license among the Bororo, while chastity is imperative in the Sherente men's house; Bororo bachelors drag in girls or women with whom they then have extraconjugal sexual relations, whereas the Sherente girls enter only to capture husbands. A comparison between the two tribes is therefore certainly justified.

Recent studies have provided new information concerning social organization and kinship. For the latter, the rich documents published by Father Albisetti show that although the dichotomy between "cross" and "parallel" relatives exists (as we should expect in a system of exogamous moieties), it does not coincide with the moiety division but, rather, cross-cuts it, since identical terms occur in both moieties. We shall limit ourselves to a few striking examples. Ego equates brother's children and sister's children, although they belong to different moieties. Although in the grandchildren's generation we find the expected dichotomy between "sons and daughters" (terms theoretically limited to grandchildren of the moiety opposite Ego's own) on the other hand and "sons-in-law" and "daughters-in-law" (terms theoretically restricted to grandchildren of Ego's moiety) on the other, the actual distribution of these terms does not correspond to the moiety division.

We know that in other tribes—for example, the Miwok of California—such anomalies indicate the presence of groupings different from, and more important than, the moieties. Furthermore, in the Bororo system, we note certain striking terminological equivalents, such as:

> mother's brother's son's son is called: daughter's husband, grandson; father's sister's daughter's daughter is called: wife's mother, grandmother;

and especially:

> mother's mother's brother's son and mother's mother's mother's brother's son's son are called: son.

These equivalents immediately bring to mind kinship structures of the Bank-Ambrym-Easter Island type. The similarities are corroborated by the possibility of marriage with the mother's brother's daughter's daughter in both cases.[3]

Regarding social organization, Father Albisetti specifies that each matrilineal moiety always consists of four clans and that there is preferential marriage not only between certain clans but between certain sections of these clans. According to him, each clan is actually divided into three matrilineal sections: Upper, Middle, and Lower. Given two clans linked by preferential marriage, unions can take place only between Upper and Upper, Middle and Middle, and Lower and Lower section members. If this description were correct (and the observations of the Salesian Fathers have always been trustworthy), we see that the classic

picture of Bororo institutions would collapse. Whatever the marriage preferences linking certain clans, the clans themselves would
lose all functional value (as we have already observed for the
Sherente), and thus Bororo society would be reduced to three
endogamous groups—Upper, Middle, and Lower—each divided
into two exogamous sections. As there are no kinship relationships between the three principal groups, these would really constitute three sub-societies (Figure 2).

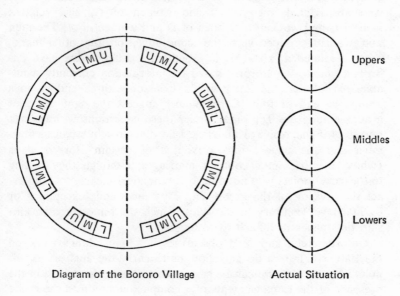

Diagram of the Bororo Village   Actual Situation

FIGURE 2

Since the kinship terminology seems explicable only in terms
of three theoretical descent groups, ultimately split into six—wife's
father, mother, daughter's husband—and linked by a system of
generalized exchange, we are led to postulate an original triadic
system transformed by the addition of a dual system, as among
the Sherente.

To regard the Bororo as an endogamous society is so startling
that we should hesitate even to consider this possibility had not
an analogous conclusion already been drawn for the Apinayé by

three different authors working independently with documents collected by Nimuendajú.

We know that the Apinayé moieties are non-exogamous and that marriage is regulated by the division of the group into four *kiyê*, as follows: a man *A* marries a woman *B*, a man *B* marries a woman *C*, a man *C* marries a woman *D*, etc. Since boys belong to the *kiyê* of their fathers and girls to that of their mothers, the apparent division into four exogamous groups masks a real division into four endogamous groups: men of *A* and women of *B*, who are related; men of *B* and women of *C*, also related; men of *C* and women of *D*; men of *D* and women of *A*. The men and women grouped into the same *kiyê*, on the other hand, are not related at all. This is exactly the situation we have described among the Bororo, based on information currently available, except that the latter would have only three endogamous groups instead of four. Certain clues suggest the same type of groups among the Tapirapé. Under these conditions we may ask ourselves if the Apinayé marriage rule that prohibits cousin marriage and the endogamous privileges of certain Bororo clans (whose members may contract marriages, although they belong to the same moiety) do not aim, by antithetical means, to counteract the division of the group, either by incestuous exceptions or by marriages contrary to the rules, which the remoteness of kinship ties makes it difficult to distinguish.

Unfortunately, gaps and obscurities in Nimuendajú's work on the Eastern Timbira do not allow us to carry the analysis to this point. At any rate, we can be certain that here again we are in the presence of the same elements of a complex common to the entire culture area. The Timbira have a systematically consecutive terminology in which:

> father's sister's son = father
> father's sister's daughter = father's sister
> mother's brother's son = brother's son
> daughter's daughter = sister's daughter

And the prohibition of cross-cousin marriage (as among the Apinayé) despite the presence of exogamous moieties; the role of the bride's maternal uncle as the protector of his niece against her husband, a situation already encountered among the Sherente; the rotating cycle of age grades, analogous to that of the Sherente associations and the Apinayé marriage classes; and, finally, the regrouping of alternate pairs of age grades in athletic contests, like that of the Sherente associations in ceremonies—all this leads us to assume that the problems raised would be quite similar.

Three conclusions emerge from this schematic presentation:

1. The study of social organization among the populations of central and eastern Brazil must be thoroughly re-examined in the field—first, because the actual functioning of these societies is quite different from its superficial appearance, which is all that has been observed until now; and second, and more important, because this study must be carried out on a comparative basis. Undoubtedly the Bororo, the Canella, the Apinayé, and the Sherente have, each in their own way, created real institutions which are strikingly similar to one another and, at the same time, simpler than their explicit formulation. Furthermore, the various types of groupings found in these societies—specifically, three forms of dual organization, clans, sub-clans, age grades, associations, etc.—do not represent, as they do in Australia, so many functional groups. They are, rather, a series of expressions, each partial and incomplete, of the same underlying structure, which they reproduce in several copies without ever completely exhausting its reality.

2. Field-workers must learn to consider their research from two different perspectives. They are always in danger of confusing the natives' theories about their social organization (and the superficial form given to these institutions to make them consistent with theory) with the actual functioning of the society. Between the two there may be as great a difference as that between the physics of Epicurus or Descartes, for example, and the knowledge derived from contemporary physics. The sociological representations of the natives are not merely a part or a reflection of their social organization. The natives may, just as in more advanced societies, be unaware of certain elements of it, or contradict it completely.

3. We have seen that, in this respect, the native representations of central and eastern Brazil, as well as the institutional language in which these are expressed, constitute an effort to regard

as basic a type of structure (moieties or exogamous classes) whose true role is quite secondary, if not totally illusory.

Behind the dualism and the apparent symmetry of the social structure we perceive a more fundamental organization which is asymmetrical and triadic;[4] the requirements of a dualist formulation lead to insuperable difficulties in the harmonious functioning of the organization.

Why do societies affected by a high degree of endogamy so urgently need to mystify themselves and see themselves as governed by exogamous institutions, classical in form, of whose existence they have no direct knowledge? This problem (to which we have elsewhere sought a solution) belongs to general anthropology. Raising it in a technical discussion and with respect to a limited geographical area at least shows the contemporary trend of anthropological research and demonstrates that henceforth in the social sciences, theory and research are indissolubly linked.

NOTES

1. By 1940, however, Lowie had cautioned against drawing false analogies to the Australian systems.

2. See C. Lévi-Strauss, *The Elementary Structures of Kinship* (1969).

3. Among the Bororo, however, marriage remains possible with the mother's brother's daughter, which indicates that we must not push the comparison too far.

4. This triadic organization had already been pointed out by A. Métraux among the Aweikoma, but it was disputed because it would have been "unique to Brazil." (For the authors cited in this argument, see the bibliography at the end of the book.)

Introduction to *A Reconsideration of Apinayé Social Morphology*

In this article Roberto Da Matta analyzes problems in Apinayé social structure that have eluded solution for some time. Da Matta's insights come as the result of extensive field research he conducted among the Apinayé as part of a program of field studies sponsored by the Harvard Central Brazil Research Project directed by Professor David Maybury-Lewis, and co-sponsored by the National Museum of Rio de Janeiro.

The Apinayé are a savanna-dwelling people who live near the confluence of the Araguaia and Tocantins rivers. Like other Gê peoples they formerly had a dual adaptation, spending part of the year as semi-nomadic hunters and gatherers, but returning each year to semi-permanent villages to reap the harvest from the manioc and maize which had been planted prior to the hunt (Nimuendajú 1939). Gradually, with the increasing encroachment of Brazilians on their hunting territories, the Apinayé lived for longer periods in their settlements and spent less time hunting. Some nineteenth-century sources report Apinayé settlements of over a thousand people, but by the 1930s the total population had shrunk to a few hundred.

Until Da Matta's work, the best source on the Apinayé had been the published work of the self-trained German ethnographer Curt Unkel, who cared so much for the people he studied that he took an indigenous name: Nimuendajú. One of the most interesting aspects of Nimuendajú's (1939) report was his description of four "marriage classes" called *kiyê* to which recruitment followed a rare pattern: girls belonged to their mother's *kiyê,* and boys to their father's. The men of each *kiyê* were said to marry women from a specific other *kiyê,* so that men from *kiyê* A married B women, B men married C women, etc.

Much of the debate over the Apinayé has focused on these marriage classes and it has now been shown (Maybury-Lewis 1960) that the system could not have functioned in the manner which Nimuendajú claimed. Da Matta has succeeded not only in showing what the *kiyê* are, but he has even reconstructed just where Nimuendajú made his error. But more importantly, Da Matta has made a significant theoretical contribution in showing that a given domain may have a relative character within a single society.

Roberto Da Matta received his Ph.D. degree from Harvard University and is presently director of the graduate program in anthropology, National Museum, Rio de Janeiro.

16. A RECONSIDERATION OF APINAYÉ
SOCIAL MORPHOLOGY

ROBERTO DA MATTA*

Since 1939, when Curt Nimuendajú published his book on *The Apinayé,* Americanists have faced difficulties in trying to relate these Northern Gê to their neighbors: the Kayapó to the west of the Tocantins and the groups known as the Eastern Timbira—the Krahó, Krĩkatí, Ramkokamkrá-Apaniekrá (Canella) and Gaviões, located to the east of the same river (v. Nimuendajú, 1946:6).

The critical difficulty involved in relating the Apinayé to these other groups was the system of four matrimonial classes which, according to Nimuendajú, governed marriage among the Apinayé. As described by Nimuendajú, the Apinayé (in contrast to all other Gê and South American groups) had developed a system of exchange of women based on four groups (termed *kiyê*). Incorporation into these groups followed a very rare type of descent: sons were incorporated into the father's group, while daughters were included in the mother's group (Nimuendajú, 1939:29 ff.).

Since Nimuendajú's publication, various anthropologists have reflected on the so-called *kiyê* and their curious method of recruiting new members. Kroeber, Lowie, Murdock, and Jules Henry have analyzed the system, and Lévi-Strauss has on several occasions taken it as a classic example of the relativity of the

* Financial aid for this research was provided by the Division of Anthropology of the Museu Nacional (FURJ), the Research Council of the same body, and the Harvard-Central Brazil Research Project. The Brazilian National Research Council and the Ford Foundation (Rio Office) assisted me with fellowships while I was finishing my studies at Harvard University. To all of the above I would like to express my deep gratitude. Early versions of this paper were read at the Congress of Americanists in 1968, Stuttgart; and at the 68th Annual Meeting of the American Anthropological Association in New Orleans, 1969. I also would like to acknowledge here the debt I owe to all of the members of the Harvard-Central Brazil Research Project (Harvard University-Museu Nacional): David Maybury-Lewis, Terry Turner, Julio C. Melatti, J. C. Crocker, J. C. Lave, Joan Bamberger and Cecil Cook, Jr.

fundamental concepts of exogamy and endogamy. Interpretations of the *kiyê* have differed widely, reflecting the differing theoretical perspectives of the anthropologists who have concerned themselves with the problem. Some, like Murdock, equated the *kiyê* marriage classes with sections of the Australian type: others, like Jules Henry, called attention the latent aspects of the matrimonial system (the inter-*kiyê* endogamy). No one, however, tried to perform a structural analysis of the system, seeking to examine all its sociological implications, until Maybury-Lewis approached the problem from precisely this point of view, in an article published in 1960 and significantly entitled "Parallel Descent and the Apinayé Anomaly."[1]

In this article, Maybury-Lewis, utilizing statistical and structural arguments, demonstrated that the *kiyê* could never have operated according to Nimuendajú's description, that parallel descent would lead to the formation of non-functional corporate groups (because they would be monosexual groups), and finally, that the *kiyê*, in the general perspective of Gê-Timbira ethnography, could not be a dominant institution of Apinayé society (Maybury-Lewis 1960:198).

Although Maybury-Lewis did not arrive at a final solution of the Apinayé system, he was correct in asserting: (a) that the *kiyê* is a secondary institution of the Apinayé social system and (b) that these groups could not regulate marriage as Nimuendajú claims.

In this paper, we shall not present a detailed study of how the *kiyê* operate in Apinayé society. This will be done in another work.[2] We shall, however, provide a description of the *kiyê* which differs from Nimuendajú's. Our intention here is to establish, using new ethnographic data as a base, a scheme of reference for Apinayé social morphology that will be able to integrate this group into the context of the other Gê groups and also account for Nimuendajú's description.

BASIC DOMAINS OF APINAYÉ SOCIETY

As with the other Northern Gê, the social universe of the Apinayé divides itself into two complementary antithetical areas:

the domain of everyday relations, primarily concentrated in the nuclear and extended uxorilocal families, located in residential groups on the periphery of the village; and a ceremonial or public domain, institutionally expressed by ceremonial groups which are always bisected and conceived as antithetical and complementary (the ceremonial moieties), and by groups of mature men (initiated, married and with children), always associated with the center of the village.

The activities of daily life are influenced by relations with close kin, or, as the Apinayé say, kinsmen (*kwóyá*) who share the same blood. Of particular importance is the nuclear family and the extended family (i.e., the residential segment as a whole). These relationships are involved with the production and transformation of natural products into social products. Thus the Apinayé relate the periphery of the village to the transformation of vegetables and game into food, and of menstrual blood and sperm into children. (In their idea of conception, the genitors of the child contribute to the formation of its body in a symmetrical manner.) This is the sphere where intimate and intense relations between persons predominate, and such relations in the Apinayé system primarily involve genitors and the individuals made by the same genitors. Here, the nuclear family is always taken as a focus. (This is the group which, according to the Apinayé, has the closest and strongest tie of common blood.) Other relatives, linked to this central group but outside it, are classified as more distant and more ambiguous in terms of obligations. For example: an Apinayé male observes dietary restrictions (*piâmgrí*) when his child is born or when his father, mother or brothers (sons of the same genitors) get sick. When asked why, he says that these are the kin who have the same blood, who live together and, consequently, are all affected when any one of them is ill. The Apinayé therefore emphasize the biological basis of the nuclear family and treat other relationships as peripheral. Extra familial relations, in proportion to their distance from the nuclear family, become more and more diffuse and open to choices and manipulation.

The biological basis of certain relationships has important implications for the understanding of Apinayé social structure. In the first place, it expresses degrees among social links on the level of social behavior, in opposition to the monolithic classification of kin on the strictly terminological plane. Thus every son of a *pam* (father, father's brother, etc.) is a *tõ* (brother) from the standpoint of the Apinayé terminological classification of kin. But if an Apinayé has to make a decision involving the choice of but one *tõ* in a group of three (for example, when he is going to decide whom he must help in clearing a forest), he can instantly distinguish between the class of *tõ* who are his *tõ kumrendy* ("real brothers" or "persons formed by the same genitor") and the *tõ kaág* ("imitation" or "false" brothers, who may be sons of the classificatory brothers of his father, sons of his adoptive father, etc.).

In the second place, the biological foundation bisects the Apinayé system of relationships into two classes: that of persons biologically connected to ego and that of persons non-biologically connected to ego, that is, kin whose blood bonds with ego are conceived as removed, weak and consequently irrelevant for serving as a point of reference for the translation and justification of mutual obligations. The Apinayé system, however, attributes ceremonial and/or public obligations to this class of relationships.[3] Where close consanguinity ceases to be fundamental and begins to allow the establishment of discontinuities in the bilateral web of relationships, a continuity is created by means of the ceremonial and public bonds.[4]

The conceptual basis of this biological distance lies in the distance between generations and in the separation of the sexes. While relatives of consecutive generations are strongly connected by biological links, as in the case of father and son, relatives of alternate generations still consider themselves biologically related, but, as the Apinayé say, the blood is weaker.[5] This is what occurs in the relationship between grandfathers and grandsons, for example. A structurally identical separation occurs between persons who possess the same genitor but are of different sex, i.e., between brother and sister. The basis of this distinction seems to be the result of the application of the opposition between men and women, since the Apinayé attribute to women a series of qualities which contrast with those of men. For them man and woman oppose each other socially, politically and ceremonially[6] as well as physically. Thus they say that man is hard, woman is soft; man is light while woman is heavy because her body has more blood.[7] For this reason she is said to be always ready to provoke conflicts.

The passage between generations is thus structurally equivalent to the passage from one sex to another, and this equivalence can only be understood in relation to the Apinayé conception of their system of relationships.

On the terminological level the cross-sex siblings of ego's father and mother are identified with his grandfathers, forming the class *geti-tui,** which opposes itself in biological and sociological terms to the class *pam-nã†* of the genitors. In this way, these two domains of the system of relationships permit the establishment of continuities. But the continuity deriving from the domestic domain is conceived of by the Apinayé in terms of blood (the emphasis falling on the biological dimension of the system and on the possibility of establishing gradations between relationships), whereas the other is frankly based on *personal names* and on the ceremonial roles which certain persons are entitled to play. The fact that the system is constituted of two domains which complement and intersect each other permits a great flexibility, because every Apinayé can utilize one or the other domain (or both) to claim a close or distant relationship with another person.[8] It is this dualism of the system of relationships that prevents the Apinayé from developing unilineal descent groups from the uxorilocal residence and the extended families. Indeed, the system is bilateral to the point of separating relationships, persons, and categories of persons according to the nature of the element which links a relative of ascending generation to one of descending generation. Thus the genitors (*pam-nã*) give blood and body to the child, while the *geti-tui* gives names and thus enlarges ego's field of relations within the community.

Seen as a totality, the Apinayé system includes as many relationships based on biological links as on social links: names, residence and frequent contacts between individuals.[9] Thus it is always possible for an Apinayé to focus on one dimension or the other in order to rationalize obligations or to settle choices in the social field. At a higher level of the system, "strangers" or non-kin can be transformed into kin (as happens in the case of affines

* *geti* = MB, MF, FF; *tui* = FZ, FM, MM.
† *pam* = F, FB, MZH; *nã* = M, MZ, FBW.

when the marriage stabilizes itself after the couple has children and thus is left, according to the Indians, "with mixed blood"), and kin into non-kin, as the social links act upon the biological links dialectically, and vice versa. This possibility of passing from the domain of nature (in which relationships are thought of as defined biologically, the paradigm for which is the nuclear family) to the domain of culture (in which kin are defined in terms of ceremonial relationships, the paradigm being given by the naming system) provides for a great manipulability in the system. This flexibility constitutes a true conceptual bridge between the two domains of the Apinayé social universe which we are describing.

Beyond this, the domestic or private domain is intimately related to "heavy work" (construction of houses, clearing of forests, construction of fences around their clearings, activities which clearly mark the status of a married man), to the difficult and crucial periods in the life of a married man and to gossip, sorcery, internal disputes and factional conflicts. In this way, the private domain is connected to the differences of power and prestige existing between groups and individuals which daily life invariably brings.

In contrast to the private domain, the Apinayé associate the public or ceremonial domain to the communal aspects of their social order. The public sphere is dominated by the *plaza* or *center of the village* (*ngo, me-i-ngo, ipôgo*) and by the most absolute equality between social groups, since there are always two and both are necessary for any collective activity. This is the area where everything is stereotyped, formal, integrated and theoretical. Indeed, remembering Curt Nimuendajú's description of the Canella and Apinayé social life (Nimuendajú 1946, 1939–56), there is no doubt that he took this domain as *the* "social structure" of both tribes, as we have suggested elsewhere (Da Matta 1967b). At this level, the system is seen as composed of discontinuous groups, recruitment into which takes place according to very well-defined principles. Whereas in the private domain an individual meets difficulties in saying where his group of kin ends, as "blood spreads throughout the village," there are no doubts about the distinctions between and composition of ceremonial groups, since the contrast between them is the essential part of their conception as entities. For example: given the name of certain individuals, the

Apinayé can confidently say to which ceremonial moiety the bearer belongs; whereas it is very difficult to separate clearly the kin groups of the same village.

Actually, it is social practice that distinguishes one group of kin from another in the domestic area, as in certain periods groups of persons associate themselves with others and thus form what Lave calls "domestic clusters" (Lave 1967). These *clusters* are particularly apparent on the political plane. In theory, however, it is always possible to relate one group to another once one takes as reference a pivotal kinsman as the focus of the common system of relationships. Public groups, on the other hand, are conceptually and practically distinct: there are no gradations between them. Passage from one to another is accomplished only through the change of names.

The public and ceremonial domain of Apinayé society divides into two pairs of moieties. There are two relationships which permit the recruitment of these pairs of social groupings. The moieties *Kolti* and *Kolre,* associated respectively with sun/moon, dry season/rainy season, east/west, red/black, etc., are transmitted with the names that each Apinayé individual receives as soon as he is born.

Apinayé names are combinations of from three to seven words, some having a translation and diverse associations. Thus some names are wholly translatable (as, for example, *Krã Kambreg* = red head), while others seem to associate themselves only with other names (Nimuendajú 1939:24). It is, however, important to observe that when the Apinayé speak of their names, they distinguish those which are used within the domestic area from those names which carry with them ceremonial roles and membership in certain groups.[10] It is these latter names that bring with them the notion of continuity between generations, because they formalize the relationship between a *geti/tamtxúa,*[11] which, after the transmission, is called *krã-tum/krã-duw* (old head/young head), in a terminological formula which certainly expresses the identity of the persons thus related. Thus the repertory of Apinayé names can be divided according to the moieties *Kolti* and *Kolre.* Besides, certain names, given the conspicuous role that their bearers play in certain ceremonies, are taken as paradigms for the moieties. This is what happens with the names *Katam* and *Wanme,* systematically identified with the moieties and seemingly cognates of the Krahó (moiety names) *Katamye* and *Wakmenye* (Melatti 1970). All the formal names can be related to one or the other of the ceremonial groups, which include both men and women (Nimuendajú 1939:21).

Among the Apinayé, however, the transmission of names does not involve only the donor and recipient of the names, as happens with the other Timbira (Nimuendajú 1946:77–78; Lave 1967; Melatti 1970), but a third position: the one who procures the name giver. The names, however, always pass between the categories *geti/tamtxúa* in the masculine case and *tui/tamtxúa* in the feminine case. The difference between the Apinayé system and that of the other Timbira resides in the role of "arranger of names" who first adopts the child, and then gets a name giver for him. Thus when one asks the Apinayé who gave names to a child, they always refer to the arranger of names, who is the child's adoptive father (*pam kaág*) in the masculine case, or adoptive mother (*nã kaág*) in the feminine case. Clearly, the emphasis on the adoptive parents tends to be confusing. In practice it means that name transmission among the Apinayé takes place through mechanisms entirely different from those that operate among the Eastern Timbira.[12]

The implications of this system of name transmission are important. In the first place, the process of incorporation of a boy (or girl) into the moieties *Kolti* and *Kolre* is not realized through his relationship with a kinsman of the category *geti* or *tui* who is related directly to the genitors. This happens among the Krahó, Canella, Krĩkatí and Gaviões, but among the Apinayé, the *geti* and *tui* are directly related to the child's *adoptive* parents. This leads to much wider possibilities for choice and variation in the relationship, as the adoptive parents may be biological, classificatory or fictive siblings of the genitors. In this way, there is among the Apinayé an exchange of children (or of parents), as if, after the emphasis on the genitors, there were a dislocation to the sociological aspects of paternity, and finally, after the transmission of names, another dislocation to a relative of a marginal category, a *geti* or a *tui*. Among the Apinayé the procurers of names (adoptive parents) and the name givers (adoptive *geti* or *tui*) are related to the child throughout his life. The former are charged with pay-ing indemnities in cases of defloration or divorce, and the latter are especially responsible for him during rites of passage. The true parents, that is, the genitors, are prohibited from giving their names to their own sons or daughters because, as some informants said, "They already made the child." Biological links thus give way to social (or ritual) links. One reason why the adoptive parents must be the principal intermediaries in disputes is because, according to the Apinayé, the whole process of settlement of conflicts can thus unfold calmly. The adoptive and ritual parents, therefore, operate in a semi-public (or semi-private) area, while the name givers (*geti-tui*) operate in an eminently public ceremonial area. Consistent with the relationship system, the naming system also avoids a contamination of one domain of social relationships with another, a basic principle of the Northern Gê social systems.

With names, the Apinayé create a considerable amplification of each individual's social network and they divide his social relationships into three categories, each one indicative of a group: (a) that of the genitors who gave him blood and body (= nuclear family), (b) that of the adoptive parents who obtained a name for him (= a domestic group different from the natal group) and (c) that of the nominators who gave him social roles (= the ceremonial moieties, *Kolti* or *Kolre*).

The second pair of moieties to which all Apinayé belong are transmitted by the formal friends (*krã-geti*), through a mechanism of filiation more or less similar to that which operates in the case of name transference. These moieties are called *Ipognotxóine* and *Krénotxóine*. The names signify, respectively, "people of the center plaza" and "people of the house or periphery." The opposition here is marked, therefore, by each group's spatial relationship of relative proximity to the section considered the most public of the village, its center. We could then say that the dualism of the moieties *Kolti/Kolre* is of the diametric type (the emphasis being placed on the symmetry and complementarity of the two opposed groups); whereas that of the *Ipognotxóine/Krénotxóine* is of the concentric type, with the emphasis on the asymmetry and hierarchy that mark the relations between the opposed groups. The Apinayé say that the *Ipognotxóine* are liars, deceptive and inconsequent, thus connecting them to the moon, night, rains, women and other elements marked by irregularity and unpredictability, while the *Krénotxóine* are associated with the opposed elements: sun, day, men, etc. When one observes that this is an inversion, as the *Ipognotxóine* ought to be related to the serious and regular things, like men, sun, etc., the Apinayé say that this is correct, but that sun and moon left things thus for men.[13]

But let us leave the symbolism of the Apinayé ceremonial groups to observe that the moieties *Ipognotxóine* and *Krénotxóine* correspond to two of the groups called *kiyê* by Curt Nimuendajú. Together with two others, the *kiyê Krā-ô-mbédy* (beautiful hair) and *Kré'kára* (eaves of the house),[14] they formed, for Nimuendajú, the four matrimonial groups of Apinayé society. Let us first note the relations between the last two groups and the first two, which we have called moieties.

When we focus upon the names of these *kiyê* a discrepancy is immediately apparent, as the names *Krā-ô-mbédy* and *Kré'kára,* in contrast to the terms *Ipognotxóine* and *Krénotxóine,* refer to the decorations used by their supposed members and not to the groups themselves. Another point is that the decorations refer respectively to the *head* and the eaves of the *house.* Now, an association made by the Apinayé is that between *head = center, plaza* and *house = periphery.* This was observed by us countless times, but it is even possible to infer such associations from Nimuendajú's data, if one keeps in mind that there are various relationships where the term *krā* (head) is fundamental, as between name donor and name recipient or between formal friends (*krā-geti/pákrā*). What marks these relationships is their ceremonial content, which is associated with the center of the village. Thus the associations of these two names lead us to consider them as references to the first two groups, a relationship which was confirmed in the field. We never heard mention of the names *Krā-ô-mbédy* or *Kré'kára* among the Aminayé. When we cited these names, the informants indicated that they were decorations of the groups *Ipog* and *Kré,* respectively. And when we made a census of the two Apinayé villages, including in our data the filiation of each individual, the former pair of names were never mentioned, whereas *Kolti* and *Kolre, Ipog* and *Kré* were invariably present. The problem of why Nimuendajú described the four groups can then be explained in the following manner: Nimuendajú probably interpreted the names of the decorations as though they were groups. The error was perpetuated because he never sought to confirm his information with other informants. We know that among the Apinayé, Nimuendajú worked only with the chief and the counselor. Moreover, the name *kiyê* means nothing to the modern Apinayé, the word for "side" or "group" being *pikiyêre*.

Let us now see how the mode of incorporation into these groups described by Nimuendajú can be explained, and also why he associated these *kiyê* with a type of matrimonial prescription. As soon as a child reaches the age of ten years, his adoptive parents (*pam kaág and nã kaág*) choose a "formal friend" for him (*krã-geti,* masc.; *krã-gedy,* fem.; reciprocals, *pá-krã*) from whom the child receives the "marks" of one of the two moieties into which he will be incorporated. His *krã-geti* is always, according to the rule, a *pá-krã* of one of his *pam* or *nã kaág,* so that the child ends up belonging to the same ceremonial group as his ceremonial parents (who, in their turn, have passed their moiety "marks" to an adoptive son or daughter of one of their *krã-geti,* perhaps the individual who now passes the same marks back to ego). All the cases I obtained among the Apinayé follow this seemingly complex rule: statistical variations are insignificant. A boy can be related either to a "formal friend" of his own sex or to a "formal friend" of the opposite sex. The same is true for a girl. Ideally the Apinayé give emphasis to the relationships between formal friends of the same sex.

There is thus a formal continuity between the recruitment of this second pair of moieties and the connections between a man with his *pá-krã* on the one hand and his adoptive son on the other, the former being the latter's future *krã-geti.* The consequence of this is that there is always a minimum of two "lines." One consists of a man and his adoptive son, and the other of his *krã-geti* and his adoptive son. The two lines, as one can see with the help of a simple diagram, exchange rights of incorporation in this second pair of moieties when one *pá-krã* becomes the *krã-geti* of his *krã-geti*'s adoptive son. There is a clear emphasis on the (adoptive) father-son relationship (or the mother-daughter relationship, as the case may be) which ends up incorporated in the same ceremonial group in an indirect fashion. In other words, adoptive father and son, in virtue of the exchanges made by their *krã-geti,* are members of the same ceremonial moiety. But it is necessary to emphasize that these "lines" are only capable of corporate actions in festivals. Their corporate character is ceremonial and they affect neither daily life nor matrimonial links.

On the basis of these facts it is possible to explain in a coherent fashion some of Nimuendajú's mistaken data and assumptions. Two facts stand out in this connection. First, Nimuendajú never fully understood the sociological significance of foster (or ceremonial) parenthood among the Apinayé. It is precisely the foster parents who act as mediators between name giver and name receiver, as well as being a point of reference for the choice of formal friends. Second, there is in fact an emphasis on the relationships between father-son/mother-daughter, but persons thus linked are bound to each other for ceremonial purposes alone. The genitors of a given ego do not establish formal friendship relations with him. Such relations properly connect only "distant" relatives and not the ones who already have a link of biological substance with a given ego. To say, then, that the Apinayé have "parallel descent" is to say very little about the true mechanisms that actually operate in this society.

There are also reasons for the association made by Nimuendajú's informant between these moieties and a supposed matrimonial prescription. One of these is that the *krã-geti* are always situated on the "other side of the village," since these formal friends govern their mutual relationships by a series of restrictions of conduct. In fact, they are only together in the ceremonials in which their groups appear. Moreover, they must avoid each other, and not speak to each other. In cases of serious conflicts or extreme ritual marginality, the *krã-geti* is always the person indicated to bring about the reincorporation of his *pá-krã* into the social structure. Now, this is precisely the situation of affines among the Apinayé, especially in the first years of marriage. Furthermore, a man goes to the other side of the village to get his wife, and it is with his affines (viz., parents and brothers of his wife) that an Apinayé establishes relationships marked by an extreme formalism. Thus the equation between marriage and the moieties *Ipognotxóine* and *Krénotxóine* is quite conceivable in the Indians' eyes on a theoretical formal level.

The so-called *kiyê* are thus ceremonial moieties which appear in festivals (the rites of passage, today about to disappear, together with the *kiyê* themselves). Their relationship with marriage can only be established analogically and indirectly. On the level of social practice, no Apinayé takes these groups as points of reference when he discusses his own or his son's marriage. In reality, they rigorously deny any suggestions that their wives must be of a particular group or even particular houses. As happens with complex systems of marriage such as ours, the Apinayé know whom they may not marry, but they do not know whom they must marry. The error of Nimuendajú was derived from the metaphorical similarities between marriage and ceremonial friendship relations that we have just discussed.

Conclusions. The example of the *kiyê* teaches two important lessons. First, it tells us that among the Apinayé (as among the other Northern Gê), social life unfolds on two levels: in a formal area and in another sphere where a great number of choices are always possible. This does not mean that a disparity exists between the plane of the code and that of the message. On the contrary, we know that these are related and that the variations and choices made by the Indians on the plane of social practice are related to a code which is very simple, and perhaps because of this, permits so many variations. The mistake of Nimuendajú's informant was to have taken one of these spheres and presented it to the anthropologist as the unique reality of social life. Nimuendajú's mistake was to have taken this formalized area as being the whole of Apinayé social structure.

The second lesson is that little by little, social anthropologists are discovering that their fundamental task is not merely to describe the formal aspects of the social systems they study, but rather to analyze the application of formal rules in specific contexts, where they become susceptible to variations and transformations. It is only by considering both of these aspects together that one can arrive at an adequate description of social reality, as the case of the Apinayé *kiyê* clearly demonstrates.

NOTES

1. As the reader will have observed, in the above part we are following the excellent history of the ethnography of the *kiyê* furnished by Maybury-Lewis in his work already mentioned (Maybury-Lewis 1960:193 ff.).

2. Da Matta 1970.

3. As may be seen, we are following the formulation developed and elegantly applied to the Krahó by Julio Cezar Melatti (1970).

4. Given these principles one cannot fail to note the similarity of the Northern Gê and the American relationship systems, as the latter is understood by Schneider (1968). A comparison of these two systems will illuminate some important aspects of the Crow-Omaha terminologies.

5. The Apinayé say that the old people are the "foot" or the "root" (*me o pó kráti*) of the kindred. An informant compared them to corn which, when planted, produces new seeds in the part above the foot or root, made of the old seeds. As one goes away from the foot, the blood proportionately grows weaker. From a strictly sociological viewpoint, the weakening of blood in the alternate generations is, without doubt, an expression of the opposition old/ young.

6. The women do not take an explicit part in the political system; they do not have initiation rituals to mark passages between age classes and changes of status within the social system. They have markedly different roles in ceremonies and they always reside in the natal residence in which they have rights by virtue of the uxorilocal rule of residence. Thus brother and sister stay separated by their natures and by their positions within the system.

7. These distinctions are fundamental because, according to the Apinayé, the entire emphasis of the seclusion of the initiates is on physical exercises (races), ingestion of meat of certain light animals (the deer, for example) and little rest, so that by means of the separation from the domestic sphere, the women, and the periphery of the village, the boys are left with little blood and, consequently, are more alert and "light."

8. The above analysis shows how important it is to consider the *ideologies* of groups in the study of relationship terms. It is not that "kinship" has nothing to do with biology. What one must take into consideration is how the system under study handles biologically given facts. In the Apinayé case this is basic for a proper understanding of their terminological system, an area left untouched by theorists of the Crow-Omaha terminologies. For a development of this point, see Da Matta 1970.

9. The reader must have noted that the categories defined with the help of the above dimensions only determine some positions of the terminological system. Thus *pam-nã* = father, father's brother, mother's mother, mother's sister, respectively. The reciprocal is *krá*. And *geti-tui* = father's father, mother's father, mother's brother and father's sister's husband; mother's mother, father's mother, father's sister and mother's brother's wife; reciprocal: *tamtxúa*. There remain, evidently, the matrilateral and patrilateral cross-

cousins. But it is precisely in the definition of these genealogical positions that the names and use of the context permit multiple solutions among the Apinayé. (Besides, this also happens among the Krahó and Krĩkatí: Melatti 1970 and Lave 1967.) Thus if the emphasis were given to the names, ego can identify himself structurally with his mother's brother (assuming that he has been the nominator) and call the latter's sons *ikrá* (sons); but if the emphasis were given in the relationship of blood between father and son, ego can identify himself structurally with his father and call his patrilateral cross-cousins *tamtxúa* ("nephews") in a solution opposite for the cross-cousins. It is the play of these two dimensions in concrete situations which provokes the differences in the terminologies presented by Nimuendajú in the American and Brazilian versions of his book on the Apinayé (Nimuendajú 1939:111–12 and 1956:141–42).

10. The distinction is fundamental because the Apinayé may possess seven names, but they are known by only one of them. Thus in the cases where the name does not bring membership in a moiety, it is necessary to mention the remaining names in order to determine the ceremonial groups. But in the rituals in which such an individual takes part, he is always referred to by his "formal" name. The implication of this distinction and the association, names = contexts, in the logic of Apinayé nomination, and that of the Timbira in general, is reexamined in Da Matta 1970.

11. *tamtxúa* = ZC, SC, DC, FZC (man speaker); BC, SC, DC, FZC (woman speaker).

12. It was his failure to understand the role of the adoptive father that led Nimuendajú to describe a totally different naming system for the Apinayé (Nimuendajú 1939:22 and 1946:78). Another recurrent error of Nimuendajú is to base his interpretation of the social implications of naming on the conception of naming relationships in terms of genealogical positions instead of categories. For a consideration of this last point, see Da Matta 1967a and 1970.

13. We are following Lévi-Strauss' use of the terms "concentric" and "diametric" (1963: Chapter VIII).

14. These terms are names for types of headdress or head decoration used by the respective groups.

Introduction to Shamanism and Political Control Among the Kuikuru

Gertrude E. Dole conducted field work among the Kuikuru Indians of Mato Grosso in 1953 and 1954, along with Robert Carneiro (see Chapter 7 in this volume). The Kuikuru are one of a number of small, independent tribes which inhabit the upper Xingú River. This area is thought to be a kind of cul-de-sac or refuge area to which peoples escaped from the north, fleeing European contact with all its depredations. Among the linguistically distinct groups living in separate villages are the Trumai (R. Murphy and B. Quain 1966), the Suyá (Schultz 1962), the Mehinacu (Gregor in Chapter 14 of this volume), the Waurá (P. E. Lima 1950), the Camayurá (Oberg 1953) and others (cf. E. Galvão 1953; C. Lévi-Strauss 1948a). Most of these participate in a common "Xinguano" culture, and trade and even intermarry with other villages. Like most of the tropical forest and savanna peoples they exhibit a low level of political development and practically no individuals or groups enjoy privileged access to strategic resources (cf. Fried 1967).

Kuikuru shamans present a partial exception to this statement in that they enjoy a special relationship with powerful spirits which no one else seems to have. People turn to shamans in times of need and believe that they can cure illnesses and solve problems. While this power is not directly converted into "political power" (cf. Fried 1967), Dole concludes that "The shaman tends to preserve the integrity of the society by reducing anxiety and conflict among its members and supporting the social norms necessary for its political existence." This conclusion would appear to characterize many other societies at this cultural level in South America. For example, Charles Wagley's classic description of Tapirapé Shamanism (orig. 1943) leads to much the same conclusion.

Given this crucial role of the shaman, it is not surprising to learn that shamans and other religious practitioners have considerable power in more highly developed societies in South America. The prestige and supernatural power attached to the shaman at this evolutionary level are then crystallized to true political power at the next level.

Gertrude E. Dole has authored numerous other articles on the Kuikuru, among which the following are particularly valuable: Dole and Carneiro 1958, Dole 1959, 1964a, 1966, 1969. Holding a doctorate from the University of Michigan, she has also carried out field research among the Amahuaca Indians of eastern Peru. She is the author of several important contributions to the study of kinship nomenclature. Gertrude Dole teaches at the State University of New York, Purchase.

17. SHAMANISM AND POLITICAL CONTROL AMONG THE KUIKURU

GERTRUDE E. DOLE

INTRODUCTION

The Kuikuru are a Carib speaking group of horticulturists in the Upper Xingú region of central Brazil. Their settlement is politically autonomous and comprises nine houses, each of which shelters several nuclear families.

The nuclear family is a self-sufficient economic unit except that the cooperation of several men is needed for a few projects such as erecting the frame of a multifamily house and carrying a newly cut canoe from the forest to water. When needed, the cooperation of friends and kinsmen is obtained through the device of throwing a party for the workers. Communal activities are rarely undertaken, but when they are, a similar device is employed to mobilize labor. Whereas in many other Tropical Forest groups in South America the headman organizes communal enterprises, among the Kuikuru the labor for such activities is paid for with food and drink provided by an individual, who is referred to as the owner of the undertaking (Dole, 1959).

As these techniques for mobilizing cooperative labor suggest, formal leadership among the Kuikuru is extremely weak. Very few special obligations and privileges are attributed to the headman. These include titular ownership of the tribal territory, making decisions about when to move the settlement, and choice of its location. In addition a strong chief may call out daily plans for work and may harangue his people about preserving tribal customs. In actual fact, however, it is questionable whether any of these

Reprinted by permission of the author and publisher from *Beiträge zur Völkerkunde Sud-Amerikas: Festgabe für Herbert Baldus*, pp. 53–62. 1964. Hannover: Münstermann.

functions was performed by the man who held the position of headman when observations for this paper were made.[1]

In theory the position of headman is inherited patrilineally, but in actuality it often happens that when a headman dies his sons are too young to assume leadership. Under these conditions the role passes to an adult male in another family, so that men from several families have assumed leadership over the past few generations and the sons of all of them now have some claim to succession.

The Kuikuru have very few restrictive rules for social behavior. Not only does the headman not control social behavior, but the ceremonial system provides very few regulations. Most of the ceremonies are primarily secular, and there is relatively little fear of the malevolent power of spirits to punish one.

The tribal settlement is agamous, but in recent years spouses have been chosen from within the settlement more frequently than from neighboring tribes. The ideal postmarital residence is virilocal with respect to both settlement and house, but there is no strict rule of residence except that a couple is expected to reside for an initial period of a few months with the parents of the bride. The several nuclear families in most of the houses are closely related to one another, constituting extended families of various types, fraternal, sororal, bilateral, patrilocal and matrilocal. However, nuclear families not infrequently change their place of residence, making the extended family organization of the community unstable as well as irregular. The kinship structure is cognatic and the kinship nomenclature is a variant of the Generation pattern. (See Dole, 1957:359 ff.)

From this brief summary it can be seen that Kuikuru society is very loosely structured. In keeping with the looseness of structure, social behavior is extremely permissive. An example of the permissiveness is the fact that most individuals have several extramarital sex partners without fear of social sanctions, even when the identities of the paramours are known or strongly suspected. (See Carneiro, 1959.) Moreover, infractions of the legal norms often go unpunished. When thefts of personal property occur, for example, the owner has no means of redressing the wrong unless he actually catches the thief in the act of stealing, which is very unlikely. And even if the thief is caught there is no prescribed punishment for such delicts.

Theoretically a person may quarrel with the miscreant, but in actuality even this action is not taken because among the Kuikuru any kind of hostility is taken as evidence of malevolence and an indication that the disgruntled individual may take revenge through witchcraft. It is dangerous to be suspected of witchcraft, because sorcery is one of the few conditions which justify homicide. A few years ago a man was killed because he was thought to be working witchcraft on a number of children. The only close kin of the victim were his two daughters, who did not avenge his death. Some years before that incident another Kuikuru had killed a man from the neighboring Kalapalu tribe who was suspected of causing deaths that led to the extinction of more than one tribal settlement in the region. This killing also went unavenged, and neither of the killers was punished.

Because suspected sorcery is punishable by death the Kuikuru try to avoid being suspected by being genial and noncombative, even when they feel they have been wronged. But the frustration that results from the virtual lack of recourse to legal sanctions in many instances may be very intense. On one occasion, in fact, the frustration was so great that a grown man wept in repressed anger because an irreplaceable item of considerable value had been stolen from him and he had no means of retrieving it or retaliating for the theft.

In view of the lack of effective social control in political and ceremonial structure, the possibility suggests itself that the Kuikuru may resort to other and less direct mechanisms to reinforce norms and preserve social cohesion. Such a mechanism is in fact to be found in shamanism. I will describe Kuikuru shamanism and discuss its function in supplying some degree of social control.

SHAMANISM

The primary function of a shaman is medical; he is hired to cure illnesses which do not respond to the herbal remedies that are common knowledge. A second important function is divining to determine the causes of illness and other misfortunes. The principal techniques used are removal of intrusive objects and trance induced by smoking native cigarettes. A shaman's services are paid for with beads, which serve as both ornament and currency among the Kuikuru.

Shamanism is not a hereditary role. In fact one shaman indicated that his son would not be a shaman, because smoking is bad for one. Rather a man may be motivated to become a shaman by receiving a "call" to do so. When a man undertakes to learn the secret techniques of shamanism he is tutored by a master shaman, who teaches him chants and the art of inducing trance by smoking. The pupil is secluded for a month in his mentor's house, where he fasts, dreams and practices smoking. In his dreams he speaks with a personal spirit helper, who is said to give him cigarettes and teach him how to smoke. The pupil also goes into the forest and communicates with one of the forest spirits which is visible only to shamans. It is thought that smoking enables shamans to see and hear things that are hidden from other people.

Finally the apprentice undergoes an arduous initiation administered by an established shaman. The body of the apprentice is anointed with a mixture of pulverized tree resin and water, which is rubbed especially on the fingernails and hair and in the ears. Then the neophyte demonstrates his ability to smoke deeply and induce a state of trance, or "die", as the Kuikuru say. When he is revived he drinks tree resin mixed with salt and water. This he must do twice, without vomiting. If he can perform this ordeal successfully he is then considered a full-fledged shaman.

There are five shamans in the Kuikuru society. These men are explicitly ranked as to their ability, and one of them, named Metsé, is said to be a far better shaman than any of the others. Although all of them frequently smoke in the evening "because they like to", only Metsé is called on to conduct shamanistic performances as a rule.

CURING

It is generally supposed by the Kuikuru that exuviae and other material of various kinds can be used to work sorcery, and that malicious persons inject objects into people in order to kill them. Illnesses of all kinds are attributed to this type of sorcery. In curing, the shaman smokes, seated on a log stool beside the patient's hammock. After inhaling very deeply he places the cigarette between his feet to free his hands, and blows smoke into his cupped hands. He then rubs his hands together and strokes the affected part of the patient's body. As he strokes the patient he says "Aakaaaaaaaah!" and then utters a sequence of noises resembling a number of rapid and uninhibited hiccups with alternately ingressive and egressive sound, "⟨ï⟩ a ⟨ï⟩ a ⟨ï⟩ a", etc. Withdrawing his hands from the patient he inspects the contents, which may be a splinter, a piece of wet matted thread, a fishscale or some other very small item. Taking the cigarette from between his feet he inhales more smoke and goes to the thatched wall of the house, where he blows smoke on the intrusive object and blows it away into the thatch. Eight or ten such performances complete the treatment.

One of the lesser shamans threw some light on the nature of intrusive objects produced by shamans during curing ceremonies. He tore a narrow strip from a piece of canvas and secreted it among his private possessions saying he would use it later in curing.

In instances of serious illness several shamans may work together, as they did on one occasion to treat the wife of a minor shaman and mother of a potential successor to the role of headman. The woman had complained of stomach disorder and pains in her legs. At times she appeared to be in a coma. When her condition did not respond to herbal medicine the principal shaman was called in to treat her. With the usual ritual Metsé "drew out" some bits of wet matted cotton thread, which he threw away in the thatch of the house. As neither this treatment nor similar treatment by her shaman husband improved her condition, it was decided that her soul had been taken from her and that this was the cause of her illness. Then all five Kuikuru shamans together with a visiting shaman conducted a curing ceremony for her. They smoked, chanted and stamped rhythmically. In this procedure a special gourd rattle was used. This rattle is so constructed that the handle is slightly loose. When properly rolled against the forearm, the gourd chamber of the rattle moves on the handle, squeaking with each stroke. The squeaking sound is apparently thought to be the voice of a spirit.

Even this performance did not cure the woman, who then became delirious. During her delirium her husband asked her where she was and what she was doing, in an attempt to learn what she was "dreaming" about. Her answers corroborated the shamans' prognosis that a spirit-being had taken her soul from her. The six shamans then went a short distance outside the settlement and conducted a seance in which they talked with the spirit people. Metsé smoked, "died" and recaptured the lost soul. He wrapped it in a ball with vegetable fibers and held it close to his chest as he returned to the house of the patient. With the ball still held close to his own chest, he placed it next to the patient's chest, in order that the soul might reenter her body.

It may be that shamans are able to convince themselves as well as others that they can hear voices when in a state of trance. I am not prepared to discuss the question of whether or not they do hear such voices. However, the techniques of drama and sleight of hand used in curing are impressive, and they serve an important function in inspiring confidence in the shaman's ability to deal with the supernatural. General belief in his supernatural power does much to determine a shaman's success as a doctor, but it does more than this. Popular faith in a shaman's ability to talk with the spirits is at the base also of his success in divining, since this is what permits him to pass judgments and suggest punitive action without engendering resentment. This fact is illustrated by instances in which Metsé was asked to determine guilt for some misdemeanors.

DIVINING

On one occasion when some stored fruit was stolen, the owner hired Metsé to smoke and divine the identity of the thief. After his smoking seance Metsé named a teen-age boy as the culprit, and the boy's supposed guilt soon became common talk in the community. Although the boy was not confronted directly with the accusation and no steps were taken to punish him formally, the gossip of course served to darken his reputation.

Guilty or not, the boy had no recourse. It is clear that members of the society are thoroughly convinced of Metsé's supernatural power. They also respect and appreciate his efforts in curing and divining. By contrast the boy named in this case was the son of a couple who were generally disliked by others in the community. In fact a number of Kuikuru thought that his father was working witchcraft against them. The marked difference in prestige of Metsé as a master shaman and the person he named undoubtedly lent support to the verdict. Hence it would have done little good for the supposedly guilty boy to protest his innocence. Moreover, if the boy had argued or openly protested the verdict the community probably would have been inclined to suspect him of witchcraft, a situation to be avoided if possible. Under these conditions the boy who was accused of stealing fruit had no choice but to be amiable in the face of adverse public sentiment.

Another and more dramatic instance of divining to determine guilt was occasioned by a fire. An account of this incident will serve to illustrate both the technique of Kuikuru divination and its sociopolitical role.

At high noon on a hot sunny day one of the nine houses in Kuikuru settlement burned to the ground, apparently set afire through careless use of a cooking fire. House fires are always a major crisis for the Kuikuru because their houses are placed very close to one another. If there is any wind, many sparks fly and the tinder-dry thatch of adjoining houses is ignited. Then the probability that all the houses will be destroyed is very high. In this instance only one house was burned because the day was calm, and the few sparks that landed on adjacent houses were successfully extinguished by beating.

Because it was impossible to save the burning house most of the men merely watched the blaze and discussed its cause as they watched. They surmised that the fire had been caused by a flaming arrow shot into the thatch by someone from another tribe. However, they were not certain of this explanation, and the threat of complete disaster was so disturbing that the shaman was asked to determine the cause of the fire.

Accordingly Metsé divined. He and four other shamans sat on log or bark stools and smoked native cigarettes. Only Metsé inhaled deeply, and as he finished one cigarette an attending shaman handed him another lighted one. Metsé inhaled all the smoke, and soon began to evince considerable physical distress. After about ten minutes his right leg began to tremble. Later his left arm began to twitch. He swallowed smoke as well as inhaling it, and soon was groaning in pain. His respiration became labored, and he groaned with every exhalation. By this time the smoke in his stomach was causing him to retch. He swallowed with audible gulps in an obvious effort to keep from vomiting.

The more he inhaled the more nervous he became. He rubbed his eyes, scratched his head and chest, blew his nose and wiped his hand on his leg. He took another cigarette and continued to inhale until he was near to collapse. A helper now supported his back as he continued to grow weaker. Suddenly he "died", flinging his arms outward and straightening his legs stiffly. At this point the log stool was removed from beneath him, and three men held his rigid body horizontal about chest high for a few moments. His tendons snapped as he writhed slowly in this position. Soon he relaxed and was lowered to a sitting position on the ground, his head hanging limply and his back again supported by the helper.

During his "death" Metsé breathed continuously, but in a very subdued manner. After some minutes his eyelids fluttered. He remained in this state of collapse nearly 15 minutes. From time to time toward the end of this period he moved his limbs slightly, breathed more deeply, and uttered some incomprehensible noises. As he began to revive, he rubbed his eyes, scratched his head several times and looked about in a startled manner as if listening for something. When Metsé had revived himself two attendant shamans rubbed his arms. One of the shamans drew on a cigarette and blew smoke gently on his chest and legs, especially on places that he indicated by stroking himself. Then Metsé began to speak.

He called to him the owner of the burned house and conversed with him with much feeling, unfolding the account of how the fire had been caused. As he did so the attending shamans, as well as several other male onlookers, commented from time to time on what Metsé had said. He drew out the account of the happenings, almost sobbing as he related parts of the story and apparently deeply moved by the tragedy. This procedure reveals two important techniques of divining which contribute to its success. First, the shaman expresses sympathy for the victims of the disaster, a technique which certainly functions to gain popular approval for his efforts. Second, he sounds out public opinion by exchanging comments with his audience. This device of course makes it possible for him to formulate a verdict which they will accept.

The gist of Metsé's narrative follows: The previous evening three men had been prowling around the settlement. When all the Kuikuru were asleep they had tried to enter Metsé's house in order to place an image of lightning inside it. (This is a form of sorcery which would have drawn lightning to his house and would have resulted in the death of Metsé himself.) Because the door was barred the men were unable to enter his house and entered the adjacent one instead,—the house that later burned. They camped nearby during the night, and about noon the next day they shot a fire arrow into that house. Metsé was unable to learn the identity of the culprits during his trance because they had shirts over their heads and spoke a language he could not understand.

Thus the cause of the fire turned out to be exactly what people had suggested earlier, with one remarkable detail added. This was Metsé's statement that the culprits had tried to enter his own house with an image of lightning in order to destroy him. Although this detail did not seem very important at the time, it suddenly took on special significance two weeks later when lightning actually did strike Metsé's house and set it afire during a thunder storm. Metsé was thrown from his hammock by the lightning bolt and was badly bruised. Within two minutes his burning house collapsed. This double disaster convinced Metsé that he was a marked man.

The next morning, unable to withstand the rigors of divining himself, he asked another shaman to divine for him and find the image of lightning which he believed must have been placed in his house and which was responsible for drawing the lightning. The performance of this shaman tells much about the skill of the primary shaman. The secondary shaman was an elderly man, as Kuikuru ages go, although he was still vigorous and healthy. He was unable to go into a trance, although he inhaled deeply and swallowed smoke. He appeared to become violently ill—hiccups and involuntary retching repeatedly preventing him from inducing trance. After several unsuccessful attempts he moved about in search of the image of lightning but with no success. Finally Metsé himself arose from his hammock, danced about the ruins of the house with a running step and then began to search also. They both failed to find the image, because, it was said, it is very difficult to find such an object in the daylight.

That evening Metsé himself divined. After reviving himself he reported that the reason the lightning image could not be found was that it had already been removed. He now stated further that the person responsible for both fires was another shaman, a Kuikuru who had left three years previously to marry a woman of the neighboring Kalapalu tribe and had never returned.

This verdict appeared to surprise some of the Kuikuru, who indicated that the culprit had been a good man. But there were social complications which may explain Metsé's reason for pointing the finger at this shaman. The accused had been expected to marry a teen-age Kuikuru girl some time before, but although the girl had waited for a very long time in puberty seclusion her fiancé had made no move to claim her. His failure to fulfill this obligation engendered some resentment among the Kuikuru, where there were several bachelors and no other marriageable girls. Finally Metsé's younger brother had proposed to the girl by leaving firewood at her parents' house. His suit was accepted, but on the very next day the house in which she was secluded burned! About 10 days later she and Metsé's brother began living together as man and wife. A few days after that Metsé's house burned also.

The man who was indicated had only one close adult relative, a very weak and effeminate brother who had recently been living in the Kuikuru settlement. But there was considerable tension between this brother and some of the other Kuikuru,—so much so that he was reluctant to go outside his house during the daylight hours. A few days before the second fire, he too had left the Kuikuru settlement and joined the Kalapalu.

As soon as Metsé disclosed the identity of the guilty person a party of avengers including Metsé's brother set out, *without consulting the headman*, to execute the supposed culprit. This mission was unsuccessful because their intended victim remained inside his house and surrounded by his family. After the return of the avenging party Metsé's fear of the malevolent power of the other shaman intensified. He predicted that fire would strike again. He became ill, seemingly unable to move about, and had his brother carry him to and from the lake to bathe. He remained in this state of debility for several days. Then a second attempt was made to destroy the other shaman. The accused was taken by surprise and killed. Thus a potential rival of both Metsé and his brother was eliminated, and Metsé recovered his strength rapidly.

No retaliation followed the killing. Among the Kuikuru there is no tradition of blood feuds. Moreover, the victim's closest relative, his own brother, did not have sufficient strength of personality to avenge his death.

DISCUSSION

It seems certain that Metsé's family felt some anxiety about taking a girl who had been spoken for by another man. The occurrence of two house fires in close association with the marriage of Metsé's brother to that girl emphasized the rivalrous aspect of the marriage and served to direct attention to the potential rival. Anxiety in this instance could have been alleviated by giving over the girl to her fiancé. But in spite of the fact that her fiancé had not released her from the engagement, there was no indication that he intended or wanted to claim her. Therefore Metsé's family chose to eliminate the source of anxiety by getting rid of the potential rival.

There is little doubt, however, that following Metsé's account of the events, the society viewed the revenge killing as a device to protect their settlement from the threat of more fires and the loss of their principal shaman through sorcery. In this instance, as in the case of the stolen fruit, there was no dissention from the shaman's verdict. From these instances of divining it becomes apparent that the focal point of whatever legal apparatus operates among the Kuikuru is not the headman but rather the principal shaman. In effect he functions as an arbiter. His effectiveness in this role is based on a belief in the operation of supernatural forces, both through sorcery and through detection by divination.

Metsé's influence as a diviner depends also on his personal ability to convince the society of his power to deal with supernatural phenomena. Without this advantage his people would be less ready to accept the judgments he makes and to follow his suggestions to the point of committing homicide. Metsé's performances in curing are indeed impressive and do much to win him the appreciation of his fellow men. Moreover his truly masterful inducement of trance has earned him their deep respect. In addition his skillful sounding of public opinion helps to make his pronouncements credible. Of course an occasional coincidence of divining which adumbrates actual events adds much prestige to the shaman's performances. Such spectacularly successful predictions are always the most clearly remembered. His impressive performances as a curer and diviner, therefore, have placed Metsé in a quasi political role, and he is regarded as a valuable social servant.

Divination exerts a direct influence on social behavior. Even when no formal punishment is meted out the drama of divination serves to demonstrate the shaman's ability to "see" the guilty one in a supernatural manner, and everyone is thereby made aware of the danger of being found guilty. Fixing blame on a person by divination places him in an uncomfortable position at the very least. Because people wish to avoid this consequence, the knowledge that misdemeanors can be detected tends to deter individuals from breaking social norms.

If a person should be accused of a serious crime, as for example killing others through sorcery, he might himself be killed as a menace to the society. And since antisocial attitudes such as anger are taken as evidence of inclination to sorcery, the Kuikuru are constrained to be genial and cooperative. The ideal Kuikuru personality is very amiable and lacking in aggressiveness. By cultivating such a personality one inspires trust rather than suspicion and is therefore less susceptible to being accused.

It should be pointed out that persons who are killed for supposed witchcraft and those who are accused of minor delicts as well are individuals who lack social support, either because they have no close kin who could avenge them or because they are not well integrated into the society, or both. Singling out such individuals as victims functions to prevent retaliation and feuding. It also fosters social integration. Of course individuals may not be able to do much to insure having strong kinsmen around them, but they can and do cultivate friendly and cooperative relations with other members of the society.

As already suggested, the suspicion of sorcery is always present as an explanation for misfortune and is a major factor in Kuikuru social control because supposed sorcerers may be killed without reprisal. But in spite of the strong belief in sorcery, the actual practice of it does not appear to exist among these people. Informants had little knowledge of how sorcery was accomplished because, they said, "those who practice it do not tell anything about it". Moreover, there was no apparent fear among the Kuikuru that their own shamans would do harm through sorcery, and when asked whether he could work counter magic on his enemy after the second fire, Metsé himself seemed at a loss for an answer. Clearly if the Kuikuru had had evidence that their very able shaman (said to be more able than his enemy) really could work magic against his enemy, they would not have killed the other man outright. Nor would Metsé have shown such unmistakable terror until his enemy was destroyed.

Reasons for the absence of sorcery among the Kuikuru probably include a high degree of freedom from stresses, which may be attributed to the general lack of either restrictive rules of social behavior or competition for subsistence resources. The Kuikuru do not practice either strict patrilocal or matrilocal residence, customs which have been shown to create special stresses on the inmarrying women and men respectively. (See Titiev, 1951; Schneider and Gough, 1962.) Moreover, their subsistence ecomomy provides an abundance of food and there is no economic oppression or exploitation to generate antagonism. (Cf. Kracke, 1963.)

But if the permissive nature of Kuikuru culture minimizes stresses, the lack of traditionally structured political leadership does create some problems. The use of divination to determine guilt may be interpreted as a substitute for adjudication and punitive action by a political leader. However, political influence such as the shaman exerts is only one of several possible solutions to problems created by a lack of traditional leadership. Another possible solution would be direct retaliatory or punitive action by individuals with or without the consent of the society. If resorted to extensively, this course of action would soon destroy the small Kuikuru society. Another solution would be the actual practice of counter sorcery to avenge antisocial acts. This also would have destructive consequences and might well lead to the disintegration of the society through fear of sorcery and the conflicts that would arise from widespread suspicion. Or, as still another solution, individual families might move away and amalgamate with other settlements in order to avoid or escape from hostility. This course would surely soon result in the disbanding of Kuikuru society.

All of these possible solutions would decrease the cohesiveness of the society if not destroy it altogether. By contrast divination by the shaman tends to preserve the integrity of the society by reducing anxiety and conflict among its members and supporting the social norms necessary for its peaceful existence. The political role of the principal shaman among the Kuikuru suggests that a comparative study of societies with very permissive social behavior might reveal a correlation between the absence of strong political leadership and the use of shamanistic divination to reinforce social norms.

NOTE

1. This paper is based on notes from field work done by Robert Carneiro and myself among the Kuikuru between August 1953 and March 1954.

PART IV: LANGUAGE

Introduction to South American Indian Linguistics at the Turn of the Seventies

Arthur P. Sorensen, Jr., has written an excellent introduction to the major problem areas of South American Indian linguistics which the alert student of anthropology will appreciate.

The author holds the Ph.D. degree from Columbia University and presently teaches ethnology and anthropological linguistics at the State University of New York in Binghamton. He is a veteran of years of linguistic and ethnographic field work among the Tukano and neighboring peoples of the Vaupés River basin.

18. SOUTH AMERICAN INDIAN LIN-GUISTICS AT THE TURN OF THE SEVENTIES

ARTHUR P. SORENSEN, JR.

INTRODUCTION

At the outset of the seventies, information on South American Indian languages is best regarded as inconsistent. Data vary in usefulness. Few languages are well described; many languages are poorly described. Figuratively speaking, the linguistic map of South America remains impressionistic at best. While individual languages can be spotted on it, and while obviously similar languages can be combined into modest language families generally acceptable to most linguists, nevertheless the data are wholly inadequate for the rigorous demonstration that they fit into more comprehensive linguistic stocks or phyla. Any large-scale solution of the classification of South American Indian languages is still really premature. This paper is, then, a survey of this shaky setting.

A brief review will be made here on the scope of South American linguistics, and on stereotypes likely to be encountered, explicitly or implicitly, in the literature or in person. The main focuses of the paper will be on some sociolinguistic areas of inquiry, and on problems underlying the description and classification of South American Indian languages. The viewpoints held are that good descriptions of phonologies and morphologies of languages are needed, and that classifications must ultimately be provable by the comparative method.

The major bibliographic sources that list the inventory of South American Indian languages are: Mason (1950), McQuown (1955), Tax (1958 and 1960), and Loukotka (1968). The few maps currently available are Mason (1950: presently unavailable except in reference rooms), Loukotka (1968: available through the Association of American Geographers, 1146 Sixteenth Street N.W., Washington, D.C. 20036; $3.00); and the Greenberg presentation of tentative phyla in the Steward and Faron textbook (1959). (See the section on basic bibliography under "Setting Up a Sample Problem" for additional sources.)

SCOPE

Two to three thousand names of languages have been reported in the archival materials. No doubt many of these are alternate names for the same languages; others are probably names of dialectal variants of already accounted languages. Loukotka cites 1492 names of languages. Perhaps 300 or 400 languages are spoken at the present time; a few more are yet to be "discovered." They are distributed among some 65 language families (following Mason 1950, who, however, leaves ambiguous statuses for language isolates—languages that form one-language families in themselves by being apparently unrelated to any other languages: see Voegelin and Voegelin 1965); or among 77 "stocks" and 44 "isolated languages" (following Loukotka as of 1968); or among 4 phyla (Greenberg, in Steward and Faron 1959). Some of these languages are disappearing, or even being eliminated through genocide; a few, such as Quechua, continue to spread to people who previously did not know them; but many—including some spoken by only a few hundred people each—appear to be "quietly holding their own."

Indian languages are spoken on the South American continent from the border of Panama (several thousand Cuna and Choco speakers) right down to Tierra del Fuego (eight people are reported still to use Selknam, the language of the Yahgan, with each other). The aboriginal languages of the Caribbean islands were of South American Indian families; one South American Indian language family (Chibchan) "spills over" into Central America. The geographic distribution of South American Indian languages ranges from a broad, continuous spread covering a sizable—and international—area of the central Andes (largely filled in by Quechua), through more regionally defined areas in Paraguay (Guaraní) and Chile (Araucanian), or along some of the upper reaches of the major rivers of South America—the Amazon, Orinoco, Paraná; to the spotty areas of enclave groups surrounded by Spanish speakers in the hilly terrain immediately away from the spine of the Andes (e.g., in southern Colombia); to the patches of more and more isolated communities in the remote headwaters of the major rivers of South America.

About the only places where Indian languages are not spoken are in the large cities (but La Paz, Cuzco, Quito, and even Lima are exceptions); coastal areas in general (again with exceptions); in the countryside around most capitals and larger cities (except in Peru, Bolivia, Ecuador, southern Colombia, and Paraguay); and in a broad belt of European settlement reaching from southern Brazil and Uruguay to Argentina—where, however, such languages as German, Italian, American English, British English are spoken in addition to Portuguese and Spanish. Even in the latter case there are some areas of heavy European settlement where Indian languages may be found after all—Guaraní in Paraguay and Araucanian in Chile being notable examples.

Although they are not Indian languages, certain other languages should be mentioned, at least in passing, for full coverage. Creolized languages are spoken in the Caribbean (including Creole French, Creole English, and Papiamentu), and a creole language, Taki Taki, is spoken in Guyana by the Djuka, a reconstituted African tribal society. There are one or two enclave communities in Brazil (and one formerly in eastern Cuba) where Yoruba and perhaps Ibo, originally brought from West Africa, are reportedly still spoken. There are also sizable communities where such languages as Hindustani, Cantonese, Hakka, and Japanese are spoken. At least one community in south central Patagonia has retained Welsh for slightly over a hundred years now. Arabic, brought by the "Sirianos" or Lebanese, has probably pretty much phased out by now. Dutch is important in parts of the Caribbean and in Surinam. English and German have phased out among some families several generations resident in South America, but still retained by others. A careful compilation of data on non-Indian, non-Latin languages remains to be done.

STEREOTYPES AND MYTHS

Information held by the non-Indian Latin American layman about Indian languages is often engulfed in stereotypes and myths, many of which have percolated through, affecting the general literature. The anthropological and linguistic fieldworker certainly has to cope with them in explaining his work there. Indian languages popularly are considered *dialectos* by non-Indians, and while the basic colloquial usage of this term refers to forms of unwritten speech spoken in restricted areas and by restricted numbers of people, the connotative extensions of this term suggest ideas of primitiveness (because the speakers have technologically primitive cultures), non-legibility (because the language has not been "reduced" to writing), no "grammar," deficient vocabulary, impreciseness of expression (witness Indians trying to speak Spanish: *"el papa, el mama"* whereas *"el"* should be used only with masculine *"papa"* and *"la"* should be used with feminine *"mama"*), inexpressibility of nuances of thought (no subjunctives), and quaint to objectionable status (*"Le confieso con toda franqueza que mi bisabuela sí sabía hablar un dialecto, y era india,"*: "I [must] in all frankness confess [admit] to you that [I had a] great-grandmother [who] did indeed know how to speak a 'dialect'— and was an Indian").

Words that are lacking in the *dialecto* are thought to be borrowed haphazardly from Spanish, grammatical forms to have been modeled from Spanish. One belief in some Colombian non-Indian folklore, for example, is that all babies originally start to speak *castellano* only to be subverted into speaking something else (perhaps, nobly, into speaking English); it is even more strongly held among some Colombians that the adequate learning of Spanish by an Indian will automatically cause him to forget his Indian *dialecto*. A few disappointed Latin American missionaries from Spanish-speaking families who had noted the unexpected clinging of Indians to Indian languages even after learning good Spanish attributed this to Indian stubbornness. This widespread, popular deprecation of unwritten, but spoken South American Indian languages in South America is probably at the base of a prevalent North American myth that the South American Indian "dialects" are nothing but kinds of underdeveloped or even deteriorated Spanish.

Some historically known facts have also provided precedents that have subsequently approached almost mythical proportions in lay thinking, but which are valuable leads for anthropologists. One precedent that influences linguistics and anthropology is based on the fact that the peaceful Arawak-speaking Indians whom Columbus encountered (though not yet called Arawaks) were actively being encroached upon and preyed upon (and eaten) by the cannibalistic Caribs, and that the Caribs had displaced or replaced the former in the Lesser Antilles during the preceding few generations. The population of a large area of northern South America was thereafter found to speak similar languages—eventually called Arawak—and this area, too, was found to be spotted with Carib intrusions. These accounts led Brinton (1891) to suggest that the attacks of the Caribs against the Arawaks must not only have forced Arawaks to retreat into the Antilles but into remote refuge areas of the continent as well. It was readily inferred that there must have been repercussions all over the lowlands right up to the borders of the highland Inca empire and Chibcha chiefdoms. Long before Brinton introduced the dynamic situation of the Arawaks and Caribs to the anthropological literature, any number of travelers in the Amazon and Orinoco had already recorded their vocabularies with the implicit intention of determining whether they had been dealing with Arawaks or with cannibalistic Caribs. To the colonial Spaniards, *carib* meant "cannibal," and was an excuse for taking slaves.

Ultimate origins of Arawaks from Polynesia (Rivet 1925a, 1925b, *et seq.*) and of Caribs from Melanesia (Gladwin 1947) remain dubious. But newer data and less speculative inferences from the distributions of the languages of both groups make the problem of tracing their origins more intriguing than ever. If the age-area hypothesis applies, then G. Kingsley Noble's survey of Arawakan languages (1965) points to the remotest headwaters of the Amazon in the Montaña of Ecuador and Peru as the area from which proto-Arawakan had spread, because that is where the most divergent (reflecting, hence, the longest isolation and concomitant development or evolution) of the Arawakan languages occur [cf. Lathrap, pp. 92–93—Ed.]. Some anthropologists and linguists might speculate instead that these languages bear witness to the earliest Arawakan-speaking populations to flee from the Caribs. Still others feel that the Montaña represents only an outlying remnant of a much larger original area of prototype Arawakan languages. The latest theoretician to deal with the Arawak and Carib question is Lathrap (1970), who, using his own first-

hand archaeological knowledge obtained in the Amazon to reinterpret Noble (1965), suggests that the Arawakan languages
spread from the region of the confluence of the Río Negro with
the Amazon near present-day Manáus (near to where Noble hy-
pothesizes that the Maipuran branch of Arawakan developed)
when the Caribs, who he thinks came from farther downriver, proceeded to attack them.

The dynamic situation of the agricultural Arawaks perennially
being chased by the Caribs has been suggested as a central theme
for tracing the possible development of agriculture and its diffusion
(e.g., among others: Brinton 1891, Meggers and Evans 1957,
Sauer 1950, Lathrap 1970).

SOCIOLINGUISTIC INQUIRIES: THE STRUCTURAL AND FUNCTIONAL ROLES OF LANGUAGES IN THEIR LARGER SOCIAL AND CULTURAL SETTINGS

South America, to be sure, holds no monopoly in its variety of
settings, but the historical background to its political development
does seem to predispose it for the stressing of certain dimensions.
In order to present a cursory overview of language and culture problems in South America, the writer will set up two dimensions with varying degrees of interplay as a scaffolding on which
to locate them. (Intense involvement at a given point in the scale
of one dimension does not necessarily mean intense involvement
at the correspondingly elaborate point in the scale of the other
dimension; rather, the two dimensions should be regarded as reference lines that are separable "near their ends" but that can define
areas of probable conflict between some of their stretches.) One
dimension will be that of the bilingualism—or *potential* bilingualism
—with which the speakers of a given Indian language may be involved: the range of variations of this are monolingualism, diglos-
sia, bilingualism proper, and poly- or multilingualism. The other
dimension could elaborately be labeled "politicosociolinguistics,"
or official policy toward Indian—and other—languages, because the
roles of Indian languages in the national societies which claim the
Indians speaking them may be presented according to the degrees

of political involvement they are allowed in those nations. The range of variations are: official statuses of suppression and repression, non-recognition, indifference, "reluctant" recognition, recognition to various degrees, full official recognition, and (perhaps in the future) even promotional recognition. Conditioning all this are the degrees of subtlety brought into play in connection with the politicoreligious statuses and activities of linguistic missionaries, which affect the role of the non-missionary anthropologist or linguist who wants to work in South America. Some linguistic missionaries have privileged positions through their private governmental contracts with some South American governments, and may be regarded by some nationals as *de facto* political parties in Indian areas.

Just as the reader may have to cope with skeptical opinions concerning the endowments of "primitive languages," or languages of people with primitive technologies, among educated laymen elsewhere, the reader should expect to encounter anachronistic stereotypes and depreciatory attitudes—and occasional romantic myths—concerning South American Indian languages in South American literature. Such ethnocentric stereotypes lie in the background of whatever political statuses may be accorded to South American Indian languages in some countries. A strong "monolingual tradition" exists in South America: the writer has heard one old-school (and non-linguistic) missionary teacher disgustedly exclaim that the Indians in this region of his country were so backward that their children came to school without even being able to speak their own "mother tongue," Spanish!

QUECHUA

Quechua is the language of the descendants of the Incas. It is spoken by at least eight million people—several times more than any other Indian language in the Americas. Its main area is in the highlands of Bolivia, Peru, and Ecuador; the periphery of its area includes southern highland Colombia and occasional spots down along the west coast of Peru; its use has spread to northernmost Chile and Argentina, and is still spreading to people who previously did not know it in the Peruvian and Bolivian lowlands east of the Andes. In its long history, Quechua displaced many other Indian languages no longer spoken (see Rowe 1954). In the highlands of Peru and Bolivia, it is estimated that 80% of the population speak it or can speak it, and that at least 90% of the population understand it. Maybe some 50% of the population know Quechua only.

The outstanding problem that the speakers of Quechua faced until recently was the refusal of their governments to give any real, operative official status to Quechua—despite the fact that more than half the population in Peru and over 80% of the population in Bolivia spoke it. But in the Bolivian revolution of 1953, Quechua was made a second national language, and speeches can be given in congress in it. And at the close of the 1970 Congress of Americanists in Lima, Peru, President Velasco announced the official beginning of a program in bilingual education—especially in the highlands—in Peru. No one is misled about the difficulties in training teachers and preparing primers for such a system, and it will take years to get it going properly, but the important factor is that now Quechua has official sanction. This does not mean that some degree of bilingual education has not already been going on, especially in the lowest grades, where children are taught Spanish by Quechuas who themselves have learned Spanish.

Quechua has been recognized as a "critical language" in the United States, because it is spoken by over a million people, while very few people in the United States speak it. There are now two or three important centers of Quechua training in the United States, and a number of specialists in it. Peace Corps training for Peru and (formerly) Bolivia includes training in Quechua.

Problems attendant with the developing of national education projects in Quechua are problems of standardization —from which dialect or dialects will the standard form be drawn? —what orthography should be used? —etc. There are already factions and partisans on these issues. There is local pride in Quechua all over the highlands; there is even a sense of a prestigious dialect, that of Cuzco (although even in Cuzco there are subdialects). What should take place is recognition of all regional forms of Quechua rather than the promulgation of a prescriptive norm. But prescription will surely be projected by educators into the problem. Quite a bit of sophisticated work is now being done in Quechua and its dialects both by Peruvians and non-Peruvians: e.g., Escribens and Proulx (1970), Lastra (1968), Parker (1965), Stark (1969).

GUARANÍ

Guaraní presents a very different situation. Guaraní is spoken by over two million people in Paraguay and in adjacent portions of Argentina and Brazil; in addition, a dialectal variant of Guaraní, called variously Tupí, Geral, or Nheengatú, is spoken in several places in Brazil—including spots along the Amazon—where it was taken by the early Jesuit missionaries and where it has not yet been entirely replaced by Portuguese. But here we will be concerned with the case of Guaraní in Paraguay.

The unique history of Paraguay lies behind the widespread use of Guaraní there. Paraguay was one place where Spaniard and Indian were compatible with each other and immediately formed a blended society—where the Spaniards actually added to the aboriginal society rather than replacing parts of it after having suppressed them (as elsewhere in South America); it was an economically unattractive area, and soon was left out of the main lines of trade and influence to become an isolated country—and even a forbidden country. In this climate, the use of Guaraní survived. It not only survived, but took a complementary position with Spanish. Almost everybody in Paraguay speaks both Guaraní and Spanish. Both languages, of course, are official; even bilingualism may be said to be officially sanctioned. People alternate between them in conversations depending on the situational context —depending on where they have met, under what auspices, and depending on the topic being discussed (see Rubin 1968). In general, Spanish tends to be used for formal affairs, such as business, and Guaraní for informal affairs, such as friendship and expression of love. Spanish may be used for the formal beginnings of courtship and Guaraní used in the later, more familiar stages. Nevertheless, some families ordinarily use Spanish at home, others Guaraní. If the alternation between using Spanish and using Guaraní in a given situation is not handled properly, the speaker can be identified as belonging to the lower class. It is interesting to note that Paraguayans who speak Spanish at home and who would otherwise greet and talk with each other largely in Spanish in Paraguay will use Guaraní when meeting each other outside of Paraguay. Paradoxically, despite its comfortably stable position in Paraguayan culture, Guaraní currently is little used on radio or television.

MULTILINGUALISM IN THE NORTHWEST AMAZON

An extensive multilingualism situation with culturally prescribed polylingualism in the individual exists among the riverine Indians found in the central northwest Amazon (Sorensen 1967, 1971). This area is here defined as the drainage system of the Vaupés River and adjacent areas in Colombia and Brazil, and perhaps southernmost Venezuela. The region is occupied by over twenty-five "tribes," each possessing its own language, e.g., Barasana, Desano, Karapana, Kubeo, Piratapuyo, Tariano, Tukano, Tuyuka, Yebamahsa, and Yurutí among others. (Many of these languages belong to the Eastern Tukanoan language family, on which the writer initiated modern descriptive work; nonetheless, some languages belong to other language families.) Each of these linguistically identifiable units is exogamous—marriage within the "tribe" would be considered incestuous (except among the Kubeo, among whom nevertheless a carefully prescribed system exists [see Goldman 1950, 1963]). This means that every husband-wife pair represents a father and a mother who come from different linguistically distinct groups who then provide their children with a minimally bilingual exposure. In addition, one of the languages, Tukano, has spread as a lingua franca (and not in pidginized form) and is generally known throughout the area. Such languages as Spanish, Portuguese, and Tupí-Guaraní also serve as linguae francae, but they are much less general and each is restricted in its distribution within the area (e.g., Spanish in Colombia and Portuguese in Brazil). There is a strong sense of identification of "tribe" with language that helps support the institutionalized multilingualism.

Sporadic attempts by old-school missionaries in the past to suppress Indian languages on the main rivers only served to reinforce the vitality of these languages. Mission policy has recently changed, due to support of vernacular languages by the Vatican II Council, and the use of Indian languages is now being encouraged; in addition, a group of linguistic missionaries of a rival religion has recently entered the area and has penetrated into the backriver areas where the established missionaries had met strong resistance, thereby intensifying the creditability of Indian languages. The fact that neither Spanish nor Portuguese serves the entire area as a lingua franca, but that Tukano, an Indian language, does, also reinforces the institution.

Incidentally, the particular patterning of language distribution in an individual's repertoire indicates some rethinking in the extant literature on what is to be implied by "mother tongue." It should be realized that almost every individual among the Indians of the Vaupés has a "father tongue" that is separately identifiable from his mother tongue; that he identifies himself with his father-tongue group; and that because of preferential classificatory cross-cousin marriage he is quite likely to acquire a spouse from his mother-tongue group. Even though a mother uses (primarily) her husband's language with her children (their father tongue)—and her own language secondarily with them—the underlying implications of the multilingual situation preclude calling this language a "mother tongue," nor is it referred to as such by a native speaker.

OTHER BILINGUAL AND MULTILINGUAL SITUATIONS

Other cases both of incidental bilingualism and of patterned bilingualism, and possibly of multilingualism, also occur in South America. The best-known of these is the historically reported case among the Carib where men spoke Carib and women spoke Arawak. Of course, each understood the other. The Arawak derived from the many women who had originated as captives taken from the Arawak. The separable use of the two languages became institutionalized along sex lines. Note, however, that the "Carib" spoken by the modern-day Caribbean descendants of these people is an Arawakan and not a Cariban language.

The occurrence of several languages among people who are in contact with each other in the upper Xingú region in Brazil has been reported. The extent of the multilingual situation, and whether its associated bilingualism or polylingualism is incidental or patterned is not known.

A trilingual situation exists in Puno, on the northwestern, Peruvian shore of Lake Titicaca. While in some areas of Peru and Bolivia such trilingualism may be the incidental result of overlap of Aymara-Spanish bilingualism with Quechua-Spanish bilingualism, in Puno it more probably represents a modern-day derivative of a more ancient Aymara-Quechua bilingualism with Spanish later added.

Bilingualism involving Quechua is not new. It is well known that the Incas brought Quechua as their governing language to the Indians whom they conquered, and that their Quechua actually replaced a number of former languages (see Rowe 1954). At the present time, as Quechua-speaking migrants continue to spread into the Montaña and lowlands of Peru and Bolivia, the use of Quechua again is spreading, and other Indians with whom Quechua-speakers come in contact can be expected to become bilingual in Quechua. Knowledge of both Spanish and English by modern Carib-speaking Indians in the Guiana highlands area of Guyana, Surinam, Venezuela, and Cayenne has been noted in recent travel stories and in occasional reports. Whether this is incidental or follows a pattern is not known.

Travel accounts indicate that the few remaining Yahgan-speakers also know good English, and that they may know Spanish as well. Southern Patagonia and Tierra del Fuego are, incidentally, areas where the use of English is widespread.

POOR STATUS OF DESCRIPTIONS

The classification of South American Indian languages and the tracing of their origins is hampered by the inadequate, underdifferentiated recordings of the data on which most language descriptions have been based. The archival and published materials which until recently have formed the bulk of these descriptions exhibit the results of falling into all the pitfalls threatening untrained linguists. And some "descriptions" merely amount to brief, poorly taken word lists. Only recently have trained or partially trained linguists begun to work in South America. But even they, while avoiding the classic pitfalls, all too often muddle their descriptions with orthographic and other methodological deviations. In general, the stage of poor, unrepresentative descriptions made by prescientific linguists is now giving way, but only to that of mediocre, programmatic descriptions by partially trained (and sometimes "mass-produced") linguists. Very few descriptions exist in which complete confidence may be placed.

The problems in poor descriptions may conveniently be etched out under three rubrics: those of phonology, morphology (and syntax), and—obfuscating these—orthography. The major problems in phonology are those of underdifferentiated phonetics, of underdifferentiated phonemics, and of transcriptions which while not narrow nevertheless are sporadically overdifferentiated. The major problems in the orthography of the transcriptions or recordings are those of projections of inconsistent spelling devices from other written languages to form three-way spelling conflicts with phonetic transcription and phonemic transcription. The major problems in morphology are "wild" morphemic cuts; grammatical categories completely missed, or misidentified, or projected from some other language; forced grammatical categories; or even categories derived from their English glosses.

The immediate major problem in phonology is "lack of ear"— the failure to discern all the sounds of a language, and the unwitting readiness to let some subtleties of sound be adjudged as mispronunciations, slurs, or slips of the informant's tongue. Aspirated consonants are regularly missed, or taken as "normal" pronunciations of the unaspirated version of the consonants when in a stressed or emphatic position: [t] and [tʰ] are, then, not distinguished. (Some languages, in the future, will be found to contain both unaspirated and aspirated series of consonants.) Consonantal length may easily be missed: [t] vs. [tt]. Some types of spirants are likely to be missed or reinterpreted as slurred pronunciations of their homorganically corresponding stop consonants: [ɸ] and [β] with [f] and [b]; [θ] and [δ] with [t] and [d]. Trills and laterals (various kinds of [r] and [l] sounds) are likely to be confused with dental and alveodental nasals (i.e., with "kinds of [n]"). That nasals may be fortis rather than lenis can be overlooked, such that fortis nasals are likely to be confused with lenis trills (the reverse of the case above): fortis [n] vs. lenis [r]; fortis voiced consonants are likely to be confused with pre-nasalized consonants (fortis [n] with [ⁿt]); etc. Central vowels are likely to be confused with rounded back vowels—what should be transcribed as [ɨ] and [ʉ] (depending on whether they are unrounded or rounded, central, high vowels) may appear as [ü] or [ö]. Some nasalized vowels may be missed, and most glottalization (or laryngealization) of vowels may be missed. Thus many languages deceptively described as having a simple five-vowel system (i, e, a, o, u) may very well really have nasalized and glottalized series of vowels as well as plain (non-nasalized) series of vowels and additional central vowels such as i and ə. Diphthongs, especially in languages having central vowels, may be completely missed. Tonal systems are notoriously missed; at most they may be very indirectly hinted at by some sort of acute and grave stressed accent system (as in English "hóthòuse"). And stress may be confused with tone.

Phonemic analysis carries its own host of problems. In the first place, more than one feasible phonemic solution is possible in any language (Chao 1956). One always has the privilege of interpreting a nasalized series of vowels, for instance, either as so many more vowels (/a/ vs. /ą/ phonemes), or as the plain vowels plus one phoneme of nasality (/a/ vs. /aN/); (the phonemicist, of course, should be able to posit theoretical reasons for his preference of one solution over the other for the given language). But for the beginning phonemicist there remain problems of unsuspected intro-jection ("interference") of phonemic and allophonic classes and subclasses from his own language—thus he may fail phonemically to distinguish /tʰ/ from /t/ if he is a native English-speaker /ɛ/ from /e/ if a native Spanish-speaker, etc.—and this may appear in his preliminary publication.

One occasional problem of phonemic underdifferentiation may occur in descriptions where the analyzer has been concerned with theoretical models of description in which a morphophonemic con-solidation of "sounds" is stressed. On the basis of a premature phonemic solution—an attitude unfortunately fostered by some lin-guistic fieldwork courses—such an analyzer may overenthusiasti-cally consolidate two phonemes into one "morphophoneme." In one published case an analyst consolidated nasals with their cor-responding voiced stops (e.g., what descriptivists would call /m/ and /b/) under the one morphophoneme //b//. Reading his "morphophonemic" transcription for the given language would be like reading English //bæn// as either /mæn/ "man" or /bæn/ "ban" depending on context. The theoretical assumption is that the native speaker-hearer of the language so described intuitively sorts the choices out according to context as he speaks. But a reader may be left unaware of the phonetic shapes of the implied phoneme-like units in such a description.

Another occasional problem, this time of phonemic overdifferentiation, may occur in descriptions when features of allophonic variation are analyzed as phonemes in their own right. The situation where there is complex allophony taking place in sequential segments may especially entice clever analysis. Such a case could be represented by setting up English aspiration as a phoneme in its own right, /H/, that phonotactically occurs only after voiceless stop consonants and has its own allophony of weaker and stronger stress in syllables of medial and strong stress. "Potato" could then phonemically be represented as /pHə̀tHéytow/ rather than the more conventional /pətéytow/ [pʰə̀théi̥tou̥]. Undoubtedly these solutions are offered as genuine insights; they may even be accepted in orthographic transcription by informants because of the enthusiasm of the linguist proffering them. But more often they are fanciful overinterpretations of the data. One such case has been explicated in a friendly, instructive way by Hockett (1959) in his criticism of the Agnew-Pike report (1957) on the phonemics of Ocaina.

Also to be viewed with caution are suprasegmental phonemic conditioning devices to account for presumed consonantal and vocalic harmony in word-length segments: statements of the sort that the addition of an affix containing a nasal will impose a feature of nasality on all vowels, or even consonants, in a word. Transcriptively this may be signaled with a nasal, prefix-like signature: /dobu/ + /-ni/ = /Ndobu-ni/ for what otherwise could be written as /dǫbų-nį/ or /nǫmų-nį/ (this example is hypothetical but based on an actual case). Such analyses may or may not be overinterpretations of the data. At any rate, their transcriptions make rough going for the reader collecting words or grammatical forms from them.

Two principal types of orthographic problems show up in descriptions. One is the adoption of unnecessary signs in the transcription—superfluous letters—presumably so as to accommodate the spelling of the Indian language to the writing system of the language of the larger society. This results in what this writer calls the "ca-que-qui-co-cu syndrome," where "c" and "qu" both stand for the same sound (conventionally /k/ or [k]).

The other type of problem is the use of digraphic devices either for sequences of dissimilar sounds or for single sounds. A good example of the former is the use of repeated vowel letters not for vowel length but for glottalized vowel, or for vowel plus glottal stop. This is what the writer calls the "Hawaii syndrome," where in the supposedly "correct" pronunciation of "Hawaii" the two *i*'s signal an intervening glottal stop. This is not to say that glottalization may not, in some languages, morphophonemically arise between repeated vowel segments, or be allophonically associated with long vowels. The problem lies in extending such an orthographic convenience to where it may not be appropriate—the usage seems to have spread uncritically as a tradition in much of American Indian linguistics.

The use of digraphic devices for single sounds is common in all the older published materials and persists even in some modern materials. A person doing research in such materials should be well aware of the use of the digraphs "th", "sh", and "ch" for θ, š, and č, respectively. Incidentally, š is likely to be represented in older materials by English speakers as "sh", by German speakers as "sch", by French speakers as "ch", and by Spanish speakers as "x" (as [š] was the conquistador pronunciation of this letter). Such problems otherwise belong to the introductory linguistics class.

In the area of morphology or grammar, the problem of its representation in descriptions is just as serious. First, of course, has been the attempt to approximate the grammar of the language being described to some familiar model for the person doing the describing. Suspiciously Latin-like, French-like, or English-like descriptions result. Unnecessary and erroneously identified categories that do not exist in the language may then have been set up, and the real ones missed, or pulled apart and partially and wrongly described.

In some cases, categories have been completely missed— inanimate "it" and "they" in an example just below; indicators of specificity; modal and other types of markers; singularizing markers or generalizers; etc. In other cases, categories have been misidentified—aspect for tense, obligatory plural for optional plural, general imperative for second person imperative, etc. In still other cases, categories have been borrowed from extraneous languages: subjunctives, for instance, where they do not exist; "here, there, and yonder" distinctions which do not really coincide with the actual systems; etc. And then there is the problem of forced categories: making forms have plurals whether in the language they have them or not; making obligatory singular and plural forms where there is optional number marking; or forcing "adjectives" into a language which does not have any identifiable adjective form class of words.

In one case, a linguist has analyzed participial suffixes in the language he was describing as relative pronouns. It is true that, because English does not have personal participles, we have to translate or gloss forms containing these suffixes as "I who, you who, he who, she who," etc. However, the linguist in question depended on working through Spanish (and consequently got no pronoun forms for inanimate "it" or "they"—forms which this writer has readily elicited for that particular language in the field), and he did not have any spoken control of the language. He certainly failed to distinguish freestanding words from bound suffixial forms in the language.

Some readers utilizing modernly published materials to draw their comparisons might balk at what they might feel to be controversial extensions of meaning. One missionary linguist, describing the "evidential forms" (indicating whether the evidence for the action being reported is known by firsthand witnessing, or by secondhand, hearsay evidence) in the verbs in the language he was analyzing and describing, insisted that verbal forms from the Bible be translated into it in direct, firsthand evidential forms because he, and his potential converts, in their admirable zeal, claimed that they had experienced the Bible firsthand, and that they were not just repeating what the Apostles had reported.

In summary, the majority of South American Indian language descriptions are inadequate. Their transcriptions imperfectly reflect the real data. Some grammatical categories are missed or unevenly reported while others are overplayed. Even modern models of descriptions well suited for languages similar to the ones from which they were developed may prove maladaptive to other languages, and engender analytic improvisations. This problem, of course, is of concern to advanced linguistic theory and its close control may not be expected of a novice linguistic fieldworker. Then, all too many descriptions are deficient in that the data on which they are based are not retrievable ("salvageable") —sufficient data are not provided for the reader to reorder the materials and develop alternate solutions. Yet these are the descriptions that subsequently serve as source data for the reader who depends on published materials. Descriptive preoccupations are prevalent—but masked to the linguistically naïve reader who is confronted by seductively simple recordings.

CLASSIFICATIONS OF SOUTH AMERICAN INDIAN LANGUAGES

REVIEW OF METHODOLOGIES

It is on these kinds of underdifferentiated source data that current classifications of South American Indian languages stand. The prospect of classification, because of the apparent abundance of data, is tantalizing; the results are premature. What can be established by inspection of similar word lists are language families; what involve increasing amounts of speculation on their establishment are stocks of language families, and then superstocks or phyla containing stocks, language families, and language isolates. Nevertheless, there remains the natural urge to take note of those languages which are obviously similar, to group them into families and stocks, and to try to see if apparently dissimilar languages and their language families aren't really somehow associated in the same phylum after all.

The conquistadores early noted that Maya was not anything like Nahuatl, the language of the Aztecs, and that neither was anything like Quechua, the language of the Incas; they further noted that the Chibcha spoke something else. Even before this they had already noted that Arawak was not like Carib, even though many Arawaks also spoke Carib. The same measure of empiricism led the academicians among the conquistadores to reject affiliations of any of these languages with Latin, Greek, or Hebrew, even though they exclaimed, for example, that Maya defied the latter three in the nature and degree of complexity of its grammar. (See Newman 1967, for the history of the earliest official Spanish reaction to vernacular languages, particularly with regard to Classic Nahuatl.) During the ensuing centuries of colonization and missionization, the academicians—usually missionaries—were able to point out groups of languages that were obviously similar to each other, and to differentiate them from other such groupings or families of languages, e.g., Chibchan, Cariban, Guaicuruan, Matacoan . . . These groupings, coupled with the observations of other language families noted by the first scientific explorers in South America during the late eighteenth and early nineteenth centuries, historically furnished the original base on which linguists could build their classifications.

With the development of more sophisticated techniques of analysis in linguistics in Europe in the late nineteenth century—and particularly of the comparative method (by which the vocabulary and grammatical forms of Indo-European languages were listed in comparison with each other, so that the languages could be set off in groups and subgroups according to their relative degrees of similarity within the group, and so that proto-languages could be hypothesized from which the later languages apparently had evolved)—the promise was there for South American Indian languages to be reviewed to see whether something like this could be done with them. The potential strength of the comparative method, which had linked Germanic, Latin, and Greek with Sanskrit, might now be used to identify possible relations between American Indian languages and the Old World languages, and clarify the problem of the origin of the American Indians.

The full use of the comparative method in American Indian linguistics did not take place until the 1930s when Bloomfield (see Bloomfield 1925, 1946; Sapir 1931; and Hockett 1948) demonstrated its applicability to the central branch of the Algonquian language family in North America. But the initial stage of collecting word lists from related languages potentially for comparative purposes had already been established. The subsequent stage of finding regular correspondences and setting up proto-forms among these word lists lagged. Powell (1891) and Brinton (1891), who made the earliest comprehensive classifications of North American and South American Indian languages, respectively, recognized that they were hampered by underdifferentiated and poorly transcribed data. Rigorous proof of proto-languages could not yet be demonstrated; in fact, some linguists wondered—a few still wonder—whether the comparative method could or even should be applied to American Indian languages at all. Worse yet, grammatical descriptions of South American Indian languages were either so sparse or so modeled on Latin or modern European languages that grammatical comparisons could not be relied on either, much less made. A divergence of opinion arose among linguists concerning the relative priorities of morphological over phonological similarities in the apparent language families and stocks being posited (see Rowe 1954, Hymes 1956, Voegelin and Voegelin 1965). Brinton "stated . . . that, when the material permitted, he preferred to classify languages primarily according to their grammatical structure because he believed that the morphology of a language is its most permanent feature" (Rowe 1954:19). Powell, instead, gave primacy to the lexicon.

As said before, Brinton's approach was severely limited because of paucity of morphological descriptions; perforce, he had to rely on lexical and phonological evidence. Because of the obscure nature of the phonological data, rigorous reconstruction work by linguists ground to a halt in language family after language family, to start anew each time new data were incorporated, only to stop again. But this approach, referred to as comparative method linguistics, was retained for the procedure it provided, for the rigorousness it promised, and for the weight it might lend to claims of correspondences among the more distant resemblances that were occasionally spotted.

Sapir sought for the reinforcement of lexical criteria by morphological criteria in positing genetic classifications. Even where lexical similarity was faint, if there were morphological similarity he hypothesized ultimate superstock (phylum) membership for the two languages or language families. Thus he was able to reduce Powell's fifty-eight North American Indian language families to six superstocks (Sapir 1929), some based on more apparent lexical similarities and some on more tenuous lexical similarities but where the languages concerned shared general or exclusive morphological features (e.g., of the sort: preponderantly polysynthetic derivational systems as opposed to stem-and-inflection systems).

The promising results of Sapir's theories had led many linguists in their search for lexical similarities to be inclined to accept even faint resemblances and to posit them as possible indicators of very distant relationships. These linguists felt that if even the faintest outlying languages of stocks and superstocks could be detected, all that it would take would be additional future data to demonstrate that these hunches were right. These collectors came to develop favorite lists of words (for example, Swadesh developed his famous 100- and 200-word lists; see Swadesh 1955); a few used very short lists (Loukotka used a list supposedly of 45, but which in operation varied down to 12 or less)—they had followed a tradition established by Brinton, who had depended on a 21-word list. Some words appeared to have correspondences in a great many language families. Cases where presumed lexical correspondences seemed to crosscut previously delimited language families were felt to provide reason enough to posit still further superordinate superstocks or phyla with the rationalization of several historical layers of borrowing and influencing as underlying the present stages of the languages involved. It seemed, in this approach—now called phylum linguistics—that the evidence worked up in this way pointed to the existence of very few phyla of languages in the New World. Several of them were confined to North America, with an outlier or two in Central America and perhaps even in northeastern Asia. A couple more were confined mostly or entirely to Central America: Azteco-Tanoan, Zoque-Mayan, Otomanguean. One spilled over from South America to Central America: Macro-Chibchan. There seemed to be relatively few more to be yielded by the still rough data in South America: Greenberg (1960) suggests Andean-Equatorial and Gê-Pano-Carib in addition to Macro-Chibchan. One, based mainly in North America, seemed to have outliers in South America as well as in Central America: Hokan. Zoque-Mayan has recently been extended to South America through evidence demonstrated by Olson (1964, 1965) that Uru and Chipaya, in highland Bolivia, are related to Mayan languages.

Divergent positions on these methodological concerns characterize the field of South American linguistics at the present time. (They are explicated in Voegelin and Voegelin 1965.) Linguists can be identified methodologically as giving basic priority to comparative method linguistics or to phylum linguistics, although any linguist is liable to work in both—and to have his own favorite word list. Anyone doing a problem in South American Indian linguistics will find himself at some point in his work forced to take a stand. However, as the Voegelins point out, the two approaches are not necessarily incompatible. A substantial increase in the demonstrations of language families by the comparative method will be made and wide-scale reconsiderations of the numbers of phyla and of their contents will follow, and we may expect that the results arrived at by either of the two methods will reinforce each other more and more during the seventies.

CURRENT CLASSIFICATIONS

The majority of linguistic families were established between the late 1800s and the 1930s by such people as Brinton, Schuller, Schmidt, and Rivet. Most of this work was further reproduced by Rivet and others in the *Journal de la Société des Américanistes de Paris,* especially between 1910 and 1940. These were the families that John Alden Mason consolidated under one cover in Volume 6 of the *Handbook of American Indians* in 1950, together with the sources that lay behind them and a map. As did Major Powell's classification of North American Indian languages long before, this compilation represents an approach in which only well-demonstrated language families are used and in which phyla are not erected. Loukotka, all during this time, independently was reworking Rivet's and other source materials and consequently presents a classification that resembles but does not always coincide with Mason's. Seen from the perspective of these two classifications, the later Greenberg and Swadesh ones may give the impression of being further reworkings and consolidations of the families already presented by Rivet, Mason, or Loukotka; but they really represent completely new passes at the literature utilizing, perhaps, the former only for their bibliographic resources. Critiques of these various classifications especially in regard to their methodologies are offered in Mason 1950, Rowe 1954, Voegelin and Voegelin 1965, and Wilbert (in Loukotka 1968).

The four classifications indicated above are the ones that currently exert influence in linguistics and anthropology. Two of them represent the comparative method linguistics approach: Mason 1950 and Loukotka 1968; the other two represent the phylum linguistics approach: Greenberg 1960 and Swadesh (see Swadesh 1967).

Of the four, anthropologists have been most inclined to adopt Greenberg's classification, for a number of reasons: because of its generalizing nature, with only four phyla to cope with; because of the reputation of Greenberg's success in consolidating the classification of African languages; because of the suggestions it presents for reconsidering migrational, diffusional, and other cultural inferences from the distributions of his phyla; and, pragmatically, because of its availability in the Steward and Faron textbook (1959) on South American Indians. Greenberg's classification is based on the technique of mass comparison which he developed (see Greenberg 1959a). It also evidences a dependency on the typological resemblances of the items being compared, while at the same time the procedure of mass comparison tends to educe this inventory of typological resemblances as its own by-product. The rationale behind mass comparison, which worked so well among languages of Africa, is that if any two languages are related to each other at all, there will be some resemblances in their vocabularies, and that if other languages related to either of them are also included in the comparison of vocabularies, even remoter resemblances stand a chance of showing up. Expressed in a slightly different way, if there are resemblances among the vocabularies of two or more languages that amount to more than a certain critical percentage (that might otherwise be due to chance resemblance) then these resemblances need some other explanation to explicate them: if they are not restricted to certain parts of the vocabulary—in which case they would be due to borrowing —then the bulk of them will be due to genetic relationship. Mass comparison is then further used to group languages into tentative groups and subgroups. Only the hard work of comparativists is needed to demonstrate these relationships rigorously.

What has happened is that Greenberg's classification, because of the inadequacies of the source data, has resulted in a typological classification skewed essentially by the underdifferentiations and other inadequacies of the source material. Greenberg claims it to be a genetic classification; he feels that eventually comparativists will validate most of his groups and subgroups. Before continuing with Greenberg, let us examine Swadesh's classification.

Swadesh's consolidation of languages and language families goes one step further. To put it in an extreme form, his opinion is that what most linguists consider "chance" resemblances between two disparate languages in two disparate language families are really not "chance" but are due to an ancient substratum upon which the relationship between the two languages then could be built. Where more than one set of such resemblances could be posited, they were due to different layers of ancient substrata. The antiquities of these substrata could be calculated through lexicostatistic techniques; again expressed in an extreme form, any two sets of word lists could be used to extract figures on the degrees of relationship between the two languages, which can then be recast in terms of centuries of separate evolution away from each other. Swadesh eventually came to view all languages of the world as essentially related; it was just the matter of establishing the degrees of relationships and of divergences that remained— and before his untimely death Swadesh was busy at this. The jigsaw puzzle-like mesh-diagrams of the less distant and the more distant relationships among groups of language families (see Swadesh 1967) suggest to comparative linguists the repeated merging at varying historical depths of family tree models with wavelike models of areal convergence and areal divergence in languages and branches of language families (see Bloomfield 1933). The closer and more recent groupings among these represent phyla, but all phyla, especially in the New World, share intricate interrelationships. Although Swadesh's later hypotheses are largely rejected by linguists because of their overly speculative nature, they are nevertheless heuristic projections of the basic problems of developing genetic models for language classification. And his development of lexicostatistics along with his classification has been of inestimable value.

Returning to Greenberg, if his classification is taken to be an adumbration of the eventual genetic distribution of languages in South America, there are certain precautions that should be voiced so as to be kept in mind. These precautions have to do with inferring cultural and migrational hypotheses from the classification. As broached above, the writer feels that Greenberg's classification is effectively a typological one, more so than a genetic one. This is not because Greenberg's methodology of mass comparison is faulty, but because he has had such poor data to work with. Greenberg's phyla represent groupings of language families and of languages that among themselves appear to share some feature that in the opinion of this writer may often more appropriately be ascribed to typological rather than to genetic similarity.

For instance, one phylum of languages, the Andean-Equatorial, seems to include or to be based on a morphological criterion of suffixation with a phonological tendency toward simple, open syllabification. Yet if the distribution of the phonological units of a given language is taken out of the phonotactic category of simple, open syllables and put into that of complex, closed syllables by the well-known and frequently opted linguistic alternative of re-interpreting suprasegmental features (e.g., nasalization, glottalization) as segmental, with their resultant effect of mounding within the syllable (e.g., -ka- vs. -kanq-, with nasalization reassessed in the second as a separate n-like phoneme and glottalization reassessed as a separate q-like phoneme), then the language phonotactically could be thrown into another grouping by having a closed-syllable CVCC pattern instead of an open-syllable CV pattern with no consonantal clusters, and would have to be classified in a different grouping of languages. Or to go to an extreme, and perhaps unkind, example, if phonemicized or semi-phonemicized (i.e., wide transcriptive) English data were listed under a non-English language name (as if a non-English-knowing linguist had taken it from an English-speaking enclave group as an Indian language) it is conceivable that it might very well serve to fit in as closely related (typologically, phonologically) to Araucanian, because of the kinds of word-medial consonant clusters shared by both (e.g., -fk-, -nč-, -tr-, -dm-, -lw-, etc.). (Of course, this possibility is unlikely, as the geographical and other known historical considerations of the language would reasonably be taken into account in a fieldwork situation.)

The writer made a cursory attempt to search for cognates between Tukano, his language of specialization (Sorensen 1969), and Quechua, with which it should be relatively closely related according to the Greenberg classification. In addition to some phonological similarities—and some clashing phonological dissimilarities (tones; glottalized vowels instead of glottalized consonants)—the two languages do have a suffixing type of morphology;

in fact, the suffixal system is even more elaborate in Tukano than in Quechua. But the concepts expressed in these suffixes and their location in the series of position classes of suffixes are utterly dissimilar. Attempts to find cognates that could be compared by form and meaning among root or suffix morphemes were unsuccessful. (This is not to say that eventually some bridging language may not be found to provide evidence for a genetic linkage between the two, or that wider bases on which to set up reconstructions for the two might not provide better evidence for their relations [as of the sort between English and Albanian].)

While he kept apart the Arawaks and Caribs by placing them in the Andean-Equatorial and Gê-Pano-Carib phyla, respectively, Greenberg surprised many people by putting together certain unlikely, culturally divergent and problematic populations such as the Gê with the Carib, and the Quechua with the Yahgan of Tierra del Fuego. The anthropologist concerned with these populations may feel more comfortable if he regards the Greenberg classification purely as a typological one. Nevertheless, Greenberg's work represents an important frontal attack on the problem of classification of South American Indian languages.

SETTING UP A SAMPLE PROBLEM

What procedure should the non-linguistic anthropologist follow who wants to gain a working knowledge of the linguistic background of the people in whom he becomes interested? What language family does their language belong to? Is there ambivalence over this? To what other language families might it eventually be proven to be related? On what kind of raw data is it based? Is it still spoken?—thriving? Who are the people who stand as authorities on this language?—on its family? Is there recent or current work going on in it? Of what caliber? Let us, in the paragraphs below, take up a case for a trial run to establish the barest of working bibliography (and let us follow it up in the last paragraphs by a resumé of a suggested working procedure).

Say that you become interested in the symbiotic social organization that existed between the Mbayá and Guaná, so much so that you want to re-examine the literature on them, and possibly visit the area to see if the situation still exists in vestigial form, or you want to follow out some other social problem such as why were the two groups seemingly predisposed to such an arrangement and where did they separately come from prior to their mingling. But first (and as a non-linguist), you would like to summon up, among other arguments, what kind of linguistic evidence may be at your disposal for defining the groups, for indicating their possible closer relationships with other social groups, for reinforcing the hypotheses you may make from your other data, or for suggesting hypotheses from possible linguistic cues; you may want to consider how these peoples linguistically may fit in with respect to the continent-wide general theory of Greenberg in case you discuss them with other people who are familiar with it, or in this same regard you may independently want to assess or evaluate the inclusion of either one of these languages in the Greenberg classification. And you stop to wonder, in recapitulating your questions, whether "Mbayá" and "Guaná" *were* actually separate languages, if the people who were called by these names lived so close together and were so dependent on each other.

The first step in the procedure is to go to a reference that serves as a general bibliography, presumably fairly full up to the time of publication. My own preferences are the J. Alden Mason survey (1950) and the Loukotka one (1968). (Rivet 1952 or Tovar 1961 may also profitably be used in these initial steps.) But they are not so exhaustive. Then I study the maps accompanying both these works in order to learn the locations of these languages and what other languages and language families are found in the vicinity. (Mason is inconvenient to use because an index of language names is not furnished in the same volume and one cannot always have the index volume at his disposal; McQuown 1955 may serve as an index.) We soon discover that Mbayá and Guaná are indeed listed as separate languages, and intriguingly as belonging to different language families. And to more than two different families, depending on which reference book we are following. Loukotka lists Mbayá as belonging to the Guaicurú Stock and Guaná to the Chané Group (Branch) of the Arawakan Stock. And we find out that while what was called Mbayá is now extinct, a form of it called Caduveo is still spoken; and that Guaná is still spoken. We go to Mason, and find "Mbya" listed as a member of the Tupí-Guaraní family, and a footnoted remark: "Distinguish from Guaicuru Mbaya" (p. 237). We excitedly take a moment and check in Loukotka and do find an "Mbyha" listed in the Guaraní Group of the Tupí Stock. This already means some serious searching in the ethnographic literature as well as in the linguistic literature to make sure of which Mbayá we want. But let us check Guaná while we have Mason open. It is not easily found. We finally locate our first "Guaná" (by using the index volume) as the previous name of a language-and-family subsequently renamed Maca, which then is part of a "probably" but not "proved" combined Macaco-Maca set of families. This reference alerts us to check Arawak and Guaná. We make a by-pass again through Guaicurú where we find a comment that "some of the scattered groups of *Guana* (q.v.), . . . apparently originally spoke *Arawakan.*" Searching further, we finally find Guaná listed geographically in the Paraná subdivision of the Southern Arawakan languages; we are tantalizingly informed of a terminological "Guana/Chana/Chane" problem. We note that in his introduction to the Arawakan grouping, Mason relies on Schmidt and Loukotka; he mentions that Rivet holds a conflicting view, so we decide we shall also have to check out Rivet in our assignment. All in all, we are well set up in a classic South American linguistic problem where we must first eliminate hypotheses of misidentification while proceeding with the appropriate ones.

Our next step is to locate some basic specialized source on the language families: let us say Noble for Arawakan; Pottier for Tupían; but who for Guaicurú and who for Chané? For the latter, we will have to decide for ourselves from investigating Mason's and Loukotka's bibliographies. We are also aware that we must build up specialized portions of our bibliographies from the above sources, and double-check on what *they* interpret as the relationships of these given languages to their respective families or stocks.

Let us for a moment reflect on what hypotheses the Greenberg classification might provide. We find a "Mbaya" and a "Chane" listed, as Tupí and Chané respectively, which are then in the same group of languages under the Equatorial Subfamily of the Andean-Equatorial family. Just in case, we note that Mataco and Guaicurú are groups under the Macro-Panoan Subfamily of the

Gê-Pano-Carib Family. (Tax 1960 may be used to correlate languages from the McQuown 1955 inventory into the Greenberg classification.)

Our single most important step at this stage of the game is to go to the original data on the two languages involved, then to the reconstructed data (if any exist) of the language families involved or to the raw data of some member of each of these families close to whom the rest of the family is supposed to be based. But of all these, the most important is to see the raw data for Mbayá and Guaná (or the various Mbayás and Guanás until we know which ones we need) and to evaluate these data impressionistically as to how usable we think they really are in the sense emphasized in this paper. Who are the sources? We know we will now find out which sources are primary and which secondary by investigating them all. We have a start in Loukotka; we need now to make longer lists of forms.

What is the recent work on these languages, and on the language families they may belong to? The best place to start checking for recent work is in the indexes of languages at the end of the volumes of the *International Journal of Linguistics*. Neither Mbayá nor Guaná are listed recently; there is no published evidence through this important source of ongoing work. You are now thrown on your own to spot references in new, and probably non-linguistic, literature. You may have to contact some individual personally who you think may be familiar with the Chaco area for leads; etc.

As in other academic problems, you will have to decide where to delimit your inquiry—how far to go in investigating possible leads in other language families—in checking out whether you will accept one interpretation over another, etc. You should not blindly follow one theory, but you should carry the inquiry at least to the first stage of contradiction, because if you don't, the next researcher may. And unless you plan to become a linguist, you must not allow your inquiry to run more than several sessions in the library over a week or two, because the problem can sabotage the rest of your work either by bogging you down in detail or by running you on endlessly into all sorts of related hypotheses to double-check.

FUTURE NEEDS

Many problems are to be found in South American Indian linguistics that need anthropological and linguistic investigation and formalization. A few have been suggested in earlier parts of this paper. A wide variety of sociolinguistic situations are to be found that need documenting: instances of bilingualism; statuses of Indian and other languages in various national settings, especially where some may emerge as politically important languages, e.g., Quechua in the central Andean highlands or Taki Taki in Guyana. More work is needed to ascertain the relationships among languages within language families and stocks so as to provide more substantial bases for critiques on their potential phylum classifications. A great deal of work needs to be done on the ethnographic circumstances of these languages. The discovery and description of language and culture problems in South America has barely begun.

But the writer insists that there are certain very basic needs. Carefully analyzed language descriptions based on skillfully collected data is foremost. (It is a shame that this can be regarded as academically unpopular.) Some fieldworkers—missionaries as well as anthropologists—for whom linguistics is of tedious, secondary interest may be too willing to settle for minimally sufficient attitudes or packaged-product models. The writer recommends that experienced linguistic fieldworkers in particular be better facilitated academically to continue collecting data.

CRITICAL ATTITUDE FOR READER

The critical attitude elaborated in this paper reflects a personal discovery of the pitfalls and shortcomings that menace a researcher particularly in dealing with the linguistic literature on South American Indian languages. It is easy to understand the impatience and enthusiasm of workers in this fascinating wide-open area. It is much harder to realize that the bulk of interpretive statements in it so far have been based on inadequate and underdifferentiated data.

PART V: RELIGION AND IDEOLOGY

Introduction to *The Supernatural World of the Jívaro Shaman*

The Jívaro Indians of Ecuador are most famous for their practice of shrinking the heads of the people they raid. Some of these heads are to be found in ethnographic exhibits of museums, or in the private collections of people with a sense of the macabre. Contrary to what may be imagined, these heads are not amulets or good luck charms to be kept by the Indian, but rather serve as the temporary prison of the *muisak* or avenging soul of the murder victim. During the brief period it is retained by the killer, the power trapped inside the shrunken head may be used to confer power on females in their agricultural work. But after this power has been transferred, the head is usually sold to a *mestizo* trader who will take it far away (Harner 1962).

The Jívaro explain much of their own behavior with reference to demons, spirits and souls, as do many other primitive peoples. The ethnographic literature is full of accounts of how South American Indians attempt to obtain the co-operation of, gain power from or avoid harm from supernatural figures represented as animals, deceased persons or demons. What has not been given great emphasis is the extent to which visions of and communications with these beings are stimulated by the use of powerful hallucinogenic drugs. Some of these are taken in quantities that would stagger a seasoned acid-head in the United States. Yąnomamö males inhale the hallucinogen *ebene* practically every afternoon and they spend several hours thereafter staggering about wild-eyed with green mucus streaming from their nostrils (Chagnon 1968c).

Michael Harner is one of the few anthropologists who has investigated the use of drugs by primitive peoples in any detail. He has shown the importance of a variety of hallucinogens in Shamanism, among them the *ayahuasca* drink of the Upper Amazon region (Harner, Ed., 1973; cf. Cooper 1947:525–48; Chagnon, Le Quesne, Cook 1971). In this article, Harner probes the supernatural world of the Jívaro shaman and documents his drug-assisted entry into the complex world of spirits and souls. For further information on the Jívaro, the reader should consult Karsten 1935 and Harner 1972.

Michael J. Harner is Associate Professor of Anthropology on the Graduate Faculty of the New School for Social Research in New York City. Formerly Assistant Director at the Lowie Museum of Anthropology, University of California, Berkeley, he has also taught at Columbia University.

19. THE SUPERNATURAL WORLD OF THE JÍVARO SHAMAN

MICHAEL J. HARNER

The Jívaro Indians of the Ecuadorian Amazon believe that witchcraft is the cause of the vast majority of illnesses and non-violent deaths. The normal waking life, for the Jívaro, is simply "a lie," or illusion, while the true forces that determine daily events are supernatural and can only be seen and manipulated with the aid of hallucinogenic drugs. A reality view of this kind creates a particularly strong demand for specialists who can cross over into the supernatural world at will to deal with the forces that influence and even determine the events of the waking life.

These specialists, called "shamans" by anthropologists, are recognized by the Jívaro as being of two types: bewitching shamans or curing shamans. Both kinds take a hallucinogenic drink, whose Jívaro name is *natema,* in order to enter the supernatural world. This brew, commonly called *yagé,* or *yajé,* in Colombia, *ayahuasca* (Inca "vine of the dead") in Ecuador and Peru, and *caapi* in Brazil, is prepared from segments of a species of the vine *Banisteriopsis,* a genus belonging to the Malpighiaceae. The Jívaro boil it with the leaves of a similar vine, which probably is also a species of *Banisteriopsis,* to produce a tea that contains the powerful hallucinogenic alkaloids harmaline, harmine, d-tetrahydroharmine, and quite possibly dimethyltryptamine (DMT). These compounds have chemical structures and effects similar, but not identical, to LSD, mescaline of the peyote cactus, and psilocybin of the psychotropic Mexican mushroom.

When I first undertook research among the Jívaro in 1956–57, I did not fully appreciate the psychological impact of the *Ban-*

Reprinted by permission of the author and publishers of *Natural History,* Vol. 77, No. 6 (1968), pp. 28–33, 60–61. © Natural History 1968. From the original article "The Sound of Rushing Water," the photographs, drawings, captions, and the first two paragraphs have been omitted.

isteriopsis drink upon the native view of reality, but in 1961 I had
occasion to drink the hallucinogen in the course of field work with
another Upper Amazon Basin tribe. For several hours after drinking the brew, I found myself, although awake, in a world literally
beyond my wildest dreams. I met bird-headed people, as well as
dragon-like creatures who explained that they were the true gods
of this world. I enlisted the services of other spirit helpers in attempting to fly through the far reaches of the Galaxy. Transported
into a trance where the supernatural seemed natural, I realized that
anthropologists, including myself, had profoundly underestimated
the importance of the drug in affecting native ideology. Therefore,
in 1964 I returned to the Jívaro to give particular attention to the
drug's use by the Jívaro shaman.

The use of the hallucinogenic *natema* drink among the Jívaro
makes it possible for almost anyone to achieve the trance state
essential for the practice of shamanism. Given the presence of the
drug and the felt need to contact the "real," or supernatural, world,
it is not surprising that approximately one out of every four Jívaro
men is a shaman. Any adult, male or female, who desires to become such a practitioner, simply presents a gift to an already practicing shaman, who administers the *Banisteriopsis* drink and gives
some of his own supernatural power—in the form of spirit helpers,
or *tsentsak*—to the apprentice. These spirit helpers, or "darts,"
are the main supernatural forces believed to cause illness and death
in daily life. To the non-shaman they are normally invisible, and
even shamans can perceive them only under the influence of
natema.

Shamans send these spirit helpers into the victims' bodies to
make them ill or to kill them. At other times, they may suck spirits
sent by enemy shamans from the bodies of tribesmen suffering
from witchcraft-induced illness. The spirit helpers also form shields
that protect their shaman masters from attacks. The following account presents the ideology of Jívaro witchcraft from the point of
view of the Indians themselves.

To give the novice some *tsentsak,* the practicing shaman regurgitates what appears to be—to those who have taken *natema*—a bril-
liant substance in which the spirit helpers are contained. He cuts
part of it off with a machete and gives it to the novice to swallow.
The recipient experiences pain upon taking it into his stomach

and stays on his bed for ten days, repeatedly drinking *natema*. The Jívaro believe they can keep magical darts in their stomachs indefinitely and regurgitate them at will. The shaman donating the *tsentsak* periodically blows and rubs all over the body of the novice, apparently to increase the power of the transfer.

The novice must remain inactive and not engage in sexual intercourse for at least three months. If he fails in self-discipline, as some do, he will not become a successful shaman. At the end of the first month, a *tsentsak* emerges from his mouth. With this magical dart at his disposal, the new shaman experiences a tremendous desire to bewitch. If he casts his *tsentsak* to fulfill this desire, he will become a bewitching shaman. If, on the other hand, the novice can control his impulse and reswallow this first *tsentsak,* he will become a curing shaman.

If the shaman who gave the *tsentsak* to the new man was primarily a bewitcher, rather than a curer, the novice likewise will tend to become a bewitcher. This is because a bewitcher's magical darts have such a desire to kill that their new owner will be strongly inclined to adopt their attitude. One informant said that the urge to kill felt by bewitching shamans came to them with a strength and frequency similar to that of hunger.

Only if the novice shaman is able to abstain from sexual intercourse for five months, will he have the power to kill a man (if he is a bewitcher) or cure a victim (if he is a curer). A full year's abstinence is considered necessary to become a really effective bewitcher or curer.

During the period of sexual abstinence, the new shaman collects all kinds of insects, plants, and other objects, which he now has the power to convert into *tsentsak*. Almost any object, including living insects and worms, can become a *tsentsak* if it is small enough to be swallowed by a shaman. Different types of *tsentsak* are used to cause different kinds and degrees of illness. The greater the variety of these objects that a shaman has in his body, the greater is his ability.

According to Jívaro concepts, each *tsentsak* has a natural and supernatural aspect. The magical dart's natural aspect is that of an ordinary material object as seen without drinking the drug *natema*. But the supernatural and "true" aspect of the *tsentsak* is revealed to the shaman by taking *natema*. When he does this, the magical darts appear in new forms as demons and with new names. In their supernatural aspects, the *tsentsak* are not simply objects but spirit helpers in various forms, such as giant butterflies, jaguars, or monkeys, who actively assist the shaman in his tasks.

Bewitching is carried out against a specific, known individual and thus is almost always done to neighbors or, at the most, fellow tribesmen. Normally, as is the case with intratribal assassination, bewitching is done to avenge a particular offense committed against one's family or friends. Both bewitching and individual assassination contrast with the large-scale headhunting raids for which the Jívaro have become famous, and which were conducted against entire neighborhoods of enemy tribes.

To bewitch, the shaman takes *natema* and secretly approaches the house of his victim. Just out of sight in the forest, he drinks green tobacco juice, enabling him to regurgitate a *tsentsak,* which he throws at his victim as he comes out of his house. If the *tsentsak* is strong enough and is thrown with sufficient force, it will pass all the way through the victim's body causing death within a period of a few days to several weeks. More often, however, the magical dart simply lodges in the victim's body. If the shaman, in his hiding place, fails to see the intended victim, he may instead bewitch any member of the intended victim's family who appears, usually a wife or child. When the shaman's mission is accomplished, he returns secretly to his own home.

One of the distinguishing characteristics of the bewitching process among the Jívaro is that, as far as I could learn, the victim is given no specific indication that someone is bewitching him. The bewitcher does not want his victim to be aware that he is being supernaturally attacked, lest he take protective measures by immediately procuring the services of a curing shaman. Nonetheless, shamans and laymen alike with whom I talked noted that illness invariably follows the bewitchment, although the degree of the illness can vary considerably.

A special kind of spirit helper, called a *pasuk,* can aid the bewitching shaman by remaining near the victim in the guise of an insect or animal of the forest after the bewitcher has left. This spirit helper has his own objects to shoot into the victim should a curing shaman succeed in sucking out the *tsentsak* sent earlier by the bewitcher who is the owner of the *pasuk.*

In addition, the bewitcher can enlist the aid of a *wakani* ("soul," or "spirit") bird. Shamans have the power to call these birds and use them as spirit helpers in bewitching victims. The shaman blows on the *wakani* birds and then sends them to the house of the victim to fly around and around the man, frightening him. This is believed to cause fever and insanity, with death resulting shortly thereafter.

After he returns home from bewitching, the shaman may send a *wakani* bird to perch near the house of the victim. Then if a curing shaman sucks out the intruding object, the bewitching shaman sends the *wakani* bird more *tsentsak* to throw from its beak into the victim. By continually resupplying the *wakani* bird with new *tsentsak,* the sorcerer makes it impossible for the curer to rid his patient permanently of the magical darts.

While the *wakani* birds are supernatural servants available to anyone who wishes to use them, the *pasuk,* chief among the spirit helpers, serves only a single shaman. Likewise a shaman possesses only one *pasuk.* The *pasuk,* being specialized for the service of bewitching, has a protective shield to guard it from counterattack by the curing shaman. The curing shaman, under the influence of *natema,* sees the *pasuk* of the bewitcher in human form and size, but "covered with iron except for its eyes." The curing shaman can kill this *pasuk* only by shooting a *tsentsak* into its eyes, the sole vulnerable area in the *pasuk*'s armor. To the person who has not taken the hallucinogenic drink, the *pasuk* usually appears to be simply a tarantula.

Shamans also may kill or injure a person by using magical darts, *anamuk,* to create supernatural animals that attack a victim. If a shaman has a small, pointed armadillo bone *tsentsak,* he can shoot this into a river while the victim is crossing it on a balsa raft or in a canoe. Under the water, this bone manifests itself in its supernatural aspect as an anaconda, which rises up and overturns the craft, causing the victim to drown. The shaman can similarly use a tooth from a killed snake as a *tsentsak,* creating a poisonous serpent to bite his victim. In more or less the same manner, shamans can create jaguars and pumas to kill their victims.

About five years after receiving his *tsentsak,* a bewitching shaman undergoes a test to see if he still retains enough *tsentsak* power to continue to kill successfully. This test involves bewitching a tree. The shaman, under the influence of *natema*, attempts to throw a *tsentsak* through the tree at the point where its two main branches join. If his strength and aim are adequate, the tree appears to split the moment the *tsentsak* is sent into it. The splitting, however, is invisible to an observer who is not under the influence of the hallucinogen. If the shaman fails, he knows that he is incapable of killing a human victim. This means that, as soon as possible, he must go to a strong shaman and purchase a new supply of *tsentsak*. Until he has the goods with which to pay for this new supply, he is in constant danger, in his proved weakened condition, of being seriously bewitched by other shamans. Therefore, each day, he drinks large quantities of *natema*, tobacco juice, and the extract of yet another drug, *pirípirí*. He also rests on his bed at home to conserve his strength, but tries to conceal his weakened condition from his enemies. When he purchases a new supply of *tsentsak,* he can safely cut down on his consumption of these other substances.

The degree of illness produced in a witchcraft victim is a function of both the force with which the *tsentsak* is shot into the body, and also of the character of the magical dart itself. If a *tsentsak* is shot all the way through the body of a victim, then "there is nothing for a curing shaman to suck out," and the patient dies. If the magical dart lodges within the body, however, it is theoretically possible to cure the victim by sucking. But in actual practice, the sucking is not always considered successful.

The work of the curing shaman is complementary to that of a bewitcher. When a curing shaman is called in to treat a patient, his first task is to see if the illness is due to witchcraft. The usual diagnosis and treatment begin with the curing shaman drinking *natema,* tobacco juice, and *pirípirí* in the late afternoon and early evening. These drugs permit him to see into the body of the patient as though it were glass. If the illness is due to sorcery, the curing shaman will see the intruding object within the patient's body clearly enough to determine whether or not he can cure the sickness.

A shaman sucks magical darts from a patient's body only at night, and in a dark area of the house, for it is only in the dark that he can perceive the drug-induced visions that are the supernatural reality. With the setting of the sun, he alerts his *tsentsak* by whistling the tune of the curing song; after about a quarter of an hour, he starts singing. When he is ready to suck, the shaman regurgitates two *tsentsak* into the sides of his throat and mouth. These must be identical to the one he has seen in the patient's body. He holds one of these in the front of the mouth and the other in the rear. They are expected to catch the supernatural aspect of the magical dart that the shaman sucks out of the patient's body. The *tsentsak* nearest the shaman's lips is supposed to incorporate the sucked-out *tsentsak* essence within itself. If, however, this supernatural essence should get past it, the second magical dart in the mouth blocks the throat so that the intruder cannot enter the interior of the shaman's body. If the curer's two *tsentsak* were to fail to catch the supernatural essence of the *tsentsak,* it would pass down into the shaman's stomach and kill him. Trapped thus within the mouth, this essence is shortly caught by, and incorporated into, the material substance of one of the curing shaman's *tsentsak*. He then "vomits" out this object and displays it to the patient and his family saying, "Now I have sucked it out. Here it is."

The non-shamans think that the material object itself is what has been sucked out, and the shaman does not disillusion them. At the same time, he is not lying, because he knows that the only important thing about a *tsentsak* is its supernatural aspect, or essence, which he sincerely believes he has removed from the patient's body. To explain to the layman that he already had these objects in his mouth would serve no fruitful purpose and would prevent him from displaying such an object as proof that he had effected the cure. Without incontrovertible evidence, he would not be able to convince the patient and his family that he had effected the cure and must be paid.

The ability of the shaman to suck depends largely upon the quantity and strength of his own *tsentsak,* of which he may have hundreds. His magical darts assume their supernatural aspect as spirit helpers when he is under the influence of *natema,* and he sees them as a variety of zoomorphic forms hovering over him, perching on his shoulders, and sticking out of his skin. He sees them helping to suck the patient's body. He must drink tobacco juice every few hours to "keep them fed" so that they will not leave him.

The curing shaman must also deal with any *pasuk* that may be in the patient's vicinity for the purpose of casting more darts. He drinks additional amounts of *natema* in order to see them and engages in *tsentsak* duels with them if they are present. While the *pasuk* is enclosed in iron armor, the shaman himself has his own armor composed of his many *tsentsak*. As long as he is under the influence of *natema,* these magical darts cover his body as a protective shield, and are on the lookout for any enemy *tsentsak* headed toward their master. When these *tsentsak* see such a missile coming, they immediately close up together at the point where the enemy dart is attempting to penetrate, and thereby repel it.

If the curer finds *tsentsak* entering the body of his patient after he has killed *pasuk,* he suspects the presence of a *wakani* bird. The shaman drinks *maikua* (*Datura* sp.), an hallucinogen even more powerful than *natema,* as well as tobacco juice, and silently sneaks into the forest to hunt and kill the bird with *tsentsak*. When he succeeds, the curer returns to the patient's home, blows all over the house to get rid of the "atmosphere" created by the numerous *tsentsak* sent by the bird, and completes his sucking of the patient. Even after all the *tsentsak* are extracted, the shaman may remain another night at the house to suck out any "dirtiness" (*pahuri*) still inside. In the cures which I have witnessed, this sucking is a most noisy process, accompanied by deep, but dry, vomiting.

After sucking out a *tsentsak,* the shaman puts it into a little container. He does not swallow it because it is not his own magical dart and would therefore kill him. Later, he throws the *tsentsak* into the air, and it flies back to the shaman who sent it originally into the patient. *Tsentsak* also fly back to a shaman at the death of a former apprentice who had originally received them from him. Besides receiving "old" magical darts unexpectedly in this manner, the shaman may have *tsentsak* thrown at him by a bewitcher. Accordingly, shamans constantly drink tobacco juice at all hours of the day and night. Although the tobacco juice is not truly hallucinogenic, it produces a narcotized state, which is believed necessary to keep one's *tsentsak* ready to repel any other magical darts. A shaman does not even dare go for a walk without taking along the green tobacco leaves with which he prepares the juice that keeps his spirit helpers alert. Less frequently, but regularly, he must drink *natema* for the same purpose and to keep in touch with the supernatural reality.

While curing under the influence of *natema,* the curing shaman "sees" the shaman who bewitched his patient. Generally, he can recognize the person, unless it is a shaman who lives far away or in another tribe. The patient's family knows this, and demands to be told the identity of the bewitcher, particularly if the sick person dies. At one curing session I attended, the shaman could not identify the person he had seen in his vision. The brother of the dead man then accused the shaman himself of being responsible. Under such pressure, there is a strong tendency for the curing shaman to attribute each case to a particular bewitcher.

Shamans gradually become weak and must purchase *tsentsak* again and again. Curers tend to become weak in power, especially after curing a patient bewitched by a shaman who has recently received a new supply of magical darts. Thus, the most powerful shamans are those who can repeatedly purchase new supplies of *tsentsak* from other shamans.

Shamans can take back *tsentsak* from others to whom they have previously given them. To accomplish this, the shaman drinks *natema,* and, using his *tsentsak,* creates a "bridge" in the form of a rainbow between himself and the other shaman. Then he shoots a *tsentsak* along this rainbow. This strikes the ground beside the other shaman with an explosion and flash likened to a lightning bolt. The purpose of this is to surprise the other shaman so that he temporarily forgets to maintain his guard over his magical darts, thus permitting the other shaman to suck them back along the rainbow. A shaman who has had his *tsentsak* taken away in this manner will discover that "nothing happens" when he drinks *natema.* The sudden loss of his *tsentsak* will tend to make him ill, but ordinarily the illness is not fatal unless a bewitcher shoots a magical dart into him while he is in this weakened condition. If he has not become disillusioned by his experience, he can again purchase *tsentsak* from some other shaman and resume his calling. Fortunately for anthropology some of these men have chosen to give up shamanism and therefore can be persuaded to reveal their knowledge, no longer having a vested interest in the profession. This divulgence, however, does not serve as a significant threat to practitioners, for words alone can never adequately convey the realities of shamanism. These can only be approached with the aid of *natema,* the chemical door to the invisible world of the Jívaro shaman.

Introduction to A Visit to God: The Account and Interpretation of a Religious Experience in the Peruvian Community of Choque-Huarcaya

The structural approach to society and myth has been pioneered by Claude Lévi-Strauss. In this selection, Zuidema and Quispe explore the structural implications of a dream recounted to them by an old lady in highland Peru. In this experience, elements appear that reflect centuries-old aspects of Inca religion and social organization. The account itself bears many of the qualities of myths, particularly its universal quality which permits the interpretation made by the authors. The editor believes that myths are born of precisely such experiences which are then recounted again and again across generations, sometimes extensively modified in the telling. The method of interpretation is of as much interest as the material itself. Readers who are interested in learning more about the particular subject matter will want to consult the works of John Murra (1956, etc.) and John Rowe (1946, etc.) as well as the monograph by R. T. Zuidema entitled *The Ceque System of Cuzco: The Social Organization of the Capital of the Inca* (1964), and Zuidema 1962 and 1969.

R. T. Zuidema holds a Ph.D. from the University of Leiden, Netherlands, and presently teaches at the University of Illinois.

20. A VISIT TO GOD: THE ACCOUNT AND INTERPRETATION OF A RELIGIOUS EXPERIENCE IN THE PERUVIAN COMMUNITY OF CHOQUE-HUARCAYA

R. T. ZUIDEMA AND U. QUISPE

During our field work in the River Pampas area, Department of Ayacucho, Peru, we were told by an old lady, Francisca Chaqiri, how she had died when 20 years old and how she had gone to God. He, however, said that He had not called for her and so He sent her back to earth and to life. We also heard elements of her religious ideas and descriptions of similar visits to God on other occasions. What makes her account so valuable is its clearly discernible structure, which relates it to similar ideas in Inca religion and social organization; ideas that still survive, as this account proves.

The Quechua text was collected and recorded in the community of Choque-Huarcaya, near the River Pampas, by R. T. Zuidema and U. Quispe and translated by the latter. The data on the modern culture were collected in Huarcaya by U. Quispe and S. Catacora and in Sarhua by S. Palomina and J. Earls, all students of the University of Ayacucho, on various occasions between April and September 1966. The two communities belong to the district of Sarhua, province of Victor Fajardo, department of Ayacucho.

After a translation of the recorded Quechua text we will give the interpretation of it.

TRANSLATION OF THE TEXT.

Sir, when I was a newly wed, I fell ill with flu; three of us got sick, two men and a woman, the first two died but I was set free by Our Lord.

Reprinted by permission of the author and Koninklijk Instituut voor Taal-, Land- en Volkenkunde, Leiden, Netherlands from *Bijdragen Tot de Taal-, Land- en Volkenkunde*, Vol. 124 (1968), pp. 22–39. Two figures and the Quechua text have been omitted.

It was as if I was sleeping, like when you dream,—I don't know what it was—I died, I don't know how it was, like when you dream, when I was . . . those who were going to take me were at my side. Straight off they took me; the one who went in front of me was white and the one that came behind was coloured *chiqchi*[1] and this one carried a *chusiq*[2] on his shoulder and was dressed in a robe. Like that with their robes and girdles they took me, Sir.

Like that I went to the centre through a bluish medium. We started off through a flower garden and then reached a village of thorns. After having passed the village of thorns with so much trouble, we entered a place of clear sky that went straight up; there I saw a lot of big dogs, black *tawañawi* with four eyes[3] above the road and coffee-coloured ones below it, they were resting. I think there were four above and four below the path—there they were, those dogs—; so I said 'can I speak?' and got answered 'no, we'll pass in silence, because if you talk they can kill us'. Although it was in such heat that I could hardly walk they told me to hurry. That, Sir, is how we got through that village, how we escaped from those dogs.

On we went then, qiqa machay?, a bit up from Ayacucho it is, Qiqapampa, there we entered; it was '*putya*'.[4] They went very easily while I could hardly walk in the heat—I felt the heat inside me. After this we started over some sand dunes, and I sank as if I were in a moor and because of this my feet got blistered. Uselessly I called: 'What heat!'.

From the sand dunes we went right up to a church, which was apparently in the sky, I was still going in between the two. There from the centre of the church I saw Hell which had a zig-zag path leading up to it. When we were going there Our Lord Himself said to them, to those who were taking me: 'hurry'. The Lord was sitting exactly in the door to Hell, with a beautiful golden beard and with a staff of silver and gold; at His left four beautiful girls were sitting, and at His right there were four gentlemen, thus with the Lord Himself there were five gentlemen. He told me to get out from where I was and to stand in a corner; there in this corner were the most beautiful polished pews, and when He said to me: 'get in' I got under a beautiful varnished pew; there I sat while those that had brought me entered. 'What have you been doing all this time?' the Lord asked them. He knocked one of them over and hit him with His staff; this one got up straight away and couldn't carry a brick that he had, neither could he get up when he was given the robe that his companion had. Then He made him climb up and enter a dark place. Now He hit the other one and said 'What have you been doing all this time, did I send you for her? I sent you for someone else. Why did you bring me a woman whom I didn't send you to get?' And He sent this one up as well; I just sat there watching.

After they had gone in, Our Lord said to me to return from here without turning my head back, so I left. When I was leaving the church . . . it all cleared up, it was wonderfully white snow, a clear world. I was at the banks of a spring which is on the path to Tomanga where there was a beautiful white china cup with which I drank some water; suddenly it all became clear to me and I spoke: 'please give me water' and they gave me more water and it all cleared up even more. Then I woke up, as from a dream; they told me to say 'Jesus' and I said 'Jesus Taytallay' (Our Lord), and there off I got back all my strength.

So I got to know the other world and came back; Our Lord Himself said to me 'I didn't get them to call you, it was another, and they mistook you for him'.

INTERPRETATION OF THE TEXT.

Something that comes to mind immediately in the study of native Andean society, either ancient or modern, is the difficulty of making a clear definition of its basic concepts. Let us take one example: the chroniclers describe the Inca ayllu equally as a group of kinsmen, a lineage, an endogamous group, an exogamous group, or a localized group unrelated to the kinship system. The same can be said for the modern ayllu. To take a few examples just within the department of Ayacucho: in Puquio we have four localized ayllus which are probably neither exogamous nor endogamous; in Huanca Sancos the four are completely unlocalized; in Sarhua there are two ayllus which divide the whole of their society into 'locals' and 'foreigners'; in Huarcaya only on certain occasions do the two ayllus come into being, and then only for ritual purposes, without any apparent relation to the kinship system, or to land or water rights. Moreover, besides these different types of ayllus, in many communities of the area of the River Pampas the concept of ayllu is known as a specific kinship grouping defined in relation to the position of Ego.

Here we have taken the ayllu as an example, but we could present many more examples taken from the social and political organization or from the economic and religious spheres. Perhaps Andean culture is nothing more than a mere amalgamation of differing types of societies, with no similarity between them. But it could also be—and this seems more probable to us—that we have not yet found the basic cultural elements—in Lévi-Strauss's sense of the words—that would enable us to see these different types of Andean societies as just so many representations of the same structure.

Such being the case, one of our tasks is to study and describe as many of these societies as possible (by means of the chronicles, colonial documents, and field work in the modern communities); choosing for strategical reasons organizations that show promise of practical possibilities for research and seem to be the most typical. At the same time we must look for these basic structural elements—if they exist—that lie behind all these organizations and which each organization illustrates in its own way. In the event of finding these elements we can then understand the differences in the organizations to be not of a basic order, but of a more superficial one, determined by the special historical circumstances of each case. Consequently, it would also be possible to compare the organizations, one to the other, as we would then know how to compare them. Finally we could then study if—and to what extent —the structure of native society has changed since the Spanish conquest.

This search for a basic structure led us to the study of the system of ceques (Zuidema 1964). Another means to arrive at it was found in the diagrams of the chroniclers Perez Bocanegra (1631) and Joan de Santacruz Pachacuti Yamqui (1613). Both diagrams depict the same order between their constituent elements, the former as to the kinship system and the latter as to the Inca religious system. Our task is now to show that the same order exists in the text of this study.

In another publication (Zuidema 1972) we shall study in greater detail just how the drawings of Perez Bocanegra and Pachacuti Yamqui express most of the basic ideas of the pre-Columbian Andean social and religious structure, but we must now indicate at least some of the conclusions we have reached. Firstly we intend to demonstrate a concordance between Perez Bocanegra, Pachacuti Yamqui and our text. The consequence of this would be—and this is our working hypothesis—that the order that we are going to point out implies a social structure still similar to that of the indigenous communities of the XVIth century. Therefore, we will also mention some elements of the modern culture that express this structure. We cannot study this in its entirety since we still lack a great amount of data, but we hope that this study will act as a beginning and will give us a basis to build on in our future field work, indicating some of the more important elements of the native culture to study.

This story of Señora Francisca Chaqiri, of some seventy years of age, was told to us by her as a true occurrence which had happened to her when she was about twenty years old. Apparently she was born in Tomanga, in the same River Pampas area, and her parents had forced her to marry a man from Huarcaya, whom she had not known before and whom she never loved. Now she is a widow and lives in Huarcaya. While she was telling us she would occasionally burst into tears and by the richness of detail in the account of her journey to God, she demonstrated that the memory of it was still very much alive in her. She had no doubt led an emotional life very much closed in upon herself, but this fact does not in any way detract from the general importance of the ideas she expressed about the religion, cosmology and society of her community. Even though her ideas may be considered personal, it is not possible that she reconstructed, consciously and sui generis, a complete cosmological model of pre-Spanish origin. On other occasions we also heard about experiences of people who had visited God. Further, the elements in this account are almost all well-known in these villages. Finally, its internal consistency, which structure is so completely comparable to the pre-Spanish social and cosmological model—as we will prove—induces us to believe that the account can help us to study and interpret the social and religious systems of Huarcaya, Tomanga and Sarhua, all belonging to the same district. We have not attempted to define this story as a dream, a myth or anything else. At any rate this is not really important; of real importance are the ideas behind it.

Finally it must be added that Señora Chaqiri, while such a good informant in this one aspect, could tell us very little about her other personal memories, or about the culture of Huarcaya in general. She had apparently forgotten. It seems that all her interests were focused on this one experience.

In her account there are three elements of special interest we want to discuss here: the ascent through the five fields, the description of God and His companions and, finally, the Tawañawi dogs. These last are also found in other descriptions of the world of the dead, thus demonstrating that our informant did employ elements belonging to her culture.

The arrangement of God with the four male saints on His right hand and four female ones on His left is also found in the diagrams of Perez Bocanegra and Pachacuti Yamqui; in the former it is seen when he describes the Inca kinship system, in the latter in his description of the religious and cosmological system. A diagram is given by the former to illustrate the type of lineage and the degrees of kinship that operated in it.

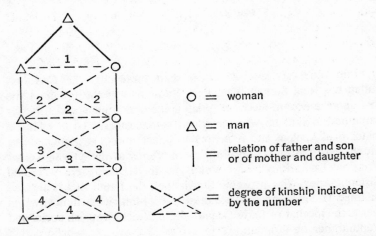

Perez Bocanegra, then, draws two lineages here, one patrilineal composed only of men, and the other matrilineal composed only of women. They consist of four generations, but the two lineages descend from one common ancestor representing an original marriage. We know that in the Inca family system only the last two people of each lineage were allowed to marry. This includes not only, negatively, the rules prohibiting incest, but in this way also forms—as we will explain elsewhere—the positive basis for the models which the Incas used in describing their social systems. In this system of marriage-regulation then lies the importance of representing four generations of descendants.

The diagram of Pachacuti Yamqui is essentially the same model, but in cosmological form:

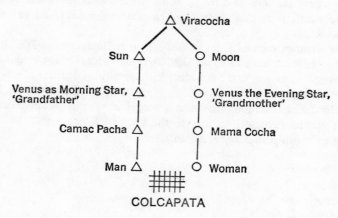

From other sources we know that Viracocha, the Creator—called the Real Sun by Pachacuti Yamqui—was the father of the Sun and the Moon. He was equally male and female, which fact is explained in that he was the founding ancestor of both a female matrilineal lineage and a male patrilineal one. The Sun and the Moon were the father and mother of Venus as the Morning Star, termed 'Grandfather', and Venus as the Evening Star, termed 'Grandmother'. The Morning Star is then the father of Lord Earth (Camac Pacha) and the grandfather of Man, while the Evening Star is the mother of Lady Ocean (Mama Cocha) and the maternal grandmother of Woman.

Besides representing the Inca kinship and religious systems, this model also reflects their system of social hierarchy. A datum with respect to this is the organization of the *panaca*. Each king founded his own panaca, which unit came to be composed of his descendants; he as the founder had married his own sister by both his father and his mother, and because of this he and his sister belonged to a lineage that was equally patrilineal and matrilineal (since all their ancestors had also married their full siblings and thus differed from all other mortal beings). The king then, within the system of social hierarchy occupied the same position as Viracocha in the cosmological hierarchy. The descendants of the king, being members of his own panaca, were pushed down a rank in the social hierarchy with every generation removed, until the great-great-grandchildren became simply nobles 'of the commons', as the chroniclers tell us. Later generations descended no more than this.

In a transformation which there is no need to describe in detail here, we recognise the same model in the way in which, according to Garcilaso de la Vega, the mummies of the kings before Huascar (the last Inca) were placed in the Temple of the Sun in Cuzco. The system behind the arrangement of the mummies was such that the older the mummies were, the lower were the positions in the social and cosmological hierarchy that they represented. Whilst every Inca started as a 'Viracocha' (as one chronicler says of the reigning Inca), with every succeeding generation after his death he represented a category lower down in the hierarchical order. This system of the mummies of the ancestors was thus a model of the society as well.

It is important to take note of this application of the model for it is in this form that we can recognise it so clearly in the art of the pre-Inca Tiahuanaco culture (Zuidema 1973) that flourished around Lake Titicaca some thousand years before the Spanish conquest.

Finally then, the model was of great importance to the calendar system of both Inca and Tiahuanaco culture.

To resume, we have good data on the existence of the model in the southern Andes area from the VIIth century up to the middle of the XVIIth century. Garcilaso de la Vega (1609) was of the royal Inca line of Cuzco. Perez Bocanegra (1631) presents the model as the kinship system of the community of Andahuaylillas near Cuzco. Pachacuti Yamqui (1613), although writing of the Incas of Cuzco, was cacique of a town half-way between Cuzco and Lake Titicaca and had Aymara as his native tongue, which language is still spoken around Lake Titicaca. He gives us the model twice, in both its social and cosmological applications, just as the chronicler Felipe Guaman Poma de Ayala (who wrote between the years 1584 and 1614). The latter writes on the basis of his knowledge of the indigenous culture of the present-day department of Ayacucho, where the communities of Huarcaya and Sarhua are found. Finally, the model can be recognised in the art of Tiahuanaco, in the Inca ancestor system and in their calendar system.

The model forms the basis and the point of departure for any theoretical study of social and religious organizations in the southern Andes region of Peru until the middle of the XVIIth century. The system of ceques which we studied in Cuzco turns out to be simply an elaboration of it. Even so, according to the chroniclers, every town and village had its own system of ceques, and in Huarcaya an elemental form of it can be recognised. If then Señora Chaqiri describes the same model in speaking of God and the four male companions at His right and the four female ones at His left, we must suppose that the model is still important in her society.

By the same token, the five fields through which the Señora passed represent an ancient concept. She mentions that she was going uphill, and the fact that the first field was the most watered and the last the driest serves to express this idea. Now the diagram of Pachacuti Yamqui contains one detail that can be compared with these fields. In the first place it is necessary to point out that, according to him, the diagram explained how the different gods were placed in the Temple of the Sun in Cuzco, i.e., his diagram represented the temple. Besides the already mentioned details, the lower part contains something that looks like a type of grid with the word 'pata' (quechua) added. This word is employed for 'anden' (terrace used for agriculture on the flanks of hills) and it seems that there he wished to draw attention to a system of andenes, i.e. a series of platforms of differing heights. These platforms can be compared to the five fields: the field of flowers, the village of thorns, the village of dogs, the Qiqapampa and the desert through which our informant passed on her ascent to God.

Nevertheless, we could ask why she describes the third field as a village of dogs and not by its geographic characteristics. Is there an explanation of why she describes exactly five fields (no more, no less), with the village of dogs on the third? We shall take the last question first. Systems of terraces, often constructed in places that defy economic explanation, also expressed in Inca culture a religious concept which was that of the pyramid. The pyramid as a construction was more important to the people on the coast than it was to those of the highlands. However, for the highland people the *concept* of pyramid was probably just as important in the sense that they transformed the mountains into pyramids by means of terraces. They also constructed artificial pyramids called *ushñu,* though these are not noteworthy for their size. The ushñu of Vilcas Huaman (an old Inca capital some 60 kms from Huarcaya) is the best example of these. Poma de Ayala gives us various drawings of ushñus, including the one at Vilcas Huaman, and they always consist of five levels. This particular number of levels would be the best reason to compare Señora Chaqiri's description of the mountain with 5 levels and the church on top to the pyramid. This conclusion is corroborated by the fact that according to the chroniclers the temples of the Sun were also constructed on top of pyramids or on top of hills, which were transformed into pyramids by terraces (the most important example of these being the so-called "fortress" of Cuzco, Sacsahuaman, which was in reality intended as another temple of the Sun).

But there are other reasons for our conclusion and here we have to answer why the village of dogs—of which first she said there were many but later specified four black ones and four coffee-coloured ones—was situated on the third level. First it must be pointed out that although she describes her journey as out of this world—through a blueish medium, as she puts it—in reality she describes the different vegetational conditions that one encounters when climbing from a hot river valley up to the cold heights of the mountains (punas). In the present-day native religion the tawañawi dogs are the guardians of the land of the dead ancestors, i.e. of the Kingdom of God and the Saints. Moreover, it is believed that one should treat one's dogs kindly, since once dead they can help their former owner on his journey to the land of the dead. In many of the pre-Spanish graves dogs were mummified and buried with people, possibly as guides to the land of the dead. The ancient Huancas believed they were descended from dogs. For these reasons we believe that the village of dogs in the story replaced in the supernatural world a village of people, perhaps even Huarcaya or Tomanga themselves. In reality, our informant is quite clear on this point, since when she describes Qiqapampa, the field after the tawañawi, she says it is like the entrance to Ayacucho from the mountains, thus comparing this city here on earth with the village of dogs in the Kingdom of God. Moreover, the communities in the region of the River Pampas are usually situated half-way up from the river to the puna, and this itself might have influenced the origin of the concept of the five levels and the village of the dogs between them. But there is something more fundamental in this.

The chronicler Cabello Valboa mentions as another name for ushñu (pyramid): 'chuqui pillaca'. Chuqui is lance, and as to pillaca Holguín (1608) says: 'Pillaca llayta, llautu (ribbon) of two colors woven in counter fashion, purple and black'. Now in his book 'Tihuanacu' Posnansky reproduces the design on an Inca k'ero (a wooden tumbler) of an ushñu in colors and of an Inca with all his royal insignia. The pyramid has six levels. Placed on the uppermost level is a lance adorned with two ribbons, one purple and one black. The same lances, also with the ribbons, are found on the four corners of the third level of the pyramid. The Inca carried a lance similar to this as a symbol of his dignity. We know that the Inca was seated on top of the ushñu when he dispensed justice (in Vilcas Huaman his seat is still there as described by Cieza de Leon), and thus seated he is depicted by Poma de Ayala. The Inca then occupied the position in the social order that was held by Viracocha in the ancient religious order and by God in the conception of Señora Chaqiri. Therefore we can conclude that the village of dogs occupies the same position as these four lances on the ushñu drawn on the k'ero. Just as the lance of the Inca represented him, so we may be sure that the other four lances also represented social entities. Later we will indicate the modern version of these lances as they still are used. What we wanted to point out here is that the position of the village of the dogs on the third level in our account is not accidental.

This connection between lance and ushñu or sacred mountain has still been preserved in Sarhua. In the department of Ayacucho these mountains and their gods are called *Hua-*

mani and are especially important in rites related to cattle high up in the puna. On San Juan (24th of June),—the most important feast in Sarhua, which replaced the old Feast of the Sun—one part of the celebration is that people go to the puna and bring from there to the village the *vaquero* who takes care of the cattle of the community. This man has a lance called Huamani. To this he speaks when he wants to communicate with the mountains.

There is still one difficulty in our comparison, however. The ushñu of the k'ero has six levels and not five. Here we note that the church in Señora Chaqiri's story was still further up than the fifth level, i.e. on a sixth level, and thus we must suppose that, in the ushñu of Vilcas Huaman and in the drawings of Poma de Ayala, the seat of the Inca, in reality, represented the sixth level.

In relation to these special ideas about the third level—in Señora Chaqiri's account and in Inca culture—we wish to observe that Paul Kosok, in his book *Life, Land and Water in Ancient Peru* gives us a model of a pyramid called 'Huaca de los Chinos' of the coastal Tiahuanaco culture in the valley of Moche. It is constructed against a hill with a series of platforms, and consists of six levels with eight houses on the third, four on each side of the stairway that climbs up to the last platform at the top. In Señora Chaqiri's experience there are equally four dogs on each side of the path on the third level.

If it is possible to relate the village of the tawañawi dogs to pre-Spanish concepts concerning the third level of a pyramid, what can be said then about the other fields—or levels—through which she passed? First let us consider the field of flowers. According to an informant in Ayacucho who lived some years in Huarcaya, children who have died go to a garden 'wayta huerta' (flower garden). There the little boys water the flowers and the little girls sweep and clean the garden. In Ayacucho, when a little girl died they used to put a little broom in her coffin so that she could sweep the garden. The field of flowers is related to children, thus making a generational distinction between them and older people who were related to other fields or levels.

The field of thorns in the story is described by the same informant as a place on the road towards God. The road to Heaven is dangerous while the road to Hell is pleasant and free of dangers.

> This idea could belong to Christian beliefs where it is said that the road to Hell is broad and that to Heaven narrow. But it is not said that the last road zig-zags and there seems to exist a pre-Spanish tradition about this concept of the two roads: the straight and the zig-zag one. We would like to remind the reader here of the form of the pyramid of Paña-marca of the north coast culture of Moche. Although this culture is older than the influence there of Tiahuanaco, it is contemporary with the classic Tiahuanaco period. The pyramid has six levels, the last of which is hardly visible. A stairway zig-zags up to the top. The pyramid is constructed around a rectangular room as high as its base to which goes a straight and horizontal path. If the top could represent the Upperworld—*Hananpacha* in Inca religion—and the room the Underworld—*Ukupacha*—then we find here the same idea as that expressed by the informant of Ayacucho. This would mean, however, that Señora Chaqiri, in whose version it is the road to Hell that zig-zags up from the church of God has confused this idea.

The importance of the concept of Qiqapampa, the fourth field in her path, can be understood if we take note of the geographic location of her birth place Tomanga. This community is also found half-way in between the river Pampas and the puna. Between the village and the river there are a number of magnificent terraces, probably of pre-Spanish origin. Further up there are pastures. Overlooking the village there is a rocky cliff called Tomanqasa on which another series of ancient terraces is found with the extensive and well preserved ruins of a pre-Spanish town. Between the modern and the ancient town are many caves with, behind walls, bones and mummies of people who were probably the ancestors of the present-day inhabitants of Tomanga. Now firstly our informant speaks of Qiqamachay instead of Qiqapampa. Machay, according to Holguín, are the caves where the dead are entombed. Comparing then the village of the dogs with Tomanga, Qiqapampa (or Qiqamachay) is situated at the altitude of the caves. This conclusion is confirmed through the comparison of the desert at the fifth level to the ruins of Tomanqasa, which is the town of the ancestors of modern Tomanga. In other parts of Peru the concept of desert is also related to ruins. Finally, the church with God can be equated with the Temple of the Sun.

More important than these explanations about the five fields is, however, the phenomenon that our story preserves integrally the old concept of the structure formed around these five fields. We have not contended ourselves with comparing odd data; on the contrary, we have shown that the whole story, with the fields and with the church, forms an organic unit, a structure equal in form to that which existed in Inca times. From this conclusion we can draw a practical result, inverting the normal procedure for structural studies. This model of a structure basic to society can be used as a guide in our research into the present-day society and culture of Huarcaya and its neighbouring communities. While the model is basic to Inca culture, as we have shown, our question is then, how has it been possible to preserve this to the present day? Or in other words, what are the elements in the modern native culture that enabled Señora Chaqiri to reconstruct, or preserve, this pre-Spanish model?

Her story proves that these elements must still be very much alive. Moreover it shows us that we still know very little of modern native society and religion. Let us mention some elements of the social organization and religion that could be of help in resolving this problem in the future.

First let us return to the diagram of Perez Bocanegra. In this are described two parallel lineages, a patrilineal one for men and a matrilineal one for women. This lineage system, peculiar to the Incas and some other South American peoples, we find described in colonial documents—including those of Huarcaya and Sarhua —up to the end of the XVIIIth century but not later. It seems that in some communities near Cuzco it still persists, but in those of our study we could not find it. However, according to one informant in Sarhua, the concept of incest prohibits marriage between the descendants of a couple up to the great-grandchildren;

the great-great-grandchildren can marry. This is the same concept of incest, then, as the Incaic one. In any case this modern concept of incest indicates that it is still important to know one's ancestors up to the third generation, i.e. up to the great-grandfather.

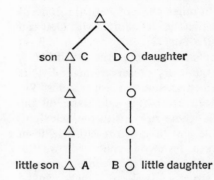

son △ C   D ○ daughter

(The last two can marry. A, according to this nomenclature, should say 'wife', not only to B but to D as well, and B will say 'husband' to C.)

little son △ A   B ○ little daughter

Another peculiarity of the diagram of Perez Bocanegra is that it describes the great-great-grandson and the great-great-granddaughter (each within his or her own lineage) as 'little son' and 'little daughter'.

Quispe and Catacora found a similar datum in Huarcaya. There a certain old lady addressed a baby, who was a distant relative of hers, as 'husband', and on another occasion a little girl said 'husband' to an old man. In both cases, the ancestor in common was the great-great-grandparent of the younger person and the parent of the elder.

Another organization that might have been the model for the representation of God with His four male and four female companions, is the system of *varayuq* (functionaries of the communities within the system of 'cargos') with the *alcalde de vara* (chief of the varayuq) called *Taytamama* 'father-mother' of the others, these latter dividing into four *regidores* and four *alguaciles*. Their distinction is the *vara* (Spanish for staff). In special ceremonies they use the *alta vara,* a very long and straight branch, with its bark stripped off and painted with ribbons in the colours purple and black. These were also the colours of the ribbons painted on the lances found on the Inca ushñu. So it results that the eight varayuq represent the community—just as the four black dogs and the four coffee-coloured ones in the account of Señora Chaqiri, or as the four lances on the Inca ushñu represent the community. The *alcalde de vara,* the father-mother, is then comparable to God or to the king in the Inca organization. But perhaps the organization of the varayuq in Sarhua, where there are two organizations, one for each ayllu, and each assigned a set position in respect to the other in the church or out of it, would be a better example.

Perhaps we should look for the Señora Chaqiri's pattern in the internal organization of the church as well, of which we have a good example in Sarhua. In this church the altar, dedicated to God, from which the priest celebrates mass, is in the centre of one end of the church and on the right there are the chapels and pictures of the male Saints and of Jesus Christ, and at the left are those of the Virgin and the female Saints. In this way it appears like the Church of God and His companions in her account. However, we have as yet only found this order in Sarhua.

We have mentioned here some facts of the modern culture in Huarcaya and Sarhua. Their kinship and political systems still preserve traces of the old Inca ones. The organization of the church of God could be related to the one in Sarhua. Also the idea of ushñu still exists, although it now refers more specifically to the bones and other remains of the 'gentiles', the pre-Spanish ancestors, which are found in the caves and on the terraces and are said to be the cause of a special kind of illness if one touches them. But in another village near Ayacucho *ushñu* refers to a heap of stones, i.e. the most elemental form of a pyramid.

We recognise that there is still a great amount to be discovered about the native kinship system, the social and political systems, and religion. The text that we studied can serve us as a guide, indicating what to look for and where. The mere description of a religious model essentially the same as an Inca one shows us that the social and cultural facts in which it is based still exist and that we can find them.

NOTES

1. A black colour with white spots, or vice versa.

2. A small nocturnal bird which announces death.

3. Black or coffee coloured dogs have often lighter coloured spots above their eyes, that give them an appearance of having four eyes; these are called tawañawi.

4. This can be translated as 'craggy', but an Ayacucho informant said that it means 'dusty'; in any case it means that some sort of trouble had to be overcome.

Introduction to Rite and Crop in the Inca State

In this intriguing selection, John Murra shows how ritual and other activities surrounding two important Andean crops reflect a dichotomy in the social life of the Inca state. The pre-Columbian Andeans lavished much more care, labor and ceremonial activity on maize and maize growing than on the lowly potato even though the latter was more likely a staple in the diet of the masses. In his interpretation, Murra emphasizes that maize, probably an intrusive crop, provided a foundation for many of the activities of the state. As an irrigated crop, it probably yielded more reliably than the potato. In addition, maize is more readily preserved, stored and transported than potatoes, facilitating the redistributive function of the state (cf. Fried 1967). Since maize and potatoes thrived in different habitats this exigency made it imperative that firm military control be established over the different ecological zones in which the different crops were cultivated.

Maize was of pre-eminent importance not only in the Andes but also elsewhere in the New World. Many of the societies of southeastern North America relied heavily on maize, and maize storehouses there were often associated with the dwellings and temples of priests and rulers. Another reason for the dominance of maize in the social and ceremonial life of these peoples might be its superior nutritional qualities to those of root crops. Consider the following data showing the nutritional value per 100-gram edible portion of dried yellow corn versus chuño (the form in which potatoes are stored):

	Food Energy	Grams Protein	Grams Fat	Grams Carbohydrate	mcg. Vitamin A
Corn:	361 cal.	9.4	4.3	74.4	70
Potatoes:	327 cal.	2.1	0.2	79.2	0

For equal edible portions, corn has nearly four and one half times more protein. Fresh corn enjoys a smaller but still significant advantage over fresh potatoes (INCAP-ICNND 1961). It need not require conscious realization of the superior nutritional qualities of a food for a people to tacitly recognize it in cultural preference.

In any case, Murra's correlation of ecological factors with ceremonial life opens new and interesting questions for study. For example, if it is the case that state formation depends in its incipient stages on central control of granaries, might we not then expect to find a rough correlation cross-culturally between the keeping qualities of staple foods and degree of stratification? Food preferences as expressed in folklore or ritual might profitably be re-examined in terms of nutritional and other advantages they confer on the population which uses them.

John V. Murra is a leading expert on the ethnohistorical study of the Inca, an Andean people who came to dominate a vast empire. His numerous publications include studies focusing on many aspects of Inca life. Murra holds the Ph.D. degree from the University of Chicago and is currently Professor of Anthropology at Cornell University.

21. RITE AND CROP IN THE INCA STATE

JOHN V. MURRA

As one reads the sixteenth-century European sources on Inca ceremonialism one becomes aware of a curious and unexpected discrepancy: the ritual crop calendar reported does not reflect either the agricultural realities of that period or the modern patterns of expressing concern over the fate of the crops. The chroniclers of the European invasion and early settlement fill many pages describing peasant- and state-sponsored ceremonies and sacrifices accompanying the planting, irrigating, weeding, and harvesting of maize; they report little if any ritual connected with the many Andean root crops.

Such a discrepancy in reporting focuses attention on the botanical and ecological differences between the two sets of crops: one a locally domesticated, high-altitude series of frost-resistant tubers, of which the potato is only the most celebrated; the other a warmweather grain, of Pan-American distribution, maize. I hope to show that the chroniclers' discrepancy is also a hint to important cultural and social differences.

At the upper levels of the Andean *altiplano* the alpine root crops —the potato, the *oca*, the *ullucu*—are the only ones at home. Juzepczuk found one wild species of potato blooming at 16,400 feet in an 18-degree frost, and many of the cultivated varieties bear tubers regularly at 14,000 feet. Without them human occupancy in this area would be impossible; "half the Indians do not have any other bread."[1] In pre-Columbian times they were the mountain peasant's staple food crops, so common in the diet that time was measured in units equivalent to a potato's boiling time. In the cold, high steppe known as the *puna*, around Lake Titicaca,

Reprinted by permission of the author and editor from *Culture and History*, edited by S. Diamond, pp. 393–407. The article has been revised by the author and a number of footnotes in the original version have been omitted.

the chroniclers were surprised to find no familiar grains; they report the area's dependence upon Andean crops. This does not condemn its inhabitants to culture-historical marginality: long before the Tiahuanaco and Inca expansions, the people of the Qollao made the most basic contributions to the possibilities of civilizational development in the Andes through the domestication of alpacas and llamas as well as the tubers.

In our time, Weston LaBarre collected over 220 named varieties of potatoes in the Qollao alone; Carlos Ochoa has more than a thousand stored live in his laboratories near Lima. Most of the names, after four hundred years of European occupation, show no trace of European influence. While some diploid varieties, which botanists consider the more primitive, stick to the *qhishwa,* the protected slopes of the Andean valleys, most of the domesticated varieties are true upland specimens—hardy, frost-resistant and closely dependent on man. In fact, the most frost-resistant, the bitter *luki,* are sterile triploids which will not grow below 8,200 feet and cannot propagate themselves without human intervention. The large number of these hybrid, high-altitude varieties would indicate that throughout most of the history of human occupancy in the Andes, the pressure has been on taming the high *puna;* the steep, lower slopes to the west, which would seem more inviting on first glance, can seriously be utilized only when public works provide terraces and irrigation.[2] As early as 1931 the German geographer Carl Troll had warned that the periods allowed at that time for the development of Andean civilizations were too short. Using botanic criteria, Troll predicted that a much longer chronology would have to be allowed for the domestication and elaboration of Andean crops.

Elsewhere in the world, root crops cannot usually be kept for any length of time. Some of the Andean varieties kept seven, ten and twelve months under *puna* conditions, which have a mummifying effect not only on vegetables but also on llama meat and other tissues. In addition, several processes were developed here which took advantage of the climate to increase storing capacity. Most potatoes could be made into *chuñu,* a substance derived from tubers alternately frozen and dried soon after harvest. The slow-ripening, bitter, high-altitude varieties are grown exclusively for *chuñu,* which can be kept for much longer periods than the potatoes themselves. The process itself is closely dependent on *puna* conditions: cold nights, warm days, and a dry climate. There is no *chuñu* in Ecuador, which lacks a true *puna,* nor was Sapper able to make it experimentally in Germany.

While potatoes have this neat zonal distribution, maize is found on both highland and coast. This has masked the essentially warm climate character of maize; it requires a good deal of humidity and warmth and has a relatively long growing season. But in Andean conditions, the regions with adequate humidity are the very ones most threatened by frosts. It is only on the *qhishwa* slopes, and then not everywhere, that corn can be found as a field crop.

We still do not know when maize reached the highlands.[3] We cannot match for the Andes MacNeish's studies of corn in Meso-America which pushed back the domestication of this crop some 2,000 years. The Peruvian botanists grouped around Alex Grobman have not been able to check through excavation their hypotheses that there was in the Andes a separate center of corn domestication.[4] But whatever their eventual discoveries, it is obvious that in the highlands maize is a vulnerable, handicapped plant.

It will not grow without irrigation in some of the hot coastal valleys where the desert climbs to over 8,000 feet, nor will it prosper where frosts can be expected eight or nine months a year.[5] There are some varieties of maize and occasional propitious ecological islands like the valleys of Chaupiwaranqa or Urubamba or the Callejón de Huaylas where corn could and still is being raised without irrigation. But generally speaking, in both Inca and present times, irrigation was considered highly desirable, even where there was no acute shortage of rainfall. Garcilaso de la Vega tells us that "not a single grain of maize was planted without irrigation," and that given steady watering and the use of fertilizers corn fields "were like a garden". Irrigated fields need no crop rotation, nor must they be left to lie fallow.

There is some indication that the famous Andean state terraces, like those at Yucay, so laboriously constructed of ceremonially dressed stone, were meant to produce maize. The terrace of Collcampata in Cuzco, the garden of the Sun, was planted to corn and Garcilaso had seen it worked in his youth. He is also specific when discussing terraces in general: "this is how industrious the Inca were in expanding the lands for maize planting." Pedro Pizarro, an eyewitness to the invasion, claims that "all were planted to corn."

While irrigation is one of the factors making it possible to raise the upper limit of corn cultivation, it was rarely used with potatoes and other Andean crops. In part, this is due to the topographic characteristics of the *puna,* with the rivers flowing in deep gorges far below it. As Garcilaso put it, where irrigation did not reach "they planted grains and vegetables of great importance . . . potatoes, *añus, oca."* Cieza de León saw no irrigation in the Qollao within twenty years of the European invasion, and most of our chroniclers similarly make no mention of Andean crops when discussing irrigation.[6] In modern times, the geographer Schwalm, who did considerable field work in the area, reports that irrigation and fertilizers were applied to maize, while potatoes were grown *de temporal,* depending on rain. La Barre tells us that in Bolivia the high-altitude *luki* receive no irrigation or fertilizers, although some of the other varieties do get such assistance today.

Such rainfall cultivation means that lands planted to tubers must rest between crops. A system of rotation, known variously as *manay, suyu* or *raymi,* had arisen to regulate which area among those controlled by a village would enter cultivation in a given year. Ideally all households had fields, if only a few furrows, in each of the *manay.* After two or three years of cultivation, the *manay* reverted to fallow and "rested" for five, six, even eight years.

Despite such adaptation and probable domestication in high altitudes, not only maize but even the Andean crops failed frequently through hail, frosts and drought. Juan Polo Ondegardo, for many years a colonial administrator in highland areas, claimed that three years in five saw crop failures. Centuries later, a Swiss observer, Tschudi, reported that one good harvest in three was normal for the *puna.* Cabello Valboa, an independent sixteenth-century witness, indicated that famine stalked the land in years when the potato crop failed. At such times the peasants ate wild roots or grasses. In the high Andes the subsistence margin was always quite narrow: fasting, sacrifices and scapegoating were all employed in an effort to mitigate frosts and water shortages.

The botanical and ecologic differences between these two sets of crops have their economic correlatives: the systems of weights and measures and of land tenure used in the two context differed as well. María Rostworowski de Diez Canseco, a Peruvian pioneer in the study of Andean weights and measures, has recently published the 1713 text recording the explanations of Guillermo Gato, an Andean surveyor, used by the colonial authorities. He tried to convey to his employers that there was one measuring unit called a *papa cancha* which

> "is used only in cold potato country where he discovered that when an Indian receives a *topo* it is understood to be multiplied seven times [when granted] in cold country . . . and sometimes by six and at times by ten. And the reason for this is that potatoes are not planted every year in the same plot because the land does not allow it but maybe five years later . . . or after seven in colder places and only after nine in the wilder uplands. If the man were to receive only a topo . . . per Indian for his annual subsistence . . . he could do it only once and the other five he would have no place to plant . . . All the Indian upland measurements must be multiplied at least sixfold."

As with measurements, so with other agricultural practices. Neither the historical sources dealing with sixteenth-century crops, nor the present day agronomists have adequately studied Andean agriculture. I would predict that we are confronting not just two kinds of crops but two distinct agricultural systems with quite different vocabularies used to describe their respective "fields" or "furrows", containers, loads or the varieties of land tenure.

A final observation before returning to the rituals. The existence of two separate agricultures, located at different end points of a vertical ecologic axis does not imply that a single ethnic group did not engage in both cultivations. On the contrary: in the Andes, each ethnic group, be they small polities of two-three thousand households like the Chupaychu of Huánuco or powerful kingdoms like the Lupaqa, on Lake Titicaca, would attempt to control through their own colonists the maximum of ecological floors, available to them depending on the energies they could mobilize. When the polity was small, the pastures, saltpans, maize or coca leaf fields could be controlled only if they were three or four days' march away from the nucleus. A kingdom with several hundred thousand souls could utilize directly resources fifteen or twenty days away. We thus get a "vertical" pattern of ecologic control, an "archipelago" of ecologic islands widely distributed through the Andes.

In such circumstances we note again how little potato or other Andean crop ritual has been recorded by our chroniclers. As indicated their ceremonial calendars dealt almost exclusively with maize. In our time there are elaborate ceremonies to protect and encourage the potato crop; these have been described in some detail by contemporary observers. Of course, it could be that such practices are post-Columbian; the absence of recorded sixteenth-century Andean crop rituals may indicate lack of anxiety over a local, well-adapted crop. However, this is unlikely since the ecclesiastic writers and idol-burners like Avila, Arriaga and others who turned their attention to the Andean peasant community after 1600, report numerous instances of ritual concern over highland crops, quite similar to modern ceremonialism. Such parallels are also present in the unique early report to have broken through the chroniclers' disinterest: only fifteen years after the invasion a European priest gave in to the urging of his communicants and allowed a potato planting ceremony in his village. There was music and dancing with digging tools and some competitive behavior between the two moieties. A llama was sacrificed, and selected large seed potatoes were dipped in its blood. At this point the padre intervened and stopped what apparently had gone too far. Soon after, Cieza de León came through the region and recorded the priest's story, but it took the chronicler consistently most sensitive to ethnographic detail to get it.

The rarity of potato rituals in our sources may perhaps be due to the fact that the Andean crops, while they may have been staples, were also low status food. In the legends from Huarochiri collected by Avila in the late sixteenth century, potato-eating was considered evidence of low status; a raggedy beggar was known as Huatyacuri, potato-eater. In another story, recorded by Cabello Valboa, the hero is hiding from his enemies among "very poor herders" who cultivate "potatoes, *ullucu,* other roots and grasses." In describing the *puna*-dwelling Qolla, the Andean writer Huaman Poma called them "Indians of little strength and courage, with large bodies, fat and tallowy because they eat only *chuñu*" and contrasted them with the Chinchaysuyus (northern and coastal Peruvians), "who although small in stature, are brave, as they are fed on maize and drink maize beer, which gives strength."

Despite such attitudes, from all we can gather potato ceremonialism was early and general in the Andes. Why then should our sources miss it?

There is no likelihood that our chroniclers would ignore maize. Grain eaters themselves, familiarized with corn in the Caribbean and Mexico, they reported early and in detail the Pan-American distribution of this crop. Its absence in any given area was noted. Some of them thought of maize as the Andean staple, which is clearly erroneous given the ecologic picture; as Sauer has pointed out, "nowhere south of Honduras is maize the staple foodstuff it was further north." In most of South America it was grown primarily for beer-making and ceremonial purposes.[7]

The chroniclers communicate the feeling that in the highland maize was a desirable, special, and even holiday food as compared with potatoes and *chuñu*. Maize was offered at village shrines. Huaman Poma recorded the text of a lament recited by the villagers "during frost or hail if it [the crop] be maize, when no water comes from the sky." At harvest time the corn was brought home amidst great celebration; men and women came singing, begging the maize to last a long time. The villagers drank and ate and sang and for three nights kept vigil over Mama Zara, Mother Maize, a shrine erected in "every house" by wrapping the best cobs in the family's best blankets.

At the village level, corn was also an integral part of life cycle rituals, even if it was not locally grown. At the initiation of a peasant youth, when his hair was ceremonially cut and his name changed, maize, llamas, and cloth were among the gifts offered by his kinfolk. At marriage, the families of the couple exchanged "seeds" along with spindles, pots and ornaments. Murúa, the sixteenth-century writer with the best information about women in the Andes, specified corncobs as gifts to the bride. At death, corn meal was sprinkled around the deceased. On the fifth day, the widow and other survivors would wash clothes at the meeting place of two rivers where sacrifices were also offered after sowing.

The real contrast between the two crops and their associated ceremonials emerges as we move from the peasant community, where both are known though differentially valued, to the state, Inca level.

A considerable effort, both technologic and magic, was made by the state and its various agencies to ensure the propagation and harvest of corn. The Inca state origin myth gives credit to the royal lineage for the introduction of this grain into the Cuzco basin and refers to it as "the seed of the [Paqaritampu] cave" from which the dynasty was supposed to have emerged. Mama Waku, the wife of the first (legendary) king, is reported to have taught the people how to plant it;[8] ever after a plot near Cuzco called Sausero was devoted to the production of maize to feed the queen's mummy and her retainers. The annual cultivating cycle was ceremonially inaugurated by the king himself, who on the appropriate day during August-September went to Mama Waku's field to break the ground for the planting, with the help of his royal kin. Poma illustrates this inauguration: the king is working, assisted by three relatives to form the usual Inca quartet; an equal number of royal women are kneeling, facing the men, to break the clods, much as peasant women are shown doing it elsewhere in the manuscript. A hunchbacked retainer is bringing refreshments to the royal workers. The king's contribution was accompanied by vigorous singing of digging songs, on a triumphal, military refrain.

The national church and its priesthood, whose top hierarchy belonged to the same royal lineage, also had many duties in and about maize agriculture. Each year the gods were asked if crops should be planted that year; "the answer was always affirmative." Priests were assigned to watch the movements of the shadow at a seasonal sundial near Cuzco to determine the right time for plowing, irrigation or planting[9] and to notify the peasantry of the approaching chore. If one missed the proper moment, the maize crop was in danger. Priests also kept *khipu,* knot records of past seasons showing the succession of wet years and dry. One group of clerics fasted from the moment maize was planted until the shoots were finger high. Cobo reports that the priests gathered at the sundial observatory and "begged the Sun to get there on time." Processions were organized, the participants armed, beating drums, and shouting war cries to scare away drought and frost which threatened the maize more than any other crop. The official state harvest began with the year's royal initiates going to reap on Mama Waku's terrace; then came the fields of the Sun, those of the king and queen. Sacrifices of llamas, fasting, thanksgiving offerings, and requests for future favors were all part of the harvest.

A perceptive observer, Polo noted that there were many more observances and anxious rituals in "advanced" areas, where the population was dense and state exactions numerous, than there were in marginal territories like Chiriguanas or Diaguita. At the symbolic center of the state, at Intiwasi, the House of the Sun, the priests had planted among the living cornstalks golden reproductions, complete with leaves and cobs, to "encourage" the maize. The temple's harvest was kept in heavy silver storage jars. Such attention and "nursery" care made it possible for the priests to cultivate maize at 12,700 feet, at the shrines near Lake Titicaca. They did not do as much for Andean crops; virtually all references to Cuzco ceremonials are about maize; there are none to potatoes in this context.[10]

The existence and survival of a sociopolitical structure like Tawantinsuyu, the Inca state, depends technologically on an agriculture capable of producing systematic surpluses beyond the subsistence needs of the peasantry. Under Andean ecologic conditions the anxiety of the state is understandable, and the solution devised is not always ceremonial. The irrigated coast was a major producer of maize and supplied an important and worry-free quota to the state warehouses. Unfortunately, we lack many details about the special features of coastal land alienation under Inca rule and the extent of the maize-growing corvée.[11] But most everybody has heard of the mitmaq colonists resettled by the Inca for what are usually considered security reasons. I have elsewhere presented the evidence that a major function of this population transfer was actually the expansion of the maize-growing area. In fact, many of these coastal oases had been settled from the highlands on the "vertical archipelago" model, long before the Inca. Such transplanted settlements remained within the jurisdiction of their traditional ethnic lords and provided their kin with corn, cotton, peppers, fruit, and other tropical produce and received llamas, jerked meat, and *chuñu*.

Terracing of the steep *qhishwa* slopes, irrigation works, and coastal fertilizer delivered to the highlands were all similar measures, providing "vertical" revenues of all kinds but with an emphasis on corn. Potatoes and other root crops may have produced the indispensable quantitative surpluses, and *chuñu* may have allowed their storage. However, the keeping qualities of maize are superior to those of potatoes; so is its higher prestige. Grains and stockpiling and the redistribution of status are basic state preoccupations everywhere. In the Inca state many factors made stockpiling a major necessity: a growing court made up of ten to twelve royal families and their thousands of retainers, a bureaucratic and ecclesiastic hierarchy, the military needs of the numerous campaigns which expanded the kingdom from Ecuador to Chile within barely a century.

It is clear that in the minds of those who encouraged the production of corn there were also those other, redistributive considerations: the higher, semi-ceremonial status of maize, inherited from pre-Inca times, would add to the state eagerness to obtain this commodity in the highlands. An issue of the rarer corn porridge would mean more than a dish of potatoes to a conscript soldier,[12] and a mug of corn beer was a morale-building dispensation in a society where patterns of reciprocal generosity were still operative.

It is my contention in this article that in dealing with Inca times in the Andes we find not only two sets of crops grown in different climatic zones, but also actually two systems of agriculture. The staple crop and mainstay of the diet is autochtonous and earlier in the highlands; grown by Andean mountaineers, it consists of plants domesticated locally, laboriously adapted to alpine conditions, grown on fallowed land and dependent on rainfall. The other crop is newer, imported; its culture is of holiday significance and centers around maize, an essentially warm weather crop, clinging to the lower and protected reaches of the highlands, handicapped though highly valued in Andean circumstances.[13]

It is my further contention that tuber cultivation was essentially a subsistence agriculture practiced by lineage (*ayllu*) members who became peasants after the Inca conquest. Maize was undoubtedly known, in a ceremonial way, through the "vertical archipelago" pattern, to the peasant *ayllu* for many hundreds of years before the Inca, but its large-scale, economic field cultivation in the highlands becomes feasible only when the emergence of a state makes possible such public works as irrigation, terraces, fertilizers from the faraway coast, and gingerly priestly concern. In Inca times maize was a state crop.

The original under-reporting of Andean highland crop ritual, which prompted this inquiry, has become under the circumstances a hint to cultural and structural matters way beyond the actual rites.

The bulk of the sixteenth-century writers associated with few Andeans beyond the royal families, the bureaucracy, the Quisling palace guards. These informants emphasized inevitably the recently obliterated glories of the past, particularly the state machinery; in the process they ignored the Andean village and the many different Andean ethnic groups. Their lack of interest matched that of most of the chroniclers. Only the most inquisitive, men like Cieza and Polo, tried to get beyond this idealized statement of bureaucratic claim. It is only later, when Andean writers begin to comment directly on their own past and when village descriptive material becomes available, that we get a glimpse of what agricultural ritual reveals: not only two systems of agriculture, but significant differences between two ways of life, one of which—the power-wielding Inca state—was in the process of incorporating and transforming the other, a process far from completed when the European invasion arrested its course.

NOTES

1. Cobo [1653]: IV, viii. Acosta reports one variety "accustomed" to coastal heat ([1590]: IV, xvii; 1940:270), and Salaman quotes Russian botanists who found wild varieties in the lowlands (1949:34). While potatoes are known on the coast and are reproduced in coastal art (Salaman 1949:15, 19; Yacovleff and Herrera 1934:299), there is no indication that they were a significant element in the food supply or the economy.

2. Our understanding of the coastal kingdoms, utterly dependent on irrigation, is still elementary. See Schaedel, 1966 and Kosok 1965.

3. In 1969, R. S. MacNeish began extensive excavations in the Ayacucho area of Perú searching for the early stages of Andean agriculture. The sug-

gestion has been made, after Tello, that maize, like the feline deity characteristic of the Chavín period, is of ultimate *montaña* derivation (Strong and Evans 1952:237; Valcárcel 1945:55–71).

4. Grobman 1965. This research was stimulated by Paul Mangelsdorf's early hypotheses that there might have been a South American center for the domestication of maize, independent of the better known Meso-American one.

5. James 1942:150. In the protected bowl of Lake Titicaca, maize was grown in Inca times even above the 12,540 foot level of the lake. In our time, José Matos Mar found thumb-size cobs cultivated for ceremonial and hospitality purposes on the island of Taquile, in the same lake (1957).

6. See the highly revealing legend collected around 1600 by Avila in Huarochiri: Collquiri, a local deity connected with maize and irrigation, tried to reward his affinal relatives by emerging as a spring near their fields. But there was too much water; it threatened to flood their fields and all their *oca* and *kinowa* which had been laid out to dry. Everybody was very mad, shouting "We are used to little water!"; his wife's folk begged him to stop. Collquiri finally stuffed some of his clothes in the spring. (Avila [1608], ch. xxxi; 1967:168–83).

7. Willey dates the beginning of the "Peruvian co-tradition" from the "advent of maize agriculture" (1953b:374). This may indicate some support for my proposed separation of Andean crops from corn agriculture, which is likely to seem artificial to some, particularly North American archeologists who used to do most of their field work on the coast and who tend to think of maize and potatoes as part of a single "complex of traits" (Bennett: 1948: 2–4).

8. Women, and particularly the queens, are credited throughout the Inca oral tradition with the invention of onerous, new obligations to the state. . . .

9. King Pachakuti (see John H. Rowe's article in Chapter 5 of this collection) is credited by most sources not only with reforming the ceremonial calendar but also with the erection of Intiwatana, the seasonal sundial in Cuzco (Polo 1940:131–32). It is likely that such sundials are pre-Inca; see Avila's text which reports that villages in the Huarochiri area had men assigned to watch the sun's shadow and notify the inhabitants. Pachakuti may have set up a *state* observatory which could ignore the different planting times varying according to altitude and ecology. In the Cuzco valley August-September was "right", and it thus assumed the special features of a national event, much as the seeds and tubers from Cuzco enjoyed special prestige in the provinces. Garcilaso [1604] III, xx; 1943, p. 171.

10. Though it may be significant that Garcilaso de la Vega does mention *kinowa*, the Andean grain, as being reproduced in the golden botanical garden of the Sun ([1604] V, i; 1943:227).

11. This point is discussed in Chapter II, "Land Tenure", of the author's unpublished dissertation, *The Economic Organization of the Inca State,* the University of Chicago.

12. Garcilaso ([1604], VII, i; 1943:86–87). In contrast Latcham states that the army ate *cocavi,* a kind of *chuñu,* but indicates no sixteenth-century sources (1936:176).

13. One should not confuse ceremonial limits, such as those achieved by the priests at Titicaca with altitude of effective cultivation. The upper limit of any given crop, and particularly maize, is affected by many factors not all

of which are ecological: the dryness of the southern Andes raises the upper limit at which annuals will grow; topographic features like protection against winds or good exposure to daylight may have a good deal to do with the effective upper limit. None of these compare with cultural motivation: if tended like a rose, maize will of course grow anywhere. See Weberbauer (1945:624); Bowman (1916:52–54); Schwalm (1927:183); Troll (1931: 270).

PART VI: SOCIAL CHANGE

Introduction to Race, Culture and Manpower

In order to explain the difference between highland and lowland patterns of race relations in South America, Marvin Harris found it necessary to don the hat of social historian. Although anthropologists by training and temperament are frequently disinclined to deal with historical documents, it has become increasingly clear that ethnohistory is a very important adjunct to anthropological explanation.

Perhaps the most striking regional contrast in South America is that between the Andean highlands (including parts of Peru, Ecuador, Bolivia, northern Chile and Colombia) and the tropical lowlands in the east of Brazil, the Guianas and Venezuela. Aside from differences in climate and topography, one notes racial and cultural differences as well. In the highlands, one encounters many people who appear to have American Indian ancestors speaking native languages exclusively (e.g., Quechua, or Aymara). These are often referred to as *indios* while others who may be phenotypically identical but who are bilingual or monolingual in Spanish may be called *ladinos, criollos* or *mestizos. Indios* typically live in small, socially ingrown, homogeneous village communities, while *mestizos* occupy a diversity of positions and live in socially differentiated towns.

In the tropical lowlands of eastern South America, by contrast, American Indian phenotypes are not predominant and there are large numbers of Afro-Americans, people of European descent and every possible mixture. These people generally all speak one language (Portuguese in Brazil, Spanish in most other places) so social differentiation cannot follow linguistic lines. Rather stratification occurs along lines of descent, political and economic status, and skin color and other "racial" characteristics. Except for unacculturated indigenous villages, "closed" communities are not found in this part of South America (cf. Wolf 1955).

To account for these systematic contrasts, Harris has dealt with the economic forces that shaped the history of colonization of South America and particularly the manpower needs and resources of the colonial economies. Ecological and social factors account for the relative scarcity of laborers in tropical eastern South America where colonizers began their extractive and agricultural enterprises. Hence African slaves were imported in great numbers. Practically no slaves were brought to the highlands, however, since large, manageable, native populations were already present to work the mines and haciendas (cf. Service 1955 for a complementary discussion of this question). Harris examines colonial Indian policies in relation to labor needs. He is careful to differentiate between restrictions spelled out in laws and codes and the concrete actions of colonizers for which documentation is much harder to obtain. Keeping the emic and etic data separate has been one of Harris' most important theoretical contributions (cf. Harris 1964a, 1968, 1971).

Marvin Harris is Professor of Anthropology at Columbia University in New York. In addition to his theoretical contributions cited above, Harris has done ethnographic research in Brazil, Moçambique, Ecuador and New York City. He has published papers on race relations, ecology, cognition and etic studies.

22. RACE, CULTURE AND MANPOWER

MARVIN HARRIS

The kinds of accommodation which have been achieved by the various racial and cultural components in Latin America are in large measure the consequence of the attempt to harness the aboriginal population on behalf of European profit-making enterprises. It is true, of course, that the New World was richly endowed by nature with fertile soils, a great spectrum of climates, and enormous reserves of precious metals. These resources, however, were in themselves worthless. In order to farm the soil, there must be farmers, and in order to mine the earth, there must be miners. Without adequate manpower, even the fabulous mines of Potosi, still producing after 500 years of intensive operation, would have served no useful purpose.[1] Lesley Simpson's (1960:94) observation that "the Conquest of Mexico was the capture of native labor" applies no less aptly to all of Latin America.

The problem of manpower in Latin America has been resolved in several radically different ways, each of which ultimately depends upon the nature of the pre-contact cultures and each of which in turn is associated in modern times with a particular pattern of race relations.

In the lowland areas the initial labor prospectus was poor indeed. The sparse aboriginal populations, semi-migratory in nature, were almost completely unaccustomed to intensive field labor, or corvée services. Just as the Inca had failed to dominate the tropical lowland peoples lying to the east of their empire, Europeans found it impossible to put the lowland Indians to work, except under a system of direct slavery. Enslavement of the lowland Amerindian groups, however, did not prove economically viable for reasons which I shall shortly recount.

The failure of the labor regime based upon the enslavement of lowland Indian groups led to the introduction into the New World of large numbers of laborers from Africa. These African contingents were localized in the tropical and semi-tropical lowlands of both North and South America and put to work on the production of plantation crops having high export value in the European markets. Meanwhile, a totally different potential for labor use was encountered in the highlands. There, once the native rulers had been removed or converted to puppets, the mass of commoners could with relative ease be put to work producing agricultural, industrial and mineral products for the benefit of the invaders. As a result, the contemporary population of the highland portions of Latin America exhibits only minute traces of Negro racial and African cultural mixtures. Let us now examine in some detail how this came about.

At the beginning of the conquest of the New World, the Spanish were optimistic about the potentialities of the lowland Indians for slave labor. Columbus himself had argued the feasibility of the enslavement of the Caribbean peoples and had envisaged a thriving slave trade between America and Europe. Enslavement of the Amerindians was easily justified on the grounds that they were not only heathens but cannibals. It was believed that many tribes could not be introduced to the virtues of Christianity or be made to work unless they were firmly controlled by their conquerors under the slave system.

Slaving expeditions ranged throughout the Caribbean Islands and along the coasts of Mexico and North and South America during the last years of the fifteenth century and the first decades of the sixteenth. It quickly became apparent, however, that Indian slavery was a doomed institution. Expeditions had to range further and further as the originally sparse population was decimated by the raiding, by disease, and by excessive toil. Indian slaves died by the thousands while engaged in labor on behalf of their conquerors. Many committed suicide; others disappeared into the forests never to be seen again. Especially devastating was their lack of immunity against European diseases such as measles, smallpox and respiratory infections. By the end of the seventeenth century, practically the entire Indian population of the Caribbean had been wiped out.[2] A similar situation prevailed in Brazil. The males no less than the females of the Brazilian coastal tribes turned out to be very poor investments. "The expenditure of human life here in Bahia these past twenty years," said one Jesuit father in 1583, "is a thing that is hard to believe; for no one could believe that so great a supply could ever be exhausted, much less in so short a time."[3]

As the supply of lowland Indian slaves diminished, the Portuguese and lowland Spanish colonists looked to Africa for their labor force. This turn of events, which was to have such long-lasting consequences for the entire world, was not due to any sudden realization that Africa contained a greater manpower pool than the American lowlands. Long before the transatlantic trade began, both the Spanish and Portuguese were well aware that Africa could be made to yield up its human treasure. But in the early part of the sixteenth century the cost of transporting large numbers of slaves across the Atlantic was excessive in relation to the profits which could be extracted from their labor. This situation changed radically when, toward the middle of the century (somewhat later in the Dutch and English Caribbean possessions), sugar cane plantings were begun in Brazil. With the introduction of chocolate (a New World crop) and the spread of the coffee-drinking habit in Europe, the world consumption of sugar had suddenly skyrocketed, and by the end of the sixteenth century sugar had become the most valuable agricultural commodity in international trade. The importation of Negroes from Africa now became economically feasible. Although the costs of transporting Africans across the Atlantic Ocean remained high, the profits which could be wrung from their labor on the sugar estates were still higher. It was thus that the craving of Europe for sweets and coffee wiped out the aboriginal population of a large portion of the New World and condemned millions from another continent to a short and toilsome life.

In seeking for an explanation of why the lowland sugar planters regarded one Negro slave as the equivalent of five Indians, one must guard against interpretations based upon biological factors.[4] It is frequently asserted, for example, that the greater adaptability of the Negro to slavery conditions on the tropical lowland plantations was a result of his ability to withstand the intense heat and humidity of the tropics. There is no reason, however, to conclude that the Indians were biologically any less adapted to life in the tropics than the Negroes were. Nor is there any reason whatsoever to conclude that the Negroes were by nature any more servile than the Indians. In the highland regions, where the culture was different, the Indians were also reduced to servility, and their semi-slave condition has endured into the present century.

There are two other factors which better explain the preference expressed by the lowland planters for Negro rather than for Indian field hands. One is that the Africans had been pre-adapted by their cultural experience to cope with the demands of regular field labor. It is well known that slavery, serfdom and corvée were on-going institutions in many sub-Saharan African societies before European contact. To be sure, the scope and intensity of slavery under African aboriginal conditions were not comparable to the system which developed after the Europeans began to promote slavery and slave-raiding on a massive scale in order to satisfy the labor requirements of the New World. But groups such as those of Yoruba, Dahomey, Ashanti, Ife, Oyo and Congo, from which the bulk of the slaves was probably brought, were societies in which considerable differences in rank existed.[5] Moreover, throughout much of Negro Africa, males made a more important contribution to agriculture than was true among the typical Amerindian lowland tribes.

The second relevant point is that the Negroes, over centuries of indirect contact with North Africa and Europe, probably had acquired immunities to certain common European disease organisms which were lethal to the American Indians. Epidemics of catastrophic proportions kept recurring all through the first centuries of contact between the Europeans and Indians. A third of the population of the Tupinamba in the vicinity of Bahia, for example, was wiped out by smallpox in 1562, and to judge from the modern experience of the Brazilian Service for the Protection of Indians, measles and the common cold were probably just as devastating (Wagley and Harris 1958:26). Recent demographic studies of central Mexico during the sixteenth century reveal that an astonishing decline in population occurred after contact. Borah and Cook (1963) claim that the people of Central Mexico were reduced in numbers from something close to 20 million to about 1 million in less than one hundred years. It is clear that this decline must be attributed in no small part to the interplay between the new diseases and the general disruption introduced by the invaders.

Also relevant here is the puzzling solicitude which many of the Spanish labor laws display on behalf of the Indians (Simpson 1938:11 ff.). The labor code of 1609, for example, prohibited the employment of Indians at certain tasks connected with sugar processing because of their alleged lack of physical stamina. Indeed, the Spanish and Portuguese generally were of the opinion that the Indians were by nature weaker than the Negroes. But this can only mean (in view of the fantastic feats of stamina characteristic of healthy Amerindian carriers and laborers) that the Indians more readily fell victim to European pathogens. A third factor might also be found in the tremendous incidence of mortality among the Negro slaves during their passage to the New World. The selective effect of this terrifying journey (following upon forced marches to the African slave entrepots) must have meant that only remarkably resistant individuals survived. Furthermore, as suggested by Gonzalo Beltrán (1946:181 ff.) for Mexico, Africans tended to be selected for youth and vitality much more systematically than was possible in the case of Indians. Thus, although African slaves cost five to ten times more than Indian slaves, they were a safer investment. Whatever the reasons for the preference for Negroes by the lowland planters, it is clear that the demography of the New World would ultimately have left them no choice in the matter. Despite their alleged physical inferiority, Indians were employed as slaves on the Brazilian plantations and they continued to be hunted until in effect there were none left except in the most remote parts of the jungle.

At the very time when the African slave trade was beginning to develop into one of the world's most important commercial ventures, the Spanish Crown passed laws prohibiting the enslavement of Indians in its New World possessions. (During the period 1580–1640, when Portugal and Spain were ruled by the same monarchs, these laws also applied to Brazil.) A great deal of romantic nonsense pervades the attempts to explain this paradox. The Spanish Crown is pictured as being influenced by the crusading religious missionary Bartolomé de Las Casas to abandon the policy of Indian slavery in its New World possessions out of humanitarian

and religious convictions. There is no doubt that men like Las
Casas, Fray Garcia de Loaisa, and Francisco de Vitoria, who were
primarily responsible for the promulgation of the famous New
Laws of 1542,[6] were motivated by sincere and deep humanitarian
convictions. There is no doubt also that the Spanish Crown was
sensitive to moral and religious arguments. However, neither the
special pleadings of the clerics nor the sensibilities of the monarchs
lacked roots in material interests. The mission of the Church was
to save souls. The power of the Church was directly related to
the number of converts and hence if for no other reason the Church
could not stand idly by while the aboriginal population of the New
World was destroyed by the colonists. Furthermore, it was not
against slavery in general that the Church fought but rather specifically against the enslavement of Indians by the colonists. On the
issue of African slavery, the Spanish Church very early adopted
an essentially hands-off position. Few churchmen expressed any
moral reservations about the slave trade with Africa. On the contrary, the enslavement of Negroes was frequently viewed as a religious duty consonant with the highest moral principles.[7] This was
equally true of the Church in Brazil, where "the Portuguese Jesuits
too often demonstrated that they would permit slavery provided
they could control it. They owned Indian as well as Negro slaves
(Diffie 1945:725)."

The most plausible explanation of the New Laws is that they represented the intersection of the interests of three power groups: the
Church, the Crown and the colonists. All three of these interests
sought to maximize their respective control over the aboriginal
populations. Outright enslavement of the Indians was the method
preferred by the colonists. But neither the Crown nor the Church
could permit this to happen without surrendering their own vested
and potential interests in the greatest resource of the New World
—its manpower.

Why then did they permit and even encourage the enslavement
of Africans? In this matter, all three power groups stood to gain.
Africans who remained in Africa were of no use to anybody, since
effective military and political domination of that continent by
Europeans was not achieved until the middle of the nineteenth
century. To make use of African manpower, the Africans had to

be removed from their homelands. The only way to accomplish this was to buy them as slaves from dealers on the coast. For both the Crown and the Church, it was better to have Africans under the control of the New World colonists than to have Africans under the control of nobody but Africans. This was especially true since the Negro slaves were destined primarily for the use of lowland planters. The importation of slaves from Africa would therefore not interfere with the *modus vivendi* worked out by Church, State and colonists in the highlands. On the contrary, the flow of Negro slaves to the lowlands helped to prevent competition between lowland planters and highland entrepreneurs for control over highland labor.

The success of the clerics in the Court of Spain on behalf of the prohibition of Indian slavery is not to be attributed to their eloquence or to the passionate conviction which they conveyed to the Spanish monarchs. The laws of 1542 were passed because slavery of the highland Indians was a political and economic threat to the sovereignty of the Spanish Crown in the New World. There is no other way to explain the benevolent, pious concern exhibited on behalf of the Indians in contrast to the indifference displayed toward the Negroes.

The New Laws were thus essentially an attempt to prevent the formation of a feudal class in Spain's American territories. This threat had arisen out of the method employed by the Spanish Crown to reward the activities and exploits of its *conquistadores*. The astonishing, almost super-human exploits of the Spanish invaders of the New World were motivated by the promise of extraordinary privileges with respect to the lands and peoples whom they were able to conquer. Although the privilege of taking slaves was of considerable importance in the system of rewards in the lowland regions, outright slavery was a relatively minor aspect of the rewards system in the highlands. In the highlands a much more effective system was employed as the dominant form of labor appropriation. This system was known as the *encomienda*. Its salient feature was that a man who had performed service on behalf of the Crown in the conquest of the new territories was rewarded with the privilege of collecting tribute and drafting labor among a stated group of Indians inhabiting a particular set of villages. Cortes, for example, received an *encomienda* consisting of twenty-two townships, inhabited by possibly as many as 115,000 people (Diffie 1945:66). The Crown was aware of the fact that such grants of privileges amounted to the establishment of a feudal noble class in the New World and hence it sought to diminish the resemblance between the *encomienda* and feudalism by hedging the grant with various restrictions. For example, theoretically the right of administering justice was to be reserved to Crown officials and to be removed from the sphere of the *encomendero's* authority. It was intended, in other words, that the Indians should remain subjects of the Crown, not of the *encomendero*. The *encomendero* was merely to have the privilege of assigning work duties to the Indians in his *encomienda* or of collecting tribute from them.

Despite these provisions, however, the great *encomenderos,* such as Cortes in Mexico and Pizarro in Peru, quickly acquired the de facto status of full feudal lords, exercising almost unrestricted, despotic control over the populations within their *encomiendas.* In practice it was impossible for the Crown and its representatives in the New World to enforce the safeguards of the *encomienda* system. Hence, the New Laws constituted a package of proposals designed to pry loose the *encomienda* and slave Indians from the tenacious grasp of the *encomenderos* and slaveholders. The laws decreed that the Indians were to be regarded as free men and as vassals of the King of Spain. They sought to prevent the inheritance of existing *encomiendas* and to reduce those of excessive dimensions. Mistreatment of the Indians, their enslavement or excessive brutality toward them were to be punished very severely. When the Crown attempted to enforce these laws in Peru and Panama, it provoked outright rebellions. As is frequently the case in colonial situations, the power of the metropolitan forces was unequal to the power, ingenuity and perseverance of the colonizers who were in direct contact with the native peoples.

Although it is true that the Spanish Crown was largely successful in eliminating Indian slavery, it must be understood that such a statement depends on a highly technical definition of slavery. The *encomienda* and the other systems of compulsory labor which followed it during the colonial and republican periods were certainly markedly different from the arrangement worked out for labor on the lowland tropical plantations. I shall try to describe these differences in a moment, but one must never lose sight of the fact that all through the colonial, republican and modern periods in the history of highland Latin America, the Indian population has been subjected to one form or another of compulsory labor.

As the Crown promulgated and attempted to enforce the laws against the *encomienda* system it introduced a new method of labor use. This system, known as *mit'a* in Peru, *minga* in Ecuador, *catequil* or *repartimiento* in Mexico, and *mandamiento* in Guatemala, was introduced about the middle of the sixteenth century. By 1600, it had become the dominant form of labor recruitment in highland Latin America (Kloosterboer 1960:90 ff.).[8] The *repartimiento* substituted Crown officials for the *encomendero* as the principal agent for labor recruitment purposes. These Crown officials were alone empowered to draw upon the labor resources of the Indian villages. Theoretically, even the owners of *encomiendas* now had to consult the royal administrators and judges with respect to the allocation of laborers on their own *encomiendas*. Although the officials in charge of labor recruitment were instructed to take precautions designed to protect the health and well-being of the Indians under their jurisdiction, there were naturally frequent abuses and disregard of the letter of the law. Private entrepreneurs undoubtedly approached the officials and curried their favor with bribes and gifts in order to avail themselves of the Indian labor under the officials' control. The result was that the *repartimiento* reform did not result in any substantial improvement from the point of view of the Indian laborers. Their situation, in effect, remained unchanged. Indeed, their plight continued to resemble pre-contact times when the rulers of the native states had carried out periodic drafts of Indian labor through the system of the aboriginal *mit'a*. Instead of a native nobility, there were now the representatives of the Spanish Crown and the private entrepreneurs who exercised the right to draw on the manpower of the Indian villages.

The *repartimiento* was probably the cheapest form of labor that has ever been invented. To begin with, and unlike slavery, the system required no initial investment of capital. True, the Crown insisted that the labor drafts be paid wages, but these wages, when they were not withheld through fraud and chicanery, were a caricature of a genuine wage system. In many instances, their only function was to permit the Indian to pay taxes to the Crown. Unlike the wages extended to even the most defenseless urban proletariat, their level was set below what was necessary to maintain the life of the workers. Indeed, this was the great advantage of the *repartimiento*. Like the modern systems of migratory labor which still exist in Mozambique and Angola, the *repartimiento* exempted the employer from any concern with the subsistence requirements of his employees.[9] This effect was achieved by permitting or compelling the work force to labor in its own *milpas* (farms) for most of the year, from whence came the food by which it subsisted and reproduced itself. In this context, the endlessly repeated refrain, common to both Africa and the New World, that the natives are lazy and do not voluntarily work for wages, acquires a peculiarly poisonous sting. In general, the highland Indian simply could not convert to full-time wage labor and eat at the same time. As J. Phelan (1958–59:191) has said, "The stereotype that the white man found he could not bribe the Indian to work for a wage and so resorted to one form or another of compulsion is false. With alacrity, the Indians took to earning a living in European fashion when they were adequately compensated."[10]

Throughout the colonial period, there were institutions at work which directly and indirectly pressured the Indians both to increase their involvement in this bastard form of wage labor and to convert part of their own agricultural product into money. The greater the involvement of the Indians in a cash economy, the more opportunities there were for other sectors of the colonial population, especially the Church and the mestizo trading class, to share the benefits enjoyed by the agricultural and industrial entrepreneurs who depended on native labor. It was to the economic advantage of everybody except the Indians, in other words, that the Indians enter the market economy to the maximum extent compatible with their primary assignment as subsistence farmers. The famous highland "fiesta complex," to be discussed in the next chapter, was one of the central devices by which this involvement was heightened. The more general ingredient in this peculiar labor syndrome was the system which permitted employers to compel Indians to discharge debts through labor services. This device was introduced at least as early as the *repartimiento*. But it was destined to acquire supreme importance during the nineteenth century in the form of debt peonage. Why this came about, we shall see in a moment.

As part of its plan to retain direct control over the Indian population, the Spanish Crown, throughout the colonial period, systematically gathered the Indians into nucleated villages called *reducciones* or *congregaciones*. Such nucleation was potentially of advantage to all three elements—Church, colonists and Crown—concerned with making profitable use of the aborigines. But the Crown did not stop at merely establishing villages. It insisted that not only ought the Indians to be gathered together, but that land be given to villages under communal tenure. Worse, from the viewpoint of the colonists, these lands were declared inviolable. They could neither be sold nor pawned. As a result of this aspect of Crown policy—one of the most fascinating counterpoints in the long colonial fugue—many fertile and well-watered lands remained in native hands until the nineteenth century. Needless to say, these lands were coveted by the *hacendados*.

In a remarkably parallel fashion, all through the highland area, one of the first actions of the nineteenth-century republican governments, after independence had been achieved from Spain, was the destruction of the safeguards preventing direct access to Indian land and labor. In the name of liberal ideologies, elevating the principle of private property and individual rights to supreme consideration, the governments of the newly established highland republics one after the other decreed the end of the communal land system. All communal properties (including those of the Church) had to be converted into private holdings. Since this conversion required legal expertise, the *hacendados* experienced no great difficulty in gaining title to the Indian properties. What the lawyers could not grab for them, they took by force. The result was that by the end of the nineteenth century practically every acre of high-quality land in Mexico, Guatemala, Ecuador, Peru and Bolivia was part of a white man's or mestizo's *hacienda*.

What happened to the Indians who had lived in these areas? For the most part, they remained in place, since the *hacendados* as usual wanted both the land *and* the labor. Having possession of one, it was easy to obtain the other. The landless Indian now had no choice. He could only gain his subsistence by working for some *hacendado*. This much was guaranteed, but which *hacendado* was it to be? The *haciendas* (which, incidentally, now that the Crown was out of the picture, had begun to attract foreign capital) could ill afford to permit the development of a mobile, free-floating agricultural proletariat. The laborers had to be fixed in one place if maximum use was to be made of them. The device needed to accomplish this was already present. Food and clothing were advanced to the Indians, and wages were set at a point low enough to insure that the debts could never be discharged. An Indian who had fallen into debt could not quit his job or leave the premises until the debt was liquidated. If a man died before his debt was paid, his children fell heir to the obligation. Thus it was that debt peonage replaced the *repartimiento* as the dominant mode of labor control.

This is not to say that other forms of forced labor more closely resembling the *repartimiento* entirely disappeared. On the contrary, numerous labor recruiting schemes based on arbitrary definitions of vagrancy, criminality and public welfare were prominent throughout the highlands, except for Mexico, well into the twentieth century. In Peru, Ecuador and Guatemala, they still enjoy a *de facto* if not legal existence. It is interesting to note that in Guatemala the influence of heavily capitalized coffee and banana plantations was sufficient to swing the pendulum almost all the way back to a system of the *repartimiento* variety. This happened when the center of agricultural production shifted to areas outside of the control of the nineteenth-century *haciendas*. In 1936, the dictator Ubico replaced debt slavery by a system based upon vagrancy, thereby prying loose the peones from the grasp of the older landed interests (Whetten 1961).

Paradoxically, the removal of the Crown's protective shield from the corporate nucleated Indian villages did not result in the total destruction of the type. Throughout the highlands there survive to this day two distinct kinds of Indians. In the first instance there are Indians who are part of a permanent labor force residing on *haciendas*. In the second instance there are Indians who live in "free" villages. The latter are usually located in the commercially worthless lands adjacent to *haciendas,* on hillsides, or in other areas which were of little use to the *hacendados* during their nineteenth-century rampage.

As Eric Wolf (1956; 1957) has suggested, the perpetuation of these free Indian communities was to a large extent a pattern thoroughly consistent with the needs of the *hacienda* system, especially in its more heavily capitalized phases in the late nineteenth and present centuries. Since the amount of land permitted the free Indian villages was strictly limited and of inferior quality, the inhabitants remained responsive to labor requests from the *hacendados*. These free villagers were also made debtors to the *hacendados* but by more subtle and intermittent methods. They thus constituted a reserve labor pool which could be drawn upon for intensive harvesting operations and for the construction of roads, canals and other public works (Wolf 1955).

What Wolf fails to make sufficiently clear is that no genuine equivalents of these highland Indian villages are to be found in any of the New World's lowland plantation areas. In lowland Latin America, the same array of powers—Crown, Church and colonists—had also been struggling for the control of cheap labor. In the lowlands, however, the balance struck was earlier and more heavily in favor of the colonists. The virtual extinction of the Indians, and the importation of Africans as slaves, meant the triumph of the colonists over Church and State. Each plantation was a political microcosm in which the slaves were ruled by an absolute despot, their owner. In this context, the development of a corporate village organization similar to that of the highland communities was clearly out of the question. The plantation was the typical lowland form of community. Out from the plantation, with its heavy capital investment, its concentration on single commercial crops, and its sensitivity to world market prices, there flowed a fundamentally different kind of peasant culture and racial prospectus. This contrast between lowland and highland community types is fundamental for an understanding of the contrast between highland and lowland race relations. It will be appropriate, therefore, to take a closer look at the cultural and social heritage of the two labor systems as they are embodied in community life.

NOTES

1. The Spanish invaders were quite aware of the centrality of the labor issue in their colonization program. Ferdinand, King of Spain, declared in 1509 with respect to Espanola: ". . . the greatest need of the island at present is more Indians, so that those who go there from these kingdoms to

mine gold may have Indians to mine it with." (Quoted in Simpson 1950:23.) In 1511, warning against bringing Indian slaves from the New World to Spain, Ferdinand again noted that "all the good of those parts lies in there being a number of Indians to work in the mines and plantations" (Ibid. 1950:27).

2. By 1585, Sir Francis Drake reported that not a single Indian was left alive on Espanola. The Indians of Puerto Rico, the Bahamas and Jamaica were also wiped out before 1600 (Rouse 1948).

3. Quoted in Freyre 1956:178.

4. In Brazil the selling price of an Indian slave was one-fifth that of a Negro (Diffie 1945:696). According to Simonsen (1937:199) Indians were worth between 4,000 and 70,000 *reis* while the Negroes were worth between 50,000 and 300,000 *reis*.

5. Classic descriptions of African stratified societies are Herskovits 1938; Meek 1931; Rattray 1923; Roscoe 1911.

6. The New Laws abolished Indian slavery and severely limited the scope of the *encomienda*. See below.

7. The Jeronymite governors of Espanola in 1517 were eager to solve the Indian problem by importing Negro slaves (Simpson 1950:48). Las Casas himself has been accused of supporting this point of view, but it is clear that the great defender of the Indians was opposed to slavery, no matter which race was concerned (Hanke 1949:95; Zavala 1944). Nonetheless, all of Las Casas' efforts were directed toward the abolition of Indian slavery. Neither he nor the Church attacked the institution vigorously enough to prevent the Jesuits from owning a not inconsiderable share of the Negro slaves in Spanish America (Diffie 1945:473).

8. For a description of *repartimiento* in Peru, see Kubler 1946 and Rowe 1957; for Mexico see Simpson 1938. Whetten 1961 provides a comparable description for Guatemala. In Peru the term *repartimiento* was also used to denote periodic allotments of goods which Crown officials obliged the Indians to buy.

9. A system very similar to the *repartimiento* is in current use in Portuguese Africa. Except for the weakened role of the Church, all the elements of the seventeenth-century situation are present. The Portuguese overseas labor code insists that all Africans are free to choose their mode of employment. Forced labor is specifically prohibited. Nonetheless, no man is permitted to remain "idle." However, the interpretation of what constitutes "idleness" is left to the government's administrators, and the latter are ill paid and remote from higher authority. In order to "civilize" the natives, the administrators must teach them the value of work. Idle "natives" can therefore be conscripted for employment on public works. It is specifically prohibited for the administration to supply such laborers to private interests, exactly as under the *repartimiento*. But the ill-paid administrators are easily subverted by the labor-hungry colonists. Every conceivable kind of "kickback" flourishes. Africans who have been caught sleeping in their houses in the middle of the night are said to be "volunteers" for employment at European enterprises. The entire fabric of laws designed to protect the "natives" turns out to be a sop to legal conscience. Most of the Africans are kept ignorant of their rights, while the unfortunate few who attempt to find remedies against temporary forced labor find themselves declared "undesirable" and are shipped off without trial to permanent forced-labor camps (Harris 1958 and 1959;

Duffy 1962; Figueiredo 1961). One would have to be fairly well out of touch with reality to suppose that native rights were any better protected in colonial Peru and Mexico. According to John Rowe (1957:162–63), ". . . the only incentive to take on the job of *corregidor* was the opportunity for graft which the post offered because of the wide powers that went with it . . . Most *corregidores* came to their jobs with one idea, to make a fortune during the brief period of their administration. The only way they could do this was at the expense of the natives." Independently, at almost the same time, I had made the following observation about the administrators of Mozambique: ". . . administrators and chiefs-of-post are notoriously underpaid . . . Obviously men upon whom such extraordinary powers are conferred, do not lack opportunity for personal gain. Although there are many administrators whose personal standards are above reproach, the system invites many others who readily succumb to its built-in temptations" (Harris 1959:10).

10. Queen Isabella wrote as far back as 1503: ". . . because of the excessive liberty enjoyed by said Indians they avoid contact and community with Spaniards to such an extent that they will not work even for wages, but wander about idle . . ." (Simpson 1950:13).

Introduction to The Highland Heritage

This chapter complements the last one and is also drawn from *Patterns of Race in the Americas* (Harris 1964c). Here Harris focuses on some particular aspects of life in the highlands of Central and South America. Much of the social and religious culture of the Indians of these regions has been regarded by anthropologists and historians as pre-Columbian in origin and serving to maintain community solidarity. Even where rituals involved the church, they were regarded as syncretic, containing mainly indigenous elements. Recent research (Foster 1960) has indicated the Iberian origin of many customs previously thought to be native. This discovery has stimulated some, including Harris, to reinterpret some customs, such as the fiesta celebrations, in the light of colonialism, both external and internal. Harris presents a hypothesis in this chapter relating these fiestas not to Indian tradition but to a long tradition of external exploitation and control of indigenous communities. More research is needed to test this hypothesis but in the meantime Harris' suggestion has given invaluable insight to all those who attempt to evaluate functionalist hypotheses. Too often, social scientists have assumed that social solidarity is enhanced by customs which otherwise seem quite costly to the community which practices them. Inability or unwillingness to operationalize concepts like social solidarity has led to skepticism of such hypotheses. The path is now clear to investigate other possibilities such as that the fiesta is essentially an adaptation to systematic exploitation. Stripped of their usual propagandistic uses, terms like exploitation and colonialism may acquire new significance in social science explanation.

23. THE HIGHLAND HERITAGE

MARVIN HARRIS

The distinctive highland Indian villages to which I have been referring have been classified by Eric Wolf as examples of the closed-corporate-peasant community. According to Wolf, the distinctive feature of these communities is that there is communal control of landholdings either through common ownership or by community-imposed sanctions against sale to outsiders. The interest in protecting the community land leads to a life which is saturated by participation in communal political and religious affairs. Other related diagnostics listed by Wolf (1955) include a tendency for an intimate interplay to take place between political and religious activities; an emphasis on prestige derived from community display; culturally recognized standards of consumption which consciously exclude cultural alternatives; defensive ignorance; a pattern of rejection of novelty; a cult of poverty; and a system of institutionalized envy leading to the restriction of consumption standards and the leveling of intra-communal economic differences.

In the highland Indian closed-corporate-peasant communities from Mexico to Bolivia, the distinctive features of the type are best illustrated through the complex of institutions known as the fiesta system. All Indian men are expected to take part in this system. In their youth they are obliged to assume certain menial offices or *cargos,* that is, "burdens," such as carrying messages for the councilmen, serving on the night watch, or cleaning the church. Eventually, each man is obliged to "volunteer" for a major *cargo.* This involves organizing and carrying out the fiesta of one of the saints who is traditionally regarded as especially significant in the

Reprinted by permission of the author and publisher from *Patterns of Race in the Americas,* Chapter 3, pp. 25–43. Copyright © 1964 Walker & Company, New York.

Social Change

life of the village. As a man moves up through this hierarchy of religious obligations, he is rewarded with increasing amounts of prestige. In addition, everywhere among the corporate Indian villages, satisfaction of religious burdens leads to or is accompanied by parallel progress up a ladder of political offices such as sheriff, councilman, mayor, etc. Thus, the *principales,* or top-ranking Indian personalities, are always individuals who have had a distinguished record as fiesta-givers and civil office holders.

The burdensome aspect of the *cargos* and political offices is that they involve considerable expenditure of time and money. Fiestas are costly affairs since large quantities of food and drink (especially drink) must be dispensed. In addition, the cost of special church services, candles, costumes for dancers and players, musicians, fireworks, bulls and bullfighters, and many other festive items must also be met. In the classic stereotype, it is alleged that the *carguero,* or burden-bearer, frequently cannot meet these expenses out of his normal income and must borrow from friends and relatives, sell or pawn land, or otherwise place himself in debt for a considerable period. "Generally, the higher offices in the hierarchy are the most costly, and economic ruin, at least temporarily, accompanies the acquired social prestige."[1] In order to meet his burden an Indian will ". . . spend all he has, go into debt, and sell his labor for trifling wages even though he ends in virtual slavery."[2]

Many anthropologists view the fiesta complex of the corporate villages as essentially a survival of allegedly aboriginal non-Western notions of economic utility and self-interest. The Indians entertain themselves, gain prestige and venerate the saints by giving the fiestas, and this is to them a more "rational" use of money than investing it in land, livestock, machinery or education. After all, what is so strange about squandering one's money on a good time? Only people suffering from a "Protestant ethic" find this a problem worth bothering about. On the other hand, there are many anthropologists who feel that the fiesta system is a bit "odd" and that it does demand a serious explanation. There are several reasons why the "burdens" simply cannot be dismissed as an example of the whimsical and quixotic (to us) things which men will do in order to achieve prestige.

First of all, recent studies have confirmed what had long been suspected about the origin of the fiesta system's ritual content, namely that it is almost wholly sixteenth-century Spanish-Catholic. Therefore, to talk about aboriginal survivals in this context is clearly out of the question (Foster 1960:167–225).[3] Secondly, and more important, the irrational, uneconomic aspects of fiesta behavior stand in marked contrast to the economic individualism, constant penny-pinching and obsessive involvement with price which is one of the most pronounced features of highland Indian life. So conspicuous is the highland Indian's dedication to the principles of thrift, investment and *caveat emptor* that Sol Tax (1953) was moved to call the Indians of Panajachel, Guatemala, "penny capitalists." In the Zapotec town in Mexico, Elsie Clews Parsons (1936:12) was overwhelmed by the same pattern: "Mitla is a business town. Trade permeates its whole life; price is of supreme interest to young and old, women and men, the poor and well to do." Once, when Parsons had finished telling a group of Indians how one of her relatives had died in a motorcycle accident, the first question which the Indians put to her was: "How much does a motorcycle cost?" In Yalalag, another Zapotecan village, Julio de la Fuente (1949:44) also gives a picture of total involvement in petty commercial activities. Here the penny-pinching is so obsessive that "brothers cheat each other," families break up over debts (p. 155), and "to ask for loans among relatives is frowned upon because they suspect that you are not going to repay them (p. 148)."

The attempt to explain the fiesta complex has recently focused on the needs of the corporate Indian community to level internal wealth differences as a protective device. Wolf (1955), for example, implies that the political-religious-prestige interplay is an aspect of the community's attempt to increase its internal solidarity in defense of the land.[4] In a somewhat similar vein, but without bothering with a material base, C. Leslie has suggested that Mitla's fiesta system is a check upon the destructive individualistic tendencies of the Mitlenos. The townspeople complain about the burdens of the fiesta system, but according to Leslie (1960:74), the vision that there could conceivably be "no law other than their desires, no limit other than that which they think advisable" inhibits would-be critics of saint's festivals and causes them to go unheeded in the community at large. "Thus families with the values of the market place, and priding themselves as experts in following its

competitive ways, Mitlenos nonetheless subordinated themselves
. . . to ideals of proper conduct which disabused all but the most
obdurate individuals of the notion that they might live whole-
heartedly in pursuit of their own self-interest."

The difficulty with viewing the fiesta complex as an egalitarian
device of the corporate peasant community is twofold: First of all,
although the fiesta system does tend to place an upper limit upon
the amount of capital which an individual Indian can accumulate,
it has never prevented the formation of rather sharp socio-
economic differences within the Indian communities. There is very
little evidence to support the stereotyped version of the *cargo*
which causes "economic ruin." In Charles Wagley's Santiago
Chimaltenango and Ruth Bunzel's Chichicastenango it was specifically established that most of the people are too poor to be able
to afford the major *cargos*.[5] According to La Farge (1947:137),
the civil-religious leaders are "in almost every village . . . extremely prosperous." Marked differences in wealth among Indians
is also characteristic of Tepotzlan (especially before the revolution), Mitla and Yalalag, and many other, if not all highland Indian
communities which have been studied by anthropologists.[6]

I do not mean to say that the fiesta system never forces any
Indians into debt. The tendency of this form of conspicuous consumption to induce many Indians to spend more than their resources allow is, as we shall see, a very important function of the
system in relationship to peonage and migratory labor. The point
is that the *cargos* do not bring economic ruin to everyone. Many
of the most burdensome fiestas are underwritten precisely by those
people who are best able to afford them. To a *principal* or *cacique,*
the *cargos* were not economically fatal. Indeed they were *principales* and *caciques*—"big shots"—precisely because, unlike lesser
mortals, they were able to buy enough *aguardiente* for the whole
village to get drunk, without having to sell their lands and animals,
and without having to work on a "foreigner's" *hacienda.*

Not only has the fiesta system failed to level the Indians into a
homogeneous solidary group, but a more inefficient defense against
outsiders could scarcely be imagined. It might be argued that the
fiesta system has helped to maintain the separate identity of the
highland communities, but this is scarcely a result which possesses
any clear adaptive advantages for the members of such communi-

ties. On the contrary, these communities themselves are the product of a colonial policy whose net result in the long run was the maintenance of the Indians in an "exploited and degraded condition." Far from protecting the Indian communities against *encomienda, repartimiento,* debt peonage, excessive taxation and tribute, the fiesta system was an integral and enduring part of the mechanisms by which these noxious influences gained access to the very heart of the village.

It seems all too often to be forgotten that the closed corporate villages fulfilled certain vital functions with respect to the larger system in which Indian life was embedded. From the point of view of this larger system the proliferation of ceremonies, the burdens of the *cargueros,* and the whole civil-religious hierarchy are nothing but direct or indirect expressions of the economic and political vassalage into which the Indians have fallen. Consider, for example, the way in which one village is closed off from other villages. All observers of highland Indian life agree that an extraordinary degree of local ethnocentrism characterizes these communities. This quaint, introverted focus, expressed in endogamy, distinctive patterns of dress, speech and other customs so dear to the hearts of certain anthropologists, has another side to it. Was this not exactly what was needed in order to stave off for the longest possible time the ultimate hour of reckoning that comes to every political system which mercilessly degrades and exploits its human resources (Rowe 1957:190)?[7] Again, it is no accident that the Indian leader who emerges from the fiesta system is typically one who has no authority beyond his own locality. The highlands had passed beyond the village level of socio-cultural organization at least a thousand years before the Europeans arrived. What else then is the closed-corporate-peasant community, if not an artifact created by the invaders to make certain that the state level of organization would never again fall under Indian control?

Also, it is all too frequently forgotten that in terms of the colonial system, the fiesta complex was a direct expression of the attempt by the Church to maintain control over the highland Indian populations and to derive wealth from them. Although this situation has been drastically modified in many highland countries today, it was clearly a dominant factor in the fiesta complex at least as far back as the eighteenth century. The famous report of Antonio de Ulloa, who was sent out by the Spanish Crown to investigate conditions in eighteenth-century Peru, contains a clear statement of the functions which the fiesta system played in relationship to the maintenance of Church income. Ulloa was astonished by the number of saint's days which were celebrated in the highland Indian villages. He noted that one of the first tasks which a newly appointed priest undertook was to create additional fiestas, requiring additional outlays for various services rendered by the Church and its representatives. Speaking of the *mayordomos* upon whom the burden of the fiesta rested, Juan and Ulloa (1826) noted that by the Indian's participation in the celebration of the saint's day, he was relieved "of all the money which he had been able to collect during the whole year and also all the fowls and animals which his wife and children have reared in their huts, so that his family is left destitute of food and reduced to wild herbs and to the grains which they cultivate in their small gardens."

To become a *carguero* was far from being a spontaneous undertaking stimulated by deep religious feeling and a sense of obligation. Juan and Ulloa (1826) observed that many of the *cargueros* were simply forced into the position of underwriting the fiesta by command from the priest. "As soon as the sermon of the day is concluded, the curate reads a paper on which he has inscribed names of those who are to be masters of ceremonies for the festivals of the following year, and if anyone does not accept it of his free will, he is forced to give his consent by dint of blows. And when his day comes there is no apology that can exonerate him from having the money ready."

The intimate relationship between the local priest, the village Indian hierarchy, the fiesta system, Church finance and politico-economic control is still clearly visible. In 1960, I had the opportunity to live in an Indian village in Chimborazo Province, Ecuador, and to observe aspects of the modern fiesta system for three months. In Ecuadorian Indian villages, nominations for the fiesta leader are submitted to the parish priest by Indian officials residing within the village. These officials are instructed by the priest, as well as by the local representative of the state, the *teniente politico*, to identify Indians in their village who have given evidence during the past year of being able to support the financial burden of the fiesta. Acting on this information, the priest, backed up by the *teniente politico,* appoints the new *cargueros* at the mass on the fiesta of the saint's day (Silverman 1960:40 ff.).

True enough, direct physical coercion is not used as it was when Ulloa observed the system. Nonetheless, the threat of material sanctions does not lie far behind the facade of persuasion and voluntary accommodation. The *teneinte politico* exercises great discretionary powers in relation to the adjudication of land claims, as well as in all processes of a legal nature requiring paperwork and reference to higher authority. Indians who are unco-operative with respect to the fiesta system earn a bad reputation among the authorities external to the village and they are subject to harassment in the form of excessive obligations placed on them for community labor and to unfair treatment in litigation.

According to Nuñez del Prado (1955:17), today in the Andes, "It should be noted that men very rarely volunteer for a *cargo.* In most cases a man is chosen against his will and persuaded to accept it when he is drunk." A poignant description of what appears to be a similar situation is provided by Ruth Bunzel (1952:181) for Guatemala:

> The conventional behavior for candidates for all offices is to refuse to serve, and to have the office thrust on them. Sometimes physical force is used in forcing the insignia of office upon unwilling candidates. At the feast of Santo Tomas I saw the candidates for office for the coming year being dragged forcibly through the streets, kicking and struggling. I saw one of the newly chosen *regidores* (councilmen) bolt for the door, after he had been brought in, like a prisoner, for the notification. All the *regidores* and *mayores* were on hand, armed with sticks to prevent the escape of the candidates. It took over an hour to persuade the candidate for First Alcade [mayor] to accept the nomination.

It should also be noted that the contemporary system depends to a great extent upon the consensus among the members of the Indian village that those who shirk their burdens as *cargueros* ought not to receive the respect to which those who have accepted the burden are entitled. If one has given a fiesta and suffered the economic consequences, he does not view with equanimity the prospect of others in the village failing to assume their proper share of the burden. Thus, a good deal of the pressure for the maintenance of the system apparently arises spontaneously from within the Indian village itself. However, this is a superficial interpretation of the forces which are at work. At the outset, to follow Antonio de Ulloa's lead, the fiestas functioned primarily to drain off a portion of the community's wealth in support of the Church bureaucracy. At the same time, the associated civil-religious hierarchy was a tool of the colonial government. The *caciques* and *principales* were puppet leaders who in return for collaboration in the work of recruiting for *mit'a* and *catequil* were vested with some semblance of local authority and power. In this context, it should be mentioned that one of the major rewards of office-holding has always been exemption from forced labor.

In modern times the draining of community wealth through the mechanism of the fiesta system is no longer primarily destined to benefit the Church. In the nineteenth century, during the course of the establishment of the liberal republican regimes, the Church suffered serious setbacks and was reduced to a position of secondary importance in the control of Indian communities. After the passing of restrictive legislation and the expropriation of Church lands, the Church ceased to be the primary direct economic beneficiary of the fiesta system. This position was now taken over by the *haciendas* and the *hacendado* class and the fiesta system became an integral part of the mechanisms by which Indians, during the nineteenth and twentieth centuries, were enticed into debt on behalf of the system of debt peonage.

Left to their own devices, the Indians were perfectly capable of maintaining a level of consumption realistically adjusted to the marginal wages which their labor commanded. The fiesta system, however, compelled them periodically to acquire goods on a scale which was far above their normal needs. In Guatemala, as recently as the 1930's, the fiesta system was deliberately used by the *haciendas* to recruit Indian labor. *Hacienda* agents were sent out to scour the countryside for prospective workers for the plantations. These labor recruiters sought out the holders of *cargos* and offered loans on deceptively friendly terms (Whetten 1961: 66 ff.). In addition, it is clear from numerous community studies carried out in the highland region that the non-Indian sectors of the population, in general, stand to gain from a continuation of the fiesta system, since the celebration of fiestas provides the principal occasion for the purchase of non-subsistence goods. Wagley's (1957:275) comment, "These days are very lucrative for the Ladinos of Chimaltenengo," is applicable to most highland fiestas. Generally speaking, throughout the highland region, fiesta buying involves the Indians in transactions with non-Indians who control the commercial sources of non-subsistence commodities. The entire non-Indian sector of the highland countries, therefore, maintains a powerful vested interest in the preservation of the fiesta system. The system prevents the rise of genuine native leaders, because it drains off the excess wealth of Indians, cutting short the prospects for the accumulation of capital resources among the Indians in the village. The wealth that is drained off is used to support the Church hierarchy and to stimulate the entrance of the Indian into the extra village labor market. It is also used as a stimulant to raise the consumption standards among the Indians and hence to increase the rate of commercial transactions between non-Indians and Indians.

Those who doubt the fundamentally repressive and abusive character of the classic fiesta complex should compare the celebration of fiestas in Indian communities with the manner in which devotion to saints is practiced in non-Indian villages. Moche, a mestizo community in Peru, also has many saint's days. The people of Moche become *cargueros,* and they give relatively expensive fiestas. However, the *carguero* in the non-Indian community is not at all subject to the financial burdens which must be shouldered by the Indian *carguero*. On the contrary, the fiesta is viewed in Moche as a means by which the saints may be venerated and the pocket of the *carguero* swelled. Far from incurring crushing financial losses, the Moche *cargueros* emerge from the fiesta with a handsome profit. This profit is gained by soliciting financial contributions from all of the townspeople by carefully gearing expenses to income (Gillin 1945). Thus, although the non-Indian fiestas are phrased in a fashion quite similar to that characteristic of the Indian fiestas, the primary functional significance is drastically different. No Moche *carguero* ever needs to be dragged screaming through the streets to the ceremony of his installation.

I have, perhaps, failed to make adequately clear that the Indian's burden in the fiesta system is not restricted merely to the expenses which must be met in the course of carrying out the celebration of the saint's day; the really critical involvement may in certain cases be the necessity of secular duties which the *carguero* is also expected to assume. In the classic form of the Indian fiesta system, appointees to *cargos* are automatically expected to serve in the village council. This requires their presence in the village away from their farms for a good portion of the year, and in many cases represents a greater sacrifice than the actual expenses of the fiesta. This aspect of the fiesta system also tends to be absent among the non-Indian communities.

It should be mentioned that many non-Indian fiesta complexes in Latin America do not derive their principal impetus from the entrepreneurial advantages accruing to the specific individuals who undertake the fiesta. There is also a very widespread pattern in which the fiesta is essentially geared to the marketing and commercial requirements of the mestizo or *ladino* community as a whole. Under such circumstances, the fiesta is advertised by the *ladino* town council in neighboring communities, and the spectacular nature of the proposed entertainments and festivities is offered as an attraction for the largest possible number of visitors to the community on the saint's day. These fiestas are really fairs, designed to stimulate the commercial life of the town, or to make the town conspicuous in the hope that its products will achieve widespread popularity. Under such circumstances, the fiesta is merely an adjunct of the market. For example, in the community of Tzintzuntzan, located in highland Mexico, the day of the town's most important fiesta is likewise the day on which the greatest market is held; since the people of Tzintzuntzan specialize in making pottery, they are most eager to have the largest possible number of prospective buyers of their wares present at their fiestas. A considerable proportion of the town's annual ceramic output is sold to the 8,000 or so people who attend the great celebration of their town's patron saint (Foster 1948). One fact which has tended to obscure the functional analysis of the fiesta system in highland Latin America is that the pattern which I have been identifying especially with the mestizos or *ladinos* actually occurs among many Indian villages as well. This is particularly true of Mexico, where after the 1910–20 Revolution, political and religious reforms made it possible for the Indians more closely to approximate the position of the mestizos within the total national economy and polity.[8]

In addition to the fiesta complex, there are many other characteristics of the corporate villages which are part of the heritage of the colonial and republican systems for making use of the labor of the highland Indians. The Indians everywhere tend to occupy the more marginal lands; they tend to produce subsistence crops rather than commercial crops; they tend to have a higher rate of illiteracy; a high rate of infant mortality; a shorter life expectancy; and a lower per capita income than the non-Indians and *ladinos* or mestizos who live in the same communities; the Indians tend to be politically subordinate, and they are subject in many instances to outright discrimination in terms of housing and social etiquette. For example, in highland Guatemala communities, it is not unusual for Indians to be obliged to step off the street in order to make way for *ladinos* (Tumin 1952). In rural highland Ecuador, it is expected that Indians will yield positions on public conveyances to *ladinos* (Ziff 1960:20), and in Peru and Ecuador it is not rare for *hacendados,* in collaboration with the local police, to use brutal methods for the suppression of Indian "deviants." In Guatemala, there is segregation in housing, street corner gatherings, recreation and leisure, local and national fiestas, social visiting and friendship units, school functions, weddings, baptisms, wakes, funerals, eating and marriage (Tumin 1952:189–208). Throughout the highland region, with the possible exception of certain social strata in Mexican urban centers, the *ladinos* or mestizos tend to regard the Indians as inferior creatures and harbor many derogatory stereotypes with respect to them. Speaking of Ecuador, Peru and Bolivia, Nuñez del Prado (1955:3) notes that "in all three countries contempt for everything Indian is habitual . . ." In Guatemala the Indians are said to be "stupid," "without shame," "like children," "dishonest" and "not deserving of respect" (Tumin 1952:117–18). I believe it could easily be shown that all of these manifestations of prejudice and discrimination against Indians are consequences of the labor policies pursued since the conquest. Certainly, the central feature of this highland pattern of prejudice and discrimination is the application of harsh labor laws exclusively to Indians.

The pattern of prejudice and discrimination against the highland Indians bears certain resemblances to the system of race relations involving whites and Negroes in the United States. As in the United States, the population is sharply divided into two major groups, one of which is subject to flagrant mistreatment at the hands of the other. Furthermore, as is true of every society in which discrimination is practiced on a systematic and intensive scale, identity in the subordinate group(s) is firmly and unambiguously established in local daily life (Harris 1964b). In the United States, one is either white or Negro, and in much of highland Latin America, one is either mestizo (*ladino, blanco,* according to the country) or Indian.[9]

The similarities between the two systems of race relations, however, do not extend much beyond this point. Several striking differences must be noted. In the first place, the two systems treat the half-castes or hybrids in diametrically opposed ways. In the United States, all persons with any demonstrable degree of Negro parentage, visible or not, fall into the subordinate caste, according to the principle which I have elsewhere labeled "hypo-descent (Harris and Kottak 1963)." This has meant that from a biological point of view, the whites in the United States have remained relatively "pure," while the Negroes have become genetically less and less like their African forebears. In the Latin American highlands, however, there has never been a time when the hybrid types were automatically lumped together with the Indian. True, there had been a time when the Crown was intent on clearly separating all three types, i.e., whites, mestizos and Indians, and on assigning special privileges and obligations to each. But this system was always more of a legal fiction than a social reality.[10] Ever since independence, the highland populations have consisted of two major groupings: Indians and non-Indians. (Negro slaves, in small numbers, would make a third group, the lowest caste of all.) The Indians were subject to the special legal disabilities relating to labor while the whites and mestizos enjoyed the benefits therefrom. The superordinate caste of non-Indians did not enjoy their superior status because they looked Caucasoid or could actually demonstrate only Caucasoid descent. On the contrary, many of those who escaped the worst features of the labor laws were genetically more Indian than the *principales* or *caciques* of the corporate villages. To be an Indian in the highlands, as we shall see in a moment, is to be someone who lives like an Indian.

Who then are the mestizos and *ladinos?* Mestizos and *ladinos* are non-Indians. They are the lower, rural, peasant portion of the superordinate caste. But they are part of that caste, not outside of it. They are not to be thought of as structurally intermediate to the European group.[11] The labor laws did not apply in halfway measure to the mestizos;[12] nor did the mestizos live in communities which were halfway between Indian and European communities. Of course, marked difference in power and style of life prevailed among the various strata and rural and urban segments of the superordinate non-Indian caste. But as far as the dominant land and labor issues in the relationship between aboriginals and invaders were concerned, the lower segment—the mestizos—was structurally aligned with the higher segments: the European—and American-born Caucasoids. The only sense in which they were intermediate was in terms of color prejudice. Caucasoid physical features were generally preferred by all strata of the dominant caste; hence the more Indian-looking, the less desirable the mestizo type. This, however, did not prevent many non-Caucasoid individuals from rising high in the colonial and republican aristocracy, although the highest economic and political positions tended everywhere to be monopolized by persons who showed the least genetic debt to the Indians. Eventually, in Mexico, the upper and lower strata of the superordinate caste came into conflict and fought a class war in which the more Caucasoid elite was defeated. The result is that in modern Mexico many of the highest economic and political positions are now in the grasp of people who could pass for Indians, if there were any reason for them to do so.

Thus racial identity in the highlands is established on quite different premises from those in the United States. The highland Indians are not usually distinguishable from non-Indians simply on the basis of physical appearance. From a purely physical point of view, most of the highland Indians could easily be taken for *ladinos* or mestizos, since the latter possess a considerable amount of Indian genetic admixture, while equally substantial frequencies of Caucasoid genes are found among the "Indians." Instead of depending upon physical appearance, Indian racial identity flows from the fact that one lives in an Indian community, speaks an Indian language, speaks Spanish with an Indian accent, wears Indian-style clothing or participates in Indian-type fiestas. The status of being an Indian, in other words, is essentially a matter of behaving according to patterns which are locally recognized as being Indian specialties.

Another contrast is that it is possible to admit that one has an Indian ancestor and still regard oneself and be regarded by others as a non-Indian. (No one can admit Negro parentage in the United States without thereby affiliating himself with the Negro group.) Indeed, in upper-middle-class Mexico City, to have an Indian ancestor is a source of considerable pride. Elsewhere, however, it is a source of amusement, and mild depreciation. As Nuñez del Prado (1955:3) suggests, "It is very nearly an insult to suggest to a mestizo that he has an Indian relative"; very nearly, but not quite.

A corollary of this difference in the mode of establishing racial identity is that "passing" is based primarily upon exposure to similar cultural conditioning rather than upon intermarriage and genetic change. Theoretically, it should be easier to "pass" under these circumstances than when marked physical differences are backed up by a rigid descent rule. Such seems to have been the case for Mexico at least, where the percentage of Indians in the population has declined from almost 99 per cent in 1600 to less than 11.5 per cent in 1950. Since the total Mexican population has risen during the same period from about 2 million to over 30 million, without appreciable foreign immigration, it would seem likely that passing from Indian to mestizo status has been largely responsible for the failure of the Indian population to keep pace with the growth of the non-Indian sectors (Wagley and Harris 1958:81–82; Lewis 1960:289–90; Kubler 1952:65–66). It is possible, however, that large-scale passing is a relatively recent phenomenon associated with the Mexican revolution and the destruction of the *hacendado* class. Elsewhere, the disparity between the enculturation experience of Indians and mestizos has led to a much slower change in the balance between the racial segments. Unfortunately this is one of the many aspects of Latin American race relations which have yet to be the object of systematic and quantitative research. Such research is needed before a clearer picture of the tendencies toward and the barriers against the assimilation of the highland Indian can be drawn. In some regions, as in central and northern Mexico, the assimilation of the Indian is proceeding at a very rapid rate, while in others, the corporate villages appear to be clinging to their Indian identity with great tenacity.

I would offer the hypothesis that these rates of assimilation reflect varying local disparities between lower-class mestizo and Indian standards of living. It must be remembered that all of highland Latin America is characterized by a rigid class structure among the mestizos themselves, in which the lower class leads a life no less degraded and precarious than that of the Indians. Although the highland Indians are surrounded by mestizo populations which in general tend to enjoy a superior standard of living, there are many specific local contexts in which the situation is reversed. In Mexico, for example, it has been estimated that at least 100,000 Indians live better than the bulk of the mestizos (Cline 1953:78–79). In Ecuador, the case of the Otavalo Indians is relevant [see Chapter 25, this volume—Ed.]; these people have become remarkably skilled in the manufacture and sale of woolen garments (Collier and Buitron 1949), and their wares have acquired a national reputation. Indeed, Otavalo Indians have been seen selling their blankets as far away as Rio de Janeiro and Panama City. Under these circumstances it would seem highly unlikely that Indians would want to exchange their identity for that of mestizos. Among the Otavalos it is the other way around. Mestizo weavers have recently been trying to pass themselves off as Otavalo Indians. Apparently many Indians could, if they wished, abandon their native village, learn to speak Spanish, and dress in the costume of the mestizo and thereby pass into the mestizo or *ladino* group. But many prefer to remain Indians. Apparently many Indians could, if they wished, abandon their native village, learn to speak Spanish, and dress in the costume of the mestizo and thereby pass into the mestizo or *ladino* group. But many prefer to remain Indians. Apparently the rate of passing is limited by the fact that in many instances there is very little improvement to be gained from such a transition.

Rather than compete with the mestizos for what must in any event be a very low rung on the ladder of the social hierarchy, many Indian communities seem to prefer instead to turn inward and to reduce social intercourse with people outside of their villages to the absolute minimum required by the fiesta system and by the apparatus of national government. It is in these intensely involuted highland Indian villages, withdrawn from effective participation in the life of the nation, that one finds the most drastic results of the 400 years of repressive systems to which the highland Indians have been subjected. Everybody who comes from outside the village, with the exception perhaps of the priest, is viewed as a potential threat to life and property. In the experience of these people everything that originates outside the village inevitably results in severe restriction of liberty and economic well-being. Many lay and professional observers forget that these fears are grounded in historical fact. It is not without historical justification that the Indians of highland Ecuador kill several census takers every time the national government attempts to count the villagers. The observer who is unfamiliar with the historical background of these villages is often perplexed by the reluctance of the Indians to accept medical and technical aid. But their caution is an adaptation that has resulted from 400 years of broken promises.

First came the *conquistadores* to liberate them from the oppressive rule of the native bureaucracy; the result was the *encomienda*. Then came the Crown, to liberate them from the oppression of the *encomienda;* the *repartimiento* followed. Then there followed the wars of independence and the promise of liberty; the result was the *hacienda* system and debt peonage. In modern times, with the abolition of formal debt peonage and the modification of the power of the *haciendas,* a considerable lapse in time must be expected before the Indians come to the point of fearlessly accepting the new offers of assistance which their national governments are now making.

Many persons in the employ of national and international development organizations are prone to regard the withdrawal of the Indians and their rejection of outside assistance as an indication of their infantilism or perversity. The friendly agronomist is rebuffed when he offers the Indians seedlings for reforestation. Why have the Indians driven him out of the village? Because they suspect, possibly with some substance in fact, that the ultimate results will be even worse than what they have now. After they have lavished care on the seedlings and after the trees have matured, how can they be sure that someone else will not come along and cut them down?

A case from highland Ecuador involving an offer of Merino sheep may perhaps illustrate this point. At first the Indians refused to listen to the advice of the foreign specialist who had been hired to improve the aboriginals' livestock. The native sheep were indeed scrawny, of little use for food, and producing only scanty amounts of wool. The specialist urged the Indians to interbreed their sheep with the sheep he would make available to them at no cost, and he promised that they would soon enjoy the benefits of animals at least twice as productive in terms of meat and wool. No one would take the offer. At last in one of the remoter villages a sole Indian who saw no danger in the situation yielded to the seductive proposition of the international expert and accepted several of the Merinos.

Returning to the village after a year had gone by, the expert was greeted by the usual shower of stones. At last, he managed to prevail upon the villagers to explain to him what had happened. It was as he had said; the sheep which had resulted from the cross with the Merino were twice as large and twice as woolly as the native flocks. They were in fact the finest sheep in the region. But this phenomenon had not gone unnoticed by the mestizos who lived in the valley below the community. They had driven up one night in a truck and had herded all of the poor fellow's sheep into it and driven off. The Indian who had departed from the ancestral patterns now found himself without any sheep at all.

Attempts to extend medical assistance to highland Indian villagers frequently result in similar disasters. With their long-established reluctance to enter into relationships with non-villagers, the Indians initially suspect the offers of medical assistance and refuse to reveal who is sick. In desperation, however, when the patient is near the point of death, the villagers will avail themselves of the offer of medical help. The doctor is then presented with a case in advanced stages of deterioration and he urges the immediate removal of the Indian to a hospital. In a high proportion of the cases such treatment is followed by the death of the patient and the spread of the myth that the hospital is a place to which the whites take Indians to die. Even when the doctor finally manages to gain the confidence of the village and is permitted to see patients whose disease is not in a terminal phase, the results are frequently unenviable. The doctor prescribes a remedy which can be purchased only at the drugstore. The drugstore, however, may be anywhere from 10 to 20 miles distant from the village. The drugs are expensive. The trip is costly in time lost from the work of the fields. But the hope of relieving the suffering of his loved one persuades the Indian to depart from his better judgment. He trudges off to town, buys the medicine and returns. He administers the medicine according to directions. When the bottle is empty he stops. The patient grows worse and dies. The next time the doctor appears, which may be anywhere from a month to half a year later, his inquiry about the welfare of the villagers is greeted by silence or else by fervent assurances that no one in the village is sick.

During 1960 a campaign was mounted in Chimborazo Province, Ecuador, to inoculate 80 per cent of the Indian villagers in the hope of eradicating smallpox. The vaccination teams were greeted in some of the villages with stones; in others they entered unmolested, only to find the houses abandoned and the Indians fled to the hills. In some villages, success was achieved only by prevailing upon the parish priest to invite the unsuspecting Indians to attend a special Mass. When everyone had entered the church, the doors were locked and the inoculations were started. Still unable to obtain the 80 per cent necessary for eliminating the disease as an endemic feature of the area, teams of vaccinators, sometimes disguised as Indians, took up stations in the various markets of the region. When an Indian passed whom they suspected of not having been treated, they seized him, and by force, if necessary, proceeded with the inoculation. This produced the counter-intelligence among the Indians who had yet to be inoculated that the whites, no longer satisfied with the theft of Indian lands and Indian waters, were now attempting to steal their blood.

NOTES

1. Camara 1952:156, speaking of Mexico.
2. Rubio Orbe quoted in Nuñez del Prado (1955:5).
3. Carrasco (1961) minimizes the cultural heritage but recognizes important structural continuities.
4. Carrasco claims that the "ladder system" has "survival value in that it holds the community together by checking the internal economic and social differentiation that tends to disrupt the community . . ." (1961:493).
5. "The high *cargos* are restricted to those who have sufficient lands and whose livelihood does not depend on wage labor." (Wagley 1957:257.) "The chief *mayordomos* [i.e. cargueros] must be chosen from wealthy families that own or have access to town houses" (Bunzel 1952:190).
6. "Class distinctions were marked" (Lewis 1951:51).
7. "Spanish colonial rule was characterized by economic exploitation and personal degradation of the natives. Both features were carried to an extreme which is difficult to credit unless one is familiar with the closely similar conditions in which the Inca of today live under the domination of the descendants of their colonial masters."
8. A study of the changes which occurred in the Mexican fiesta system after the 1910–20 Revolution is badly needed.
9. Historically, the situation was much more complex. In Mexico, for example, there was official concern with the problem of distinguishing Spanish-born whites from American-born whites; whites from both Indians and Negroes; and Negroes from Indians (see Beltrán 1946:199 ff.). Neither in the United States, nor in highland Latin America, are there only two racial segments to be considered. Nonetheless, the evolution of these systems has been in the direction of a clash between two large, well defined social groups with identity in one or the other associated with marked differences in political, economic and social behavior. It is the sharpness of this division and the social consequences of belonging which need to be stressed. In local situations, there is no doubt about who is or is not an Indian, and there is no significant status which is intermediate between Indian and non-Indian. I admit, however, that this pattern may be changing in some highland countries where the emergence of an intermediate group called *cholos* is reported (cf. J. Fried 1959). Greater ambiguity of identity will probably follow upon the achievement of social reform everywhere in the highlands, but this is a field in which there has been little methodical inquiry.
10. Beltrán (1946:175 ff.) describes how the Spanish attempted to keep track of all the permutations and combinations of the "castas" without success.
11. This is a mistake made by Ralph Beals (1955:417) and others who try to analyze the highland racial situation. The mestizos are rural, economically depressed and closer to the Indian physical type. Structurally, however, the greatest social cleavage has always been between Indians on the one hand, and mestizos and Europeans on the other.
12. Referring to Guatemala's vagrancy law of 1936, Whetten notes that the law was interpreted as applicable mainly to Indians (1961:66 ff.).

Introduction to The Karajá and the Brazilian Frontier

The following article analyzes the contact between a moderately acculturated Indian group, the Karajá of central Brazil, and Brazilian national society. In exploring his subject, Tavener provides us with an objective look at the motivations, goals and behavior of all the significant actors in the drama of contact. In many respects he follows a model developed by a number of Brazilian anthropologists in the last decade (Oliveira 1964, 1972; Laraia 1965; Laraia and Da Matta 1967; Da Matta 1963; Melatti 1967; Ribeiro 1970, *inter alia*). In these studies they have established several important points. First, one should not only talk of Indian/non-Indian relations in general. Such relations actually differ from region to region, as both traditional Indian cultures and national fronts vary (cf. Service 1955). Secondly, today one can rarely analyze contact as a simple confrontation of two distinct groups. Regional interethnic sociocultural systems have emerged in which the culture of the component ethnic groups reflects considerable borrowing and other forms of mutual adjustment, co-operation and competition. Finally, in characterizing much contact as a form of "internal colonialism," R. C. de Oliveira (1972: ch. 6–8) emphasizes that contact cannot be adequately explained if we regard it simply as a product of the immediate actors —Indians, frontierspeople, a handful of government agents. The situation is invariably more complex, and the domination of the local scene does not end with the activity of the frontiersmen. The presence of Indian agents, for example, intimates that the policies of remote governmental agencies may have decisive influence upon the local scene and the life and death of the Indians. Other pressures derive from commercial enterprises, typically based in distant cities and responsive primarily to the exigencies of international trade. They may be interested in exploiting territory occupied by Indians for agriculture, cattle raising, mining, extraction of wild produce or communication links. Sometimes they want land, sometimes Indian labor, as for collecting rubber (Murphy 1960) or Brazil nuts (Laraia and Da Matta 1967).

This third point raises certain methodological problems. At the same time that these field studies have refined our understanding of contact, they have increasingly emphasized the impact of such remote influences. These are hard to investigate fully from the field, and harder still to predict and account for within a model of a regional interethnic system.[1] While Tavener's study recognizes the important effects of outside influences, we must place it alongside other articles in this section in order to approach a better model of what must be known to understand the pervasive and practically ubiquitous changes going on in South American societies. The two articles by Marvin Harris provide a global outlook from the point of view of political economy on relations between colonizers and indigenous peoples.

But all the facts of a particular contact situation cannot be generated from this higher level of analysis. An examination of global political economy gives us a glimpse of an inevitable future which we can use to predict the direction of cultural change and acculturation. However, in order to understand the content of a given system we need to look also to the past, to the influence of traditional culture. Following Tavener's article, which examines a lowland society on the basis of contemporary ethnography, Frank Salomon treats sociocultural change in a specific highland society from an ethnohistorical point of view (Chapter 25).

Finally, it is necessary to go *below* the level of analysis that is used in many studies of contact. While the Brazilian anthropologists mentioned above have broken down the phenomenon of

[1] In this respect it is interesting that Roberto Cardoso de Oliveira notes (1972:9) that it was not so much the work of Brazilian anthropologists so much as the scandal in the national and international press in 1967–68 over the record of the S.P.I. that made Brazilians realize that the Indian problem is not a mere backwoods affair but a national problem.

contact into regional varieties, they have nevertheless depended largely on one accepted anthropological view of culture. This view emphasizes the shared and learned qualities that characterize human culture. Tavener's study, by contrast, emphasizes variation within a single culture, and regards the acceptance of this fact as necessary to the understanding of the particular contact situation with which he is concerned. Perhaps this approach entails the danger of overparticularization, but it reflects certain truths. If we are to understand culture as behavior which, among other things, has adaptive value, then it follows that a society's potential for future survival depends as much on the maintenance and multiplication of diversity as on the reproduction of uniformity (cf. Wallace 1970). Furthermore, in a situation of contact and acculturation, where much is new to both societies and especially when the participants may literally be fighting for survival, perhaps it is particularly appropriate that culture should be regarded less as a tradition and more as a means of adaptation.

We badly need further careful comparative and particular studies of contact, integrating the various levels of analysis outlined here. Not only will such work provide us with an improved basis for explanations and predictions regarding culture change, one also hopes that such studies will serve as lessons to those empowered to direct or oversee situations of contact and change. The failure to adopt humane solutions in the near future will surely result in the cultural or even physical destruction of most of the surviving native peoples of South America.

Christopher Tavener studied social anthropology at Cambridge, England, then came to the United States for graduate work at Columbia University. He has carried out field work among Brazilian peasant fishermen, and has spent eighteen months working among the Karajá. He presently teaches at New York University College.

24. THE KARAJÁ AND THE BRAZILIAN FRONTIER

CHRISTOPHER J. TAVENER

This article examines the impact of Brazilian national society on the Karajá Indians of the Araguaia River in central Brazil, and focuses in particular on the role of the government agency charged with responsibility for Indian affairs. It is based on fieldwork done in 1966, 1968, and 1969.[1] I mention the dates because in 1967 this agency ceased to be called the Indian Protection Service (S.P.I.) and was reconstituted as the National Indian Foundation (FUNAI). I will generally refer to it as the S.P.I., which, after all, played the major part in the region up to 1969, rather than use both acronyms with chronological exactitude. I am not doing this for simplicity alone. By April 1969 (which was perhaps too early to judge) I could see little change in government activity or personnel on the Araguaia. Obviously the disassociation of the present Brazilian regime and its agency, FUNAI, from the sorry record of the S.P.I. must depend not on the mere extinction of a name and the replacement of some incumbent bureaucrats, but on visible achievements for and among the Indians.

The S.P.I., which was founded in 1910, established a post among the Karajá only after it had gained more than twenty years of experience among other Indian groups. But in 1932 Peter Fleming passed St. Isabel on the west bank of Bananal Island in his search for Colonel Fawcett and found this post, with its sewing school, deserted (Fleming 1942). This might have been taken as an omen, but President Vargas, apparently touched by the Karajá children whom he saw on his extraordinary visit to St. Isabel in 1940, decided to strengthen the Service (Ribeiro 1970:147). Another post was built for the Karajá at the mouth of the Tapirapé River. Today there are more than a dozen personnel at five posts, since two have been set up among the Javaé, the branch of the tribe now found on the eastern bank of Bananal, and one far to the north in the one remaining village of the other branch, called Ixãbiawa by the Karajá proper.

For a century now, the Karajá have been neither hostile nor particularly remote. The middle reaches of the Araguaia valley are flat and open, easily traversed on foot or horseback and even by jeep. Although they may be flooded at the height of the six-month rainy season, at this time one can use the river, which, lacking rapids, is never difficult to navigate. Civilian and government planes arrive weekly at St. Isabel from Goiânia and Brasília, and there are airstrips near three other posts. The climate is tolerable; in the dry season it is splendid enough to attract tourists from São Paulo and even New York.

Since there are a few more than one thousand Karajá, almost all concentrated in eight villages around Bananal, it might seem that sufficient time and opportunity have been available for the S.P.I. to have achieved something for them. But when FUNAI took over, even local officials who stayed on acted, and with reason, as if they would have to create new programs rather than continue with any old ones.

One can regard the lack of services rendered to the Karajá as a local expression of inherent weaknesses in the ideology and structure of the S.P.I. as a whole. These have been admirably examined by Darcy Ribeiro (1962, 1970: part 2) and Roberto Cardoso de Oliveira (1972: ch. 1–5) so my analysis of them here will be purposefully summary. Almost from its inception the S.P.I. has been hamstrung by lack of funds, and since 1934 it has lacked political autonomy, having been subordinated to the interests of the ministries of the army, labor, or agriculture. This subordination has continually hampered the development and efficacy of a group of experts, so that the successes of dedicated individuals, such as José da Gama Malcher, who fought for the creation of the Xingú National Park, appear as the exception rather than the rule. Besides, the mandate of the S.P.I. itself has never extended beyond the Indians despite the fact that in dealing with pacified groups it faces social systems and problems that include Indians and non-Indians alike. This last point brings us to the ideological contradictions of S.P.I. policy, which might hinder the development of effective action even if the requisite human, political, and financial resources were available. The Service was founded upon the ideal of respecting Indian culture, both by preventing incursions upon their traditional habitat and by limiting the activity of the S.P.I. among the Indians only to such humanitarian assistance as might maintain or ameliorate their standard of living without disruptive sociocultural consequences. Yet, at the same time, due first to Positivist philosophy and later perhaps to the necessity of appeasing those from whom it must obtain a mandate and funds, the S.P.I. accepted the premise that any Indian, given time and opportunity, would inevitably develop into a good Brazilian citizen. Thus, it follows that the best Indian program must be almost no program—and one that would take generations to implement at that—and the process by which an Indian becomes a citizen remains, like the S.P.I. philosophy, something of a mystery.

Let me illustrate what these basic weaknesses in policy and structure mean at the local level. The first example shows the relationship between the lack of sufficient legislative and executive power and the S.P.I.'s duty to defend the Indians' traditional habitat. Karajá villages are situated on both banks of the Araguaia and were before Brazilians settled the area. But only one post has been built on the western side, and for some years it has been under pressure from a powerful real estate and cattle company, which bought the land on which the post had been established despite Article 216 of the Brazilian Constitution. And despite pleas from the agent in charge of this post, the S.P.I. had not, by 1969, effectively established the Indian patrimony. Only on Bananal do the Karajá seem to enjoy protection under the law. In 1959 it was made a national park (Decree 47-470), and as such is administered under the New Forest Code of 1965 (Law 4.7771). This code establishes the principle (Article 3, ¶1) of maintaining the environment necessary to the life of Indian populations. Since Indians in Brazil are not legal persons, but wards of the S.P.I. acting for the federal government, the application of such a principle ultimately depends on the authority or local power of the S.P.I.[2] Unfortunately, the decree of 1959 gives authority over the park not to the S.P.I. but to the Parks Section of the Forest Service. Only these functionaries have the authority to punish the exploitation of the natural resources of national parks, which is expressly

prohibited in Article 5 of the Code. Since there are only two officials of the Parks Section on this island of almost eight thousand
square miles and they have no transportation, they can do precious
little. The cattle of Brazilian ranchers graze the savannas with impunity in their tens of thousands, and the fish in the island's lakes
and streams are similarly exploited, sometimes by dynamite. One
would think that fish were both a natural resource and part of
the environment necessary to maintain the life of the Indians, since
the Karajá depend on them for protein and income. However, being
neither man nor beast, the fish are protected neither by the S.P.I.
nor the Forest Service but, I was told, by a Department of Inland
Fisheries, which has never to my knowledge made its presence
known on the island. Furthermore, it happens that the only people
living within walking distance of the station of the Parks Section
are the Karajá of a large mission village, and they, unlike any
Brazilians, are prevented from exploiting certain natural resources.
The trees they wish to cut down are part of a riverine forest. Such
forest is specially protected under Article 2 of the New Forest
Code. Unfortunately there is only riverine forest on Bananal. I
think this amply demonstrates how the lack of authority hinders
the S.P.I. in their basic task of preserving an environment in
which Indians might survive. Furthermore, it suggests that without
a corps of functionaries expert in local conditions, the promulgation
of appropriate laws and systems of administration is unlikely.

Similar shortcomings limit the ability of the S.P.I. to maintain
or improve the Karajá's standard of living. For more than a generation, commercial fishing has flourished on the Araguaia. The
Karajá have developed this traditional expertise rather than gardening[3] to provide them with most of their small cash income. With
this they buy cloth, tools, and items valued by Brazilians such
as shoes and coffee cups, which not only give them pleasure but
allow them to save face. Although they still depend on their gardens
for root crops and fruit, for them commercial fishing has become
a way of life. But it is a livelihood that they do not control because,
since the fish is destined for urban markets, the enterprise demands
considerable investment by middlemen in riverboats, storage facilities, and trucks. Because of this the middlemen must operate on
a considerable volume, so they buy from both Brazilians and
Karajá, and not only fish, chiefly *pirarucú* (*Arapaima gigas*) and

some giant catfish, but also the skins of two species of caiman (*Melanosuchus niger* and *Caiman sclerops?*) and jaguars and wild-cats, which command relatively higher prices. Although I do not have exact figures, it is clear that the enterprise depends on Brazilian participation, since there are only about two hundred adult Karajá men and the Brazilian population of the riverine counties of this area is over forty thousand.[4]

It is a classic example of what Cardoso de Oliveira calls regional interethnic systems, and with reference to the role of the S.P.I. in such a system, it is interesting that he notes that they often reflect the phenomenon of "internal colonialism" (1972:97–100 and ch. VI).[5] In this case the development of a new frontier fails to raise the local standard of living because it is dependent upon, and ultimately controlled by, the more developed, metropolitan sector of Brazil.

Although local officials can and often do protect the Karajá in their transactions with middlemen, at least at the posts, the organization in no way controls the system as a whole. The point here, however, is not that the relative weakness of the S.P.I. at the federal level contradicts the thesis of "internal colonialism." In fact, in June 1968 yet another branch of the Ministry of Agriculture, the Brazilian Institute of Forest Development, passed down an executive order (No. 253) which may seriously affect the economy of the Araguaia. It was directed to an admirable national goal—that of limiting hunting of all fauna to authorized areas, species, and quantities (which remained unspecified), and strengthening animal husbandry as a means of deriving income and protein from animals. Such a goal makes ecological and financial sense in the long run, and it should be remembered that at the time the world press was suddenly concerned with vanishing animal species, and the Brazilian press with the declining proportion of meat in the Brazilian urban diet at a time when the economy was apparently developing.

But the final beauty of the order, from an administrative point of view, may also be the ruin of this local fishing industry, for the funds for the development of animal husbandry are to come from a 10% tax on income derived from hunting. It is not clear whether all involved—the hunter/fisherman, the local collector, and the middleman-trucker—must register and pay the tax. There is no doubt about the latter, since those who demonstrate investments in the legal hunting zones ("natural nurseries") can discount them against the tax. But middlemen were talking in 1968–69 of turning to other pursuits, as such tax advantages would be blunted by the further stipulation that any authorized zone must, after a specified period, remain a biological reserve for three consecutive years.

I think one could safely predict that without middlemen the industry must die, and that Karajá and Brazilian fishermen would probably suffer a diminished standard of living. Unfortunately I left the field before the hunting season of 1969, when the order was due to take effect. It is possible that the rumors and the threat died in the face of the difficulty or corruptibility of administration. Further research would be interesting. In any case, I saw no efforts to develop an alternative, such as animal husbandry, for those involved in the industry. It is hard to see how this could be accomplished. If the hunting and fishing complex is stricken here and in other similar situations, where will the money for such development come from? Furthermore, I would estimate that such investment as occurs will tend, for economic and political reasons, to remain close to the cities in projects like intensive pig and cattle raising.

So it seems that the Karajá standard of living is threatened by forces beyond the control of the S.P.I., by choices made by different interest groups in the federal government. Local officials were mostly unaware of the order, although one paragraph refers specifically to Indians. It says that "Indian populations are permitted to sell animal products and sub-products through the S.P.I. posts." If "through" is liberally interpreted as "under the moderately blind eye of" the posts, then in theory the Karajá could go on as before. But we have seen that this looks like a hollow concession. If it is interpreted narrowly as "only to" the posts—and the S.P.I. has often attempted to run posts as commercial enterprises (cf. Cardoso de Oliveira 1972: ch. VIII)—then the onus is squarely on the S.P.I. to provide the means for the Karajá to continue commercial fishing. Again, I saw no signs of any such activity one month before the fishing season of 1969 was due to begin.

However, it is true that in the spring of that year officials at St. Isabel, but at no other Karajá village, were spending considerable sums to create non-fishing jobs. Two characteristics of these jobs deserve to be noted. First, they seemed temporary. The Karajá were immediately involved in providing materials for, and building, sheds for a sawmill and a tile plant. One wonders what will happen when the buildings have been constructed and the scant supply of local timber and the small local market for tiles exhausted. This program resembles the schools which have been opened at several posts only to be closed, except when run by missionaries, because the S.P.I. seems unable to find a use for a literate Karajá. In sum, this new program seems like another example of my point that for the S.P.I., trying to resolve or avoid the contradictions inherent in its basic philosophy, too often the best program is no program at all. The second point is that within a month these jobs were creating considerable resentment among local Brazilians as rumors and facts circulated about the wages paid. Although they were rarely higher than the legal state minimum, wage work is scarce on the Araguaia. Undoubtedly, these two facets of the program are connected. Had the S.P.I. mounted a more significant program for the Karajá, local Brazilian resentment would have been stronger. As Cardoso de Oliveira has pointed out, any administration divided on ethnic lines will inevitably run into this problem in the face of an interethnic regional system, as we know in the United States (1972: ch. III and pp. 115–20). But the response of the S.P.I. must not be to minimize its Indian programs. It must struggle to find a solution for both Indians and local Brazilians alike, and in this case I believe that commercial fishing could be the best answer.

My final example illustrating the basic weaknesses of the S.P.I. as they affect local situations is in the fundamental field of medical care. If indeed it is committed to sensitive programs of acculturation and integration that might take generations to fulfill, then knowing full well the pitiful lack of tolerance for Old World diseases that Brazilian Indians suffer, the S.P.I. must surely be committed to a sound medical program. But among the Karajá the same masterful inactivity prevails in health care. In an emergency, in 1950, the S.P.I. called in a doctor who diagnosed the presence of tuberculosis and gonorrhea at St. Isabel (Cândido de Oliveira 1952). He recommended a regular visiting doctor, better medical supplies and facilities for isolation at the posts. In 1952, Dr. Noel Nutels recorded 71.1% positive reactions to tuberculosis tests at the same village, and recommended a national program to defend the Brazilian Indian against tuberculosis (Nutels 1952). In 1956, Darcy Ribeiro, once an official of the S.P.I., published his horrifying and detailed account of the medical and demographic effects of contact, which included data on the Karajá. The Protestant mission near the station of the park officials keeps excellent medical records which they willingly let me read. Of thirty-seven deaths recorded at the village between 1958 and 1968, ten were due to tuberculosis. Fifteen were ascribed to "causes unknown." It is possible that many of these were complications of malaria, which is the disease most frequently recorded in their treatment book, but is not identified as a cause of death. Of the thirty-seven who died, eighteen had come from other villages for treatment, occasionally from villages with S.P.I. posts. All these facts and recommendations were available to the S.P.I., but by 1969 only St. Isabel had received medically trained personnel, and these intermittently. Only St. Isabel had facilities for isolation. Two other posts lacked malaria pills. Their stock, apart from worm medicines, consisted almost entirely of free samples meant for urban practitioners and mainly appropriate for the treatment of nervous disorders. The results of such inattention are that in the thirty years since Lipkind conducted his census (Lipkind 1945) and the S.P.I. established its permanent presence, the Karajá population has diminished by almost exactly one third. Most of this loss has occurred among the Javaé where there are no mission villages. The population of the Karajá proper has remained stable, although it has been replenished by Javaé immigrants. It is not enough for local officials to argue that the Karajá are difficult to treat, because the missions have achieved somewhat better results. For instance, the proportion of children to women of reproductive age in the three Karajá villages of more than one hundred Indians is higher at the two mission villages than at the S.P.I. post of St. Isabel. One mission even supports a launch stocked with medicines that makes periodic trips up and down the Araguaia, offering some treatment to Indians and Brazilians. The failure of the S.P.I. in this field extends beyond the local level, in failing to use available information and to obtain adequate funds and personnel.

One might also measure the failure of the S.P.I. to fulfill its mandate by noting the fact that in the same period a large part of Karajá religious and ceremonial life, described by Lipkind (op. cit.) as the cult of the dead, has withered away or disappeared. Since these rituals are not actively discouraged, except at one mission, one could argue that their desuetude indicates that they no longer stand in a sensible relationship to the rest of Karajá life whereas until recently they were of central importance. *Heto-hokā* (big house), the most important of the four feasts which Lipkind regards as comprising this cult, served to symbolize and validate not only the ideal relations between the living and the dead, but also those between shamans, leaders, and ordinary men, between men's groups, between adults and initiates to the men's house, men and women, village and village, and people and animals. It involved a large number of people, including visitors from several villages, the elaborate use of body-painting, costume, dance, singing, buffoonery, and ritualized fighting, the building of special houses and enclosures, the preparation and consumption of a feast, the exchange of goods and services, including the lip-piercing of a set of young boys and the haircutting of the age set they were replacing, and many other things. The preparations took several weeks, the feasting at least two days, and the *rites de passage* of the latter set of boys into the men's house several days more.[6] This feast took place only once, in one village, during the time I was in the field. There were no visitors, costumes, feasting, or lip-piercings, and it was all accomplished in two hours. Admittedly this festival probably took place once in about four years in any one village, but the others in the cult were apparently annual. Of these, I witnessed an attenuated version of but one. The other Karajá ritual complex, the masked *aruanā* dances (Karajá, *ijaso*), survives. I do not think that these dance festivals, unlike the *heto-hokā,* ever *necessarily* involved inter-village cooperation (but see below, p. 450). The masks represent animal supernaturals, but for many Karajá today the significance of the festivals is limited to the manipulation of relations with women to the advantage of men. In other words, although the form remains and the dances still provide Karajá men with enormous physical exhilaration, here too their area of meaning has diminished. It should also be noted that the *aruanā* dance ceases when there is a death in the village, so in this case one can see that there could be a direct relationship between its continuity, both immediately and in a larger sense, and the quality of medical attention provided in any particular village. I found the *aruanā* dances extraordinarily beautiful, and so I regret the disappearance of Karajá ritual, probably more, I realize, than many Karajá for whom it has lost its meaning. But I am not arguing that the S.P.I. should do better for the Karajá in order to preserve their rituals, for they would become artificial.[7] I have discussed the decline of traditional ritual for two reasons. First, it is simply another part of the whole complex of rapid change that has occurred in Karajá culture since the arrival of the S.P.I. Secondly, I believe it is some measure of Karajá awareness of other changes, as those who no longer find sense in the rituals fail to participate.

It should not be any surprise, at this point, to learn that the typical Karajá opinion of the S.P.I. is *"não presta."* In view of my characterization of the basic failings of the S.P.I., the best translation of this phrase might be "good for nothing." Certainly I never heard a positive evaluation. I did hear the Karajá, not only when drunk, curse out all *torí* (non-Indians) in the area. However, despite their low opinion of it, I never heard them calling for the S.P.I. specifically to withdraw. Evidently it offers them something.

The answer to this paradox lies in the complexity of the total contact situation. The Karajá are no longer in a position to choose between life under the S.P.I. and their traditional independence.

This might seem surprising, as the Araguaia valley between Barra do Garças and Conceição encompasses some fifty thousand square miles, and the non-Indian population density is probably a little less than one person per square mile.[8] But the river dominates the settlement patterns of both populations. Any location on its banks provides competitive advantage, not only in terms of trade, transportation, and communication, but also in access to garden lands. All settlements of any size are situated on the riverbanks. However, every rainy season the Araguaia floods the countryside in all directions, so that the sites on its banks dry enough for permanent habitation are few and generally far between. Today each of these permanent sites is occupied, with the result that almost all Karajá settlements must be attached to some distinct segment of the Brazilian front—not only to S.P.I. posts, but also to missions, townships, and cattle farms.

The structure and designs of these Brazilian communities differ considerably, each affording different opportunities and problems for the Karajá. Consequently, while they cannot avoid contact they can at least, or perhaps I should say at most, choose between a variety of face-to-face contact situations. An analysis of shifts of residence has shown that most Karajá prefer missions and S.P.I. posts to cattle farms and townships, but when missions and posts are equally available, more choose the missions.[9] If, as the examples already given ought to have shown, the posts offer little, then perhaps one should conclude that the Karajá tolerate the Service either for its effects on the rest of the contact situation, i.e. outside the posts, or because the little offered at the posts is better than what must be suffered elsewhere. I am suggesting, in other words, that an evaluation of the S.P.I. as "good for nothing" may have another meaning beyond the two I have already illustrated. The second part of this paper will be concerned with demonstrating and analyzing the facts and opinions contained in this paragraph.

In support of my assertion that the Karajá seem to prefer the missions and the posts to townships and ranches, it is necessary to review some historical and cultural facts.[10] If the situation is hard for the Karajá today, they have suffered more in the past from private individuals, government agencies, and missions. In the eighteenth century the Karajá were raided for slaves by *bandeirantes* from the south. In the early nineteenth century, military posts were established along the Araguaia to hold political prisoners and common criminals and to control the relations between the Karajá and the *bandeirantes*. They often failed to control the latter, but decimated the Indians with diseases. When the posts were withdrawn, only a few hundred of perhaps more than ten thousand Karajá survived. When the first mission on the Araguaia was founded at Conceição by the Dominicans, many Karajá migrated there only to find that the mission was not able to protect them from raids by the Kayapó. Disease again was a serious problem. Records indicate that after the Karajá population reached its nadir around 1820, it probably increased quite rapidly during the rest of the nineteenth century when there was only intermittent contact, only to be cut back again around the turn of the century when permanent settlers, on whose heels the Dominican mission had followed, first drifted in from the north.[11] Since the current posts and missions have been established at least the Karajá have been free of concerted raids by Brazilians or other Indian groups, and the medical picture, while far from satisfactory, is undoubtedly better than it was.[12]

To say that the missions and posts do better today than missions and government agencies of former time does not demonstrate that the Karajá prefer them to the townships or ranches. But this can be inferred from other facts. Again, the historical record is illuminating. Despite the attacks they suffered, there is only one recorded instance of open hostility. Otherwise the Karajá seem to have sought out Brazilian settlements. Eighteenth-century accounts place the Karajá and the Javaé on the banks of Bananal and nowhere to the south of the island. In the second half of the nineteenth century, a steamship began to run down the Araguaia in an attempt to open up an internal trade route for Brazil. It was based in a town now called Aruanã, far to the south of Bananal. Many Karajá came to attend a school built there, and new villages sprang up all along the river, presumably at the fueling points between Bananal and Aruanã. Apparently the Karajá freely offered their services, acting as pilots and providing wood and material for repairs. Later, as I have mentioned, others moved north to the mission at Conceição. This was situated on a stretch of the Araguaia previously dominated by the Kayapó, or at least not occupied by the Karajá and separating them from the northern branch of the tribe, the Ixãbiawa. Many Ixãbiawa moved south to attend school at the mission, and when I visited them in 1966 I found some who knew even some Latin.

One can discern similar patterns in the more recent Karajá migrations. The villages established in the south remained there until very recently, becoming attached to small Brazilian townships on the riverbanks as peasant farmers, fishermen, and diamond panners slowly pushed downriver from the headwaters of the Araguaia in Goiás and Minas Gerais. In the north, however, no other villages were established much beyond Bananal, and when the activity of the mission at Conceição was curtailed the Karajá left the area and returned to Bananal. The difference between the south and the north followed from the different character of the Brazilian front in each zone. In the south, Brazilians engaged in mixed subsistence farming and diamond panning and so settled along the river. Thus they were accessible to the Karajá, and it was here that commercial fishing began. In the north the front was based on cattle raising, which demands little labor and encourages a dispersed pattern of settlement over the savanna regions away from the river.[13] Furthermore the Karajá retreat from the north coincided with the meeting of both fronts at the center of Karajá territory along the island of Bananal, so this move need not be seen as a retreat but as a continuing search for new opportunities. I think it is clear that the Karajá have actively sought out such opportunities throughout a century of contact, so their presence at missions and posts today need not be interpreted as a passive acceptance of inevitable necessity.

The current distribution of the Karajá population also indicates Karajá preferences. There are five S.P.I. posts and two mission villages, but there are more than a dozen small townships between Aruaná and Conceição and many more cattle farms and ranches. Between the two Javaé posts alone there are ten cattle farms. But there are few more than one hundred Karajá in the townships and less than half that number at cattle ranches, i.e. a total of about 15% of their population.

The Karajá only settle at large cattle stations. Since one or two men can manage up to five hundred head during most of the year and each animal needs up to fifty acres of pasture, there is little demand for Brazilian, let alone Karajá, labor, especially where cattle are only raised in small numbers in conjunction with subsistence agriculture (i.e. on cattle farms). At the ranches, which are typically financed with metropolitan capital and are rapidly displacing the mixed farms of the unprotected Brazilian peasant-squatters, there are enough cattle to create at least a seasonal demand for Karajá labor in such tasks as branding and repairing corrals. There is also a nucleus of ranch hands ready to buy fish from the Karajá for immediate consumption, since these cattle are never slaughtered locally but saved for the urban markets. Moreover it is only at the ranches that the owners find it pays to fence the cattle at all, so that it is only here that Karajá gardens and settlement sites can enjoy some protection from the cattle without considerable extra effort. It is doubtful that a large independent village could be set up at a private cattle ranch. There would be too many con-flicts over the use of the pockets of forest above the level of the floods, which are necessary for both gardens and cattle pasture in the wet season. I heard several such disputes at cattle ranches where there were but a few Karajá, and it was a frequent issue at the larger villages at the posts and missions. These also raise cattle, although unlike the private and secular establishments, they recognize some obligation to put Karajá interests on a par with those of the cattle. Finally, the owners of the cattle ranches tend to treat other resources such as timber and fish as private property, often so that they can hunt and fish for sport. Although as we have seen the legal right to such tenure in traditional Indian ter-ritory is dubious, the S.P.I. has never challenged such *de facto* control of large areas of the Araguaia valley. Moreover, though they probably do not know it, the owners of private rural proper-ties are entitled under Article 15 of another executive order of the Brazilian Institute for Forest Development (No. 252, June 1968) to prohibit any hunting on their lands. So it is no won-der that there are no large Karajá villages on such cattle ranches, and that all Karajá who choose such a place of residence are either refugees fleeing the threat of assassination in other Karajá villages, or marginal Javaé who have only recently moved to the main stream of the Araguaia.

The townships at which the Karajá live are, with the exception of Mato Verde, also on the fringes of Karajá territory. The Karajá living at such sites consistently have strong reasons for avoiding other Karajá, like fear of vengeance by witchcraft or assassination, or even of particular Brazilians living around Bananal. As on a ranch, the number of Karajá at any one township is small. The problem is competition for dry land for housing, since the resident Brazilian population is larger. Karajá houses tend to be at the end of the street where the levee begins to drop, and if there are more than one or two they are noticeably crowded. A feature that makes some townships unattractive is the frequent lack of medical help, and especially the fact that the available medicines are not free.[14] That the townships as a whole attract more Karajá than the ranches must be explained by the larger market for fresh fish, the greater opportunities for day labor throughout the year, and the easier access to the goods of civilization, from canned food to prostitutes.

The townships are also the only true Brazilian communities in the area with churches, elementary schools, stores, political activity, and so on. They lack the "greenhouse" atmosphere of the posts and missions (cf. Cardoso de Oliveira 1972:135), the cultural desolation of the ranches, and the obvious subordination to the limited interests of a few *torí* that characterize all three. Karajá residents generally take part in the *movimento* of the townships, and while some Brazilians are derisive and hostile, others act as good neighbors.

Ultimately it is not the missions nor the S.P.I. posts, but the townships and the ranches that represent the future of the Araguaia. So they must be regarded as a significant resource for the Karajá. Not surprisingly, the Karajá resident at the latter locations are more Brazilian in their dress, manner, and speech. The fact that they are often refugees should not mislead us; many other Karajá refugees simply move to other post and mission villages. Those that have chosen the townships and cattle ranches often struck me as more than usually industrious and enterprising. There are a few drunkards and some whom the townspeople regard as parasites, but it should be remembered that even in the townships job opportunities for anyone are not great.

I hope that in the last few paragraphs I have not only shown that the Karajá believe that the missions and posts offer them something—or at least that nearly 85% have good reason not to opt for the ranches and townships. There is still a handful living on isolated sites free of any Brazilians, but even these are engaged in commercial fishing, and because of the flooding and Brazilian immigration, such isolation is no longer an option for any significant number of Karajá. As I have said, today they can only choose between a variety of contact situations.

I also hope it is becoming clear that it would be wrong to evaluate the role of the S.P.I. by considering the S.P.I. and the Karajá alone. A few other local institutions should be mentioned at this point. There are airstrips not only at the posts, but also at some townships. Occasionally tourists and buyers arrive from the city, to whom the Karajá are able to sell clay dolls, feather headdresses, and miniature canoes and weapons as exotic souvenirs. The center of this activity is St. Isabel, where there is a surprising first-class hotel complete with air conditioning. The Karajá provide the hotel with fish and occasionally act as guides on fishing parties. St. Isabel, the original and senior post among the Karajá of a service dedicated to gradual change, is also an air force base, a stop for the National Airmail (CAN), and a base for the Central Brazil Foundation. This last was set up under Vargas (the president who is said to have wanted to strengthen the S.P.I.) as part of a campaign to open up the interior for Brazilian use. The Foundation now comprises a small colony of Brazilians right next to the Karajá village. Finally, a strange echo of the nineteenth-century steamboat can be found in the Botel, a floating hotel carrying mostly North American tourists gently downriver for a week of adventure and hours of importunity from Karajá souvenir salesmen. So the Karajá and the S.P.I. are not alone in a tropical paradise, but are bit players in a Wild West drama—complete with cowboys and fortune hunters, revivalists and renegades, homesteads and large ranches owned by absentee landlords, dame schools and whorehouses, with an occasional twentieth-century audience of tourists and the Brazilian armed forces, but largely without the law.

The diversity of the Brazilian front is matched to some degree by diversity within Karajá culture. Some of this variation has arisen out of the contact situation. In order to earn cash the Ixãbiawa, unlike any other Karajá, have turned to gardening. Remote from the established trade routes for dried fish, the Ixãbiawa produce manioc flour, which is less perishable, and fruit for the local market. Since trading is a male role on the Araguaia, Ixãbiawa men are more involved in gardening than even their Javaé counterparts, who have been regarded as the gardeners of the Karajá. Even unmarried men make gardens, to the amusement and consternation of Karajá bachelors. Their village is devoid of "traditional" artifacts; instead of making combs or dolls, women weave hammocks, again for the local Brazilians. This should be explained by the lack of tourists and buyers, for they exhibit a lively interest in non-salable traditions such as recounting myths. In St. Isabel, by way of contrast, one finds a false archaism. Much time is devoted to making dolls and feather headdresses and other decorative items. Here there are the largest numbers of tourists and buyers, but it was at St. Isabel that I observed the impoverished version of the *heto-hokã* feast (at which none of the participants wore costumes) and found the largest number of males engaged in non-traditional pursuits, acting as cooks, motorists, and odd-job men for the sundry local Brazilian interests.

Other differences between Karajá villages seem to have an autochthonous origin. As local natural resources vary, so does the advantage of developing certain skills and specializations. One finds larger and more elaborate sleeping mats in the northern part of Bananal, where informants say the *buriti* palm (*Mauritia flexuosa*) is easier to find. Since mat making is extremely time-consuming and *buriti* fibers much finer than alternative materials, one can safely say that women in this area devote much more time to it than any others. The Karajá say that it is only near the mouth of the Tapirapé that there are stands of *taquari* (*Chusquea* spp.), which they regard as better for arrow shafts than the more common *taboca* (gen. *Guadua*), and also supplies of *imbé,* an aroid, which makes the best binding for arrows. Here Karajá will lay up stores of these materials when they plan to visit other villages. Farther upstream there are the best supplies of canoe wood, and here men will make surplus canoes for sale or exchange. The quality of the oil-producing *babaçú* nut (*Orbignya oleifera*), of clay and coloring materials, of bow wood and bowstring fiber all vary from place to place, leading to a degree of village specialization and inter-village trade and thus affecting the allocation of time to other pursuits.

Thus Karajá in different villages have rather different interests, depending on the character of the natural and social resources. At the same time as we have seen, there is considerable migration from village to village, from post to mission, from township to cattle ranch, and so on. This suggests that while every site has a distinct potential, each site can tolerate only a small number of permanent inhabitants.

Nor is this situation merely a contemporary and transient phenomenon. Certain traditional aspects of Karajá culture indicate that the Araguaian environment has long discouraged permanent local settlements of any considerable size, even when fewer demands have been made on it. One can surmise that Karajá culture has contributed to the successful adaptation of the Karajá within the Araguaian ecosystem over many generations. Linguistic evidence shows that the Karajá have been a distinct population for more than a thousand years,[15] reflecting perhaps their specialization in

fishing when compared to the other more closely interrelated tribes
of the Macro-Gê stock who, while also horticulturalists, hunt in
the surrounding savannas. When contacted, the Karajá were numbered in the tens of thousands. However, their villages were limited
to a maximum of a few hundred inhabitants, divided into temporary fishing parties every dry season and relocated permanently
at least at the death of certain ceremonial leaders. Individuals and
related family groups must have moved more frequently. The
Karajá like to move away for at least a season when there is a
death in the family, or even before, since they tend to have more
respect for a shaman's curing abilities the farther he lives from
them. They lacked leaders with permanent secular authority, so
leaving the village was the easiest and often the only way to resolve
individual or factional disputes without bloodshed. Delicate rituals
of hospitality indicate that the reception of visitors and political
refugees was a common and critical occurrence. One could even
argue that the elaborate intermittent inter-village *heto-hokã* feast
on the one hand and the fastidiously replicated, continual, role-
providing character of intra-village *aruanã* ritual on the other facilitated the exchange not only of goods but also of *personae* between
villages differing in resources and opportunities, thereby creating
a larger and more resilient socio-economic system. All this points
to the conclusion that on the Araguaia where the flood waters
limit and separate habitable sites, permanent and peaceful settlement at any one location is not likely to be viable in the long
run without reliable ties to other populations, which can be acti-
vated in times of stress to provide refuge or materials or some
other means of relieving pressure by abuse or population growth
upon local ecosystems. Like the dominant feature of the natural
environment, population movement must be fluid and escape valves
must exist to relieve temporary blocks in the system.[16] This may
sound more like plumbing theory than anthropology, but I think
the simile is apt.

It is now possible to evaluate the role of the S.P.I. posts. What
is the major concern of the *encarregado,* the head of the post?
Not Indians, but cattle. Although we have seen that the interests
of the resident Karajá vary, at each and every post the *encarregado*
is responsible for a herd of cattle which is expected to raise money

for the S.P.I. Perhaps the herd was originally meant to provide work for the Karajá, but it would take an enormous herd to employ a significant number of Karajá, and they have preferred to earn money by fishing, making artifacts, or even gardening, in all of which ventures the S.P.I. has remained totally uninvolved. The failure of the S.P.I. to support rationalized commercial fishing is particularly unfortunate. It is of passionate interest to the Karajá, it has involved both Indians and Brazilians, it has encouraged the development of trade throughout the Araguaia valley, and finally it is the one area in which Brazilians show interest in and respect for Karajá skills since nets, guns, and motors demand more capital than a bow and arrow and a canoe and have disastrous ecological side effects which soon lead to diminishing returns.[17] Meanwhile, unfortunately, the lesser *encarregados* often show more than professional devotion to the cattle. Since their pay is miserable and never delivered to the post, they must find some local source of income. Some therefore raise their own cattle among or even out of the S.P.I. herd. This is hardly their fault, but it gives the Karajá a pretext for cynicism. So the Karajá and the S.P.I. are separated and not united by their labor. Cattle raising also serves to exacerbate relations between the posts and local Brazilian peasant farmers, most of whom are engaged in the same pursuit and are in competition for pasture.

As a junior member of a bureaucracy, the *encarregado* must also do paper work. It not only takes time, but tends to make the *encarregado* more attentive to the demands of his superiors and less so to the desires of the Karajá. This is especially true at St. Isabel, through which messages from the smaller posts must pass. Such work serves again to oppose the *civilizado* to the Indian since it has not occurred to the S.P.I. to train literate Karajá for such tasks, thus giving their spasmodic school programs some point. After all, at the age they finish school Karajá youths would not be required to work at traditional tasks, but they often desire income before their marriage, so it is possible that such jobs would be welcomed.

At the larger posts the *encarregado* is freed from some tasks by assistants such as cowhands and mechanics. But so long as they fail to attract Karajá to these jobs and have to bring in other Brazilians, the *encarregados* have to worry about making extra gardens to feed them or at least about obtaining land for the employees to work. When only swidden agriculture is possible and there is little suitable forest away from the riverbanks, every additional resident at a post makes considerable demands on local resources. Again, this can only serve to create hostility between Indians and S.P.I. officials, which will grow in proportion to the size of each population. At St. Isabel this is especially clear because there are many other Brazilian residents beyond the S.P.I.

It is fortunate then, in some respects, that the S.P.I. does provide but few personnel. But this is no advantage unless these few are extraordinarily trained in medicine, anthropology, agronomy, etc., so that a number of necessary roles can be performed by one or two individuals. Experience in cattle raising or estate management, which were the only obvious qualifications apart from connections of FUNAI appointees at St. Isabel in 1968–69, are simply not enough.

Even if it manages by default to limit its own population to a tolerable size at most posts, the S.P.I. tends to attract too many Karajá to reside permanently at a given site. This is a characteristic which they share with the missions and seems to arise out of their similar institutional structure. It is not simply because they are both there to attend to the Indians, and that doing a good job is easily confused with dealing with the largest possible number, which of course is easier if the Indians can be attracted to the posts. It also derives from the fact that for a post or mission, personnel are necessary. To keep the personnel, a certain minimum of facilities is necessary. The less the personnel have in common with the Karajá, i.e. to the degree that they come from the city or even the United States, the more expensive these facilities. Having tied up appreciable capital in fixed assets, neither the S.P.I. nor a mission is anxious for the Karajá to move away. The S.P.I. can use some legal authority to this end, if necessary, having little else to offer than the occasional slaughter of a cow from the post's herd. Missionaries may appeal to personal Christian ethics, and for those whom they cannot reach in this manner they too have cattle but more importantly good, free medicine. As of 1969 the S.P.I. posts had no mobile services; the Karajá had to come to them, and not vice versa.

To the degree that posts and missions remain fixed, there are and will be undesirable ecological, economic, and political side effects. At one mission garden land is almost exhausted and the situation can only deteriorate as the population grows. As long as the mission stays put, fresh forest land will be difficult to acquire because on one bank it is protected by the neighboring Parks Service (see above, p. 435), and on the other it has been cleared for pasture for a vast cattle ranch, driving local peasants onto the nearest available sites up- and downstream. At St. Isabel, some Karajá must be transported to their gardens by truck as they are now so far from the village. Here fishing too is becoming difficult; the Karajá eat species that elsewhere are passed over and buy and sell fish among themselves whereas in other villages they are freely exchanged. One ceremonial leader, in order to honor the request of guests for turtles, could only get them by sending trade goods by government plane to the Xingú! Another point that the S.P.I. does not seem to consider is that as it concentrates Karajá in one place, it becomes hard to find jobs for them all either at the posts or in local townships, and this generates conflict among the Karajá. Also as long as the posts remain fixed, the *encarregados* concerned with their cattle, and the Service as a whole without adequate transportation, communications and authority, it is very hard for S.P.I. officials to devote time to the delicate business of discouraging the settlement and growth of Brazilian populations on neighboring or distant sites, with reserves of forest for garden land, that might act as safety valves against some future crisis.

The *encarregados* actually worry with more immediate problems such as fencing cattle. The cattle must be kept out of the gardens and the village. There are never funds to fence the pasture. The only cheap solution is to fence the village, giving it the air of an internment camp designed to keep the Karajá in rather than the cattle out. The fence also serves as a visible barrier between the Indians and the local Brazilians, and symbolizes the S.P.I. tendency to treat Indians as exotic growths even in well-established interethnic regional systems. Cardoso de Oliveira has described this tendency as the "greenhouse" syndrome (1972:120).[18] I would like to draw attention here to something I shall call the "greenroom effect." These transparent yet significant barriers remind me of the theater. Some S.P.I. villages have the air of a row of dressing rooms as the Karajá, hearing a boat or jeep approach, rapidly don their showiest clothing and emerge ready to play some appropriate role. These roles are frequently more embarrassingly false if the Indians come out through the gates, like actors in the modern theater stepping into the audience. For us, the barbed wire backdrop would seem to denote a stark tragedy. But the Karajá play such scenes as if they were a comedy of manners, with reason, as we shall see, for the barrier is an accepted convention and this one is simply in the wrong place. For the outsider, however, their traditional life within the new confines of the village now seems, by contrast, less real, a worn-out convention, or, remembering Kroeber's famous opinion of Gê culture, as impalpable as a play within a play.

The *encarregados* see the fences as a tolerable necessity and point out with pride that they have encouraged the Karajá to maintain the traditional village plan. This is a long straight line of dwelling houses running parallel to the river, with an isolated men's house lying a good fifty yards behind, connected only by a dance track running back perpendicularly from the village. In effect it is a simple T-shape, but it is also a grid which provides the Karajá with what one might call a sense of moral geography. While men move freely up and down its vertical axis (the dance track), such movement is dangerous to women, who may not enter or even approach the men's house under pain of rape or of being ascribed the status of a village wanton. It is this danger and opposition which gives the *aruanã* dance its character and excitement, as women, respecting the authority of the spirit-masks, are enticed farther and farther away from the village. On the other hand, the horizontal axis of the T (the line of dwellings and the street running between it and the riverbank) is the one along which only women freely move.[19] If a Karajá man cannot conduct his business with other men at the men's house and finds it necessary to visit a home down the street, he finds it easier to approach via the men's house taking two perpendicular paths rather than a direct horizontal one.[20] This symbolizes that his business in the other home is purely business, i.e. a male activity, and that he is not there for amorous reasons. So when the *encarregado* for economy or his convenience decides to run the fence between the village and the men's house or to place the only gate at the end of the village street near his home, he is unwittingly complicating the maintenance of traditional

Karajá values even though the alignment of the village maintains its original form.[21] This is unfortunate, for S.P.I. officials often show an easy tolerance for Karajá rituals, values, and institutions such as the dances of the animal spirits, the village wantons, and the greater use of the sexes at the expense of the nuclear family as a basis for the organization of economic and ritual activity, all of which some missionaries openly regard as heathen abominations. But by their practice *encarregados* become less easily distinguished from missionaries, despite their good intentions.

What then is the answer to the original question of why the Karajá tolerate the S.P.I. despite their low opinion of it? Is it because of the quality of life at the posts, or because of the effect of the S.P.I. on the over-all quality of the contact situation? Framing the question more theoretically, is it the manifest or the latent function of the institution which offers the Karajá more? The posts do provide space for a greater number of Karajá than the townships and cattle ranches, so that some semblance of traditional village life, which demands at least about fifty people, is possible. And despite their lack of funds and training, some personnel demonstrate a level of sympathy and concern without equal among their local Brazilian counterparts. The posts also offer a minimum of medical and legal protection and occasionally other goods and services, at least more than the Karajá can find in the towns and ranches. But in all these qualities, with the exception of their tolerance and legal authority, the posts are outclassed by missions, and in other fields, as we have seen, the posts are far from perfect.

Is the manifest function of the posts more valuable? This might seem improbable. I have characterized the situation that they face as, broadly, a society of considerable diversity, delicately integrated in some respects and full of antagonism in others. One can summarize the activity of the posts within this system as an inappropriate replication of uniformity, a uniformity based on cattle raising and inadequate management that seems only to separate and antagonize the various participants in this interethnic system. While I believe all this is true, I would still maintain that the S.P.I. has a certain value for the Karajá and a function within a larger system, simply *because it is there* or rather because it is there and so are the missions. These two institutions are basically similar in structure and in their relations with the Indians, for whom therefore they must compete. For instance, missionaries seem to grow more tolerant in time. Undoubtedly there are human reasons for this, but I think the missionaries also fear losing the Karajá to the posts, where, as I have said, the personnel are more tolerant of, if only unconcerned by, certain aspects of traditional Karajá culture. At the same time the missions provide a level of services which the S.P.I. must try to emulate, for this is a cheaper solution than taking over the missions entirely.

One must not forget, however, that both institutions are ecologically, economically, and politically inadequate, whatever one may think of their values. So it is unwise to rest upon the conclusion that at least they do better for the Karajá than the townships and the cattle ranches. Unfortunately the latter, with all their poverty and injustice, represent the future of the Araguaia, as far as one can see. Brazil must achieve a major transformation of its rural sector. Otherwise the prospects for the Karajá and millions of others look extremely bleak, and the idea of regarding the transformation of Indians into Brazilian citizens as progress seems like a horrible joke.

NOTES

1. The research was funded first by the Frontier Research Project of the Latin American Institute, Columbia University, and then by the Doherty Foundation. I would like to thank all those whose help and encouragement made my fieldwork possible: Charles Wagley, my sponsor, and Robert Murphy, my advisor at Columbia, Eduardo Galvão and the staff of the ethnology section of the Museu Goêldi, Belém, Roberto Cardoso de Oliveira of the Museu Nacional, Rio de Janeiro, George Kimon of the Brazilian Foreign Office, and above all David and Gretchen Fortune of the Summer Institute of Linguistics, Brasília, and those friends on the Araguaia who would prefer to remain anonymous. I would also like to acknowledge the helpful discussion and criticism of all the members of the New York Seminar on South American Indians of an earlier version of this paper, especially that of Daniel Gross.

2. Under Law 5-484 of 1928. For a discussion of the confusion surrounding the civil rights of Indians, and their guaranteed and inalienable possession of traditional territory (Art. 216 of the Federal Constitution of 1946), see Ribeiro 1970, pp. 197–214. In October 1970, the President of Brazil

handed down a new Statute of the Indian, which while it may clarify Indian rights, does so largely by limiting them much further in the interests of national development. At the time of writing this statute had not yet been ratified by the Congress.

3. With the exception of the Ixãbiawa; see p. 448.

4. Based on figures from the 1960 census kindly provided by Sra. Magdalena Viera Pinto and the Information and Documentation Office of the Brazilian Institute of Geography and Statistics.

5. For ethnographic accounts of such systems see Melatti 1967, Laraia and Da Matta 1967, and Cardoso de Oliveira 1964.

6. Baxter n.d., which is based on the field notes of Kozak, who witnessed a *heto-hokã* feast in February 1954. See also Dietschy 1959 and 1962 for analyses of this feast based apparently on informants' accounts; and Dietschy 1960 for a rather different approach to the *aruanã* dance.

7. The S.P.I. has encouraged the Karajá to perform the *aruanã* dance for a Brazilian audience in Brasília. This I would regard as a doubly artificial form of the preservation of ritual.

8. See p. 437. Official figures actually indicate a population density considerably less than one person per square mile.

9. Tavener 1966. For instance, as an old village in the north of Bananal broke up, three quarters moved to a mission, one quarter to a post less than a day's journey away. In the central reaches of Bananal, villages average only thirty miles apart; I have known a couple paddle their sick family more than seventy miles downstream by nightfall. Neither inaccessibility, nor lack of resources (see p. 449 ff.), nor the persistence of old quarrels can explain this choice, since the mission village is split into factions. It seems that the explanation must be sought in the differences between posts and missions. Farther south, about three times as many Karajá have moved recently to Fontoura rather than St. Isabel, which again are close to each other, from other sites. The total number of inhabitants does not differ so widely. There are only three Karajá villages which have maintained a more or less continuous existence around one local site, or series of such sites; all the rest are recent settlements and resettlements.

10. These are taken from Krause 1911:173 ff., and the inferences on population growth and decline come from his sources and census, and also that of Lipkind 1945.

11. For an account of the early days at Conceição and particularly their effect on the Karajá see Ribeiro da Cunha 1945.

12. With the exception of the Javaé. I believe that, unlike the rest of the Karajá, the Javaé avoided contact during the nineteenth century, moving away from the banks of the eastern branch of the Araguaia into the center of Bananal. Thus it is only recently, as they have returned to the riverbanks to take part in commercial fishing, that they have been heavily exposed to non-Indian diseases, and are now suffering the sort of population decline suffered by the rest of the Karajá some generations ago.

13. For a sociological and historical account of this northern front, see Moreira Neto 1960, which is especially interesting for its description and analysis of the antagonism between townspeople/creditors and outback cowhand/debtors.

14. The Karajá who have recently arrived in St. Isabel from southern villages are often sick and seeking treatment. Cf. Cândido de Oliveira 1952.

15. David Fortune, in a personal communication, has told me that this can be calculated by glotto-chronology. For further information on the relationship of Karajá to Gê languages see Greenberg 1960, and on the interrelatedness of Gê, see Wilbert 1962.

16. In discussing the interethnic situation which involves the Tukuna, another Indian group living on a large river, Cardoso de Oliveira also introduces the concept of the S.P.I. posts as safety valves (1972: ch. III).

17. *Pirarucú* take five years to mature sexually, and lay relatively few eggs. The survival of the next generation depends a great deal on protection of the young by at least one parent. Shallow water is preferred for breeding, so on the Araguaia *pirarucú* are often found not in the main stream but in closed lakes or small inlets. For all these reasons, and of course their size, only a few will be found, and even fewer must be taken, at any one location. See Fontenelle n.d. The Karajá did use nets when the *pirarucú* was consumed at *aruanã* feasts. Presumably this was suitable when the demand was so limited. Since the advent of competitive commercial fishing, which lacks such ritual controls on demands, they have not used these nets. See Schultz 1953.

18. Cardoso de Oliveira implies earlier in the same article (1972: ch. VII "Problems and Hypotheses Concerning Inter-ethnic Friction") that such a greenhouse is, of course, the creation of the gardener, not the plant, with the implication that the significant differences to be seen inside a post greenhouse do not derive from the variety of exotic Indian institutions, but rather from the culture of the Brazilian authorities/gardeners. Thus as a mission or post grows, and becomes more of a Brazilian community, institutions like the patron-client relationship appear, implying of course a number of competing patrons, each with his subordinate and competing clients. At St. Isabel, where this is most developed, there must be at least half a dozen Karajá clients, each looking to his particular patron for support and to other Karajá for followers. Even in the smaller villages, the appointed chief can be seen as a client of the *torí*, competing with traditional officeholders and their factions. Cf. Cardoso de Oliveira 1972: ch. VII, 93–97, and ch. VIII, 136 for a fuller discussion of the problems of patronage, power, and conflict in these situations, and for Brazil in general see Leeds 1964. Leeds mentions the crucial importance of journalists in the informal Brazilian political system: it was a journalist who was the patron of the Karajá Arutana in the following story, whose implications I shall allow to speak for themselves:

THE NEW YORK TIMES
SUNDAY, FEBRUARY 19, 1967

BRAZILIAN INDIANS
OUST TRIBAL CHIEF

BRASILIA (Reuters)—The world's most unpublicized coup d'état has taken place on Bananal, a jungle island deep in the interior of Brazil.

Arutana, a tribal leader, ousted his cousin, Ataualpa, "dictator" of the Caraja Indian tribe for the last 26 years, as ruler of the island.

Brazilians learned about the change when Chief Arutana described the coup on a television program.

He said that the Caraja tribe had a tradition of choosing its leaders for skill in hunting and fishing, but Ataualpa was old and almost blind.

Ataualpa, he added, was appointed chief in 1940 by the late Getulio D. Vargas, then President of Brazil.

Arutana said that he had been voted into office on a three-point program—no drinking of cachaca, a fiery cane spirit, good relations with white men, and no exploitation of the island by outsiders.

Bananal, with a population of 1,500, lies in the Araguaya River, a tributary of the Amazon.

19. Residence upon marriage tends toward matrilocality. Karajá women are not only more likely to be related by ties of kinship than the men of any one village, but they will emphasize that they are related in this way, whereas the men play down their kinship ties, and validate their membership in a particular village by emphasizing their participation in non-kin-based men's groups and men's house activities. Cf. Murphy and Da Matta in this volume.

20. For discussion of the deceptive use of pathways for similar reasons among a Xingú tribe, see Gregor 1969.

21. For discussions of the significance of village shape among South American Indians see A. G. James 1949; among the Gê, Lévi-Strauss 1963: ch. VIII, and among the Karajá, Dietschy 1962.

Introduction to Weavers of Otavalo

Too often when we read about native peoples in South America and elsewhere, we are confronted with a virtual obituary of that people as a distinct entity or we learn of the factors which are leading to its imminent demise. Many readers will be pleased by this relatively optimistic report on the Otavalo people of Ecuador, a highland group which has exhibited great vitality and strength against seemingly insuperable forces. In his original article, Frank Salomon gives us a sensitive and very complete account of this people from the earliest known sources to the present. In his conclusion he not only challenges some commonly held notions regarding the inevitability of assimilation or destruction, but he also suggests some of the reasons why the Otavalo have been able to survive as a cultural entity. He also injects some very relevant opinions regarding the nature of contemporary culture change.

When dealing with the indigenous societies of South America, just about the only thing of which we can be absolutely certain is change. This applies as much to societies like the Otavalo who have been incorporated within state-organized societies for hundreds of years as to tribal Indians living deep in isolated jungle areas in the Amazon basin. All anthropologists accept the notion that the nature of a particular culture is intimately bound up with the environment in which it lives. Some believe that culture itself is best explained as an adaptation to environment taken in its broadest sense, including not only the natural habitat but also surrounding societies and technology.

It is now evident that environmental change is taking place at an unprecedented rate throughout the length and breadth of South

America. These changes include sociopolitical changes at the national level, the expansion and intensification of agricultural and extractive economies, the construction of new communications and transportation links, the increasing availability of manufactured items, changes in diet and the transmission of communicable diseases. There is not a single region of South America untouched by one or more such changes. Insofar then as their cultures are adaptive to environment, all the peoples of South America, primitive and modern, urban and rural, are undergoing cultural change.

For those societies remote from urban centers still organized primarily as tribal peoples these changes are often abrupt and brutal. The very physical survival of the culture bearers is often threatened and outrageous incidents of exploitation, official indifference and even massacre have been reported. In those areas where traditional peoples are living in permanent contact with national societies, speak the national language and are enmeshed in the national economic system, the impact of change is different. In addition to incidents of discrimination and exploitation, traditional societies are undergoing a process of assimilation whereby they become a part of the national rural lower class. Along with this comes a process of cultural homogenization in which centuries-old traditions and customs are set aside in favor of "modern" customs.

The modification of distinctive native lifeways is, to a large extent, irresistible, given the inevitability of environmental change just mentioned. But a few voices now raise the question of whether *complete* assimilation and the resulting extinction of native lifeways is desirable or beneficial to the peoples involved. Curiously, strong arguments for the preservation of diversity have more frequently been made by environmentalists concerned with the extinction of non-human species. The question of cultural survival is scarcely touched in much of what is written about South America or the environment in general. Are there any arguments in favor of striving to maintain cultural diversity and autonomy among human populations for their own sake? Do we count among basic human rights the right of a people to remain different? The rapid spread of a relatively homogeneous culture associated with urban-industrial society poses this question very urgently. How shall we respond as anthropologists and as human beings?

Frank Salomon was an undergraduate at Columbia University and did graduate work in sociology at the University of Michigan. Salomon became interested in Otavalo while staying at the Universidad Central del Ecuador in Quito during 1967. Primarily interested in ethnohistorical research, he is now pursuing further graduate studies at Cornell University.

25. WEAVERS OF OTAVALO

FRANK SALOMON

"I never saw a race of finer looking people than an assembly of Otavaleños on a Sunday," wrote an English visitor to the Ecuador of a century and a half ago (Stevenson 1825: vii, 347), and many other travelers in the Ecuadorean highlands, from Cieza de León in conquest times up to the anthropologists of our own, have likewise admired Canton Otavalo as the home of a people whose prosperity and ethnic pride stand out handsomely amid the Andean spectacle of misery. Today textile merchants from Otavalo, neatly dressed in white pants and shirts under gray or blue ponchos, wearing broad-brimmed hats over long braids, travel as far as Argentina, Colombia, Panama, and even Miami in the conduct of a weaving economy which has distinguished Otavalo as far back as documentation reaches. Yet Canton Otavalo, a spacious, fertile valley about thirty-five miles north of the capital city of Quito, looks like anything but a modern manufacturing center; its textile economy remains firmly embedded in an indigenous ("Indian" by the local criteria, Quechua speech and dress) peasant culture which cottage industry has strengthened rather than supplanted.

This symbiosis of a manufacturing economy tied into national and even international market structures with a localistic agricultural system and a community structure that resists out-marriage, permanent out-migration, and the erosion of native norms, is not entirely unique. Several other peoples of the Ecuadorean sierra have invented functionally parallel adaptations to repeated conquest (Salz 1955:128; Casagrande 1969:6–7) and, like the Otavalans, have intermittently resisted Hispanic domination with violence. But this best-studied and best-developed example of a smallholding-cum-cottage industry adaptation offers a particularly impressive instance of the occasional ability of small-scale social and economic formations to survive, and even take advantage of, a ponderous succession of superimposed large-scale systems of domination.

So Otavalo is of double interest to the people of the world's richest nation. First, it serves as a counterexample to the popular stereotype of Indian societies as hermetically sealed, static, and historically doomed, a stereotype which the anthropologists' preference for remote and unacculturated societies has done little to erase. Otavalans, like the vast majority of both South and North American Indians, belie this notion. They are not a tribe but a regionally distinct ethnic group with a four-century history of intimate culture contact; to study them is to see that, increasingly, indigenist studies must belong to the social anthropology of complex societies. Second, Otavalo contradicts the steamroller image of modernization, the assumption that traditional societies are critically vulnerable to the slightest touch of outside influence and wholly passive under its impact, devoid of policy for coping with it beyond a futile initial resistance. The view of modern forms of social organizations as a dynamic force acting on the inert mass of older societies, however benevolently voiced, is a reflection of imperialist ideologies of "progress." A post-imperialist social science must embody the view from the village as well as that from the metropolis; it must recognize the possibility that what looks like irrationality or conservatism from the master's point of view may be, from the victim's, an activist response to the social problem posed by conquest. Otavalo demonstrates particularly clearly the dynamism of some outwardly traditional societies.

My study of the Otavalan adaptation began with an attempt to gather from ethnographic sources more than what my short visits could teach me about the textile industry in its present form, and the resulting synchronic view forms the first part of this article. But in following up the origins of market weaving it became clear that the Otavalan market of today is a successor to a long history of local textile economies. The region's cottage industry has been drafted into the service of each of the imperial and national systems that have in turn subjugated native Ecuador. Yet in certain ways Otavalo's productivity, at the same time as it has beckoned exploiters, has enabled it to endure oppression and contempt more successfully than most Indian cultures. This history is the subject of the rest of this paper; the emphasis of the historical presentation is upon pointing out events which have contributed uniquely to Otavalo's integral survival and on suggesting the conditions of its relative good fortune in recent times.

THE VILLAGE IN THE NATION

Aníbal Buitrón, Gonzalo Rubio Orbe, Elsie Clews Parsons, and the collaborators of the Instituto Ecuatoriano de Antropología y Geografía have supplied a quartet of thorough Otavalan village ethnographies; the first two are native sons of the area, and, by their sensitivity to the differences among the Canton's villages (*parcialidades*), afford not only representative or typical community portraits, but also explain the directions and range of variation among communities. Joseph Casagrande and his associates have, since 1966, been furthering the comparative study of highland Ecuadorean villages. From these and many less comprehensive sources there emerges a composite picture of the Canton as a many-sided reality. Depending on what interests us, we can see it as a vast multitude of tiny family subsistence units, each striving for autonomy, or as a constellation of village communities, each an endogamous band of families, or as a single centralized market system in which all the villages act as specialists in a regional economy, or as a regional unit, political or economic, integrated into overarching national and international institutions. To accommodate all these realities, I have pictured it as a nest of systems-within-systems, a set of concentric productive and political units with the nuclear family at the center.

It is a commonplace of political science that the building of national political and economic institutions demands the integration of old, local systems into bigger, newer ones, even at the price of violent and politically explosive breakup and reconstitution. If we look at the process from the point of view of the traditional peasant, however, and not from that of the state-building elite, the problem appears quite different: how can local collectivities—the family, the village—arrange their relations with the spreading and deepening national institutions in such a way as to protect their own independence and security? What appears to urbanites as traditionalism, stubbornness, or irrational identification with the land is simply the peasants' way of doing exactly what the nation-builders are also trying to do, namely, restrict their dependence to resources over which they have some influence. This is the question to which the Otavalan farming-manufacturing complex is an answer. In the terms of the nest analogy, how is the tiny central unit to relate to the changing demands of the larger systems around it?

I. The Farming-Weaving Household. Canton Otavalo comprises a high, well-watered valley, walled by extinct volcanoes and freshened by deep, cold lakes. A railroad and a highway connect the city of Otavalo, administrative seat of the region, with Quito to the south and Colombia to the north. Most of the city's 8,600-odd people are white (*blanco,* more a cultural than a racial designation) or mestizo. The remaining 37,000 Otavaleños form an overwhelmingly agricultural and Indian population dwelling on family farms in rural *parcialidades* (Jed Cooper 1965:15).

The farming-weaving household, at the center of the nest of structures, is the smallest and the most enduring of Indian socio-economic institutions. Almost as in Incaic times, families cultivate their plots with wooden spades, digging sticks, and hoes that differ from their ancient prototypes only in their metal sheathing. Dependent on the plot for all their food except spices and a few vegetables, they devote tireless labor to its intensive cultivation. The commitment to land is fundamental; other involvements in larger systems "succeed" only insofar as they enhance and protect the family holding. Husband and wife own the plot jointly and each wills half of it to his or her chosen heirs. Land is alienable property in a sense similar to the white understanding of property, but its emotional and prestige value is so great that families almost never sell out. Children live with parents until they inherit land or marry an inheritor. Those who lack land or cannot farm attach themselves to landed households in a variety of adoption relationships appropriate to paupers, orphans, infirm people, or the very old (Rubio Orbe 1956:372–76; Parsons 1945:33–38).

The farming household, which we have been considering as the smallest unit of the subsistence economy, is also the unit of textile production; weaving takes place almost exclusively within the walls of the home. In weaving, unlike farming, technology is varied and as modern as circumstances allow. For traditional-style woolens weavers use a belt loom of pre-Hispanic design, but families which weave for the market as well as for village consumption also own wooden frame looms, and most augment the portable spindle with Spanish-style spinning wheels. Families divide the labor roughly by sex and age (for instance, spinning on the wheel is a masculine job, while spindles are women's tools), but each individual can do several tasks. The day's work consists of many short shifts at various textile and agricultural jobs: "for them, rest consists of exchanging one task for another" (Buitrón 1947:52). (A fine photographic record of weaving technique appears in a children's book by Bernard Wolf, *The Little Weaver of Agato*.) Some families especially active in the textile trade hire help, usually landless neighbors, to do piecework, and a few maintain workshops in town near the market, but the true textile factories (Otavalo has had three in recent times) are always *blanco*-owned. Indian factory hands also own or rent family plots; there is as yet no Otavalan textile proletariat.

Technical arrangements and the division of labor within the family do not vary much from place to place within the region, but the prosperity of families and the degree of their involvement in textile trade do vary a great deal, not only between *parcialidades,* but even within them. In some places the typical home is a spacious building with a tile roof and broad fields, while in others the landscape of thatched huts and exhausted plots hardly differs from the scenes of misery characteristic of debt peon settlements. The overall differences between Otavalo and poorer regions, as well as the differences in wealth between and within its settlements, all arise from Otavalo's complex land tenure situation.

The parts of the valley vary sharply in the extent and quality of farmlands. Valley-floor land is the most fertile, producing squash, vegetables, corn, and beans; higher slopes yield wheat and barley, while the cold, foggy grasslands over 11,000 feet are good only for quinoa, tiny potatoes, and pasture. Nowhere is land abundant enough for weavers to grow their own wool; it is brought from regions farther south (Parsons 1945:16–26; Collier and Buitrón 1949:33). Position in the valley powerfully affects the fortunes of a family or village, specifically, the degree to which it can enter into the cottage manufacturing economy. Farmers whose holdings extend up the poorer slopes must sow and harvest different fields at different times. Extra work then consumes time potentially useful for weaving, and poverty precludes saving money for investment in crafts supplies (Buitrón 1947:45–67). Buitrón holds this to be the chief determinant of the growth of cottage industry. Within the single parish of Ilumán, the weaving industry sorts itself out into weaving households dwelling on the lower, richer fields and families upon the higher slopes who spin thread to sell to weavers (IEAG 1953:163).

Although the area overall can be considered a zone of small-holding peasantry, land is far from uniformly distributed, and the quantity as well as the quality of land a family owns affects its place in the textile economy. Not all Otavalan farmers own the land they cultivate, and although nearly all those who do own land fall into the *minifundio* bracket—holdings too small to yield a complete livelihood for a family—there is plenty of variation within that bracket. For instance, Gonzalo Rubio Orbe found that in Punyaro, a *parcialidad* where land is scarce, "the distribution of lands is irregular: while there are families having two, two and a half, or three *cuadras* [that is, 1.4 to 2.1 hectares], many have a quarter, or less than a quarter, of a *solar* [that is, under .04 of an acre]." There are 23 landless families (in Punyaro), sixteen of them homeless and dwelling two or three families to a roof (Rubio Orbe 1956:31 and 108n). Seventy-six percent of Punyaro families have less than half a *cuadra,* that is, under .36 hectare (Rubio Orbe 1956:108).

Those who own only *microparcelas* too tiny to live off make do with a variety of other tenures. Some rent extra plots; a more common arrangement is *partido,* sharecropping for an absentee owner. "Collective or communal property is completely unknown in regard to land," Rubio Orbe reports, because, given the custom that only landholders or renters are marriageable, "there is not enough land to provide any. Punyareños consider some brushland in the ravines communal, so as to avail themselves of the firewood. But it's not unusual for a neighbor to declare himself the owner" (p. 31). Pasture land must be sought afar, usually at a price.

In Otavalo as elsewhere minifundism goes hand in hand with latifundism. Yet Otavalo's latifundia appear scarce and precarious when compared to those farther south in the Andes. Several big farms employing landless Indians do own tracts of the valley's finest land; in Punyaro when Rubio Orbe studied it, for instance, absentees owned (but did not cultivate) fields so rich and convenient to the city of Otavalo that Punyareños had no hope of buying them (Rubio Orbe 1956:110–11). And in the 1940's even Peguche, among the most prosperous *parcialidades,* had a few families that farmed only *huasipungos,* small plots of hacienda property allotted in payment for heavy hacienda labor obligations (Parsons 1945:8). In spite of these facts, however, big valley farms stand out by their growing weakness more than their power. Buitrón (n.d.:36) sums up this situation, so contrary to Ecuadorean and foreign stereotypes of highland agriculture: "A good part of the most fertile and best situated lands still belong to the haciendas. But little by little the Indians are buying them up, first the high grasslands, later the hillsides around the valley, and finally the valleys themselves, in short, the whole hacienda . . . abandoned and uncultivated for a long time, [hacienda lands] have been plowed and sown at once on passing into Indian hands." In another study (Buitrón and Buitrón 1945:196) the same observer illustrates the momentum of advancing minifundism: "The Indians of Pucará (another *parcialidad*), with a white man from Otavalo as an intermediary and backer, tried to buy the hacienda of Santa Rosa. They had already offered the hacienda owners 130,000 sucres, a pretty high price in the opinion of everyone. While the sale was being negotiated, to the intermediary's great surprise, about a hundred Indians came to his house to see him one afternoon. They had come from the *parcialidad* of Cumbas, near the hacienda in question, to tell him that they did not want Indians from other places in their territory, much less whites. Each of the hundred had contributed 2,000 sucres and they had already bought the hacienda for 200,000 sucres." In Punyaro, on the other hand, local bidders lost out to people from the textile-wealthy *parcialidades* of Peguche and Ilumán in nearly all of the seven hundred transactions that dismantled a neighboring hacienda; this suggests, as we will see later, that the wealth generated by weaving produces social stratification among localities. Otavalo has moved so far in the direction of minifundism that, in 1946, only 31% of residents surveyed did any work on land other than their own, while for the highlands as a whole, about one third of the population works *exclusively* on land owned by others; many more work both their own and rented fields (Salz 1955:32, 36). But the reasons for the breakup of haciendas, a tendency of which Otavalo is only the most conspicuous example, are not well understood. Beate Salz (1955:41) offers three explanations. First, haciendas are in general low-profit businesses because of high irrigation and other service costs, hazardous production, and scarce labor (crafts, urban labor, and seasonal work in the lowlands all compete for the land-hungry worker's time). Second, the farm products market is unstable (less stable, for instance, than income from city rental properties). For instance, in 1942 the coincidence of new price controls on meat with rising corn prices gave incentive for a shift in land use from pasture to crops, but, since an independent farmer can hardly be persuaded to turn peon, hacienda owners failed to raise from the countryside labor forces adequate to the greater need for field hands. Third, cultural change has demoted the hacienda owner; today, "everyone wants to have a Chevrolet and live in Quito." The knowledge that Indians will pay high prices for land encourages landowners to follow this impulse. It might be added as a fourth reason that Ecuadorean legislation now mandates the government to redistribute underused lands, a law which, even when not immediately applied, acts as an incentive for absentees to sell while the selling is good.

The flow of land from latifundists to Indians has taken place through money transactions, typically with *blanco* intermediaries such as lawyers, banks, or government agencies. Thus land hunger, an expression of desires for local autonomy, has paradoxically brought Otavaleños into closer contact with the large-scale institutions of the nation-state. It has put them in need of large amounts of cash and given a seeming incentive to mestization or abandonment of the community. It has erased all possibility of a retreatist or enclave adaptation. Yet, unlike similar encounters in other places, it has not weakened the land-based household by draining its manpower or vitiating the commitment to Indian-ness; and this rare outcome, as we will see later, arises from the historical opportunity to turn a craft tradition of long standing to a new end, the piecemeal reconquest of the land.

II. The Parcialidad. Although it approaches economic independence, the farming household has economic as well as purely social ties to the *parcialidad* (village, a local usage) of which it

forms a part. At harvests and house-raisings it depends on cooperative work parties. Reciprocal arrangements also take care of
many smaller tasks. The *parcialidad* is an inward-looking system.
Buitrón and Buitrón (1945:205) found that, of civilly registered
marriages (which include virtually all marriages), 93% of those
contracted between two Indians united a man and a woman of
the same parish, while the comparable figure for *blancos* was 45%
and for mestizos 25%. The parish (*parroquia*) encloses several
parcialidades, but most marriages occur within one village or
between contiguous ones. By contrast relations between non-
neighboring *parcialidades* are remote; the weekly market in
Otavalo City affords an exchange of greetings and specialty products, but villages have ideological traditions of localism, and the
entire history of the region is full of intervillage conflicts, some
legalistic, some violent. Ritualized fighting between villages is a
feature of the largest annual festival.

The *parcialidad* as such is not an administrative unit, but an
unofficial subdivision of the *parroquia;* the nine parochial towns
in Canton Otavalo form subsidiary centers of non-Indian population and minor governmental and commercial centers. The bulk
of Indians live in *parcialidades* of eighty people to several thousand, each consisting of a tract of land with houses scattered
among the fields rather than forming a nucleated village. Foot-
paths, ravines, or rows of cabuya plants demarcate *parcialidad*
and property boundaries. Buitrón and Buitrón (1945:192) takes
a rigidly indigenist approach in defining the *parcialidad* as "a portion of territory perfectly delimited, whose inhabitants form perfectly homogeneous groups, not only in regard to material culture,
but also in social and economic organization." In fact, however,
many *parcialidades* also house a culturally distinct mestizo minority which rarely joins Indian families in marriage or cooperative
labor. In many places, the mestizos are poorer than Indians and
looked down on with the same contempt that Indians endure in
most of Ecuador.

The *parcialidad* is held together largely by kinship and cooperation; its authority structures are few and not mandated to exercise
control outside their narrow specialties. In no single individual are
power and authority decisively combined; even the landlord, if
the area is one where much land is rented, exercises domain only

in specifically economic dealings, a sharp contrast to the status of the *hacendado* ["landlord"] as ultimate secular authority observed in other parts of Ecuador (Casagrande 1969:5). The magic power of the *brujo* ["healer"] commands respect in personal matters, but he is no politician. Insofar as the *parcialidad* has any general authority roles, they are representative of more encompassing social structures, the state and the church. Traditionally, each village had at least two *alcaldes* ["mayors"], *"de doctrina"* or religious, and *"de justicia"* or political. These unpaid part-time officials, appointed by the priest of the parish and the *teniente político* ["political chief"] respectively, were to extract labor for various imposed duties such as maintaining churches and roads, and intervene as justices of the peace in minor disputes, tasks which earn more opprobrium than authority. The village *cabildo* or council of aldermen, which the *alcaldes* were supposed to organize, rarely functioned well and in some places became a dead letter (Rubio Orbe 1956:337, 341).

III. Regional and National Integration. Looking at the social location of the Otavalan as a spot in the center of several nested systems of trust, power, and authority, there appears a discontinuity between arrangements at the village and at the regional and national level. Even when deeply enmeshed in extralocal markets, the locality functions not as a political subsystem of the bigger system, but, as much as possible, in isolation from it. This preference finds face-to-face expression in the social distance norms Indians uphold (and which white Ecuadoreans are in no hurry to ease) in dealing with white officials and buyers at market: stiff, taciturn courtesy and a complete absence of spontaneity or joking prevail. The relation of local community to the state remains passive and peripheral.

So long as land supplies could meet the demand posed by natural increase, this preference for enclave living was non-problematic. However, land hunger profoundly endangers autonomy, and the *minifundio* complex here, as in many parts of Latin America, seems to generate irreversible social change. New plots can be obtained in only a few ways: increasing sharecropping and peonage; land invasions and political revolution, as occurred in Cochabamba, Bolivia; or purchase of lands on the open market. The first implies loss of autonomy; the second a gamble on the chances of violence or politics, and, in the event of victory, a commitment to national political institutions; the third a commitment to whatever will give the community a reliable source of cash. The first of these alternatives has been the commonest all over the Andes, while the second stands out much less in Ecuadorean history than in that of Boliva or Perú. But Indians in several parts of the highlands besides Otavalo have moved in the third direction. Ralph Beals (1966:78) describes a village near Quito which adapted to a land squeeze early in the twentieth century by turning to the growing of fruit and vegetables for the city market, so as to expand enough to remain self-sufficient. In Cañar and Azuay provinces during the 1940s Indians developed the manufacture of what the world knows as Panama hats in order to escape from desperate landless poverty (Salz 1955:104n). Throughout the Ecuadorean sierra, Indians have entered onto the stage of national history almost exclusively in economic roles.

In contrast to its weakness as a political center, the city of Otavalo, and especially its market place, has long acted as an economic nexus unifying the whole Canton. Before dawn every Saturday, families from every *parcialidad* hike into town with their week's production of textiles, basketry, pots, and produce to do a few intense hours of business and then enjoy an afternoon of drinking, dancing, watching medicine shows, socializing, and eating meats or other delicacies at the stalls in the plaza. Insofar as this exhaustingly lively gathering exchanges mostly local specialty products, it functions as what Eric Wolf calls a sectional market (Wolf 1966:40), a central point among interdependent but autonomous villages "scattered around it in a radial fashion, like the planets of the solar system around the sun." Like planets with satellites of their own, the parochial towns conduct smaller markets, partly remnant sales, the day after the Otavalo City market (IEAG 1953:65). But the weekly market also works as a link integrating the villages into the larger economic system from which they are politically and socially separated by a racial animosity even more intense than that familiar to North Americans, as well as by class and language barriers and the Indians' own disinclination to take part. Buyers of Otavalan craft products include Ecuadorean mestizos, both as consumers and as middlemen, some *blancos,* and an ever-increasing number of foreign, chiefly

North American, tourists. In turn, manufactured goods from other countries and other parts of Ecuador—pots and pans, glazed stoneware, dyes, sewing machines—find Indian buyers, although the average rural family buys only one of each item per generation (Rubio Orbe 1956:49–58). Most prominent among extralocal goods are the raw materials of weaving, tools, and trimmings.

At the market the display of village-made products far exceeds that of manufactured goods; Indians have not followed the mestizos in becoming eager consumers of *blanco*-style goods. Money made at market tends to be saved for land buying. Otavalans deal regularly with mestizos and *blancos* of all classes. They travel all over Ecuador and into neighboring countries, even overseas, as traders and lately as textile experts; in 1950 a delegation from Peguche visited UN headquarters in New York to speak for and about Ecuador (Rubio Orbe 1957:331). Hardly any indigenous people has had more opportunity to become acculturated, at least in terms of consumption patterns; yet the one point on which all accounts of the region agree is that Otavaleños have adopted a limited body of *blanco* material culture and, aside from religion, little of the non-material. Often traits actively promoted by whites are taken in only reluctantly and slowly. Indeed those writers who, like Rubio Orbe, believe that a quicker pace of acculturation would be to the Indians' advantage find this reluctance problematic and explainable only in terms of a generalized traditionalism. Yet how can one attribute generally conservative attitudes to a social system which has innovated so aggressively in its external relations?

In "Tappers and Trappers" Robert Murphy and Julian Steward (1956:353) have posited what they consider to be a universal rule: "When goods manufactured by industrialized nations with modern techniques become available through trade to the aboriginal populations, the native people increasingly give up their home crafts in order to devote their efforts to producing specialized cash crops or other trade items in order to obtain more of the industrially made articles. The consequences of this simple though world-wide factor are enormous, even though they vary in local manifestation. The phenomenon is of such a high order of regularity that special explanations must be sought for the few departures from it." Apparently Otavalo is such an exception.

Buitrón (1962:315) remarks on the Otavalans' "great attach-
ment to their traditional garments . . . The young Indians
who have been drafted and who for a year have worn military
uniforms, on returning home abandon all these new garments
. . . to return to their pants and shirts of white cotton and
their ponchos." But is the explanation needed special, or can we
take the Otavalan experience to mean that Murphy and Steward's
generalization is true only given conditions which need to be
specified?

Manufactured goods as such possess no special virtue. Sol Tax,
working from Guatemalan highland evidence, holds that even
when Indians accept many non-indigenous practices, "they have
nevertheless maintained a total pattern that is distinctively their
own. The evidence appears to be that the major changes occurred
in the first generation after the sixteenth-century conquest, and
that the new pattern crystallized early and has maintained itself
since with relatively minor changes. It seems easiest to explain
this history on the hypotheses that alternatives were presented in
large numbers when the Spanish first came, that the Indians
adopted many, and that in the ensuing hundreds of years few
new alternatives appeared. Colonial Guatemala settled down to a
fairly stable set of Indian cultures coexisting with an equally
stable Ladino culture" (1957:150). We cannot account for acculturation by reading into Indian behavior pro or con value judgments about white practices as things in themselves; rather, we
have to interpret selection and rejection of practices as expressing
estimates of their usefulness in living out already held values. If
a change seems useful, Tax observes, it will take hold fast, not
slowly.

Otavalans too show a "total pattern that is distinctively their
own" in production and consumption. The list of definitely exog-
enous practices, gathered from several writers, is not very long:

Government by *alcaldes* and *cabildo;* recognition of state
power.

Baptism and *compadrazgo;* other sacraments; certain religious beliefs.

Civil registry of marriages.

Use of European-design looms and other weaving techniques; chemical dyes.

Settlement of disputes in court.

Free choice of spouse (not always practiced).

Divorce (very rare, perhaps deviant from the Indian point of view).

Certain children's games.

Residence in towns (rare).

Tile roofing of houses and use of furniture within.

Ownership of certain manufactured goods: metalware and pottery are common, radios, bicycles, sewing machines are rarer. Rental of automobiles.

Attendance at schools.

Some folk tales.

Use of manufactured textiles for home-made clothes. The factory-made reversible poncho. Manufactured beads.

Bilingualism.

> (Rubio Orbe 1956:389–91 and 1959: 318–34; Buitrón 1962:314–20; IEAG 1953:143; Parsons 1945:181, 190)

If one accepts Murphy and Steward's generalization it becomes hard to see how the lines between acceptable and deviant acculturation are drawn, or why different populations in similar situations of culture contact draw them differently. In Nayón, a formerly Quechua-speaking community near Quito, land-poor Indians turned to truck farming, trading, and outside wage labor in the early twentieth century, and since then have acculturated so rapidly that Ralph Beals (1952:73) sees them as virtually bypassing the mestizo stage altogether. Men of Nayón wear suits and short hair, while in Otavalo, which has been in at least as favorable a position to buy into *blanco* culture, Indians draw the line at the use of factory-made ponchos of characteristically Indian design. Apparently the desirability of white-style goods cannot be considered self-evident, even when, as in Ecuador, fidelity to indigenous culture invites oppression.

The most parsimonious explanation of the Otavalans' choices among available innovations (excluding the first three listed, which have a history of compulsion), as well as of the persistence of villages as enclaves in the political and social nation in spite of their economic involvements, is that economic security and autonomy in the form of land ownership is paramount over the enjoyment of consumer goods. Historically, the reason is not hard to see; the loss of lands to *blancos* has almost always left Indians dependent and defenseless. Given this criterion of usefulness, Tax's theory yields cogent explanation of the choices. In an example from Rubio Orbe (1956:216), a young man who could have supported his future wife well in the city was refused until he agreed to go back to farming. Innovations which further the quest for land are welcome, on the other hand; Buitrón (1956:228–93) reports that when a North American textile expert introduced a simple device for making wide cloths more easily, it was not Indian conservatism that prevented wide distribution of the invention—the device was eagerly received—but the non-cooperation of Ecuadorean and foreign officials.

The harnessing of cottage industry to the national market for the purpose of buying land is the current solution to problems of long standing, the problems of achieving independence in the face of subjugation. Twentieth-century circumstances, as we will see later, have made the craft-marketing adaptation outstandingly successful in recent times; but even in the region's worst periods of oppression, its ancient preeminence in textile-making has paradoxically acted as a buffer against total cultural demise at the same time that it has invited exploitation. The historical record, incomplete as it is, allows us to glimpse several successive relationships between Otavalo and its conquerors.

WEAVING IN OTAVALAN HISTORY

Archaeological evidence shows that Otavalo between A.D. 500 and 1500 was the home of a people dwelling in small city-states, socially stratified to about the same extent and in the same manner as the Chibchans to the north (Murra 1944:792): "The chief and his retainers, priests, and various craftsmen probably lived in a town supported by the produce of farmers scattered over the surrounding countryside. The latter came to town to exchange goods at the market, to participate in festivals, and to offer prayers and sacrifices at the temple" (Meggers 1966:159). This population, known historically as the Cara tribe or nation, was linguistically similar to the Cayapa-Colorado Indians to its west; both peoples' tongues are of the Barbácoa Chibchan group, related to Colombian, not Peruvian, speech (Loukotka 1968:250).

Incaic and Spanish superimpositions have made it hard to reconstruct Cara socio-political arrangements. The only history of Cara territory written before the extinction of the Cara language in the eighteenth century, that of the Jesuit Juan de Velasco, sets forth a picture so rich in extravagant but undocumented detail that its portrait of the Cara as empire-building centralizers must be discounted as mostly regional chauvinism (Szászdi 1964).

One of the few aspects of Cara civilization of which we can be fairly sure, however, is its craft life. "The textile culture of the Otavaleños goes back to the earliest history of the Andean Indians. Before the conquest, before the coming of the Incas, the Otavalo . . . were weaving blankets and cloaks from cotton they obtained in trade with the people of the Amazon jungle" (Collier and Buitrón 1949:163). John Murra writes (1944:794) that "Trade relations were maintained with the peoples of the eastern lowlands, who brought achiote (a red coloring powder), parrots, monkeys, and even children to exchange for blankets, salt, and dogs. Cotton was also imported from the east." The corregidor Sancho de Paz Ponce de León, whose 1573 report to the crown is the best early Otavalan document, says that Indians of the area carried on trade with "pagan Indians from lands which have not yet been conquered." Traders enjoyed special prestige, according to Ponce de León: "In the old days, the people of each town or village in this entire *corregimiento* (of Otavalo) had their *cacique* who governed them as a tyrant, because he was the most able and valiant. They had him for a master, and obeyed and respected him and paid tribute; and the Indians owned no more than what the *cacique* might let them have, so that he was the master of all that the Indians possessed as well as of their wives and children. They served him as if they were his slaves, *except the merchant Indians, who did not serve their chief like the others, but only paid a tribute of gold, blankets, and red or white bone beads"* (Ponce de León 1897:111; italics added).

No single pre-Incaic political unit ever dominated the area north of Quito; even after the Incaic conquest, wars between localities persisted (Cieza de León 1959:22). Nonetheless this region resisted the Peruvians' offensive more tenaciously than any other except Araucanian Chile. Inca invasion of the area began about 1450, but when Huayna Capac's troops finally subjugated it, forty-five years had elapsed and Columbus had already set foot on Hispaniola. As a result, the Inca period in Otavalo lasted only some forty years, and although the Inca empire concentrated much manpower and administrative attention on integrating this rich area—a much more fertile and inviting zone than Cuzco, the seat of the empire—its impact proved, in some respects, shallow.

Among towns in the Cara region, only Sarance—the modern city of Otavalo—and Caranqui became Inca administrative centers. Accounts of the building of a formidable temple and a northward extension of the imperial road through Sarance (which must have meant mobilizing large numbers of locals in labor brigades), the removal of local nobles to Cuzco to be trained in Quechua language and imperial ideology, and the reshuffling of land tenures in order to impose the famous tripartite management basic to the integrated Andean economy all suggest that conquest must have completely rebuilt Cara society. But some indicators point in the opposite direction. The large-scale killing of captives suggests an uncertain hold on the political structure, as do the introduction of *mitimaes,* transplanted labor forces, from long-subdued Bolivia and the erection of a fortress in Sarance "to deal with revolts in time of war and peace" (Cieza de León 1959: 21). Quechua language did not fully replace Cara for another two hundred years, and the ideology and mythology expressed in it never took root at all; Otavalan folk tales mix pre-Incaic with Spanish, but not Inca, content (Buitrón and Buitrón 1966:55–79). It is true that the region paid tribute heavily and regularly, and that the upper levels of Cara stratification merged with the middle levels of the Inca hierarchy. Yet, "The Inca conquest had not caused major changes in the autochthonous nuclei of population . . . [or] destroyed the social and economic organization of the conquered peoples" (Vargas 1957:71). Apparently, as one descends from wider levels of coordination to local structures Inca control becomes weaker, so that while Sarance became an Incaic outpost, villages bought relative autonomy by rendering tributes in kind. The introduction of wool-bearing llamas by the Incas must have greatly enhanced Otavalo's productivity in this period (Buitrón 1956:287) and its value as a revenue source. There is a parallel to the modern system in this acquiescence to the material demands of large-scale structures as a proxy for social involvement in them. The price of the accommodation in both cases is the yielding up of whatever is produced beyond subsistence, whether to a market as today, or to a fully managed economy as under the Incas. Otavalo has worked hard to remain on the periphery of the political world.

The demands of the next wave of invaders, the Spanish, were far harsher. Aside from the most obvious causes of misery, disease, and brutality, the Spanish conquest created a situation which, even with the best intentions, had to hurt. A fast-growing Spanish immigrant population, largely urban, had to be fed by a labor force which at the same time was being drained by the headlong expansion of mining enterprises. Moreover, the system contained the seeds of its own deterioration in that it drained off in the form of goods and metal exports to Spain much of the value created by Indian labor. The exploitation of the natives did not even succeed in capitalizing the colonial economy with money or social-overhead goods; instead it created a society addicted to the buying of European products. As a result the answer to every economic problem was to squeeze still greater production from Indian labor. Otavalo fared better in this bind than many other places, but colonial times brought terrible suffering to the region (Reyes 1938: vol. 1, 345–57), first through the exploitation of its labor and later through the piecemeal theft of its lands.

Sebastián de Benalcázar and his followers, who conquered modern Ecuador in 1534 in the wake of Pizarro's assault on the war-torn Inca empire, were disappointed in their hopes of finding another gold-rich Perú. Throughout colonial history Ecuador remained politically an appendage to the viceroyalties, first of Perú and after 1720 of New Granada (modern Colombia). This reflected its economic status as supplier of goods to other parts of the empire. Nonetheless the institutions of conquest, and many of their results, resembled those in more politically potent colonies: the evolution of land tenures from usufruct grants to latifundia, and of Indian labor obligations from *encomienda* to *mita* to debt peonage, parallels Peruvian developments.

The newly founded *cabildo* (city council) of Quito granted three forms of agricultural land tenures, limited, from 1535 onward, to fairly small holdings: *solares,* gardens in or near the city; *estancias* for the encouragement of livestock growing (which proved so successful that seventeenth-century Quito was famous for cheap livestock); and *tierras para sembradura,* land for crops. Not landholding proper, however, but rather the exploitation of a non-territorial grant, the *encomienda,* yielded up early colonial fortunes. The *encomienda,* consisting of the assignment to a Spanish *encomendero* of a varying number of Indians to be protected and catechized, and, in payment for these services, to pay him tribute in goods or labor, specifically required that the *encomendero* should not live on the lands of his *encomendados.* But many managed to acquire land grants neighboring their *encomendado* villages and to extort excessive labor from them under the name of tribute. Otavalo fell into the hands of a violent and adventurous conquistador, Rodrigo de Salazar, in one of the earliest and largest *encomiendas,* and the surrounding *parcialidades* were divided into a series of much smaller ones. Because the terms of *encomienda* granted the privilege for only two generations, these first grants reverted to the crown relatively early (Salazar's in 1581). The crown chose to set aside this community, so rich in skilled labor, as a crown tributary area. That Otavalan Indians became workers for the Spanish state instead of being reassigned in new *encomiendas* is one reason for their relative good fortune in this era (Reyes 1938: vol. 1, 315–22; Vargas 1957: 160–62).

Since the Otavalo area is poor in minerals and under preautomotive conditions not advantageously placed for truck farming, *encomenderos* and officials extracted private wealth and crown revenue from the area chiefly by putting the yoke of forced labor on the indigenous textile culture. The highly successful introduction of sheep to the Andes and the expansion of cotton growing and other fiber culture in the lowlands supplied Otavalo with the raw materials for making a very large part of the colonial world's supply of textiles, from rope and sackcloth to fine handkerchiefs, but above all, of ordinary shirt cloth, woolen blankets, and ponchos. Tribute laws of 1612 required every man of eighteen through fifty years to render two white cotton cloaks to the crown as well as money and livestock payments (Municipalidad de Otavalo 1909:35–36). Textiles from the Ecuadorean highlands clothed the mine labor forces of Peru and Colombia and paid for the wine and imported goods that Quiteño Spaniards enjoyed; indeed the cloth trade, as John Phelan explains in his admirable history *The Kingdom of Quito in the Seventeenth Century* (1967: 66–85), became the backbone of Ecuador's colonial economy and made it "the sweatshop of South America."

The Spanish achieved the expansion of weaving from a local craft to an export industry not chiefly through technological reorganization (although the use of the Spanish frame loom did take root quickly throughout the Andes) but through the concentration and merciless overworking of Indians in primitive factories, or *obrajes,* where amid filth, darkness, and hunger, overseers forced them to work hours far beyond what royal legislation theoretically permitted. *Obrajes* ranged downward in size and quality from those operated as crown enterprises (later leased to contractors); to viceroyally-licensed private shops, some of which were assigned quotas of forced *mita* labor while others hired weavers; to unlicensed shops run by *encomenderos,* city entrepreneurs, powerful Indians, and not uncommonly, religious orders. A few *obrajes* belonged to corporate Indian communities which used them to pay their tributes. The most concentrated area of *obraje* production was not Otavalo but Riobamba, a region south of Quito where sheep raising flourished. After the *encomienda* including Otavalo reverted to the crown in 1581 the large *obraje* in Otavalo City was reorganized as a crown enterprise and under corrupt management declined; but when a change of royal policy in 1620 put it on the market as a leased concession, it quickly appreciated and by 1623 had become the most valuable in Ecuador (Phelan 1967:69–74; Vargas 1957:235, 303). Also in 1620, another crown *obraje* was opened at Peguche.

The continuing struggle which crown officials waged to put limits to the abuse and wastage of life that colonists were always ready to visit on the King's Indian subjects was resisted tirelessly by colonists who saw no other way to wring a decent living from Ecuador's soil. Amid this conflict, conditions in the *obrajes* proved a perennial bone of contention. From the earliest times of the Ecuadorean *Audiencia* (the ruling body immediately subject to the Viceroy of Perú), royal correspondence deals with the issues of non-payment of weavers, overwork, child labor, the question of whether *obrajes* should serve as debtor's prisons, usurpation of Indian lands by *obraje* owners, and myriad forms of cruelty, starvation, and neglect (Landazuri Soto 1959:28, 31, 32, 75–76, 82). Otavalo, by virtue of its status as a crown holding, repeatedly had the good luck to become a test case in *obraje* reform, the decision to lease it in 1620 being one such experiment.

The Otavalo reforms of 1620, planned by the dynamic president of the *Audiencia,* Dr. Antonio de Morga, constituted one of the earliest and wisest plans for Indian reconstruction. Its terms included the restoration of all lands whether stolen or bought, provision of a plot and a house for every Indian, exemption from the forced labor of the *mita,* segregation of non-Indians and traders in the town of Ibarra, and a number of measures to insure administrative honesty and efficiency (Phelan 1967:76). But subsequent presidents could not make them stick, and abuses recurred; a 1648 royal order refers to Otavalo Indians fleeing to the mountains for fear of debtor's prison or because their lands had been stolen (Vargas 1957:95). By 1680 mounting protest prodded the Bourbon king Charles II to a Draconian reform which would have decimated textile production by destroying all unlicensed shops. President Munive of the Quito *Audiencia* convinced the crown that this reform could only wreck the economy (Phelan 1967:78–79), but in doing so he admitted that the crown tributary areas once again needed protection if they were to prosper: "[Weavers at Otavalo] live in and are accustomed to the city of Otavalo with their homes and their families there, going to work without any coercion or violence, which condition does not prevail at the *obraje* of Peguche because of the inconvenient distance of 6 to 9 miles from the villages where they live to the workshops, where they enter at four in the morning and leave at six in the evening, resulting in the harm and nuisance of having to walk 18 miles every day to and from work, without a chance to rest . . . they despair . . . three of them threw themselves under a bridge and were pulled out dead, and so I propose to Your Majesty that the only remedy is to demolish this *obraje* . . ." (Landazuri Soto 1959:144–45). The crown *obraje* at Peguche employed 200 workers; that at Otavalo, 498. The abuses which these workers suffered were far less horrible than those inflicted on inmates of some private shops (Landazuri Soto 1959:171–72).

During the same period, the crown, by cumulative partial measures, was abolishing the *encomienda*. Earlier measures such as the (rarely enforced) ban on tributes payable only in labor and the non-redistribution of *encomiendas* had not brought labor conditions up to the standards of Spanish law, and during the period 1690–1720 the remaining holdings were reclaimed as crown lands or sold and the institution liquidated (Vargas 1957:163–65). Instead of relieving the Indians of their exploiters, however, this change gave Spaniards and *criollos* ["mixed bloods"] an incentive to invest the profits from *obrajes* in land purchases or to indulge in seizures of land which the increasingly corrupt *corregidores* (officials charged with the protection of Indians) could be persuaded to tolerate. It is in this period—not the conquest—that we find the seeds of latifundism. Otavalo had and still has some sizable latifundia, but these did not, as happened farther south in the Andes, convert whole villages into captive colonies of landless debt peons; rather they have bordered on freehold *parcialidades,* so that *huasipungeros* of the big farm nonetheless remained socially attached to independently landed neighbors. Possibly because Otavalo's relatively gentle climate allows farming high up on the mountainsides, and consequently permits victims of land-grabbing to resettle, latifundia of the Otavalo region have had to rely on hired labor done part time by *minifundistas* and less on fixed colonies of indebted Indians than those elsewhere.

The decline of the *encomienda* also heightened the demand for *mita* labor. The *mita,* an Incaic institution of which nothing Incaic but the name remained by 1700, had become a form of slavery.

Every village had to supply a quota of workers conscripted for a fixed period (six months was the legal limit) who were marched off to mines or *obrajes,* usually far from their homes, and exploited mercilessly. According to Jorge Juan and Antonio de Ulloa (1918: vol. 1, 288–316), visitors to Ecuador in 1736, few survived the hunger, brutality, and exposure to cold inflicted on *mitayos;* and although a minor debt or offense might incur conscription, it amounted to a sentence of death. "Often on the roads one meets Indians with their braids tied to the tail of a horse, on which a mounted mestizo leads them to the *obrajes;* and this perhaps for the slight offense of having fled . . . for fear of the cruelties (their masters) inflict on them" (Juan and Ulloa 1918: vol. 1, 311). *Mita* gangs had long been assigned to some licensed *obrajes,* but after 1700 the abolition of the *encomienda* obligation created pressure on the authorities to grant many more operators conscript labor, pressure which they could hardly resist without endangering Quito's place in intercolonial trade.

Even while *obraje* production and the *mita* drained their work force, however, eighteenth-century Otavalans were able to do independent business, and it is in another report of Juan and Ulloa (1806: vol. 1, 301–2) that we first hear of Otavalans as adapting to domination and the theft of their resources by becoming suppliers to a supra-local open market: ". . . a multitude of Indians residing in its villages . . . seem to have an innate inclination to weaving; for besides the stuffs made at the common manufactories (i.e. *obrajes*), such Indians as are not Mitayos, or who are independent, make, on their own account, a variety of goods, as cottons, carpets, pavillions for beds, quilts in damask work, wholly of cotton, either white, blue, or variegated with different colours; but all in great repute, both in the province of Quito and other parts, where they are sold to great advantage."

During the century following Juan and Ulloa's visit latifundism sank deep roots in the highlands. The traveler William Bennett Stevenson (1825: vol. 2, 348) tells of haciendas with four or five hundred Indians attached either to their fields or *obrajes,* and reports that near Otavalo the Count of Casa Xijón had "brought several mechanics and artisans from Europe for the purpose of establishing a manufactory of fine cloths, woolens, and cottons;

also for printing calicoes, and other goods," but the *Real Audiencia* forbade his plan and forced him to send the mechanics home.

The Creole elites of the Otavalo area sided for the most part with the forces of independence in the war against Napoleonic Spain, and "from its famous workshops came the cloaks that warmed the army in its campaigns" (Jaramillo 1953:4, 22). From them also came the porters of the independence armies' cargoes, abducted from their villages in what is still remembered as the *cogida de gente*—the seizure of people—(Rubio Orbe 1956: 29) which caused a mass flight to the mountains.

Newly independent and until 1830 a part of the federation of Gran Colombia, Ecuador suddenly became an open market for imports from England, and the resulting flood of cheap factory-made cloth dealt a blow to the *obraje* industry from which, Phelan says (1967:68), it never recovered. Nonetheless several nineteenth-century land magnates tried to revive local weaving in competition with English industry by combining technical modernization with the cheap labor which debt peons provided. Among these was the grandson of the Count of Casa Xijón, Don José Manuel Jijón y Carrión, whose prosperous Peguche hacienda the United States diplomat Friedrich Hassaurek visited in 1863. Here hacienda peasants made ponchos and shawls for Indians as well as material for European vests and pants on modern looms, all for shipment to Colombia or the Pacific coast (Vargas 1957: 122; Hassaurek 1967:151). Two other latifundia, the Quinta Otavalo and the Quinta de San Pedro, were equipped with European machines, for weaving and for thread-making respectively; an earthquake in 1864 destroyed much of this machinery (Municipalidad de Otavalo, 1909:294). An unmodernized *parcialidad,* Cotacachi, was doing well with coarse ponchos and silks (products without industrial competition) for sale in other parts of Gran Colombia, while nearby a landowner had imported an industrial cotton mill from New Jersey, but gone bankrupt on the venture (Hassaurek 1967:175–77). Thus in the later nineteenth century Indian weavers working outside hacienda workshops could profit by the making of clothes for other Indians, but the technologically fortified vestiges of the *obraje* system still dominated whatever share of the city clothing market had not fallen to the English.

The farming-weaving complex in its modern form did not arise until the early twentieth century, when villagers found that the duplication of machine-made luxury textiles on primitive equipment enabled them to undersell the quality import trade even though they could not compete in the making of cheap stuffs. Once introduced, this business became the mainstay of cottage industry. The weaving boom of this period reflected the mounting urgency of land problems and signals the beginning of the land-hunger dynamic described above.

For Otavaleños to own land has double importance: first, it is the only reliable and autonomous way of earning a living; and second, it is a *sine qua non* of full participation in Indian society, since the alternatives are to abandon the community, become a permanent debtor, or live as a burden on another household. In order to provide every family with a plot, parents will their land partibly, that is, divide it among all the children. We do not know when this practice began, though Murra (1944:794) thinks the system "was greatly influenced by post conquest ideas." But we do know how it worked in the time of the childhood of Elsie Parsons' informant Rosita Lema, when quarter shares of already tiny plots might be all a person inherited. And we know from her testimony how partible inheritance, after centuries of slow population increase, produced a land crisis: "Formerly, my mother tells as her parents tell her, there were not as many families as today, and only two or three little straw houses. The families cultivated land according to their capacity, the rest was common land, untilled, unenclosed, an enormous plain. As the families increased it was customary to upturn land as a kind of deed, always with witnesses or the *curaca* (village headman) to direct it. This made a man owner and lord of this land where he built a house and lived independently of his parents. In the course of time, ambitious for land, families spread over the whole plain, becoming landowners, *and there was no longer common land to turn up*" (Parsons 1945:186; italics added).

This must have occurred in the middle or late nineteenth century. From the time when lands gave out, the ability to save cash and buy land became the prerequisite for survival as a free peasant: "Then those who had too much land or for other reasons would sell land, a cuadra for five pesos, ten pesos, twenty pesos according to the situation or fertility. Today (1945), if the lot is located on the main street and the soil is fertile, it costs 1,500 sucres; a lot less fertile and far from the main street will cost as little as 400 sucres" (Ibid.). By 1909 the trend toward land-buying by Indians had gone far enough to alarm the anonymous author of Otavalo's municipal history, who saw things from the latifundists' point of view: "By forming societies they have bought *fundos* of the value of twenty-three thousand sucres, of twenty thousand, et cetera . . . Day by day, the Indian is taking over the lands of the Canton, albeit by fair purchase; having taken possession of them on a larger scale, by cultivating them with care he will achieve a well-being that will make him scorn the laborer's wage. Then who will till [the latifundists'] fields? . . . Even now . . . the Indians do not volunteer for government works; it is necessary to round them up with the *alcaldes* or the police, or take their belongings hostage [*quitarles prendas,* an abuse still practiced by townsmen], or threaten to throw them in jail, in order to force them to work" (Municipalidad de Otavalo 1909:254–57).

Into this environment of land hunger and rising prices, local *blancos* in 1917 introduced the germ of the modern textile trade. A lady of the hacienda of Cusín, bordering on Peguche, gave her Quiteño son-in-law, F. A. Uribe, a beautifully woven poncho as a wedding gift. Impressed with its quality, rivaling that of costly imported clothes, Uribe sought out its maker, a Peguche native named José Cajas, and offered him the use of a Spanish loom to try his skill at making fine fabric after Scottish patterns. Cajas found that he could profitably undersell imports with his imitation tweeds (*casimires*), and soon had a business in Quito; his descendants are still among the leading weavers of the area (Parsons 1945:25–26).

Thus Otavalo smallholders found a major entrée into the money economy at the precise time when it served to defend, not supplant, the bases of the local economy (IEAG 1953:98). In subsequent decades the *casimir* trade has spread to many other villages, although by no means all (in reading Collier and Buitrón's 1949 optimistic account of the weaving renaissance one must bear in mind that the weaving boom has left some *parcialidades* still land-poor and overworked). Since the Second World War the growth of Ecuadorean textile factories has greatly weakened

Otavalo's position in the market for suit fabrics; but the burgeoning of the tourist market in autochthonous and not so autochthonous designs has offset this damage considerably.

Both the Ecuadorean indigenist movement and United States foreign aid agencies have sought to encourage cottage industry in capturing foreign money, the former through the programs of the Instituto Ecuatoriano de Antropología y Geografía, which have encouraged the weaving of authentic rather than imitative designs for the market (Salinas 1954:315–26), and the latter through the *Centro Textil* in Otavalo City, which Ecuadoreans have consistently criticized as poorly integrated with village life and in fact of use only to mestizos. (Rubio Orbe 1957:335–60 offers a detailed critique.) Other recent innovations in textile economy center on marketing; Otavaleños own several shops in downtown Quito while others crisscross the country as traveling merchants.

Because of this interest in modernizing business technique, the children of weaving families have begun to appear in public schools (though the great majority of families still prefer home training). Travel needs have involved some villagers in local transportation businesses; others have learned skilled and semiskilled agricultural jobs, or become mechanics in textile factories; and the first generation of Indian nurses, teachers, and lawyers is starting to emerge from universities (Jed Cooper 1965:45–56; Buitrón 1962; Casagrande 1966:9). Most of these changes, large or small, can be understood in the light of Sol Tax's observation that "traditional" populations will innovate readily, provided that innovation promises to be useful within the context of already accepted norms.

But can Otavalo continue to turn large-scale societal conditions to its own local advantage without suffering unintended consequences that will gradually take the pace and direction of change out of the reach of its own mechanisms of social policy? Points of stress are already visible. It may be true that the organization of production in household units sets limits on the scale and complexity of production (Nash 1966:71), but nothing has prevented some families from developing as adjuncts to the household workshops approaching a factory form of organization (Casagrande 1969:4). As a result the textile industry has probably increased rather than moderated the inequality of landholdings and standards of living. It is true that the employment of land-poor villagers by other Indians as spinners, weavers, or farm helpers may share out some of the wealth, but the ascendancy of a few entrepreneurially active families in business is conspicuous. If most textile wealth continues to go into the buying-up of lands, partible inheritance and the deprecation of greed central to Otavalan ethics may not prevail against the dynamics of private ownership, and the Indian communities will have agrarian problems of their own. Second, although Otavalans have usually relied on judicial rather than political resolution of power and property struggles, both the increased integration and visibility of the community and the trend in law toward the inclusion of Indians in the effective electorate will bring the area more, though not necessarily more beneficial, government attention. Can the combination of market integration with socio-political isolation endure this?

It is by no means a foregone conclusion that any such change would do the *parcialidades* harm, or at any rate harm enough to outbalance the enriching benefits to an impoverished country that ideally follow from the modernization of production and the penetration of the nation-state into previously isolated localities. But the human costs of these changes weigh heavy on every people that has undergone them. Early industrial society everywhere seems to be inseparably connected with traumatic reorganizations, brutal demands on workers, and wholesale loss of much of what men live for. Humanly satisfying and varied labor, the solidarity and continuity of small communities, and the preservation of old, local cultures whose rationality is not that of maximizing production at the expense of everything else are the first casualties of every industrial revolution. While the "Awakening Valley" looks poor in the eyes of visitors from the United States, it is not only a fortunate place compared to almost every other Andean region, but also compared to areas in the throes of early industrialization. The pride of manner and handsome appearance of its men and women testify to a relation to the modern world that deserves more recognition. It is a great feat to modernize rapidly and dynamically; it is also a great feat not to.

Both sides of this paradox find expression in North American youth politics, a politics growing in response to the apparent exhaustion in our country of the very same notion of development that the United States government promotes in places like Ecuador. The Marxist left, proclaiming itself an ally of the Third World, advocates the redistribution of industrial wealth and the seizure of control over its machinery and resource bases by neo-colonized peoples within and without the U.S.A.; the central aim is to counteract the growth of inequality between rich and proletarized countries and make of the industrial revolution a worldwide egalitarian revolution. But, uneasily in step with the Third World movement, cultural revolutionaries follow a post- or even anti-industrial vision. Seeing industrial society as a Frankenstein monster capable only of following an inflexible track to complete wastage of man and earth, they concentrate on ways of liberating people from the life of economic rationality itself by inventing social forms which can break production into decentralized operations, automate and cleanse industry, and make room for those who want to subsist outside the orbit of modernity altogether. Their mutual lack of confidence reflects a real dilemma; given industry as we know it, how are we to put machines at our service without becoming servants of machines?

Equations of the North American new left with Latin American revolutionary nationalism, and of neo-tribal communes with indigenous peoples, are obviously specious. Yet the comparison is of some interest. Ecuador is still far from facing any post-industrial problems; but already the question arises of how Ecuador's Indians—nearly half the nation—can be enlisted in the struggle to raise national productivity (under any political regime) without making the supposed beneficiaries mere tools of the effort. Beate Salz (1955:215–19) has answered by proposing, as an alternative to a smallhold agrarian reform which would still further restrict productivity to household subsistence, the implanting of "interstitial industry"—small industrial enterprises which would fit into the "interstices" of rural economy by employing the land-poor while giving them plots as a job benefit. This plan seeks to avoid abruptly destroying rooted social units and agrarian bases, the guaranteed availability of which would form an incentive for workers to stay "until they have sloughed off a traditional predilection for cultivation of land." Thus from a modernist point of view the idea is to uproot tradition in a humane way.

But the Otavaleños have, in effect, carried out Salz's plan of their own accord, for the reverse purpose; they have used an "interstitial" industry, weaving, as a way of preserving their rooted way of life. It may come to pass that the dynamics of their industrialism will eventually weaken land-based organization, as Salz foresees. But this would not signify the loss of local society, for the change could be achieved at least in part on the people's own terms. The significant point is that Otavalans have found an alternative to exploitation and cultural extinction on the one hand and dire poverty on the other, by creating a nationally integrated small industry distinct from the *Gesellschaft* model. From this both the Marxist and the culture-radical may have something to learn.

In the development-versus-stagnation stereotype, too much is taken for granted. Otavalo, with a minimum of technological aid and little outside sympathy, has succeeded in creating a flexible technology tailored to the changing needs of small groups. Once technologists produce a range of tools suited to small projects, and revolutionaries make their use a high priority, places less historically fortunate may have similar opportunities, as may communal alternatives in rich nations; a broader conception of industry will afford broader alternatives of engagement and autonomy. In both the most advanced and the newest industrial economies, smallness of scale, far from signifying obsolescence, has rationality of its own, based on the social satisfactions of the producers and an economic flexibility that can withstand certain hazards of early interdependence such as market and supply fluctuations. In the economies of rich nations communal forms have begun to find a niche by providing labor-intensive products (crafts) and, increasingly, services (such as experimental and special education) to the larger whole on a basis of partial autonomy; the technical and economic possibilities of these forms are just now coming into view. For revolutionists and technicians, it will be time to cease thinking of how to manage other peoples' livelihoods, and to begin thinking how livelihood can become less a matter of management and more a fruit of local creativity.

SUGGESTED READINGS

Researchers and teachers frequently decry the lack of adequate published ethnographic material on South American Indians. However, great progress has been made in filling this gap. Any program of reading devoted to a particular region or people should include one or more detailed ethnographic studies. The following is a partial list of such studies, available in English, most of them in print, many of them available in inexpensive paperbound editions (indicated by a p, preceding the author's name):

p N. Chagnon (1968a)
p L. Faron (1961c)
    L. Faron (1964)
p L. Faron (1968)
p Garcilaso de la Vega (1961)
p I. Goldman (1963)
p M. Harner (1972)
p J. Henry (1964, orig. 1941)
p A. Holmberg (1969, orig. 1950)
p F. Huxley (1966, orig. 1956)
    D. Maybury-Lewis (1967)
    R. Murphy (1960)
    G. Reichel-Dolmatoff (1971)
    P. Rivière (1969)
p E. Thurn (1967, orig. 1883)
p J. Wilbert (1972)
p P. Young (1971)

The following, while not specific case studies, will be of great value as well:

p J. H. Hopper (Ed. and Trans.) (1967)
p C. Lévi-Strauss (1963, 1964, 1969a, 1969b)
p D. Maybury-Lewis (1968, orig. 1965)
p B. J. Meggers (1971)
    J. Steward and L. Faron (1959)
    H. Valero (1971)

A number of studies in prehistory are also available:

p W. Bennett and J. Bird (1964)
p G. H. S. Bushnell (1963)

p   E. Lanning (1967)
    D. Lathrap (1970)
p   K. Macgowan and J. A. Hester, Jr. (1962)
p   J. A. Mason (1968)
p   J. Rowe and D. Menzel (Eds.) (1967)
    G. Willey (1971)

A NOTE ON THE BIBLIOGRAPHY

This bibliography is by no means exhaustive on any aspect of South American Indians, but I hope that it will be of use to students and scholars interested in further reading on some of the topics presented in this book. Most of the references listed here are citations from the articles reprinted and constitute documentation of some specific point. Others are of more general interest. These include both works cited by the authors of articles and by me in my introductions.

If the reader is particularly interested in a particular people or question discussed by one of the articles in this volume, I suggest that he first consult the items that were cited by the author of the article and then the suggested readings below. If the reader is interested in deepening his knowledge of a particular society, I suggest that he consult one of the specialized bibliographies, O'Leary (1963) or Baldus (1968). O'Leary's bibliography is very thorough up to about 1962 with listings by tribal names subdivided into regions. Readers who are familiar with Portuguese (often a knowledge of Spanish is a help) can profit from Baldus' annotated bibliography. Baldus frequently summarizes the article. The bibliographies in the *Handbook of South American Indians* (Steward 1944–49) will also be of great use to serious students, although, of course, they are now far out of date. The reader is also urged to consult the references cited by recent books and journal articles on the subject or people he wants to investigate.

Bibliography

Acosta, Joaquin
   1848   *Compendio Histórico del Descubrimiento y Colonización de la Nueva Granada en el Siglo Décimo Sexto*. Paris: Beau.
Acosta, José de
   1940 (orig. 1590)   *Historia Natural y Moral de las Indias* . . . México: Fonda de Cultura Económica.
Adams, Robert M.
   1966   *The Evolution of Urban Society: Early Mesopotamia and Prehispanic Mexico*. Chicago: Aldine Publishing Co.
Agnew, Arlene, and Evelyn G. Pike
   1957   "Phonemes of Ocaina (Huitoto)." *International Journal of American Linguistics* 23:24–27.
Aguado, Pedro de
   1906   "Recopilación Historial." *Biblioteca de Historia Nacional*, Vol. V, Bogotá.
———
   1930   *Historia de la Provincia de Sancta Marta y Nuevo Reino de Granada*. 3 vols., Espasa Calpe, Madrid.
———
   1950   *Historia de Venezuela*. 2 vols., Madrid.
Albo, Xavier
   1970   *Social Constraints on Cochabamba Quechua*. Cornell University Latin American Studies Program Dissertation Series, No. 19, Ithaca, New York.
Alchian, Armen, and William R. Allen
   1965   *Economics*. Belmont, California: Wadsworth Publishing Co., Inc.
Anchieta
   1846   "Informação dos Casamentos dos Indios do Brasil." *Revista*

Trimensal do Instituto Histórico e Geográfico Brasileiro, 2ª série, 1(8):259.

Anderson, W., G. Burmeister, N. P. Guidry, R. G. Hainsworth, A. G. Kevorkian, C. M. Purves, R. P. Schottroff and K. H. Wylie.
1958 *Agricultural Geography of Latin America*. Washington, D.C.: United States Department of Agriculture, Miscellaneous Publication No. 743.

Anonymous
1938 "Varias Noticias Curiosas Sobre la Provincia de Popayán." Jijón y Caamaño: *Sebastián de Benalcázar* II:179–82, Quito.

Anuario General de Estadistica
1957 *Lluvias, Humedad, Temperatura y Vientos*. Pp. 4–20, Bogotá, Colombia.

Arends, T., G. Brewer, N. Chagnon, M. Gallango, H. Gershowitz, M. Layrisse, J. Neel, D. Shreffler, R. Tashian and L. Weitkamp
1967 "Intratribal Genetic Differentiation Among the Yanomama Indians of Southern Venezuela." *Proceedings of the National Academy of Sciences* 57:1252–59.

Arnaud, Expedito C.
1963 "A Terminologia do Parentesco dos Indios Asuriní." *Revista do Museu Paulista*, São Paulo, nova série, 14:105–19.

Asch, T., and N. A. Chagnon
1970 *The Feast*. A 30-minute, 16-millimeter color film, synchronous sound. Washington, National Audiovisual Center.

Ascher, Robert
1962 "Ethnography for Archaeology: A Case from the Seri Indians." *Ethnology* 1(3):360–69.

Auer, V.
1956 "The Pleistocene of Fuego-Patagonia, Part I, The Ice and Interglacial Ages." *Ann. Acad. Sci. Fenn.*, Ser. A, III, No. 45.

———
1958 "The Pleistocene of Fuego-Patagonia, Part II, The History of the Flora and Vegetation." *Ann. Acad. Sci. Fenn.*, Ser. A, III, No. 50.

———
1959 "The Pleistocene of Fuego-Patagonia, Part III, Shoreline Displacements." *Ann. Acad. Sci. Fenn.*, Ser. A, III, No. 60.

Baldus, Herbert
Ms. "Caracterização da Cultura Tapirapé." *Proceedings of the 29th International Congress of Americanists*, New York, 1949.

———
1937 "Os Grupos de Comer e os Grupos de Trabalho dos

Tapirapé." *Ensaios de Etnologia Brasileira,* Brasiliana, ser. 5, 101:86–111.

——— 1944–49   "Os Tapirapé, Tribo Tupí no Brasil Central." *Revista do Arquivo Municipal,* vols. 96–105, 107–24, 127, São Paulo.

——— 1948   "Tribos da Bacia do Araguaia e o Serviço de Proteção aos Indios." *Revista do Museu Paulista,* nova série, 2:137–68, São Paulo.

——— 1949   "Akkulturation im Araguaya-Bebiet." *Anthropos* 41–44: 889–91.

——— 1967   "Synopsis of the Critical Bibliography of Brazilian Ethnology, 1953–1960," in Hopper (Ed.), *Indians of Brazil in the Twentieth Century.* Washington, D.C.: Institute for Cross-Cultural Research.

——— 1968   *Bibliografia Crítica da Etnologia Brasileira.* Völkerkundliche Abhandlungen, Band 4, Hannover: Niedersächsiche Landesmuseum.

——— 1970   *Tapirapé: Tribo Tupí no Brasil Central.* São Paulo: Companhia Editora Nacional.

Bamburger, Joan
1968   "The Adequacy of Kayapó Ecological Adjustment." Paper presented to the 38th Congress of Americanists, August 1968, Stuttgart.

Bandelier, Adolph Francis Alphonse
1910   *The Islands of Titicaca and Koati.* New York: The Hispanic Society of America.

Banner, Horace
1961   "O Indio Kayapó em seu acampamento." *Boletim do Museu Paraense Emílio Goeldi,* 12, Belém.

Barrau, Jacques
1958   *Subsistence Agriculture in Melanesia.* Bernice P. Bishop Museum Bulletin 219.

Barrett, Otis W.
1928   *The Tropical Crops.* New York: Macmillan.

Bates, Henry Walter
1864   *The Naturalist on the River Amazons.* Second edition, London: John Murray.

Baudin, Louis
1961   *A Socialist Empire: The Incas of Peru.* Princeton: D. Van

Nostrand and Co. Katherine Woods (Trans.), Arthur Goddard (Ed.).

Baxter, David
n.d.   *The True People*. Ms.

Beals, Ralph L.
1952   "Acculturation, Economics, and Social Change," in Sol Tax (Ed.), *Acculturation in the Americas. Proceedings and Selected Papers of the XXIX International Congress of Americanists*, Chicago, 2:67–73.

————
1955   "Indian-Mestizo-White Relations in Spanish America," in Andrew W. Lind (Ed.), *Race Relations in World Perspective*. Pp. 412–32, Honolulu: University of Hawaii Press.

————
1966   *Community in Transition: Nayón-Ecuador*. Latin American Center of the University of California, Los Angeles: University of California Press.

Becher, Hans
1957   "A Importância de Banana Entro os Indios Surará e Pakidai." *Revista de Antropologia*, São Paulo, 5(2).

————
1960   *Die Surara und Pakidai: Zwei Yanonami-Stamme in Nordwestbrasiliens*. Hamburg: Mitteilungen aus dem Museum für Völkerkunde, Hamburg.

Beltrán, Gonzalo Aguirre
1946   *La Población Negra de México*. Mexico: Ediciones Fuente Cultural.

Bennet, Charles F.
1962   "The Bayano Cuna Indians, Panama: An Ecological Study of Diet and Livelihood." *Annals of the Association of American Geographers* 52:32–50.

Bennett, Wendell Clark
1934   *Excavations at Tiahunaco*. Anthropological Papers of the American Museum of Natural History, Vol. 34, Part 3:329–494.

————
1936   *Excavations in Bolivia*. Anthropological Papers of the American Museum of Natural History, Vol. 35, Part 4:329–507.

————
1950   *The Gallinazo Group, Viru Valley, Peru*. New Haven: Yale University Publications in Anthropology, No. 43.

————
1953   *Excavations at Wari, Ayacucho, Peru*. New Haven: Yale University Publications in Anthropology, No. 49.

—— (Ed.)

1948   *A Reappraisal of Peruvian Archaeology.* Memoir, *American Antiquity,* Vol. 13 (4), Part 2.

Bennett, Wendell C., and Junius B. Bird

1964   *Andean Culture History.* 2nd revised edition, New York: Natural History Press, American Museum Science Books.

Bettelheim, Bruno

1954   *Symbolic Wounds.* Glencoe, Illinois.

Bingham, Hiram

1930   *Machu Picchu, a Citadel of the Incas.* Memoirs of the National Geographic Society, New Haven: Yale University Press.

Bird, J.

1938   "Antiquity and Migrations of the Early Inhabitants of Patagonia." *Geographical Review* 28:250–75.

Blanton, Richard E.

1972   "Prehispanic Adaptation in the Ixtapalapa Region." *Science* 175(4028):1317–26.

Bloomfield, Leonard

1925   "On the Sound System of Central Algonquian." *Language* 1:130–56.

——

1933   *Language.* New York: Holt.

——

1946   "Algonquian." *Linguistic Structures of Native America,* New York: Viking Fund Publications in Anthropology No. 6:85–129.

Boggiani, Guido

1895   "Vocabulario dell'Idioma Caduveu," in *Viaggi d'un Artista nell' America Meridionale. I Caduvei.* Roma.

——

1945   *Os Caduveu.* Biblioteca Histórica Brasileira, São Paulo: Livraria Martins Editora.

Borah, Woodrow, and Sherburne Cook

1963   "The Aboriginal Population of Central Mexico on the Eve of the Spanish Conquest." *Ibero-Americana* 45:1–155.

Bowman, Isaiah

1916   *The Andes of Southern Peru.* New York.

Bram, Joseph

1941   *An Analysis of Inca Militarism.* Monograph 4, New York: American Ethnological Society.

Brass, L. J.

1941   "Stone Age Agriculture in New Guinea." *Geographical Review* 31:555–69.

Breton, Raymond
1965 *Dictionnaire Caraibe-François.* Auxerre: G. Bouquet.
Bridges, Esteban Lucas
1949 *The Uttermost Part of the Earth.* New York: E. P. Dutton.
Brinton, Daniel Garrison
1891 *The American Race: A Linguistic Classification and Ethnographic Description of the Native Tribes of North and South America.* New York.
Brown, Paula, and H. C. Brookfield
1959 "Chimbu Land and Society." *Oceania* 30:1–75.
Bruzzi Alves Da Silva, Alcionilio
Ms. *The Indian Civilization of the Uaupes River.*
Buitrón, Aníbal
1947 "Situación Económica y Social del Indio Otavaleño." *America Indígena* 7:45–67.

1956 "La Tecnificación de la Industria Textil Manual de los Indios del Ecuador," in *Estudios Antropologicos Publicados en Homenaje al Dr. Manuel Gamio.* Mexico D. F.

n.d. *Taita Imbabura, Vida Indígena en los Andes.* Quito: Missión Andina.

1962 "Panorama de la Aculturación en Otavalo, Ecuador." *America Indígena* 22:313–22.
Buitrón, Aníbal, and Barbara Salisbury Buitrón
1945 "Indios, Blancos, y Mestizos en Otavalo, Ecuador." *Acta Americana* 3:190–216.

1966 "Leyendas y Supersticiones Indígenas de Otavalo." *America Indígena* 26:53–79.
Bunzel, Ruth
1952 *Chichicastenango: A Guatemalan Village.* New York: J. J. Augustin.
Burnet, F. M.
1966 "Man or Molecules." *Lancet* 1:37–39.
Bushnell, G. H. S.
1963 *Peru,* revised edition. New York: Frederick A. Praeger, Ancient Peoples and Places.
Butt, Audrey J.
1970 "Land Use and Social Organization of Tropical Forest Peoples of the Guianas," in J. P. Garlick and R. W. J. Keay (Eds.), *Human Ecology in the Tropics.* Pp. 33–50, Oxford: Pergamon Press.

502   Bibliography

Cabello Valboa, Miguel
  1951 (orig. 1586)   Miscelánea Antártica. Ed. Instituto de Etnología,
    Facultad de Letras, Lima: Universidad Nacional Mayor de San
    Marcos.
Cámara, Fernando
  1952   "Religious and Political Organization," in Sol Tax (Ed.),
    Heritage of Conquest. Pp. 142–73, Glencoe, Illinois: The Free
    Press.
Cândido de Oliveira, Haroldo
  1952   "O Estado de Saúde dos Índios Karajá em 1950." Revista do
    Museu Paulista, São Paulo, n.s., 6:498–508.
Cardim, Fernão
  1925   Tratados da Terra e Gente do Brasil. [Biblioteda Pedagogic
    Brasileira, ser. 5a., Vol. 168?]:169–70, Rio de Janeiro.
Carneiro, Robert L.
  1958   "Extra-Marital Sex Freedom Among the Kuikuru Indians of
    Mato-Grosso." Revista do Museu Paulista, São Paulo, 10:135–42.

  ———
  1960   "Slash and Burn Agriculture: A Closer Look at Its Implica-
    tions for Settlement Patterns." Men and Cultures (Selected Papers
    of the Fifth International Congress of Anthropological and Ethno-
    logical Sciences), Anthony F. C. Wallace (Ed.), pp. 229–34, Phila-
    delphia (available as Bobbs-Merrill Reprint #A-26).

  ———
  1961   "Slash-and-Burn Cultivation Among the Kuikuru and Its Im-
    plications for Cultural Development in the Amazon Basin," in
    J. Wilbert (Ed.), The Evolution of Horticultural Systems in Native
    South America, Causes and Consequences: A Symposium. Antro-
    pologica, Caracas, 47–67, Supplement Publication No. 2.

  ———
  1964   "Shifting Cultivation Among the Amahuaca of Eastern Peru."
    Völkerkundliche Abhandlungen, Hannover, 1:9–18.

  ———
  1970a   "The Transition from Hunting to Horticulture in the Ama-
    zon Basin," in Eighth Congress of Anthropological and Ethnologi-
    cal Sciences. Pp. 244–48, Tokyo: Science Council of Japan.

  ———
  1970b   "A Theory of the Origin of the State." Science 169:733–38.
Carr-Saunders, A. M.
  1922   The Population Problem. Oxford: The Clarendon Press.
Carrasco, Pedro
  1961   "The Civil-Religious Hierarchy in Mesoamerican Communi-

ties: Pre-Spanish Background and Colonial Development." *American Anthropologist* 63:483–97.

Casagrande, Joseph B.
1966 *Proposal for Research on Intergroup Relations in Ecuador.* Unpublished.

——— 1969 *The Implications of Community Differences for Development Programs: An Ecuadorean Example.* Paper presented at the Society for Applied Anthropology Meetings, Mexico City, April 9–16.

Cassidy, N. G., and S. D. Pahalad
1953 "The Maintenance of Soil Fertility in Fiji." *Agricultural Journal,* Fiji, 24:82–86.

Castellanos, Juan de
1955 "Elegías de Varones Ilustres de Indias." *Biblioteca de la Presidencia de Colombia,* 4 vols., Bogotá.

Cavalle-Sforza, L. L., and A. W. F. Edwards
1967 "Phylogenetic Analysis: Models and Estimation Procedures." *American Journal of Human Genetics* 19:233–57.

Chagnon, Napoleon A.
1966 *Yanomamo Warfare: Social Organization and Marriage Alliances.* Ph.D. dissertation, University of Michigan.

——— 1967 "Yanomamö: The Fierce People" *Natural History* 76:22–31.

——— 1968a *Yanomamö: The Fierce People.* New York: Holt, Rinehart & Winston, Case Studies in Cultural Anthropology.

——— 1968b "Yanamamö Social Organization and Warfare," in M. Fried, M. Harris, R. Murphy (Eds.), *War: The Anthropology of Armed Conflict and Aggression.* Pp. 109–59, Garden City: The Natural History Press.

——— 1968c "The Feast." *Natural History* 77:34–41.

——— in press *Doing Anthropological Fieldwork Among the Yanomamö Indians.* New York: Holt, Rinehart & Winston.

Chagnon, Napoleon A., Philip Le Quesne and James M. Cook
1971 "Yanomamö Hallucinogens: Anthropological, Botanical, and Chemical Findings." *Current Anthropology* 12(1):72–74.

Chandless, W.
1866 "Ascent of the River Purús." *Journal of the Royal Geographic Society* 35:86–118.

Chao, Yuen-Ren
1956 "The Non-Uniqueness of Phonemic Solutions of Phonetics

504   *Bibliography*

Systems," in Martin Joos (Ed.), *Readings in Linguistics I: The Development of Descriptive Linguistics in America 1925–56.* Chicago: University of Chicago Press.

Chapple, Eliot D., and Carleton S. Coon
1942 *Principles of Anthropology.* New York: Henry Holt & Company.

Childe, V. Gordon
1953 "Old World Prehistory: Neolithic," in A. L. Kroeber (Ed.), *Anthropology Today.* Pp. 193–210, Chicago: University of Chicago Press.

Cieza de León, Pedro
1941 *La Crónica del Perú.* Madrid: Espasa Calpe.

———
1945 (orig. 1551) *La Crónica del Perú.* Buenos Aires: Colección Austral.

———
1959 *The Incas of Pedro de Cieza de León,* Harriet de Onis (Trans.), Victor Wolfgang von Hagen (Ed.). Norman: University of Oklahoma Press.

Clark, George L.
1954 *Elements of Ecology.* New York: John Wiley & Sons, Inc.

Clastres, Pierre
1972 "The Guayaki," in M. G. Bicchieri (Ed.), *Hunters and Gatherers Today.* Pp. 138–74, New York: Holt, Rinehart & Winston.

Cline, Howard
1953 *The United States and Mexico.* Cambridge: Harvard University Press.

Cobo, Bernabé
1890–93 (orig. 1653) *Historia del Nuevo Mundo,* Marcos Jiménez de la Espada (Ed.). Seville: Sociedad de Bibliófilos Andaluces.

———
1956 *Historia del Nuevo Mundo.* Biblioteca de Autores Españoles Desde la Formacion del Lengua je Hasta Nuestros Dias (Continuacion), Tomo 91:1–427; Tomo 92:5–275. Madrid: Ediciones Atlas.

Coe, Michael
1966 *The Maya.* New York: Praeger, Ancient Peoples and Places Series.

Coe, William R.
1957 "Environmental Limitation on Maya Culture: A Re-examination." *American Anthropologist* 59:328–35.

Colbacchini, A., and C. Albisetti
1942 *Os Bororos Orientais Orarimogodogue do Planalto Oriental*

de Mato Grosso. Brasiliana, Serie Grande, Formato 4, São Paulo.
Collier, Donald
1958   "El Desarrollo de la Civilizacion Peruana." *Revista Colombiana de Antropología* 7:271–87.

────   1962   "The Central Andes." *Viking Fund Publications in Anthropology* No. 32, pp. 162–76.
Collier, John, and Aníbal Buitrón
1949   *The Awakening Valley.* Chicago: University of Chicago Press.
Conklin, Harold C.
1957   *Hanunóo Agriculture: A Report of an Integral System of Shifting Cultivation in the Philippines.* Rome: Food and Agriculture Organization of the United Nations.

────   1961   "The Study of Shifting Cultivation." *Current Anthropology* 2(1):27–61.
Conolly, J. R., and M. Ewing
1965   "Ice Rafted Detritus as a Climatic Indicator in Antarctic Deep-Sea Cores." *Science* 150:1822–24.
Cooper, Jed Arthur
1965   *The School in Otavalo Indian Society.* Tucson: Panguitch Publications.
Cooper, John M.
1942   "Areal and Temporal Aspects of Aboriginal South American Culture." *Primitive Man* 15(1–2):1–38.

────   1946   "The Yahgan," in Julian Steward (Ed.), *Handbook of South American Indians.* Vol. 1:94, Washington, D.C.: Smithsonian Institution.

────   1947   "Stimulants and Narcotics," in Julian Steward (Ed.), *Handbook of South American Indians.* Vol. 5:525–58, Washington, D.C.: Smithsonian Institution.
Crocker, J. Christopher
1969a   "Men's House Associates Among the Eastern Bororo." *Southwestern Journal of Anthropology* 25(3):236–60.

────   1969b   "Reciprocity and Hierarchy Among the Eastern Bororo." *Man* 4(1):44–58.
Crocker, William
1958   "Os Indios Canelas de Hoje. Nota Prévia." *Boletim do Museu Paraense Emílio Goeldi,* nova série, Antropologia, 2:1–9.

1961   "The Canela Since Nimuendajú." *Anthropological Quarterly*
        34:69–84.
Cruxent, J. M.
1968   "Theses for Meditation on the Origin and Distribution of
        Man in South America," in *Biomedical Challenges Presented by
        the American Indian.* Washington, D.C.: Pan American Health
        Organization Publication 165, pp. 11–16.
Cruxent, José M., and Irving Rouse
1959   *An Archaeological Chronology of Venezuela.* Pan American
        Union of Social Science Monographs No. 6, Vols. 1 and 2.

d'Abbeville, Claude
1614   *Histoire de las Mission* . . . Paris: F. Huby.
Da Matta, Roberto
1963   "Notas Sôbre o Contato e a Extinção dos Indios Gaviões do
        Médio Rio Tocantins." *Revista do Museu Paulista* 14.

1967a   "Grupos Jê do Tocantins." *Atas do Simpósio sôbre a Biota
        Amazônica,* Rio de Janeiro: Conselho Nacional de Pesquisas.

1967b   "Mito e Autoridade Doméstica: Uma Tentative de Análise
        de um Mito Timbira em Suas Relações com a Estrutura Social."
        Revista do Instituto de Ciências Sociais, Rio de Janeiro, 4(1).

1970   *Apinayé Social Structure.* Unpublished Ph.D. dissertation,
        Harvard University.

1971   "Myth and Anti-Myth Among the Timbira," in P. Maranda
        and E. Kongas Maranda (Eds.), *The Structural Analysis of Oral
        Tradition.* Philadelphia: University of Pennsylvania Press.
Dancis, J.
1968   "Antepartum Diagnosis of Genetic Diseases." *Journal of
        Pediatrics* 72:301.
d'Andretta Jr., C., R. G. Baruzzi, M. F. Sarmento, I. Kameyama,
L. C. Souza Dias and H. Pewteado, Jr.
1969   "Estudo da Prevalencia da Malaria em Índios do Parque
        Nacional do Xingu Determinação dos Indices Parasitário e
        Esplénico." *Revista Brasileira de Medicina Tropical* 3(1):12.
Deevey, E. S.
1960   "The Human Population." *Scientific American* 203:195–201.
De Mars, R., G. Sarto, J. S. Felix and P. Benke

1969 "Lesch-Nythan Mutation: Prenatal Detection with Amniotic Fluid Cells." *Science* 164:1303–5.

Denevan, W. M.
1971 "Campa Subsistence in the Gran Pajonal, Eastern Peru." *Geographical Review* 61(4):496–518.

Descobar, Fray Geronimo
1938 "Relación de . . . de la Orden de San Agustín Sobre el Carácter e Costumbres de los Yndios de la Provincia de Popayán." Jijón y Caamaño: *Sebastián de Benalcázar* II:149–76, Quito.

d'Evreux, Yves
1864 *Voyage dans le Nord du Brésil*, F. Denis (Ed.). Leipzig et Paris.

Dietschy, Hans
1959 *Das Häuptlingswesen bei den Karajá*. Mitteilungen aus den Museum für Völkerkunde im Hamburg 25 (Amerikanische Miszellen). Hamburg: Komissionsverlag Ludwig Appel.

——— 1960 "Notes à propos des Dances des Caraja." *Bulletin de la Société des Americanistes* 19:1–5, Geneva: Musée et Institut d'Ethnographie.

——— 1962 "Männerhäuser, Heiliger Pfahl und Männerplatz bei den Karajá-Indianern Zentralbrasiliens." *Anthropos*, Freiburg, 57: 454–64.

Diffie, Bailey Wallys
1945 *Latin American Civilization: Colonial Period*. Harrisburg: The Telegraph Press.

Diniz, Edson Soares
1962 *Os Kayapó-Gogotire; Aspectos Socio-Culturais do Momento Atual*. Belém: Instituto Nacional de Pesquisas da Amazonia.

Dobrizhoffer, Martin
1822 *An Account of the Abipones, an Equestrian People of Paraguay*. 3 vols., London.

Dobyns, Henry F.
1966 "Estimating Aboriginal American Population: An Appraisal of Techniques with a New Hemispheric Estimate." *Current Anthropology* 7(4):395–449.

Dole, Gertrude E.
1956 "Ownership and Exchange Among the Kuikuru Indians." *Revista do Museu Paulista*, São Paulo, 10:125–33.

——— 1957 *The Development of Patterns of Kinship Nomenclature*. Ph.D.

dissertation, University of Michigan, Ann Arbor: University Microfilms.

――――

1959   "La Cultura de los Indios Kuikuru del Brasil Central: La Organización Social." *RUNA* 8(2):185–202 (1956–57), Buenos Aires.

――――

1960   "Techniques of Preparing Manioc Flour as a Key to Culture History in Tropical America," in Anthony F. C. Wallace (Ed.), *Men and Cultures*. Selected Papers of the Fifth International Congress of Anthropological and Ethnological Sciences, Philadelphia: University of Pennsylvania Press, 241–48.

――――

1964a   "The Development of Hawaiian Kinship Nomenclature as Exemplified by the Kuikuru" (summary). *Proceedings of the 35th International Congress of Americanists*, 1962, Vol. 2:95.

――――

1964b   "A Preliminary Consideration of the Prehistory of the Upper Xingú Basin." *Revista do Museu Paulista* 13:399–423 (1961–62).

――――

1966   "Anarchy Without Chaos: Alternatives to Political Authority Among the Kuikuru," in Marc J. Swartz, Victor W. Turner and Arthur Tuden (Eds.), *Political Anthropology* 73–87, Chicago: Aldine Publishing Company.

――――

1969   "Generation Kinship Nomenclature as an Adaptation to Endogamy." *Southwestern Journal of Anthropology* 25(2):105–23.

Dole, Gertrude, and Robert Carneiro

1958   "A Mechanism for Mobilizing Labor Among the Kuikuru." *Transactions* of the New York Academy of Sciences 21:58–60.

Donahue, J. G.

1965   "Diatoms as Indicators of Pleistocene Climatic Fluctuations in the Pacific Sector of the Southern Ocean." *Abstracts, VII Inqua Congr.*, Boulder, Colorado, p. 103.

Donn, W. L., W. R. Farrand and M. Ewing

1962   "Pleistocene Ice Volumes and Sea Level Lowering." *Journal of Geology* 70:206–14.

Dreyfus, Simone

1963   *Les Kayapó du Nord, État de Para, Brésil: Contribution a l'Étude des Indiens Gé.* Paris: Mouton & Co.

Dubos, R.

1969a   "Human Ecology." *WHO Chronicle* 23:499–504.

1969b "Lasting Biological Effects of Early Influences." *Perspectives in Biology and Medicine* 12:479–91.

Duffy, James
1962 *Portugal in Africa.* Cambridge: Harvard University Press.

Dumond, D. E.
1961 "Swidden Agriculture and the Rise of Maya Civilization." *Southwestern Journal of Anthropology* 17:301–16.

Dumont, Louis
1957 *Hierarchie et Alliance: Notes Comparatives sur la Parenté dans l'Inde du Sud.* Paris: Mouton.

Dunn, F. L.
1965 "On the Antiquity of Malaria in the Western Hemisphere." *Human Biology* 37:385–93.

1968 "Epidemiological Factors: Health and Disease in Hunter-Gatherers," in R. B. Lee and I. DeVore (Eds.), *Man the Hunter.* Chicago, Illinois: Aldine Publishing Co.

Eggan, Fred (Ed.)
1955 *The Social Anthropology of North American Tribes.* 2nd edition, Chicago: University of Chicago Press.

1966 *The American Indian: Perspectives for the Study of Social Change.* Chicago.

Ehrlich, P. R., and J. P. Holdran
1970 "Population and Process: A Technological Perspective." *Bio-Science* 19:1065–71.

Emery, K. O.
1965 "Submerged Shore Deposits of the Atlantic Continental Shelf." *Abstracts, VII Inqua Cong.,* Boulder, Colorado, p. 127.

Engel, Frédéric
1958 "Sites et Établissements sans Céramique de la Côte Péruvienne." *Journal de la Société des Americanistes,* Paris, n.s., Tome 46:67–155.

Escribens, Augusto, and Paul Proulx
1970 *Gramatic del Quechua de Huaylas.* Lima: Universidad Nacional Mayor de San Marcos.

Estete, Muguel
1938 La Relación del Viaje que Hizo el Señor Capitán Hernando Pizarro por Mandado del Señor Gobernador, Su Hermano, Desde el Pueblo de Caxamalca a Pachacama y de Alli a Jauja. Los Cronistas de la Conquista; Selección, Prologo, Notas y Con-

cordancias de Horacio H. Urteaga. *Biblioteca de Cultura Peruana,* primera serie, No. 2:77–98, Paris: Desclee, De Brouwer.

Evans, Clifford

1955   "New Archeological Interpretations in Northeastern South America." *New Interpretations of Aboriginal American Culture History,* 75th Anniversary Volume of the Anthropological Society of Washington, Washington, D.C.

———   1965   "Lowland South America," in Jesse Jennings and Edward Norbeck (Eds.), *Prehistoric Man in the New World.* Chicago: University of Chicago Press, pp. 419–50.

Evans, Clifford, and Betty J. Meggers

1968   *Archeological Investigations on the Rio Napo, Eastern Ecuador.* Washington: Smithsonian Contributions to Anthropology 6.

Eyde, David B., and P. M. Postal

1963   "Matrilineality and Matrilocality Among the Siriono: A Reply to Needham." *Bijdragen tot de Taal-, Land- en Volkenkunde* 119:284–85.

Farabee, W. C.

1918   *The Central Arawaks.* Philadelphia: University of Pennsylvania Museum Publications in Anthropology, No. 9.

———   1922   *Indian Tribes of Eastern Peru.* Cambridge: Peabody Museum Paper in American Archeology and Ethnology No. 10.

———   1924   *The Central Caribs.* Philadelphia: University of Pennsylvania Museum Publications in Anthropology, Vol. 10.

Faron, Louis C.

1956   "Araucanian Patri-Organization and the Omaha System." *American Anthropologist* 58:435–56.

———   1961a   "On Ancestor Propitiation Among the Mapuche of Central Chile." *American Anthropologist* 63:824–30.

———   1961b   "The Dakota Omaha System in Mapuche Society." *Journal of the Royal Anthropological Institute* 91:11–22.

———   1961c   *Mapuche Social Structure.* Illinois Studies in Anthropology, No. 1, Urbana: University of Illinois Press.

———   1961d   "A Reinterpretation of Choco Society." *Southwestern Journal of Anthropology* 17:94–102.

1962a "Marriage Residence and Domestic Groups Among the Panamanian Choco." *Ethnology* 1:13–38.

1962b "Matrilateral Marriage Among the Mapuche." *Sociologus,* Berlin, n.s., 12:54–56.

1962c "Symbolic Values and the Integration of Society." *American Anthropologist* 64:1151–64.

1964 *Hawks of the Sun: Mapuche Morality and Its Ritual Attributes.* Pittsburgh: University of Pittsburgh Press.

1968 *The Mapuche Indians of Chile.* New York: Holt, Rinehart & Winston.

Fejos, Paul
1943 *Ethnography of the Yagua.* Viking Fund Publications in Anthropology 3:1–144.

Ferdon, Edwin N., Jr.
1959 "Agricultural Potential and the Development of Cultures." *Southwestern Journal of Anthropology* 15(1):1–19.

Fernandes, Florestan
1949a "A Análise Funcionalista da Guerra: Possibilidade de Aplicação à Sociedade Tupinambá." *Revista do Museu Paulista,* nova série 3:7–128, São Paulo.

1949b "A Economia Tupinamba." *Revista do Arquivo Municipal,* São Paulo, 122:7–77.

1952 "A Função Social da Guerra na Sociedade Tupinambá." *Revista do Museu Paulista* 6:7–425.

Figueiredo, Antônio de
1961 *Portugal and the Empire: The Truth.* London: V. Gollancz.

Firth, Raymond
1939 *A Primitive Polynesian Economy.* London.

1958 *We, the Tikopia.* New York: Macmillan.

Fitch, W., and J. V. Neel
1969 "The Phylogenetic Relationships of Some Indian Tribes of Central and South America." *American Journal of Human Genetics* 21:384–97.

Fittgokau, et al.
  1968 *Biogeography and Ecology of South America.* 2 vols., The
       Hague: Junk, #18 in Monographiae Biologiciae.
Fleming, Peter
  1942 *Brazilian Adventure.* London: Readers Club Press.
Flint, R. F.
  1963 "Status of the Pleistocene Wisconsin Stage in Central North
       America." *Science* 139:402–4.
Fock, N.
  1963 *Waiwai: Religion and Society of an Amazon Tribe.* Copen-
       hagen: Etnografisk Roekke 8.
Fontenelle, Osmar
  n.d.   "Contribution to the Biology of the Pirarucu, *Arapaima gigas*
       —(Cuvier), in Captivity." Fortaleza, Ceará: M.V.O.P.-D.N.O.C.S.,
       Serviço de Pisicultura, Trabalhos Técnicos, Série 1-c, Publication
       No. 177.
Ford, A. B.
  1970 "Casualties of Our Time." *Science* 167:256–63.
Foster, George
  1948 *Empire's Children: The People of Tzintzuntán.* Washington,
       D.C.: Smithsonian Institution.
——
  1960 *Culture and Conquest: America's Spanish Heritage.* Chicago:
       Quadrangle Books.
Fray, C., and M. Ewing
  1963 "Wisconsin Sea Level as Indicated in Argentine Continental
       Shelf Sediments." *Proceedings* of the Academy of Natural Science
       of Philadelphia 115(6):113–26.
Freeman, J. D.
  1955 *Iban Agriculture: A Report on the Shifting Cultivation of Hill
       Rice by the Iban of Sarawak.* Colonial Research Studies, Vol. 18,
       London: Her Majesty's Stationery Office.
Freud, Sigmund
  1952 *Totem and Taboo.* New York.
Freyre, Gilberto
  1956 *The Masters and the Slaves.* New York: Alfred A. Knopf.
Fried, Jacob
  1959 "The Indian and Mestizaje in Peru." Paper read at the Mexico
       City Meeting of the American Anthropological Association.
Fried, Morton H.
  1967 *The Evolution of Political Society: An Essay in Political An-
       thropology.* New York: Random House.

Friede, Juan (Ed.)
1955–57   *Documentos Inéditos para la Historia de Colombia.* 5 vols., Bogotá: Academia Colombiana de Historia.

Frikel, Protásio
1968   *Os Xikrín: Equipamento e Técnicas de Subsistência.* Belém: Museu Paraense Emílio Goeldi, Publicações Avulsas No. 7.

Fuente, Julio de la
1949   *Yalalag: Una Villa Zapoteca Serrana.* Mexico: Museo Nacional de Antropologia.

Galvão, Eduardo
1953   "Cultura e Sistema de Parentesco dos Tribus do Alto Rio Xingú." *Boletim do Museu Nacional (Antropologia)*, Rio de Janeiro, n.s., 14:1–56.

———   1963a   "O Cavalo na America Indígena: Nota Prévia a um Estudo de Mudança Cultural." *Revista do Museu Paulista*, São Paulo, n.s., 14:220–32.

———   1963b   "Elementos Básicos da Horticultura de Subsistência Indígena." *Revista do Museu Paulista*, São Paulo, 14:120–44.

———   1967   "Indigenous Culture Areas of Brazil, 1900–1959," in Janice Hopper (Ed. and Trans.), *Indians of Brazil in the Twentieth Century.* Washington, D.C.: Institute for Cross-Cultural Research.

Gandavo, Pedro de Magalhães de
1922   *The Histories of Brazil.* Vol. II, New York: The Cortes Society.

Garcilaso de la Vega
1943 (orig. 1604)   *Comentarios Reales*, Angel Rosenblatt (Ed.). Buenos Aires.

———   1945 (orig. 1609)   *Comentarios Reales de los Incas*, Angel Rosenblatt (Ed.). 2nd Edition, Buenos Aires.

———   1961   *The Incas: The Royal Commentaries of the Inca*, Alain Gheerbrant (Ed.), Maria Jolas (Trans.). New York: Avon Books.

Gillin, John N.
1936   *The Barama River Caribs of British Guiana.* Cambridge, Mass.: Papers of the Peabody Museum of Archeology and Ethnology, Harvard University, Vol. 14(2).

1940   "Tropical Forest Area of South America." *American Anthropologist* 42:642.

1945   *Moche: A Peruvian Coastal Community.* Washington, D.C.: Smithsonian Institution.

Gilmore, Raymond M.
1950   "Fauna and Ethnozoology of South America," in Julian Steward (Ed.), *Handbook of South American Indians,* Vol. 6: *Physical Anthropology, Linguistics, and Cultural Geography of South American Indians.* Pp. 345–464, Washington, D.C.: Smithsonian Institution.

Gladwin, Harold S.
1947   *Men Out of Asia.* New York: Whittlesey House.

Goffman, Erving
1959   *The Presentation of Self in Everyday Life.* New York: Anchor Books.

Goldman, Irving
1948   "Tribes of the Uapés-Caquetá Region," in Julian Steward (Ed.), *Handbook of South American Indians,* Vol. 3. Pp. 763–98, Washington, D.C.: Smithsonian Institution.

1963   *The Cubeo: Indians of the Northwest Amazon.* Illinois Studies in Anthropology No. 2, Urbana: University of Illinois Press.

Gonzalez Holguín, Diego
1608   *Vocabulario de la Lengua General de Todo el Peru Llamada Lengua Quichua o del Inca.* Lima.

Gourou, Pierre
1953   *The Tropical World.* London: Longmans, Green and Co.

Greenberg, Joseph H.
1960   "The General Classification of Central and South American Languages," in A. F. C. Wallace (Ed.), *Men and Cultures.* Selected Papers of the 5th International Congress of Anthropological and Ethnological Sciences, Philadelphia: University of Pennsylvania Press.

Gregor, Thomas
1969   *Social Relationships in a Small Society: A Study of the Mehinacu Indians of Central Brazil.* Ph.D. dissertation, Columbia University.

1970   "Exposure and Seclusion: A Study of Institutionalized Isolation Among the Mehinacu Indians of Brazil." *Ethnology* 9:234–50.

Grobman, Paul
1965   *Races of Maize in Perú.* Washington, D.C.: National Academy of Sciences, publication 915.

Groot, J. J.
1964   "Quaternary Stratigraphy of Sediments of the Argentine Basin." *Transactions of the New York Academy of Sciences Series II* (26):881–86.

Groot, J. J., C. R. Groot, M. Ewing and L. Burckle
1965   "Stratigraphy and Provenance of Quaternary Sediments of the Argentine Basin." *Abstracts, VII Inqua Congr.,* Boulder, Colorado, p. 179.

Grubb, W. B.
1911   *An Unknown People in an Unknown Land, the Indians of the Paraguayan Chaco.* London.

Guillen Chaparro, Francisco
1898   "Memoria de los Pueblos de la Gobernación de Popayán y Cosas y Constelaciones que Hay en Ellos." *Anales de la Instrucción Pública* 15:144–56, Bogotá.

Guppy, N.
1958   *Wai-wai.* New York.

Gusinde, Martin
1961   *The Yamana* (English translation). New Haven: Human Relations Area Files Press.

Guyot, Mireille
1968   *Les Mythes chez les Selk'nam et les Yamana de la Terre de Feu.* Université de Paris Travaux et Memoires de l'Institut d'Ethnologie, No. 75, Paris: Institut d'Ethnologie.

Hafsten, U.
1961   "Pleistocene Development of Vegetation and Climate in the Southern High Plains as Evidenced by Pollen Analysis." D. F. Wendorf (comp.), *Paleoecology of the Llano Estacado,* Ft. Burgwin Res. Center Publ. 1:59–91.

Hanke, Lewis
1949   *Bartolomé de las Casas.* Havana.

Harding, Thomas
1960   "Adaptation and Stability," in M. D. Sahlins and E. R. Service (Eds.), *Evolution and Culture,* 45–68. Ann Arbor: University of Michigan Press.

Hardy, F.
1945   "The Soils of South America," in *Plants and Plant Science in Latin America.* Vol. 2:322–26.

Harner, Michael J.

    1962   "Jívaro Souls." *American Anthropologist* 64:258–72. Also in P. B. Hammond (Ed.), *Cultural and Social Anthropology: Selected Readings.* Pp. 299–308, New York: Macmillan.

    ———

    1963   *Machetes, Shotguns and Society.* University of California, doctoral dissertation.

    ———

    1970   "Population Pressure and the Social Evolution of Agriculturalists." *Southwestern Journal of Anthropology* 26:67–86.

    ———

    1972   *The Jívaro: People of the Sacred Waterfalls.* New York: Doubleday-Natural History.

    ———

    1973   (Ed.) *Hallucinogens and Shamanisms.* New York: Oxford University Press.

Harris, Marvin

    1958   *Portugal's African "Wards."* New York: The American Committee on Africa.

    ———

    1959   "Labour-Emigration Among the Mozambique Thonga." *Africa* 29:50–66.

    ———

    1964a   *The Nature of Cultural Things.* New York: Random House.

    ———

    1964b   "Racial Identity in Brazil." *Luso-Brazilian Review.*

    ———

    1964c   *Patterns of Race in the Americas.* New York: Walker & Company.

    ———

    1968   *The Rise of Anthropological Theory.* New York: T. Y. Crowell.

    ———

    1971   *Culture, Man and Nature.* New York: T. Y. Crowell.

Harris, Marvin, and Conrad Kottak

    1963   "The Structural Significance of Brazilian Racial Categories." *Sociologia,* São Paulo, 25:203–9.

Hassaurek, Friedrich

    1967   *Four Years Among the Ecuadoreans,* C. Harvey Gardner (Ed.). Carbondale: Southern Illinois University Press.

Hawkes, J. G.

    1944   *Potato Collecting Expeditions in Mexico and South America, Vol. 2, Systematic Classification of the Collections.* Cambridge:

Imperial Bureau of Plant Breeding and Genetics, School of Agriculture.

――――
1947 "Some Observations on South American Potatoes." *Annals of Applied Biology* 34(4):622–33.

Hays, J. D.
1965 "Radiolaria and Late Tertiary and Quaternary History of Antarctic Seas." *Biology of the Antarctic Seas II*, Amer. Geophys. Union, Ant. Res. Ser. 5.

Henry, Jules
1941 *Jungle People: A Kaingáng Tribe of the Highlands of Brazil.* New York (reprinted with an added note by the author in 1964, New York: Alfred A. Knopf, Random House, Vintage Books).

Heredia, Pedro de
1916 "Cartas Inéditas." *Boletin Historial,* Cartagena, Tomo I.

Herrera, Antonio de
1944 (orig. 1601) *Historia General de los Hechos de los Castellanos en las Islas y Tierra-Firme de el Mar Oceano.* 10 vols., Asunción.

Herskovits, M. J.
1938 *Dahomey, an Ancient West African Kingdom.* 2 vols., New York: J. J. Augustin.

Heusser, C. J.
1965 "Late-Pleistocene Pollen Diagrams from Southern Chile." Revised abstract of paper presented at VII Inqua Congr., Boulder, Colorado.

Hilbert, Peter Paul
1962a "Preliminary Results of Archaeological Research of the Japurá River, Middle Amazon." *Akten des Internationalen Amerikanistenkongresses, Wien 1960:*465–70.

――――
1962b "New Stratigraphic Evidence of Culture Change on the Middle Amazon (Solimões)." *Akten des Internationalen Amerikanistenkongress, Wien 1960:*471–76.

――――
1968 *Archäologische Untersuchungen im Mittleren Amazonas.* Berlin: Marburger Studien zur Völkerkunde 1.

Hockett, Charles F.
1948 "Implications of Bloomfield's Algonquian Studies." *Language* 24:117–31.

――――
1959 "On the Format of Phonemic Reports, with Restatement of Ocaina." *International Journal of American Linguistics* 25:59–62.

Hoijer, Harry, Eric P. Hamp and William Bright
  1965   "Contributions to a Bibliography of Comparative Amerindian." *International Journal of American Linguistics* 31:346–53.
Holmberg, Allan R.
  1950   *Nomads of the Long Bow: The Sirionó of Eastern Bolivia.* Smithsonian Institution, Publications of the Institute of Social Anthropology, No. 10 (reprinted 1969, Garden City: Natural History Press).
Hopper, Janice (Ed. and Trans.)
  1967   *Indians of Brazil in the Twentieth Century.* Washington, D.C.: Institute for Cross-Cultural Research.
Hulett, H. R.
  1970   "Optimum World Population." *BioScience* 20:160–61.
Huxley, Francis
  1956   *Affable Savages: An Anthropologist Among the Urubu Indians of Brazil.* New York: Capricorn Books.
Hymes, Dell
  1956   "Review on Rowe, J. H., 'Linguistic Classification Problems in South America.' " *Language* 32:591–96.

INCAP-ICNND
  1961   *Food Composition Table for Use in Latin America.* Bethesda, Maryland: Interdepartmental Committee on Nutrition for National Defense.
Instituto Ecuatoriano de Antropología y Geografía (IEAG)
  1953   *Ilumán, una Comunidad Indígena Aculturada.* Quito: Instituto Nacional de Prevision, serie informes, No. 3.
International Journal of American Indian Linguistics. Indiana University, Baltimore: Waverly Press.
Ishida, Eiichiro, and others
  1960   *Tōkyō Daigaku Andesu Chitai Gakujutusu Chōsa dan 1958 Nendo Hōkokusho.* The report of the University of Tokyo Scientific Expedition to the Andes in 1958, Tokyo: Bijutsu Shuppan Sha.

James, A. G.
  1949   *Village Arrangement and Social Organization Among Some Amazon Tribes.* Ph.D. dissertation, Columbia University.
James, Preston
  1959   *Latin America.* 3rd Edition, New York: The Odyssey Press.
Jaramillo, Victor Alejandro
  1953   *Participación de Otavalo en la Guerra de Independencia.* Otavalo: Editorial Cultura.

Jijon y Caamaño, J.
 1936 *Sebastián de Benalcázar.* 2 vols., Quito.
Journal de la Société des Américanistes de Paris. Paris, France.
Juan, Jorge, and Antonio de Ulloa
 1806 *A Voyage to South America: Describing at Large the Spanish Cities, Towns, Provinces, etc., on That Extensive Continent.* Vol. I, London.

_____

 1918 *Noticias Secretas de America (Siglo XVIII).* Tomo I, Madrid: Editorial America, Serie "Biblioteca Ayacucho."
Juan y Santacillia and Antonio de Ulloa
 1826 *Noticias Secretas de América.* London.

Karsten, R.
 1935 *The Headhunters of Western Amazonas.* Helsingfor: Commentationes Humanarum Litterarum, Societas Scientarum Fennica.
Kidder, Alfred II
 1943 *Some Early Sites in the Northern Lake Titicaca Basin.* Papers of the Peabody Museum of American Archaeology and Ethnology, Vol. XXVII, No. 1, Cambridge.
Kietzman, Dale W.
 1967 "Indians and Culture Areas of Twentieth-Century Brazil," in J. Hopper (Ed.), *Indians of Brazil in the Twentieth Century.* Washington, D.C.: Institute for Cross-Cultural Research.
Kigoshi, Kunihiko, and others
 1962 *Gakushuin Natural Radiocarbon Measurements I.* Kunihiko Kigoshi, Yoshio Tomikura and Kunihiko Endo, *Radiocarbon* 4:84–94, New Haven.
Kimura, M.
 1968 "Evolutionary Rate at the Molecular Level." *Nature* 217:624–26.

_____

 1969 "The Rate of Molecular Evolution Considered from the Standpoint of Population Genetics." *Proceedings of the National Academy of Sciences* 63:1181–88.
King, J. L., and T. H. Jukes
 1969 "Non-Darwinian Evolution." *Science* 164:788–98.
Kirchhoff, Paul
 1931 "Die Verwandschaftsorganisation der Urwaldstämme Südamerikas." *Zeitschrift für Ethnologie* 63(15):182.
Kloosterboer, W.
 1960 *Involuntary Labour Since the Abolition of Slavery.* Leiden: E. J. Brill.

520 *Bibliography*

Koch-Grunberg, Theodor
1922 "Die Völkergruppierung zwischen Rio Branco, Orinoco, Rio Negro und Yapura." *Festschrift Eduard Seler,* Stuttgart.
———
1923 *Vom Roroima zum Orinoco.* Vol. 3, *Ethnographie,* Stuttgart.
Kosok, Paul
1960 *El Valle de Lambayeque.* Actas y Trabajos del II Congreso Nacional de Historia del Perú (Epoca Pre-Hispánica), 4–9 de Agosto de 1958, I:49–67, Lima: Centro de Estudios Historico-Militares del Peru.
———
1965 *Life, Land and Water in Ancient Peru.* Brooklyn: Long Island University Press.
Kottak, Conrad
1963 "Race Relations in Arembepe." Columbia-Cornell-Harvard-Illinois Summer Field Studies Program (Mimeographed).
Kozak, V.
1963 "Ritual of a Bororo Funeral." *Natural History* 72(1):38–49.
Kracke, Waud H.
1963 "The Dual Role of Witchcraft in Trobriand Social Structure." *Anthropology Tomorrow* 9:23–31.
Krause, Fritz
1911 *In den Wildnessen Brasiliens.* Leipzig.
Krieger, Alex D.
1964 "Early Man in the New World," in Jesse Jennings and Edward Norbeck (Eds.), *Prehistoric Man in the New World.* Chicago: University of Chicago Press, pp. 23–81.
Kroeber, Alfred Louis
1944 *Configurations of Culture Growth.* Berkeley: University of California Press.
———
1948 *Anthropology.* New York.
Kubler, George
1946 "The Quechua in the Colonial World," in Julian Steward (Ed.), *Handbook of South American Indians.* Vol. 2, Washington, D.C.: Smithsonian Institution.
———
1952 *The Indian Caste of Peru, 1795–1940.* Washington, D.C.: Smithsonian Institution.
———
1962 *The Art and Architecture of Ancient America; the Mexican, Maya, and Andean Peoples.* The Pelican History of Art, Z21, Baltimore: Penguin Books.

LaBarre, Weston
1948 *The Aymara Indians of the Lake Titicaca Plateau, Bolivia.*
Memoir No. 68, Washington, D.C.: American Anthropological
Association.
Lack, David
1954 *The Natural Regulation of Animal Numbers.* Oxford: The
Clarendon Press.
LaFarge, Oliver
1947 *Santa Eulalia.* Chicago: University of Chicago Press.
Landar, Herbert
1968 "The Karankawa Invasion of Texas." *International Journal of
American Linguistics* 34:242–58.
Landazuri Soto, Alberto
1959 *El Regimen Indígena Laboral en la Real Audiencia de Quito.*
Madrid.
Lanning, E. P.
1965 "Preceramic Archaeology of the Andes." *Abstracts, VII Inqua
Congr.,* Boulder, Colorado, p. 281.

———
1967 *Peru Before the Incas.* Englewood Cliffs, New Jersey: Prentice-
Hall.
Lanning, E. P., and E. A. Hammel
1961 "Early Lithic Industries of Western South America." *American Antiquity* 27:139–54.
Laraia, Roque de Barros
1965 "A Fricção Interétnica no Médio Tocantins." *América Latina*
7(2).
Laraia, Roque de Barros, and Roberto Da Matta
1967 *Indios e Castanheiros: A Impresa Extrativa dos Indios do
Médio Tocantins.* São Paulo: Difusão Europeia do Livro.
Lastra, Yolanda
1968 "Cochabamba Quechua Syntax." *Janua Linguarum,* Series
Practica 40, The Hague: Mouton.
Latcham, Ricardo E.
1936 *La Agricultura Pre-Colombina en Chile.* Chile: Santiago.
Lathrap, Donald W.
1958 "The Cultural Sequence at Yarinacocha, Eastern Peru."
American Antiquity 23(4):379–88.

———
1962 *Yarinacocha: Stratigraphic Excavations in the Peruvian Montaña.* Unpublished doctoral dissertation, Harvard University.

1963   "Possible Affiliations of the Macalilla Complex of Coastal Ecuador." *American Antiquity* 29(2):239–41.

1965a   "Origins of Central Andean Civilization: New Evidence." (Review of *Andes 2: Excavations at Kotosh, Peru, 1960,* by Izumi and Sono) *Science* 148(3671):796–98.

1965b   "Investigaciones en la Selva Peruana, 1964–1965." *Boletín del Museo Nacional de Anthropología y Arqueología,* Lima, 4:9–12.

1970   *The Upper Amazon.* New York: Praeger.

Lave, Jean Carter
1967   *Social Taxonomy Among the Krikati (Gê) of Central Brazil.* Unpublished Ph.D. dissertation, Harvard University.

Lawes, J. B., and J. Gilbert
1895   *The Rothamsted Experiments.* Edinburgh: William Blackwood and Sons.

Leacock, Seth
1964   "Economic Life of the Maue Indians." *Boletim do Museu Paraense Emilio Goeldi,* Belém, Antropologia, No. 19.

Lederberg, J.
1964   In G. Wolstenholme (Ed.), *Man and His Future.* Boston: Little, Brown & Company, 263–73.

1969   "Biological Warfare and the Extinction of Man." Statement before the Subcommittee on National Security Policy and Scientific Developments, House Committee on Foreign Affairs (2 December).

Lee, Richard B., and Irven DeVore (Eds.)
1968   *Man the Hunter.* Chicago: Aldine Publishing Co.

Leeds, Anthony
1960   "The Ideology of the Yaruru Indians in Relation to Socio-economic Organization." *Antropologica* 9:1–10, Caracas.

1961   "Yaruru Incipient Tropical Forest Horticulture," in J. Wilbert (Ed.), *The Evolution of Horticultural Systems in Native South America, Causes and Consequences: A Symposium. Antropologica,* Caracas, Supplement Publication No. 2:13–46.

1964   "Brazilian Careers and Social Structure." *American Anthropologist* 66:1321–47.

1969   "Ecological Determinants of Chieftainship Among the Yaruru Indians of Venezuela," in A. P. Vayda (Ed.), *Environment and Cultural Behavior: Ecological Studies in Cultural Anthropology.* Garden City: Natural History Press.

Léry, Jean
1880   *Voyage Faict en la Terre du Bresil.* 2(17):85, Paris: Gaffarel.

Leslie, Charles M.
1960   *Now We Are Civilized.* Detroit: Wayne State University Press.

Lévi-Strauss, Claude
1943a   "Guerre et Commerce chez les Indiens de l'Amerique du Sud." *Renaissance, Revue Trimestrelle Publiée par l'École Libre des Hautes Etudes* 1:122–39.

1943b   "The Social Use of Kinship Terms Among the Brazilian Indians." *American Anthropologist* 45:398–409.

1944   "The Social and Psychological Aspects of Chieftainship in a Primitive Tribe: The Nambikwara." *Transactions* of the New York Academy of Sciences, Series 2, 7(1).

1948a   "Tribes of the Upper Xingú River," in Julian Steward (Ed.), *Handbook of South American Indians.* Vol. 3, Washington, D.C.: Smithsonian Institution.

1948b   "La Vie Familiale et Sociale des Indiens Nambikwara." *Journal de la Societée des Americanistes,* Paris, n.s., 37:1–132.

1963   *Structural Anthropology.* New York: Basic Books.

1964   *Tristes Tropiques,* Trans. by John Russell. New York: Atheneum.

1966   *The Savage Mind.* Chicago: University of Chicago Press.

Lewis, Oscar
1951   *Life in a Mexican Villiage: Tepotzlan Restudied.* Urbana: University of Illinois Press.

1960   "Mexico Since Cárdenas," in Richard Adams et al., *Social Change in Latin America Today.* Pp. 285–345, Council on Foreign Relations, New York: Harper.

Lima, Pedro E. de
1950   "Os Indios Waurá: Observações Gerais. A. Ceramica."

Boletim do Museu Nacional, nova série, Antropologia 9, Rio de Janeiro.

Lipkind, William
1945 "The Caraja," in Julian Steward (Ed.), *Handbook of South American Indians.* Vol. 3:179–91. Washington, D.C.: Smithsonian Institution.

Littlefield, J. W.
1969 "Prenatal Diagnosis and Therapeutic Abortion." *New England Journal of Medicine* 280:722–23.

Loriot, James
1964 "A Selected Bibliography of Comparative American Indian Linguistics." *International Journal of American Linguistics* 30:62–80.

Lothrop, S. K.
1961 "Early Migrations to Central and South America: An Anthropological Problem in the Light of Other Sciences." *Journal of the Royal Anthropological Institute* 91:97–123.

Loukotka, Cestmir
1967 "Map: Ethno-Linguistic Distribution of South American Indians." *Annals of the Association of American Geographers,* Map Supplement No. 8, Washington, D.C.

———
1968 *Classification of South American Indian Languages,* Johannes Wilbert (Ed.). Los Angeles: Latin American Center, University of California.

Lowie, Robert H.
1919 "Family and Sib." *American Anthropologist* 21:28.

———
1947 *Primitive Society.* New York.

———
1948 "The Tropical Forests, an Introduction," in Julian Steward (Ed.), *Handbook of South American Indians,* Vol. 3: *The Tropical Forest Tribes.* Pp. 1–56, Washington, D.C.: Smithsonian Institution.

Macdonald, J. Frederick
1965 "Some Considerations About Tupi-Guarani Kinship Structures." *Boletim do Museu Paraense Emilio Goeldi,* Belém, n.s., Antropologia, 26.

Macgowan, Kenneth, and Joseph A. Hester, Jr.
1962 *Early Man in the New World.* Garden City: Anchor Books.

Marcoy, Paul (pseud. Laurent Saint-Cricq)
1873 *A Journey Across South America from the Pacific Ocean to*

the Atlantic Ocean, Elihu Rich (Trans.). 2 vols., London: Bladkie and Son.

Martin, M. Kay
1969 "South American Foragers: A Case Study in Cultural Devolution." *American Anthropologist* 71(2):243–60.

Martir de Angleria, Pedro
1944 *Décadas del Nuevo Mundo.* Buenos Aires.

Mason, James A.
1950 "The Languages of South America," in Julian Steward (Ed.), *Handbook of South American Indians.* Vol. 6:157–318, Washington, D.C.: Smithsonian Institution.

—— 1968 *The Ancient Civilizations of Peru.* Revised edition, London: Pelican Books.

Matthiessen, Peter
1961 *The Cloud Forest: A Vivid Journey into One of the Unknown Regions of the World.* New York: Pyramid Publications.

Maybury-Lewis, David
1956 "Kinship and Social Organization in Central Brazil." *Proceedings of the 32nd International Congress of Americanists,* 123–35.

—— 1960 "Parallel Descent and the Apinayé Anomaly." *Southwestern Journal of Anthropology* 16(2).

—— 1967 *Akwẽ-Shavante Society.* London: Oxford University Press.

—— 1968 (orig. 1965) *The Savage and the Innocent.* Boston: Beacon Press (paperback).

McConnell, Campbell
1966 *Economics.* New York: McGraw-Hill.

McCown, Theodore Doney
1945 *Pre-Incaic Huamachuco; Survey and Excavations in the Region of Huamachuco and Cajabamba.* University of California Publications in American Archaeology and Ethnology 39(4):i–x, 223–400, Berkeley and Los Angeles.

McQuown, Norman A.
1955 "The Indigenous Languages of Latin America." *American Anthropologist* 57:501–70.

Mead, Margaret
1932 *The Changing Culture of an Indian Tribe.* New York.

—— 1935 *Sex and Temperament in Three Primitive Societies.* New York: Morrow.

1940 *The Mountain Arapesh: II. Supernaturalism.* Anthropological Papers 37: Part 2, New York: American Museum of Natural History.

1949 *Male and Female.* New York: Morrow.
Meek, C. K.
1931 *A Sudanese Kingdom.* London: Kegan, Paul.
Meggers, Betty J.
1954 "Environmental Limitation on the Development of Culture." *American Anthropologist* 56:801–24 (also Bobbs-Merrill S-189).

1957a "Environmental Limitation on Maya Culture: A Reply to Coe." *American Anthropologist,* n.s., 59:888–90.

1957b "Environment and Culture in the Amazon Basin: An Appraisal of the Theory of Environmental Determinism." *Studies in Human Ecology. Social Science Monograph,* No. 3, Washington, D.C.: Panamerican Union.

1966 *Ecuador.* New York: Praeger.

1971 *Amazonia: Man and Culture in a Counterfeit Paradise.* Chicago: Aldine.
—— (Ed.)
1956 "Functional and Evolutionary Implications of Community Patterning," with Richard K. Beardsley, Preston Holder and Alex D. Kutsche. *Seminars in Archaeology,* R. Wauchope (Ed.), Memoir 11 1955, Menasha: Society for American Archaeology.
Meggers, Betty J., and Clifford Evans, Jr.
1956 "The Reconstruction of Settlement Pattern in the South American Tropical Forest," in Gordon R. Willey (Ed.), *Prehistoric Settlement Patterns in the New World.* Viking Fund Publications in Anthropology No. 23.

1957 "Archaeological Investigations at the Mouth of the Amazon." Washington, D.C., Bureau of American Ethnology Bulletin 167.

1961 "An Experimental Formulation of Horizon Styles in the Tropical Forest Area of South America," in S. K. Lothrop et al. (Eds.), *Essays in Pre-Columbian Art and Archaeology.* Cambridge: Harvard University Press.

―――
1963   "Aboriginal Cultural Development in Latin America: An Interpretative Review." *Smithsonian Institute Miscellaneous Collection,* Vol. 146, No. 1.

Meillet, Antoine, and Marcel Cohen
1952   *Les Langues du Monde.* New edition, Centre National de la Recherche Scientifique: H. Champion, dépositaire, Paris, France.

Mejia Xesspe, M. Toribio
1931   "Kausay: Alimentación de los Indios." *Wira Kocha* 1(1):9–24.

Melatti, Julio Cezar
1967   *Indios e Criadores: A Situação dos Kraho na Área Pastoril do Tocantins.* Monografia No. 3, Rio de Janeiro: Universidade Federal de Rio de Janeiro, Instituto de Ciências Sociais.

―――
1970   *O Sistema Social Kraho.* Unpublished doctoral dissertation, Universidade de São Paulo.

Menzel, Dorothy
1958   "Problemas en el Estudio del Horizonte Medio en la Arqueologia Peruana." *Revista del Museo Regional de Ica,* ano IX, No. 10, 20 de junio, pp. 24–57, Ica.

―――
1959   "The Inca Occupation of the South Coast of Peru." *Southwestern Journal of Anthropology* 15(2):125–42.

―――
1964   "Style and Time in the Middle Horizon." *Ñawpa Pacha* 2:1–105.

Menzel, Dorothy, John H. Rowe, and Lawrence E. Dawson
1964   *The Paracas Pottery of Ica; A Study in Style and Time.* Vol. 50 of University of California Publications in American Archaeology and Ethnology. Berkeley: University of California Press.

Merton, Robert K.
1957   "Continuities in the Theory of Reference Groups and Social Structure," in R. K. Merton, *Social Theory and Social Structure.* New York: The Free Press.

Métraux, Alfred
1928   *La Religion des Tupinambas.* Paris: Leroux.

―――
1948a   "The Hunting and Gathering Tribes of the Rio Negro Basin," in Julian Steward (Ed.), *Handbook of South American Indians,* Vol. 3: *The Tropical Forest Tribes.* Pp. 861–67, Washington, D.C.: Smithsonian Institution.

―――
1948b   "Tribes of the Middle and Upper Amazon River," in Julian

Steward (Ed.), *Handbook of South American Indians,* Vol. 3: *The Tropical Forest Tribes.* Pp. 687–712, Washington, D.C.: Smithsonian Institution.

1948c   "The Tupinamba," in Julian Steward (Ed.), *Handbook of South American Indians.* Vol. 3:95–133, Washington, D.C.: Smithsonian Institution.

1950   *A Religião dos Tupinambas e Suas Relações com a das Demais Tribos Tupi-Guaranis,* trans. by Estevão Pinto. São Paulo: Brasiliana, Series 5, Vol. 267.

1967   *Religions et Magies Indiennes d'Amérique du Sud.* Paris: Editions Gallimard.

Miller, M. F., and R. R. Hudelson
1921   *Thirty Years of Field Experiments with Crop Rotation, Manure and Fertilizers.* University of Missouri Agricultural Experiment Station Bulletin, No. 182, Columbia, Missouri.

Mishkin, Bernard
1946   "The Contemporary Quechua," in Julian Steward (Ed.), *Handbook of South American Indians.* Vol. 2:411–70, Washington, D.C.: Smithsonian Institution.

Momsen, Richard P., Jr.
1964   "The Isconahua Indians: A Study of Change and Diversity in the Peruvian Amazon." *Revista Geográfica* 32(60):59–81.

Monzon, Luis de
1881   *Descripción de la Tierra del Repartimiento de los Rucanas Antamarcas de la Corona Real, Jurisdicion de la Ciudad de Guamanga—Ano de 1586 Relaciones Geográficas de Indias.* Publícalas el Ministerio de Fomento, Perú, Tomo I:197–215, Madrid: Tipografía de Manuel G. Hernandez.

Moreira Neto, C. A.
1960   "A Cultura Pastoril do Páu d'Arco." *Boletim do Museu Paraense Emílio Goeldi,* Belém, n.s., Antropologia, 10.

Morley, Sylvanus G.
1947   *The Ancient Maya.* 2nd edition, Stanford: Stanford University Press.

Muller, J.
1959   "Palynology of Recent Orinoco Delta and Shelf Sediments: Reports of the Orinoco Shelf Expedition: 5." *Micropaleontal* 5:1–32.

Municipalidad de Otavalo
1909   *Monografía del Cantón de Otavalo, Edición Costeada por la Municipalidad.* Quito: Tipografía Salesiana.
Murdock, George P.
1949   *Social Structure.* New York: Macmillan.

1951   "South American Culture Areas." *Southwestern Journal of Anthropology* 4:415–36.

1960   *Social Structure in Southeast Asia.* New York: Viking Fund Publications in Anthropology, No. 29.
Murphy, Robert F.
1956   "Matrilocality and Patrilineality in Mundurucu Society." *American Anthropologist* 56:414–34.

1957   "Intergroup Hostility and Social Cohesion." *American Anthropologist* 59:1018–35.

1958   *Mundurucu Religion.* Vol. 49, University of California Publications in American Archeology and Ethnology, Berkeley: University of California Press.

1960   *Headhunters' Heritage.* Berkeley: University of California Press.

1964   "Social Distance and the Veil." *American Anthropologist* 66:1257–74.

1967   "Tuareg Kinship." *American Anthropologist* 69:163–70.

1971   *The Dialectics of Social Life: Alarms and Excursions in Anthropological Theory.* New York: Basic Books.
Murphy, R. F., and L. Kasdan
1959   "The Structure of Parallel Cousin Marriage." *American Anthropologist* 61:17–29.
Murphy, Robert F., and Buell Quain
1966   *The Trumai Indians of Brazil.* Seattle: The University of Washington Press. The American Ethnological Society Monograph #24.
Murphy, Robert, and Julian Steward
1956   "Tappers and Trappers: Parallel Processes in Acculturation." *Economic Development and Culture Change* 4:335–55. [Bobbs-Merrill Reprint #A-167.]

Murra, John V.
1944   "The Historic Tribes of Ecuador," in Julian Steward (Ed.), *Handbook of South American Indians*. Vol. 2:785–821, Washington, D.C.: Smithsonian Institution.

——   1956   *The Economic Organization of the Inca State*. Ph.D. dissertation, University of Chicago.

——   1958   "On Inca Political Structure," in Verne Ray (Ed.), *Systems of Political Control and Bureaucracy in Human Society*. Seattle: University of Washington Press.

——   1961   "Social Structure and Economic Themes in Andean Ethnohistory." *Anthropological Quarterly* 34:47–59.

Musters, G. C.
1873   *At Home with the Patagonians*. London: John Murray.

Nadler, H. L., and A. B. Gerbie
1969   "Enzymes in Noncultured Amniotic Fluid Cells." *American Journal of Obstetric Gynecology* 103:710–12.

Nash, Manning
1966   *Primitive and Peasant Economic Systems*. San Francisco: Chandler Publishing Co.

Needham, Rodney
1954   "Sioriono and Penan: A Test of Some Hypotheses." *Southwestern Journal of Anthropology* 10:228–32.

——   1961   "An Analytical Note on the Structure of Sirionó Society." *Southwestern Journal of Anthropology* 17(3):239–55.

——   1964   "Descent, Category, and Alliance in Sirionó Society." *Southwestern Journal of Anthropology* 20:229–40.

Neel, J. V.
n.d.   "Genetic Aspects of the Ecology of Disease in the American Indian," in F. M. Salzano (Ed.), *The Ongoing Evolution of Latin American Populations*. Springfield, Illinois: Thomas.

——   1961a   "A Geneticist Looks at Modern Medicine." *Harvey Lectures* 56:127–50.

——   1961b   "Thoughts on the Future of Human Genetics." *Medical Clinics of North America* 33:1001–11.

1967 "The Genetic Structure of Primitive Human Populations." *Japanese Journal of Human Genetics* 12:1–16.

1968 "Some Aspects of Differential Fertility in Two American Indian Tribes." *Proceedings, VII International Congress of Anthropological and Ethnological Sciences* 1:356–61.

1969 "Some Changing Constraints on the Human Evolutionary Process." *Proceedings, XII International Congress of Genetics, 1968,* Tokyo: Science Council of Japan, 3:389–403.

1970 "Lessons from a 'Primitive' People." *Science* 170:815–22. [Reprinted herein—Ed.]

Neel, J. V., and A. D. Bloom
1969 "The Detection of Environmental Mutagens." *Medical Clinics of North America* 53:1243–57.

Neel, J. V., W. R. Centerwall, N. A. Chagnon and H. L. Casey
1970 "Notes on the Effect of Measles and Measles Vaccine in a Virgin Soil Population of South American Indians." *American Journal of Epidemiology* 91:418.

Neel, J. V., and N. A. Chagnon
1968 "The Demography of Two Tribes of Primitive Relatively Unacculturated American Indians." *Proceedings of the National Academy of Sciences* 57:1252–59.

Neel, J. V., W. M. Mikkelsen, D. L. Rucknagel, E. D. Weinstein, R. A. Goyer and S. H. Abadie
1968 "Further Studies of the Xavante Indians, VIII. Some Observations on Blood, Urine and Stool Specimens." *American Journal of Tropical Medical Hygiene* 17:474–85.

Neel, J. V., and F. M. Salzano
1964 "A Prospectus for Genetic Studies of the American Indian." *Cold Spring Harbor Symposium on Quantitative Biology* 29:85–98.

1967 "Further Studies on the Xavante Indians, X. Some Hypotheses-Generalizations Resulting from These Studies." *American Journal of Human Genetics* 19:554–74.

Neel, J. V., F. M. Salzano, P. C. Junqueira, F. Keiter and D. Maybury-Lewis
1964 "Studies on the Xavante Indians of the Brazilian Mato Grosso." *American Journal of Human Genetics* 16:52–140.

Neel, J. V., and W. J. Schull
  1968   "On Some Trends in Understanding the Genetics of Man."
          Perspectives in Biology and Medicine 11:565–602.
Neel, J. V., and R. H. Ward
  1970   "Village and Tribal Genetic Distances Among American In-
          dians and the Possible Implications for Human Evolution." *Pro-
          ceedings of the National Academy of Science* 65:323–30.
Newman, M. T.
  1951   "The Sequence of Indian Physical Types in South America,"
          in W. S. Laughlin (Ed.), *Papers on the Physical Anthropology of
          the American Indian*. Pp. 69–97, New York: Viking Fund.
  ————
  1953   "The Application of Ecological Rules to the Racial Anthro-
          pology of the Aboriginal New World." *American Anthropologist*
          55:311–27.
  ————
  1960   "Blood Groups Systems in Latin America." *American Jour-
          nal of Physical Anthropology*, n.s. 18:334–35.
Newman, Stanley
  1967   "Classical Nahuatl." *Handbook of Middle American Indians*.
          Vol. 5, *Linguistics:* 179–200, Austin: University of Texas Press.
Newsletter
  1970   "The Fellow Newsletter of the American Anthropological
          Association." Special Edition, 69th Annual Meetings, San Diego,
          California.
Nimuendajú, Curt
  1939   *The Apinayé*. Washington, D.C.: The Catholic University of
          America, Anthropological Series, No. 8.
  ————
  1942   *The Šerente*. Los Angeles: Publications of the Frederick Webb
          Hodge Anniversary Publications Fund.
  ————
  1946   *The Eastern Timbira*. University of California Publications
          in American Archeology and Ethnology, 41, Berkeley: University
          of California Press.
  ————
  1952a *The Tapajo*, J. H. Rowe (Trans. and Ed.). Kroeber Anthro-
          pological Society Paper No. 6.
  ————
  1952b *The Tukuna*, W. D. Hohenthal (Trans.) and Robert Lowie
          (Ed.). University of California Publications in American Archae-
          ology and Ethnology, Berkeley, 45.

1956 "Os Apinayé." *Boletim do Museu Paraense Emílio Goeldi,* Belém, 12.

Noble, G. Kingsley
1965 "Proto-Arawakan and Its Descendants." *International Journal of American Linguistics* 31(3), Part 2, Publication 38 of the Indiana University Research Center in Anthropology, Folklore and Linguistics.

Nóbrega, Manoel de
1931 *Cartas do Brasil 1549–1560, Cartas Jesuiticas I.* Rio de Janeiro: Academia Brasileira.

Nuñez del Prado, Oscar
1955 "Aspects of Andean Native Life." *Kroeber Anthropological Society Papers* 12:1–21.

Nutels, Noel
1952 "Plano para uma Campanha de Defesa do Indio Brasileiro Contra a Tuberculose." *Revista Brasileira de Tuberculose,* Rio de Janeiro, 20:3–28.

Oberg, Kalervo
1949 *The Terena and Caduveo of Southern Matto Grosso.* Washington, D.C.: Smithsonian Institution, Institute of Social Anthropology, Publication No. 9.

1953 "Indian Tribes of Northern Mato Grosso." Washington, D.C.: Smithsonian Institution, Institute of Social Anthropology, Publication No. 15.

1955 "Types of Social Structure Among the Lowland Tribes of South and Central America." *American Anthropologist* 57:472–87. [Reprinted herein—Ed.]

O'Leary, Timothy J.
1963 *Ethnographic Bibliography of South America.* New Haven: Human Relations Area Files Behavior Science Bibliographies.

Oliveira, Roberto Cardoso de
1959 "A Situação Atual dos Tapirapé." *Boletim do Museu Paraense Emílio Goeldi,* Belém, n.s., Antropologia, 3.

1960 "The Role of Indian Posts in the Process of Assimilation: Two Case Studies." *American Indígena* 20(2):89–95.

1964 *O Índio e o Mundo dos Brancos: A Situação dos Tukuna do Alto Solimões.* São Paulo: Difusão Européia do Livro.

1968 *Urbanização e Tribalismo: A Integração dos Indios Terêna Numa Sociedade de Classes*. Rio de Janeiro: Zahar Editores.

1972 *A Sociologia do Brasil Indígena*. Rio de Janeiro: Tempo Brasileira.

Olson, Ronald D.
1964 "Mayan Affinities with Chipaya of Bolivia I: Correspondences." *International Journal of American Linguistics* 30:313–24.

1965 "Mayan Affinities with Chipaya of Bolivia II: Cognates." *International Journal of American Linguistics* 31:29–38.

Pachacuti Yamqui, Joan de Santacruz
1950 (orig. 1613) *Tres Relaciones de Antigüedades Peruanas*. Asunción del Paraguay.

Palerm, Angel
1955 "The Agricultural Base of Urban Civilization in Mesopotamia," in Julian Steward (Ed.), *Irrigation Civilizations: A Comparative Study*. Washington, D.C.: Pan American Union, Social Science Monograph No. 1.

Palmatary, Helen Constance
1960 *The Archaeology of the Lower Tapajos Valley, Brazil*. Transactions of the American Philosophical Society, n.s., 50(3).

1965 *The River of the Amazons*. New York: Carlton Press.

Pan American Health Organization
1969 *Perinatal Factors Affecting Human Development, Scientific Publication 185*. Washington, D.C.: Pan American Health Organization.

Parker, Gary
1965 "Gramatica del Guechua Ayachuchano." *Plan de Fomento Linguistico*, Lima: Universidad de San Marchos.

Parsons, Elsie Clews
1936 *Mitla: Town of All Souls*. Chicago: University of Chicago Press.

1945 *Peguche, Canton of Otavalo, Province of Imbabura, Ecuador: A Study of Andean Indians*. Chicago: University of Chicago Press, The University of Chicago Publications in Anthropology, Ethnological Series.

Patiño, Victor Manuel
1958 "El Cachipay o Pijibay (Guilielma Gasipaes Baily), y Su

Papel en la Cultura y en la Economía de los Pueblos Indígenas de América Tropical." *América Indígena* 18(3):177–204; 18(4): 299–332.

Perez Bocanegra, Juan
1631   *Ritual Formulario; e Institucion de Cura, para Administrar a los Naturales de Este Reyno, etc.* Lima.

Phelan, John L.
1958–59   "Free Versus Compulsory Labor: Mexico and the Philippines 1540–1648." *Comparative Studies in Society and History* 1:189–201.

1967   *The Kingdom of Quito in the Seventeenth Century, Bureaucratic Politics in the Spanish Empire.* Madison: University of Wisconsin Press.

Philipson, J.
1945   "O Parentesco Tupi Guaraní." *Sociologia,* São Paulo, 8(1):53–62.

Piedrahita, Lucas Fernandez de
1881   *Historia General de las Conquistas del Nuevo Reino de Granada.* Bogotá.

Polo de Ondegardo, Juan
1940   "Report to Briviesca de Muñatones [1561]," Carlos Romero (Ed.). *Revista Historica,* Vol. 8, Lima.

Poma de Ayala, Felipe Guaman
1936 (orig. 1584–1614)   *Nueva Corónica y Buen Gobierno.* Paris: Institut d'Ethnologie.

Ponce de León, Sancho de Paz
1897   "Relación y Descripción de los Pueblos del Partido de Otavalo . . . 1582," in *Relaciones Geográficas de Indias* 3:105–20, Madrid: Ministerio de Fomento.

Ponce Sanginés, Carlos
1961   *Informe de Labores, Octubre 1957–Febrero 1961.* Centro de Investigaciones Argueológicas en Tiwanaku, Publicación No. 1, La Paz.

Popenoe, Hugh
1964   "The Pre-Industrial Cultivator in the Tropics," in *The Ecology of Man in the Tropical Environment.* Morges, Switzerland: International Union for the Conservation of Nature and Natural Resources Publications, n.s., No. 4.

Posnansky, Arthur
1957   *Tihuanacu.* Vol. III, La Paz.

Post, R. H., J. V. Neel and W. J. Schull
1968   "Tabulations of Phenotype and Gene Frequencies for Eleven

Different Genetic Systems Studied in the American Indian," in *Biomedical Challenges Presented by the American Indian.* Washington, D.C.: Pan American Health Organization Publication 165.

Powell, J. W.
1891 "Indian Linguistic Families of America North of Mexico." Washington, D.C.: Bureau of American Ethnology, 7th Annual Report: 1885–86:1–142.

Price, P. David, and Cecil E. Cook, Jr.
1969 "The Present Situation of the Nambiquara." *American Anthropologist* 71(4):688–93.

PRONAPA
1970 "Brazilian Archeology in 1968, an Interim Report on the National Program of Archeological Research." *American Antiquity* 35(1).

Pulgar Vidal, Javier
1954 "La Quinua o Suba: Alimento Básico de los Chibchas." *Economia Colombiana,* Bogotá, 1(3):549–60.

Quevedo, Lafone
1919 "Guaraní Kinship Terms as an Index of Social Organization." *American Anthropologist* 21:421–40.

Radcliffe-Brown, A. R.
1952 *Structure and Function in Primitive Society.* New York: The Free Press.

Ralph, Elizabeth K.
1959 "University of Pennsylvania Radiocarbon Dates III." *American Journal of Science Radiocarbon Supplement,* New Haven, 1:45–58.

Rappaport, Roy A.
1968 *Pigs for the Ancestors.* New Haven: Yale University Press.

Rattray, R. S.
1923 *The Ashanti.* Oxford: Clarendon Press.

Redfield, R.
1953 *The Primitive World and Its Transformations.* Ithaca, New York: Cornell University Press.

Reichel-Dolmatoff, Gerardo
1951a "Datos Histórico-Culturales Sobre las Tribus de la Antigua Gobernación de Santa Marta." *Banco de la República,* Bogotá.

———
1951b *Los Kogi.* 2 vols., Bogotá.

———
1958 "Recientes Investigaciones Arqueológicas en el Norte de

Colombia." *Miscellanea Paul Rivet Octogenario Dicata* II:471–86, Mexico: Universidad Nacional Autónoma.

1959 "The Formative Stage: An Appraisal from the Colombian Perspective." *Actas del XXXIII Congreso Internacional de Americanistas, San José de Costa Rica,* 1958, I:152–64, San José.

1965 *Colombia: Ancient Peoples and Places.*

1971 *Amazonian Cosmos: The Sexual and Religious Symbolism of the Tukano Indians.* Chicago: University of Chicago Press.

Reichel-Dolmatoff, Gerardo and Alicia
1961 *The People of Aritama: The Cultural Personality of a Colombian Mestizo Village.* Chicago: University of Chicago Press.

Reyes, Oscar Efren
1938 *Breve Historia General del Ecuador.* Vol. 1, Quito: Imprensa de la Universidad Central.

Reynolds, Phillip Keep
1927 *The Banana: Its History, Cultivation, and Place Among Staple Foods.* Boston.

Ribeiro, Darcy
1956 "Convívio e Contaminação: Efeitos Dissociativos da Depopulação Provocada por Epidemias em Grupos Indígenas." *Sociologia,* São Paulo, 17(1):3–50.

1962 *A Política Indigenista Brasileira.* Rio de Janeiro: Ministério da Agricultura, Serviço de Informação Agrícola *(Atualidade Agraria,* 1), 178 pp.

1967 "Indigenous Cultures and Languages of Brazil," in J. Hopper (Ed.), *Indians of Brazil in the Twentieth Century.* Washington, D.C.: Institute for Cross-Cultural Research.

1970 *Os Indios e a Civilização.* Rio de Janeiro: Civilização Brasileira.

Ribeiro da Cunha, Boaventura
1953 "Indios Carajá e Javaé," in Candido Rondon (Ed.), *Indios do Brasil,* Vol. 2:165–98, Rio de Janeiro: Ministério de Agricultura: Conselho Nacional de Proteção aos Indios.

Rivers, W. H. R.
1914a *Kinship and Social Organization.* London.

1914b *The History of Melanesian Society.* Cambridge.

Rivet, Paul
1925a "Les Origines de l'Homme Americain." *L'Anthropologie* 35:293–319.

———

1925b "Les Melano-Polynesians et les Australiens en Amerique." *Anthropos* 20:51–54.

Rivet, Paul, and Cestmir Loukotka
1952 "South American Indian Languages," in A. Meillet and M. Cohen (Eds.), *Les Langues du Monde*. Pp. 1160–9.

Rivière, Peter
1969 *Marriage Among the Trio: A Principle of Social Organization.* Oxford: Clarendon Press, 353 pp.

Roberts, John M., and Thomas Gregor
1970 "Privacy: A Cultural View," in *Nomos*, the Yearbook of the American Society for Political and Legal Philosophy.

Robledo, Jorge
1892 "Relación de las Provincias de Ancerma y Quimbaya," in Antonio B. Cueruo (Ed.), *Colección de Documentos Inéditos Sobre la Geografia y la Historia de Colombia*. 2:437–52, Bogotá.

Rodrigues, Arion D.
1958 "Classification of Tupi-Guarani." *International Journal of American Linguistics* 24(3):231–34.

Rodriguez Fresle, Juan
1884 *Conquista y Descubrimiento del Nuevo Reino de Granada.* Bogotá.

Rodriguez de Medina, Antonio et al.
1919 "Relación Geográfica de San Miguel de las Palmas de Tamalameque, Gobernación de Santa Marta, Audiencia de Nueva Granada, Virreinato del Perú." *Boletin de Estudios Americanistas,* Año 6, Febrero–Marzo, Sevilla.

Roheim, Geza
1934 *The Riddle of the Sphinx or Human Origins.* London.

Roscoe, J.
1911 *The Baganda.* London: Macmillan & Co.

Rostovtzeff, Michael Ivanovitch
1957 *The Social and Economic History of the Roman Empire.* 2nd edition, revised by P. M. Fraser, 2 vols., Oxford: Clarendon Press.

Rouse, Irving
1948 "The Arawak," in Julian Steward (Ed.), *Handbook of South American Indians*. Vol. 4:507–46, Washington, D.C.: Smithsonian Institution.

———

1962 "The Intermediate Area: Amazonia and the Caribbean Area," in R. Braidwood and G. Willey (Eds.), *Courses Toward Urban Life*. Pp. 34–59, Chicago: Aldine Press.

Rouse, Irving, and José M. Cruxent

1963a   "Some Recent Radiocarbon Dates for Western Venezuela." *American Antiquity* 28(4):537–40.

1963b   *Venezuelan Archaeology*. Yale Caribbean Series No. 6, New Haven: Yale University Press.

Rowe, John Howland

1944   *An Introduction to the Archaeology of Cuzco*. Papers of the Peabody Museum of American Archaeology and Ethnology XXII(2), Cambridge.

1946   "Inca Culture at the Time of the Spanish Conquest," in Julian Steward (Ed.), *Handbook of South American Indians*, Vol. 2, *The Andean Civilizations*. Pp. 183–330, Washington, D.C.: Smithsonian Institution.

1952   "Introduction," in Curt Nimuendajú, *The Tapajo*. Kroeber Anthropological Society Papers 6:1–25.

1954a   "Linguistic Classification Problems in South America." *University of California Publications in Linguistics* 10:13–26.

1954b   *Max Uhle, 1856–1944; a Memoir of the Father of Peruvian Archaeology*. University of California Publications in American Archaeology and Ethnology 46(1):i–viii, 1–134, Berkeley and Los Angeles: University of California Press.

1956   "Archaeological Explorations in Southern Peru, 1954–1955; a Preliminary Report of the Fourth University of California Archaeological Expedition to Peru." *American Antiquity* 22(2):135–51.

1957   "The Incas Under Spanish Colonial Institutions." *Hispanic-American Historical Review* 37:155–91.

1958   "The Adventures of Two Pucara Statues." *Archaeology* 2(4):255–61, Brattleboro, Vermont.

1960a   "La Arqueología de Ica." *Revista de la Facultad de Letras*, Universidad Nacional "San Luís Gonzaga" de Ica, 1(1):113–31.

1960b   *Tiempo, Estilo y Proceso Cultural en la Arqueología Peruana.* Segunda edición, corregida. Tawantinsuyu K'uzkiy Paqarichisqa, Instituto de Estudios Andinos, Berkeley: Institute of Andean Studies.

1962a   "La Arqueología de Ica." *Revista de la Facultad de Letras,* Universidad Nacional "San Luís Gonzaga" de Ica, 1(1):113–31.

1962b   "Stages and Periods in Archaeological Interpretation." *Southwestern Journal of Anthropology* 18(1):40–54.

1967   "What Kind of a Settlement was Inca Cuzco?" *Ñawpa Pacha* 5:59–76.

Rowe, J. H., and D. Menzel (Eds.)
1967   *Peruvian Archeology: Selected Readings.* Palo Alto: Peek Publications.

Royo y Gomez, J.
1956   "Cuaternario en Venezuela." Ministerio de Minas y Hidrocarburos, Direccion de Geologia, Bol. de Geol. Publ. Espec. 1:199–209.

Rubin, Joan
1968   *National Bilingualism in Paraguay.* The Hague: Mouton.

Rubio Orbe, Gonzalo
1956   *Punyaro, Estudio de Antropología Social y Cultural de Una Comunidad Indígena y Mestiza.* Quito: Casa de la Cultura Ecuatoriana.

1957   *Promociones Indígenas en America.* Quito: Casa de la Cultura Ecuatoriana.

Russell, W. M. S.
1968   "The Slash-and-Burn Technique." *Natural History* 77(3):58–65.

Sahlins, Marshall D.
1964   "Culture and Environment," in Sol Tax (Ed.), *Horizons of Anthropology.* Pp. 132–47, Chicago: Aldine Press.

Salaman, Redcliffe N.
1949   *The History and Social Influence of the Potato.* Cambridge, England.

Salinas, Raul
1954   "Manual Arts in Ecuador." *America Indígena* 14:315–26.

Salz, Beate R.
1955   *The Human Element in Industrialization, a Hypothetical Case*

Study of Ecuadorean Indians. Washington, D.C.: American Anthropological Association Memoir No. 85.

Sanders, W. T., and B. J. Price
  1968 *Mesoamerica: The Evolution of a Civilization.* New York: Random House.

Sapir, Edward
  1929 "Central and North American Languages," *Encyclopædia Britannica* (14th ed.) 5:138–41.

———
  1931 "The Concept of Phonetic Law as Tested in Primitive Languages by Leonard Bloomfield," in Stuart A. Rice (Ed.), *Methods in Social Science: A Case Book.* Chicago: University of Chicago Press.

Sardella, Juan Bautista
  1892 "Descubrimiento de las Provincias de Antioquia," in Antonio B. Cuervo (Ed.), *Colección de Documentos Inéditos Sobre la Geografía y la Historia de Colombia.* 2:437–52, Bogotá.

Sauer, C. D.
  1944 "A Geographic Sketch of Early Man in America." *Geographical Review* 34(4).

Sauer, Carl O.
  1950 "Cultivated Plants of South and Central America," in Julian Steward (Ed.), *Handbook of South American Indians.* Vol. 6:319–45, Washington, D.C.: Smithsonian Institution.

———
  1952 *Agricultural Origins and Dispersals.* New York: American Geographical Society.

———
  1959 "Age and Area of American Cultivated Plants." *International Congress of Americanists* 33:215–29.

Schaedel, Richard Paul
  1951a "The Lost Cities of Peru." *Scientific American* 185(2): 18–23, New York.

———
  1951b "Major Ceremonial and Population Centers in Northern Peru." *Civilizations of Ancient America,* Selected Papers of the XXIXth International Congress of Americanists, pp. 232–43, Chicago: University of Chicago Press.

———
  1966 "Incipient Urbanization and Secularization in Tiahuanacoid Peru." *American Antiquity* 31(3).

Schauensee, Rudolphe Meyer de
  1970 *Guide to the Birds of South America.* Wynnewood, Pennsyl-

vania: Livingstone Publishing Company (for the Academy of Natural Sciences of Philadelphia).

Schneider, David
1968 *American Kinship.* New Jersey: Prentice-Hall.

Schneider, David M., and Kathleen Gough
1962 *Matrilineal Kinship.* Berkeley: University of California Press.

Schomburgk, Robert H.
1841 *Reisen in Guiana und am Orinoco während der Jahre 1835 bis 1839.* Leipzig.

Schultz, Harald
1953 "A Pesca Tradicional do Pirarucú Entre os Indios Karajá." *Revista do Museu Paulista,* São Paulo, n.s., 7:149–55.

——— 1962 "Brazil's Big-Lipped Indians." *National Geographic Magazine* 121:118–33.

Schuster, Meinhard
1958 "Die Soziologie der Waika." *Proceedings of the 32nd International Congress of Americanists,* 114–22, Copenhagen.

Schwalm, H.
1927 "Klima, Besiedlung und Landwirtschaft in den Peru-Nord Bolivianischen Anden." *Ibero-Amerikanisches Archiv* 2:17–74, 150–96.

Schwartz, Barry
1968 "The Social Psychology of Privacy." *American Journal of Sociology,* 741–52.

Scrimshaw, N. S., and J. E. Gordon (Eds.)
1968 *Malnutrition, Learning, and Behavior, Proceedings of an International Conference.* Cambridge: MIT Press.

Seitz, Georg J.
1967 "Epene, the Intoxicating Snuff Powder of the Waika Indians and the Tucano Medicine Man, Agostino," in D. H. Efron, B. Holmstedt, and N. S. Kline (Eds.), *Ethnopharmacologic Search for Psychoactive Drugs.* Public Health Service Publication No. 1645, 315–38, Washington, D.C.

Service, Elman
1955 "Indian-European Relations in Colonial Latin America." *American Anthropologist* 57(3):411–25.

——— 1960 "The Law of Evolutionary Potential," in M. D. Sahlins and E. Service (Eds.), *Evolution and Culture.* Pp. 93–122, Ann Arbor: University of Michigan Press.

Service, Helen and Elman
1954 *Tobatí, a Paraguayan Village*. Chicago: University of Chicago Press.

Shapiro, Judith
1968 "Ceremonial Redistribution in Tapirapé Society." *Boletim do Museu Paraense Emílio Goeldi*, Antropología, 38.

Sievers, W.
1914 "Reise in Peru und Ecuador Ausgefuhrt 1909, Wissenschaftliche Veröffentlichungen der Gesellschaft für Erdkunde zu Leipzig, Achter Band." Munchen und Leipzig: Duncker und Humblot.

Silva, P. Alcionílio Bruzzi Alves da
1962 *A Civilização Indígena do Uapés*. São Paulo: Centro de Pesquisas Iauareté.

Silverman, Martin
1960 "Community, State and Church." Columbia-Cornell-Harvard-Illinois Summer Field Studies Program (Mimeographed).

Simmel, Georg
1950 "The Sociology of Secrecy and Secret Societies," in K. Wolf (Ed.), *The Sociology of Georg Simmel*. New York: The Free Press.

Simmonds, N. W.
1959 *Bananas*. New York: Longmans, Green & Co.

Simões, Mário F.
1969 "The Castanheira Site: New Evidence on the Antiquity and History of Ananatuba Phase." *American Antiquity* 34:402–10.

Simon, Fray Pedro
1882 *Noticias Historiales de las Conquistas de Tierra Firme en las Indias Occidentales*. 5 vols., Bogotá.

Simonsen, R.
1937 *História Econômica do Brasil*. Vol. 1, São Paulo: Companhia Editôra Nacional.

Simpson, Lesley B.
1938 *The Repartimiento System of Native Labor in New Spain and Guatemala*. Berkeley: University of California Press.

———
1950 *The Encomienda in New Spain*. Berkeley: University of California Press.

———
1960 *Many Mexicos*. Berkeley: University of California Press.

Siskind, Janet
1968 *Reluctant Hunters*. Doctoral dissertation, Columbia University.

Soares de Sousa, Gabriel
1851 "Roteiro do Brasil." *Revista do Instituto Histórico e Geographico Brasileiro* 14:316–17.

———

1938 (orig. 1587) *Tratado Descriptivo do Brasil em 1587.* Nova Edição, São Paulo.
Sorensen, Arthur P., Jr.
1965 *The Phonology of Tukano.* Columbia University Master's essay.

———

1967 "Multilingualism in the Northwest Amazon." *American Anthropologist* 69:670–84.

———

1969 *The Morphology of Tukano.* Ph.D. dissertation, Columbia University.

———

1970 "Multilingualism in the Northwest Amazon: Papurí and Pira-Paraná Regions." Paper read at the 39th Annual Congress of Americanists at Lima, Peru.
Soustelle, Jacques
1937 *La Famille Otomi-Pame du Mexique Central.* Paris: Institut d'Ethnologie.
Spath, Carl
1971 "Manioc as a Determinant of Settlement Patterns." Paper delivered at the Annual Meeting of the American Anthropological Association, New York City.
Staden, Hans
n.d. *The True History of His Captivity,* Malcolm Letts (Ed.). II(18):146, London.
Stark, Louisa R.
1968 *Mayan Affinities with Yunga of Peru.* Doctoral dissertation, New York University.

———

1969 *Bolivian Quechua Dictionary* (first draft). Madison: University of Wisconsin, Dept. of Anthropology.
Steinen
1897 *Unter der Naturvölkern Zentral Brasiliens.* P. 286, Berlin.
Sternberg, Hilgard O'Reilly
1964 "Land and Man in the Tropics." *Proceedings of the Academy of Political Science* 27(4):319–29.
Stevenson, William Bennett
1825 *A Historical and Descriptive Narrative of Twenty Years' Resi-*

dence in South America. Vol. II, London: Hurst, Robinson, and Co.

Steward, Julian H.

1947 "American Culture History in the Light of South America." *Southwestern Journal of Anthropology* 3:85–107.

——

1948a "The Circum-Caribbean Tribes: An Introduction," in Julian Steward (Ed.), *Handbook of South American Indians.* Vol. 4:1–41, Washington, D.C.: Smithsonian Institution.

——

1948b "Culture Areas of the Tropical Forest," in Julian Steward (Ed.), *Handbook of South American Indians.* Vol. 3: *The Tropical Forest Tribes.* Pp. 883–99, Washington, D.C.: Smithsonian Institution.

——

1948c "Tribes of the Montaña," in Julian Steward (Ed.), *Handbook of South American Indians.* Vol. 3:507–33, Washington, D.C.: Smithsonian Institution.

——

1949 "South American Cultures: An Interpretative Summary," in Julian Steward (Ed.), *Handbook of South American Indians.* Vol. 5:669–72, Washington, D.C.: Smithsonian Institution.

——

1955 *Theory of Culture Change.* Urbana, Illinois: University of Illinois Press.

——

1970 "Cultural Evolution in South America," in W. Goldschmidt and H. Hoijer (Eds.), *The Social Anthropology of Latin America.* Los Angeles: Latin American Center, University of California, pp. 199–223.

—— (Ed.)

1944–49 *Handbook of South American Indians.* 7 vols., Bureau of American Ethnology Bulletin No. 143, Washington, D.C.: Smithsonian Institution.

Steward, Julian H., and Louis C. Faron

1959 *Native Peoples of South America.* New York: McGraw-Hill.

Stini, William A.

1971 "Evolutionary Implications of Changing Nutrition Patterns in Human Populations." *American Anthropologist* 73(5):1019–30.

Stout, David B.

1938 "Culture Types and Culture Areas in South America." *Papers of the Michigan Academy of Sciences, Arts, and Letters* 23:73–86.

Strong, William Duncan
1957 *Paracas, Nazca, and Tiahuanacoid Cultural Relationships in South Coastal Peru.* Memoirs of the Society for American Archaeology, No. 13, Salt Lake City.
Strong, W. Duncan, and Clifford Evans, Jr.
1952 *Cultural Stratigraphy in the Virú Valley.* Columbia Studies in Archaeology and Ethnology, Vol. IV, New York.
Stumer, Louis Michael
1953 "Playa Grande: Primitive Elegance in Pre-Tiahuanaco Peru." *Archaeology* 6(1):42–48, Brattleboro, Vermont.
Sussman, Robert W.
1972 "Child Transport, Family Size, and Increase in Human Population During the Neolithic." *Current Anthropology* 13(2):258.
Suttles, Wayne
1960 "Affinal Ties, Subsistence, and Prestige Among the Coast Salish." *American Anthropologist* 62:296–305.
Swadesh, Morris
1955 "Towards Greater Accuracy in Lexicostatistic Dating." *International Journal of American Linguistics* 21:121–37.

1959 "Mapas de Clasificacion Linguistica de Mexico y las Americas." *Cuadernos del Instituto de Historia, Serie Antropologica, No. 8,* Universidad Nacional Autonoma de Mexico, Mexico.

1967 "Lexicostatistic Classification," in Norman A. McQuown (Ed.), *Linguistics,* Vol. 5 of *Handbook of Middle American Indians.* Austin: University of Texas Press.
Swanton, John R.
1911 *Indian Tribes of the Lower Mississippi Valley and Adjacent Coast of Gulf of Mexico.* Washington, D.C.: Bureau of American Ethnology Bulletin No. 43, Smithsonian Institution.
Szászdi, Adam
1964 "The Historiography of the Republic of Ecuador." *Hispanic American Historical Review* 44:503–50.

Tabio, Ernesto E.
1957 *Excavaciones en Playa Grande, Costa Central del Peru, 1955.* Arqueológicas; publicaciones del Instituto de Investigaciones Antropologicas I–1, Pueblo Libre, Lima: Museo Nacional de Antropologiá y Arqueología.
Tavener, Christopher J.
1966ms. "Report of a Preliminary Survey Among the Karajá." On file at the Institute for Latin American Studies, Columbia University.

Tax, Sol

1953   *Penny Capitalism: A Guatemalan Indian Community.* Washington, D.C.: Smithsonian Institution Institute of Social Anthropology.

1957   "Changing Consumption in Indian Guatemala." *Economic Development and Culture Change* 5:147–58.

1960   "Aboriginal Languages of Latin America." *Current Anthropology* 1:431–36.

Tello, Julio C.

1920   Introduction to Peruvian Translation of C. R. Markham's *The Incas of Perú.* Lima.

1942   *Orígen y Desarrollo de las Civilizaciones Prehistóricas Andinas.* Actas y Trabajos Científicos del XXVII Congreso Internacional de Americanistas (Lima, 1939), Tomo 1:589–720, Lima.

1956   *Arqueologia del Valle de Casma; Culturas: Chavin, Santa o Huaylas Yunga y Sub-Chimú.* Informe de los Trabajos de la Expedición Arqueológica al Marañón de 1937, Publicación Antropológica del Archivo "Julio C. Tello" de la Universidad Nacional Mayor de San Marcos, Vol. I, Lima: Editorial San Marcos.

Textor, Robert B.

1967   *A Cross-Cultural Summary.* New Haven: Human Relations Area Files Press.

Thevet

Cosmogonie Universelle.

Thurn, Everard F. IM.

1967 (orig. 1883)   *Among the Indians of Guiana, Being Sketches Chiefly Anthropologic from the Interior of British Guiana.* New York: Dover Publications.

Tippett, A. R.

1958   "The Nature and Social Function of Fijian War." *Transactions and Proceedings of the Fiji Society* 5:137–55, 1951–54.

Titiev, Mischa

1951   *Araucanian Culture in Transition.* Occasional Contributions, Museum of Anthropology, No. 15, Ann Arbor: The University of Michigan.

Tovar, Antonio

1961   *Catalogo de las Lenguas de America del Sur.* Buenos Aires.

548   *Bibliography*

Trimborn, Hermann
  1928   "Die Kultur-historische Stellung der Lamazucht." *Anthropos*
          pp. 656–64.
Trojer, Hans
  1954   "El Tiempo Reinante en Colombia: Sus Características y
          Desarrollo." *Boletín Técnico, Centro Nacional de Investigaciones
          de Café* 2:1–43, Chinchina.
Troll, Karl
  1931–32   "Die Geografische Grundlagen der Andinen Kulturen und
             des Inka-reiches." *Ibero-Amerikanisches Archiv* 5:258–94.
Tschopik, Harry
  1951   *The Aymara of Chucuito, Peru, I: Magic.* New York: Anthro-
          pological Papers of the American Museum of Natural History,
          Vol. 44, Pt. 2.
Tumin, Melvin
  1952   *Caste in a Peasant Society.* Princeton: Princeton University
          Press.

Ubbelohde-Doering, Heinrich
  1959   "Bericht über Arcäologische Feldarbeiten in Perú: II."
          Ethnos (Stockholm) 1–2:1–32.
United Nations
  1962   "Report of the United Nations Scientific Committee on the
          Effects of Atomic Radiation." Supplement No. 16 (A/5216),
          New York: United Nations.
Urien, C. M.
  1965   "Old Beach Levels in the Littoral of Argentina." *Abstracts,
          VII Inqua Congr.*, Boulder, Colorado, p. 477.

Valcárcel, Luis E.
  1925a   *De la vida Incaica.* Lima.

  ———
  1925b   *Del Aillu al Imperio.* Lima.

  ———
  1937–41   *Mirador Indio: Apuntes para una Filosofía de la Cultura
             Incaica.* Lima.

  ———
  1943–48   *Historia de la Cultura Antigua del Perú.* 2 vols., Lima.

  ———
  1945   *La Ruta Cultural del Perú.* Mexico.
Valero, Helena
  1970   *Yanoáma: The Narrative of a White Girl Kidnapped by*

Amazonian Indians, E. Biocca (Ed.), D. Rhodes (Trans.). New York: E. P. Dutton.

Vallois, H. V.
1961 "The Social Life of Early Man: The Evidence of Skeletons," in S. L. Washburn (Ed.), *The Social Life of Early Man.* Chicago: Aldine Publishing Co.

Valory, Dale
1967 "Bibliography of Fuegian Folklore." *Behavioral Science Notes* 2,3:175–202.

Van der Hammen, T.
1965 "Palynological Data on the History of Savannas in Northern South America." *Abstracts, VII Inqua Congr.,* Boulder, Colorado, p. 480.

Van der Hammen, T., and E. Gonzalez
1960 "Upper Pleistocene and Holocene Climate and Vegetation of the 'Sabana de Bogotá.' " *Leidse Geol. Mede.* 25:261–315.

Van Loon, H.
1966 "Characteristics of the Distribution of Average Temperature in the Sea Surface and Adjacent Air over the Southern Oceans." *Geographical Review.*

Vargas, José María
1957 *La Economía Política del Ecuador Durante la Colonia.* Quito: Editorial Universitaria.

Vasconcellos, Simão de
1865 *Chronica da Companhia de Jesus do Estado do Brasil.* I(82):133, Lisboa.

Vasquez de Espinosa, Antonio
1948 "Compendio y Descripción de las Indias Occidentales." *Smithsonian Miscellaneous Collections,* Vol. 108, Washington.

Vayda, Andrew P.
1961a "A Re-examination of Northwest Coast Economic Systems." *Transactions of the New York Academy of Sciences* 23:618–24.

———
1961b "Expansion and Warfare Among Swidden Agriculturalists." *American Anthropologist* 63:346–58.

Vayda, Andrew P., Anthony P. Leeds and David B. Smith
1961 "The Place of Pigs in Melanesian Subsistence." *Proceedings of the 1961 Annual Spring Meeting of the American Ethnological Society* (ed. by V. Garfield), Seattle: University of Washington Press.

Vellard, J.
1939 *Une Civilisation du Miel: Les Indiens Guayakis du Paraguay.* Librairie Gallimard.

1956 "Causas Biológicas de la Desaparición de los Indios Americanos." Boletin del Instituto Riva-Aguero 2:77–93.

1965 *Histoire du Curare: Le Poisons de Chasee en Amerique du Sud*. Paris: Editions Gallimard.

Viertler, Renate Brigitte
1969 *Os Kamayurá e o Alto Xingú: Análise do Processo de Integração de Uma Tribo Numa Área de Aculturação Intertribal*. São Paulo: Instituto de Estudos Brasileiros.

Villas Boas, Orlando and Claudio
1970 *Xingú: Os Indios, Seus Mitos*. Rio de Janeiro: Zahar Editores.

Vine, H.
1953 "Experiments on the Maintenance of Soil Fertility at Ibadan, Nigeria, 1922–51." *The Empire Journal of Experimental Agriculture* 21:65–85.

Voegelin, C. F. and F. M.
1965 "Languages of the World: Native America, Fascicle Two." *Anthropological Linguistics* 7, Part 1.

Wagley, Charles
1940a "The Effects of Depopulation upon Social Organization as Illustrated by the Tapirapé Indians." *Transactions of the New York Academy of Sciences, Series II* 3(1):12–16.

1940b "World View of the Tapirapé Indians." *Journal of American Folklore* 53(210):252–60.

1943 "Tapirapé Shamanism." *Boletim do Museu Nacional*, Rio de Janeiro, Antropología 3:61–92. (Also in M. Fried [Ed.], *Readings in Anthropology*, 2nd edition, 1968, Vol. II, pp. 617–35, New York: Thomas Y. Crowell.)

1957 *Santiago Chimaltenango*. Guatemala City: Seminario de Integración Social Guatemalteca.

1964 *Amazon Town: A Study of Man in the Tropics*. New York: Alfred A. Knopf.

1971 *An Introduction to Brazil*. Revised edition. New York: Columbia University Press.

—— (Ed.)
1952 *Race and Class in Rural Brazil*. Paris: UNESCO.

Wagley, Charles, and Eduardo Galvão
1946a "O Parentesco Tupi-Guarani (Tupi Guarani Kinship)."
Boletim do Museu Nacional, Rio de Janeiro, n.s., Antropología, 6.

—— 1946b "O Parentesco Tupi-Guarani (Cosiderações a Margem de Uma Crítica)." *Sociologia,* São Paulo, 8(4):305–8.

—— 1948a "The Tapirapé." *Handbook of South American Indians* 3:167–78, Washington.

—— 1948b "The Tenetehara." *Handbook of South American Indians* 3:137–48, Washington.

—— 1949 *The Tenetehara Indians of Brazil.* New York.
Wagley, Charles, and Marvin Harris
1955 "A Typology of Latin American Subcultures." *American Anthropologist* 57:428–51.

—— 1958 *Minorities in the New World.* New York: Columbia University Press.
Wallace, Anthony F. C.
1970 *Culture and Personality.* 2nd edition, New York: Random House.
Ward, R. H., and J. V. Neel
1970 "Gene Frequencies and Micro-differentiation Among the Makiritane Indians: IV. A Comparison of a Genetic Network with Ethnohistory and Migration Matrices: A New Index of Genetic Isolation." *American Journal of Human Genetics* 22:538–61.
Watson, J.
1952 *Cayuá Culture Change.* Memoir No. 73 of the American Anthropological Association.
Watt, George
1908 *The Commercial Products of India.* London: John Murray.
Weberbauer, August
1945 *El Mundo Vegetal de los Andes Peruanos.* Lima.
Webster, Hutton
1908 *Primitive Secret Societies.* New York.
Weinstein, E. D., J. V. Neel and F. M. Salzano
1967 "Further Studies in the Xavante Indians, VI. The Physical Status of the Xavantes of Simoes Lopes." *American Journal of Human Genetics* 19:532–42.
Westin, Alan F.
1967 *Privacy and Freedom.* New York: Atheneum.

Whetten, Nathan Laselle
  1948   *Rural Mexico.* Chicago: University of Chicago Press.

——
  1961   *Guatemala: The Land and the People.* New Haven: Yale University Press.
White, Leslie A.
  1959   *The Evolution of Culture.* New York: McGraw-Hill.
White, L., Jr.
  1967   "The Historical Roots of our Ecological Crisis." *Science* 155:1203–7.
Whiton, Louis C., H. Bruce Greene and Richard P. Momsen, Jr.
  1964   "The Isconahua of the Remo." *Journal de la Société des Américanistes,* Paris, 53:85–124.
Wilbert, J.
  1958   "Kinship and Social Organization of the Yekuána and Goajiro." *Southwestern Journal of Anthropology* 14:51–60.

——
  1962   "A Preliminary Glotto-Chronology of Gê." *Anthropological Linguistics* 4(2):17–25.

——
  1968   "Loukotka's Classification of South American Indian Languages." Preface to Cestmir Loukotka, *Classification of South American Indian Languages:* 7–23, Los Angeles: Latin American Center, University of California.

——
  1972   *Survivors of Eldorado: Four Indian Cultures of South America.* New York: Praeger.
Willey, Gordon R.
  1949   "Ceramics," in Julian Steward (Ed.), *Handbook of South American Indians.* Vol. 5:139–204, Washington, D.C.: Smithsonian Institution.

——
  1951   "Peruvian Settlement and Socio-economic Patterns," in *Civilizations of Ancient America: Selected Papers of the XXIXth International Congress of Americanists.* Pp. 195–200, Chicago: University of Chicago Press.

——
  1953a   "Archaeological Theories and Interpretations: New World," in Kroeber et al., *Anthropology Today,* pp. 361–85.

——
  1953b   *Prehistoric Settlement Patterns in the Virú Valley.* Washington, D.C.: Bureau of American Ethnology Bulletin.

1971   *An Introduction to American Archeology, Vol. 2: South America.* Englewood Cliffs: Prentice-Hall.

Willey, Gordon R., and Demitri B. Shimkin
1971   "The Collapse of Classic Maya Civilization in the Southern Lowlands: A Symposium Summary Statement." *Southwestern Journal of Anthropology* 27(1):1–18.

Wilmsen, Edwin N.
1968   "Paleo-Indian Site Utilization," in Betty J. Meggers (Ed.), *Anthropological Archeology in the Americas.* Washington: The Anthropological Society of Washington.

Wilson, H. Clyde
1958   "Regarding the Causes of Mundurucú Warfare." *American Anthropologist* 60:1193–99.

Wissler, Clark
1917   *The American Indian: An Introduction to the Anthropology of the New World.* New York: Oxford University Press.

Wolf, Bernard
1969   *The Little Weaver of Agato.* New York: Cowles Book Co.

Wolf, Eric R.
1955   "Types of Latin American Peasantry: A Preliminary Discussion." *American Anthropologist* 57(3):452–71. (Also a Bobbs-Merrill reprint.)

1956   "Aspects of Group Relations in a Complex Society: Mexico." *American Anthropologist* 58:1065–78.

1957   "Closed Corporate Peasant Communities in Mesoamerica and Central Java." *Southwestern Journal of Anthropology* 13:1–18.

1966   *Peasants.* Englewood Cliffs: Prentice-Hall.

Wright, S.
1931   "Evolution in Mendelian Populations." *Genetics* 16:97–159.

Wynne-Edwards, V. C.
1962   *Animal Dispersion in Relation to Social Behavior.* Edinburgh: Oliver and Boyd.

Yacovleff, Eugenio, and F. L. Herrera
1934   "El Mundo Vegetal de los Antiguos Peruanos." *Revista del Museo Nacional de Lima* 3(3):241–322.

Yarnell, Richard A.
1970   Review of *Environment and Cultural Behavior,* edited by A. P. Vayda. *American Anthropologist* 72(5):1105–7.

554   *Bibliography*

Young, Philip D.
 1971   *Ngawbe: Tradition and Change Among the Western Guaymí
        of Panama*. Urbana: University of Illinois Press.

Zavala, Silvio
 1944   "Las Casas, Esclavista?" *Cuadernos Americanos* 3:149–54.
Zerries, Otto
 1958   "Kultur im Übergang: Die Waika-Indianer des Oberen
        Orinoco—Wilbeuter oder Pflanzer?" *Die Umschau in Wissenschaft
        und Technik,* LVIII, 177–80.

 1964   *Waika: Die Kulturgeschichtliche Stellung der Waika-Indiener
        des Oberen Orinoco in Rahmen der Völkerkunde Sudamerikas.*
        Vol. 1 of *Ergebnisse der Frobenius—Expedition 1954/1955 nach
        Sudost Venezuela.* Munich: Klaus Renner.
Ziff, David
 1960   "The Interaction of a Spanish Village with Indian Villages
        in the Sierra of Ecuador." Columbia-Cornell-Harvard-Illinois Sum-
        mer Field Studies Program (Mimeographed).
Zuidema, R. T.
 1962   "The Relationship Between Mountains and Coast in Ancient
        Peru," in *The Wonders of Man's Ingenuity, Being a Series of
        Studies in Archeology, Material Culture and Social Anthropology
        by Members of the Staff of the National Museum of Ethnology,
        Published on the Occasion of the Museum's 125th Anniversary.*
        Leyden: Mededelingen van het Rijksmuseum voor Volkenkunde
        No. 15.

 1964   *The Ceque System of Cuzco: The Social Organization of the
        Capital of the Inca.* International Archives of Ethnography, Leiden:
        E. J. Brill.

 1969   "Hierarchy in Symmetric Alliance Systems." *Bijdragen Tot
        de Taal-Land en Volkenkunde* 11(1):134–39.

 1972   "The Inca Kinship System: A New Theoretical View." Paper
        presented at the Annual Meeting of the American Anthropological
        Association, Toronto, Canada.

 1973   "Un modelo Incaico para el Estudio del Arte y de la Arquitec-
        tura Prehispanicas del Perú." *38 Internationalen Amerikanisten
        Kongress, Stuttgart,* Munich.

INDEX